GARY DONELL

Byrd & Chen's
Canadian
Tax
Principles

2021–2022 EDITION

Volume II

CONTENTS

(Continued)

(Continued)

Chapter 19 - Continued

CHAPTER 20

International Issues in Taxation

CHAPTER 21

GST/HST

Study Guide

Your two volume textbook is accompanied by a separate Study Guide that is available in print and online.

The chapters of this Study Guide correspond to the chapters of *Byrd & Chen's Canadian Tax Principles.*

Each of these Study Guide chapters contains the following:

- Detailed guidance on how to work through the text and problems in the chapter.
- Detailed solutions to the Exercises and Self-Study Problems in the textbook for the chapter.
- A list of learning objectives for the material in the chapter.

In addition, the Study Guide contains:

- Two sample personal tax returns and two Self-Study Tax Software Problems in Chapters 4 and 11.
- A sample corporate tax return in Chapter 13.
- An extensive glossary.

PREFACE

Complete Preface In Volume I

The complete preface to this three volume set of **Byrd & Chen's Canadian Tax Principles** can be found in Volume I.

MyLab

MyLab is the teaching and learning platform that empowers you to reach every student. By combining trusted author content with digital tools and a flexible platform, MyLab personalizes the learning experience and improves results for each student. Learn more about MyLab at https://mlm.pearson.com/northamerica/myaccountinglab/.

Resources available on MyLab include:

- Pearson eText
- Data Analytics Project
- Self-Study Problems
- CPA Competency Alignment Map
- Practice Examinations and Solutions
- PowerPoint Presentations
- Tax Returns for Examples and Self-Study Tax Return Problems
- 2021 Tax Rates, Credits, and Common CCA Classes
- ProFile Tax Return Preparation Software access
- Glossary Flashcards

2021 Rates, Credits, and Other Data

> A downloadable version of this document is available
> as a PDF from MyLab.

Information Applicable to Individuals
Federal Tax Rates for Individuals

Taxable Income in Excess of	Federal Tax	Marginal Rate on Excess
$ -0-	$ -0-	15.0%
49,020	7,353	20.5%
98,040	17,402	26.0%
151,978	31,426	29.0%
216,511	50,141	33.0%

Federal Tax Credits for Individuals—Personal Tax Credits (ITA 118)

Reference

118(1.1)   **Basic Personal Amount (BPA)**   There are three alternatives dependent on net income. (1) For individuals with net income of $151,978 or less the BPA is $13,808, (2) for individuals with net income of $216,511 or higher the BPA is $12,421, and (3) for individuals with net income between $151,978 and $216,511 the BPA is calculated as $13,808 − [$1,387][(net income − $151,978) ÷ $64,533]

118(1)(a)   **Married Persons**   15% the of **BPA** for the individual

118(1)(a)   **Spousal**   15% of the **BPA** for the individual and:

> if the spouse of the married individual is dependent because of a mental or physical infirmity, there is an additional amount of $2,295 added to the **BPA**. The total of these two amounts ($16,103) is reduced by the income of the individual's spouse.

118(1)(b)   **Eligible Dependant**   15% of **BPA** for the individual and:

> if the dependent person is dependent because of a mental or physical infirmity, there is an additional amount of $2,295 added to the **BPA**. The total of these two amounts ($16,103) is reduced by the income of the dependent person.

118(1)(b.1)   **Canada Caregiver for Child under 18**   15% of $2,295 ($344).

118(1)(c)   **Single Persons**   15% of the **BPA**.

118(1)(d)   **Canada Caregiver**   15% of $7,348 ($1,102), reduced by 15% of the dependant's income in excess of $17,256.

118(2)   **Age**   The age credit base is $7,713. The base for this credit is reduced by 15% of the amount by which the individual's net income exceeds $38,893. Not available when income reaches $90,313. This credit is available to be transferred to a spouse or common-law partner.

118(3)   **Pension**   15% of up to $2,000 of eligible pension income for a maximum credit of $300 [(15%) ($2,000)]. This credit is available to be transferred to a spouse or common-law partner.

118(10)   **Canada Employment Credit**   15% of up to $1,257. This produces a maximum credit of $189.

Other Common Federal Personal Credits (Various ITA)

118.01 **Adoption Expenses Credit** 15% of eligible expenses (reduced by any reimbursements) up to a maximum of $16,729 per adoption. This results in a maximum credit of $2,509.

118.02 **Digital News Subscriptions** 15% of the lesser of $500 and the cost of qualifying subscription expenses.

118.041 **Home Accessibility Credit** 15% of the lesser of $10,000 and the amount of qualifying expenditures for the year.

118.05 **First Time Home Buyers' Credit** 15% of $5,000 ($750) of the cost of an eligible home.

118.06 **Volunteer Firefighters Credit** 15% of $3,000 ($450) for qualifying volunteers.

118.07 **Volunteer Search and Rescue Workers Credit** 15% of $3,000 ($450) for qualifying volunteers.

118.1 **Charitable Donations—Regular** The general limit on amounts for this credit is 75% of net income. There is an addition to this general limit equal to 25% of any taxable capital gains and 25% of any recapture of CCA resulting from a gift of capital property. In addition, the income inclusion on capital gains arising from a gift of some publicly traded shares is reduced from one-half to nil. For individuals, the credit is equal to:

$$\mathbf{[(15\%)(A)] + [(33\%)(B)] + [(29\%)(C)]}\ \text{where:}$$

A = The first $200 of eligible gifts.
B = The lesser of:
   • total gifts, less $200; and
   • taxable income, less $216,511.
C = The excess, if any, by which the individual's total gifts exceed the sum of $200 plus the amount determined in B.

118.2 **Medical Expenses** The medical expense tax credit is determined by the following formula:

$$\mathbf{[15\%]\ [(B - C) + D]},\ \ \text{where:}$$

B is the total of an individual's medical expenses for him- or herself, his or her spouse or common-law partner, and any of his or her children who have not reached 18 years of age at the end of the year.
C is the lesser of 3% of the individual's net income and $2,421.
D is the total of all amounts each of which is, in respect of a dependant of the individual (other than a child of the individual who has not attained the age of 18 years before the end of the taxation year), an amount determined by the formula:

$$\mathbf{E - F},\ \text{where:}$$

E is the total of the dependant's medical expenses.
F is the lesser of 3% of the dependant's net income and $2,421.

118.3 **Disability—All Ages** 15% of $8,662 ($1,299). If not used by the disabled individual, it can be transferred to a person claiming that individual as a dependant.

118.3 **Disability Supplement—Under 18 and Qualifies for the Disability Tax Credit** 15% of $5,053 ($758), reduced by the total of amounts paid for attendant care or supervision in excess of $2,959 that are deducted as child care costs, deducted as a disability support amount, or claimed as a medical expense in calculating the medical expense tax credit.

Education-Related Credits

118.5
- **Tuition Fees, which Includes Examination and Ancillary Fees**
  - 15% of qualifying tuition fees
  - 15% of examination fees for both post-secondary examinations and examinations required in a professional program
  - 15% of ancillary fees that are imposed by a post-secondary educational institution on all of their full- or part-time students. Up to $250 in such ancillary fees can be claimed even if not required of all students.

118.62
- **Interest on Student Loans**
  15% of interest paid on qualifying student loans.

118.9
- **Transfer of Tuition Credit**
  If the individual cannot use the credit, is not claimed as a dependant by a spouse or common-law partner, and does not transfer the unused credit to a spouse or common-law partner, then a parent or grandparent of the individual can claim up to $750 [(15%)($5,000)] of any unused tuition credit. The amount that can be transferred is reduced by the amount of the credit required to reduce the student's federal tax payable to nil.

118.7
Employment Insurance   15% of amounts paid by employees up to the maximum Employment Insurance premium of $890 (1.58% of $56,300). This produces a maximum tax credit of $134 [(15%)($890)].

118.7
Canada Pension Plan   The maximum credit base for all individuals is $2,876 [(4.95%)($61,600 maximum pensionable earnings - $3,500 exemption)]. This produces a maximum tax credit of $431 [(15%)($2,876)]. The actual maximum CPP contributions for those individuals with pensionable earnings of $61,600 or more is $3,166 [(5.45%)($61,600 maximum pensionable earnings - $3,500 exemption)]. The difference of $290 [$3,166 - $2,876] is treated as a deduction under ITA 60(e.1) and reduces net income.

122.51
Refundable Medical Expense Supplement   The individual claiming this amount must be over 17 and have earned income of at least $3,751. The amount is equal to the lesser of $1,285 and 25/15 of the medical expense tax credit. The refundable amount is then reduced by 5% of family net income in excess of $28,446. Not available when family income is more than $54,146.

122.9
Refundable Teacher and Early Childhood Educator School Supply Tax Credit   A maximum of 15% of up to $1,000 ($150) of eligible expenditures that are made by eligible educators.

122.91
Canada Training Credit   The lesser of training amount limit and 50% of eligible training costs incurred in the previous year. Minimum required working income must be $10,100 and maximum net income is $150,473.

127(3)
Political Donations   Three-quarters of the first $400, one-half of the next $350, one-third of the next $525, to a maximum credit of $650 on donations of $1,275.

127.4
Labour Sponsored Venture Capital Corporations (LSVCC) Credit   The federal credit is equal to 15% of acquisitions of provincially registered LSVCCs.

ITA 82 and
ITA 121

Dividend Tax Credit

- **Eligible Dividends**   These dividends are grossed up by 38%. The federal dividend tax credit is equal to 6/11 of the gross up. The credit can also be calculated as 15.02% of the grossed up dividends, or 20.7272% of the actual dividends received.

- **Non-Eligible Dividends**   These dividends are grossed up by 15%. The federal dividend tax credit is equal to 9/13 of the gross up. The credit can also be calculated as 9.0301% of the grossed up dividends, or 10.3846% of the actual dividends received.

Other Data for Individuals

ITA 82

Dividend Gross Up

Eligible Dividends   For these dividends, the gross up is 38% of dividends received.

Non-Eligible Dividends   For these dividends, the gross up is 15% of dividends received.

Chapter 4

OAS Clawback Limits   The tax (clawback) on Old Age Security (OAS) benefits is based on the lesser of 100% of OAS benefits received and 15% of the amount by which "threshold income" (net income calculated without the OAS clawback) exceeds $79,845.

Chapter 4

EI Clawback Limits   The tax (clawback) on Employment Insurance (EI) benefits under the *Employment Insurance Act* is based on the lesser of 30% of the EI benefits received and 30% of the amount by which "threshold income" exceeds $70,375 (1.25 times the maximum insurable earnings of $56,300). For this purpose, "threshold income" is net income calculated without the OAS or EI clawbacks.

Chapter 9

Child Care Expenses   The least of three amounts:

1. The amount actually paid for child care services. If the child is at a camp or boarding school, this amount is limited to a weekly amount $275 (any age if eligible for disability tax credit), $200 (under 7 year of age), or $125 (age 7 through 16 or over 16 with a mental or physical impairment).

2. The sum of the **annual child care expense amounts** for the taxpayer's eligible children. The per child amounts are $11,000 (any age if eligible for disability tax credit), $8,000 (under 7 year of age), or $5,000 (age 7 through 16 or over 16 with a mental or physical impairment).

3. 2/3 of the taxpayer's **earned income** (for child care expenses purposes).

Chapter 10

RRSP Deduction Room   For 2021, the addition to RRSP deduction room is equal to:

- the lesser of $27,830 and 18% of 2020 earned income,
- reduced by the 2020 pension adjustment and any 2021 past service pension adjustment, and
- increased by any 2021 pension adjustment reversal.

Chapter 11

Capital Gains Deduction   For 2021, the deduction limit for dispositions of shares of qualified small business corporations is $892,218. There is an additional amount for farm or fishing properties of $107,782, providing a total of $1,000,000 for such properties.

Provincial Tax Rates and Provincial Credits for Individuals   Provincial taxes are based on taxable income, with most provinces adopting multiple rates. The number of brackets range from three to five. Provincial tax credits are generally based on the minimum provincial rate applied to a credit base that is similar to that used for federal credits. In addition to regular rates, two provinces, Ontario and Prince Edward Island, use surtaxes.

Information Applicable to Individuals and Corporations

ITR 4301 **Prescribed Rate** The following figures show the base rate that would be used in calculations such as imputed interest on loans. It also shows the rates applicable on amounts owing to and from the CRA. For recent quarters, the interest rates were as follows:

Year	Quarter	Base Rate	Owing From*	Owing To
2018	I	1%	3%	5%
2018	II to IV	2%	4%	6%
2019	**All**	**2%**	**4%**	**6%**
2020	**I, II**	**2%**	**4%**	**6%**
2020	**III, IV**	**1%**	**3%**	**5%**
2021	**I**	**1%**	**3%**	**5%**

*The rate on refunds to corporations is limited to the base rate, without the additional 2%.

Automobile Deduction Limits

- CCA is limited to the first $30,000 of the automobile's cost, plus applicable GST/HST & PST (not including amounts that will be refunded through input tax credits).
- Interest on financing of automobiles is limited to $10 per day.
- Deductible leasing costs are limited to $800 per month (other constraints apply).
- Operating cost benefit = $0.27 per kilometre.
- Deductible rates = $0.59 for first 5,000 kilometres, $0.53 for additional kilometres.

CCA Rates See Appendix to Chapter 5.

Quick Method Rates (GST Only)

	Percentage on GST Included Sales	
	First $30,000	On Excess
Retailers and Wholesalers	0.8%	1.8%
Service Providers and Manufacturers	2.6%	3.6%

Note Different rates apply in the provinces that have adopted an HST system.

Information Applicable to Corporations

Federal Corporate Tax Rates are as follows (federal tax abatement removed):

General Business (Basic 38% - 10% Abatement)	28%
General Business (After General Rate Reduction of 13%)	15%
Income Eligible for M&P Deduction	15%
Income Eligible for Small Business Deduction (28% - 19%)	9%
Part IV Refundable Tax	38 1/3%
Part I Refundable Tax on Investment Income of CCPC (ART)	10 2/3%

Reference
89(1) **General Rate Income Pool** A CCPC's general rate income pool (GRIP) is defined as follows:

- The GRIP balance at the end of the preceding year; plus
- 72% of the CCPC's taxable income after it has been reduced by amounts eligible for the small business deduction and aggregate investment income; plus
- 100% of eligible dividends received during the year; plus
- adjustments related to amalgamations and wind-ups; less
- eligible dividends paid during the preceding year.

125(1)   **Small Business Deduction**   is equal to 19% of the least of:

  A. Net Canadian active business income.

  B. Taxable income, less:

  1. 100/28 times the ITA 126(1) credit for taxes paid on foreign non-business income, calculated without consideration of the additional refundable tax under ITA 123.3 or the general rate reduction under ITA 123.4; and

  2. 4 times the ITA 126(2) credit for taxes paid on foreign business income, calculated without consideration of the general rate reduction under ITA 123.4.

  C. The annual business limit of $500,000, less any portion allocated to associated corporations, less the grinds for large corporations and passive income.

123.3   **Additional Refundable Tax on Investment Income (ART)**   is equal to 10 2/3% of the lesser of:

  • the corporation's "aggregate investment income" for the year [as defined in ITA 129(4)]; and

  • the amount, if any, by which the corporation's taxable income for the year exceeds the amount upon which the the small business deduction is determined.

123.4(2)   **General Rate Reduction**   is equal to 13% of full rate taxable income. This is taxable income reduced by the amount upon which the small business deduction is determined, income eligible for the M&P deduction, and the corporation's "aggregate investment income" for the year.

125.1   **Manufacturing and Processing Deduction**   is equal to 13% of the lesser of:

  A. manufacturing and processing profits, less the amount upon which the small business deduction is determined; and

  B. taxable income, less the sum of:

  1. the amount upon which the small business deduction is determined;
  2. 4 times the foreign tax credit for business income calculated without consideration of the ITA 123.4 general rate reduction; and
  3. "aggregate investment income" (of CCPCs) as defined in ITA 129(4).

126(1)   **Foreign Tax Credits for Corporations**   The foreign non-business income tax credit is the lesser of:

  • the tax paid to the foreign government (for corporations, there is no 15% limit on the foreign non-business taxes paid); and

  • an amount determined by the following formula:

$$\left[\frac{\text{Foreign Non-Business Income}}{\text{Adjusted Division B Income}} \right] [\text{Tax Otherwise Payable}]$$

126(2)   The foreign business income tax credit is equal to the least of:

  • the tax paid to the foreign government;

  • an amount determined by the following formula:

$$\left[\frac{\text{Foreign Business Income}}{\text{Adjusted Division B Income}} \right] [\text{Tax Otherwise Payable}]; \text{ and}$$

  • tax otherwise payable for the year, less any foreign tax credit taken on non-business income under ITA 126(1).

129(4)   **Refundable Portion of Part I Tax Payable**   is defined as the least of three items:

1. the amount determined by the formula

$$A - B, \text{ where}$$

A   is 30 2/3% of the corporation's aggregate investment income for the year, and

B   is the amount, if any, by which the foreign non-business income tax credit exceeds 8% of its foreign investment income for the year.

2. 30 2/3% of the amount, if any, by which the corporation's taxable income for the year exceeds the total of:

   - the amount upon which the small business deduction is determined;
   - 100 ÷ 38 2/3 of the tax credit for foreign non-business income; and
   - 4 times the tax credit for foreign business income.

3. the corporation's tax for the year payable under Part I.

129(4)   **Aggregate Investment Income**   is the sum of:

- net taxable capital gains for the year, reduced by any net capital loss carry overs deducted during the year; and

- income from property including interest, rents, and royalties, but excluding dividends that are deductible in computing taxable income. Since foreign dividends are generally not deductible, they would be included in aggregate investment income.

129(4)   **ELIGIBLE 2021 Refundable Dividend Tax on Hand**   (RDTOH) is defined as follows:

Beginning Balance   The balance in the eligible RDTOH at the end of the preceding taxation year.

Additions

- Part IV taxes paid on eligible dividends from non-connected taxable Canadian corporations. These are commonly referred to as portfolio dividends.
- Part IV taxes paid on eligible dividends from connected corporations to the extent that such dividends included a refund from the paying corporation's eligible RDTOH.

Deduction   Dividend refund claimed from the eligible RDTOH account for the previous taxation year.

NON-ELIGIBLE 2019 Refundable Dividend Tax on Hand   (RDTOH) is defined as follows:

Beginning Balance   The balance in the non-eligible RDTOH at the end of the preceding taxation year.

Additions   There are three items that are added to the non-eligible RDTOH beginning balance:

- The Part I refundable tax for the year.
- Part IV taxes paid on non-eligible dividends from connected corporations to the extent that such dividends included a refund from the paying corporation's non-eligible RDTOH.
- Part IV taxes paid on non-eligible dividends from non-connected taxable Canadian corporations.

Deduction   Dividend refund claimed from the non-eligible RDTOH account for the previous taxation year.

186(1)   **Part IV Tax**   is assessed at a rate of 38 1/3% of portfolio dividends, plus dividends received from a connected company where that connected company was entitled to a dividend refund as a result of the dividend payment.

Tax Related Websites

GOVERNMENT

Canada Revenue Agency   www.canada.ca/en/revenue-agency
Department of Finance Canada   www.canada.ca/en/department-finance.html

CPA FIRMS

BDO   www.bdo.ca/en-ca/services/tax/domestic-tax-services/overview/
Deloitte.   www2.deloitte.com/ca/en/pages/tax/topics/tax.html
Ernst & Young   www.ey.com/CA/en/Services/Tax
KPMG   www.kpmg.com/ca/en/services/tax
PricewaterhouseCoopers   www.pwc.com/ca/en/services/tax.html

OTHER

CPA Canada   www.CPAcanada.ca
Canadian Tax Foundation   www.ctf.ca
ProFile Tax Suite   profile.intuit.ca

Taxable Income and Tax Payable for Individuals Revisited

Learning Objectives

After completing Chapter 11, you should be able to:

1. Describe the four-step process used to determine net federal tax payable for individuals, the common taxable income deductions, and their place in that process (Paragraph [P hereafter] 11-1 to 11-8).
2. Describe the purpose of the rules related to lump-sum payments and how they apply (P 11-9 to 11-14).
3. Explain how transaction-based losses differ from source-based losses, the exceptions to transaction-based losses, how they fit into net income under ITA 3, and what happens when there is insufficient income to apply them in a year (P 11-15 to 11-29).
4. Explain how personal tax credits play a role in loss planning (P 11-30 to 11-31).
5. Explain and be able to apply how current-year losses become loss carry overs and the importance of ITA 3 in that process (P 11-32).
6. Describe the various types of loss carry overs, their carry over period, and their restrictions, if any (P 11-33).
7. Calculate and apply the loss carry over provisions applicable to non-capital losses (P 11-34 to 11-38).
8. Calculate and apply the loss carry over provisions applicable to net capital losses, including the conversion of a net capital loss carry over to a non-capital loss carry over (P 11-39 to 11-45).
9. Explain the special rules for applying net capital losses on the death of an individual (P 11-46 to 11-49).
10. Describe the circumstances under which an ABIL can occur, how it is treated in determining net and taxable income, and the interaction with the capital gains deduction (P 11-50 to 11-60).
11. Explain the difference between a restricted farm loss and a non-restricted farm loss and the loss carry overs that apply when there is insufficient net income to apply them in the year they arise (P 11-61 to 11-65).
12. Explain the purpose of the capital gains deduction together with the type of property to which it applies (P 11-66 to 11-73)
13. Apply the provisions of the capital gains deduction (P 11-74 to 11-89).

14. Explain the importance of selectively applying loss carry overs in the optimum way possible and describe some of the basic tax planning points to keep in mind when choosing which losses to apply (P 11-90 to 11-94).
15. Describe basic federal tax payable (P 11-95 to 11-100).
16. Explain why income splitting is such a concern to the federal government and the types of transactions that were identfied as problematic (P 11-101 to 11-105).
17. Describe the kiddy tax and how it applies (P 11-106 to 11-110).
18. Describe the TOSI and how it differs from the kiddy tax (P 11-111 to 11-114).
19. Describe and apply the TOSI analysis to a basic fact pattern (P 11-115 to 11-130).
20. Explain the circumstances under which dividends can be transferred between spouses or common-law partners. Apply the transfer and determine whether it is beneficial in specific cases (P 11-131).
21. Explain how the eligible amount of donation is determined, the impact of an "advantage," and how the legal concept of a donation differs from that of the ITA (P 11-132 to 11-140)
22. Explain how the ITA treats donations of property to registered charities, how it affects the 75% annual limit and any special treatment to certain property donations such as publicly listed shares, and calculate the charitable donations tax credit for donations of these various types of property (P 11-141 to 11-157).
23. Explain the purpose of the foreign tax credit, the tax treatment of the payment of foreign taxes, and be able to calculate both the foreign business and non-business income tax credits (P 11-158 to 11-168).
24. Explain the purpose and reasons for the AMT and the circumstances under which it is likely to apply (P 11-169 to 11-171).
25. Apply the provisions of the AMT (P 11-172 to 11-182)
26. Review a personal tax return completed using the ProFile T1 tax preparation software program.

Introduction

11-1. In Chapter 1 we set out the following four-step process to determine whether an individual would, for a specific year, owe federal income tax or expect a refund:

Step 1 – net income = Division B (predominantly Subdivisions a to e)

Step 2 – taxable income = Division C

Step 3 – Gross tax = Division E (Subdivision a)

Step 4 – Personal tax credits = Division E (Subdivision a)

Result = Net tax payable or refund

In the first 10 chapters of Volume 1 of the text our primary focus was on steps 1, 3, and 4. Chapters 3 and 5 to 10 were devoted to unravelling the various components of net income, while Chapter 4 was devoted to determining federal income tax payable and the many personal tax credits available to individual taxpayers. In those earlier chapters there was some limited cursory exposure to taxable income such as the employee stock option deduction discussed in Chapter 3 on employment income and the determination of loss carry overs that were discussed in Chapter 1.

11-2. To this point we have covered many of the rules necessary to develop a solid understanding of the income tax principles and concepts that are important to applying the ITA with the goal of meeting the CPA standards as well being able to prepare one's own income tax return, including those of others such as family members and friends. Unfortunately our journey of individual income tax is not quite complete. There are a few remaining rules that affect taxable income, tax payable, and certain tax credits that we could not cover in sufficient detail until the first 10 chapters had been covered. Our goal in this chapter is to complete the picture that will take you to the bottom line of determining an individual's federal income tax result for a specific year.

11-3.   The determination of net income is quite extensive, requiring seven chapters to discuss the many rules. On the other hand, taxable income is much more limited in nature, providing a handful of rules that can, for the most part, be covered in this one chapter. As a result, this chapter will revisit step 2 in a much more meaningful way with the goal of providing a practical and working understanding of taxable income with a focus on the more common deductions available, such as the various loss carry overs and the capital gains deduction.

11-4.   Once we have covered taxable income we will return to step 3 to discuss two special sets of rules that can change the amount owed in certain situations. The two sets of rules that will be discussed are the alternative minimum tax, or AMT, and the tax on split income, or TOSI. The TOSI has received considerable attention within the income tax community over the last few years.

11-5.   Finally, we will conclude the chapter by revisiting two tax credits and adding one new tax credit. In Chapter 4 we discussed the charitable donation credit, and in Chapters 6 and 7 we touched on the foreign tax credit but did not go into much detail. In this chapter we will revisit the charitable donation tax credit by discussing the income tax implications of donating certain types of property. We will also provide the necessary detail concerning the application of foreign tax credits. Finally, we will add a credit not previously discussed that allows, in limited circumstances, dividends to be shifted from one spouse or common-law partner to another.

Taxable Income Overview

11-6.   Once net income has been determined, the next step is to calculate taxable income. ITA 2(2) defines taxable income as net income (ITA 3) plus any additions and minus any deductions found in Division C. The taxable income definition refers to both additions and deductions within Division C. However, the only addition is for ITA 110.5, which is a special rule that applies to corporations only. There are no Division C additions for taxpayers who are individuals.

11-7.   Division C technically includes provisions starting with ITA 109 and ending with ITA 114.2. ITA 109 used to contain the rules for personal tax deductions that were converted to tax credits decades ago, and therefore ITA 109 no longer applies to current years. ITA 112 and 113 apply special rules for corporations, and ITA 114 to 114.2, which apply to individuals, covers special rules for part-year residents. What this means is that the only Division C deductions that are of concern are those found in ITA 110 to 111.1, the most common of which are the following:

ITA 110(1)(d), (d.01), and (d.1)—Employee Stock Option Deduction   The basic coverage of stock options and stock option deductions was included in Chapter 3. In this chapter, we discuss the implications where stock option shares are donated to a charitable organization. This will integrate the donation tax credit coverage with the stock option deduction rules.

ITA 110(1)(f)—Deductions for Payments   This provision is designed to recognize that certain amounts that are required to be included in net income are not to be subject to income tax. ITA 110(1)(f) provides the legislative authority by allowing a deduction in computing taxable income of the amount included in net income. The end result is that the particular net income amount is excluded from taxable income. The short list of qualifying amounts include workers' compensation, amounts exempted by income tax treaties with other countries, and certain social assistance payments. Additional detail is provided in Chapter 4 at Paragraphs 4-6 to 4-8.

ITA 110.2—Lump-Sum Payments   This provision recognizes that individuals are generally required to include amounts in net income based on when the amounts are received. This means that lump-sum amounts received in a year that represent many years of income are subject to income tax all at once. Where the amounts are significant the result could be that much higher tax brackets will apply than would have been the case had the amounts been received in the year to which they relate. This provision offers an option to spread the lump-sum receipt over the years to which they relate. Caution must be exercised, however, since allocating an amount to an earlier year will result in interest charges for that year, which could offset any income tax savings. The provision is generally applied to retroactive settlements (often as a result of a court order or an arbitration award) of spousal support, EI benefits, pension benefits, and termination negotiations with employers. Lump-sum payments as a result of collective bargaining would not qualify. This topic will be discussed briefly in this chapter.

ITA 110.6—Capital Gains Deduction The capital gains deduction, sometimes inaccurately referred to as the capital gains exemption, provides a deduction to offset certain capital gains that have been included in net income. The result is that the capital gains in question avoid being included in taxable income and are therefore not subject to income tax. This valuable deduction can be quite complex and requires a solid understanding of capital gains. The capital gains deduction will be discussed in detail in this chapter.

ITA 110.7—Northern Residents Deduction This provision allows a deduction for certain travel benefits and living costs of individuals who have lived in certain northern and isolated regions for a period of at least six consecutive months. The deduction is designed to assist those individuals with the higher costs of living in those regions of Canada. The topic was briefly discussed in Chapter 4 and will not be covered in any further detail in this chapter.

ITA 111—Loss Carry overs There are five specific taxable income deductions allowed for loss carry overs of other years. The deductions are found in ITA 111(1)(a) to (e) and cover non-capital losses (ITA 111(1)(a)), net capital losses (ITA 111(1)(b)), restricted farm losses (ITA 111(1)(c)), farm and fishing losses (ITA 111(1)(d)), and limited partnership losses (ITA 111(1)(e)). These loss carry overs are either available to deduct against any type of income or are "streamed," meaning they are only deductible against certain types of income. Only non-capital and farm and fishing losses can be deducted against any type of income. Net capital losses, restricted farm losses, and limited partnership losses are subject to streaming and are therefore only deductible if certain types of income are present. Loss carry overs will be discussed in detail in this chapter.

11-8.   Figure 11-1 reproduces that part of the T1 individual Income Tax and Benefit Return that calculates taxable income. The figure begins with net income and subtracts certain amounts. We have inserted the ITA references to each line.

Figure 11-1
Step 4 of the T1 Individual Income Tax and Benefit Return, with Correlating ITA References Added

ITA References	Step 4 – Taxable income			
	Enter your **net income** from line 50 on the previous page.		23600	51
110(1)(f)	Canadian Forces personnel and police deduction (box 43 of all T4 slips)	24400	52	
110(1)(d),(d.1),(d.01)	Security options deductions (boxes 39 and 41 of T4 slips or see Form T1212)	24900 +	53	
110(1)(c)	Other payments deduction (claim the amount from line 27, unless it includes an amount at line 26. If so, see line 25000 in the guide)	25000 +	54	
111(1)(e)	Limited partnership losses of other years	25100 +	55	
111(1)(a),(c),(d)	Non-capital losses of other years	25200 +	56	
111(1)(b)	Net capital losses of other years	25300 +	57	
110.6	Capital gains deduction (complete Form T657)	25400 +	58	
110.7	Northern residents deductions (complete Form T2222)	25500 +	59	
110(1)(f) and	Additional deductions Specify:	25600 +	60	
110.2(2)	Add lines 52 to 60.	25700 =	▶ –	61
	Line 51 minus line 61 (if negative, enter "0") This is your **taxable income.**	26000 =		62

Lump-Sum Payments—ITA 110.2

The Problem

11-9.   Individuals sometimes receive lump-sum payments that relate to one or more previous years. An example of this would be an employment termination payment, retroactive spousal support payments, or retroactive pension payments. In general terms, individuals are only required to include amounts in income when received and not accrued. Therefore, the lump-sum receipt of several years of income would be included in the income for the year of receipt, which causes potential issues.

11-10.   There may be some limited advantage in such situations in that there has been some deferral of the income tax on these amounts. However, our graduated tax rate system may cause part of the lump-sum payment to be taxed at a higher rate. For example, an individual with $58,000 of annual taxable income would be subject to a federal income tax rate of 20.5% on additional income of approximately $40,000 in 2021. If that individual were to receive a lump-sum payment of $120,000 in 2021 representing $40,000 for each of 2019, 2020, and 2021, then the first $40,000 would be taxed at 20.5%, the next estimated $54,000 [$151,978 - $98,040] would be taxed at 26.0%, and the remaining $26,000 (the amount above $151,978) would be taxed at 29.0%. The additional tax above the 20.5% rate as a result of the lump-sum payment would total approximately $5,180 [($54,000)(.026 - 0.205) + ($26,000)(0.29-0.205)]. ITA 110.2 offers an opportunity to spread the amounts over the years to which they relate, which in our example would effectively mean adding $40,000 to each of the three years so that taxable income was $98,000 in each year.

Qualifying Amounts

11-11.   This optional relief can be applied to payments that are referred to as "qualifying amounts," an expression defined in ITA 110.2(1). In the explanatory notes that accompany the legislation, the following more general description is found:

> A **qualifying amount** is the principal portion (e.g., not including interest) of certain amounts included in income. Those amounts are: spousal support amounts, superannuation or pension benefits otherwise payable on a periodic basis, employment insurance benefits and benefits paid under wage loss replacement plans. Also included is the income received from an office or employment (or because of a termination of an office or employment) under the terms of a court order or judgment, an arbitration award or in settlement of a lawsuit.

Relief Mechanism

11-12.   ITA 110.2(2) provides a deduction for the "specified portion" of a "qualifying amount" that was received by an individual during a particular taxation year. The "specified portion" is the portion of the receipt that relates to a different taxation year referred to as an "eligible taxation year." An "eligible taxation year" is any prior year after 1977 in which the individual was a resident of Canada throughout the year and during which the individual did not become bankrupt. No deduction is available if the qualifying amount is less than $3,000. In somewhat simplified terms, this means that an individual can remove the types of payments described as qualifying amounts from the current year's income, to the extent that they relate to prior years. In our example in Paragraph 11-10, the individual would have included $120,000 in net income for 2021. ITA 110.2(2) would allow a deduction of $80,000, representing the amounts related to 2019 and 2020. If this were the only income of the individual for 2021 then net income would be $120,000 and taxable income would be $40,000.

11-13.   Interestingly, the ITA does not require amending the previous years' income tax returns. In our example the taxable income for each of 2019 and 2020 would remain unchanged at $58,000. Instead, ITA 120.31 calculates a "notional tax payable," which recalculates what the income tax would have been had the additional amount been added to taxable income for that year. As a result there are no changes made to any tax credits or any other amounts for the previous years. This may or may not be of benefit depending on the facts. The resulting tax calculation is then considered owing with interest accruing from May 1 of each of the following years. Continuing with our example, the notional tax for 2019 would be considered due May 1, 2020, and interest will accrue until paid. The same would occur for the 2020 taxation year.

11-14.   Since ITA 110.2 is optional, the CRA requires individuals who wish to take advantage of this provision to file form T1198 setting out the details so that the tax calculations can be made.

Loss Basics

General Transaction-Based Losses

11-15.   Throughout this next section we will explain basic loss concepts using a combination of Figure 1-5 from Chapter 1, which graphically displays net income (ITA 3), and Figure 11-2 in this chapter. Understanding losses begins with current-year losses. Current-year losses can be divided into two types of losses: the first are transaction-based losses and the second are source-based losses.

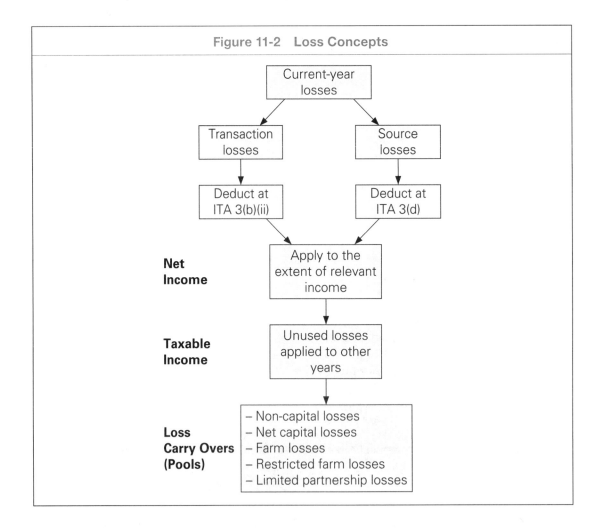

Figure 11-2   Loss Concepts

11-16.   Transaction-based losses generally refer to the disposition of non-depreciable capital property that results in a capital loss. Examples would include the sale of land not held as inventory in a business or the sale of various investments such as shares of corporations, bonds, or interests in mutual funds. Remember that the ITA does not allow capital losses on depreciable property or personal-use property (except where the property is also considered listed personal-use property). Such transaction-based losses are factored into net income through ITA 3(b), which is divided into two separate parts: ITA 3(b)(i) and ITA 3(b)(ii).

11-17.   Taxable capital gains are added to ITA 3(b)(i) and allowable capital losses are added to ITA 3(b)(ii). The effect on net income depends on whether the ITA 3(b)(i) amount exceeds the ITA 3(b)(ii) amount. If it does, then the positive difference is added to net income for that year. We generally refer to this as the "net taxable capital gains" for the year. If the ITA 3(b)(i) amount does not exceed the ITA 3(b)(ii) amount, then the difference is automatically considered to be nil. The ITA rarely recognizes negative numbers as a result of a special rule found in ITA 257.

> **EXAMPLE 1**   In 2021 you sold shares in three separate transactions. The result was a taxable capital gain of $9,000 and two allowable capital losses of $10,000 and $17,000 for a total of $27,000.

> **ANALYSIS 1**   In calculating your net income for 2021 you would show the following with respect to the three capital transactions:

> ITA 3(b)(i) taxable capital gains $9,000
> Less:
> ITA 3(b)(ii) allowable capital losses $27,000
> ITA 3(b) = Nil

> You can see that because the taxable capital gains did not exceed the allowable capital losses the impact on net income is nil for 2021. You will also notice that the full amount of the allowable capital losses were entered. ITA 3 simply asks you to input the actual allowable capital loss, providing no choice to include a different amount. This is important to ensure that any excess amounts be available to other years as a loss carry over.

11-18.   We can continue the analysis of our example in Paragraph 11-17 by turning to Figure 11-2. We began with two 2021 allowable capital losses totalling $27,000. These two transaction-based losses take us to ITA 3(b)(ii), as indicated. The next step is to apply those current-year losses to the extent of the relevant income, which in this case is the taxable capital gain of $9,000. Before continuing you can see that allowable capital losses are streamed, meaning they are only deductible to the extent there are taxable capital gains. Had there been no taxable capital gains the net income impact would be unchanged at nil.

11-19.   From the initial example we can readily determine that only $9,000 of the allowable capital losses were actually used to offset the $9,000 of taxable capital gains. Figure 11-2 directs us next to the unused losses, the five categories of which are listed at the bottom of the figure. In this case we turn our attention to the "net capital loss" category. ITA 111(8) defines a net capital loss as a formula. The first two components of that formula are A – B. "A" is equal to the ITA 3(b)(ii) amount and "B" is equal to the ITA 3(b)(i) amount. The result is as follows:

> 2021 net capital loss = $18,000 [$27,000 ITA 3(b)(ii)] - $9,000 ITA 3(b)(i)]

11-20.   The 2021 net capital loss is deductible in any of the three preceding years (2018, 2019, or 2020) and in any future year (2022 and subsequent years) as long as the individual lives. ITA 111(1.1) adds a condition consistent with the streaming concept that only allows net capital losses to be deducted to the extent that there is a positive ITA 3(b) amount for the year to which the net capital is applied and deducted.

> **EXAMPLE 2**   Continuing with our example, assume that in 2020 your net income and taxable income were both $72,000. The ITA 3(b)(i) amount was $5,000 of taxable capital gains and the ITA 3(b)(ii) was nil as there were no allowable capital losses. In other words, the "net taxable capital gains" for 2020 (the ITA 3(b)) amount was $5,000. You want to apply the 2021 net capital loss to the 2020 year to the extent possible.

ANALYSIS 2   The 2021 net capital loss can be carried back three years and forward until the year of death. However, it is only deductible to the extent of the ITA 3(b) amount for the year to which it is applied (ITA 111(1.1)). Since the ITA 3(b) amount for 2020 is only $5,000, the net capital loss that can be deducted is restricted to that amount. The result would be as follows:

Net income for 2020	$ 72,000
Less:	
ITA 111(1)(b)	
2021 net capital loss	5,000
Taxable income for 2020	$68,000

11-21.   Finally, there is a tracking and ordering rule for loss carry overs found in ITA 111(3) that reduces each of the five loss categories shown in Figure 11-2 by the amount deducted in other years. As a result, the 2021 net capital loss balance would be $13,000 [$18,000 - $5,000].

11-22.   The above examples demonstrate the interaction between net income and taxable income, the importance of the ITA 3 calculation, and the basic loss concept that begins with a current-year loss that potentially moves into a loss carry over category if there is insufficient income to apply against the current-year loss. In terms of transaction-based losses, it is important to remember that the transaction-based loss that finds its way into the ITA 3 calculation is the loss that is allowed by the provisions of the ITA. If, for example, a loss on the sale of investments is a superficial loss, then part or all of the loss may be disallowed.

Transaction-Based Losses—Exceptions

11-23.   There are three exceptions to the application of ITA 3(b) to transaction-based losses:

Listed Personal Property (LPP) Losses   In Chapter 8 we discussed both personal-use property and listed personal property. When capital gains from LPP exceed capital losses from LPP in the same year, the difference is generally referred to as a "net LPP gain." The net LPP gain is separately added to ITA 3(b)(i). However, when capital losses from LPP exceed capital gains from LPP the difference is generally referred to as a "net LPP loss," which is a loss carry over with some unusual features. While net LPP losses are streamed (meaning they can only be applied to the extent of capital gains from LPP), the loss carry over does not affect taxable income but instead the loss is self-contained within net income, specifically ITA 3(b). You may have noticed that net LPP losses are not mentioned in Figure 11-2. If we assumed that all of the capital gains and capital losses in our examples starting at Paragraph 11-17 were from LPP, the results would be the same except that 2020 net income (after applying the 2021 LPP loss carry over) would be $68,000 with no taxable income deduction (see Paragraph 11-20). LPP losses can be carried back three years and forward seven years.

Adventure or Concern in the Nature of Trade (Adventure)   In Chapter 6 we briefly discussed adventures, which we described as single transactions in which an individual acts in a manner similar to that of a business person intent on making a profit. A common example would be an individual purchasing real estate one day and selling it the next day at a gain. On occasion a loss is realized. When the activity is considered an adventure it is treated as a business. The result is that instead of a capital loss there would be a business loss. In other words, the loss is not part of ITA 3(b), which we have described as transaction-based losses, but instead is considered a source-based loss and factored into net income at ITA 3(d), which will be discussed in the next section of this chapter.

Allowable Business Investment Loss (ABIL)   An ABIL is an allowable capital loss that receives special treatment. An ABIL occurs when those who have invested in certain private corporations by either acquiring shares or by loaning money have realized a loss on the disposition of the shares or as a result of an inability to fully collect amounts owed to them. As we have seen, allowable capital losses are generally streamed, meaning they can only be deducted to the extent there are taxable capital gains. ABILs, however, are not subjected to the same streaming and can be deducted against any type of income. ITA 3 achieves this result by allowing ABILs to be deducted under ITA 3(d) instead of ITA 3(b)(ii). In Figure 1-5 you should see the addition of ABILs at ITA 3(d).

Source-Based Losses

11-24.   In Volume 1 of this text we extensively discussed the source concept of income, noting there are three main sources of income: employment (Chapter 3), business (Chapter 6), and property (Chapter 7). Source-based losses are differentiated from transaction-based losses by the fact that a source has a continuity with ongoing effort, resulting in numerous transactions that together determine the annual income or loss. Current-year source-based losses (including ABILs) are factored into net income through ITA 3(d). The ability to reduce net income through ITA 3(d) is advantageous in that there is no streaming required, meaning that source-based losses can be deducted against all sources of income.

11-25.   We can illustrate the application of current-year source losses with the following example:

EXAMPLE 3   In 2021 you had employment income of $53,000, interest income of $1,000, and taxable capital gains of $7,000. In addition, you made an RRSP contribution that entitled you to a deduction of $2,400. You also carried on a business as a sole proprietor in which you reported a business loss of $70,000.

ANALYSIS 3   Net income for 2021 would be determined as follows:

ITA 3(a) Employment income + interest	$54,000
ITA 3(b) Net taxable capital gains	7,000
ITA 3(c) [(ITA 3(a) + 3(b)) less RRSP deduction of $2,400	$58,600
ITA 3(d) Business loss	(70,000)
2021 Net income	Nil

The first thing to notice is that the business loss is applied against all types of income without restriction. You will also notice that the full amount of the business loss is included at ITA 3(d), and finally that net income is either positive or nil. Once again, negatives are not recognized. The same results would have occurred had the business loss been an employment loss, a property loss, or an ABIL alone or in any combination.

11-26.   Using Figure 11-2, the loss calculation begins with the 2021 business loss. The business loss was deducted at ITA 3(d) and was applied to the extent of all relevant income ($58,600), which can be referred to (for now) as the "ITA 3(c) amount." In this case there was insufficient income to absorb all of the business loss, so a portion of unused losses leads to the carry over categories. If the business loss was from farming or fishing, the loss carry over category would be called a "farm loss" as a result of ITA 111(8). If the business is anything other than a farming or fishing business, the loss carry over category is called a "non-capital loss."

11-27.   ITA 111(8) also defines a non-capital loss as a formula similar in some respects to net capital losses. In this instance the formula is somewhat more complicated for reasons we will explain later in this chapter. The main part of the formula is straightforward, however, and is described as "E – F" where the E component is the ITA 3(d) current-year losses and the F component is the ITA 3(c) amount. Applying this part of the formula results in the following non-capital loss for 2021:

Business loss $70,000 (ITA 3(d)) – ITA 3(c) amount of $58,600 = $11,400

11-28.   The 2021 non-capital loss is deductible in any of the three preceding years (2018, 2019, and 2020) and in the next 20 years (2022 to 2041) as long as the individual lives.

EXAMPLE 4   Continuing with Example 3, assume that in 2020 your net income and taxable income were both $72,000. You want to apply the 2021 non-capital loss of $11,400 back to the 2020 year to the extent possible.

ANALYSIS 4   The 2021 non-capital loss can be carried back to 2020 as it is within the carry back period. In addition, it is fully deductible against all types of income. Since there is sufficient net income, the full non-capital loss can be applied as follows:

Net income for 2020	$ 72,000	
Less:		
ITA 111(1)(a)		
2021 Non-capital loss	11,400	
Taxable income for 2020	$60,600	

As was the case with the net capital loss in Example 2, ITA 111(3) tracks the remaining 2021 non-capital loss balance, which would be nil after the application to 2020.

11-29.   Only farm losses (not restricted farm losses) and non-capital losses can be deducted against any type of income. The four remaining loss categories are streamed as follows:

- Net capital losses can only be applied against net taxable capital gains (the ITA 3(b) amount).

- Net listed personal property losses (see Chapter 8) can only be applied against listed personal property gains.

- Restricted farm losses (see Chapter 6) can only be applied against income from any farming business.

- Limited partnership losses are only deductible against income from the same partnership.

Exercise 11-1

Subject: Listed Personal Property Losses

During 2020, Mr. Ronald Smothers was unemployed and had no income of any kind. In order to survive, he sold a painting on December 1, 2020, for $89,000. This painting had been gifted to Mr. Smothers by his mother at a time when the FMV was $100,000. During 2021, Mr. Smothers finds a job and has employment income of $62,000. In June of 2021 he sells a second painting for $5,000. He had purchased this painting several years earlier for $1,000. Determine Mr. Smothers' minimum net income and taxable income for 2021. Indicate the amount and type of any losses available for carry forward at the end of the year. Assume the December 1, 2020, sale had been of publicly traded shares instead of a painting. How would this change your solution?

Solutions to Exercises are available in the Study Guide.

Loss Carry Overs and Tax Credits

11-30.   In Chapter 4 we discussed the various types of non-refundable tax credits that are available each year to individual taxpayers. The basic personal tax credit for 2021 is set at $13,808 for an individual with net income that is not greater than $151,978 and reduced to $12,421 for an individual with net income of $216,511 or greater. This means that taxable income equal to the maximum basic personal credit amount will be free of federal income tax since income tax of 15% of $13,808 is offset by the tax credit of the same amount.

11-31.   In terms of applying losses it therefore becomes important to ensure that loss applications leave sufficient income to offset the tax credits. It is therefore not advisable to use loss carry overs to reduce taxable income to nil in a loss application year.

> **EXAMPLE**   In 2020, Jan Teason had employment income of $25,000 and a rental loss of $55,000. She had no reported income in the three preceding years. In 2021, she has no employment income and rental income of $25,000. Ms. Teason's only 2020 tax credit is the basic personal credit of $13,808.

> **ANALYSIS**   In 2020, Ms. Teason's net income is nil. In 2020 she will have a non-capital loss of $30,000 [$55,000 ITA 3(d) - $25,000 ITA 3(c)]. Note that the ITA requires that the full amount of the 2020 current-year rental loss of $55,000 be included in ITA 3(d). She did not have the option of including a lesser amount in order to use her basic personal tax credit for that year. Her net income and taxable income for 2021 are both initially $25,000.

> If she wished to do so, Ms. Teason could reduce her 2021 taxable income to nil by applying $25,000 of her $30,000 2020 non-capital loss. However, if she limits her carry forward deduction to $11,192 ($25,000 - $13,808), her taxable income will be reduced to $13,808. The gross tax payable on this would be $2,071 [(15%)($13,808)], an amount that would be completely offset by her basic personal credit of the same amount. This approach leaves an unused carry forward balance of $16,192 ($30,000 - $13,808). If filing electronically, most tax software would automatically advise the tax filer that a lesser amount should be claimed because of the existence of tax credits.

Summary—Interaction between ITA 3 and Loss Carry Overs

11-32.   The following example summarizes the importance of the interaction between ITA 3 and loss carry overs.

> **EXAMPLE**   In 2021 James had employment income of $37,000, taxable eligible dividends of $6,900 [($5,000 dividends received + gross up of 38%), or $1,900]. James also had taxable capital gains of $3,800 and allowable capital losses of $9,000, none of which are ABILs. None of the capital gains or capital losses are from listed personal property. James also had a rental loss of $17,000 and a business loss of $42,000. Finally, James deducted $2,300 of moving expenses.

> **ANALYSIS**   Net income for 2021 would be determined as follows:

ITA 3(a) Employment income + taxable dividends	$43,900
ITA 3(b)(i) Taxable capital gains $ 3,800	
ITA 3(b)(ii) Allowable capital losses $9,000	Nil
ITA 3(a) + 3(b)	$43,900
Subdivision e moving expenses	(2,300)
ITA 3(c)	$41,600
ITA 3(d) Business loss + rental loss	(59,000)
2021 Net income	Nil

We can draw a few observations from this example. First, ITA 3(d) includes the full amount of current-year losses. The second is that no negative numbers are allowed. A third observation is that determining the 2021 net capital loss and non-capital loss becomes a simple matter in this case. The 2021 net capital loss is equal to the difference between the ITA 3(b)(ii) amount of $9,000 and the ITA 3(b)(i) amount of $3,800, resulting in $5,200. In addition, the 2021 non-capital loss is similarly straightforward when working with the details of ITA 3. The non-capital loss equals the ITA 3(d) amount of $59,000 minus the ITA 3(c) amount of $41,600, resulting in $17,400. This example illustrates why the details of the ITA 3 calculation are so important.

Types of Loss Carry Overs

11-33.   In Figure 11-2 we described the process of how current-year losses impact net income and how any unused current-year losses become loss carry overs that can then be applied in other years. Figure 11-3 summarizes the six types of loss carry overs together with ITA provisions that authorize a deduction, the carry over period (the first number is the years the loss can be carried back to and the second the years the loss can be carried forward) and whether the losses are streamed or can be applied against any type of income.

Figure 11-3 Loss Carry Overs			
Type of Loss	**ITA**	**Carry Over Period (Years)**	**Streamed***
Non-capital	111(1)(a)	3 and 20	No
Net capital	111(1)(b) 111(1.1)	3 and indefinite	Yes
Farm	111(1)(d)	3 and 20	No
Restricted farm	111(1)(c)	3 and 20	Yes
Limited partnership	111(1)(e)	0 and indefinite	Yes
Listed personal property	41(2)	3 and 7	Yes

*Streamed means the loss can only be deducted against certain types of income.

Non-Capital Losses—ITA 111(8)

11-34.   As previously mentioned, there are two general types of loss categories: transaction based and source based. Technically only net capital losses and net listed personal property losses are transaction-based losses and both types are streamed. Source-based losses can be further subdivided into those loss categories that are streamed and those that are not. The only loss categories that are not streamed and that are both source based are non-capital losses and farm losses. In our examples, exercises, and problems we will focus on the more common loss category, which is the non-capital loss. Non-capital losses begin with the ITA 3(d) amounts of the net income calculation that includes losses from employment, business, and property as well as ABILs.

11-35.   In Paragraph 11-27 we provided an introduction to the non-capital loss formula-based definition. We will now turn our attention to a more complete but somewhat simplified version:

ITA 111(8)   The non-capital loss of a taxpayer for a taxation year means the amount determined by the formula:

$$A - D, \text{ where}$$

A   is the amount determined by the formula:

$$E - F, \text{ where}$$

E   is the total of all amounts that make up the taxpayer's loss for the year from an office, employment, business, or property, the taxpayer's ABIL for the year, plus certain taxable income deductions such as net capital losses (ITA 111(1)(b)) deducted in the year, capital gains deduction (ITA 110.6) claimed in the year, and deductions such as the stock option deduction (ITA 110(1)(d)) and deduction for tax-free amounts (ITA 110(1)(f)), both of which were briefly discussed at Paragraph 11-7

F   is the ITA 3(c) amount

D   is the taxpayer's farm loss for the year (amount included in E)

11-36.   We had mentioned earlier that there are two source-based losses that are not subject to streaming. In terms of a business loss there are farm and fishing losses and all other types of business losses. You will note that the "E" component technically requires including all business losses. Therefore, if the only current-year loss is a loss from a farming or fishing business you would first determine the non-capital loss then subtract the farm loss at "D" with the result that the non-capital loss would be nil and there would be a farm loss category equal to the current-year farm loss that could not be completely used because there was insufficient income. In the unlikely event that there is both a farm loss and a non-farm loss, the ITA effectively applies the ITA 3(c) amount against the non-farm business loss first. For example, if the ITA 3(c) amount was $10,000 in 2021 and there was a farm business loss of $20,000 and a non-farm business loss of $20,000, the 2021 farm loss would be $20,000 and the 2021 non-capital loss would be $10,000.

11-37.   In Paragraph 11-32 we provided a basic example that determined that the non-capital loss was the difference between the ITA 3(d) and ITA 3(c) amounts; however, the "E" component includes amounts other than the ITA 3(d) amount. The amounts that are added represent taxable income deductions that offset amounts already included in the ITA 3(c) amount. The following example will help clarify the reasoning for these adjustments.

EXAMPLE   In 2021 you received workers' compensation of $35,000 and you had a rental loss of $50,000. There were no taxable capital gains or allowable capital losses and no Subdivision e deductions (e.g., RRSP, child care, moving).

ANALYSIS   Net income for 2021 would be determined as follows:

ITA 3(a) Workers' compensation ITA 56(1)(v)	$35,000
ITA 3(b)(i) Taxable capital gains $Nil	
ITA 3(b)(ii) Allowable capital losses $Nil	Nil
ITA 3(a) + 3(b)	$35,000
Subdivision e expenses	Nil
ITA 3(c)	$35,000
ITA 3(d) Rental loss	(50,000)
2021 Net income	Nil

If we subtract the ITA 3(d) rental loss of $50,000 from the ITA 3(c) amount of $35,000 it appears that the 2021 non-capital loss would be $15,000. This result would seem unfair, since the workers' compensation amount is not actually subject to income tax because of the taxable income deduction of ITA 110(1)(f). If there was no rental loss, the net income for 2021 would have been $35,000 and the taxable income nil. In recognition of the fact that the $35,000 included in the ITA 3(c) amount is not taxable, the non-capital loss definition is adjusted to neutralize its impact. As a result, the 2021 non-capital loss would be determined as follows:

"E" component rental loss	$50,000	
Plus ITA 110(1)(f) deduction	35,000	$85,000
Less:		
"F" component ITA 3(c) amount		$35,000
2021 non-capital loss		$50,000

11-38.   All of the adjustments serve the same purpose. ITA 110(1)(d) and (d.1) allow 50% of an employee stock option deduction, meaning that only half of the stock option finds its way to taxable income. If a deduction is claimed for the capital gains deduction or as a net capital loss, both offset net taxable capital gains included in ITA 3(b) and therefore the ITA 3(c) amount. What this means is that non-capital losses are only reduced by the part of the ITA 3(c) amount that makes it through to taxable income and is therefore actually subject to income tax.

Exercise 11-2

Subject: Non-Capital Losses

During 2021, Janice McMann has employment income of $35,000 and net taxable capital gains of $13,000. In addition, she has a non-farm business loss of $58,000 and an unrestricted farm business loss of $2,200. Determine her 2021 non-capital loss.

Solutions to Exercises are available in the Study Guide.

Net Capital Losses—ITA 111(8)

General Rules—Summary

11-39.   At Paragraph 11-19 we looked at the most important part of the basic formula of the ITA 111(8) net capital loss definition that is described as "A" (the ITA 3(b)(ii) amount) less "B" (the ITA 3(b)(i) amount). While there are a few other components to the formula, they are not common and are beyond the scope of an introductory course on federal income tax.

11-40.   We had also discussed that a net capital loss for a year can be carried back three years and forward to the year an individual dies. In addition, net capital losses are streamed and can only be applied to the extent there are net taxable capital gains for the year (a positive ITA 3(b) amount). ITA 111(1.1) establishes the streaming concept.

Conversion of a Net Capital Loss to a Non-Capital Loss

11-41.   In our discussion of non-capital losses we noted that component "E" added certain taxable income deductions to neutralize amounts included as part of the ITA 3(c) amount. One of those taxable income deductions was to adjust for any net capital losses deducted in the year since they would offset any ITA 3(b) amount. At Paragraph 11-37 we illustrated the process using workers' compensation payments. To explain this next topic we have modified the example as follows:

ITA 3(a)	$ Nil
ITA 3(b)(i) Taxable capital gains $35,000	
ITA 3(b)(ii) Allowable capital losses $Nil	35,000
ITA 3(a) + 3(b)	$35,000
Subdivision e expenses	Nil
ITA 3(c)	$35,000
ITA 3(d) Rental loss	(50,000)
2021 Net income	Nil

We will further assume that the individual has a 2019 net capital loss balance of $35,000.

11-42.   Taxable income deductions, including loss carry overs, are optional. In our example, at first glance, it appears that there would be no benefit to applying the 2019 net capital loss against 2021 net income since it is already nil. If no such claim is made then the 2019 net capital loss balance would remain available to be deducted in other years. In addition, the 2021 non-capital loss would be $15,000 [ITA 3(d) amount of $50,000 (with no other adjustments) minus the ITA 3(c) amount of $35,000]. As a result, the individual would have $50,000 of loss carry overs, comprising a $35,000 net capital loss from 2019 and a $15,000 non-capital loss from 2021.

11-43.   Can we improve on that result? The answer is yes, by claiming the 2019 net capital loss to the extent possible, which in this case is up to the 2021 ITA 3(b) amount of $35,000. If we claim the net capital loss, 2021 net income and taxable income remain unchanged at nil but the loss carry over results change.

11-44.   By applying the 2019 net capital loss in 2021, the net capital loss balance would be nil. The 2021 non-capital balance now changes to $50,000 and is calculated as follows:

"E" component rental loss	$50,000	
plus ITA 111(1)(b) deduction	35,000	$85,000
Less:		
"F" component ITA 3(c) amount		$35,000
2021 Non-capital loss		$50,000

The result is that the individual still has $50,000 of loss carry overs but they are all non-capital losses. This type of strategy is important for many reasons, such as the fact that net capital losses are streamed to net taxable capital gains whereas non-capital losses are fully deductible against any type of income. The consensus is that if you have net capital losses they should be used when there is an ITA 3(b) amount. The exception is where some or all of the net taxable capital gains are eligible for the capital gains deduction, which we will discuss in this chapter. As a rule of thumb, any loss carry overs that are streamed should be claimed before losses that are not streamed.

11-45.   One final point to keep in mind with this tax planning strategy is that it is not all that common. It only works where there are both net taxable capital gains (a positive ITA 3(b) amount), current-year losses (an ITA 3)(d) amount), and the existence of net capital losses all in the same year.

Exercise 11-3

Subject: Net Capital Loss Carry Overs

During 2020, Ms. Laura Macky had an allowable capital loss of $15,000 and as a result has a 2020 net capital loss of the same amount of $15,000. Prior to 2021, she had no taxable capital gains and, as a consequence, she has not been able to deduct this 2020 net capital loss. In 2021, her income consists of a taxable capital gain of $40,000 and a rental loss of $30,000. She does not anticipate any future capital gains. Determine Ms. Macky's minimum 2021 net income and minimum 2021 taxable income, as well as the amount and type of any loss carry overs at the end of the year if (1) she chooses to claim enough of her 2020 net capital loss to reduce 2021 taxable income to nil and (2) she deducts the maximum amount of her 2020 net capital loss. Ignore the effects of her tax credits.

Solutions to Exercises are available in the Study Guide.

Net Capital Losses at Death—ITA 111(2)

11-46.   One of the difficulties with net capital losses is that they are streamed, limiting their deduction to the extent there are net taxable capital gains in a particular year. Even with a carry forward period that extends to the end of one's lifetime there remains the distinct possibility that an individual could die with substantial net capital loss balances. While this may be mitigated to some extent by deemed dispositions on death that result in taxable capital gains and elective options to trigger capital gains, these deemed dispositions may also add to the problem if such disposition results in additional capital losses.

11-47.   In recognition of this difficulty ITA 111(2) provides some potential relief by allowing net capital losses that occur in the year of death and in the immediately preceding year to be claimed against other income. The net capital losses must first be applied to the maximum extent possible against net taxable capital gains for both years. Remaining amounts are further reduced by any capital gains deductions claimed by the individual during his or her lifetime. Any remaining balance can then be applied against any other type of income.

11-48.   An example will illustrate these provisions.

EXAMPLE   Ms. Vincent dies in December 2021. She has a 2018 net capital loss balance of $35,300. Her 2021 final income tax return shows net income of $40,000, which includes a taxable capital gain of $4,500. The only tax credit available to her for 2021 is the basic personal amount (BPA) credit of $13,808. Ms. Vincent has never claimed the capital gains deduction.

ANALYSIS   If Ms. Vincent had not died in 2021, her 2018 net capital loss could have been deducted to the extent of the net taxable capital gains of $4,500. This would result in taxable income of $35,500 ($40,000 - $4,500).

However, the net capital loss limitation does not apply in the year of death as a result of ITA 111(2), which would allow the remaining portion of her 2018 net capital loss of $30,800 [$35,300 - $4,500] to be applied against any other type of income. As explained in Paragraph 11-30, she should limit her net capital loss deduction to an amount that would reduce her taxable income to the BPA. For 2021, this amount would be $13,808, requiring that she use $21,692 ($35,500 - $13,808) of her remaining net capital loss balance against other income.

This would leave a net capital loss balance of $9,108 ($35,300 - $4,500 - $21,692), which could be carried back and applied against any type of income for the 2020 taxation year.

11-49.   If the property of an individual has been transferred to an estate to be administered by executors with subsequent distributions to beneficiaries additional complications arise. The estate is considered a taxpayer separate from the deceased individual. If the estate (referred to as a graduated rate estate or GRE) disposes of property and has capital losses that exceed its capital gains in its first year it may be unable to use the excess as a net capital loss in its short lifespan if no capital gains are realized in a subsequent year. However, relief is provided by ITA 164(6), which effectively allows any portion of the excess capital losses to be considered capital losses of the deceased in the final return. Note, however, that a timely election must be filed in a prescribed manner by the legal representative of the estate.

Exercise 11-4

Subject: Net Capital Losses at Death

Mr. Derek Barnes dies during 2021. He has a 2017 net capital loss balance of $20,000 at the time of his death. His final return reports net income of $23,800, which includes a taxable capital gain of $9,200. The only tax credit on his final return is his basic personal tax credit of $13,808. Describe the optimal income tax treatment of Derek's 2017 net capital loss balance.

Solutions to Exercises are available in the Study Guide.

Allowable Business Investment Losses (ABIL) — ITA 39(1)(c)

11-50.   In terms of terminology we saw that 50% of a capital loss is an allowable capital loss. A business investment loss, or BIL, is a special type of capital loss, and an ABIL is a special type of allowable capital loss. We will use the two acronyms (BIL and ABIL) to discuss these special rules.

11-51.   At Paragraph 11-23, we briefly described an ABIL as a special type of allowable capital loss that is not subject to streaming and, in the calculation of net income, is deducted at ITA 3(d) and not ITA 3(b). This means that if there is insufficient income to offset the ABIL it becomes a non-capital loss for that year. It is clearly preferable to have an ABIL rather than a regular allowable capital loss.

11-52.   ABILs were added to the ITA for the purpose of encouraging investment in small business corporations (SBCs) by providing favourable income tax treatment should investors suffer a loss. An ABIL occurs when an individual taxpayer owns either shares or debt of an SBC that is disposed of at a loss.

11-53.   An SBC is defined in ITA 248(1) as a Canadian controlled private corporation (CCPC) of which "all or substantially all" of the fair market value (FMV) of its assets are used principally in an active business carried on "primarily" in Canada. The expression "all or substantially all" is considered by the CRA to have been met where the use is at least 90%, and the word "primarily" is considered to have been met where use is more than 50%.

11-54.   There are many potential issues concerning the definition of an SBC, but in general terms it is a private corporation (not publicly listed) where resident Canadians own the majority of the voting shares. In summary, the definition requires meeting three tests: qualifying as a CCPC, meeting the 90% asset test, and meeting the 50% "active business in Canada" test. The test that often receives the most attention is the 90% asset test. If a CCPC owns investments or excess cash reserves not required for its business, this can jeopardize its standing as an SBC, which requires ongoing monitoring to ensure that the 90% thresholds are respected. Failure to meet these tests means that investors suffering a loss will have regular capital losses and not BILs.

11-55.   Assets that qualify for the 90% test include shares or debt (e.g., loans receivable) of another corporation that would meet the SBC definition on its own as long as the CCPC owns more than 10% of its voting shares, and the shares that it owns represent more than 10% of the FMV of all of that corporation's outstanding shares. Assume, for example, that a private corporation meets all three tests mentioned in Paragraph 11-54 to qualify as an SBC. All of its shares are owned by its parent company, which is also a CCPC. The only assets of the parent company are the shares of the subsidiary. The parent company would also be considered an SBC since 90% or more of its assets are shares of another company that qualifies as an SBC and the parent company owns more than 10% of the subsidiary's shares in terms of voting shares and FMV.

11-56.   ITA 39(1)(c), however, only treats a capital loss as an ABIL in one of two situations. The first requires that the shares or debt be disposed of to an arm's-length person. A "related person" is not an arm's-length person. The result is that an arm's-length person is generally a person who is not a family member or a corporation in which the individual does not have a controlling interest alone or together with family members. A capital loss realized in the first situation will be a BIL. It is important to be aware that the relationship between an individual and a corporation can be non-arm's length when the individual acquires shares or loans funds to an SBC. However, recognizing a capital loss as a BIL requires that the relationship between the individual selling the shares or debt and the buyer be arm's length.

11-57.   The second situation occurs when an SBC is in financial difficulty, including insolvency or bankruptcy and, as a result, a debt owing is considered uncollectible or a share owned has lost all of its value. This situation is somewhat more problematic since shares or debt are not actually considered to have been disposed of until the corporation is dissolved or a settlement has been reached as to some form of compensation, both of which can take years after the loss in value has occurred. ITA 50(1) resolves this situation with a deemed disposition rule that allows investors to elect to have disposed of the shares or debt at the end of the year for nil proceeds of disposition and to have reacquired the shares or debt for a cost of nil. This then allows the investor to recognize the loss immediately rather than wait until an actual disposition takes place. If the investor subsequently recovers any additional amounts they would be treated as capital gains.

Special Treatment

11-58.   As mentioned, allowable capital losses can only be deducted against taxable capital gains. However, ABILs are given special treatment in that the individual is permitted to deduct these amounts from any type of income. The following example will illustrate the different treatment.

> **EXAMPLE**   An individual with employment income of $50,000 has an ABIL of $10,500 [(1/2)($21,000)].

> **ANALYSIS**   This individual would be able to deduct the $10,500 ABIL against the employment income, resulting in net income of $39,500. If this had been an ordinary allowable capital loss, the individual's net income would be $50,000 and the unapplied allowable capital loss would become a net capital loss of $10,500 for the year, which would be available for carry over to other years.

Effect of the ITA 110.6 Capital Gains Deduction—ITA 39(9)

11-59.   The tax policy of capital gains and capital losses generally requires that they should be netted during one's lifetime. This means that capital losses should only be permitted to the extent there are capital gains. The capital gains deduction (which will be discussed next in this chapter), however, alters the economics of that tax policy. This can be explained with the following example.

Assume that in 2021 an individual realized a taxable capital gain of $100. That taxable capital gain is eligible for the capital gains deduction. The result is that the $100 taxable capital gain is added to net income but a taxable income deduction of the same amount is allowed through ITA 110.6. As a result, that gain would not be subject to income tax. If the individual also had an ABIL of $100 then there would appear to be a reduction in both net income and taxable income. In effect the result would be a $100 addition for the taxable capital gain and $200 worth of deductions (the ABIL of $100 + the $100 capital gains deduction).

The government believed that this result was unacceptable and contrary to the tax policy that capital gains and capital losses should be netted during one's lifetime. Two main rules were added to the ITA to eliminate this result. The first reduces the potential capital gains deduction that can be claimed in a year by the amount of any ABIL realized in the same year. In our example this would mean that there would be no capital gains deduction of $100 in 2021 as a result. Economically this leaves the $100 taxable capital gain and the $100 ABIL that offset it to nil. This is described in greater detail in this chapter's coverage of the capital gains deduction.

The second can be explained with a modification of our example. Assume that in 2020 an individual had a taxable capital gain of $100 that was eligible for the capital gains deduction. The net result is nil because the taxable capital gain is completely offset by the capital gains deduction. In 2021 the individual has an allowable capital loss of $100 that meets the conditions necessary to qualify as an ABIL. If the ITA allows ABIL treatment, we again have an issue because the two-year result is that there is a $100 taxable capital gain and $200 of deductions (the ABIL of $100 and the $100 capital gains deduction). The ITA resolves this issue with the addition of ITA 39(9), which requires that the ABIL be reduced on a dollar-for-dollar basis by any capital gains deduction claimed in previous years. The result is that the 2021 $100 allowable capital loss that would have been considered an ABIL is reduced by the $100 capital gains deduction claimed in 2020. This means that no part of the $100 allowable capital loss qualifies as an ABIL but remains an ordinary allowable capital loss. As an ordinary capital loss it is added to the ITA 3(b)(ii) amount where, in our example, it becomes a 2021 net capital loss of $100 and can only be deducted in a year in which there are net taxable capital gains (a positive ITA 3(b) amount).

> **EXAMPLE**   Mr. Mercer had a taxable capital gain in 2015 of $8,000 and claimed a capital gains deduction for the same amount under ITA 110.6. In July 2021, Mr. Mercer realizes a $60,000 capital loss on the arm's-length sale of shares of an SBC. Mr. Mercer has no capital gains or capital losses in 2021 and no net capital losses from other years.

> **ANALYSIS**   If Mr. Mercer had not previously claimed a capital gains deduction, he would have an ABIL of $30,000 [(1/2)($60,000)] in 2021. However, the previous use of the capital gains deduction results in the following BIL:

Actual capital loss	$60,000
ITA 39(9) reduction for previous capital gains deduction	(16,000)
BIL	$44,000
Inclusion rate	1/2
Allowable business investment loss (ABIL)	$22,000

11-60.   ITA 39(1)(c) determines that only $44,000 of the $60,000 capital loss is a BIL. The remaining $16,000 retains its character as a regular capital loss. In calculating net income for the 2021 year, $22,000 would be an ABIL deducted at ITA 3(d) while $8,000 would be an ordinary allowable capital loss that would be deductible at ITA 3(b)(ii), as previously discussed. ITA 39(9) tracks the history of the capital gains deduction and reduces any potential BIL. In our example, since all of the previous capital gains deductions have been applied to reduce a BIL, there will be no further reductions of BILs in subsequent years unless there are further capital gains deduction claims.

Exercise 11-5

Subject: Business Investment Losses

During 2020, Mr. Lawrence Latvik used his capital gains deduction to offset a taxable capital gain of $13,000 [(1/2)($26,000)]. During 2021, he has capital gains on publicly traded shares of $18,000 and a capital loss of $50,000 on the disposition of shares of an SBC. His employment income for 2021 is over $200,000. Determine the amount of the ABIL in 2021, as well as the amount and type of any losses available for carry over at the end of the year.

Solutions to Exercises are available in the Study Guide.

We suggest you complete SSP 11-1 at this point.

Farm Losses

Regular Farm Losses

11-61.   For full-time farmers, losses from carrying on a farming business are not restricted, meaning they are deductible against any type of income. Restricted farm losses, however, are streamed and allowed to be deducted only against farming business income. Both types of farm losses can be carried back three years and forward 20 years.

Restricted Farm Losses

11-62.   As noted in Chapter 6, if farming activity is not undertaken in the pursuit of profit none of the losses would be deductible since there is no source of income. This type of farming activity is commonly referred to as a hobby farm. If the farming activity meets the criteria necessary to establish a source of income, farming losses are subject to restrictions imposed by ITA 31. More specifically, farm losses are restricted if:

> ... a farmer's chief source of income for a taxation year is neither farming nor a combination of farming and some other source of income that **is a subordinate source of income** for the taxpayer ...

11-63.   The reference to a subordinate source of income is meant to recognize that full-time farmers may at times be required to supplement their income by taking employment, particularly where weather, market, or other conditions have occurred that have negatively impacted the profits of the farming business. Assume, for example, that a full-time farmer experiences losses due to adverse weather conditions. The farmer accepts employment at a local hardware store to be able to pay the bills. While the farming activity would arguably not be considered to be the chief source of income given the employment, the combination of the two activities would ensure that the individual remained a full-time farmer and that any farm losses would not be restricted.

11-64.   In effect, if farming is only a secondary source of income, farm losses will be restricted. The restriction limits losses that can be deducted against other sources of income to the first $2,500 of such losses, plus one-half of the next $30,000, for a maximum deduction of $17,500 [$2,500 + (1/2) ($30,000)]. This maximum is reached when farm losses are $32,500 or more. In effect, ITA 31 divides the farm loss into a restricted and unrestricted portion. The unrestricted portion is treated in the same manner as a farm loss to a full-time farmer and the restricted part is streamed and therefore only deductible in the carry over period to the extent there is farming income in a carry over year.

> **EXAMPLE**   In 2021 an individual has employment income of $80,000 and a farm loss of $60,000. The farming business is a secondary source of income to the employment. In 2022 the individual has employment income of $84,000 and farming income of $7,000.

> **ANALYSIS**   In 2021 the farm loss would be subject to ITA 31, which divides the farm loss between an unrestricted portion of $17,500 (which is the maximum because the farm loss exceeds $32,500) and a restricted farm loss of the remaining $42,500 ($60,000 - $17,500 ITA 31(1.1)]. The 2021 net income would be $62,500 [ITA 3(a) $80,000 - ITA 3(d) $17,500]. In addition there would be a 2021 restricted farm loss of $42,500. In 2022 net income would be $91,000 [ITA 3(a) $84,000 + $7,000]. Taxable income in 2022 would be $84,000 [net income $91,000 - ITA 111(1)(c) $7,000]. There would be a restricted farm loss balance of $35,500 [$42,500 - $7,000].

11-65.   If land used in a farming business is disposed of before the taxpayer has an opportunity to fully usee restricted farm losses, a part of the undeducted losses can be used to increase the ACB of the farm land (ITA 53(1)(i)). This would have the effect of reducing any capital gains or increasing capital losses arising on a subsequent disposition of the farm land. This treatment is only possible to the extent that property taxes and interest payments on the land were included in any restricted farm loss.

Exercise 11-6

Subject: Farm Losses

Ms. Elena Bodkin has a full-time appointment as a professor at a Canadian university. In her free time, she is developing an organic vegetable farm. In 2020, the first year of operation, she had a farm loss of $36,000 and deducted the maximum allowable amount. In 2021, in addition to her employment income of $85,000, her farming operation showed a profit of $3,500. Determine Ms. Bodkin's minimum 2021 net income and taxable income, as well as the amount and type of any losses available for carry forward at the end of the year.

Solutions to Exercises are available in the Study Guide.

We suggest you complete SSP 11-2 at this point.

Capital Gains Deduction—ITA 110.6

Background

The Original Legislation

11-66.   The capital gains deduction was first introduced in 1985 and, in its original form, it allowed every individual resident in Canada to enjoy up to $100,000 in tax-free capital gains during the course of their lifetime. This privilege was available without regard to the type of capital property on which the gain accrued. The original legislation was modified in 1988, limiting the scope of the deduction to shares in qualified small business corporations (QSBC shares) and for qualified farm properties. Some further modifications were made to add qualified fishing properties (QFP for both farming and fishing properties).

Current and Future Limits

11-67.   As of 2021, the deduction limit for dispositions of QSBC shares is $892,218. This is an indexed figure that was established at $800,000 in 2014 and is indexed each year for inflation. The available deduction for QFP was increased to $1,000,000 for dispositions after April 20, 2015. The $1,000,000 limit will remain unchanged until the indexed limit for QSBC shares reaches $1,000,000. At that time the same indexed figure will apply to all types of qualified property. For 2021, the extra amount for QFP is $107,782 ($1,000,000 - $892,218).

11-68.   You should note that the limits are cumulative for all three types of qualified property. That is, you do not get $892,218 for QSBC shares and an additional $1,000,000 for QFP. Given that we have two different limits, there is a problem in applying a cumulative limit. The solution is that gains on all three types of qualified property are accumulated until they reach the indexed figure ($892,218 for 2021). To go beyond this to the $1,000,000 limit, only gains on dispositions of QFP are eligible, even if gains on these types of property are included in the first $892,218.

> **EXAMPLE**   In 2020, Mary Geary had a $300,000 gain on QSBC shares and a $500,000 gain on QFP. In October 2021, Mary had a $100,000 gain on QSBC shares and a $75,000 gain on QFP. Mary never used the capital gains deduction prior to 2020.

> **ANALYSIS**   In 2020, both the QSBC and QFP gains would qualify for the capital gains deduction as they are within the 2020 limit of $883,384. In 2021, only $92,218 of the gain on the QSBC shares would qualify for the capital gains deduction. The remaining $7,782 ($100,000 - $92,218) would not be eligible because it exceeds the indexed limit for QSBC shares. However, the $75,000 gain on the QFP would qualify, bringing the total claimed to $967,218 ($800,000 + $92,218 + $75,000).

Qualified Property—ITA 110.6(1)

Qualified Farm and Fishing Property (QFP)

11-69.   The ITA 110.6 capital gains deduction is available on a disposition of QSBC shares and QFP. We will focus our attention on QSBC shares as they are much more common than QFP dispositions. QFP can generally be described as follows:

> **Qualified Farm or Fishing Property**   Qualified farm property and qualified fishing property are defined in ITA 110.6(1). They include real property such as land and buildings, fishing boats, and class 14.1 property such as milk and egg quotas and fishing licences used in the course of carrying on a farming or fishing business in Canada by an individual, the individual's spouse, their children, or a corporation or partnership in which any of the individuals have an interest. In recognition that farming and fishing businesses can be carried on by corporations or partnerships, QFP also includes a share of a family farm or fishing corporation and an interest in a family farm or fishing partnership. Additional conditions are attached to interests in family farm or fishing corporations and partnerships. These include a requirement that throughout the 24-month period prior to the disposition that assets of the corporation or partnership are principally used in the business and at the time of the disposition 90% or more of the value of the assets are attributable to the farming or fishing business. These additional conditions are similar to those of QSBC shares and are covered in that section.

Qualified Small Business Corporation Shares (QSBC Shares)

11-70.   As noted in our discussion of ABILs in Paragraph 11-53, ITA 248(1) defines an SBC as a Canadian controlled private corporation (CCPC) of which all, or substantially all (90% or more), of the FMV of its assets are used in an active business carried on primarily (more than 50%) in

Canada. For the purposes of claiming the capital gains deduction for QSBC shares, SBC status is only required at the time at which the shares are disposed of (i.e., sold).

11-71.   One of the most troublesome aspects of SBC status is ensuring that the 90% FMV active business asset test is met. If the test is not met then transactions prior to the disposition are undertaken to "purify" the corporation by ensuring that the threshold is met. If, for example, a corporation has investments that account for 30% of the FMV of its assets, then steps can be taken to sell the investments and use the cash to pay off debt and make dividend distributions to shareholders before selling the shares. In addition, there are standard purification planning transactions that involve creating new companies and then using rollovers to remove the non-qualifying assets while minimizing income tax consequences. These type of transactions are discussed in the chapters on corporate income tax.

11-72.   Not all shares of SBCs qualify as QSBC shares. This is because SBC status is only one of the conditions necessary for the shares to qualify for the capital gains deduction. In addition, SBC status is modified for the purposes of the capital gains deduction by special valuation rules set out in ITA 110.6(15) that apply for the purposes of both the 50% and 90% FMV asset test by deeming certain assets such as intercompany shares and loans to be valued at nil and life insurance policies to be valued at the cash surrender value. Needless to say the capital gains deduction rules contain a significant amount of complexity that frequently requires the assistance of tax professionals. There are, however, two additional rules to be aware of in determining whether shares qualify for the capital gains deduction. In somewhat simplified terms, they are as follows:

- The shares must not be owned by anyone other than the individual or a related person for at least 24 months preceding the disposition. With few exceptions the shares must be owned for a continuous period of 24 months.

- Throughout this 24-month period, more than 50% of the FMV of the corporation's assets must be mainly used in an active business carried on primarily in Canada. Active business assets would include goodwill.

11-73.   Planning to meet the 90% asset value test on the day of the disposition of the shares is often relatively straightforward and this is frequently the focus of the CRA when they investigate such matters. It is much more difficult to address the two 24-month tests since they are a function of the passage of time.

Determining the Deductible Amount

General Rules

11-74.   The determination of the amount of the capital gains deduction that can be deducted in a year involves calculations that can be complex. In general terms, the available deduction is the least of the following three amounts:

- Capital gains deduction available
- Annual gains limit (AGL)
- Cumulative gains limit (CGL)

11-75.   These items will be explained in detail in the following material.

Capital Gains Deduction Available

11-76.   The "capital gains deduction available" is the indexed annual maximum less any amounts that have been claimed in previous years. As discussed and illustrated with an example in Paragraph 11-68, there are two limits:

- For QSBC shares, the 2021 limit is $446,109 [(1/2)($892,218)].

- For QFP the 2021 limit is $500,000 [(1/2)($1,000,000)].

11-77.   Capital gains deductions began to be available in 1985. At that time the capital gains inclusion rate was one-half, or 50%. The inclusion rate changed to two-thirds, or 66.7%, in 1988 and 1989, then increased to three-quarters, or 75%, from 1990 until partway through 2000. In 2000 the rates went from 75% to 66.7% and back to 50% where the rate has remained to this day. Since the capital gains deduction works with the actual taxable income deduction there are complications in determining the amount available where an individual has claimed the capital gains deduction in years with different inclusion rates.

> **EXAMPLE**   You claimed a capital gains deduction in 1998 of $75,000 (which is 75% of a capital gain of $100,000 for that year) then next claimed a capital gains deduction of $50,000 in 2020 (which is 50% of a capital gain of $100,000 using 2020 inclusion rates).

> **ANALYSIS**   In 2021 it would appear that the capital gains deduction available would be $321,109 [$446,109 - $75,000 from 1998 - $50,000 from 2020]. In fact, it is actually $346,109 because the ITA adjusts the 1998 claim to the 50% inclusion rate by multiplying $75,000 by two-thirds. The actual calculation in the ITA would be $346,109 [$446,109 - (2/3)($75,000) from 1998 - $50,000 from 2020]. A much simpler way of determining the available amount is to start with the full indexed 2021 amount of $892,218 then subtract the capital gains upon which the capital gains deduction was claimed of $200,000 [$100,000 capital gains for each of 1998 and 2020], which leaves a difference of $692,218. When the difference is multiplied by the 2021 inclusion rate of 50% the amount available becomes $346,109.

We avoid using different inclusion rates in our exercises and problems. However, from a practical perspective verifying the history of an individual's capital gains deduction claims can be important at times.

Annual Gains Limit (AGL)—ITA 110.6(1)

11-78.   The AGL is defined in ITA 110.6(1) as follows:

> **AGL** of an individual for a taxation year means the amount determined by the formula

$$A - B, \text{ where}$$

> **A** is equal to the lesser of:

> - net taxable capital gains for the current year on all capital property dispositions [ITA 3(b) amount]; and
> - a modified ITA 3(b) amount only including dispositions from QFP and QSBC shares.

> **B** is equal to the total of:

> - the amount, if any, by which net capital losses deducted for the year under ITA 111(1)(b) exceeds the excess that is the difference between the ITA 3(b) amount and the amount determined in part A of this formula; and
> - ABILs realized during the current year.

11-79.   The AGL formula contemplates the possibility of there being both a taxable capital gain that is not eligible for the capital gains deduction in the same year that there is a taxable capital gain that does qualify. In a year in which there is a taxable capital gain that qualifies for the capital gains deduction and no other taxable capital gain, the formula can be stated more simply as follows:

> **AGL** is equal to the taxable capital gains on QFP or QSBC shares, less:

> - Allowable capital losses realized
> - Net capital loss carry overs deducted
> - ABILs realized

11-80.   We will make use of this abbreviated formula when the only taxable capital gains during the year are those on QFP or QSBC shares.

11-81.   Additional noteworthy points include the following:

- ABILs reduce the AGL regardless of whether there is sufficient income to absorb them. Remember that any unused ABILs form part of a non-capital loss. Also keep in mind that an ABIL is only that part of an allowable capital loss that meets the conditions to qualify as an ABIL including a reduction for previous capital gains deductions, as discussed at Paragraph 11-59.

- The deduction of net capital losses is discretionary. This means that careful consideration is required in deciding whether to claim the capital gains deduction or a net capital loss. The effect of the AGL formula is to allow one of the two taxable income deductions but not both. The reason for this is the underlying tax policy that was discussed at Paragraph 11-59.

- While the choice between a capital gains deduction and a net capital loss does not generally change taxable income, there is a preference for using the capital gains deduction. There is no time limit on using the net capital loss carry forward and, more importantly, it can be used when any type of taxable capital gain is realized. In contrast, the capital gains deduction can only be used for taxable capital gains on QFP or QSBC shares.

Exercise 11-7

Subject: Annual Gains Limit

On January 1, 2021, your client, Miss Jana Slovena, has a 2018 net capital loss of $45,000. During 2021, Miss Slovena has the following:

- Taxable capital gains on sales of real estate in the amount of $114,000
- Allowable capital losses of $82,000, none of which are ABILs
- A taxable capital gain of $42,000 on the sale of QSBC shares
- An ABIL of $3,000 on sales of shares of an SBC that would not have qualified for the capital gains deduction had there been a taxable capital gain.

As she does not expect to have additional capital gains in the near future, Miss Slovena has asked you to deduct the maximum amount of the 2018 net capital loss during 2021. Determine her AGL for 2021 using this approach. What advice would you give Ms. Slovena regarding her 2018 net capital loss?

Solutions to Exercises are available in the Study Guide.

Cumulative Net Investment Loss (CNIL)—ITA 110.6(1)

11-82.   Many high-income individuals invest in products that offer tax advantages commonly referred to as tax shelters. Such products include limited partnerships, certain types of investments in resource properties, and in some situations real estate. These investments, while producing positive overall results for investors, also generate significant income tax savings. The government concluded that it was inequitable for individuals to simultaneously deduct such investment losses while sheltering capital gains through the use of the capital gains deduction. To prevent the multiplication of this generous tax savings the concept of cumulative net investment losses (CNIL) was introduced.

11-83.   CNIL is defined as the amount by which the aggregate of "investment expenses" for the current year and prior years ending after 1987 exceeds the aggregate of "investment income" for that same period. That is, the CNIL consists of post-1987 investment expenses minus investment income. You should note that, in this context, both of the expressions "investment income" and "investment expense" are defined in *ITA 110.6(1)*. As a consequence, they have a meaning that can be different from the meaning associated with the everyday use of these expressions.

11-84.   As will be explained in the following section, a CNIL will reduce access to the capital gains deduction. As a result, from a planning perspective it is advantageous to minimize any CNIL if an individual is anticipating capital gains that would qualify for the capital gains deduction. Some examples of ways in which the impact of the CNIL can be reduced are as follows:

- Realizing taxable capital gains on QFP and QSBC shares early, if a CNIL is anticipated in future years.

- Delaying the disposition of QFP and QSBC shares with accrued capital gains until the CNIL has been eliminated or reduced to the extent possible.

- For owners/managers, having their corporation pay dividends or interest on shareholder loan accounts, rather than salaries, to increase investment income which then reduces the CNIL.

Cumulative Gains Limit (CGL)—ITA 110.6(1)

11-85.   In somewhat simplified form, the CGL can be defined as follows:

The sum of all of the AGL for current and previous years. This total is reduced by:

- the sum of all amounts deducted under the capital gains deduction provision in computing the individual's taxable incomes for preceding taxation years; and
- the individual's CNIL at the end of the year.

11-86.   In the absence of a CNIL balance, this formula would simply be the sum of all AGL reduced by all of the capital gains deductions made in previous years. As individuals will normally deduct the full amount of their AGL (if it is below the capital gains deduction available for that year), this balance will usually be equal to the AGL for the current year. The result will be different if an individual chooses to deduct a lesser amount as a tax planning choice or as the result of a CNIL balance.

11-87.   The following is a simple example of the CGL calculations.

EXAMPLE   In 2021, Ms. Nolan has $5,600 of deductible interest on loans for investment purposes and $2,600 of net rental income. She has had no investment income or investment expenses in years prior to 2021, so her CNIL is $3,000 ($5,600 - $2,600) at the end of 2021. During August 2021, she has a $60,000 taxable capital gain on the sale of QSBC shares. Ms. Nolan has no other taxable capital gains or allowable capital losses in 2021 or in years prior to 2021.

ANALYSIS   As she has made no previous use of her capital gains deduction, her available unused limit for QSBC shares is $446,109. While her AGL would be $60,000, the amount of the taxable capital gain, her ability to use the capital gains deduction would be reduced by her CNIL resulting in a CGL of $57,000 ($60,000 - $3,000).

Comprehensive Example

11-88.   The example that follows illustrates the basic rules involved in the application of the capital gains deduction.

EXAMPLE   Dwight Treadway's 2021 net income is as follows:

Employment income	$ 60,000
Taxable capital gain on the sale of QSBC shares (ITA 3(b))	
Shares in a qualified small business corporation	200,000
Net income	$260,000

In 2015, Mr. Treadway had a $20,000 taxable capital gain [(1/2)($40,000)] from the sale of QSBC shares and claimed capital gains deduction for the same amount. In 2014, Mr. Treadway had an allowable capital loss of $9,000 [(1/2)($18,000)]. No part of that loss qualified as an ABIL. He had no taxable capital gains in that year, therefore the $9,000 became a 2014 net capital loss. He intends to deduct the 2014 net capital loss in 2021. Other than the 2015 taxable capital gain of $20,000 and the 2014 allowable capital loss of $9,000, Mr. Treadway had no taxable capital gains, allowable capital losses, other net capital loss carry overs, or ABILs from 2014 to and including 2021. He has no CNIL balance at the end of 2021.

ANALYSIS For 2021, the maximum capital deduction would be the least of the following amounts:

- **Capital gains deduction available = $426,109** ($446,109 - $20,000).

- **AGL = $191,000** As Mr. Treadway has had no other taxable capital gains that qualified for the capital gains deduction in 2021, we can use the simplified version of this calculation (see Paragraph 11-79). This would result in an AGL of $191,000, the $200,000 taxable capital gain for the year, less the taxable income deduction of the 2014 net capital loss of $9,000 under ITA 111(1)(b).

- **CGL = $191,000** As the AGL for 2014 would be equal to the $20,000 taxable capital gain on QSBC shares, the sum of the AGL would be $211,000 ($20,000 + $191,000). Subtracting from this the $20,000 capital gains deduction for 2014 leaves a CGL at the end of 2021 of $191,000.

11-89. Given these calculations, the maximum capital gains deduction for 2021 would be $191,000, the amount of both the AGL and the CGL. The full $200,000 gain on the shares could have been deducted if Mr. Treadway had not chosen to deduct the 2014 net capital loss. The deduction of this amount reduced both the AGL and the CGL by $9,000. It would be advisable for Mr. Treadway not to deduct any of the net capital loss carry forward. If he did this, his AGL would increase to $200,000. Although he would have used $9,000 more of his capital gains deduction, his taxable income and tax liability for 2021 would not change and he would still have a net capital loss carry forward of $9,000 that could be applied against any type of capital gain for an unlimited period of time. In this example a $200,000 taxable capital gain is offset by either (1) a capital gains deduction of $191,000 plus a net capital deduction of $9,000 or (2) a $200,000 of capital gains deduction.

Exercise 11-8

Subject: Capital Gains Deduction

Mr. Edwin Loussier had a 2014 taxable capital gain on QSBC shares of $5,000 [(1/2)($10,000)] and a 2016 taxable capital gain on QSBC shares of $13,000 [(1/2)($26,000)]. He used his ITA 110.6 capital gains deduction to offset both of the taxable capital gains. He has no other taxable capital gains, allowable capital losses, or ABILs in the period 2014 through 2019. In December 2020, he has a $31,500 allowable capital loss [(1/2)($63,000)], which, because he has no taxable capital gains in that year, he cannot deduct. As a result he has a 2020 net capital loss of $31,500. In 2021, he has a $255,000 [(1/2)($510,000)]taxable capital gain on the sale of QSBC shares. In addition, he deducts the $31,500 2020 net capital loss. Mr. Loussier does not have a CNIL balance at the end of 2021. Determine Mr. Loussier's maximum capital gains deduction for 2021. Provide all of the calculations required to determine the maximum capital gains deduction.

Solutions to Exercises are available in the Study Guide.

We suggest you complete SSP 11-3 at this point.

Ordering of Deductions and Losses

Significance of Ordering

11-90.   When an individual has determined net income for a given year and there are multiple sources of income and multiple loss carry overs there is a decision to be made as to which deductions to claim. In this chapter we have seen that there is overlap between claiming the capital gains deduction versus claiming net capital losses. In addition there are multiple loss carry over categories, most of which are streamed, such as net capital losses and restricted farm losses, whereas there are those loss carry over categories, such as non-capital and farm losses, that are deductible against all types of income. In other words, an individual may have a number of choices to make as to which deduction to claim in a given year.

11-91.   Technically there is an ordering rule in ITA 111.1 for individuals in determining taxable income. The rule currently requires individuals who are claiming taxable income deductions for amounts such as stock options, loss carry overs, and the capital gains deductions to apply them in that specific order when all are claimed for the same year. There is no ordering rule, however, for the claiming of different loss carry over categories. The only significant general loss rule is found in ITA 111(3) that tracks loss carry over balances and requires older losses to be applied before newer ones. ITA 111.1 was somewhat important in the early 1980s when personal tax credits were taxable income deductions, but its relevance currently is insignificant and largely irrelevant.

11-92.   The ultimate decision as to which deductions and loss carry overs to claim is dependent on the facts, including remaining time limits with respect to loss carry overs. As a general rule the capital gains deduction is best claimed when there are taxable capital gains from QFP and QSBC shares rather than using net capital losses or non-capital losses to reduce taxable income. In addition, if there are streamed losses, such as restricted farm losses and limited partnership losses, they should be deducted when the restricted type of income is present, saving the unstreamed non-capital losses and farm losses for another day. Finally, as mentioned earlier, taxable income deductions should avoid reducing taxable income to nil and instead leave enough taxable income to fully offset non-refundable tax credits that would otherwise be lost.

Example

11-93.   The following is an example of the appropriate choices when deciding which taxable income deductions to claim.

> **EXAMPLE**   At the beginning of 2021, Miss Farnum had the following loss carry forwards available:
>
> | | |
> |---|---|
> | 2016 Restricted farm loss | $ 5,000 |
> | 2017 Non-capital loss [(1/2)($20,000)] | 40,000 |
> | 2019 Net capital loss [(1/2)($20,000)] | 10,000 |
>
> For 2021, her only non-refundable tax credit is the basic personal amount of $13,808. Also during 2021, she has no available Subdivision e deductions such as RRSP contributions, spousal support, child care expenses, or moving expenses. She had the following income for 2021:
>
> | | |
> |---|---|
> | Employment income | $15,000 |
> | Interest income | 4,000 |
> | Business income from farming | 2,000 |
> | Non-farming business Income | 15,000 |
> | Taxable capital gains [(1/2)($12,000)] | 6,000 |

ANALYSIS   Miss Farnum's 2021 net income and taxable income would be calculated as follows:

Income under ITA 3(a):			
Employment income	$ 15,000		
Interest income	4,000		
Income from a farming business	2,000		
Non-farming business income	15,000	$	36,000
Income under ITA 3(b):			
Taxable capital gains (ITA 3(b)(i))			6,000
2021 Net income		**$**	**42,000**
2016 Restricted farm loss ITA 111(1)(c) (limited to farming income)		(	2,000)
2019 Net capital loss ITA 111(1)(b) (limited to ITA 3(b) net			
taxable capital gains)		(	6,000)
Subtotal		$	34,000
2017 Non-capital loss carry forward ($34,000 - $13,808)		(	20,192)
Taxable income = Basic personal amount		**$**	**13,808**

Loss carry forwards:

• 2016 Restricted farm loss balance ($5,000 - $2,000)	$ 3,000
• 2019 Net capital loss balance ($10,000 - $6,000)	4,000
• 2017 Non-capital loss balance ($40,000 - $20,192)	19,808

11-94.   Note that, in this example, the amount of net capital and restricted farm losses deducted was limited by the amount of the net taxable capital gains (the ITA 3(b) amount) and income from a farming business. The non-capital loss deducted was limited to the amount that would reduce taxable income to an amount sufficient to offset the basic personal amount of $13,808. Since tax payable will be nil, there is no reason to deduct any non-capital loss above that amount. With taxable income of $13,808, gross tax payable will be $2,071 [(15%)($13,808)] and tax credits will equal the same amount, resulting a net tax payable amount of nil.

Exercise 11-9

Subject: Ordering of Losses

At the beginning of 2021, Alan Barter had the following loss carry forwards available:

2015 Net capital losses [(1/2)($40,000)]	$20,000
2018 Restricted farm loss	8,000
2020 Non-capital losses	36,000

During 2021, he had the following amounts of income:

Taxable capital gains [(1/2)($18,000)]	$ 9,000
Business income	12,000
Employment income	56,000
Farm income	3,500

Determine Alan's net income, as well as his minimum taxable income for 2021. Indicate the amount and type of any losses available for carry forward at the end of the year.

Solutions to Exercises are available in the Study Guide.

Tax Payable Overview

General

11-95.   Chapter 4 provided detailed coverage of the application of federal tax rates to taxable income in order to determine federal gross tax payable. In addition, coverage of most of the tax credits available to individuals was provided. The coverage of tax credits was extended in Chapter 7 with the addition of the dividend tax credit and the foreign tax credit.

11-96.   Many of the Self-Study and Assignment Problems that accompany this chapter are comprehensive and require tax calculations and applications of credits based on these earlier chapters.

11-97.   As was the case with the material on taxable income, there are additional issues involved with the determination of gross and net tax payable for individuals that could not be dealt with in Chapter 4 because of the need to understand income concepts not presented until subsequent chapters. As a result, additional coverage of net tax payable is included in this chapter. Specifically, the following topics will be discussed:

Tax on Split Income (TOSI)   This is a special tax assessed at the maximum federal rate of 33% on certain types of income.

Transfer of Dividends to a Spouse or Common-Law Partner   The calculations related to this tax credit require an understanding of the dividend gross up and dividend tax credit, which were not introduced until Chapter 7.

Charitable Donations   The basic calculation of this tax credit was presented in Chapter 4. However, it was not possible to deal with donations of property until the material in Chapters 5 through 8 on business income, property income, and capital gains had been covered.

Foreign Tax Credits   These credits were introduced in Chapter 7. However, completing the intricacies of the calculations requires the additional material on taxable income that is included in this chapter.

11-98.   Having completed the material in Chapters 5 to 10, we are now in a position to complete our coverage of the determination of net tax payable for individuals.

Basic Federal Tax Payable

11-99.   Throughout this text we have used the expression "gross tax payable" to refer to the federal income taxes calculated on taxable income and the expression "net federal income tax payable" to refer to the net result once personal tax credits and other amounts have been applied (e.g., OAS clawback, taxes withheld by an employer, and CPP overpayments). The ITA, however, uses different expressions, such as "tax otherwise payable under this Part" or "tax payable under this Part" and modifications to those expressions in select areas, such as the foreign tax credit provisions.

11-100.   The income tax return, however, uses the expressions "basic federal tax," "federal tax," and "net federal tax" in place of the actual legislative expressions found in the ITA. Basic federal tax is a figure from which some but not all tax credits have been deducted. At one time, this was an important figure in that it was the base that the provinces and territories used in calculating their respective provincial tax payable. Since the provinces now base provincial taxes on taxable income, the basic federal tax figure is no longer of general importance. The most important use of basic federal tax is that it is used to calculate the additional federal tax payable that must be paid by individuals who are deemed Canadian residents but do not reside in a province (e.g., members of the Canadian Armed Forces stationed outside of Canada). However, other than indicating that this concept exists, we will give basic federal tax payable no further consideration and will continue to use the expressions "gross federal tax" and "net federal tax."

Tax on Split Income (TOSI)

Introduction—Income Splitting

11-101.   There have been attribution rules in place since 1985 the purpose of which was to address income splitting, which are transactions designed to shift income within a family from high-income earners to those family members with little or no income. These transactions typically involved the gifting of investments to spouses, common-law partners, and minor children. The investment returns, most commonly in the form of dividends, interest, and capital gains, would be included in the income of the low-income earners as opposed to the high-income earner where there would be little to no income tax because of a combination of low tax rates and availability of non-refundable tax credits. The attribution rules designed to deal with these situations simply redirected the income back to the original property owner, being the high-income-earning family member. We discussed those attribution rules in Chapter 9.

11-102.   From the introduction of the basic attribution rules, tax planners used other income splitting strategies to save income taxes within a family. Two of the most common were (1) dividend sprinkling and (2) management services structures. Dividend sprinkling involves a corporation that carries on a business in which one or both spouses or common-law partners are actively involved. Minor children are added as shareholders either from the initial incorporation or by adding them after the fact through structural planning referred to as estate freezes, which are discussed in the chapters on corporate and trust taxation. Once the children have become shareholders, dividends may be declared on their shares at the discretion of the board of directors, who are frequently the parents. Because of income tax credits, including the dividend tax credit, approximately $55,000 of eligible dividends or $30,000 of non-eligible dividends can be received tax free by an individual with no other income.

11-103.   Management services structures typically involved an individual who was either carrying on a business as a sole proprietor or as a member of a professional partnership. Arrangements would be made to create a corporation, trust, or another partnership effectively controlled by the same individual to provide management or other services to the business. Family members of the individual would have an ownership interest in the service provider entity as a shareholder, beneficiary of a trust, or as a partner where legally possible. The business would be entitled to an expense for the service fees paid, and the service fee income would be included in the entity providing the services. That income would then be used to make various income distributions to the low- or no-income family members.

11-104.   During the years 1985 to 1999 the federal government challenged hundreds of taxpayers involved in these income splitting arrangements, convinced that they would succeed on the premise that, in terms of tax policy, income splitting was offensive and therefore unacceptable. The government challenges included a wide range of arguments and use of numerous anti-avoidance rules in the ITA, all to no avail. The two Supreme Court of Canada decisions in *McClurg* ([1990] 3 SCR 1020) and *Neuman* ([1998] 1 SCR 770) that dealt with dividend sprinkling resulted in wins for the taxpayers. To add insult to injury, the Supreme Court in *Neuman* at paragraph 35 of the decision added that "There is no general scheme to prevent income splitting in the ITA."

11-105.   While the CRA was making their arguments in the *Neuman* case they were fighting another battle dealing with income splitting in management services structures in the Federal Court of Appeal case in *Ferrel* ([1999] 2 CTC 101). The Tax Court of Canada had ruled against the CRA, and the Federal Court of Appeal upheld that decision. Given the comments of the Supreme Court of Canada in *Neuman*, the federal government decided not to appeal the decision but chose instead to deal with the issue head on by adding legislation to address their concerns.

The 2000 TOSI (Kiddy Tax)

11-106.   The first and original version of the TOSI became effective in 2000. This anti-avoidance legislation was aimed at certain types of passive income earned by individuals under 18 years of age. Because of the application to minors it was commonly referred to by the tax community as the "kiddy tax." The rules applied to taxable dividends declared and paid by private companies and shareholder benefits conferred by private companies whether received directly or through trusts or partnerships. This first part of the kiddy tax addressed the CRA's concern of dividend sprinkling with minor children.

11-107. The second part of the kiddy tax addressed the management services structures. Income received by a minor child with an interest in a trust or partnership would be subject to the kiddy tax where the income of the trust or partnership was derived from a business of providing goods or services to a business carried on by a relative of the minor child or a business in which the relative participated. These structures commonly used family trusts in which minor children are beneficiaries.

11-108. The income subject to the kiddy tax is called "split income," which is defined in ITA 120.4(1). The split income is included in the income of the minor child but then fully subtracted under ITA 20(1)(ww). As a result, none of the split income is actually included in net income or taxable income under Part I. The reason is that taxable income applies graduated rates of income tax starting at 15%. The kiddy tax is designed to be punitive, therefore the kiddy tax (ITA 120.4(2)) contains its own separate income tax calculation, which starts with the split income and then applies the highest federal tax rate of 33%. You should also be aware that the highest provincial tax rate also applies (see Chart C of TOSI Form T1206). The rules also limit the tax credits that can be claimed against the kiddy tax to the dividend tax credit or foreign tax credit that relates to the split income plus the disability tax credit. As a result of this tax credit restriction the minor is unable to use his or her basic personal credit to reduce income taxes. ITA 160(1.2) was also added to make the parents jointly liable for the kiddy tax.

> **EXAMPLE**   Tom Fleming and his spouse, Janice, both have taxable income in excess of $300,000. They own all of the voting shares of their privately owned company, Fleming Co. Tom and Janice have two children, Jonathan who is 7 years old and Marissa who is 9 years old. The two children own non-voting shares in Fleming Co. that they purchased with cash gifts they had received from family friends over the years. In 2021 the company declares and pays eligible dividends of $50,000 to each of the two children, which are then held in trust for them. Were it not for the kiddy tax the hypothetical income tax consequences would have been as follows:

Taxable eligible dividends [($50,000)(1.38)]	$69,000
Tax payable [(15%)($49,020) + (20.5%)($19,980)]	$11,449
Personal tax credit [(15%)($13,808)]	(2,071)
Dividend tax credit [(6/11)(38%)($50,000)]	(10,364)
Part I tax payable without the kiddy tax	$ Nil

The kiddy tax would be calculated as follows:

Split income—Taxable eligible dividends	$69,000
Tax rate	33%
Tax payable before dividend tax credit	$22,770
Dividend tax credit [(6/11)(38%)($50,000)]	(10,364)
TOSI federal tax payable (kiddy tax)	$12,406

When the kiddy tax applies, the addition to net income is nil. In this case it would be calculated as $69,000 of taxable dividends from resident corporations (ITA 12(1)(j)) minus split income of $69,000 (ITA 20(1)(ww)). An additional example is presented at Paragraph 11-130.

11-109.   The kiddy tax did not result in the immediate end of income splitting with minors. It quickly became apparent to the CRA that tax planning was underway where minor children would sell shares of private companies to non-arm's-length persons. The children would include the taxable capital gains in their income subject to the regular Part I graduated tax rates. In the Tax Court of Canada decision in *Gwartz* (2013 TCC 86), the CRA reassessed taxable capital gains reported by minor children for the 2003, 2004, and 2005 taxation years as dividends that should have been subjected to the kiddy tax applying the GAAR (general anti-avoidance rule; see Chapter 2). The GAAR argument was that the tax planning circumvented the kiddy tax in a manner contrary to the scheme and purpose of the ITA and therefore the tax should be equivalent to what it would have been had the kiddy tax applied. The court disagreed with the CRA and gave the win to the taxpayers.

11-110.   In response the federal government added ITA 120.4(4) and (5) to block this type of planning by expanding the scope of the kiddy tax. As of March 23, 2011, taxable capital gains of minor children realized in non-arm's-length transactions are deemed to be non-eligible dividends equal to two times the taxable capital gain. This would mean that a $10,000 taxable capital gain would be deemed to be a $20,000 non-eligible dividend subject to the 33% kiddy tax. As a result the dividend gross up and dividend tax credit rules would also apply with the following results:

Split income—Taxable non-eligible dividend [($20,000)(1.15)]	$23,000
Tax rate	33%
Tax payable before dividend tax credit	$ 7,590
Dividend tax credit [(9/13)(15%)($20,000)]	(2,077)
TOSI federal tax payable	$ 5,513

In Paragraph 11-118 there is mention of an exemption from the TOSI rules where there is a capital gain on property that would have qualified for the capital gains deduction. That exception, however, does not apply to the kiddy tax where a capital gain is realized by a minor child as a result of a non-arm's-length disposition.

Part 2: The 2018 TOSI (Adults 18 Years of Age and Older)

11-111.   For the most part, attribution concepts have not applied to adult children as was clear in both the regular attribution rules and the kiddy tax. All of that changed beginning in 2018 when the federal government, after the release of a discussion paper in 2017, some initial draft legislation, consultation with the public, followed by some limited modifications, introduced the TOSI. In our discussions we will use the expression "kiddy tax" to refer to the initial 2000 TOSI rules, which only applied to children under 18 years of age, and the expression "TOSI" (tax on split income) to refer to those rules that apply to adults 18 years of age and older.

11-112.   A common theme that runs through the TOSI rules has some similarity to the kiddy tax. The basic premise is that if an individual receives income that can be traced to the activities of a related person and that the individual has contributed little or nothing toward earning that income there is a presumption of income splitting. Applying this basic premise you can see that if an adult receives salary from a company owned and controlled by a family member the TOSI would not apply because the individual has presumably contributed employment services equal to the salary received. If the same individual is a shareholder and receives dividends the TOSI should not apply if the individual worked in the business or contributed capital that contributed to the ability of the business to earn profits that would fund the dividends. On the other hand, if the individual was a shareholder only and never made any contributions of labour or capital toward the business then the premise is that the TOSI rules should apply.

11-113.   The TOSI rules are unique in that they draw a line between different age groups. The contemplated age groups are (1) between 18 and 24, (2) between 25 and 64, and (3) 65 and over. The categorization by age is designed to be lenient in applying the TOSI to individuals with a spouse or common-law partner 65 years of age or older. The rationale is that if the TOSI does not apply to an individual 65 or older then it should also not apply to that individual's spouse or common-law partner. This income splitting opportunity in the TOSI is supported in principle by the pension income splitting concepts allowed to individuals 65 and older.

11-114.   The age group of 18 to 24 was carefully chosen since it represents individuals such as adult children who are likely attending college, university, or other educational institutions. The concern is that parents are using income splitting opportunities to fund their adult children's education and related costs such as meals and accommodation. Until the introduction of the TOSI in 2018 it had been standard tax planning practice to structure one's affairs to have individuals in this age group as shareholders, partners, or beneficiaries of trusts with connections to a source of business income in which parents were actively involved. In other words, the activities of the parents that were responsible for generating business profits were being used to make income distributions to adult children to fund their education with little or no income tax. Dividends were frequently the income of choice given how they are taxed.

Applying the TOSI

The Basic Analysis

11-115.   It is not our objective to provide comprehensive coverage of the TOSI but rather to provide a general awareness of the operation of these rules to be able to identify potential risk. The legislation can be quite complex, often requiring the assistance of income tax professionals to carefully analyze complex structures. Our focus, however, will be on the basic analysis with a slightly modified example put together by the CRA to assist in understanding how these rules apply in general. You can access the complete set of examples and further information provided by the CRA at https://www.canada.ca/en/revenue-agency/programs/about-canada-revenue-agency-cra/federal-government-budgets/income-sprinkling/guidance-split-income-rules-adults.html.

11-116.   The TOSI analysis begins with the receipt of "split income" by a "specified individual." A specified individual is an individual who is resident in Canada at the end of the year in which the split income is received. Split income includes the following:

- Taxable dividends from a private company

- Shareholder benefits or loans from a private company

- Income from a partnership or trust including from a related business and from rental properties

- Capital gains on the disposition of private company shares

11-117.   The next part of the analysis is whether the split income received is an "excluded amount," which is also a defined expression (ITA 120.4(1)). There are two general types of excluded amounts. The first are general exclusions and then there are those that require further analysis, which we will refer to as specific exclusions. It is the specific exclusions that are critical to the analysis as will be demonstrated in the example presented at Paragraph 11-128.

General Exclusions

11-118.   The following are some of the more common amounts that we refer to as general exclusions:

Capital gains eligible for the capital gains deduction: If a taxable capital gain would have been eligible for the capital gains deduction because the property sold was QFP or QSBC shares, then the capital gain is excluded from split income and is therefore not subject to the TOSI. The capital gains deduction does not have to actually be claimed; the gain just needs to be eligible for this exclusion to apply.

Property acquired as a result of the breakdown of a marriage or common-law partnership.

Property acquired as the result of the death of a parent if the individual is between 18 and 24 years of age.

Applying the TOSI

Specific Exclusions Overview

11-119. Paragraph 11-112 explained that the reason for the TOSI is to trace split income of a specified individual to an income earning activity of a related person. Even if the split income can be so traced, the TOSI may not apply as long as the specified individual has made some contribution to the business or activity. The ITA applies this notion by adding definitions for the following concepts:

- Related business

- Excluded business

- Excluded shares

- Reasonable return, safe harbour capital return, and arm's-length capital

Related Business

11-120. A related business in respect of a specified individual means a business carried on by

- a related individual as a sole proprietor;

- a partnership, corporation, or trust where a related individual is actively and regularly engaged in the business;

- a partnership if the related individual is a partner; or

- a corporation where a related individual owns 10% or more of the FMV of all issued and outstanding shares of the corporation at any time in the year.

Excluded Business

11-121. One of the most important of the specific exclusions is the concept of an excluded business. This concept can be described as follows:

> A business in which the specified individual is actively engaged on a regular, continuous, and substantial basis in the relevant year or in any five previous taxation years. The five years do not have to be consecutive and can include years prior to the 2018 introduction of the TOSI.

> ITA 120.4(1.1)(a) was added to deem an individual to have met the active engagement test if the individual works in the business an average of at least 20 hours per week during the time the business is in operation. Note that if the business is seasonal (e.g., a landscaping business), the 20 hours per week requirement is only required for the portion of the year during which the business operates.

A failure to meet this 20-hour per week test does not necessarily prevent an individual from relying on the excluded business exception. Whether or not an individual is actively engaged in a business will depend on the facts and circumstances in individual cases. If, for example, the business is internet-based and requires only 10 hours of work weekly, then a specified individual who works in that business perhaps half the time at 5 hours per week would be sufficient.

Excluded Shares

11-122. The legislation allows individuals who have reached 25 years of age at the end of a year to avoid the TOSI on dividends or capital gains on shares of private corporations that meet the definition of "excluded shares." This particular exception recognizes that not all private corporations are problematic in terms of potential for income splitting. The private companies that have historically been used in income splitting are (1) professional corporations, (2) service-based corporations, and (3) management services companies that earn their income from related businesses. These three concerns are embedded in the definition of excluded shares, which can be described as follows:

For shares to be classified as excluded shares, all of the following conditions must be met:

- It must not be a professional corporation. ITA 248(1) defines a professional corporation as a corporation that carries on the professional practice of an accountant, dentist, lawyer, medical doctor, veterinarian, or chiropractor. Corporations carrying on the practice of other professionals, for example architects, do not fall within this definition.
- Less than 90% of the gross business income is from providing services.
- Less than 10% of its income is from a related business.
- When the split income is received the individual must own shares of the corporation that represent 10% or more of the FMV of all issued and outstanding shares of the corporation and the shares owned by the individual must give the individual the ability to cast 10% or more of the votes in an annual shareholders meeting.

Reasonable Return, Safe Harbour Capital Return, and Arm's-Length Capital
11-123.   The final part of the specific exception recognizes the actual contributions a specified individual has made that may justify earning the split income. While there are three return concepts, the "safe harbour capital return" and "arm's-length capital" apply to specified individuals between 18 and 24, whereas the "reasonable return" concept applies to those specified individuals 25 years and older.

Safe Harbour Capital Return   This return is based on the FMV of property contributed in support of the related business. The return is quantified as the highest of the lowest quarterly prescribed rate in the year applied to the FMV of the contributed property at the time it was contributed and prorated based on the number of days the property is used in support of the business. This would mean that if an individual agrees to use his or her automobile or other property in the business, there is a value to that contribution that reduces the amount subject to the TOSI.

Arm's-Length Capital (Taxpayers Aged 18 to 24)   This second test is based on a reasonable return on contributed arm's-length capital only. According to the explanatory notes to the legislation the only property that would be considered would generally be inherited property and salary earned by the individual.

11-124.   For individuals 25 years of age and older the TOSI will not apply to split income where the amount represents a reasonable return based on the following factors:

- The work the individual performed in support of the related business

- The property contributed in support of the related business

- The risks the person assumed in respect of the related business

- The total of all amounts that were paid to the individual in respect of the related business

- Any other relevant factors

The reasonableness test can be quite subjective, but the goal is to attempt to determine whether the contributions by a specified individual to a business in terms of labour and capital justify the split income amounts paid to him or her. It is only split income amounts in excess of these reasonably determined amounts that would be subject to the TOSI.

TOSI—Analytical Summary

11-125.   Once it has been determined that a resident Canadian individual is in receipt of split income there are five general ways to avoid the TOSI:

Exception 1   There is no related business.

Exception 2   The business is an excluded business.

Exception 3   The shares are excluded shares (25 years and older only).

Exception 4   The safe harbour capital return or a reasonable return on arm's-length capital exceeds the split income (18 to 24 years of age only).

Exception 5   The amount of the reasonable return based on labour, capital contributions, and other factors exceeds the split income (25 years and older only).

11-126.   We can summarize the application of the TOSI as follows:

Step 1   Is there an individual resident in Canada at the end of the year? If yes, continue. If no, then the TOSI does not apply.

Step 2   Has the individual received split income? If yes, continue. If no, then the TOSI does not apply.

Step 3   Do any of the general exclusions listed in Paragraph 11-118 apply? If no, continue. If yes, the TOSI does not apply.

Step 4   Is there a related business? If yes, continue. If no, then the TOSI does not apply.

Step 5   Is there an excluded business? If no, continue. If yes, then the TOSI does not apply.

Step 6   If the individual is 25 or older, are the shares excluded shares? If no, continue. If yes, then the TOSI does not apply.

Step 7   Do any of the reasonableness tests apply, including the safe harbour capital return and arm's-length capital? If no, then the TOSI applies. If they do apply, then the amount subject to the TOSI is reduced by the relevant amount.

TOSI Example

Dividends to an Adult Child Away at School

11-127.   Figure 11-4 displays the business structure and transactions of Opco, a Canadian controlled private corporation.

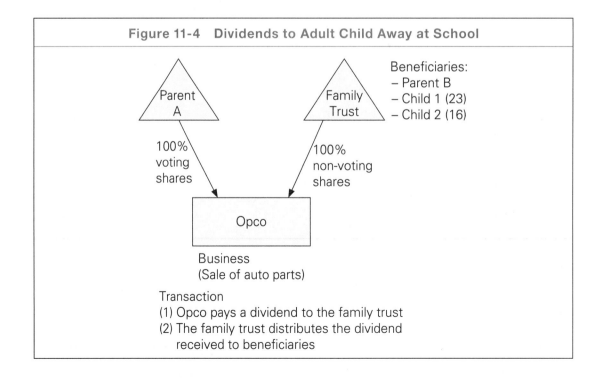

Figure 11-4   Dividends to Adult Child Away at School

FACTS   Opco carries on an active business supplying parts to an auto parts manufacturer. Parent A and Family Trust each owns a separate class of shares of Opco. Parent A is the founder of Opco's business and is the controlling shareholder of Opco. Family Trust is a discretionary trust established for the benefit of its beneficiaries, Parent B, Child 1, and Child 2. All individuals are residents of Canada.

Child 1 is age 23 and is a full-time graduate student at a university and is away from home for most of the year either attending classes during the school term or working part time as a research assistant during the summer. Child 1 has never performed any functions for Opco and has not made any other contribution to Opco and its business.

Child 2 is age 16 and is a high school student.

Opco pays a dividend on the class of shares held by Family Trust. Family Trust distributes the full amount of the dividend to Child 1 and that amount is included in computing the income of Child 1.

ANALYSIS   Following the steps described in Paragraph 11-126 results in the following analysis for Child 1:

Step 1   Is there an individual resident in Canada at the end of the year? YES

Step 2   Has the individual received split income? YES. In this case the trust taxation rules allow the trust to effectively flow the taxable dividend through to Child 1. A taxable dividend originating from a private company is split income.

Step 3   Do any of the general exclusions listed in Paragraph 11-118 apply? NO

Step 4   Is there a related business? YES. Child 1's parent is actively involved in the business carried on by Opco. The business is a related business. Since Parent A owns 10% or more of the FMV of the Opco shares, that fact is also sufficient to cause the Opco business to be a related business.

Step 5   Is there an excluded business? NO. Child 1 has never worked in the Opco business.

Step 6   If the individual is 25 or older are the shares excluded shares? Not applicable since Child 1 is only 23 years old.

Step 7   Do any of the reasonableness tests apply, including the safe harbour capital return and arm's-length capital? NO. Child 1 never made any contribution in support of Opco's business.

CONCLUSION   The dividends received by Child 1 through Family Trust are split income that are not excluded amounts. Had Child 2 received dividends through Family Trust he or she would have been subject to the kiddy tax. Had Parent B received dividends through Family Trust the parent could not have relied on the excluded share exception because the shares were not owned by Parent B but by Family Trust. Parent B would have to rely on one of the other exceptions listed in Paragraph 11-125 to avoid the TOSI.

NOTE   We would add that it is not uncommon to avoid having shares owned by family members, particularly minor children. Family trust situations are discussed in Chapter 19.

Calculation of the TOSI Tax

The Tax Credit Problem

11-128.   When a specified individual has received split income, the income tax is determined under the TOSI rules applying the highest tax rates rather than the regular tax payable calculations under Part I of the ITA. We mentioned at Paragraph 11-108 that there is no addition to net income or taxable income of split income as a result of ITA 20(1)(ww), which subtracts the full amount of the split income. This can create a problem in determining dependent tax credits that are income tested.

EXAMPLE   Josh Browning has net income of $250,000, while his spouse, Maria, has net income of $15,000, all of which is split income. When the deduction is claimed under ITA 20(1)(ww), Maria's net income will be nil.

ANALYSIS   The problem with this result is that if the nil amount was used for calculating personal tax credits, the result would be to allow a spousal tax credit for Josh of $1,863 [(15%)($12,421 - nil)]. In contrast, if there had been no split income, Maria's net income of $15,000 would have exceeded the 2021 base for the spousal tax credit of $12,421, resulting in no spousal tax credit for Josh. Note that because Josh's net income for 2021 exceeds the highest tax bracket of $216,511 his basic personal amount is $12,421. This is explained in the 2021 Rates, Credits, and Other Data at the beginning of each volume of the text as well as in Chapter 4.

The government did not believe that this was an appropriate result and added ITA 118(4)(a.2). This provision requires that the ITA 20(1)(ww) deduction be ignored for the purposes of determining personal tax credits. This means that Josh's spousal tax credit would be nil ($12,421 - $15,000).

Two Components

11-129.   With the ITA 20(1)(ww) split income deduction, an individual's net income is made up of two components where he or she has both split income and other income:

Split Income Component   This component will be subject to a federal flat rate of 33%. The only credits allowed against this tax will be dividend tax credits and foreign tax credits that relate to the amounts included in split income plus the disability tax credit.

Regular Income Component   This component will be subject to the regular graduated rates and will be eligible for the usual tax credits, subject to ITA 118(4)(a.2).

11-130.   The following example will serve to illustrate these calculations.

EXAMPLE   Helen, who is 25 years old, receives non-eligible dividends of $20,000 from a private company controlled by her father. In addition, she has interest income of $5,500 from a savings account funded by an inheritance. Her only tax credits are the basic personal credit and the dividend tax credit. None of the TOSI exceptions apply.

ANALYSIS   The initial calculation involves the determination of net income, taking the ITA 20(1)(ww) split income deduction into consideration. All of the usual tax credits can be claimed in this calculation.

Taxable non-eligible dividends [(115%)($20,000)]	$23,000
Interest income	5,500
Deduction for split income—ITA 20(1)(ww)	(23,000)
Net income = Taxable income	$ 5,500
Tax rate	15%
Tax payable before credits	$ 825
Basic personal credit [(15%)($13,808)]	(2,071)
Federal tax payable on regular income	Nil

The TOSI payable would be calculated as follows:

Split income—Taxable non-eligible dividends	$23,000
Tax rate	33%
Tax payable before dividend tax credit	$ 7,590
Dividend tax credit [(9/13)(15%)($20,000)]	(2,077)
TOSI federal tax payable	$ 5,513

With the regular component being nil, the total federal tax payable will be $5,513, the amount attributable to split income.

Exercise 11-10

Subject: Tax on Split Income

During 2021, Norton James, who is 16 years old, receives non-eligible dividends of $15,000 from a private corporation controlled by his mother. He also has income of $15,200 from contracts to create computer games. As he has used the income that he has earned from these contracts in previous years to invest in the stock market, he has eligible dividends from publicly traded companies of $8,600. Assume his only tax credits are his basic personal credit and dividend tax credits on the shares that he owns. Determine Norton's federal tax payable for 2021.

Solutions to Exercises are available in the Study Guide.

We suggest you complete SSP 11-4 at this point.

Tax Credits Revisited

Transfer of Dividends to a Spouse or Common-Law Partner—ITA 82(3)

11-131.   There may be situations in which an individual's spousal credit has been reduced or eliminated altogether as a result of taxable dividends received by that spouse or common-law partner. The ITA 82(3) election permits a transfer of all of the dividends from the spouse or common-law partner's income to that of the taxpayer if it creates or increases the spousal credit. Consider the following example.

EXAMPLE   Mr. Barba is in the highest federal income tax bracket of 33%. As a result the maximum spousal credit available to him for 2021 would be $12,421. Mrs. Barba's total income for 2021 consists of $12,000 in eligible dividends received from taxable Canadian corporations, which would be grossed up to $16,560 [(1.38)($12,000)]. No federal income tax would be payable by her because of the combination of the basic personal tax credit and the dividend tax credit. However, because her net income exceeds the maximum spousal credit of $12,421 that could be claimed by Mr. Barba, the spousal credit would not be available.

ANALYSIS   In this case, an election under ITA 82(3) would result in the taxable dividends of Mrs. Barba being included in Mr. Barba's income, which would then enable Mr. Barba to claim the full spousal credit of $12,421. Mr. Barba would be required to include the grossed up dividends of $16,560 in his income, but he would also be able to claim the dividend tax credit with respect to these dividends. Determining whether the election is beneficial requires a comparative analysis, which is shown in the following calculations. The calculations compare the benefits of the election if Mr. Barba was in the 15% and 33% federal tax bracket. Where his tax bracket is 15%, the maximum spousal credit for 2021 would be $13,808.

Mr. Barba's tax bracket	15%	33%
Increase in taxable income	$16,560	$16,560
Tax on $16,560	$ 2,484	$ 5,465
Increase in spousal credit [(15%)($13,808)]	(2,071)	
Increase in spousal credit [(15%)($12,421)]		(1,863)
Dividend tax credit [(6/11)(38%)($12,000)]	(2,487)	(2,487)
Increase (decrease) in tax payable	($ 2,074)	$ 1,115

As can be seen in the table, if Mr. Barba is in the 15% federal income tax bracket, his federal income tax would be decreased by $2,074. Alternatively, if he is in the 33% bracket, the transfer would not be beneficial as his federal income tax would be increased by $1,115.

Exercise 11-11

Subject: Transfer of Dividends to a Spouse

Mr. Albert Ho is 38 years old and has over $250,000 in 2021 net and taxable income. His spouse's only 2021 income is $8,500 in eligible dividends received from taxable Canadian corporations. In terms of federal tax payable, would Mr. Ho benefit from the use of the ITA 82(3) election to include the eligible dividends received by his spouse in his net income? Justify your conclusion.

Solutions to Exercises are available in the Study Guide.

We suggest you complete SSP 11-5 and 11-6 at this point.

Charitable Donations Credit Revisited

Introduction
11-132.   The basics of the charitable donations tax credit were covered in Chapter 4. In that chapter, we noted that, for individuals, the first $200 of donations were eligible for a tax credit of 15%. The rate applicable to amounts in excess of $200 was either 29% or 33% depending on whether all or part of the individual's taxable income was within the 33% tax bracket, which, for 2021, begins when taxable income reaches $216,511. In general, the donation tax credit base for calculating the credit was limited to 75% of the taxpayer's net income.

11-133.   In Chapter 4, we covered cash donations. Coverage of more complex issues involving donations of various types of capital property was purposefully deferred until this chapter. The justification for this deferral was because there are income tax consequences when capital property is disposed of by donation that we had yet to cover. Now that we have covered all the necessary income tax implications of property dispositions we can discuss the consequences of donating capital property.

Donations Classified
11-134.   ITA 118.1 defines four types of charitable donations:

1. **Total Charitable Gifts** is defined to include all eligible amounts donated by an individual to a registered charity, a registered Canadian amateur athletic association, a Canadian municipality, the United Nations or an agency thereof, a university outside of Canada that normally

enrolls Canadian students, and a charitable organization outside of Canada to which Her Majesty in right of Canada has made a gift in the year or in the immediately preceding year.

2. **Total Crown Gifts** is defined as the aggregate of eligible amounts donated to Her Majesty in right of Canada or a province.

3. **Total Cultural Gifts** is defined as the aggregate of all eligible gifts of objects that the Canadian Cultural Property Export Review Board has determined meet the criteria of the *Cultural Property and Import Act*.

4. **Total Ecological Gifts** is defined as all eligible gifts of land certified by the Minister of the Environment to be ecologically sensitive land, the conservation and protection of which is important to the preservation of Canada's environmental heritage. The beneficiary of the gift can be any level of government. The beneficiary can also be a registered charity, provided its primary purpose is the conservation and protection of Canada's environmental heritage.

11-135.   In addition to the items specified in the Act, under the U.S./Canada tax treaty, Canadians can claim donations to any qualifying U.S. charity in amounts up to 75% of their net U.S. income (75% of their net worldwide income if the Canadian resident lives near the U.S. border and commutes to a U.S. place of business or employment).

Eligible Amounts

11-136.   Donations (e.g., a gift) have a legal meaning in both common-law jurisdictions (all provinces and territories except Quebec)and civil law jurisdictions (Quebec). The legal meaning of a gift requires a voluntary transfer of property without the receipt of any valuable consideration. In addition, there must be what is referred to as a donative intent. The receipt of any kind of consideration in exchange for a "gift," including an intent to enrich one's self through an underlying income tax or other scheme, would negate a donative intent. The result would mean that no gift had been made. This means that donation income tax schemes would never succeed on that basis. Although the government viewed this as a positive result that would assist in challenging tax-motivated donation schemes it presented other problems. Fundraising events, for example, would often include free entertainment, travel, accommodation, or meals and sometimes an opportunity to win prizes. All of these benefits or advantages would negate the existence of donations upon which many Canadian charities relied.

11-137.   In order to ensure that donations would qualify for donation credits, which often fuelled the raising of funds for charities, the federal government was obliged to change the rules of donations/gifts for income tax purposes. ITA 248(30) to (41) were added to the ITA in 2012 to add the necessary flexibility.

11-138.   In the preceding material on the classification of donations, each of the definitions contains the expression "eligible amounts." The expression is defined as follows:

ITA 248(31)   The eligible amount of a gift or monetary contribution is the amount by which the FMV of the property that is the subject of the gift or monetary contribution exceeds the amount of the advantage, if any, in respect of the gift or monetary contribution.

11-139.   ITA 248(32) defines "advantage" very broadly to include a benefit to the taxpayer that is in any way related to the gift, including benefits that are contingent on future events.

EXAMPLE 1   As an example of an advantage, consider a gift of real property with a FMV of $300,000. If the charity receiving the gift were to assume a $100,000 mortgage on the property, this would be considered an advantage because the donor would no longer be responsible for the repayment. The resulting eligible amount of the donation is $200,000 ($300,000 - $100,000).

EXAMPLE 2   A second example is a fundraising dinner. Assume that tickets cost $250 each and a dinner is provided, the value of which is estimated at $100. In addition, each individual receives a ticket for a draw to win $3,500 estimated to be worth $7. Finally, a logo pen worth $10 is also given to each ticketholder. The CRA administratively provides a "nominal threshold" that disregards the value of any consideration as long as it is less than $75 and represents no more than 10% of the gift. In this case the pen and ticket for the draw are ignored since their combined $17 value is less than $75 and less than 10% of the $250 gift or $25. The donation tax credit is therefore based on the price of the fundraising ticket of $250 less the $100 value of the meal or $150.

EXAMPLE 3 The third example is lottery tickets with the proceeds to raise funds for various charities. These tickets, which are often in excess of $100, are frequently used by hospitals and medical research, giving away top prizes that include million dollar homes and other luxury prizes. The CRA position is outlined at paragraph 1.19 of Folio S7-F1-C1 titled "Split Receipting and Deemed Fair Market Value." It is the CRA's view that since the primary motivation is to purchase a lottery ticket, no part of the cost of such tickets is considered a donation for income tax purposes.

11-140.   While the ITA has been modified to allow individuals to receive consideration (i.e., an advantage), ITA 248(30) caps the consideration. Specifically, if the advantage to an individual resulting from making the gift exceeds 80% of the value of the gift, the gift will be disqualified from benefiting from the donation tax credit unless the individual can convince the minister that the transfer was made with a true donative intent.

Deemed Fair Market Value

11-141.   In order to further reduce incentives to participate in income tax-motivated donation schemes, ITA 248(35) introduces the concept of "deemed fair market value." The purpose of this provision is to potentially reduce the "eligible amount" of a gift of property if the property was acquired less than three years prior to the time it was donated or, if an individual acquires a property less than 10 years before the gift is made and it is reasonable to conclude that the property was acquired with an intent to make a gift, the eligible amount of the gift will be based on the lesser of its cost and the actual FMV at the time of the gift. There is a lengthy list of exceptions to this at ITA 248(37), including where a gift is made as a consequence of the death of an individual.

Gifts of Capital Property—Transfer at Elected Value

11-142.   When an individual makes a charitable, Crown (i.e., government), or ecological (but not cultural) gift of capital property, an election is available under ITA 118.1(6). On such properties, there will usually be a difference between the tax cost of the property (i.e., ACB for non-depreciable capital property or UCC for depreciable property) and its FMV. If the FMV is the higher value, the taxpayer can elect to designate the proceeds of the disposition at any amount between the relevant tax cost of the property and its FMV. There are special rules that apply where donated property is publicly traded shares and ecologically sensitive land. This will be covered in Paragraph 11-146.

11-143.   In the case of non-depreciable capital property, if the FMV of the donated property exceeds its ACB it is advisable to elect the FMV. Any amount of elected value in excess of $200 will be eligible for a tax credit at either 29% or 33%. In contrast, only one-half of any capital gain that results from the disposition will be included in net income and subject to income tax.

EXAMPLE   Mr. Vignesh Menan owns land (not ecologically sensitive land) with an ACB of $100,000 and a FMV of $150,000. During 2021, he intends to donate this land to a registered Canadian charity and would like to know whether he should elect to make the donation at $100,000 or alternatively at $150,000. Before consideration of any income resulting from making the gift, Mr. Menan has taxable income of more than $400,000. Given this, any amount of donations in excess of $200 will receive a credit based on the maximum tax rate of 33%.

ANALYSIS The income tax consequences of the two alternatives are as follows:

Elected value	$100,000	$150,000
Tax credit [(15%)($200) + (33%)($99,800)]	$ 32,964	
Tax credit [(15%)($200) + (33%)($149,800)]		$49,464
Tax on gain [(1/2)(POD $100,000 - ACB $100,000)(33%)]	N/A	
Tax on gain [(1/2)(POD $150,000 - ACB $100,000)(33%)]		(8,250)
Credit net of tax	$ 32,964	$41,214

11-144. It should be noted that ITA 118.1(6) places a floor or minimum amount that can be elected. The elected value cannot be below the amount of any advantage received by the tax-payer as a consequence of the donation.

EXAMPLE—Extended Mr. Vignesh Menan owns land (not ecologically sensitive land) with an ACB of $100,000 and a FMV of $150,000. In return for the donation, he receives a cash payment from the registered charity of $110,000.

ANALYSIS Mr. Menan cannot elect an amount that is less than $110,000. Assuming he elects to designate the proceeds of the land at the maximum value of $150,000, the eligible amount of his gift will be $40,000 ($150,000 - $110,000).

11-145. The situation is somewhat more complicated when depreciable property is involved, as a disposition at FMV may result in recapture. The income taxes on recapture may offset the tax savings of the donation credit. The analysis is further complicated by provincial tax rates and donation credits.

Gifts of Capital Property—Income Limits

11-146. In most cases, an individual's eligible donations are not allowed to exceed 75% of their net income for the year of the donation. A potential problem with electing an amount that results in additional income is that the income tax on this additional income may not be completely offset by the donation tax credit. In other words, making a gift could result in the payment of additional income taxes. To reduce this potential problem, two other components are added to the net income base for charitable donations, resulting in a total donation base equal to

- 75% of net income for the year; plus
- 25% of any taxable capital gain resulting from a gift; plus
- 25% of any recaptured CCA resulting from a gift.

11-147. An example will illustrate the importance of these modifications to the overall donation limit.

EXAMPLE In July 2021, Jonas Anderson gifts a customized bus that was used in a business he carried on as a sole proprietor to a registered Canadian charity. The bus has a FMV of $130,000, a capital cost and ACB of $100,000, and a UCC of $65,000. He elects to designate the proceeds of the gift at the FMV of $130,000. He has no other income in 2021, other than any amounts arising as a result of the gift.

ANALYSIS The election to designate the donation at the FMV of $130,000 will result in a total increase in his 2021 net income of $50,000. This is composed of a taxable capital gain of $15,000 [(1/2)(POD $130,000 - ACB $100,000)] and recaptured CCA of $35,000 [$100,000 (lesser of proceeds of $130,000 and capital cost $100,000) - UCC of $65,000].

As Mr. Anderson has no other income, his basic 2021 donation limit would be $37,500 [(75%)($50,000)]. If his limit were only $37,500, the income resulting from the donation exceeds what is permitted as a donation credit with respect to that donation. The modifications to the donation limit are designed to match the income related to the donation. The modified donation limit is determined as follows:

75% of net income [(75%)($50,000)]	$37,500
25% of taxable capital gain [(25%)($15,000)]	3,750
25% of recaptured CCA [(25%)($35,000)]	8,750
Total donation limit (equals income from donation)	$50,000

11-148.   The additions to the limit create a base for charitable donations that includes 100% of any income resulting from gifts of capital property. Note, however, that Mr. Anderson will not want to use the full $50,000 in 2021. As amounts over $200 will generate a credit at a rate of 29% and all of Mr. Anderson's income will be taxed at a lower rate, use of the full $50,000 would produce a credit that exceeds his gross federal tax payable. In addition, he will want to make use of any non-refundable tax credits that are available for 2021. Note that the 33% charitable donations rate is not relevant in this example as Mr. Anderson's taxable income is well below the income threshold for that rate.

Exercise 11-12

Subject: Donation of Depreciable Property

Ms. Sally Felder donates some food preparation equipment to the local food bank, a registered Canadian charity. The depreciable property has a FMV of $85,000, a capital cost and ACB of $62,000, and a UCC of $28,000. She elects to designate the proceeds of the donation at the FMV of $85,000. She has no other income during the year and her only tax credit other than the charitable donations tax credit is her basic personal credit of $13,808. Determine her maximum charitable donations tax credit for 2021. In addition, determine the amount of the donation she should claim in 2021 in order to reduce her net federal tax payable to nil. Calculate any unused donations that can be carried forward to future years.

Solutions to Exercises are available in the Study Guide.

Gifts of Publicly Traded Securities and Ecologically Sensitive Land
11-149.   Gifts of publicly traded securities (shares and debt obligations) and ecologically sensitive land benefit from special rules that make donations particularly attractive. While a donor can receive a donations tax credit based on the full FMV, ITA 38(a.1) deems the taxable capital gain on donations of publicly traded securities to be nil and ITA 38(a.2) deems the taxable capital gain on gifts of ecologically sensitive land to be nil.

Exercise 11-13

Subject: Donation of Listed Shares

Mr. Saheed Radeem has employment income of $90,000. He owns shares that are listed on the Toronto Stock Exchange. These shares have a FMV of $110,000 and an ACB of $30,000. During 2021, these shares are donated to a registered Canadian charity. Mr. Radeem has no taxable income deductions (i.e., his taxable income is equal to his net income). Assume that his tax credits, other than the charitable donations credit, total $4,000. Determine Mr. Radeem's maximum charitable donations tax credit for 2021, the amount of the donation he should claim in 2021 in order to reduce his federal tax payable to nil and the balance of any unused donations that can be carried forward to future years.

Solutions to Exercises are available in the Study Guide.

Gifts of Publicly Traded Securities Acquired through Stock Options
11-150.   Without special rules, there is a potential problem for donations of publicly traded shares acquired as a result of employee stock options. You will recall from Chapter 3 that, in the case of these shares, any accrued gain that is present at the time the options are exercised is treated as employment income (ITA 7(1)). The tax policy is, in general, to only subject half of the employee stock option benefit to income tax in a manner similar to the taxation of capital gains. As a result, a taxable income deduction equal to 50% of the employee stock option amount is deducted under ITA 110(1)(d) or (d.1).

> **EXAMPLE**   Roberto Cerutti is provided with options to buy 1,000 of his employer's shares at an option price of $20 per share, the FMV of the shares at the time the options are granted. Roberto exercises these options when the shares are trading at $32 per share. He gifts the shares immediately to a registered charity.
>
> **ANALYSIS**   Roberto will have an increase in taxable income calculated as follows:

Employment income [(1,000)($32 - $20)]	$12,000
Deduction under ITA 110(1)(d) [(1/2)($12,000)]	(6,000)
Increase in taxable income	$ 6,000

11-151.   As this increase in taxable income is not a capital gain, it will not be deemed to be nil as a result of ITA 38(a.1). In the absence of any relief, this $6,000 amount would then be subject to income tax. ITA 110(1)(d.01), however, was added to equalize the treatment when stock option shares are donated. This taxable income deduction allows an additional one-half of the employee stock option benefit to be deducted, which then ensures there is no income tax as a result. This is comparable to a situation in which an individual would acquire shares at $20 and then subsequently donated them when their FMV had increased to $32. ITA 38(a.1) would deem the taxable capital gain to be nil. ITA 110(1)(d.01) achieves the same result as follows:

Employment income [(1,000)($32 - $20)]	$12,000
Deduction under ITA 110(1)(d) [(1/2)($12,000)]	(6,000)
Deduction under ITA 110(1)(d.01) [(1/2)($12,000)]	(6,000)
Increase in taxable income	Nil

11-152.   In the Fall Economic Statement of November 30, 2020, the federal government released draft legislation to modify the taxation of employee stock options. These rules are designed to limit the ability of certain employees to claim the stock option taxable income deductions. The rules are generally restricted to employees of publicly listed corporations but are to come into effect for new stock options granted beginning July 1, 2021. If the stock option taxable income deduction of ITA 110(1)(d) is not available because of the restrictions, then the stock option taxable income deduction of ITA 110(1)(d.01) will also not be available.

Canadian Cultural Property
11-153.   We have noted that, when an individual makes a charitable, Crown, or ecological gift of capital property, they can elect to designate the proceeds of disposition to be any amount between the tax cost and the FMV of the donated property. In the case of cultural gifts of capital property the proceeds of disposition must be the FMV of the property in all cases. ITA 118.1(10) clarifies that the FMV is to be determined by the Canadian Cultural Property Export Review Board. There is also an appeal process that allows the FMV to be redetermined within a 24-month period. CRA pamphlet P113, "Gifts and Income Tax," provides additional information.

11-154.   The income tax treatment of a disposition of Canadian cultural property is quite advantageous. ITA 39(1)(a)(i.1) provides that there can be no capital gains on the donation of such properties. This means that if the FMV exceeds the ACB there are no amounts required to be included in net income. If, however, the ACB exceeds the FMV the ITA permits the recognition of capital losses.

Limits on Amount Claimed and Carry Forward Provisions

11-155.   As noted in Chapter 4, it is the policy of the government to limit charitable donations that are eligible for the tax credit to a portion of a taxpayer's net income. Note that, while corporations claim a taxable income deduction under ITA 110.1 as opposed to receiving a credit against tax payable as individuals do under ITA 118.1, the annual donation limits are the same for corporations as they are for individuals.

11-156.   The limit on eligible amounts of charitable gifts is 75% of net income, but there are exceptions to this general limit. For individuals, this limit is increased to 100% of net income in the year of death and the preceding year. This treatment on death is similar in many respects to the flexibility provided in using net capital losses on death, as discussed earlier in this chapter. There is no income limit on the amount of cultural or ecological gifts. Credits can be claimed for these gifts up to their full eligible amounts.

11-157.   The ITA does not require that charitable donations be claimed in the year they are made. Unused charitable donations can be carried forward and claimed in the subsequent five-year period (10 years for ecological gifts). Unused donations cannot be carried back. In the carry forward period, the same annual income-based limits will apply in determining the amounts that can actually be deducted.

Foreign Tax Credits Revisited
Foreign Non-Business (Property) Income Tax Credit for Individuals—ITA 126(1)

11-158.   ITA 126(1) provides for a tax credit in situations where a Canadian resident has paid foreign income or profits tax on non-business income. We introduced coverage of foreign tax credits in Chapter 7, but could not fully discuss the calculations as we had not yet covered loss carry overs and the capital gains deduction, both of which are relevant to the calculation of the foreign tax credit.

11-159.   As was noted in Chapter 7, the full amount of foreign non-business income earned must be added to the taxpayer's net income. This amount is then subject to Canadian income taxes, with the amount withheld by the foreign jurisdiction being allowed as a credit against Canadian income tax payable. The objective of this is to tax non-business income earned in a foreign jurisdiction at the same overall rate as would have applied to non-business income earned in Canada while recognizing that the foreign jurisdiction also has a right to tax that same income.

11-160.   There are a few issues with respect to foreign non-business income earned by resident Canadian individuals. The first is that ITA 126(1) only permits a foreign tax credit to a maximum of 15% of the non-business income. Any foreign tax in excess of 15% must be deducted under ITA 20(11). If, for example, an individual earned $1,000 in a foreign country that withheld $200, $150 of this amount would serve as a foreign tax with the remaining $50 deducted under ITA 20(11).

11-161.   A further issue is that the federal government wants to ensure that taxpayers do not receive a foreign tax credit that exceeds the Canadian income tax that would have been payable on the foreign non-business income. This is accomplished by limiting the foreign non-business tax credit to the lesser of the amount withheld in the foreign country and an amount designed to approximate the Canadian income tax equivalent, which is determined by multiplying the ratio of one's foreign non-business income to their total income by their Canadian income tax payable. This approach is reflected in the following formula:

The **foreign non-business tax credit** is the lesser of:

- the tax paid to the foreign government converted to Canadian currency. For individuals, this is limited to 15% of foreign non-business income, or
- an amount determined by the following formula:

$$\left[\frac{\text{Foreign Non} - \text{Business Income}}{\text{Adjusted Division B Income}} \right] [\text{Tax Otherwise Payable}]$$

11-162.   The "Adjusted Division B Income" in this formula is defined as follows:

> Division B income (i.e., net income without subtracting TOSI under ITA 20(1)(ww)) less the following taxable income deductions:
> - net capital loss carry overs deducted under ITA 111(1)(b);
> - any capital gains deduction (ITA 110.6);
> - any amounts deductible for stock options under ITA 110(1)(d) and (d.1); and
> - any amounts deductible under ITA 110(1)(f) for workers' compensation, social assistance, or exempt foreign income.

The objective is to determine the amount of net income that is actually subject to income tax and has made it through to taxable income.

11-163.   "Tax Otherwise Payable" in this calculation consists of:

> Part I tax payable before the deduction of:
> - dividend tax credits;
> - employment outside of Canada tax credits;
> - political contributions tax credits;
> - investment tax credits; and
> - labour sponsored funds tax credits.

11-164.   You should note that the preceding definition of Adjusted Division B income is unique to the calculation of foreign tax credits. It starts with net income without allowing the TOSI deduction under ITA 20(1)(ww) (Division B income) and proceeds to deduct some, but not all, of an individual's taxable income deductions. The most important exclusions are loss carry overs with the exception of net capital losses.

11-165.   The foreign tax credit rules apply on a country-by-country basis, therefore if non-business income were received from more than one foreign country, multiple foreign tax credit calculations would be required. If the amount of foreign non-business taxes withheld exceeds the amount determined by the formula, there is no carry over of the unused amount as a tax credit. However, ITA 20(12) allows a taxpayer to deduct such excess amounts in the determination of net income.

Foreign Business Income Tax Credit for Individuals — ITA 126(2)

11-166.   If a Canadian resident carries on business in a foreign country as a sole proprietor or as a member of a partnership that carries on a business in that foreign country, ITA 126(2) provides for a tax credit for foreign income or profits taxes paid that is similar to that for non-business income.

11-167.   The amount of the business foreign tax credit that can be used is not restricted to a set percentage as it is with respect to the foreign non-business 15% limitation. However, it is limited by a formula similar to the formula applicable to the foreign non-business foreign income tax credit. One of the main differences between the two formulas is that the "tax otherwise payable" for foreign business income tax credit purposes is reduced by any foreign non-business income tax credit deducted, meaning that one would first have to calculate the non-business foreign tax credit before the business foreign tax credit. The calculation of the foreign business income tax credit is as follows:

The **foreign business income tax credit** is the least of:

- the income or profits tax paid for the year to a foreign country converted to Canadian currency;

- an amount determined by the following formula:

$$\left[\frac{\text{Foreign Business Income}}{\text{Adjusted Division B Income}} \right] [\text{Tax Otherwise Payable}]$$

- tax otherwise payable for the year, less any foreign tax credit taken on non-business income under ITA 126(1).

11-168.   A further important difference between the two foreign tax credits is that when foreign business income taxes paid exceed the amount that can be used as a credit during the current year, there is a three-year carry back and 10-year carry forward available. That is, if a taxpayer does not have sufficient tax payable to use all of the foreign business income tax credit during the current year, the excess can be claimed against tax payable in any of the three preceding years or in any of the 10 subsequent years. Note, however, that it can only be used in those years within the constraints provided by the formula in Paragraph 11-167 and must be applied on a country-by-country basis. In other words, foreign tax credits in respect of a business in one country cannot be applied against income and profits taxes in a different foreign country.

Exercise 11-14

Subject: Foreign Tax Credits

During 2021, Sarah Cheung has rental income of $44,000, net taxable capital gains of $2,500 (ITA 3(b) amount), and foreign non-business income of $3,500. The foreign country withheld 11% of this amount as an income and profits tax, resulting in a net receipt of $3,115. In calculating taxable income, she deducts a $4,000 non-capital loss carry forward (ITA 111(1)(a)) and a $1,000 net capital loss carry forward (ITA 111(1)(b)). Her only tax credits are the basic personal credit and any credit for foreign taxes paid. Calculate her federal tax payable for 2021. Include a detailed calculation of her foreign non-business income tax credit. Ignore the fact that Ms. Cheung could deduct any excess of the withholding amount ($385) over the actual credit in the determination of her 2021 net income.

Solutions to Exercises are available in the Study Guide.

Alternative Minimum Tax—ITA 127.5 (Division E.1)

General Concept

11-169.   The alternative minimum tax, or AMT, is a tax that was first introduced in 1986 in response to headline news that divulged a lengthy list of wealthy Canadians and trusts that were paying little to no income tax. The cause was individuals taking advantage of certain tax shelter-type deductions authorized by the ITA, including involvement in acceptable tax planning, that relied on additional incentive-based deductions that frequently created losses that were then applied against other income. While there was nothing offensive to the government in these situations, the strong public outcry necessitated a federal government response that led to the AMT.

11-170.   This tax is directed at individuals who take advantage of tax shelters and certain other "tax preference" items. The AMT looks to individuals who have certain types of income, deductions, or credits and requires that an adjusted taxable income be determined by adding back part or all of these "tax preferences." The AMT applies to individuals and most trusts although our focus will be on individuals.

11-171.   After deducting a basic $40,000 exemption from the adjusted taxable income, a flat rate of 15% is applied to the remaining amount. The resulting tax payable is reduced by some, but not all, of the individual's regular income tax credits to arrive at a minimum tax. The individual then compares the AMT to the regular income tax payable for the year. If the regular income tax payable is higher than the AMT then there is no AMT. If, however, the AMT is higher then it will be this higher amount that will be payable. The excess of the AMT over the regular tax payable is recoverable in a carry over period to a year in which the regular tax payable exceeds the AMT in that year. We would add that the $40,000 exemption is available to individuals and only those trusts designated as a graduated rate estate.

Minimum Tax Calculation

Definition

11-172.   The minimum tax is specified in ITA 127.51 as follows:

An individual's minimum amount for a taxation year is the amount determined by the formula

$$A (B - C) - D, \text{ where}$$

A   is the appropriate percentage for the year (15% for 2021);
B   is the adjusted taxable income for the year determined under ITA 127.52;
C   is basic exemption for the year (currently $40,000); and
D   is the basic minimum tax credit for the year determined under ITA 127.531.

Adjusted Taxable Income

11-173.   The calculation of adjusted taxable income that is described in ITA 127.52 is illustrated in a somewhat more comprehensible manner in Form T691. The idea behind adjusted taxable income is to add to regular taxable income certain "tax preferences." Examples of such preference items would include losses on tax shelters and the non-taxable portion of capital gains.

11-174.   The calculation of adjusted taxable income described in ITA 127.52 is as follows:

Regular taxable income

Plus additions:
- 60% of the excess of taxable capital gains over allowable capital losses (see Paragraph 11-175).
- 60% of the employee stock option deductions under ITA 110(1)(d) and (d.1).
- Amounts of CCA on certified Canadian films.
- The excess of CCA and interest charges claimed on rental and leasing property, over the income or loss reported for such property.
- Resource expenditure deductions for Canadian exploration expense (CEE), Canadian development expense (CDE), or depletion, net of certain resource-related income.
- Losses deducted by limited partners and members of a partnership who have been specified members (i.e., not actively involved in the businesses) at all times since becoming partners in respect of their partnership interests, net of certain gains allocated from the same partnership.
- Deductions related to investments identified or required to be identified under the tax shelter identification rules.

Less deductions:
- The gross up of Canadian taxable dividends.
- 60% of ABILs deducted (see Paragraph 11-176).
- 60% of net capital loss carry overs deducted.

Equals: Adjusted taxable income for AMT purposes

11-175.   Rather than require that all of the non-taxable component of capital gains be added back, which could result in an excessive number of individuals being exposed to the AMT, only 30% of the total capital gain or 60% of the taxable capital gain is added in the adjusted taxable income calculation. This brings the total inclusion of the excess of capital gains over capital losses to 80% (50% is already included in regular income, plus the additional 30%). If, for example, there was a capital gain of $100 the taxable part of the gain would be $50 [(50%)($100)]. If we add 60% of the taxable capital gain, or $30, then the total amount added for AMT purposes is $80, or 80% of the capital gain.

11-176.   The government also decided that this 80% treatment was appropriate for both ABILs and net capital losses. The adjusted taxable income calculation requires an additional deduction of 60% of ABILs or net capital losses deducted in the year.

Tax Payable before Credits

11-177.   A basic exemption of $40,000 is subtracted from the adjusted taxable income amount. As noted, this $40,000 exemption is only available to individuals and to trusts designated as graduated rate estates.

11-178.   After subtraction of the basic exemption, a flat rate of 15% is applied to the resulting balance. The resulting figure could be described as the AMT before the deduction of tax credits.

Tax Credits for AMT

11-179.   ITA 127.531 specifies the tax credits, as calculated for the determination of regular tax payable, that can be applied against the alternative minimum tax. The credits specified are as follows:

- Personal credits under ITA 118(1)
- Age credit under ITA 118(2), but not the transfer from a spouse
- Canada employment credit under ITA 118(10)
- Adoption expenses credit under ITA 118.01
- Home accessibility credit under ITA 118.041
- First-time home buyers credit under ITA 118.05
- Volunteer firefighters credit under ITA 118.06
- Volunteer search and rescue workers credit under ITA 118.07
- Charitable donations credit under ITA 118.1
- Medical expense credit under ITA 118.2
- Disability credit under ITA 118.3, but not the transfer from a spouse or other dependant
- Tuition credit under ITA 118.5, but not the transfer from a spouse or other dependant
- Interest on student loans credit under 118.62
- CPP and EI credits under ITA 118.7

11-180.   The deduction of these credits will produce the AMT payable. If this amount exceeds the regular taxes that are payable on the regular taxable income, the AMT must be paid.

AMT Carry Forward—ITA 120.2

11-181.   There will be individuals who become subject to the AMT in only some taxation years. The most common example of this situation is the realization of a large taxable capital gain that was offset by the use of the capital gains deduction. Other examples include large interest expenses on certain investment loans and large employee stock option deductions. Many years ago RRSP deductions used to be adjusted as part of the AMT calculations, but this is no longer the case.

11-182.   To provide for this, an excess of AMT over regular tax payable can be carried forward for up to seven years to be applied against any future excess of regular tax payable over the AMT. This credit acts as a recovery of an overpayment of income tax, however the refund of these amounts does not include interest.

Exercise 11-15

Subject: Alternative Minimum Tax (AMT)

Mr. Norton Blouson has taxable income for 2021 of $85,000. This includes taxable capital gains of $22,500 and taxable eligible dividends of $27,600 [(138%)($20,000)]. In addition, he received a $50,000 retiring allowance that was contributed to his RRSP.

The full contribution was deductible. His only tax credits are the basic personal credit of $13,808 for 2021 and the dividend tax credit. Determine whether Mr. Blouson would be subject to the AMT and, if so, the total amount of such tax.

How would your answer change if the taxable capital gains totalled $222,500 instead of $22,500 with $200,000 deductible as a capital gains deduction?

Solutions to Exercises are available in the Study Guide.

Sample Comprehensive Personal Tax Return

11-183.   In the Study Guide, there is a comprehensive example containing a completed individual income tax return, as well as a Tax Software Self-Study Problem included in the material for Chapter 11. The sample return illustrates the income tax savings that are possible with pension income splitting.

We suggest you complete SSP 11-7 through 11-11.

Key Terms

A full glossary with definitions is provided at the end of the Study Guide.

Active Business	Loss Carry Forward
Active Business Income	Lump-Sum Payments
Adjusted Taxable Income	Net Capital Loss
Allowable Business Investment Loss (ABIL)	Net Income
Alternative Minimum Tax (AMT)	Non-Capital Loss
Annual Gains Limit (AGL)	Ordering Rule
Business Investment Loss (BIL)	Personal-Use Property
Carry Over	Purification of a Small Business
Charitable Donations Tax Credit	Corporation
Charitable Gifts	Professional Corporation
Crown Gifts	Qualified Farm Property (QFP)
Cultural Gifts	Qualified Fishing Property (QFP)
Cumulative Gains Limit (CGL)	Qualified Small Business Corporation
Cumulative Net Investment Loss (CNIL)	Shares (QSBC)
Ecological Gifts	Restricted Farm Loss
Excluded Business	Small Business Corporation
Excluded Shares	Source Individual
Farm Property	Specified Individual
Fishing Property	Split Income
Foreign Tax Credit	Stock Option
Capital Gains Deduction	Taxable Income
Listed Personal Property	TOSI
Loss Carry Back	

References

For more detailed study of the material in this chapter, we refer you to the following:

ITA 82(3)	Dividends Received by Spouse or Common-Law Partner
ITA 110	Deductions Permitted
ITA 110.6	Lifetime Capital Gains Deduction
ITA 111	Losses Deductible
ITA 111.1	Order of Applying Provisions
ITA 118.1	Charitable Gifts
ITA 120.2	Minimum Tax Carry Over
ITA 127.5-.55	Obligation to Pay Minimum Tax
IC 75-23	Tuition Fees and Charitable Donations Paid to Privately Supported Secular and Religious Schools
S4-F8-C1	Business Investment Losses
S5-F2-C1	Foreign Tax Credit
S7-F1-C1	Split Receipting and Deemed Fair Market Value
IT-113R4	Benefits to Employees—Stock Options
IT-226R	Gift to a Charity of a Residual Interest in Real Property or an Equitable Interest in a Trust
IT-232R3	Losses—Their Deductibility in the Loss Years or in Other Years
IT-244R3	Gifts by Individuals of Life Insurance Policies as Charitable Donations
IT-288R2	Gifts of Capital Properties to a Charity and Others
IT-295R4	Taxable Dividends Received after 1987 by a Spouse
IT-322R	Farm Losses
IT-523	Order of Provisions Applicable in Computing an Individual's Taxable Income and Tax Payable

Appendix—Returns for Deceased Taxpayers

Special Rules at Death

Coverage In Text

11A-1.   Filing requirements on the death of an individual can be very complicated and complex, especially if the individual left a significant amount of various types of property. There are a number of special rules that are applicable when an individual dies. Some of these are covered in various chapters in the text. The following is a short summary of the special rules covered in the text, as well as where more information related to the rules can be found in the text. This appendix also covers the special filing requirements and elective returns for deceased individuals. Note that death benefits are income of the recipient and have no effect on the final return of the deceased. Death benefits are covered in Chapter 9.

Charitable Donations—Special Rules at Death

11A-2.   Charitable donations made in the year of death, or through bequests in the will and carried out by the executors of the will, can be claimed for tax credit purposes subject to a limit of 100% of net income, as opposed to the normal limit of 75%. Any charitable donations that are not claimed in the final return can be carried back to the immediately preceding year, subject to the 100% of net income limit.

Medical Expenses—Special Rules at Death

11A-3.   Medical expenses paid can normally be claimed for any 12-month period ending in the year to the extent they exceed a threshold amount (see Chapter 4). In the year of death, the time period is extended to a 24-month period prior to death.

Deemed Disposition of Capital Property at Death

11A-4.   The deceased individual is deemed to have disposed of capital property at FMV immediately before death. When the capital cost of a depreciable property for the deceased individual exceeds its FMV, the beneficiary is required to retain the original capital cost, with the difference being treated as deemed CCA.

11A-5.   An exception to the general rules is available where the transfer is to a spouse, a common-law partner, or a testamentary spousal or common-law partner trust. This is a rollover provision that allows the transfer of non-depreciable capital property at its ACB and depreciable property at its UCC. There are other tax-free transfers involving specific types of farm and fishing property. Deemed dispositions at death are covered in Chapter 9.

Deferred Income Plans at Death

11A-6.   In many cases, a deceased individual will have a TFSA, an RRSP, or a RRIF at the time of death. There are a number of special rules associated with this situation and these are covered in Chapter 9 (TFSA) and Chapter 10 (RRSP and RRIF).

Capital Losses — Special Rules at Death

11A-7.   There are special rules that apply to both net capital losses from years prior to death and to allowable capital losses arising in the year of death. These losses can be applied against any type of income in the year of death or the immediately preceding year. Any capital gains deductions claimed to the date of death reduce the net capital losses that can be claimed in this manner. The treatment of capital losses at death is covered in this chapter.

Representation

11A-8.   The deceased do not, of course, file income tax returns. However, numerous filing requirements may need to be done by the legal representative of the deceased. This legal representative may be an executor. This is an individual or institution appointed in the will to act as the legal representative of the deceased in handling the estate.

11A-9.   In the absence of a will, or in situations where an executor is not appointed in the will, a court will generally appoint an administrator as the legal representative of the deceased. This administrator will normally be the spouse or other family members of the deceased.

11A-10.   The basic tax-related responsibilities of the legal representative of an estate are as follows:

- Filing all necessary income tax returns;
- Paying all taxes owing;
- Obtaining a clearance certificate from the CRA that confirms that all outstanding amounts owing for income taxes, interest, and penalties have been paid at the time the certificate is issued. This then allows the legal represetative to distribute estate property without the risk of being personally liable for amounts owed by the deceased or the estate
- Advising beneficiaries of the amounts of income from the estate that will be required to be included in their income

11A-11.   In order to deal with the CRA in these matters, the legal representative will have to provide a copy of the deceased individual's death certificate, as well as a copy of the will or other document identifying him or her as the legal representative of the deceased. Without this documentation, the CRA will not divulge any of the deceased person's income tax information.

Procedures for Specific Returns

Ordinary Return(s)

11A-12.   As noted previously, the legal representative of the deceased is responsible for filing an income tax return for the year of death (a.k.a., final return) and, if required, any other unfiled or amended income tax returns. The final return would include the usual income—employment income, business income, property income, and net taxable capital gains. With respect to employment income, it would include salary or wages to the date of death.

> **EXAMPLE**   An individual dies on June 4. The last pay period is from May 16 through May 31, with the amount being payable on June 7.

> **ANALYSIS**   The accrual for the period from June 1, the first day after the end of the last pay period, through the June 4 date of death must be included in the final return for the year of death. With respect to the amount that is accrued but unpaid at death, this can either be included in the final ordinary return or, alternatively, in a separate "rights or things" return.

Rights or Things Return

11A-13.   Rights or things are defined as unpaid amounts that would have been included in income had they been received by the individual prior to their death. Included would be:

- unpaid salaries, commissions, and vacation pay for pay periods that ended before the date of death (e.g., the salary for the period May 16 through May 31 in the example in Paragraph 11A-12);
- uncashed matured bond coupons, provided they were not required to be included in a previous year's income;
- harvested farm crops and livestock on hand;
- inventory and accounts receivable of taxpayers using the cash method; and
- declared but unpaid dividends.

> **NOTE**   Declared but unpaid dividends can provide a significant tax savings in the case of an individual who controls a CCPC. Dividends in an amount of up to the beginning of the top tax bracket ($216,511 for 2021) can be declared just prior to the individual's death and paid subsequent to death. This amount can then be included in a separate "rights or things" return, with none of it being subject to the maximum 33% federal rate.

11A-14.   While some of these amounts could be included in the final return of the individual, it is generally advisable, provided the amounts are material, to file a separate return as it permits a doubling up of certain tax credits and, in many cases, will result in additional amounts being taxed at the lowest federal rate.

11A-15.   Interest accrued at the time of death is somewhat problematic. If, at the time of death, an individual owns a term deposit or similar investment that pays interest on a periodic basis, ITA 70(1)(a) requires that interest accrued to the date of death be included in the final return. This would be the case even if the individual ordinarily used the cash basis to report interest income. Under ITA 70(2), any accrued interest that is required to be included in the final ordinary return cannot be included in the rights or things return.

11A-16.   In contrast, if a debt investment does not pay periodic interest, the accrued interest can be treated as a right or thing. As examples of this, IT-210R2, "Income of Deceased Persons—Periodic Payments," paragraph 2, refers to a matured treasury bill that has not been realized and to matured but uncashed bond coupons as follows:

> If a deceased taxpayer owned a term deposit or other similar investment on which interest was payable periodically, interest accrued from the last date on which interest was payable up to the date of death would be included in income for the year of death under paragraph 70(1)(a). However, if the taxpayer also had on hand a matured investment (such as a matured Treasury Bill or uncashed matured bond interest coupons) at the date of death, any interest that was owing to the deceased taxpayer on the matured investment immediately before the date of death would be considered a right or thing for the purposes of subsection 70(2) to the extent the amount was not included or required to be included in the deceased's income for the year or a preceding year.

> For information about the tax treatment of "rights or things," refer to IT-212R3, "Income of Deceased Persons—Rights or Things."

11A-17.   As a final point, note that rights or things can be transferred to a beneficiary, provided this is done within the time limit for filing a separate rights or things return. If this election is made, the amounts will be included in the beneficiary's income when they are realized and not in either the final ordinary return or the rights or things return of the deceased.

Other Elective Returns

11A-18.   There are other elective returns that will be given limited coverage in the following paragraphs.

Filing Requirements

Prior-Year Returns

11A-19.   If an individual dies between November 1 of the prior year and the normal due date for the prior year's return (April 30 of the current year or, if the individual or his or her spouse or common-law partner had business income, June 15 of the current year), it is likely that the deceased will not have filed the return for the prior year. In this situation, the due date for the prior year's return is the later of six months after the date of death and the normal filing date. For example, if an individual dies on January 31, 2021, it is unlikely that his or her 2020 income tax return would have been filed. If the normal filing date was either April 30 or June 15, the legal representative would have until July 31, 2021, to file the 2020 income tax return.

11A-20.   Under ITA 111(2), a deceased individual is allowed to deduct unused net capital losses against any type of income in the year of death and the immediately preceding year. However, any capital gains deductions claimed to the date of death reduce the net capital losses that can be claimed in this manner. Charitable donations can also be carried back to the preceding year if not needed on the final return. If either of these amounts are applied to the year preceding death, the prior year's income tax return must be amended if it has already been filed.

Multiple Returns

11A-21.   Filing the appropriate income tax returns in the most advantageous manner for a deceased individual can be complicated as there are a number of exceptions to the normal rules. In addition, there are special rules for final returns.

11A-22.   In fact, in some situations, more than one return will be filed on behalf of a deceased individual. Some of these are required by the ordinary provisions of the *ITA*. Other returns can be filed on the basis of an election and may or may not be filed in particular cases. The potential returns and their deadlines can be described as follows:

- **Ordinary Return—Year of Death**   The ordinary return for the year of death, also referred to as the final or terminal return, will be due on April 30 or June 15 of the following year. However, if the death occurs between November 1 and December 31 of the current year, the deceased individual's legal representative has until the later of the normal filing date and six months after the date of death to file the current year's return. For example, if an individual died on December 1, 2021, and the normal filing date was April 30, 2022, the representative would have until June 1, 2022, to file the 2021 final return. Alternatively, if the deceased individual's return included business income, the normal filing date of June 15, 2022, would be applicable.

- **Elective Return—Rights or Things**   Under ITA 70(2), this special return is due the later of one year from the date of death or 90 days after the mailing date of the notice of assessment of the final return. (See Paragraph 11A-13, which explains rights or things.)

- **Elective Return—Non-Calendar Fiscal Year End**   If the deceased had business income from a partnership or as a sole proprietor with a non-calendar fiscal period, the individual's death may create a fiscal year end for the business that ends in the same calendar year. ITA 150(4) provides for an elective return to include the income of the business for the period between the end of the first fiscal period that ended in the calendar year to the end of that calendar year in a separate return. This avoids having up to two years of business income accruing in a single taxation year. Note that when an individual carries on a business as a sole proprietor the business ends on the individual's death. If the individual was a member of a partnership that carried on a business, technically the partnership would come to an end on the death of the partner and a new partnership begins with a change of partners.

For example, if Mr. Samuel Rosen had a proprietorship with a June 30 year end and he died on November 23, 2021, his representative could file a separate return for the period July 1 through November 23, 2021. This would allow the representative to limit the business income in his final return to the 12-month period ending June 30, 2021. The filing deadline for this return is the same as the final return.

- **Elective Return—Graduated Rate Estate**   Under ITA 104(23)(d), if the deceased is an income beneficiary of a graduated rate estate that has a non-calendar taxation year, the representative may elect to file a separate return for the period between the end of the trust's fiscal year and the date of the taxpayer's death. The filing deadline is the same as the final return.

11A-23.   There are two basic reasons for filing as many tax returns as possible. The first relates to the fact that the income tax rates are progressive and income starts at nil in each return. This means that the first $49,020 (for 2021) in each return has the advantage of being taxed at the lowest federal rate of 15%. If multiple returns are not filed, there may be amounts taxed at rates higher than 15% that would have been taxed at the lower rate if multiple returns had been filed.

11A-24.   The second advantage of filing multiple returns is that some personal tax credits can be deducted in each return. As will be discussed in the following material, this could save the deceased taxpayer's estate several thousand dollars for each income tax return filed.

Use of Deductions and Credits

Multiple Usage

11A-25.   The full amount of applicable personal credits is claimed, regardless of when the individual died in the year. As previously noted, one of the major advantages of being able to file multiple returns is that some personal tax credits can be used in each of the returns filed. It appears that the rationale for claiming certain tax credits on multiple returns is to recognize the fact that the income reported on the different returns could have been included in a later year's income tax return if the individual had not died. In that later year, personal tax credits would have been available to reduce tax payable.

11A-26.   The CRA's Guide "Preparing Returns for Deceased Persons" (T4011) provides a great deal of information relevant to the returns of deceased individuals. In the guide, it notes that there are three groups of amounts that can be claimed on optional returns. More specifically, the following non-refundable credits can be claimed in the final return and in each optional return filed:

- Basic personal credit
- Age credit
- Spousal credit (including the infirm amount)
- Credit for an eligible dependant (including infirm amount)
- Canada caregiver credit for a child under 18 years of age
- Canada caregiver credit

11A-27.   The combined value of these federal tax credits can represent a significant tax savings if multiple tax returns can be filed. There are similar credits available in the various provinces. Achieving these savings is, of course, conditional on each of the individual returns having sufficient tax payable to make use of the credits.

Elective Usage

11A-28. Other non-refundable credits can be split between, or deducted in full, in any of the returns filed. However, the total claimed cannot exceed the amount that would be included in the final return for the year of death. These credits include the following:

- Adoption expenses
- Disability amount for the deceased
- Disability amount for a dependant other than a spouse
- Tuition amount for the deceased
- Tuition amount transferred from a child
- Interest paid on certain student loans
- Charitable donations, including amounts gifted in the will (limited to 100% of net income)
- First-time home buyers' amount
- Medical expenses (note that the total expenses must be reduced by the lesser of $2,421 (2021 figure) and 3% of the total net income reported on all returns)

Usage with Related Income

11A-29. With respect to the following deductions and non-refundable credits, they can only be claimed in the return in which the related income is reported:

- Canada or Quebec Pension Plan contributions credit
- Employment Insurance premiums credit
- Canada employment credit
- Pension income credit
- Dividend tax credits
- Stock option deduction
- Social benefits repayment (OAS clawback)

Usage with Ordinary Return

11A-30. Deductions and credits that cannot be claimed on elective returns are claimed on the final return. The following deductions and non-refundable credits are listed in the CRA guide as amounts that cannot be claimed on an optional return but can only be claimed in the final return (it is not a complete list):

- Registered pension plan deduction
- RRSP deduction
- Annual union or professional dues
- Amounts transferred from a spouse or common-law partner
- Child care expenses
- Carrying charges and interest expenses
- Disability supports deduction
- ABILs
- Moving expenses
- Support payments made
- Loss carry overs
- Capital gains deduction
- Northern residents deduction
- Exploration and development expenses

Payment of Taxes

11A-31. Regardless of the extension of filing dates for the final and elective returns, the income tax owing is normally due on April 30 of the year following the year of death. We would also remind you that the due date for payment of taxes is unchanged by the deferral of the normal filing date to June 15 for individuals with business income.

11A-32.   However, if death occurs between November 1 and December 31, any amount owing with respect to the final return is due six months after the date of death. For deaths that occur between January 1 and October 31, the due date for paying any balance owing on the final return is April 30 of the following year.

11A-33.   With respect to income from the value of rights or things and from deemed dispositions of capital property at death, the legal representative for the deceased individual can elect to defer the payment of taxes by filing form T2075. Under ITA 159(5), payment can be made in 10 equal annual instalments, with the first payment due on the regular payment due date of the final return. Security acceptable to the minister must be furnished to guarantee payment of the deferred taxes. Interest will be charged on amounts outstanding and, as is the usual case, such interest is not deductible (ITA 18(1)(t)).

Sample Tax Return and Tax Software SS Problem

The Sample Tax Return and the Tax Software Self-Study Problem for Chapter 11 can be found in the Study Guide.

Self-Study Problems (SSPs)

Self-Study Problems (SSPs) provide practice in problem solving. Within the chapters, we have indicated where it would be appropriate to stop and work on each SSP. The problems can be downloaded by chapter from MyLab Accounting. Solutions are available in the Study Guide. Select problems can also be completed directly in MyLab and auto-graded.

Assignment Problems

Solutions to Assignment Problems (APs) are available to instructors only.

AP 11-1   (Loss Carry Overs—Individual)

Over a four-year period ending on December 31, 2021, Ms. Brenda Breau had the following financial data:

	2018	2019	2020	2021
Non-farming business income (loss)	$18,000	($14,000)	$30,000	($19,000)
Farming business income (loss)	(10,000)	2,000	3,150	(2,000)
Taxable (grossed up) dividends	2,360	2,950	3,963	6,450
Taxable capital gains	600	1,000	2,000	2,250
Allowable capital losses	(2,100)	Nil	Nil	(7,250)

Because of the nature of her farming activities, Ms. Breau's farm losses are restricted and are therefore subject to ITA 31. The dividend income is from taxable Canadian corporations and the amount includes the gross up.

When she has a choice, she would like to deduct the maximum amount of any net capital loss carry overs and carry back any losses to the earliest possible year. None of Ms. Breau's losses can be carried back before 2018.

Assume that Ms. Breau requires $14,000 in taxable income in each year to fully use her available tax credits.

Required: Calculate Ms. Breau's minimum net income and taxable income for each of the four years. In applying carry over amounts, do not reduce Ms. Breau's taxable income below $14,000, the amount required to fully use her tax credits. Indicate the amended figures for any years to which losses are carried back. Also indicate the amount and types of loss carry overs that would be available at the end of each year.

AP 11-2 *Allowable Business Investment Losses (ABIL)*

In 2018, after several years of working part time, Lucinda McIvor won a lottery prize of more than $1,000,000.

She embarked on a program of actively investing in rental properties and in the shares and debt of small private companies. Her investment income during the three years 2019 through 2021 were as follows:

2019 During this year she realized a large capital gain on the sale of shares in a successful small business corporation. The shares were eligible for the capital gains deduction as QSBC shares. She used $156,000 of her capital gains deduction (actual capital gains deduction was $78,000 [(50%)($156,000)]) to reduce her 2019 taxable income to an amount that allowed her to claim all of her available tax credits and reduce her federal tax payable to nil.

2020 During this year she had the following amounts of income:

Taxable capital gains	$ 17,300
Rental income	91,450
Interest income	38,275
Total	$147,025

2021 Income amounts during this year were as follows:

Taxable capital gains	$ 18,620
Rental income	86,300
Interest income	27,438
Total	$132,358

During 2021, Recovery Inc., a small business corporation to which she had extended a loan of $675,000, began bankruptcy proceedings. Lucinda has been advised that it is extremely unlikely that she will recover any of this amount. Given this, Lucinda will file an election under ITA 50(1) to deem the debt to have been disposed of for nil proceeds.

The only tax credit available to Lucinda in 2020 or 2021 is the basic personal credit (basic personal amount of $13,229 in 2020 and $13,808 in 2021). For several years prior to 2019, Lucinda's tax payable was eliminated by various credits. She did not have any loss carry overs from years prior to 2021.

Required: Determine Lucinda's optimum taxable income for the years ending December 31, 2020, and December 31, 2021. In your solution, consider the effect of the basic personal credit. Indicate any loss carry over balance that is available at the end of either year, and the rules applicable to claiming the loss carry over.

AP 11-3 *(ABILs and the Capital Gains Deduction)*

The following information is for David Foster for the taxation year ending December 31, 2021:

- David has been carrying on a business of custom residential painting as a sole proprietor since 2010. His business income for 2021 is $110,000.

- David purchased common shares of Abacus Ltd. for $33,000 in 2016 and sold the shares to an arm's-length individual in December 2021 for $167,000. Selling expenses totalled $2,000. The shares met the definition of QSBC shares and therefore qualify for the capital gains deduction.

- Abacus Ltd. regularly declared annual dividends and David received $8,000 of non-eligible dividends in November 2021.

- David purchased common shares in Calculatrix Inc. in May 2019 for $82,000. He sold the shares for $21,000 in September 2020. Selling costs were $200. Calculatrix never paid any dividends during the time that David owned the shares. The shares met the definition of a small business corporation, which would qualify the shares for ABIL treatment. Had there been a capital gain the shares would not have qualified as QSBC shares eligible for the capital gains deduction since David did not own the shares for at least 24 months prior to the disposition.

- David's CNIL at the end of 2020 was $12,000. In 2021 there are no additions to the investment expense and the non-eligible dividend is the only addition to investment income.

- David has a 2017 net capital loss of $5,500 [(1/2)($11,000)], which he has never deducted.

- David has used the capital gains deduction twice in his lifetime—once in 2012 to shelter a capital gain of $20,000 and a second time in 2016 to shelter a capital gain of $14,000. The capital gains deduction claimed was equal to the annual gains limit in each of those two years.

Required: Calculate David's net income and taxable income for 2021, minimizing taxable income to the extent possible. Provide all supporting calculations. In addition, provide the necessary calculations to support the maximum deduction that can be claimed for the capital gains deduction under each of the following scenarios:

A. David would prefer to maximize the use of his 2017 net capital loss balance before using the capital gains deduction.

B. David would prefer to maximize use of the capital gains deduction only.

AP 11-4 (Tax on Split Income)

In the following five cases, one or more individuals receive dividends from a private company. For each individual, determine whether the dividends are split income. Explain your conclusion.

CASE 1 Sam and Sandra are both 23 years old and have been married for five years. They each own 50% of the voting shares of the same class of Mobus, a corporation that is carries on a mobile applications business. The shares were acquired, in return for a nominal investment, when the corporation was formed.

Sam works full time for another corporation, while Sandra has a part-time job in health care. They both spend time managing and operating Mobus. Neither Sam nor Sandra work more than 20 hours per week in the business. However, the nature of the corporation's business is such that additional employees are not required.

During 2021, because one of its applications has been very successful, Mobus is able to pay dividends of $200,000, with Sam and Sandra each receiving $100,000.

CASE 2 GoGreen is a private corporation that carries on a seasonal landscaping business. The business operates for five months from May 1 through September 30. John Go owns 90% of the shares, with his twin children, Max and Mary Go, owning the remaining 10% (5% each).

The twins are 22 years old and attending university in another city during the period from mid-September until the end of April. During the period May through mid-September, they work full time with their father in the GoGreen business.

During 2021, each twin receives $10,000 in dividends from GoGreen.

CASE 3 Edward and Elsie Cole were married in 2008. Elsie owns all of the shares of Cole Industries, a private company that carries on a business in which she is actively involved on a continuous basis. In late 2020, citing irreconcilable differences, the couple divorced.

As part of the settlement agreement, Elsie was required to have Cole Industries issue a separate class of shares to Edward. During 2021, as required by the terms of the divorce settlement, dividends of $50,000 were declared and paid to Edward.

CASE 4   Larry and Louise Martin own, respectively, 95% and 5% of the shares of Musken Enterprises, a private company. Larry is 66 years old and Louise is 59 years old. They have been married for over 20 years.

From 2008, when Musken commenced to carry on business, until 2020, Larry worked full time in the business. In 2020, Larry retired and turned the operation of the business over to a salaried manager. Louise has never been involved in the business.

During 2021, Musken pays dividends of $190,000 to Larry and $10,000 to Louise.

CASE 5   Donald Rump owned all of the shares of Dontar during the period 2013 through 2020. Dontar is a private Canadian company that carries on a manufacturing business. Donald has worked full time in the business since its inception in 2013.

After graduating from high school at 18 years of age, Donald's son David worked full time in the business during the years 2018 through 2020. However, in January 2021 he enrolled in a full-time university program and no longer spends any time working in the business. He was 22 years old at the end of 2021.

In late 2020, in order to assist David with the cost of attending university, Donald authorizes the company to issue a separate class of shares to his son. David used his personal savings to acquire the shares. These new shares have a FMV equal to 20% of the total value of all outstanding shares, pay dividends at an annual rate of 5%, and are non-voting. Assume that the highest quarterly prescribed rate in 2021 was 2%.

During 2021, Dontar pays $105,000 in dividends to Donald and $6,000 in dividends to David.

AP 11-5   (Transfer of Credits and Pension Income Splitting)

Mr. and Mrs. Bahry have been retired for several years. They are both in their early seventies, residents of Canada, and rely on pension income to provide for most of their needs. More specifically, the components of their income for the year ending December 31, 2021, are as follows:

	Mr. Bahry	Mrs. Bahry
Old Age Security (OAS)	$ 7,400	$7,400
Receipts from registered pension plan (RPP)	12,340	820
Receipts from RRIF	N/A	1,000
CPP receipts	3,690	830
Eligible dividends received from Canadian public corporations (100%)	1,600	336
Interest on savings accounts	1,239	3,500
Charitable donations	1,210	300
Capital gain on sale of painting	N/A	500
Capital loss on sale of public company shares	3,975	820

Required:

A. Assume that Mr. and Mrs. Bahry do not elect to use the pension income splitting provisions. Determine the taxable income for both Mr. and Mrs. Bahry and the maximum federal tax credits that will be available to Mr. Bahry for the 2021 taxation year. Also indicate the amount and types of any loss carry overs that would be available to Mr. and Mrs. Bahry at the end of 2021.

B. If Mr. and Mrs. Bahry jointly elect to split the pension income, what objectives should they try to accomplish with the pension income split? (No calculations are required.)

AP 11-6   (Alternative Minimum Tax [AMT], RRSP Calculations, and Tax Planning)

Carol Duncan has been teaching introductory federal income tax at a college in Alberta for the last 10 years. At tax time, family and friends inundate her with requests for assistance with their personal income tax returns. As a rule, aside from answering a question or two, she has avoided involvement with assisting in preparing income tax returns. For 2021, however, she changed her mind and agreed to prepare the returns of two part-time students (Milana and Albert) and one family member (Therese) on condition that she can use the results as case studies in her income tax classes. She carefully selected the three individuals given their unique circumstances that allow her to focus on the AMT, RRSPs, and related tax planning. The following information has been presented to Carol for the three individuals:

	Milana	**Albert**	**Therese**
Business income	$120,000	$ Nil	$ Nil
Employment income	Nil	$26,000	$60,000
Eligible dividends received	Nil	Nil	25,000
Dividend gross up (38%)	Nil	Nil	9,500
Non-eligible dividends received	Nil	94,000	Nil
Dividend gross up (15%)	Nil	14,100	Nil
Taxable capital gains	140,000	180,000	500,000
Capital gains deduction allowable	Nil	100,000	440,000[1]
Retiring allowance	80,000	Nil	Nil
RRSP contributions	46,000	5,000	24,000
ABIL	Nil	Nil	60,000
Non-capital losses available	173,000	50,000	Nil

[1]The capital gains deduction is limited by the annual gains limit, which is equal to the ITA 3(b) amount of $500,000 less the ABIL realized of $60,000.

After 30 years of service, Milana retired from her employment in December 2020 and went into business for herself in January 2021. The terms of her employment provided her with a retiring allowance of $80,000, only part of which ($46,000) was eligible for a tax-free rollover to her RRSP.

Albert had no unused RRSP deduction room or undeducted RRSP contributions at the end of 2020. His 2020 earned income was only $22,000.

Therese's T4 for 2020 indicates a pension adjustment (PA) of $11,600. Her earned income for 2020 was $120,000. In addition, at the end of 2020 she has unused RRSP deduction room of $21,000 and undeducted RRSP contributions of $8,000,

Albert and Therese's taxable capital gains relate to the sale of QSBC shares. Albert has used his capital gains deduction extensively in previous years and only had an available amount remaining of $200,000 of the maximum of $892,218. Milana's taxable capital gain arose as a result of the sale of a cottage that was not eligible for either the principal residence exemption or the capital gains deduction.

Albert is the sole shareholder of a Canadian controlled private corporation (CCPC) that is very profitable. He is flexible in terms of determining how he will be compensated by his company. Annually he requires $120,000 of income, which in 2021 he has decided should be paid as salary of $26,000 and dividends of $94,000.

Therese has been involved in searching for investment opportunities since she inherited a large sum of money years ago when her parents passed away. Most of her investments are in public companies, but a few years ago she decided to invest in up and coming CCPCs that qualify as small business corporations. While she experienced substantial capital gains on the sale of shares of one company, she suffered a sizable loss on the sale of another, which fortunately qualified as an ABIL.

Ignore the EI, CPP, and Canada employment tax credits. Assume that the only tax credits available to each of the three individuals are their basic personal credit and dividend tax credits.

Required: Calculate the minimum Part 1 net federal tax payable for the 2021 year for each of the three individuals as well as each of their respective AMT liabilities, if any.

Bonus Question: What could Albert, Milana, and Therese have done differently to reduce or eliminate their AMT liability?

AP 11-7 *(Death of an Individual)*

Family Information

On July 7, 2021, Mrs. Rachelle Flax was killed in an automobile accident. At the time of her death, Rachelle was 47 years old. She is survived by her 44-year-old husband, Martin Flax, and her 24-year-old daughter, Roxanne Flax.

Martin has spent most of his adult life volunteering for worthy causes. During 2021, he has employment income of $2,100 that was paid to him for services performed for a business that Rachelle carried on as a sole proprietor prior to her death, as well as $1,700 in interest income. This interest was earned on a guaranteed investment certificate that had been given to him by Rachelle several years ago.

Roxanne is a very successful home decorator and is not a dependant of Rachelle.

Business Income

For several years, Rachelle has been the sole proprietor of a restaurant. The business had a December 31 fiscal year end. Until the date of her death, the proprietorship had business income for income tax purposes of $69,400. At the time of her death, the FMV of the depreciable properties was $5,900 greater than their UCC. The FMV of the depreciable properties did not exceed their ACB (e.g., capital cost).

As noted, prior to her death, the business had paid Martin a total of $2,100. This was for serving as bartender in the restaurant. As Martin did not feel capable of carrying on the business on his own, he immediately sold the the depreciable property for FMV to a regular customer.

Rental Property

Rachelle had owned a residential rental property for five years prior to her death. In 2021, prior to her death, the property had gross rents of $46,300 and expenses other than CCA of $31,400. The rental property had been purchased for $312,000, of which $210,000 was allocated to the building and $102,000 to the land. An appraisal indicated that, at the time of her death, the total value of the property was $355,000, which was allocated $243,000 to the building and $112,000 to the land. At January 1, 2021, the UCC of the property was $174,795.

Rachelle's will leaves this property to her daughter, Roxanne.

Investments and Other Property

Information related to other property that Rachelle owned at the time of her death is as follows:

Art Collection Rachelle had collected Inuit art for a number of years. Her collection had an ACB of $23,400. At the time of her death, the FMV of the collection was $57,000. The collection was left to her daughter, who immediately sold the collection for its FMV of $57,000.

Jewellery Over the years, Rachelle had spent $32,000 on various pieces of jewellery. At the time of her death, their FMV was only $8,300. The collection was left to her daughter who immediately sold them for their FMV of $8,300.

Shares in RAF Ltd. RAF Ltd. is a Canadian public company. The shares were purchased for $12,400 and, prior to her death, paid Rachelle eligible dividends of $860. At the time of her death, the FMV was $28,600. Her will leaves these shares to the Humane Society. The Humane Society issues a charitable donation receipt for $28,600 on receiving the shares.

Shares in Flax Fittings Inc. This is a company that was started by Rachelle's father with an investment of $20,000. He left all of the shares to Rachelle in his will. At the time she acquired the shares they were valued at $72,000. Prior to her death, the shares paid Rachelle non-eligible dividends of $6,200. At the time of her death, the FMV was $104,000. The shares are not eligible for the capital gains deduction. Her will leaves these shares to Martin.

RRSP   At the time of her death, Rachelle had an RRSP with a total FMV of $1,123,000. Martin is named as beneficiary of the RRSP.

Family Residence   The family home is in Rachelle's name only. It had been purchased at a cost of $382,600. At the time of her death, the appraised value of the property was $507,000. This property is left to Martin.

Other Information

At the time of her death, Rachelle had a 2018 listed personal property loss (100%) of $5,400 and a 2019 net capital loss balance of $89,400. Rachelle has never claimed the capital gains deduction in a year prior to her death.

Due to her business income, Rachelle will pay the maximum CPP contributions for a self-employed proprietor.

The terms of Rachelle's will require that the executor of her estate elect out of the ITA 70(6) spousal rollover in the case of all properties bequeathed to Martin.

Required: Calculate Rachelle's minimum net income, taxable income, and net federal tax payable for the 2021 taxation year.

AP 11-8   *(Comprehensive Tax Payable with Donations)*

Family Information

Lyla and Clark Beaston are both 45 years of age. They have been happily married for 23 years. They have no children.

Both of them are lawyers and have had very successful careers in a variety of jobs. At this point, their net worth is over $5 million. Lyla is currently employed by a large public company. While Clark has been an employee in the past, he currently spends his time managing the family's investments. For a variety of reasons, all of these investments are solely owned by Clark.

While both Lyla and Clark enjoy generally good health, Clark has significant back problems related to a childhood accident. As these have worsened in recent years, in 2021 he decides to go to a clinic in the U.S. for surgery. The total cost of this surgery is US$52,000. At the time of this surgery, the exchange rate was US$1.00 = C$1.35, providing a Candian doilar equivalent of $70,200. The travel costs associated with this surgery were US$8,000, resulting in a Canadian dollar equivalent of $10,800. Clark's Canadian doctor has provided a letter indicating that a similar surgery would have required a wait time of at least two years in Canada.

The couple have qualifying medical expenses in Canada consisting of prescriptions and regular dental work of $4,800.

Because they attribute much of their success to the excellent education they received at the University of Toronto, they make a 2021 donation of $175,000 to this institution when Clark receives a large and unexpected inheritance. No other donations are made during the year.

Lyla's Employment Information

Lyla's gross salary for 2021 is $270,000. Her employer withholds the maximum 2021 contributions of Employment Insurance ($890) and the Canada Pension Plan ($3,166). She does all of her work in her employer's office and is not required to travel. Given this, she has no deductible travel or other employment-related expenses.

Her employer sponsors a defined benefit registered pension plan. Her contribution, which is withheld from her salary, is $12,450. Her employer makes a matching contribution.

Her employer provides a group disability plan for its employees. The 2021 premium on this plan is $2,500, one-half of which is paid by Lyla through withholdings. Her employer also provides for a generous medical insurance plan that covers 100% of any prescription costs and dental fees paid in Canada by employees for themselves or their families.

Clark's Investment Results

During 2021, the results for the investments that Clark manages are as follows:

Interest	$ 28,600
Eligible dividends from Canadian public companies	136,000
Net taxable capital gains	77,000

In order to increase his investment holdings, Clark assumed a mortgage on the family residence. The residence had been purchased for cash and, at the time the mortgage was arranged, there was no debt on the property. The proceeds of the mortgage were immediately invested in shares of Canadian public companies. Interest on the mortgage for 2021 was $12,000.

Required:

A. Determine the combined net federal tax payable for Lyla and Clark, assuming that Lyla claims all of the medical expenses and all of the charitable donations.

B. Determine the combined net federal tax payable for Lyla and Clark, assuming that Clark claims all of the medical expenses and all of the charitable donations.

C. Determine whether there is an allocation of medical expenses and charitable donations that would produce a lower combined net federal tax payable than either the Part A results or the Part B results. Show your calculations.

AP 11-9 (Comprehensive Personal Tax Payable)

On January 10, 2021, Ms. Arlene Arsenault formally separated from her husband and retained custody of her 15-year-old son, Jerry. Jerry has no income during 2021. Ms. Arsenault is also responsible for her 21-year-old daughter, Janine, who has a severe and prolonged disability (a medical doctor has certified her disability on Form T2201). Janine has 2021 income of $6,000, resulting from income on investments that were left to her by her grandmother.

In order to get a fresh start in life, Ms. Arsenault found a new job. She resigned from her position in Ottawa and moved to a similar position in Toronto. The move took place on October 31, 2021. She has asked for your assistance in preparing an estimate of her 2021 personal income tax liability and, in order to assist you with your calculations, she has prepared the following list of transactions that occurred during 2021:

1. Her gross salary from her Ottawa employer, a large public company, for the first 10 months of the year was $82,000. Her employer withheld from this amount CPP contributions of $3,166, EI premiums of $890, and RPP contributions of $2,500. The employer also contributed $2,500 to the company's RPP on her behalf.

2. Before leaving her Ottawa employer, she exercised stock options to acquire 2,000 of the company's shares at a price of $15 per share. The options were issued in 2020, when the market price of the shares was $12 per share. On August 12, 2021, the day that she exercised the options, the shares were trading at $20 per share. Ms. Arsenault sells the shares as soon as she acquires them. Brokerage fees totalled $350 on the sale.

3. During November and December, her gross wages with her Toronto employer amounted to $13,000. Her new employer withheld CPP contributions of $500, EI premiums of $390, and $650 in RPP contributions. Her Toronto employer also contributed $650 to the company's money purchase RPP on her behalf.

4. Ms. Arsenault found a new home in Toronto during her September house hunting trip there. The legal arrangements for the house purchase were finalized on October 10. In Ottawa,

she and her husband had lived for 10 years in a home that they rented. Her agreement with her new employer requires that they pay her moving costs. In order to simplify the record keeping, the employer paid her an allowance of $7,500 and did not require a detailed accounting of expenses. Her actual expenses were as follows:

Moving company charges	$3,800
Airfare for September Toronto trip to acquire new home	350
Meals and lodging on September Toronto trip	275
Gas for October 31 move to Toronto	65
Lodging in Ottawa on October 30	110
Meals on October 30 and October 31 while moving	250
Charges for cancellation of lease on Ottawa home	935
Legal and other fees on acquisition of Toronto home	1,500
Total	$7,285

Ms. Arsenault did not use the simplified method of calculating vehicle expenses and moving costs.

5. In 2018, Ms. Arsenault's mother died, leaving her 5,000 shares of Linz Industries, a private company. These shares had cost her mother $50,000 and had a FMV at the time of her death of $95,000. Ms. Arsenault received non-eligible dividends of $7,500 on these shares in May of 2021 and, in December, she sells the shares for $105,000. Selling costs were $850.

6. Ms. Arsenault made $1,500 in donations to a registered Canadian charity and $900 in contributions to the Libcon Rebloc Party, a registered federal political party.

7. Ms. Arsenault incurred the following child care costs:

Payments to individuals for Jerry and Janine	$ 7,160
Fees for Jerry to attend camp (4 weeks at $200 per week)	800
Food and clothing for the children	6,400
Total	$14,360

8. Ms. Arsenault paid the following medical expenses:

For Herself	$ 9,700
Jerry	900
Janine	7,250
Total	$17,850

9. In previous years, Ms. Arsenault's husband took care of her financial affairs. She has no understanding of either RPPs or RRSPs, but will make the maximum deductible RRSP contribution for 2021 as soon as you have calculated it. Her RRSP deduction limit statement from the CRA states that her 2020 earned income was $81,100 and that, at the end of 2020, she had no unused RRSP deduction room. Her 2020 T4 from her employer indicates a pension adjustment of $4,500. There are no undeducted contributions in her RRSP.

10. During the year, Ms. Arsenault paid legal fees of $2,500 in connection with her separation agreement. This settlement requires her husband to make a lump-sum payment of $25,000 on March 1, 2021, in settlement of any future payments, as well as child support payments of $4,000 at the end of each month beginning on January 31, 2021. All required payments were received for the year.

11. In addition to her employment income, Ms. Arsenault carries on a mail-order business as a sole proprietor with a December 31 year end. Her 2021 business income for income tax

purposes totalled $22,500. Included in this amount is a deduction of $950 for interest that she paid on a demand loan taken out to finance inventory purchases. During the year ending December 31, 2021, Ms. Arsenault withdraws $27,000 from the bank account maintained by the business.

12. Ms. Arsenault's father owns a controlling interest in a successful CCPC that carries on a business that he is actively involved with. In 2021, he gave Arlene a block of non-voting shares in his company. During 2021, these shares paid non-eligible dividends to Arlene in the amount of $10,000. Arlene has never been involved in this company's activities.

Required:

A. Determine Ms. Arsenault's minimum net income and her taxable income for 2021. Ignore any GST/HST considerations. In the determination of net income, provide separate calculations of:

- employment income,
- business and property income,
- net taxable capital gains,
- other types of income, and
- other deductions from income.

B. Based on your answer to Part A, calculate Ms. Arsenault's minimum 2021 net federal income tax payable and any other amounts owing to (refundable from) the CRA for 2021. Ignore any income tax withholdings that her employers would have made.

AP 11-10 (Comprehensive Tax Payable)

Jody Simpson turned 40 years of age in 2021. She has one child, Bert, who was 11 years of age at December 31, 2021. Jody was married in 2010 to her high school sweetheart, Michael Burns, but the marriage ended with a divorce that was finalized in November 2020. Jody obtained full custody of Bert following a court order issued shortly after the divorce. The court order entitles her to both child support in the amount of $15,000 annually and spousal support in the amount of $25,000 annually beginning January 1, 2021. All of the 2021 support payments were paid directly to her on a monthly basis throughout the year.

Jody provides you with the following information concerning her 2021 income and expenses:

1. Jody's parents have been owner-managers of a CCPC for over 30 years that carries on a successful business commonly referred to as "pickers"—the company name is Pickers Ltd. The business involves travel across the country to identified locations where old items and collectibles can be found, including advertising signs, paintings, furniture, toys, cars, motor-cycles, bicycles, comic books, and other various decades old items. When the business was incorporated, Jody and her three siblings were all made shareholders. Each of them owns common voting shares that represent 12.0% of all of the voting shares and 12.0% of the value of the company. Jody has never been actively involved in Pickers Ltd.'s business nor has she made any financial or other contributions. In 2021 Jody received a non-eligible dividend of $40,000 from Pickers Ltd.

2. In 2017 Jody obtained an MBA and immediately decided to start a pawn shop business. Her parents agreed to sell her some of their surplus inventory on an ongoing basis at a discount and provided her with their many contacts, allowing her to establish her own network for goods that her parents' company was not interested in. In 2020 Pickers Ltd. gross sales to Jody's business accounted for only 1.5% of their total gross sales. Jody operated the pawn shop as a sole proprietor until early 2020, at which time she incorporated the business in a CCPC she named PS World Inc. The company's taxation year is January 1 to December 31. Jody owns all of the 100 issued and outstanding common shares and Bert owns all 10 of the non-voting preferred shares. The ACB of Jody's common shares equal $100 ($1 per share). The ACB of Bert's shares are $10 ($1 per share), which he acquired with his own money earned mowing the lawns of neighbours.

3. Jody had learned in her MBA program that it was best to avoid incorporation until the business profits were sizable enough to warrant taking advantage of low corporate tax rates. As a result, Jody has non-capital losses in each of 2017 to 2019 in the amounts of $32,000, $21,000, and $7,800, respectively. None of these losses have been claimed prior to 2021.

4. In 2021 PS World declared and paid non-eligible dividends in the amount of $84,000 to Jody and $34,000 to Bert. Jody also received a weekly salary of $1,500 on which the maximum CPP of $3,166 was paid. Since Jody's shareholding exceeds 40% of the voting shares she is ineligible for Employment Insurance and therefore pays no EI premiums nor does her company, except for other employees.

5. The company regularly declares year-end bonuses based on sales performance. A bonus of $50,000 had been declared by the company at the end of 2020 and was paid to Jody on April 2, 2021. A bonus of $60,000 was declared on December 31, 2021, and was paid to Jody on April 15, 2022.

6. In August 2021 Jody met Joe Abernathy, a like-minded individual who was very much interested in the pawn shop. He offered to purchase an interest in the company and Jody accepted, agreeing to sell him 25 of her common shares for $400,000 with half due at the signing on August 1, 2021, and the balance due July 31, 2022. Interest was charged on the outstanding balance at the rate of 5%. Selling costs were $4,000.

7. In 2020 Jody received dividends from a U.S. public company in the amount of US$10,000. The exchange rate at the time was 1.282. U.S. withholding taxes were 15%, or US$1,500. Jody and her other siblings had inherited the shares on the passing of their grandmother in 2018.

8. Since Judy frequently travels to the U.S. she maintained, in Canada, a personal U.S. currency bank account from which she would draw sufficient funds when necessary. Due to ongoing cash needs she decided to transfer $20,000 of U.S. funds that had cost her C$26,100 to her Canadian currency account at a time when the exchange rate was 1.25.

9. Medical expenses for prescriptions and dental services (including braces for Bert) totalled $23,000 in 2021. Jody established a medical and dental plan in her company shortly after it was incorporated. The plans are equally available to all employees and their families. The plans covered 60% of the submitted claims or $13,800. In addition Jody personally paid total premiums of $2,400 for both plans for the year.

10. In prior years Jody has claimed the capital gains deduction using $160,000 of the currently available $892,218 for 2021. Her CNIL account at the end of 2021 is $19,000.

11. In addition to the non-capital losses in #3, Jody has a 2018 net capital loss of $4,500 [(1/2) ($9,000)] and a 2019 listed personal property loss of $1,200 (100%).

12. Jody paid child care costs for Bert in the amount of $6,200. The costs cover daycare before and after school on weekdays throughout the year.

13. Jody learned at an early age to enjoy collectibles and is an avid collector to this day. When purchasing items for her company's pawn ship business she often comes across items that are perfect additions to her personal collections that are not suited for the business. As a result, purchasing excursions often result in a combination of personal and business purchases. To ensure she had additional funds to make new purchases Jody decided to let go of some of her collection and sold the following items: (1) a painting that had cost her $1,700 was sold for $8,700; (2) a stamp collection that cost her $9,500 was sold for $11,000; and (3) a rare book about medical practices in the 1700s and 1800s that had cost her $250 was sold for $5,000.

14. Jody donates $1,000 every year to Plan Canada and another $1,000 to the Humane Society. In 2021 a local hospital was asking for donations to expand the Intensive Care Unit. Jody decided to donate a coin collection that she had acquired in 2013 for $19,000. An appraiser who works for her company determined that the fair market value of the collection was only $11,000 and was unlikely to increase in value. Jody received charitable donation receipts for all three donations, including an $11,000 receipt for the coin collection.

Jody currently lives with her son, Bert, in a spacious waterfront property that she has been renting since her divorce. The owner wants to sell and has offered her the opportunity to buy before the property is officially listed. The purchase price of $550,000 is a little more than she wants to spend, but she does not want to pass up the opportunity. She asks you for advice. She currently has $69,500 in her TFSA and $210,000 in her RRSP. She contributed $11,300 to her RRSP for the 2021 taxation year, all of which is fully deductible. She is not interested in carrying any debt and has asked you whether it is better to withdraw funds from her TFSA or RRSP should she require any additional cash to either avoid a mortgage altogether or to keep it as low as possible.

Required:

A. Determine Bert's minimum net income, taxable income, and net federal tax payable for 2021. Where there is a potential TOSI (tax on split income), indicate whether or not it would apply and why.

B. Determine Jody's minimum net income, taxable income, and net federal tax payable for 2021 including the AMT. Where there is a potential TOSI (tax on split income), indicate whether or not it would apply and why.

C. In addition, detail the advice you would give to Jody regarding her questions to you about potential additional cash requirements should she go ahead and purchase the house she is currently living in.

AP 11-11 *(Comprehensive Case Covering Chapters 1 to 11)*
Family Information
Adam Huffer is 42 years old. His wife, Estelle Huffer, is 38 years old. They have been married for 19 years. They have a daughter, Portia, who is 16 years old and in good health.

Portia, who is very precocious, began attending university on a full-time basis in September 2021. Her only income for the year is $3,400 that she earned in various part-time jobs. Adam has paid her $5,400 tuition fee for the fall semester, as well as $450 for required textbooks and $2,400 for her residence fees. As her income is less than the basic personal tax credit, she has agreed to transfer her tuition credit to her father.

Adam and Estelle's only surviving parent is Adam's father, Jack. While he does not qualify for the disability tax credit, he is dependent on Adam and Estelle because of his limited mobility. He is 69 years old and lives with them. His 2021 net income is equal to $12,300, including OAS payments and a small pension from a former employer. Adam claims any available personal credit for Jack.

Adam serves as a volunteer firefighter. During 2021 he spent over 300 hours in this work, for which he received no compensation. Because he was convicted of arson when he was a juvenile, he feels that this volunteer work at least partially makes up for some of the damage he did in his teen years.

For many years, Adam has owned a small office building that he rented to the Red Cross. On January 1, 2021, he donates this building to that organization, receiving a tax receipt from them for its FMV of $325,000. This estimated value is made up of $250,000 for the building and $75,000 for the land. Adam's capital cost for the property of $210,000 was made up of $150,000 for the building and $60,000 for the land. On January 1, 2021, the UCC of the building was $119,859. Adam would like to use the maximum amount of this credit during the current taxation year.

During 2021, Adam paid for medical and dental services as follows:

Root canal fee—Adam	$ 1,350
Teeth cleaning—Adam and Estelle	360
Psychological counselling for Portia	820
Teeth whitening for Portia	625
Cosmetic surgery for Portia	8,450
Prescription glasses for Estelle and Portia	500
Electric wheelchair for Jack	4,200
Total	$16,305

Estelle will claim the credit for qualifying medical expenses.

Adam's Employment Information

Adam works for a large Canadian public company. As CEO, his 2021 salary is $350,000, none of which is commissions. The amounts withheld by his employer during 2021 are as follows:

Registered pension plan contributions*	$12,300
EI premiums	890
CPP contributions	3,166

   *Adam's employer makes a matching contribution of $12,300.

As CEO, Adam is required to travel extensively by his employer. He uses his own vehicle for this travel. He purchased his current automobile, a BMW 750i, for $132,000 on January 1, 2021. During the year, he drove the automobile a total of 63,000 kilometres, of which 59,000 were employment related and the remaining 4,000 were for personal use. Operating costs paid for the year totalled $11,300.

In addition to his automobile costs, his other 2021 employment-related travel costs were as follows:

Hotels	$16,000
Food	7,200

His employer provides him with the following allowances for his travel:

Hotels and food ($700 per day)	$21,000
Use of personal automobile ($300 per week)	15,600

On a regular annual basis in January of each year, Adam's employer grants him options to buy the shares of the company at their trading value on the grant date. During 2021, he exercises options to acquire 1,000 shares at a price of $25 per share. On the exercise date the shares are trading at $28 per share. These shares paid no dividends during the year and Adam still owns the shares on December 31, 2021.

All of the family's other stock investments are owned by Estelle. As a consequence, Adam has no income other than his employment-related income and income that results from his charitable donation of real property.

Estelle's Investment Information

When Estelle's father died six years ago, he left her with shares in several CCPCs that qualifiy as small business corporations. Prior to 2021, she had the following two dispositions of these shares, which qualified as QSBC shares for capital gains deduction purposes:

2016   In this year she sold QSBC shares in ABC for $500,000. The ACB of the shares was $275,000, resulting in a capital gain of $225,000. The taxable amount of the gain was fully offset by the capital gains deduction.

2018   In this year she sold QSBC shares in DEF for $623,000. The ACB of the shares was $216,000, resulting in a capital gain of $407,000. Once again, the taxable amount of the gain was fully offset by the capital gains deduction.

Estelle had no other dispositions of capital property prior to 2021.

All of Estelle's investment income is derived from corporate shares. During 2021, she received a total of $32,000 in non-eligible dividends from these corporations.

In 2021, she had the following dispositions:

- Sale of QSBC shares of GHI for $662,000. The ACB of the shares was $360,000, resulting in a capital gain of $302,000.

- Sale of QSBC shares of JKL for $230,000. The ACB of the shares was $250,000, resulting in a capital loss of $20,000. The shares were sold to an arm's-length person and would potentially qualify for ABIL treatment.

For several years, Estelle has been carrying forward a $15,000 net capital loss from 2015. In previous years, she has chosen not to use this carry forward to maximize her capital gains deduction. She would like to use this deduction in 2021, regardless of whether her capital gains deduction is maximized. Estelle has never had a CNIL balance.

Required: Ignore GST/HST/PST considerations in your solution.

A.   Determine Adam's net income, taxable income, and net federal tax payable for 2021. Indicate whether there are any carry forward amounts available at the end of 2021.

B.   Determine Estelle's net income, taxable income, and net federal tax payable, including AMT for 2021. Indicate whether there are any carry forward amounts available at the end of 2021.

Tax Software Assignment Problems

Tax Software AP 11-1

This problem is an expansion of the Chapter 4 problem.

DISCLAIMER: All characters appearing in this problem are fictitious. Any resemblance to real persons, living or dead, is purely coincidental.

Mr. Buddy Musician (SIN 527-000-061) was born in Vancouver on August 28, 1953. He has spent most of his working life as a pianist and song writer. He and his family live at 111 WWW Street, Vancouver, B.C. V4H 3W4, phone (604) 111-1111.

Mr. Musician's wife, Natasha (SIN 527-000-129), was born on June 6, 1995. She and Mr. Musician have four children. Each child was born on April 1 of the following years: Linda, 2015; Larry, 2016; Donna, 2017; and Donald, 2018. None of the four children have any income of their own for 2020. Natasha's only income during 2020 is $3,200 from singing engagements.

Buddy and Natasha Musician have two adopted children. Richard (SIN 527-000-285) was born on March 15, 2003, and has income of $2,800 for the year. Due to his accelerated schooling, he started full-time attendance at university in September of 2020 at the age of 17. His first semester tuition fee is $3,000. These amounts are paid by Mr. Musician.

The other adopted child, Sarah, was born on September 2, 2000, and was in full-time attendance at university for all of 2020 (including a four-month summer session). Her tuition is $9,600. These amounts are also paid by Mr. Musician. Sarah has no income during the year.

Neither Richard nor Sarah will have any income in the next three years. They both have agreed that the maximum tuition amount should be transferred to their father. Assume that they will not file income tax returns to take advantage of the Canada training credit.

Tax Software Assignment Problems

Mr. Musician's mother, Eunice, was born on April 10, 1933, and his father, Earl, was born on November 16, 1931. They both live with Mr. Musician and his wife. While his father has some mobility issues, he is not infirm. His mother is legally blind. Eunice Musician had income of $9,500 for the year, while Earl Musician had income of $7,500.

Other information concerning Mr. Musician and his family for 2020 is as follows:

1. Mr. Musician earned $16,500 for work as the house pianist at the Loose Moose Pub. His T4 showed that his employer withheld $500 for income taxes and $280.70 for EI.

2. During the year, Mr. Musician made his annual $3,000 donation to Planned Parenthood of Canada, a registered Canadian charity.

3. Mr. Musician has been married before to Lori Musician (SIN 527-000-319). Lori is 52 years old and lives in Fort Erie, Ontario.

4. Mr. Musician has two additional children who live with their mother, Ms. Dolly Nurse (SIN 527-000-582), in Burnaby, British Columbia. The children are Megan Nurse, aged 12, and Andrew Nurse, aged 14. Neither child has any income during 2020. While Ms. Nurse and Mr. Musician were never married, Mr. Musician acknowledges that he is the father of both children. Although Buddy has provided limited financial aid by paying their dental and medical expenses, the children are not dependent on Buddy for support.

5. Mr. Musician wishes to claim all his medical expenses on a calendar-year basis. On December 2, 2020, Mr. Musician paid dental expenses to Canada Wide Dental Clinics for the following individuals:

Himself	$1,200
Natasha (wife)	700
Richard (adopted son)	800
Sarah (adopted daughter)	300
Linda (daughter)	100
Earl (father)	1,050
Lori (ex-wife)	300
Dolly Nurse (mother of two of his children)	675
Megan Nurse (daughter of Dolly Nurse)	550
Total	$5,675

6. Mr. Musician signed a contract with Fred Nesbitt on January 13, 2020, to do permanent modifications to his house. The contract was for the installation of ramps with sturdy hand railings outside his front and back doors to give his parents easier access to the house and modifications to their bathroom so they would be less likely to fall when using the shower. The contract price was $5,800. As neither of his parents has a severe and prolonged mobility impairment, these expenditures are not eligible medical expenses.

7. Mr. Musician paid four quarterly instalments of $1,000 each (total of $4,000) for 2020, as requested on his instalment reminders from the CRA. He paid each instalment on the due date.

8. Mr. Musician receives $7,271.67 in OAS payments and $5,500 in CPP "retirement benefit" payments over 12 months. There was no tax shown as withheld on his T4A(OAS) or his T4A(P).

9. Mr. Musician builds a state-of-the-art home theatre in a new extension of his home. In order to finance it, he sells stock in his RRSP and withdraws the funds from his RRSP. His T4RSP showed $52,000 in withdrawals from the House of Rock Bank (Box 22) and total tax of $15,600 deducted from these payments.

10. Several of Mr. Musician's songs, including his outstanding hit "Drop Kick Me, Jesus, through the Goal Posts of Life", have provided him with substantial royalty payments over the years. In 2020, the Never Say Die Record Company paid him $78,000 in royalty payments. No T5 was issued by the company.

11. Mr. Musician had carried on a songwriting business for many years but had gradually reduced the time devoted to the endeavour. However, in order to ensure the financial security of his family, Mr. Musician decided to accelerate his involvement by committing additional time to songwriting. On November 1, 2020, he rented a small, quiet studio for $700 a month and purchased a Roland electric piano for $7,750 that was delivered there. He does not plan to use the space or piano for personal enjoyment, only for composing.

12. The previous year, on January 2, 2019, Mr. Musician elected not to make any further CPP contributions on his income from carrying on a business.

13. Mr. Musician is required by a court order to pay spousal support of $400 per month to his former spouse, Lori Musician. Mr. Musician made spousal support payments of $4,800 during 2020.

14. Mr. Musician is required by a court order to make child support payments of $350 per month to Dolly Nurse for his two children, Megan and Andrew Nurse. A total of $4,200 was paid during the year.

15. Mr. Musician made contributions to the federal Liberal Party in the amount of $610 during the year.

16. Mr. Musician made a $5,000 contribution to his TFSA during the year. Thanks to the excellent investing advice of his gardener, the balance in his TFSA account has grown to more than $175,000 by the end of the year.

Required: With the objective of minimizing Mr. Musician's tax payable, prepare Mr. Musician's 2020 income tax return using the ProFile tax software program assuming Natasha does not file an income tax return. List any assumptions you have made and any notes and tax planning issues you feel should be placed in the file.

Tax Software AP 11-2

This problem is an expansion of the Chapter 4 problem.

DISCLAIMER: All characters appearing in this problem are fictitious. Any resemblance to real persons, living or dead, is purely coincidental.

George Pharmacy is a pharmaceutical sales rep who has been very successful at his job in the last few years. Unfortunately, his family life has not been very happy. Three years ago, his only child, Anna, was driving a car that was hit by a drunk driver. She and her husband were killed and their 14-year-old son, Kevin, was blinded in the accident. He also suffered extensive injuries to his jaw that have required major and prolonged dental work.

George and his wife, Valerie, adopted Kevin. Valerie quit her part-time job to care for him. She also cares for her mother, Joan Drugstore, who lives with them. Joan suffers from dementia, Parkinson's, and severe depression. The family doctor has signed a letter stating that she is dependent on George and Valerie because of her impairments. Joan does not meet the residency requirements necessary to qualify for Canadian OAS payments.

Valerie's parents separated two years ago in Scotland after her father, David Drugstore, suffered enormous losses in the stock market. They were forced to sell their home and David moved to Chile. David phones periodically to request that money be deposited in his online bank account.

George's brother, Martin, completed an alcohol rehabilitation program after being fired for drinking on the job. He is also living with George and Valerie while he is enrolled as a full-time student at Western University. George is paying his tuition, and Martin has agreed to transfer any available education-related amounts to George. Although Martin plans to file his 2020 income tax return, he has not done so yet.

Kevin is taking several undergraduate psychology courses at Western University. After hearing a talk given by an expert blind echolocator (a person who uses sound to locate objects),

Tax Software Assignment Problems

his goal is to become a researcher at the Brain and Mind Institute and study the use of echolocation. Kevin has agreed to transfer the maximum tuition credit to George.

Other information concerning George for 2020 is provided on the following pages.

Required: Prepare the 2020 income tax return of George Pharmacy using the ProFile tax software program assuming Valerie does not file a tax return. List any assumptions you have made and any notes and tax planning issues you feel should be placed in the file. Ignore GST/HST implications in your solution by assuming that George does not qualify for the GST/HST rebate.

Personal Information	Taxpayer
Title	Mr.
First Name	George
Last Name	Pharmacy
SIN	527-000-509
Date of birth (Y/M/D)	1956-07-02
Marital Status	Married
Canadian citizen?	Yes
Provide information to Elections Canada?	Yes
Own foreign property of more than $100,000 Canadian?	No

Taxpayer's Address
123 ZZZ Street, London, Ontario, N0Z 0Z0
Phone number (519) 111-1111

Family Members	Spouse	Child	Mother-in-Law
First Name	Valerie	Kevin	Joan
Last Name	Pharmacy	Pharmacy	Drugstore
SIN	527-000-483	527-000-517	None
Date of birth (Y/M/D)	1955-12-30	2004-10-17	1935-02-24
Net income	$6,520 in CPP	Nil	$500

Family Members	Father-in-Law	Brother
First Name	David	Martin
Last Name	Drugstore	Pharmacy
SIN	None	527-000-533
Date of birth (Y/M/D)	1936-01-12	1973-06-02
Net income	Nil	$8,300

During September, David was arrested in Chile. Valerie had to spend three weeks in Chile and pay $2,000 in bribes before she could get him released from jail. George had to pay Nannies On Call $3,500 for in-home help to take care of Kevin while she was gone.

T2202—(Martin)	Box	Amount
Tuition fees—for Martin Pharmacy (brother)	A	8,000
Number of months in school—part time	B	0
Number of months in school—full time	C	8

T2202—(Kevin)	Box	Amount
Tuition fees—for Kevin	A	3,600
Number of months in school—part time	B	8
Number of months in school—full time	C	0

Donor	Charitable Donation Receipts	Am't
Valerie	Mothers Against Drunk Drivers (MADD)	1,000
George	Canadian Institute for the Blind (CNIB)	3,000

T4	Box	Amount
Issuer—Mega Pharma Inc.		
Employment income	14	378,000.00
Employee's CPP contributions	16	2,898.00
Employee's EI premiums	18	856.36
Income tax deducted	22	114,000.00
Employment commissions	42	82,000.00
Charitable donations	46	400.00

During 2020, Mega reimbursed George $3,788 for meals and entertainment with clients, $2,268 for hotels, and $4,925 for airline tickets.

In addition to George's salary, he also earns commissions. His employer requires him to have an office in his home and has signed the form T2200 each year to this effect.

On October 1, 2020, George purchased a new computer and software that will be used solely in his home office for employment-related uses. The computer cost $3,600 and the various software programs cost $1,250.

House Costs	
Area of home used for home office (square feet)	650
Total area of home (square feet)	5,000
Telephone line including high speed internet connection	620
Hydro	3,200
Insurance—House	4,000
Maintenance and repairs	3,800
Mortgage interest	6,200
Mortgage life insurance premiums	400
Property taxes	6,700

Tax Software Assignment Problems

(Y/M/D)	Patient	Medical Expenses	Description	Amount
2020-12-31	George	Johnson Inc.	Out of Canada insurance	731.00
2020-08-31	George	Dr. Smith	Dental fees	155.40
2020-09-19	George	Optician	Prescription glasses	109.00
2020-11-07	Valerie	Pharmacy	Prescription	66.84
2020-06-07	Joan	Dr. Wong	Psychiatric counselling	2,050.00
2020-03-22	David	Tropical Disease Centre	Prescription	390.00
2020-12-20	Martin	Dr. Walker	Group therapy	6,000.00
2020-10-01	Kevin	Dr. Takarabe	Orthodontics and dental	30,000.00

George paid $800 for the care and feeding of Kevin's seeing eye dog, Isis, during 2020.

At the beginning of 2020, George had a 2019 net capital loss balance of $10,500 from the sale of shares in 2019. He had not disposed of any capital property prior to 2019.

Dispositions of Property	Asset 1	Asset 2	Asset 3
Description	Molson Inc. shares	Imperial Oil shares	Sailboat
Number of units	150	387	N/A
Year of acquisition	2017	2018	2018
Date of disposition	February 14	June 6	October 1
Proceeds of disposition	37,000	9,600	74,000
Adjusted cost base	27,600	12,100	72,000
Outlays and expenses	35	29	N/A

Dispositions of Property	Asset 4	Asset 5	Asset 6
Description	Motorcycle	Painting	Coin collection
Year of acquisition	2020	2013	2017
Date of disposition	November 17	August 28	March 24
Proceeds of disposition	14,000	1,100	700
Adjusted cost base	21,000	450	1,800
Outlays and expenses	N/A	N/A	N/A

Real Estate Rental—Commercial Property	Amount
Address—888 YYZ Drive, Toronto, Ontario, M0M 0M0	
Year of purchase	2016
Gross rents	16,000
Property taxes	5,128
Insurance	1,890
Interest on mortgage	3,175
Payment on principal	2,200
Furnace repairs	550
Maintenance contract	3,469
Building purchased for $120,100—UCC beginning of year	107,441
Fixtures purchased for $8,500—UCC beginning of year	4,651

The building and fixtures were purchased on August 28, 2016. At the time the building and fixtures were being used as a drugstore and Mr. Pharmacy has retained the same tenant.

George knows he should have been contributing to various savings plans over the years, but his increasing number of needy dependants required he spend all of his take-home pay to support them and he has contributed to none. It was only in 2020 that his compensation had increased enough so that he had sufficient funds to consider savings plans.

His daughter had made contributions totalling more than $10,000 to an RESP for Kevin prior to her death, but George has made no RESP contributions to the plan since then.

George's 2020 RRSP deduction limit is $285,550.

Tax Software AP 11-3

This problem is an expansion of the Chapter 4 problem.

DISCLAIMER: All characters appearing in all versions of this problem are fictitious. Any resemblance to real persons, living or dead, is purely coincidental.

Information Related to Chapter 4 Material

Seymour Career and Mary Career are your tax clients. They have been married for two years. Mary has progressed quickly in MoreCorp, the large, publicly traded firm she is working for, due to her strong tax and accounting background. Her firm has an excellent health and dental plan that reimburses 100% of all medical and dental expenses.

Personal Information	Taxpayer	Spouse
Title	Ms.	Mr.
First Name	Mary	Seymour
Last Name	Career	Career
SIN	527-000-129	527-000-079
Date of birth (Y/M/D)	1982-12-08	1961-01-29
Marital status	Married	Married
Canadian citizen?	Yes	Yes
Provide information to Elections Canada?	Yes	Yes
Own foreign property of more than $100,000 Canadian?	No	No

Taxpayer's Address
123 ABC Street, Saint John, N.B. E0E 0E0
Phone number (506) 111-1111
Spouse's address same as taxpayer? Yes

Dependant	Child
First Name	William
Last Name	Career
SIN	527-000-319
Date of birth (Y/M/D)	2013-02-24
Net Income	Nil

T4—Mary	Box	Amount
Issuer—MoreCorp		
Employment income	14	152,866.08
Employee's CPP contributions	16	2,898.00
Employee's EI premiums	18	856.36
RPP contributions	20	Nil
Income tax ceducted	22	48,665.11
Charitable donations	46	1,000.00

Donor	Charitable Donation Receipts	Amount
Seymour	Canadian Cancer Foundation	500
Seymour	Salvation Army	250

Information Related to Chapter 6 Material

Tax Software Note To create a return for Seymour that is coupled to Mary's, hit the F5 key with Mary's return open.

Seymour earns business income writing and editing instruction manuals on a contract basis. He has six different clients and operates under the business name Crystal Clear Communications from an office in their home. One of his clients issues him a T4A for the work that he has done for them.

During the year, Seymour is a part-time student at Dalhousie University for three months. He is enrolled in the musicology program. Seymour's 2019 assessment notice indicates that his Canada training credit available for 2020 is $250.

Business or Professional Income—Seymour	
Revenues without T4A	41,603.17
T4As issued (see T4A information)	20,000.00
Membership dues—Business Writers Association	231.00
Business insurance	126.16
Bank service charges	156.20
Cell phone air time	485.27
Postage and courier charges	110.00
Supplies	2,982.17
Separate business phone line charge	577.86
Fees for accounting and tax advice	500.00
Air fare (business travel)	526.97
Hotels (business travel)	1,240.91
Meals when travelling on business	607.14
Meals and drinks when entertaining clients	887.12
UCC of furniture—Beginning of year	2,254.94
UCC of computer application software—Beginning of year	219.15
UCC of computer hardware (class 50)—Beginning of year	426.00
Application software purchased May 12, 2020	525.00
Laptop computer purchased May 12, 2020	2,048.00

The mortgagee of Seymour's house, the Royal Bank, does not require life insurance.

House Costs	
Area of home used for business (square feet)	160
Total area of home (square feet)	1,500
Gas for heating	1,712.86
Hydro	1,641.18
Insurance—House	757.55
Snow plowing contract	440.00
Installation of new gas furnace	3,675.00
Painting of house interior	2,548.05
Mortgage interest paid to Royal Bank	8,456.22
Mortgage life insurance premiums	375.00
Mortgage principal paid	1,279.58
Property taxes	2,533.01
Interest on late property taxes	122.52

Tax Software Note   As the problem requires that you ignore GST/HST implications, enter all motor vehicle expenses as non-eligible for GST or HST.

Car Costs—Seymour	
Description—Subaru, cost = $35,000, bought 2017-02-15	
January 1 odometer	89,726
December 23 odometer	124,701
Business kilometres driven	8,412
Parking	321.71
Gas	2,582.12
Maintenance and repairs	458.63
Car insurance	779.00
Licence and registration fees	49.87
Interest on four-year car loan granted on purchase date	597.89
UCC of class 10.1—Beginning of year	15,470.00

T2202 - Seymour	Box	Amount
Tuition fees	A	2,200
Number of months in school—part time	B	3
Number of months in school—full time	C	0

T4A—Seymour	Box	Amount
Issuer—3065 Canada Inc.		
Fee for services (professional)	48	20,000.00

Information Related to Chapter 7 Material

Seymour was previously married and has a 19-year-old daughter from the previous marriage. As part of the property settlement, he received the house that he and his family had lived in. Since Mary already owned a much nicer home, he moved in with her when they were married in 2018 and rented out the property.

Seymour believed that in June he had paid an income tax instalment of $2,400 for 2020, but could find no record of it. You call the CRA and find that the June payment was toward his 2019 income tax liability. Seymour had tax owing of more than $10,000 for 2019 and has not completely paid off the liability yet. He has paid no instalments for 2020.

Mary also paid no instalments for 2020. She has received tax refunds in the last two years.

During 2018, one of his clients convinced Seymour to take out a demand loan to purchase shares in the public company EEE Art Films Ltd. for $37,000. Later that year, the company's president was indicted for fraud. In 2019, Seymour sold his shares for $2,000 and used the proceeds to pay down his demand loan. During 2019 the capital loss of $35,000 was the only capital loss transaction. There were no capital gains realized by Seymour in 2019. During 2020, Seymour did not have sufficient funds to pay off the demand loan, but managed to reduce the principal by $10,000.

The interest and penalties paid by Seymour during 2020 were as follows:

Interest on credit cards for business expenses	$ 627.27
Interest on loan to buy laptop and software	104.24
Interest on loan to make 2018 RRSP contribution	162.15
Interest on loan to purchase EEE Art Films securities	1,372.52
Interest on late payment of 2019 income tax	233.72
Interest on insufficient tax instalments for 2019	52.81
Interest on late GST/HST payments	212.82
Penalty for late filing of 2019 income tax return	303.92
Total	$3,069.45

Mary has invested in the stock market over the years and has done well. Seymour held no securities outside of his RRSP during 2020. Mary has received her T3 and T5 information slips from her stockbroker and bank. The interest from the TD Bank is from a joint chequing account in the name of both Mary and Seymour.

Tax Software Note   By inputting the joint T5 on Mary's return, the T5 information will appear as "Other Income" on Seymour's income tax return.

T5	Box	Slip 1	Slip 2
Issuer		Power Corp.	TD Bank
Recipient (input both on Mary's return)		Mary	Joint 50% each
Actual amount of eligible dividends	24	950.00	
Taxable amount of eligible dividends	25	1,311.00	
Interest from Canadian sources	13		236.12

T3	Box	Amount
Issuer—TD Asset Management		
Recipient—Mary Career		
Foreign country—United States		
Foreign non-business income (Canadian dollars)	25	1,553.10
Foreign income tax paid—Investment (Canadian dollars)	34	37.00
Other income—Investment	26	214.50
Actual amount of eligible dividends	49	346.00
Taxable amount of eligible dividends	50	477.48

Real Estate Rental—Seymour	Amount
Address—555 KKK Street, Moncton, NB, E0E 0E0	
Gross rents	12,000.00
Property taxes	3,610.00
Insurance	650.00
Interest on mortgage	4,207.25
Payment on principal	1,511.92
Wiring and furnace repairs	2,282.71
Snow removal and landscaping annual contract	1,070.00
Building purchased May 1, 2007 for $150,000—UCC beginning of year	150,000.00
Appliances purchased June 6, 2018 for $1,700—UCC beginning of year	1,350.00

Tax Software Assignment Problems

Information Related to Chapter 8 Material

When Mary's grandmother died in 2018, she inherited some pieces of jewellery as well as a dining room set and a chandelier. Since the jewellery is not suited to Mary's relaxed style of dress, she sold some pieces during 2020. She sold the dining room set and chandelier to two colleagues from work.

Mary has purchased Extreme Wi-Fi Technologies stock over the years. Her transactions in this stock are as follows:

Acquisition Date	Shares Purchased (Sold)	Cost per Share	Total Cost
April 1, 2018	1,500	$ 2	$ 3,000
October 1, 2018	2,000	12	24,000
April 1, 2019	(1,000)	?	
June 1, 2019	400	25	10,000
January 6, 2020	(800)	?	
February 1, 2020	800	20	16,000
March 14, 2020	(600)	?	

Mary Career provides you with the following information about her sales of securities and other items.

Dispositions of Property	Disposition 1	Disposition 2	Disposition 3
(All owned by Mary) Description	Extreme Wi-Fi Technologies	Extreme Wi-Fi Technologies	Fidelity Small Cap Fund
Number of units	800	600	258.92
Year of acquisition	2018	2018	2018
Date of disposition	January 6	March 14	February 17
Proceeds of disposition	11,806	13,465	2,982.31
Adjusted cost base	?	?	5,300.33
Outlays and expenses	29	29	Nil

Dispositions of Property	Disposition 4	Disposition 5	Disposition 6
Description	Diamond Pendant	Gold Ring	Pearl Broach
Year of acquisition	2018	2018	2018
Date of disposition	July 20	July 20	July 20
Proceeds of disposition	4,000	750	1,300
FMV at grandmother's death	5,800	600	850

Dispositions of Property	Disposition 7	Disposition 8
Description	Dining Room Set	Crystal Chandelier
Year of acquisition	2018	2018
Date of disposition	July 20	July 20
Proceeds of disposition	200	1,500
FMV at grandmother's death	3,000	800

Information Related to Chapter 9 Material

Seymour has made all of the required payments to his ex-wife, Monica DeWitch (SIN 527-000-186), in 2020. In your files, you have noted that his 2017 divorce agreement requires Seymour to pay spousal support to his ex-wife of $200 per month. He also pays her child support of $250 per month for his 19-year-old daughter, Faith.

Mary tells you that her parents have established an RESP for William in 2020 and are the sole contributors. They have contributed $300 in lieu of Christmas and birthday presents.

Mary has learned that Seymour's mother purchased a guaranteed investment certificate (GIC) in William's name in 2020. The GIC paid interest of $120 in 2020, which Seymour had spent without advising her. She expects a T5 to be issued in William's name.

Mary registered William for art classes at the Da Vinci Institute on Saturdays. She provides you with the following receipts:

Child	Child-Related Expenses (Organization or Name and SIN)	No. of weeks	Amount
William	No Worries Childcare (after school and summer)		3,100
William	Da Vinci Institute	16	1,000

On December 23, 2020, you receive a call from Mary Career with the terrible news that Seymour has just suffered a massive heart attack and died. Mary, his executor, inherits all of his property except for the rental property and appliances in Moncton, which he has left to his daughter, Faith. Assume the transfer of the property and appliances takes place in 2020.

As Seymour was thinking of selling the property, he had it appraised in early December. The appraisal valued the land at $60,000, the building at $180,000, and the appliances at $700. Seymour had purchased the property on May 1, 2007, for $195,000 (land of $45,000 and building of $150,000) and lived in it until his marriage to Mary in 2018.

Tax Software Notes   On Seymour's "Info" page, input his date of death (under his birth date). Answer No to the question "Is this an Early Filed ...?" On Mary's return, check that her marital status has been changed to widowed and the date of change is included.

Answer Yes on the Info page on Seymour's return to the question "Did you dispose of a property ...?"

Complete the T2091, "Designation of Property as a Principal Residence," for Seymour's Moncton property and S3, "Principal Residence Detail."

Information Related to Chapter 10 Material

On January 10, 2021, you receive a phone call from Mary Career. She has just received a T4RSP in the mail showing that Seymour had withdrawn virtually all the funds from his RRSP without her knowledge. She knows this could substantially increase Seymour's income tax liability and is very concerned. At the moment, she cannot find any trace of the funds that were withdrawn.

Her stockbroker has told her that a spousal contribution can be made to her RRSP to use Seymour's unused contribution room. She would like you to calculate the maximum RRSP contribution that can be deducted on Seymour's return so that she can contribute that amount to her RRSP and have the RRSP receipt issued with Seymour's name as the contributor.

She would also like you to calculate the maximum RRSP contribution that can be deducted on her own return for 2020 and 2021. Since Mary has received more than $1 million in life insurance benefits, she will make the maximum RRSP contributions for Seymour and herself that you have calculated immediately (before the beginning of March 2021).

She provides you with the following T4RSP and RRSP receipts for the contributions that she has already made, as well as information related to her and Seymour's RRSP limits.

RRSP Information—Mary	(Y/M/D)	Amount
Issuer of receipt—TD Asset Management	2020-12-10	5,400
Issuer of receipt—TD Asset Management	2021-01-05	35,191
Contributions made prior to 2020/03/02 and not deducted		Nil
Unused deduction room at the end of 2019		13,361
Earned income for 2019		180,000

Tax Software Assignment Problems

T4RSP—Seymour	Box	Amount
Issuer of receipt—Royal Bank		
Withdrawal payments (in amounts of < $5,000 each)	22	126,000
Income tax deducted	30	12,600

RRSP information—Seymour	(Y/M/D)	Amount
Issuer of receipt—TD Asset Management		Maximum ?
Contributions made prior to 2020/03/02 and not deducted		Nil
Unused deduction room at the end of 2019		19,762
Earned income for 2019		45,000

Information Related to Chapter 11 Material

In checking Seymour's file, you find he has a 2019 net capital loss carry forward of $17,500 from the sale of his EEE Art Films Ltd shares. Mary has informed you that she has made all of the RRSP contributions as you had calculated.

On February 14, 2021, you receive a call from a very upset Mary Career. She has just received an amended T4. The original T4 had not included information on the stock options in her employer, MoreCorp (a public company), that she had exercised.

Mary had options to purchase 500 shares of MoreCorp at $42 per share. When she received the options, the shares were trading at $40 per share. On December 20, 2020, when the shares were trading at $125 per share, she exercised her options for 200 shares. She left verbal instructions for MoreCorp to immediately donate all of the shares to Tax Behind Bars, a Canadian registered charity whose volunteers provide extensive tax education to inmates in prisons across Canada.

Unfortunately for Mary, the employee she had given the donation instructions to was fired for falsifying her credentials so the donation was not done and she did not receive a 2020 charitable donation receipt.

Amended T4—Mary	Box	Original Amount	Amended Amount
Issuer—MoreCorp			
Employment income	14	152,866.08	169,466.08
Employee's CPP contributions	16	2,898.00	2,898.00
Employee's EI premiums	18	856.36	856.36
RPP contributions	20	Nil	Nil
Income tax deducted	22	48,665.11	48,665.11
Stock option deduction 110(1)(d)	39	Nil	8,300.00
Charitable donations	46	1,000.00	1,000.00

Required: With the objective of minimizing the income tax liability for the family, prepare Mary's 2020 income tax return and Seymour's final 2020 income tax return. List any assumptions you have made and provide any explanatory notes and tax planning issues you feel should be placed in the files. Include in your solution Mary's maximum RRSP deduction for 2021.

CHAPTER 12

Taxable Income and Tax Payable for Corporations

Learning Objectives

After completing Chapter 12, you should be able to:

1. Explain the basic differences or similarities in determining net income, taxable income, and taxes payable for corporations and individuals (Paragraph [P hereafter] 12-1 to 12-7).
2. Briefly describe the four general tax payable deductions available to Canadian corporations and how these deductions contribute toward identfying general corporate tax rates by type of income and corporation (P 12-8 to 12-13)
3. Calculate a corporation's net income for ITA purposes (P 12-14 to 12-17).
4. List the deductions that are available to corporations in calculating taxable income (P 12-18 to 12-19).
5. Explain the purpose of ITA 112 in terms of integration and the impact on a corporation's net income and taxable income (P 12-20 to 12-24).
6. Explain the purpose of ITA 112(3), how it applies, and the circumstances under which it would not apply (P 12-25 to 12-28).
7. Describe the general income tax treatment when foreign dividends are received (P 12-29).
8. Apply and calculate the non-capital losses rules to a corporation (P 12-30 to 12-36).
9. Explain the factors that are relevant in deciding the optimum ordering of the taxable income deductions (P 12-37 to 12-42).
10. Describe and apply the rules that allocate corporate income to specific provinces (P 12-43 to 12-50).
11. Apply the basic corporate tax rate and explain the effect of the federal tax abatement and the general rate reduction (P 12-51 to 12-57).
12. Calculate provincial tax payable for a corporation using a supplied schedule of rates and other data (P 12-58 to 12-68).
13. List the important non-revenue-raising goals of the corporate tax system (P 12-69 and 12-70).
14. Explain the rules for determining which corporations and what amounts of income are eligible for the small business deduction (P 12-71 to 12-80).
15. Describe the main characteristics of a CCPC and the circumstances where CCPC status could change (P 12-81 to 12-84).

16. Explain the meaning of an "active business," including the interaction with income from property and the meaning and implications of a "specified investment business" (P 12-85 to 12-98).

17. Describe and calculate the amount of the small business deduction (P 12-99 to 12-109).

18. Explain why the government introduced the TCEC and AAII grinds to the small business limit. Calculate and apply the reduction to the small business deduction (P 12-110 to 12-127).

19. Describe a personal services business, explain why the concept was added to the ITA, and describe the tax treatment (P 12-128 to 12-137).

20. Explain the meaning of a professional corporation and why corporations are created to provide management services (P 12-138 and 12-139).

21. Calculate the M&P deduction for all types of corporations and explain whether the M&P deduction is still relevant and why (P 12-140 to 12-157).

22. Calculate the general rate reduction that is available to all corporations and the specific application of the general rate reduction to CCPCs (P 12-158 to 12-171).

23. Calculate the foreign non-business (property) and business income tax credits for corporations and explain and apply the rules that deal with any excess of foreign tax withheld over the allowable foreign tax credit (P 12-172 to 12-182).

24. Describe the basic concept of the refundable journalism labour tax credit (P 12-183 to 12-186).

Introduction

12-1.   In Volume 1 of the text we discussed the rules of the ITA that apply to individuals, noting a four-step process. We described that process as (1) determining net income (ITA 3); (2) determining taxable income (ITA 2(3)); (3) applying the graduated income tax rates to taxable income to determine the gross federal income tax payable; and (4) determining the available income tax credits (both refundable and non-refundable) and applying the relevant amount of those credits against gross federal income tax payable. The end result of that process was the determination of net federal income tax owing or whether there was a refund for a given taxation year.

12-2.   Determining corporate federal income tax is similar. The first step of net income is the same. There is a reconciliation process required when accounting standards generate a net income figure that employs accounting rules that are inconsistent with what is allowed for income tax purposes. Schedule 1 of the T2 corporate income tax return is designed to reconcile accounting-based financial statements with income tax.

12-3.   The second step of determining taxable income is also similar, but there are some notable differences. The most common differences are that individuals are allowed taxable income deductions for capital gains and stock options. These deductions are not available to corporations, but corporations can deduct certain dividends received as income from other corporations and can deduct donations, unlike individuals who must claim a non-refundable income tax credit. The treatment of loss carry overs as taxable income deductions, however, are generally the same for both corporations and individuals.

12-4.   The third and fourth steps are where the real differences between the taxation of individuals and corporations can be found. Individuals first determine gross tax payable, which is done by applying graduated income tax rates to taxable income. Personal tax credits are then separately determined, many by applying a 15% rate to a predetermined amount, most of which are indexed annually, such as the basic personal tax credit, which varies from $12,421 to $13,808 for 2021. Other credits apply different rates, such as the political contributions credit, the donations credit, dividend tax credits, and foreign tax credits. Once the total credits are determined the total amount plus income tax withheld or paid as instalments for the year is subtracted from the gross tax payable to determine whether an amount remains to be paid or an individual is entitled to a refund. Other adjustments are made for OAS and other clawbacks, excess CPP and EI contributions, and potentially the alternative minimum tax.

12-5.   Corporations are not subject to graduated income tax rates. In addition, rather than a separate determination of a number of personal tax credits the corporate income tax rules allow special deductions against tax payable that often depend on the type of income earned, whether the income is earned within or outside of Canada, and the nature of the corporate business activity. These tax payable deductions mirror the income tax credits available to individuals in that they reduce the federal income tax for a taxation year. As in the case with individuals, further adjustments are made to take into account income tax paid by instalments. In addition, corporations are able to recover certain income taxes and are subject to additional types of income tax that will be discussed in subsequent chapters.

12-6.   Canadian corporations are subject to a flat 38% rate on taxable income plus an additional flat rate of 10 2/3% on investment-type income included in taxable income if the corporation is a Canadian controlled private corporation (CCPC). In brief, a CCPC is a corporation incorporated in Canada that is not controlled by non-residents or publicly listed companies or a combination of the two. This means that most corporations incorporated in Canada by resident Canadian individuals to carry on small to medium-sized businesses would be CCPCs.

12-7.   Provincial income taxes can add another 10 to 16% on corporate investment income. While the combined income tax rates on investment income are quite high, a significant portion of these additional taxes imposed on a CCPC are refundable. In effect, once the additional taxes have been refunded the net result is a tax rate on investment income of a CCPC that is much lower than the highest income tax rates that would apply to individuals. The high corporate income tax rates are designed to discourage individuals from using corporations to defer income tax on investment income that would have been taxable at much higher individual tax rates had the income been earned by the individual rather than a corporation controlled by that same individual. This is discussed in detail in Chapter 13.

Corporate Income Tax Payable — The Basics

12-8.   The main federal corporate tax deductions, all of which will be discussed in this chapter, are the small business deduction (ITA 125), the manufacturing and processing profits deduction (ITA 125.1), the general rate reduction (ITA 123.4), and the federal abatement (ITA 124). A brief summary of each of these major tax payable deductions follows:

Small Business Deduction (SBD)   The small business deduction allows a deduction against tax payable for a CCPC that earns active business income (ABI) in Canada. The maximum deduction for 2021 is equal to 19% of ABI up to $500,000. This generates a potential annual income tax savings of $95,000 [(19%)($500,000)]. The $500,000 limit is shared where there are associated corporations, a topic discussed in Chapter 14.

Manufacturing and Processing Profits Deduction (M&P)   The M&P deduction allows a deduction against tax payable for any corporation that carries on the manufacturing or processing of goods for sale or lease in Canada as long as at least 10% of its gross revenues is from that activity. The maximum deduction for 2021 is 13% of its manufacturing and processing profits less any of those profits that were eligible for the small business deduction. There are further limitations based on a modified taxable income amount.

General Rate Reduction (GRR)   This deduction against tax payable applies to taxable income that is not eligible for preferential treatment, such as taxable income eligible for the small business deduction, the manufacturing and processing profits deduction, or refundable tax treatment for certain investment income. The maximum deduction for 2021 is equal to 13% of a modified taxable income figure.

Federal Abatement   The federal abatement provides a flat-rate 10% reduction in income taxes based on the proportion of corporate taxable income earned in Canada. If all of a corporation's taxable income is earned in Canada, the reduction is the full 10%. If only 75% of taxable income is earned in Canada then the reduction would equal 7.5% [(10%)(75%)].

Corporate Income Tax Payable—The Basics

12-9.   Each of the four corporate tax deductions mentioned in the preceding paragraph are complicated by extensive rules designed to address numerous situations, including avoiding abuse and, at times, restricting the deductions in certain instances. For example, in 2019, access to the SBD began to be restricted where a CCPC used too much of its after-tax profits to acquire investments rather than to grow its business. This subject will be discussed in this chapter.

12-10.   The corporate tax deductions mentioned allow one to get an appreciation for the general corporate tax rates that are applicable in a number of situations. This awareness assists in evaluating the effectiveness of establishing a corporation to earn certain types of income. A description of general corporate tax rates follows:

A CCPC that only earns active business income in Canada of $500,000 or less: The federal corporate tax rate would be 9% calculated as the 38% general rate - 10% abatement - 19% small business deduction.

A CCPC that only earns active business income in Canada of more than $500,000: The federal corporate tax rate would be 9% on the first $500,000 and 15% on the remainder, calculated as the 38% general rate - 10% abatement - 13% general rate reduction.

A non-CCPC that only earns manufacturing income in Canada: The federal corporate tax rate would be 15%, calculated as the 38% general rate - 10% abatement - 13% manufacturing and processing profits deduction or the general rate reduction. Note that the M&P deduction is not necessary given that the GRR tax deduction is the same 13%. The M&P deduction, however, remains important in determining provincial/territorial income taxes that rely on the federal M&P, such as Saskatchewan and Yukon.

A CCPC that earns investment income: The federal corporate tax rate would be 38 2/3%, calculated as the 38% general rate + the additional refundable tax on investment income of 10 2/3% - 10% abatement.

12-11.   In general, understanding and applying corporate income tax requires (1) identifying the type of corporation for Canadian income tax purposes, such as a CCPC or publicly listed corporation (generally meaning that its shares are listed on a stock exchange), and (2) categorizing the income of the corporation into Canadian business income (manufacturing and non-manufacturing), foreign business income, Canadian and foreign investment income (including capital gains and losses but excluding dividend income), and dividend income.

12-12.   The following example will illustrate the importance of these concepts together with the application of the general corporate tax rates.

EXAMPLE   For the year ending December 31, 2021, Aberdeen Ltd., a CCPC, has $1,000,000 in taxable income. Taxable income comprises $900,000 in non-manufacturing business income and $100,000 of investment income. No dividend income was received in 2021. Aberdeen is not associated with any other company.

ANALYSIS   The federal tax payable for Aberdeen Ltd. applying the general corporate rates to specific types of income as mentioned in Paragraph 12-10 would be calculated as follows:

CCPC rate on the first $500,000 of non-manufacturing business income [(9%)($500,000)]	$ 45,000
CCPC rate on non-manufacturing business income in excess of $500,000 [(15%)($900,000 - $500,000)]	(60,000)
CCPC rate on investment income [(38 2/3%)($100,000)]	(38,667)
Federal corporate income tax payable	$143,667

ANALYSIS   In applying the provisions of the ITA, the federal corporate income tax payable would be calculated as follows:

Base amount of Part I tax [(38%)($1,000,000)]	$380,000
Additional tax on investment income [(10 2/3%)($100,000)	10,667
Federal tax abatement [(10%)($1,000,000)]	(100,000)
Small business deduction [(19%)($500,000)]	(95,000)
General rate reduction [(13%)($1,000,000 - SBD amount $500,000) - Investment income $100,000]]	(52,000)
Federal corporate income tax payable	$143,667

12-13.   The example demonstrates two analyses that are used for two different purposes. In the first analysis, knowledge of the general corporate rates that apply to specific types of corporate income allows for a quick estimate of corporate income tax in a given situation. Provincial taxes can be added easily. This information assists in helping others decide whether to incorporate or not. The second analysis is required when completing a corporate income tax return, which follows the specific rules of the ITA. In this chapter we will focus on corporate income tax under Part I, the rules of which are found in Division E titled "Computation of Tax," specifically Subdivision b titled "Rules Applicable to Corporations" (ITA 123 to 125.7) and Subdivision c titled "Rules Applicable to All Taxpayers" (ITA 126 to 127.41).

Computation of Net Income

12-14.   The day-to-day books and records of most Canadian corporations are maintained and apply accounting standards and principles that are often referred to as generally accepted accounting principles (GAAP), which includes both ASPE (Accounting Standards for Private Enterprises) and IFRS (International Financial Reporting Standards). As noted in Chapter 6 on business income, many of the rules for computing business income under the *ITA* are identical to those used under GAAP. However, there are a number of differences. Throughout the text we have emphasized that accounting concepts are generally not relevant to income tax and therefore any different treatment of income or expenses must be adjusted to produce a net income in accordance with the rules of the ITA. Therefore, the first step in the process of determining a corporation's income tax liability or refund begins with a reconciliation process to convert accounting net income into net income for purposes of the ITA. Once that process is complete we can then move to determining taxable income.

12-15.   In the reconciliation process, there are many potential adjustments that could be required. Some adjustments are necessary because of different allocation patterns that result in timing differences between accounting and income tax. Examples of this would be differences between accounting depreciation and CCA, as well as alternative approaches to the determination of pension cost deductions. Other adjustments involve permanent differences between accounting and income tax amounts. An example of this type of difference would be the non-taxable one-half of capital gains. While accounting principles include 100% of such gains, one-half of such gains will never be included in net income for ITA purposes.

12-16.   A reconciliation between accounting net income and net income for ITA purposes is a required part of the corporate income tax return. As previously mentioned, Schedule 1 of the T2 corporate income tax return is specifically designed for the purposes of the reconciliation process. The most common adjustments from Schedule 1 are listed in Figure 6-3 in Chapter 6, and that list has been duplicated as Figure 12-1.

Figure 12-1
Conversion of Accounting Net Income to Net Income for Tax Purposes

Additions to Accounting Income:
- Income tax expense
- Amortization, depreciation, and depletion of tangible and intangible assets (accounting amounts)
- Recapture of CCA
- Tax reserves deducted in the prior year
- Losses on the disposition of capital assets (accounting amounts)
- Pension expense (accounting amounts)
- Scientific research expenditures (accounting amounts)
- Warranty expense (accounting amounts)
- Amortization of discount on long-term debt issued (see discussion in Chapter 7)
- Foreign tax paid (accounting amounts)
- Excess of taxable capital gains over allowable capital losses
- Interest and penalties on income tax assessments
- Non-deductible automobile costs
- 50% of business meals and entertainment expenses
- Club dues and cost of recreational facilities
- Non-deductible reserves (accounting amounts)
- Charitable donations
- Asset write-downs, including impairment losses on intangibles
- Fines, penalties, and illegal payments

Deductions from Accounting Income:
- Capital cost allowances (CCA)
- Incorporation costs (first $3,000)
- Terminal losses
- Tax reserves claimed for the current year
- Gains on the disposition of capital assets (accounting amounts)
- Pension funding contributions
- Deductible scientific research expenditures
- Deductible warranty expenditures
- Amortization of premium on long-term debt issued
- Foreign non-business tax deduction [ITA 20 (12)]
- Allowable business investment losses
- Landscaping costs

12-17.   Chapter 6 on business income provided a detailed discussion of the reconciliation process together with examples that demonstrate the methodology and analysis (see Paragraphs 6-165 to 6-170). This reconciliation process applies to convert business income from accounting to income tax regardless of whether the business is carried on by a corporation, a partnership, or through a sole proprietorship. In addition to Exercise 12-1, which provides a fairly simple illustration of how this reconciliation process works, we encourage students to review the coverage in Chapter 6.

Exercise 12-1

Subject: Schedule 1 Reconciliation

Available information for the S1 Company for the year includes the following:

1.   A depreciable property was sold for $48,300. It had a capital cost and ACB of $120,700 and a carrying value for accounting purposes of $53,900. It was the last property in its CCA class and the UCC balance was $34,600 immediately before the disposition. There were no other additions or dispositions during the year such that no property remained in the class on the last day of the taxation year.

2. During the year, the company acquired goodwill at a cost of $180,000. Since there was no impairment of the goodwill during the year, no write-down was required for accounting purposes.
3. During the year, the company expensed charitable donations of $15,000.
4. Premium amortization on the company's bonds payable was $4,500 for the year.

You have been asked to prepare a reconciliation of accounting net income and net income for purposes of the ITA. Determine the addition and/or deduction that would be made for each of the four items.

Solutions to Exercises are available in the Study Guide.

We suggest you complete SSP 12-1 at this point.

Computation of Taxable Income

Deductions Available to Corporations

12-18.   The reconciliation schedule illustrated in Figure 12-1 is used to establish a corporation's net income for ITA purposes. When this task is completed, certain taxable income deductions are available. There are three main types of deductions available to corporations, as set out in Figure 12-2.

Charitable Donations   Unlike the situation for individuals where charitable donations are the basis for a tax credit, corporations deduct charitable donations when determining taxable income. The rules for determining which donations can be deducted by a corporation are essentially the same as the rules for determining which donations qualify for the tax credit for individuals. The five-year carry forward provision is also applicable to corporations. These matters are given detailed consideration in Chapters 4 and 11 and will not be repeated here.

Dividends   As noted in previous chapters, individuals must gross up dividends received from taxable Canadian corporations by 15% for non-eligible dividends and 38% for eligible dividends. This is accompanied by a federal dividend tax credit equal to either 9/13 of the gross up for non-eligible dividends and 6/11 of the gross up for eligible dividends. Canadian corporations do not gross up taxable dividends received. However, a corporation is permitted to deduct the full amount of taxable dividends received from taxable Canadian corporations from taxable income. This means that these intercompany

---

**Figure 12-2
Conversion of Corporate Net Income to Taxable Income**

Net Income (Loss)

Less:
- Charitable donations (limited to 75% of net income with a five-year carry forward of unused amounts)—ITA 110.1
- Taxable dividends received from taxable Canadian corporations—ITA 112(1)
- Loss carry overs from subsequent or prior taxation years—ITA 111(1)

Equals Taxable Income (Loss)

taxable dividends are not subject to Part I income tax. If, for example, a corporation received $100,000 in taxable dividends from another taxable Canadian corporation, and had no other income, its net income would be $100,000 but its taxable income would be nil as a result of a taxable income deduction of $100,000 (ITA 112(1)). As a result, no Part I tax would be payable.

12-19.   In addition, corporations are allowed to deduct loss carry overs from previous or subsequent years in the calculation of taxable income. Other than in situations where a corporation has been the subject of an acquisition of control (see Chapter 14), the rules related to the deduction of loss carry overs by corporations are basically the same as those applicable to individuals. These general rules are covered in Chapter 11 and will not be repeated here.

Taxable Dividends from Taxable Canadian Corporations

Deduction from Taxable Income—ITA 112(1)

12-20.   ITA 112(1) permits a corporation to deduct, in the determination of taxable income, taxable dividends that are received from taxable Canadian corporations. A "Taxable Canadian Corporation" is a corporation that is resident in Canada, incorporated in Canada, and is not exempt from Part I tax. All three conditions must be met.

12-21.   The Canadian taxation of taxable dividends is guided by the process of integration. Integration requires that income earned by a corporation that funds dividends will be subject to corporate income tax. When the after-tax funds are distributed to individual shareholders as taxable dividends, then a second level of income tax applies. The gross up and dividend tax credit process is designed to ensure that the income tax paid by individual shareholders is reduced by any income tax paid by the corporation. The hypothetical result is that the income taxes paid by both the corporation and the individual are equivalent to what the individual would have paid had the underlying income been earned directly by the individual. The integration concept only works if the income is first subject to corporate income tax and then taxed to individual shareholders when a taxable dividend distribution is made to them. If, however, the initial after-tax corporate funds are paid to an intermediary corporation before dividends are paid to individuals it is imperative that no additional Part I corporate income taxes are charged to that intermediary corporation. If corporate taxes were charged at each level of intermediary corporations, the total income taxes would be excessive and would neutralize the integration concept.

EXAMPLE   Mr. X owns 100% of the shares of Company X, and Company X owns 100% of the shares of Company Y. Both companies pay out all of their after-tax income as dividends. Company Y has income of $1,000 for the year and Company X has no income other than dividends from Company Y. Assume both Company X and Company Y are subject to a combined federal/provincial tax rate of 30% and that Mr. X is subject to a combined federal/provincial tax rate on non-eligible dividends received of 33%.

ANALYSIS   A comparison of the after-tax cash flow, with and without the ITA 112(1) intercompany dividend deduction, would be as follows:

	No Deduction	Deduction
Company Y income	$1,000	$1,000
Corporate taxes at 30%	(300)	(300)
Dividends to Company X	$ 700	$ 700
Corporate taxes at 30%	(210)	Nil
Dividends to Mr. X	$ 490	$ 700
Personal taxes at 33%	(162)	(231)
After-tax retention	$ 328	$ 469

12-22.   Without the ITA 112(1) taxable income deduction, the after-tax retention is only $328. This means that the total tax rate on the $1,000 of income earned by Company Y is a very high 67.2% [($1,000 - $328)/$1,000)]. While the application of the dividend deduction provides a more reasonable level of taxation, you should note that the combined corporate and personal tax on the $1,000 of income is $531 ($300 + $231).

Exercise 12-2

Subject: Corporate Taxable Income

The Chapman Company had net income for ITA purposes for the year ending December 31, 2021, of $263,000. This amount included $14,250 in taxable capital gains, as well as $14,200 in taxable dividends received from taxable Canadian corporations. Also during 2021, the company made donations to registered charities of $8,600. At the beginning of the year, the company had available a 2018 non-capital loss carry forward of $82,000, as well as a 2019 net capital loss carry forward of $18,000. Determine the company's minimum taxable income for the year ending December 31, 2021, and the amount and type of any carry forwards available at the end of the year.

Solutions to Exercises are available in the Study Guide.

Taxable Dividends—Problems with Integration
12-23.   There is a presumption built into the integration concept that corporate income tax has been paid and it is the after-tax funds that are distributed as a taxable dividend to individual shareholders. This then justifies a dividend tax credit that is based on a presumed level of corporate income tax. This presumption is not always met, particularly where a corporation experiences losses but the accounting income indicates a profit or where the basis for a dividend distribution are unrealized gains on corporate property.

12-24.   There is no mechanism in the ITA to track corporate income taxes in connection to a taxable dividend distribution. The income tax system, however, contains complex rules that either deny the ITA 112(1) deduction or impose special income taxes on corporations to ensure that the integration process works as intended. These additional rules include specialized taxes under Part II.1, IV.1, and VI.1, which go beyond the scope of an introductory course on income taxation.

Dividend Stop Loss Rule—ITA 112(3)
12-25.   The declaration and payment of dividends by a corporation reduces the value of the corporation by the amount of the dividend. The decline in value would be reflected in the value of the shares of that company that would experience a proportional decline in value. Given this, it would be possible for one corporation to acquire shares in another corporation at a time when it was anticipated that a dividend would be paid on the acquired shares. The dividends on these shares could be received tax free because of the intercorporate taxable income deduction of ITA 112(1). A subsequent sale would result in a capital loss attributable to the dividend. In effect, the corporate recipient of the dividend would have recovered its cost as a combination of a tax-free dividend and the sale proceeds of the shares. The income tax result, however, would be to realize a capital loss even though no economic loss took place. The following example illustrates the problem.

EXAMPLE   On June 30, 2021, Brian Company acquires 1,000 shares of Leader Company, a public company, at a cost of $20 per share. On July 1, 2021, Leader Company declares and pays its regular $3 per share taxable dividend. Because this dividend had been anticipated by the market, the value of the Leader Company shares falls by $3 per share to $17. On July 15, 2021, Brian Company sells all of its Leader Company shares at a price of $17 per share.

ANALYSIS In the absence of a special rule, Brian Company would have received $3,000 in dividends that are not subject to Part I tax because of the ITA 112(1) deduction for intercorporate dividends. In addition, they would realize a capital loss of $3,000 on the disposition of the shares [POD ($17)(1,000) - ACB ($20)($1000)]. Brian Company would have recovered its full $20,000 cost as $3,000 of tax-free dividends plus $17,000 on the sale of the shares.

12-26. To prevent this result, ITA 112(3) and (3.01) together contain an anti-avoidance rule referred to as a "stop loss" rule, which applies to reduce the capital loss where shares are held as capital property, and ITA 112(4) and (4.01) contain similar rules where shares are held as inventory as would be the case for an adventure or concern in the nature of trade or for a trader or dealer in securities. Under these rules, any loss resulting from a disposition of shares by a corporation must be reduced by the amount of all taxable dividends received that are eligible for a taxable income deduction under ITA 112(1) or that are capital dividends . Capital dividends are discussed in Chapter 14

12-27. There is an exception to this stop loss rule under ITA 112(3.01) that excludes a dividend from reducing a capital loss if either of the following conditions are met:

- The dividend was received on shares that were held for less than one full year (365 days).
- The corporate owner of the shares together with other non-arm's-length shareholders owned more than 5% of the shares of any class of shares of the corporation that paid the dividend at the time the dividend was received.

12-28. In the preceding example, since Brian Company owned the shares for less than one full year, the $3,000 capital loss would be reduced by the $3,000 dividend that was received. Since the one-year test was not met, the second test is irrelevant in this case.

Exercise 12-3

Subject: Stop Loss Rules

On June 16, 2020, Loren Ltd. acquires 1,000 of the 10,000 issued and outstanding shares of Manon Inc. at a cost of $25.30 per share. On July 1, 2021, these shares pay a taxable dividend of $2.16 per share. These are the only dividends that were received on these shares. Loren sells the shares on July 29, 2021, for $21.15 per share. Loren Ltd. has taxable capital gains of $50,000 in the year. What is the amount of the allowable capital loss that Loren Ltd. can recognize for its taxation year ending December 31, 2021?

Solutions to Exercises are available in the Study Guide.

We suggest you complete SSP 12-2 at this point.

Foreign Source Dividends Received

12-29. The situation for dividends received from non-resident corporations is more complex. The general rules are discussed in Chapter 7, which notes that foreign source dividends are included in income on a gross basis, before the deduction of any foreign taxes withheld. However, in Chapter 11 we introduced the foreign non-business tax credit provisions. These credits against federal Canadian tax payable are designed to compensate the recipient of foreign source non-business income for foreign taxes withheld at source, provided the dividend income has been subject to foreign income taxes comparable to what would have been charged had the dividends been received from a Canadian source. You will recall that, in many situations, the credit against Canadian tax payable will be equal to the amount of foreign taxes withheld at the source unless the foreign jurisdiction tax rate exceeds that of Canada or where losses and other amounts are applied to reduce Canadian income taxes for the year. Note that foreign source dividends are generally not deducted in the determination of taxable income (the exception to this general rule is foreign affiliate dividends, which are covered in Chapter 20).

Non-Capital Loss Carry Over for a corporation

Additional Issues

12-30.   As the general rules for loss carry overs are the same for all taxpayers, most of the relevant material on this subject is dealt with in Chapter 11 where we discuss the determination of taxable income for individuals. There is, however, an additional problem in calculating the amount of the current-year non-capital loss carry over for a corporation. This problem relates to the fact that dividends received from taxable Canadian corporations can be deducted by a corporation in the determination of its taxable income. To illustrate this problem, consider the following example.

> **EXAMPLE**   During 2021 Marco Inc. has net taxable capital gains of $30,000 [(1/2) ($60,000)], dividends of $25,000 received from taxable Canadian corporations, and a business loss of $60,000. The company also has a 2019 net capital loss carry forward of $50,000 [(1/2)($100,000)].
>
> **ANALYSIS**   Using the ITA 3 rules for calculating net income, the result would be as follows:

ITA 3(a)	Dividends received	$25,000
ITA 3(b)	Net taxable capital gains	30,000
ITA 3(c)	Subtotal	$55,000
ITA 3(d)	Business loss	(60,000)
2021 Net income and taxable income		Nil

2021 Net income	$ Nil
ITA 112(1)	(25,000)
ITA 111(1)(b) 2019 Net capital loss	(30,000)
2021 Taxable income	Nil

12-31.   From an intuitive point of view, it would appear that the non-capital loss for the year is $5,000, the business loss of $60,000 minus the ITA 3(c) amount of $55,000. Further, as net income is nil, it appears that none of the net capital loss carry forward can be deducted, despite the $30,000 ITA 3(b) amount. In addition, it does not appear that the company will get any benefit from the potential deduction of the $25,000 in dividends that were received during the year. As discussed in Chapter 11, the difficulty lies with the basic loss carry over definitions, which begin by measuring the difference between the current-year business loss and the ITA 3(c) amount. However, there is a presumption that the ITA 3(c) amount includes income that flows through to taxable income. In the example, the $25,000 dividends that are included in income do not make it through to taxable income because of the ITA 112(1) deduction. In a similar manner, the net taxable capital gains also do not make it to taxable income because of the net capital loss deduction. As a result, modifications are made to the loss carry over definition to recognize this difficulty, which is explained in the following paragraphs.

An Expanded Definition

12-32.   You may recall that the ITA 111(8) definition was discussed previously in Chapter 11. In that chapter, we explained how the definition provides for the deduction of a net capital loss to be claimed even when net income would otherwise be nil. In effect, the non-capital loss definition allows an adjustment to be made for the net capital loss claimed, which increases the non-capital loss.

12-33.   The expanded definition is as follows:

ITA 111(8)   The non-capital loss of a taxpayer for a taxation year means the amount determined by the formula:

$$A - D, \text{ where}$$

A   is the amount determined by the formula:

$$E - F, \text{ where}$$

E   is the total of all amounts each of which is the taxpayer's loss for the year from an office, employment, business, or property; the taxpayer's allowable business investment loss for the year; net capital loss carry overs deducted in the calculation of taxable income for the year (this amount cannot exceed the net taxable capital gains for the year [the ITA 3(b) amount]); and **dividends received from taxable Canadian corporations and deducted in computing taxable income.**

F   is the amount of income determined under ITA 3(c). (Sum of ITA 3(a) non-capital positive sources and ITA 3(b) net taxable capital gains, less Division B, Subdivision e deductions.)

D   is the taxpayer's farm loss for the year.

12-34.   The only difference in this definition from the one that was presented in Chapter 11 is the addition of "dividends received from taxable Canadian corporations and deducted in computing taxable income" in the E component. However, it is an important change in that it allows dividends that are deductible to be adjusted to the non-capital loss carry over balance.

Example

12-35.   All of these points can be illustrated by returning to the example presented in Paragraph 12-30. If we assume that Marco Inc. wishes to deduct the maximum amount of the net capital loss carry forward in 2021, net income and taxable income would both remain at nil. The 2021 non-capital loss would be calculated as follows:

Amount E:		
Business loss		$ 60,000
Dividend deduction ITA 112(1)		25,000
2019 Net capital loss deducted ITA 111(1)(b)		
(limited to net taxable capital gains for the year)		30,000
Total for amount E		$115,000
Amount F—ITA 3(c) income:		
Dividends received	($25,000)	
Net taxable capital gains	(30,000)	(55,000)
Non-capital loss for the year		$ 60,000
2019 Net capital loss balance ($50,000 - $30,000)		$ 20,000

12-36.   The method used in the ITA adjusts for the $55,000 of income included in ITA 3(c) that never makes it through to taxable income, thus preserving the $60,000 business loss as a non-capital loss for 2021. The 2021 non-capital loss can be carried back three years to 2018 and forward 20 years to 2040 assuming full taxation years.

Exercise 12-4

Subject: Non-Capital Loss with ABIL

For the taxation year ending December 31, 2021, Hacker Inc. has business and property income of $63,500. Also during this year, dispositions of capital property result in taxable capital gains of $11,550 and allowable capital losses of $19,200. The company experiences a further capital loss on the arm's-length sale of shares of a small business corporation in the amount of $151,500. The result is an allowable business investment loss (ABIL) of half of that amount or $75,750. Determine Hacker Inc.'s 2021 net income. Indicate the amount and type of any loss carry overs available for the year.

Exercise 12-5

Subject: Non-Capital Loss

The following information is for Laser Ltd., a Canadian public company, for the taxation year ending December 31, 2021:

Taxable capital gains	$55,500
Allowable capital losses	42,000
Allowable business investment loss (ABIL)	5,250
Dividends received from taxable Canadian corporations	48,000
Canadian source interest income	27,200
Business loss	273,000

The company has a 2020 net capital loss balance of $19,000. It would like to deduct this loss for 2021. Determine the 2021 non-capital loss and 2020 net capital loss balance remaining for Laser Ltd. after the maximum claim for 2021.

Solutions to Exercises are available in the Study Guide.

Ordering of Taxable Income Deductions

12-37.　In the calculation of taxable income for individuals there are specific ordering rules for claiming deductions that are provided in ITA 111.1. These rules are directed at individuals and do not apply to corporations. The ITA does not contain an equivalent provision for corporations and, as a consequence, there is a question as to how deductions should be ordered for a corporation. The answer is determined on the basis of practicality, which takes many factors into consideration.

12-38.　Charitable donations in excess of 75% of net income are not deductible in the current year but can be carried forward for five years, subject to the same 75% limitation in each of the carry over years. As this is shorter than the carry forward period for any other type of loss, this would suggest using these amounts prior to claiming loss carry forwards. However, in reaching this conclusion, it should also be noted that these donations can be deducted against any type of income.

12-39.　Turning to the deduction of loss carry overs, ITA 111(3) requires that losses within any single category must be deducted in chronological order. That is, if a corporation chooses to deduct a non-capital loss during the current year, the oldest non-capital losses must be deducted first. However, there are no rules with respect to the order in which different types of loss carry forwards must be deducted.

12-40.　Farm loss carry forwards and non-capital losses have restrictions on the time for which they are available. This would suggest that they be deducted first. However, while there is no restriction on the period of availability for net capital loss carry forwards, these amounts can only be used to the extent that there are net taxable capital gains during the period.

12-41.   For a corporation that experiences only limited capital gains, these restrictions may be a more important consideration than the period of time during which the loss will be available. With the carry forward period for non-capital losses lasting 20 taxation years, this would appear to leave plenty of time to recover this type of loss.

12-42.   An additional factor in making decisions on whether to deduct non-capital or farm losses is the period left to their expiry. Clearly, losses carry overs that expire in the current year should be deducted immediately, with additional consideration given to losses near the end of their life.

We suggest you complete SSP 12-3 and SSP 12-4 at this point.

Geographical Allocation of Income

Permanent Establishments

12-43.   Once taxable income is determined, an allocation process becomes necessary to determine the amount of provincial taxes that are payable and the province(s) to which they are due. Given the variations in provincial corporate tax rates, this can be a matter of considerable significance.

12-44.   The key concept is the notion of a "permanent establishment." This concept is defined as follows:

> **ITR 400(2)**   Permanent establishment means a fixed place of business of the corporation, including an office, a branch, a mine, an oil well, a farm, a timberland, a factory, a workshop, or a warehouse.

12-45.   This meaning is extended to include having an agent or employee in a province, if that agent or employee has the general authority to contract for a corporation or carries a stock of merchandise from which orders are regularly filled. The mere presence of a commissioned salesperson or an independent agent without the requisite authority to contract on behalf of the corporation is not considered evidence of a permanent establishment. In addition, the presence of a controlled subsidiary of a corporation in a province is not, by itself, considered a permanent establishment of that corporation. Some provinces, such as Alberta, deem a corporation incorporated in the province to have a permanent establishment in that province.

12-46.   Additional rules further extend the permanent establishment concept. For example, ITR 400(2)(d) indicates that where a corporation that has a permanent establishment anywhere in Canada owns land in a province, such land will be deemed to be a permanent establishment of the corporate owner. In addition, ITR 400(2)(e) indicates that where a corporation uses substantial machinery or equipment in a particular place, that corporation shall be deemed to have a permanent establishment in that province.

Activity at Permanent Establishments

12-47.   Once the location of permanent establishments has been determined, income will be allocated on the basis of two variables. These are gross revenues attributable to the permanent establishment and salaries and wages paid by the establishment.

12-48.   After these values are established, ITR 402(3) provides a formula for using these variables to allocate taxable income to provinces. It requires calculating, for each province, that province's gross revenues as a percentage of total corporate gross revenues, and that province's salaries and wages as a percentage of total corporate salaries and wages. A simple average of these two percentages, without regard to the relative dollar values associated with the corporate totals, is then applied to corporate taxable income to determine the amount of taxable income that will be allocated to that province.

12-49.   Note that, if the corporation has permanent establishments outside of Canada, not all of its taxable income will be allocated to a province. The presence of these foreign permanent establishments will be reflected in the calculation of the federal tax abatement (see Paragraph 12-52). If there are no permanent establishments outside of Canada, the federal tax abatement will be the full 10%, even if there is foreign investment income.

Example — Permanent Establishments

12-50.   The following example illustrates the process of allocating taxable income on a geographic basis:

EXAMPLE Linford Company has permanent establishments in Alberta, Manitoba, and Ontario. The company's taxable income for the current year totalled $100,000, with gross revenues of $1,000,000 and salaries and wages of $500,000.

The following allocation of the gross revenues and the salaries and wages among the provinces occurred during the current year:

	Gross Revenues		Salaries and Wages	
Province	Amount	Percent	Amount	Percent
Alberta	$ 250,000	25.0	$100,000	20.0
Manitoba	400,000	40.0	200,000	40.0
Ontario	350,000	35.0	200,000	40.0
Totals	$1,000,000	100.0	$500,000	100.0

ANALYSIS Using the average of the two percentages for each province, Linford Company's taxable income would be allocated to the three provinces as follows:

Province	Average Percent	Taxable Income	Amount Allocated
Alberta	22.5	$100,000	$ 22,500
Manitoba	40.0	100,000	40,000
Ontario	37.5	100,000	37,500
Totals	100.0	N/A	$100,000

We suggest you complete SSP 12-5 at this point.

Federal Tax Payable

Basic Rate — ITA 123(1)

12-51.   All corporations are initially subject to the same basic tax rate. This rate is specified in ITA 123 and is set at 38%.

Federal Tax Abatement — ITA 124(1)

12-52.   ITA 124(1) provides a reduction of 10% in the federal tax rate. This is normally referred to as the federal tax abatement and it is designed to leave room for the provinces to apply their respective tax rates. When deducted from the basic rate of 38%, this leaves a net federal rate of 28%.

12-53.   Note that this 10% reduction in the federal tax rate is only applicable to income earned in a Canadian province or territory. When a corporation carries on a business through permanent establishments situated outside of Canada, less than 100% of its taxable income will be allocated to the various provinces and territories. When this is the case, the amount of the abatement to be deducted is reduced by multiplying the 10% abatement by the total percentage of taxable income that was allocated to the provinces and territories. For example, if only 80% of a corporation's taxable income was allocated to one or more provinces, the abatement would be reduced to 8% [(10%)(80%)].

General Rate Reduction—ITA 123.4(2)

General Rate Reduction Percentage

12-54.   In implementing changes in the federal rate on corporations, the government has decided to use a process that maintains the basic flat rate of 38%. When changes are required, the desired result is accomplished by using a "general rate reduction percentage." This percentage is applied to what is referred to as "full rate taxable income" (see explanation that follows). The general rate reduction percentage has been 13% since 2011.

12-55.   As discussed at Paragraph 12-10 on general corporate rates, where all of a corporation's income is both allocated to a province and eligible for the general rate reduction, the general corporate rate at the federal level is 15%:

Basic corporate rate	38%
Less: Federal tax abatement	(10%)
Balance	28%
Less: General rate reduction	(13%)
General federal corporate rate	15%

Full Rate Taxable Income—ITA 123.4(1)

12-56.   As noted, the "general rate reduction percentage" must be applied to "full rate taxable income." In fairly simple terms, full rate taxable income is income that does not benefit from certain other tax payable preferences. The most common of these preferences are the small business deduction (SBD), the manufacturing and processing profits deduction (M&P deduction), and the refundability of certain types of taxes on the investment income of private companies, particularly CCPCs.

12-57.   Both the SBD and the M&P deduction are discussed later in this chapter. The general rate reduction and the concept of full rate taxable income will also be considered in this chapter. The coverage of refundable taxes on the investment income of private companies will not be covered until Chapter 13.

Exercise 12-6

Subject: Geographical Allocation and Federal Tax Payable

Sundown Ltd., a Canadian public company, has taxable income for its taxation year ending December 31, 2021, in the amount of $226,000. It has Canadian permanent establishments in Ontario and Manitoba. The company's gross revenues for the 2021 taxation year are $2,923,000, with $1,303,000 of this accruing at the permanent establishment in Ontario and $896,000 accruing at the permanent establishment in Manitoba. Wages and salaries total $165,000 for the year. Of this total, $52,000 is at the permanent establishment in Ontario and $94,000 is at the permanent establishment in Manitoba. Sundown has sales to the U.S. through a U.S. permanent establishment that account for the remaining gross revenues and salaries and wages not attributable to Canadian permanent establishments. Calculate federal tax payable for the taxation year ending December 31, 2021. Ignore any foreign tax implications

---

Solutions to Exercises are available in the Study Guide.

Provincial/Territorial Tax Payable

General Rules

12-58.   In calculating income tax payable for individuals, a graduated rate structure is involved at both the federal and provincial/territorial levels. While limits on the brackets may differ from those used at the federal level, all of the provinces and territories assess income taxes on individuals using graduated rates applied to taxable income.

12-59.   In contrast, provincial/territorial corporate taxes are based on a flat rate applied to a taxable income figure. With the exception of Alberta and Quebec, the federal taxable income figure is used. While these two provinces collect their own corporate taxes, the taxable income figure that they use is normally similar to that used at the federal level.

General Rate

12-60.   As calculated in Paragraph 12-55, the general federal corporate rate is 15%. When the varying provincial/territorial rates are added to this percentage, Figure 12-3 shows that the general corporate tax rate ranges from a low of 23.0% in Alberta to a high of 31% in Prince Edward Island.

Manufacturing and Processing Rate

12-61.   For many years, manufacturing and processing (M&P) income has been eligible for a 13% deduction from tax payable at the federal level. More recently, a general rate reduction, providing the same 13% reduction in tax payable, was made available. As the base for the general rate reduction is reduced by any amounts on which the M&P deduction is claimed, there is little point in claiming the M&P deduction at the federal level. This situation is reflected in Figure 12-3, which indicates that, at the federal level, the general rate and the M&P rate are identical.

	General Rate	M&P Rate	Small Business Rate
Figure 12-3 **Combined Federal/Provincial/Territorial Corporate Rates—February 2021**			
Federal tax only	15.0%	15.0%	9.0%
Combined federal/provincial			
Alberta	23.0%	23.0%	11.0%
British Columbia	27.0%	27.0%	11.0%
Manitoba	27.0%	27.0%	9.0%
New Brunswick	29.0%	29.0%	11.5%
Newfoundland	30.0%	30.0%	12.0%
Northwest Territories	26.5%	26.5%	11.0%
Nova Scotia	29.0%	29.0%	11.5%
Nunavut	27.0%	27.0%	12.0%
Ontario	26.5%	25.0%	12.2%
Prince Edward Island	31.0%	31.0%	11.0%
Quebec	26.5%	26.5%	13.0%
Saskatchewan	27.0%	25.0%	11.0%
Yukon	27.0%	17.5%	9.0%

12-62.   This is also the situation with all but four of the provinces. At one time, there were more provinces with reduced M&P rates, but now only Ontario, Quebec, and Saskatchewan apply reduced rates to this type of income. Because of this provincial relevance we continue to provide coverage of the M&P deduction in this chapter.

Small Business Rate

12-63.   The lowest rates in Figure 12-3 are referred to as the small business rates. As was mentioned in Paragraph 12-10 and as will be discussed in greater detail in this chapter, CCPCs are eligible for a small business deduction that lowers the federal rate to 9% on a limited amount of income. In general, the availability of this reduced rate is limited to the first $500,000 of active business income earned in a year.

12-64.   All of the provinces, with the exception of Saskatchewan, also apply their small business rate to the first $500,000 of active business income. Saskatchewan uses a limit of $600,000.

12-65.   When the reduced federal and provincial rates are combined, the resulting rates range from a low of 9% in Manitoba to a high of 13% in Quebec.

Investment Income Rates

12-66.   While this is not illustrated in Figure 12-3, different rates are applicable to certain types of investment income. We will provide additional coverage of these rates in Chapter 13.

Other Provincial Taxes

12-67.   At one time, provincial taxes on corporate capital were fairly common. The taxes were determined applying a fixed percentage rate to capital such as retained earnings, long-term debt, and share capital. However, though some provinces levy capital taxes on specific types of entities (e.g., financial institutions), provinces no longer apply a general tax on corporate capital.

12-68.   Several provinces currently levy payroll taxes, often to fund the provincial health care system. For example, Ontario has a payroll tax referred to as the EHT (Employer Health Tax). The EHT is based on annual payroll, however an exemption applies to the first $1,000,000 of payroll costs. Certain Ontario employers with annual payroll in excess of $5,000,000 are not entitled to the exemption.

Other Goals of the Corporate Tax System

12-69.   If raising revenues was the only goal of the corporate taxation system, there would be nothing much to discuss with respect to this matter, and there would be little need for the chapters on corporate taxation that follow. However, in addition to raising revenues, the Canadian corporate taxation system has been structured to accomplish a number of other objectives, including the following:

- **Incentives for Small Business**   While there are several features of the tax system directed at encouraging small businesses, the major tax incentive for these organizations is the small business deduction, which allows a significant deferral of income tax that can be used to grow a business.
- **Incentives for Certain Business Activities**   The Canadian tax system provides generous investment incentives offered in the form of tax credits for scientific research as well as for the employment of apprentices, some of which are refundable.
- **Incentives for Certain Regions**   Certain regions of Canada are given assistance through targeted investment incentives offered as investment tax credits and other assistance programs, including low-rate and forgivable loans.
- **Integration**   One of the goals of the Canadian tax system is to keep the level of income taxes paid on income the same regardless of whether or not a corporation is placed between the original source of the income and the ultimate individual recipient.

12-70.   The small business deduction and the manufacturing and processing profits deduction will be examined in this chapter. Integration will be dealt with in further detail in Chapter 13. Our material on scientific research and experimental development expenditures and investment tax credits can be found in Chapter 14.

Small Business Deduction—ITA 125

Introduction

12-71.   Since its introduction in 1972, the small business deduction has been a targeted incentive to incorporated Canadian small to medium-sized businesses in recognition that such businesses do not have access to raise capital as do companies such as large private corporations or publicly listed companies. The small business deduction is designed to lower the tax rate on business income, leaving business owners with increased after-tax funds to reinvest and grow the business.

12-72.   Generous incentives such as the small business deduction, however, require safeguards to ensure they are properly targeted and not abused. Three principal policy goals of the small business deduction are (1) the economic entity notion, (2) a single business notion, and (3) a reinvestment notion.

> The economic notion provides that there should be no more than one $500,000 small business deduction for each economic entity. Therefore, if one individual owns all of the shares of three different corporations that each carry on a different business, there should be only one small business deduction allowed. The associated corporation rules, which are discussed in Chapter 14, are designed to address this notion. The association rules require the sharing of the $500,000 small business limit among the three companies. Associated corporations are free to choose the amount of the business limit allocated to each such corporation (ITA 125(2) and (3)).

> The business notion strives to ensure that each business should be entitled to no more than one small business limit of $500,000. Attempts to multiply the small business deduction for a single business would generally be contrary to that notion. Tax planning strategies that serve to increase or multiply access to the small business deduction, not corrected with the associated corporation rules, would fall into this category.. An example would be four unassociated CCPCs that are equal partners in a partnership carrying on a business that earns $2,000,000 annually of active business income. Each would be allocated one-quarter of the business income, or $500,000, resulting in four small business deductions. This is contrary to the single business notion. Rules were established to limit the small business deduction of each CCPC to one-quarter of the $500,000 small business limit, or $125,000, to address this multiplication issue.

> The reinvestment notion looks to determine whether a given CCPC needs the additional after-tax funds or is actually using those funds to reinvest in the business. If not, then the policy would be to limit or restrict access to the small business deduction by that CCPC. Additional rules examine the amount of corporate capital and whether the CCPC has passive investment income as indicators that the small business deduction is no longer accomplishing its objectives. In such cases the business limit of $500,000 may be reduced.

12-73.   Historically the SBD rules have been relatively straightforward to apply with the exception of situations involving associated corporations, which are discussed in Chapter 14. In recent years, however (beginning in 2016), additional legislative constraints have been added to restrict access to the SBD. This additional legislation has greatly increased the complexity.

12-74.   The legislative changes have included reductions in what can be claimed as a small business deduction for CCPCs that have used after-tax funds to acquire investments with no or little connection to the active business. These rules are commonly referred to as the "passive investment income limitations" and are added in support of the reinvestment notion discussed.

12-75.   In addition, rules relating to certain corporate and partnership structures have been added to address tax planning designed to multiply access to the small business deduction. These latter rules are referred to as the "specified partnership income" and "specified corporate income" rules. These relatively new rules were added in support of the notion that a single business should be entitled to no more than one small business limit of $500,000.

12-76.   In this chapter we will focus on the general rules together with the restrictions imposed on large CCPCs that have sufficient capital resources of their own and CCPCs that are using after-tax funds to acquire passive investments. New rules that focus on more sophisticated partnership and corporate structures designed to multiply access to the small business limit are beyond the scope of an introductory text on federal income tax.

General Rules

12-77.   The small business deduction was introduced in 1972 and the small business deduction rate (ITA 125(1.1)) has varied ever since. The current rate of 19% has been in effect since 2019. The small business deduction rate establishes the general rate on active business income of up to $500,000 at 9% [38% general rate - 10% abatement - 19% small business rate]. This rate is six percentage points lower than the general business rate of 15% [38% general rate - 10% abatement - 13% general rate reduction]. All of the provinces allow a small business deduction rate between zero and 4% (see Paragraph 12-61) based on $500,000 of active business income with the exception of Saskatchewan, which allows a deduction based on $600,000 of active business income.

12-78.   A simple example will serve to illustrate the application of this deduction.

EXAMPLE   A CCPC has taxable income of $500,000 for the year ending December 31, 2021. All of this income is earned in Canada and is eligible for the small business deduction. The provincial tax rate applicable to income eligible for the small business deduction is 2%.

ANALYSIS   The corporation's tax payable would be calculated as follows:

Base amount of Part I Tax [(38%)($100,000)]	$38,000
Federal tax abatement [(10%)($100,000)]	(10,000)
Small business deduction [(19%)($100,000)]	(19,000)
Federal tax payable	$ 9,000
Provincial tax payable [(2%)($100,000)]	2,000
Total tax payable	$ 11,000

12-79.   The small business deduction provides a significant incentive to businesses that qualify. Only certain types of corporations qualify for this deduction and it is only available on certain amounts and types of income. The criteria for qualification can be described in non-technical terms as follows:

Type of Corporation   The availability of the small business deduction is restricted to CCPCs.

Type of Income   The deduction is only available with respect to income from "active businesses" carried on in Canada. This would include the income of professional corporations and management companies, provided they are CCPCs. If the active business meets the definition of a "specified investment business" or a "personal services business" (see definitions later in this chapter), the income would not qualify for the small business deduction.

Limit on Amount   The federal deduction is available on up to $500,000 of active business income earned in a year. This amount is referred to as the business limit for the year and may be reduced for a number of reasons, including a short taxation year (less than 365 days—ITA 125(5)(b)).

Associated Corporations The $500,000 business limit must be shared among associated corporations even if the corporations carry on different businesses. The associated corporation rules are based on an economic entity notion identifying two or more corporations that are commonly controlled by the same person or group of persons.

12-80.   The issues associated with these criteria are discussed in the material that follows.

Canadian Controlled Private Corporation (CCPC)—ITA 125(7)

12-81.   CCPCs are defined in ITA 125(7) as "private corporations" (ITA 89(1)) that are "Canadian corporations" (ITA 89(1)). Private corporations are companies that are resident in Canada, are not public corporations, and are not controlled by public corporations. Canadian corporations are corporations that are both incorporated in Canada and resident in Canada. "Public corporations" (ITA 89(1)) are corporations resident in Canada and whose shares are listed on designated stock exchanges in Canada, such as the Toronto Stock Exchange (TSX).

12-82.   The effect of this first part of the definition is that corporations incorporated in Canada that are resident in Canada and are not controlled by public companies would be CCPCs as long as the shares of the company are not listed on a designated stock exchange in Canada. An additional rule denies CCPC status if the shares of a corporation are listed on certain designated foreign stock exchanges, such as the New York Stock Exchange. The practical result is that private corporations incorporated in Canada by Canadian resident individuals would be a CCPC. Companies incorporated outside of Canada, public companies, and corporations controlled by a public company would not meet the definition of a CCPC.

12-83.   The CCPC definition, however, goes beyond identifying the type of corporation, including where it is resident and incorporated, to an examination of the shareholders. The general rules are that if a corporation that would otherwise meet the definition of a CCPC becomes controlled by non-residents, public companies, or a combination of non-residents and public companies it would not be considered a CCPC at that time. In other words, it would lose its CCPC status.

12-84.   In summary, a CCPC is a private company incorporated in Canada, resident in Canada, and controlled by Canadian residents (other than Canadian public companies). There are numerous ITA rules that impact the status of a Canadian corporation as a CCPC, but many are beyond the scope of an introductory text on federal income tax.

> **EXAMPLE 1**   Anika is a Canadian resident. She incorporated a company in Manitoba in 2015 and owns all of the shares of the company. The company uses a calendar-based taxation year from January 1 to December 31. The company carries on an active business in Canada. On October 10, 2021, Anika sells all of the shares to a non-resident that is a foreign company in France.
>
> **ANALYSIS 1**   Since the company was incorporated in Canada and is resident in Canada (ITA 250(4)(a) deems a company incorporated in Canada after April 26, 1965, to be a resident of Canada), the company is both a private company and a Canadian corporation. In addition, since prior to October 10, 2021, it was not controlled by non-residents or public companies or a combination of the two it meets the definition of a CCPC and would be entitled to the SBD. On October 10, 2021, however, the company would lose its CCPC status since it would be controlled by non-residents. From that moment it would no longer be eligible for the SBD even though it would continue to carry on an active business in Canada. When a corporations' status changes from or to a CCPC, ITA 249(3.1) deems the company's taxation year to have ended before that time. As a result of the sale, the company would have a short taxation year beginning January 1, 2021, and ending October 9, 2021. This will be discussed in Chapter 14. Any small business limit would be prorated by the number of days in that period (282 days) over 365. Therefore, if the company had active business income of $500,000 for the short taxation year ending October 9, 2021, its business limit would only be $386,301 [($500,000)(282/365)].

EXAMPLE 2   Anika is a Canadian resident. She incorporated a company in Manitoba in 2015 and owns all of the shares of the company. The company uses a calendar-based taxation year from January 1 to December 31. The company carries on an active business in Canada. On October 10, 2021, Anika emigrates from Canada, severing her Canadian residency.

ANALYSIS 2   Since the company was incorporated in Canada and is resident in Canada (ITA 250(4)(a) deems a company incorporated in Canada after April 26, 1965 to be a resident of Canada) the company is both a private company and a Canadian corporation. In addition, since prior to October 10, 2021, it was not controlled by non-residents or public companies or a combination of the two it would meet the definition of a CCPC and would be entitled to the SBD. As of October 10, 2021, Anika is a non-resident of Canada and continues to control the company. While the company remains a private company that is both incorporated and resident in Canada, it no longer qualifies as a CCPC since it is controlled by a non-resident. In this instance, terminating Canadian residency caused the corporation to lose its CCPC status. The income tax consequences are identical to the analysis in the first example. It is noteworthy that Anika would be deemed by ITA 128.1(4)(b) to have disposed of her shares in the company at their fair market value immediately prior to her departure from Canada. If the shares qualified for the capital gains deduction, a reduction in Canadian income tax could eliminate tax on all or part of the capital gain.

Active Business Income

The General Idea

12-85.   When the legislation was first introduced decades ago it simply referred to "active business income" without qualification. Courts that were called upon to address the meaning of an active business simply determined that all businesses would be active businesses. This meant that investment activity that met the threshold of a business and business income earned by a corporation that represented an employee charging an employer for their employment services through the company were entitled to claim the SBD on that income. In response, and to ensure that the small business deduction was targeted to genuine businesses that did not involve investments or a previous employment relationship, definitions were added to clarify the meaning of an active business. ITA 125(7) added a few definitions to refine the active business concept:

> **Active business carried on by a corporation** means any business carried on by the corporation other than a "specified investment business" or a "personal services business" and includes an adventure or concern in the nature of trade.

12-86.   While the preceding defines active business, a further definition in ITA 125(7) defines "income from an active business" as follows:

> **Income of the corporation for the year from an active business** means ... the income of the corporation for the year from an active business carried on by it, including any income for the year pertaining to or incident to that business, other than income for the year from a source in Canada that is a property ...

12-87.   Based on these definitions, an active business will generally exclude businesses that earn investment-type income ("specified investment business") and businesses that represent a corporation acting as an intermediary between an employer and employee ("personal services business") but will include any income that is incidental to an active business but generally not income from property.

12-88.   Income that is incidental or pertains to an active business ensures that certain income that is not directly linked to the active business will be considered active business income as long as there is some connection to the business. A common example of this would be an active business selling goods on credit. Any interest earned on the accounts receivable would normally be considered income from property (e.g., interest income), but the connection to the business results in a categorization as business income. Another common example is an active business with fluctuating cash balances. If the cash is required to meet business needs then any interest earned on these cash balances would be considered business income. The CRA typically examines the cash needs of a business by verifying fluctuations in cash reserves throughout a period of time. Assume, for example, that a business has excess cash reserves that generate considerable interest. The cash balance, however, never drops below $100,000. This would imply that only cash in excess of $100,000 is necessary for the business. Only interest earned on cash balances above $100,000 would be considered active business income. Interest earned on the $100,000 cash base would be investment income subject to the additional tax on investment income of 10 2/3% mentioned in Paragraph 12-10.

The Problem with Defining Property Income

12-89.   Chapter 6 examined income from a business and Chapter 7 looked at what constitutes income from property. In general terms income from property would include interest, dividends, rents, and royalties. Interest and dividends earned on bonds and shares purchased solely for investment purposes would normally be categorized as income from property. However, if one were to spend considerable time and effort continuously monitoring, buying, and selling shares, bonds, and other investments the nature of the activity, at some point, crosses the line from a passive investment activity to a business activity. The same could be said of an individual who owns one rental property as opposed to a second individual who owns a hundred rental properties. In other words, while interest, dividends, rents, and royalties are often considered property income, it is possible for such income to be the product of a business and to be considered business income.

12-90.   The definitions of an active business and income of an active business make it abundantly clear that, as a rule, business income that is primarily composed of investment-type income should not be able to access the SBD. The government concern is that individuals could incorporate a CCPC, inject it with sufficient capital with the result that investments that the individual would normally own, the income of which would be subject to high individual income tax rates, would be owned by a CCPC that would be eligible for low corporate tax rates with access to the SBD. The income tax deferral advantages would be substantial.

12-91.   The government could have simply excluded businesses that earn investment-type income from the SBD altogether. Instead, the government settled for a compromise that would allow such businesses to access the small business deduction as long as the nature of the activity is a business and that the scope of the business justifies the hiring of more than five full-time employees.

The Solution—Specified Investment Business—ITA 125(7)

12-92.   The concept of a "specified investment business" was added to address this compromise. The term is defined in ITA 125(7) as follows:

> **Specified Investment Business** carried on by a corporation in a taxation year, means a business (other than a business carried on by a credit union or a business of leasing property other than real or immovable property) the principal purpose of which is to derive income (including interest, dividends, rents and royalties) from property but, except where the corporation was a prescribed labour-sponsored venture capital corporation at any time in the year, does not include a business carried on by the corporation in the year where
>
> (i)   the corporation employs in the business throughout the year more than five full-time employees, or
>
> (ii)   any other corporation associated with the corporation provides, in the course of carrying on an active business, managerial, administrative, financial, maintenance or other similar services to the corporation in the year and the corporation could reasonably be expected to require more than five full-time employees if those services had not been provided.

12-93.   If a CCPC carries on a business the principal or main purpose of which is to earn income from property of the corporation, then the business will be a specified investment business unless the CCPC employs more than five full-time employees throughout the relevant taxation year. If the CCPC does not meet the more than five full-time employee test itself, the specified investment business rules would also not apply where a separate associated corporation provides services to the CCPC that would have required the CCPC to employ more than five full-time employees were that service not provided. This latter test recognizes that in practice it is not uncommon to create multiple corporations to provide service and financing to the company that carries on the main business. This is often done to limit corporate liability.

12-94.   Since 2016 the CRA has challenged claims to the SBD for storage businesses, campground businesses, and businesses that provide seasonal campsites. Typically these businesses principally earn rental income from the use of land and other property with incidental service fees. The nature of the businesses generally requires few employees, and as a result the CRA has been quite successful in these challenges.

12-95.   There have also been a few court decisions that have considered the meaning of the phrase "more than five full-time employees." Historically the CRA took the view that the phrase meant at least six full-time employees, but the courts ruled that the phrase meant five full-time employees plus one more employee, whether part time or full time. The CRA has since accepted that interpretation.

Property Income Received from an Associated Corporation—ITA 129(6)

12-96.   Income from a specified investment business and non-incidental property income earned by a CCPC do not qualify for the SBD. However, when a corporation derives income from property, and the income is received from an associated company that deducted the amounts in computing its active business income, ITA 129(6)(b) deems the income to be active business income to the recipient and not income from property.

12-97.   The justification for this treatment in ITA 129(6) can be explained with the following example.

EXAMPLE   Lardin Ltd. and Dwarm Ltd. are associated corporations. Lardin carries on an active business and expects to earn $500,000 in active business income in 2021. Dwarm Ltd.'s sole purpose is to finance Lardin Ltd. Dwarm has one full-time employee. At the beginning of the year Dwarm lends $750,000 to Lardin with interest. Interest charges for 2021 total $31,000. Lardin reports active business income of $461,000 [$500,000 less $31,000 of interest] and Dwarm reports $31,000 of interest income.

ANALYSIS   Lardin carries on an active business and would be entitled to the SBD of $87,590 [(19%)($461,000)] for 2021. Technically Dwarm's income would appear to be income from property and not income from a business. If it were possible to argue that the activity of Dwarm was a business, that activity would fall under the definition of a specified investment business and would not qualify for the SBD due to the failure to meet the five full-time employee test. However, regardless of whether the $31,000 of interest earned by Dwarm is income from property (e.g., the loan receivable) or business income, ITA 129(6) overrides the SBD rules by deeming the interest to be active business income of Dwarm. The effect is to provide symmetry in recognizing that there is really $500,000 of active business income globally, and therefore companies should not be penalized for having separate finance companies when the purpose is to finance or provide other services to support an active business among associated corporations. In this case, Dwarm could claim a small business deduction of $5,890 [(19%)($31,000)].

Annual Business Limit

12-98.   The federal limit on the amount of active business income that is eligible for the SBD is $500,000 per taxation year. As discussed in the paragraph that follows, this annual limit must be shared among associated corporations. In addition, as will be discussed beginning at

Paragraph 12-116, this $500,000 limit will be reduced for CCPCs with either "taxable capital employed in Canada" (TCEC) in excess of $10 million in the preceding year or "adjusted aggregate investment income" (AAII) in excess of $50,000 in the preceding year. These adjustments are made in support of the reinvestment notion (see Paragraph 12-72) recognizing that the SBD incentive is no longer meeting its objectives.

Calculating the Small Business Deduction

The General Formula

12-99.   In this paragraph we present a modified calculation that excludes references to specified corporate income, specified partnership income, and specified partnership losses. This simplified calculation is included at the front of this text in "Rates, Credits, and Other Data—Information Applicable to Corporations"). ITA 125(1) specifies that the SBD is equal to 19% of the least of three amounts:

(a)   Net Canadian active business income.

(b)   Taxable income, less:

   (i)   100/28 times the ITA 126(1) credit for foreign taxes paid on foreign non-business income, calculated without consideration of the additional refundable tax under ITA 123.3 (see Chapter 13) or the general rate reduction under ITA 123.4; and

   (ii)   4 times the ITA 126(2) credit for taxes paid on foreign business income, calculated without consideration of the general rate reduction under ITA 123.4 (see Note).

(c)   The annual business limit of $500,000, less any portion allocated to associated corporations, less any reduction for TCEC or AAII. (These reductions are explained later in this chapter.)

> **Note**   ITA 125(1)(b)(ii) actually has a more complicated calculation as follows:
>
> ... the amount determined by the formula
>
> $$1 \div (A - B), \text{ where}$$
>
> **A**   is the percentage set out in paragraph 123(1)(a) [the basic federal rate of 38%], and
>
> **B**   is the percentage that is the corporation's general rate reduction percentage (as defined by section 123.4) for the taxation year [13%].
>
> Given these numbers, ITA 125(1)(b)(ii) is calculated as $[1 \div (.38 - .13)] = 4$. We will use this number 4 in all of our examples and problems, without repeating this calculation.

Constraints—Type of Income and Business Limit

12-100.   We have already noted that the deduction is only available on net active business income earned in Canada (ITA 125(1)(a)). Net active business income considers a situation in which a corporation carries on two or more active businesses in a year. Net active business income is the difference between income in one active business minus any losses in the other active businesses. The ITA 125(1)(c) amount is the business limit of $500,000 or a lesser allocated amount where there are associated corporations.

Constraints—Taxable Income

12-101.   ITA 125(1)(b) applies a constraint based on taxable income. Net active business income is included in net income but may be offset by taxable income deductions discussed in Paragraph 12-18. Examples of such taxable income deductions would be as follows:

- Charitable donations
- Non-capital loss carry overs
- Farm loss carry overs

12-102.   You will notice that neither taxable dividends nor net capital losses are included in this list. This reflects the fact that these amounts can only be deducted to the extent that either taxable dividends or net taxable capital gains are included in net income. Given this, they cannot offset amounts of net active business income that are included in net income.

12-103.   A simple example will illustrate the need for this taxable income constraint on the SBD:

> **EXAMPLE**   During the current year, Allard Ltd. has active business income of $123,000, taxable capital gains of $15,000, and dividends received from taxable Canadian corporations of $50,000. Allard Ltd. has a 2019 net capital loss balance of $35,000 and a 2018 non-capital loss balance of $105,000. The company will use the loss carry forward balances to the extent possible during the current year. The calculation of Allard's net income and taxable income would be as follows:

2021 Net income	
($123,000 + $15,000 + $50,000)	$188,000
Dividends received—ITA 112(1)	(50,000)
2019 Net capital loss—ITA 111(1)(b)	(15,000)
Subtotal (equal to active business income)	$123,000
2018 Non-capital loss—ITA 111(1)(a)	(105,000)
2021 Taxable income	$ 18,000

12-104.   Note that if only the net capital loss carry forward and dividends were deducted, taxable income would have been equal to the $123,000 in active business income. The problem is the non-capital loss carry forward. It has further reduced taxable income to $18,000, offsetting a large portion of the active business income.

12-105.   If, in this case, the SBD were based on active business income, the amount would be $23,370 [(19%)($123,000)]. As this deduction is in excess of the tax payable on $18,000 of taxable income, this is not a reasonable outcome. The effect is that the SBD is only available with respect to active business income that is actually subject to income tax. In this case that amount would only be $18,000.

Constraints—Foreign Tax Credits

12-106.   Another concern of the federal government is to ensure that the SBD is not provided on income that has not been taxed in Canada. To prevent this from happening, ITA 125(1)(b) further reduces taxable income by:

- 100/28 times the ITA 126(1) credit for foreign taxes paid on foreign non-business income, calculated without consideration of the additional refundable tax of 10 2/3% under ITA 123.3 (see Chapter 13) or the general rate reduction of 13% under ITA 123.4; and
- 4 times the ITA 126(2) credit for foreign taxes paid on foreign business income, calculated without consideration of the general rate reduction of 13% under ITA 123.4.

The actual foreign tax credits under ITA 126(1) and 126(2) may be different than the amounts used in the small business deduction formula. The references to "without consideration of ..." is designed to modify those foreign tax credits to avoid overly complex situations of circularity and other issues. This is discussed in Chapter 13. In the examples and problems throughout this text it is assumed that the amount of foreign tax credits provided has taken these modified calculations into consideration.

12-107.   The 100/28 figure is based on the notional assumption that foreign non-business income will be subject to a federal corporate tax rate of 28% (i.e., if the credit is equal to the taxes paid at 28%, 100/28 times the credit will equal the notional amount of income received). The 28% rate represents the 38% basic corporate rate minus the 10% abatement since no part of the non-business income would be connected to a permanent establishment outside of Canada. The intention is to identify and remove from taxable income a portion of income that relates to the foreign tax credit allowed.

> **EXAMPLE** A CCPC earns foreign non-business income of $100, which should be subject to Canadian tax of 28%, or $28. The foreign income was taxed in the foreign jurisdiction with the result that a foreign tax credit of $21 was provided. This means that there should be $7 of Canadian tax to make up the $28 difference. There are two general ways to address this issue. The first is to add $100 to income, charge $28 of tax but allow a foreign tax credit of $21 so that the net Canadian tax is $7. The second way is to only include in taxable income enough income that would result in $7 of Canadian tax. In this case that would mean that only $25 should be added, which at 28% equals $7. The calculations begin with the foreign income of $100, which is reduced by the amount of income that would have resulted in income tax of $21 at 28%. This amount is $75, which is calculated as [(100/28)($21)]. This is the approach used in the SBD and in many other corporate income tax rules.

12-108.   In similar fashion, the 4 times figure that is applicable to foreign business income is based on the notional assumption that this income will be subject to a federal corporate tax rate of 25% (1 ÷ 4). The corporate tax rate of 25% is determined as the 38% basic corporate tax rate minus the 13% general rate reduction. No amount would be allowed for the federal abatement since, as a rule, a foreign jurisdiction is only permitted to tax business income if the income is attributable to a permanent establishment in that foreign jurisdiction, which would prevent a claim for the federal abatement of 10% with respect to that foreign income. The purpose of this reduction is identical to that of foreign non-business income mentioned in Paragraph 12-107.

12-109.   Based on the preceding analysis, subtracting these amounts from taxable income has the effect of removing foreign income on which the foreign tax credit has offset the Canadian corporate income tax at the assumed rates of 28% and 25%. The following further example will help clarify this point.

> **EXAMPLE** A CCPC earns $100,000 in foreign non-business income, with $18,000 being withheld by the foreign government as foreign income tax.
>
> If this income had been earned in Canada, it is assumed that the tax would be $28,000 (using the notional rate on this type of income of 28%). The assumed $28,000 in Canadian tax payable will be offset by a foreign tax credit of $18,000. This will leave a net Canadian tax payable of $10,000.
>
> Using the foreign non-business tax credit of $18,000 and an assumed tax rate of 28%, the formula removes $64,286 [(100/28)($18,000)] from taxable income, leaving $35,714 ($100,000 - $64,286). If we multiply this $35,714 by the notional rate of 28%, the result is $10,000, the amount of the net Canadian corporate income tax that would have been charged after consideration of the foreign tax credit. This demonstrates how the formula ensures that the small business deduction is not available on taxable income on which foreign tax credits have eliminated any Canadian corporate tax. Another way to look at this is that $18,000 of foreign taxes is the equivalent to 28% of $64,286. This approach hypothetically implies that no tax was imposed on the remaining $35,714.
>
> If the foreign tax withheld and the foreign tax credit had both been $28,000 [(28%)($100,000)], the formula would have removed $100,000 [(100/28)($28,000)], or all of the foreign non-business income.

Exercise 12-7

Subject: Amount Eligible for the Small Business Deduction

Kartoom Ltd. is a CCPC that began operations on January 1, 2019, when it was first incorporated. A calendar-based fiscal period was chosen. It is not associated with any other corporation. For its year ending December 31, 2021, Kartoom has net income of $570,000. This amount is made up of taxable dividends from taxable Canadian corporations of $85,000, net active business income of $425,000, and foreign non-business income of $60,000. The foreign income was subject to foreign income tax of 15%, or $9,000 [(15%)($60,000)]. The foreign tax credit allowed Kartoom under ITA 126(1) is equal to the foreign tax withheld of $9,000. Kartoom has a 2019 non-capital loss carry forward of $160,000, which it intends to deduct in full in 2021.

Determine the amount eligible for the small business deduction for the year ending December 31, 2021.

Solutions to Exercises are available in the Study Guide.

Business Limit Reduction — ITA 125(5.1)

Problem I

12-110.   As the name implies, the small business deduction was designed to provide assistance to CCPCs carrying on small to medium-sized businesses. For a variety of reasons, including the fact that such businesses are responsible for a considerable portion of employment in Canada and that these businesses often experience financing difficulties in their formative years, the generous tax advantages provided by this deduction were thought to be appropriate.

12-111.   However, in the initial design of the SBD, eligibility was based on the type of income earned (active business income) and the type of corporation (CCPCs). No consideration was given to the size of the corporation in terms of income or capital. As a consequence, some large CCPCs received the benefit of the SBD on amounts of active business income up to the small business limit. This was clearly not in keeping with the tax policy intent of the legislation.

12-112.   To deal with this problem, the government introduced legislation to reduce access to the SBD by grinding down the $500,000 business limit for CCPCs where the taxable capital employed in Canada (TCEC) of that CCPC together with associated companies exceeds $10 million. This grind eliminates all of the small business limit when TCEC reaches $15 million. A proportional reduction in the business limit occurs where TCEC is between $10 and $15 million.

Problem II

12-113.   A second and more recently identified problem was briefly described in Paragraph 12-72. This is the fact that the low small business rate provides additional funds that are sometimes being used to purchase portfolios of passive investments. In other words, the implication is that the low small business rate is no longer necessary to support and grow the business.

12-114.   For taxation years of CCPCs that begin after December 31, 2018, a second business limit grind applies. This grind is based on a CCPC's adjusted aggregate investment income (AAII). This version of investment income, defined in ITA 125(7), is used only for purposes of determining the reduction or grind in the small business limit. In somewhat simplified terms the AAII includes:

- income from property such as interest, rents, and royalties (if ITA 129(6) applies, these amounts would be deemed to be active business income and would therefore not be included);

- net taxable capital gains on the disposition of capital property other than "active assets" defined as property principally used in the active business of the corporation and shares of connected corporations if the shares would have qualified for the capital gains deduction if they had been owned by an individual;
- dividends received from taxable Canadian corporations with the exception of those from connected corporations (discussed in Chapter 13);
- income from a specified investment business; and
- dividends from foreign corporations with the exception of those from foreign affiliates (discussed in Chapter 20).

12-115.   Only one of the two small business limit grinds can apply to a CCPC in a given taxation year. ITA 125(5.1) requires that the overall grind be based on the greater of the TCEC grind and the AAII grind. Once you have determined the TCEC and the AAII you can then determine the grinds for the taxation year. The TCEC and AAII of the CCPC and associated corporations must be considered. If the TCEC is less than $10 million, this grind does not apply. If the TCEC is $15 million or more the business limit is reduced to nil. If the TCEC is between $10 and $15 million a proportional reduction in the business limit occurs. If the AAII is $50,000 or less there is no grind. If the AAII is $150,000 or more the business limit is reduced to nil. If the AAII is between $50,000 and $150,000 there is a proportional reduction in the business limit.

Taxable Capital Employed in Canada (TCEC) Grind—ITA 125(5.1)(a)
12-116.   The legislative formula for this component of the annual business limit grind is as follows:

TCEC REDUCTION where,

A   is the amount of the corporation's business limit for the year ($500,000 or less if shared with associated corporations).

B   is 0.225% (.00225) of the excess over $10 million of the previous year end's total taxable capital employed in Canada of the corporation and any associated companies.

NOTE   This formula is for the **reduction** of the business limit only.

12-117.   "TCEC" is defined in ITA 181.2. In somewhat simplified terms, it has the following meaning:

Taxable Capital Employed in Canada (TCEC)   Long-term debt and equity capital of the corporation, less certain types of debt and equity investments in other corporations. The dollar amounts used are those amounts that appear in a year-end balance sheet prepared using generally accepted accounting principles (ASPE or IFRS). The "in Canada" portion is determined applying the same percentage used in calculating the 10% federal abatement that was discussed beginning at Paragraph 12-43.

12-118.   The mechanics of this formula are easily understood. If a corporation has $10 million or less TCEC, B will equal nil ($10 million or less minus the $10 million specified deduction). This means the formula amount will be nil and there will be no reduction in the corporation's business limit.

12-119.   When the amount of TCEC for the previous year reaches $15 million, B in the formula will be equal to $11,250 [(.00225)($15,000,000 - $10,000,000)]. The annual business limit will then be multiplied by one ($11,250 ÷ $11,250) and the reduction in the business limit will be 100%.

12-120.   Not surprisingly, a CCPC that is associated with one or more corporations in a taxation year will be required to take into account the TCEC of all associated corporations. The rules apply different TCEC bases depending on a CCPCs history with associated corporations.

Example of the TCEC Grind

12-121.   The following example illustrates the TCEC grind of the small business deduction for a large CCPC.

EXAMPLE   Largess Inc. is a CCPC with a December 31 year end. All of its income is earned in Canada, and it is has never been associated with any other corporation. On December 31, 2021, the following information is available:

2021 Net active business income	$ 523,000
2021 Taxable income	550,000
2020 TCEC	13,700,000
2020 AAII	Nil

ANALYSIS   For the preceding year, 2020, B in the reduction formula would be equal to $8,325 [(.00225)($13,700,000 - $10,000,000)]. Using this in the ITA 125(5.1) formula would produce the following reduction in the 2021 business limit:

$$\$500,000 \times \frac{\$8,325}{\$11,250} = \$370,000 \text{ \textbf{Reduction}}$$

Given this, the reduced business limit would be $130,000 ($500,000 - $370,000) and the SBD for 2021 would be 19% of the least of:

Net active business income	$523,000
Taxable income	550,000
Reduced business limit ($500,000 - $370,000)	130,000

The reduced annual business limit is the least of the three amounts, and the 2021 SBD would be $24,700 [(19%)($130,000)], a significant reduction from the $95,000 [(19%)($500,000)] that would have been available in the absence of the TCEC grind. You will note that since the AAII was less than $50,000 in the 2020 preceding year there is no AAII grind. ITA 125(5.1) requires applying the greater of the two grinds, which in this case is $370,000. TIP: You can double check your calculation of the TCEC grind by applying a simple method. The TCEC of $13,700,000 is 74% of the way between $10 and $15 million [($3,700,000 ÷ $5,000,000)]. The TCEC grind is therefore 74% of the 2021 business limit of $500,000, or $370,000.

Exercise 12-8

Subject: Taxable Capital Employed in Canada (TCEC) Grind

Largely Small Inc. is a CCPC. For the year ending December 31, 2021, its net income is $1,233,000, of which $1,197,000 is Canadian active business income and $36,000 is foreign source non-business income. Foreign income tax of 15%, or $5,400, was withheld. The foreign non-business income tax credit under ITA 126(1) is equal to $5,400. The corporation's only deduction in the calculation of taxable income is for a 2020 non-capital loss carry forward balance of $914,000. The corporation's TCEC was $11,300,000 for the year ending December 31, 2020, and $11,600,000 for the current year ending December 31, 2021. The corporation's AAII for 2020 was nil. The corporation has never been associated with any other corporation. Determine the amount of Largely Small Inc.'s small business deduction for the year ending December 31, 2021.

Solutions to Exercises are available in the Study Guide.

Adjusted Aggregate Investment Income (AAII) Grind—ITA 125(5.1)(b)

12-122.   The legislative formula for the AAII grind is as follows:

AAII REDUCTION

$$= \left[\frac{D}{\$500,000} \right] [(5)(E - \$50,000)] \text{ where,}$$

D   is the amount of the corporation's business limit for the year ($500,000 or less if shared with associated corporations).

E   is the total of all amounts each of which is the AAII of the corporation or of any corporation with which it is associated for the preceding year.

12-123.   As was the case with the TCEC grind formula, the AAII grind formula is fairly easy to understand. If the CCPC's AAII for the previous year is $50,000 or less, there is no reduction in the business limit.

EXAMPLE   Before the grind, DOC Inc. has a business limit of $500,000 and the AAII for the previous year of $50,000. Its TCEC for the previous year is less than $10 million.

ANALYSIS   The required reduction would be calculated as follows:

[($500,000/$500,000)][(5)($50,000 - $50,000)] = Nil

This would leave the company's annual business limit at $500,000.

12-124.   Alternatively, for every dollar of AAII in excess of $50,000, the company's annual business limit will be reduced by $5 where the business limit would otherwise be $500,000.

EXAMPLE   Before the grind, Arc Ltd. has a business limit of $500,000 and AAII for the previous year of $75,000. Its TCEC for the previous year is less than $10 million.

ANALYSIS   The required reduction would be calculated as follows:

[($500,000/$500,000)][(5)($75,000 - $50,000)] = $125,000 **Reduction**

This would leave an annual business limit of $375,000 ($500,000 - $125,000).

TIP: There is a proportional reduction in the business limit where the previous year's AAII is between $50,000 and $150,000. You can double check the reduction formula calculation in a manner similar to that for the TCEC reduction tip provided at Paragraph 12-121. An AAII of $75,000 is 25% of the way between $50,000 and $150,000. Therefore, the AAII reduction would be 25% of $500,000 or $125,000. The modified business limit would be $375,000.

Exercise 12-9

Subject: Adjusted Aggregate Investment Income (AAII) Grind

Investco Ltd. is a CCPC. For the taxation year ending December 31, 2021, its net income and taxable income is made up of active business income of $350,000 plus investment income of $125,000, all of which is AAII. For 2020, its AAII was $95,000. Its TCEC for 2020 was $9 million and for 2021 is $8 million. The company is associated with Subco Ltd. Investco's 2021 business limit allocation is $300,000. Subco's TCEC is $200,000 for each of 2020 and 2021. Subco's AAII for 2020 is $10,000 and nil for 2021.

Determine the amount of Investco's small business deduction for the year ending December 31, 2021.

Solutions to Exercises are available in the Study Guide.

Economic Impact

12-125.   As indicated previously, the actual reduction in the business limit will be the greater of the TCEC and AAII grind. With respect to the TCEC grind, it will only have an effect on CCPCs that have TCEC in excess of $10 million in the preceding year. This means that the great majority of CCPCs would not be affected.

12-126.   With respect to the new AAII grind, in the explanatory notes to the legislation the Department of Finance has indicated that only about 3% percent of CCPCs claiming the SBD would be impacted.

12-127.   Even in those situations where there would be a reduction in the business limit, this may have no impact on the company's SBD. There are many CCPCs that do not have sufficient active business income to fully use their annual business limit. In such situations, the application of these grinds will only effect the SBD where the annual business limit is reduced below the CCPC's active business income.

Exercise 12-10

Subject: Annual Business Limit Reduction

Reduco Inc. is a CCPC. For the taxation year ending December 31, 2021, its net income of $540,000 is made up of active business income of $450,000 and investment income of $90,000, all of which qualifies as AAII. For 2020, Reduco's AAII was $72,000. Its only deduction in the determination of 2021 taxable income is a 2018 non-capital loss carry forward balance of $60,000. Because of its association with another company, Reduco's share of the 2021 business limit is $350,000. The associated company's AAII in each of 2020 and 2021 is nil.

Determine Reduco's small business deduction for the year ending December 31, 2021, assuming that the combined TCEC of Reduco and its associated company was:

Case 1 $11,000,000 for 2021 and $13,500,000 for 2020.

Case 2 $13,500,000 for 2021 and $11,000,000 for 2020.

Solutions to Exercises are available in the Study Guide.

Personal Services Business—ITA 125(7)

12-128.   The small business deduction represents a significant reduction in corporate income taxes and, as a consequence, individuals have a strong incentive to structure their affairs to take advantage of these low corporate tax rates.

12-129.   At one point in time, this could be accomplished by having an employee resign, incorporate a new company, and immediately have the newly created company sign a contract with the former employer to provide the same employment services to that employer. The employee would sign a contract with her own corporation to provide employment services to that company in fulfillment of the services to be provided to the former employer. In substance, the newly created company would represent an intermediary between the employee and the former employer. The important income tax difference, however, would be that instead of receiving employment income directly from the former employer, the newly created company would receive fees (economically representing the former employee's salary) in the form of business income. The newly created company would pay a lesser amount to the employee in salary and retain the remainder, which would be subject to low corporate income tax.

12-130.   Since this new corporation could then qualify for the SBD, the use of such incorporated personal services businesses provided significant tax deferral and, in some cases, significant tax avoidance for individuals such as executives, professional athletes, and entertainers.

12-131.   Under the current legislation, rules are in place to make such structuring costly. The central provision that discourages these practices is found in the definition of a "personal services business" (ITA 125(7)), which reads as follows:

... a business of providing services where

(a)   an individual who performs services on behalf of the corporation (referred to as an incorporated employee), or
(b)   any person related to the incorporated employee

is a specified shareholder of the corporation and the incorporated employee would reasonably be regarded as an officer or employee of the person or partnership to whom or to which the services were provided but for the existence of the corporation, unless

(a)   the corporation employs in the business throughout the year more than five full-time employees, or
(b)   the amount paid or payable to the corporation in the year for the services is received or receivable by it from a corporation with which it was associated in the year.

12-132.   In less technical language, a business of a corporation (e.g., the newly created company) is considered to be carrying on a personal services business when a "specified shareholder" (generally an individual who owns 10% or more of the shares of any class of the intermediary corporation providing the services) and the individual who is performing the services for the intermediary corporation would reasonably be regarded as an employee of the former employer. When an individual was an employee of an employer and the same employment services are being provided to that employer through the newly created company it will be difficult to argue that the intermediary corporation is not carrying on a personal services business.

12-133.   It is clear from the exceptions to the definition that this type of restructuring is not always considered offensive. If the business employs more than five full-time employees throughout the year it would not be a personal services business. A second exception recognizes that if the services are provided between associated corporations that the business will also not be considered a personal services business.

12-134.   Carrying on a personal services business through a corporation is costly in terms of income tax. Income from such a business is not eligible for the SBD or the 13% general rate reduction. In addition, corporations carrying on a personal services business are subject to an additional tax of 5% (ITA 123.5) on that income. The result is that the federal tax rate on such income is 33% [38% basic rate - 10% federal abatement + 5% additional tax]. This rate is designed to equal the highest income tax rate for individuals.

12-135.   In addition to this high rate, personal services businesses, as a result of ITA 18(1)(p), are only allowed to deduct expenses that are:

• salaries, wages, or other remuneration and benefits paid in the year to the individual who performed the services on behalf of the corporation; and
• other expenses that would normally be deductible against employment income, for example, travel expenses incurred to earn employment income.

12-136.   Recently, the CRA publicly cautioned truck drivers who were participating in an industry trend to acquire the truck used in their employment from their employer, resign, create a new company, and enter into a long-term contract with the same employer to provide the same employment services through the new company. Such arrangements would likely be considered personal services businesses with the detrimental income tax consequences noted in Paragraphs 12-134 and 12-135. If, however, these former employed individuals provide expanded services through their company, including providing services to other businesses (not just the former employer), the likelihood of arguing that the business is not a personal services business increases.

12-137.   However, certain individuals, such as athletes, entertainers, and consultants, may still find it attractive to incorporate. In many cases, they will qualify for the SBD either because they have sufficient diversity of income or more than five full-time employees. In addition, there is an advantage in that all of the income of a personal services business is added to the GRIP balance (see Chapter 13), meaning that all of the income can be paid out as eligible dividends, which are taxed to individuals at very favourable rates.

Professional Corporations and Management Companies

12-138.　In general terms, these two types of private corporations can be described as follows:

Professional Corporations　This term is used where a corporation is established to carry on the practice of a profession specified in ITA 248(1). The ITA definition includes a corporation that carries on the professional practice of an accountant, dentist, lawyer, medical doctor, veterinarian, or chiropractor. Each province has different laws and rules as to which professions are allowed to incorporate. The incorporation of the professional practice of an engineer or architect would not meet the ITA definition.

Management Companies　This is a generic term that is not separately defined in the ITA. The expression refers to corporations whose function is to provide supportive services such as various management, administrative, and clerical services to another business, primarily to unincorporated business carried on as sole proprietorships or as partnerships. Common examples include the business of pharmacists, doctors, or dentists where incorporation is not allowed.

The specific types of services provided by this type of company include various personnel functions, such as payroll and accounting services, purchasing all supplies and equipment necessary to carry on the business, and providing the necessary office space required by the professional practice. The goal of these companies is to effectively carve out a portion of the profit of the main business and subject it to low corporate income tax rates.

The unincorporated business pays fees to the management company to cover the cost of providing management services and to provide for some income. Historically, the CRA has stated that a markup of 15% would generally be considered reasonable as long as actual necessary services are being provided, the individuals providing the services possess the necessary skills and expertise to provide that service, and the charge for such services is representative of what would have been charged by arm's-length persons. The reference to arm's-length persons recognizes that management companies are almost always non-arm's length. Services are often provided on behalf of the management corporations by family members of the professionals carrying on the main business.

12-139.　Both professional and management companies are generally eligible for the SBD as long as they are CCPCs with active business income. However, the fact that medical services are exempt goods under the GST/HST legislation has made management companies unattractive for doctors and dentists. While GST/HST must be paid on services billed by the management company, these amounts cannot be recovered by medical professionals because their services are GST/HST exempt. (For coverage of GST/HST exempt services, see Chapter 21, "GST/HST.") Given this situation, and the fact that professionals can incorporate, management companies for medical professionals delivering GST/HST exempt services are not as common.

Manufacturing and Processing Profits Deduction—ITA 125.1

Introduction

12-140.　Given the importance of manufacturing to the Canadian economy, it is not surprising that the federal government has provided income tax incentives to corporations that carry on an active business in Canada that involves manufacturing and processing in Canada of goods for sale or lease (M&P). As an example of this, in Chapter 5, "Capital Cost Allowance," we noted that the government is providing significantly enhanced CCA rates on both buildings used for M&P and for M&P machinery and equipment.

12-141.   A more general incentive is the M&P deduction available to some corporations for their M&P profits. IT Folio S4-F15-C1, "Manufacturing and Processing," discusses the calculation of this deduction and activities that are and are not considered to be manufacturing or processing.

12-142.   As was explained previously, the rate for this deduction is the same as the percentage for the general rate reduction. Since the general rate reduction does not apply to income that is eligible for the M&P deduction, the use of the M&P deduction does not provide any direct corporate income tax benefits at the federal level. Given this situation, it would seem logical for the government to eliminate the complex legislation related to the M&P deduction. However, this has not happened. One of the reasons for this is that the three provinces of Ontario, Quebec, and Saskatchewan together with Yukon territory continue to provide special income tax incentives for income that would qualify for the federal M&P deduction. Each province and territory has their own income tax legislation that relies on the provisions of the federal ITA. The M&P rules of ITA 125.1 are the base used in determining provincial or territorial M&P incentives.

12-143.   The provincial and territorial M&P tax incentives, however, are not the only reasons why the M&P concept remains important. In Chapter 5 we discussed the AccII that allows accelerated CCA in the first year of the purchase of depreciable property. Depreciable property that is used in M&P activity may be entitled to CCA of 100% in the year of purchase. In addition, federal investment tax credit incentives are also available in certain regions of Canada that help offset the costs of purchasing property used for M&P. Because of these other purposes we will continue to provide some limited coverage of the M&P rules.

12-144.   There are two important points to keep in mind in determining whether a corporation manufactures or processes goods for sale or lease in Canada. The first is a rule found in ITA 125.1(3)(l). This rule requires that gross revenues from M&P activity (goods manufactured or processed for sale or lease) account for at least 10% of all gross revenues from all active businesses carried on in Canada in any year. This is referred to as a *de minimus* rule. The second point is whether goods are being manufactured or processed for sale or lease. The relevance of this point became important in 2000 when the Supreme Court in *Will-Kare Paving and Contracting Ltd.* ([2001] 1 SCR 915) clarified the meaning of the words "goods for sale or lease." In that case, Wilkare carried on a paving business and manufactured the asphalt used in fulfilling its various service contracts. The Supreme Court distinguished goods that are directly sold from goods that are indirectly provided through a service contract. The court ruled that manufactured goods are not considered sold when provided through a service contract (see paragraph 1.7 of Folio S4-F15-C1, "Manufacturing and Processing"). This has become an important consideration in determining whether depreciable property qualifies for maximum CCA write-offs in the first year as a result of the AccII.

Calculating the Deduction

General Formula

12-145.   ITA 125.1 provides for a deduction from tax payable equal to the rate of 13% applied to M&P profits. There are, however, a number of constraints on the amount that is eligible for this deduction. ITA 125.1(1) specifies that the deduction will be based on the lesser of:

A   manufacturing and processing profits, less amounts eligible for the small business deduction; or

B   taxable income, less the sum of:

1.   the amount eligible for the small business deduction;

Manufacturing and Processing Profits Deduction—ITA 125.1

2. the relevant factor (see Note) multiplied by the foreign tax credit for business income calculated without consideration of the general rate reduction of 13% under ITA 123.4; and

3. where the corporation is a CCPC throughout the year, aggregate investment income as defined in ITA 129(4). Note that this is not the same as the AAII discussed as a reduction of the business limit for small business deduction purposes.

Note   The relevant factor is the same for both the small business deduction and the M&P deduction. While this is a simplification, we will use 4 as the relevant factor in our examples and problems (see Paragraph 12-99 for an explanation).

12-146.   Part A of this formula provides the basic limit based on the amount of M&P profits earned during the year. As will be noted subsequently, M&P profits is a technical term and must be calculated by a formula established in ITR 5200. In many cases, particularly for large public companies, this will be the limiting factor in determining the M&P deduction.

12-147.   Like the small business deduction formula, for ease of reference this M&P deduction formula is included at the front of this text in "Rates, Credits, and Other Data."

Constraints—Small Business Deduction

12-148.   As was previously discussed, the small business deduction provides CCPCs with a deduction equal to 19% of the first $500,000 of active business income. It appears that the government believes that granting both the 13% M&P deduction and the 19% small business deduction on the same income would be overly generous. As a consequence, any amount of active business income eligible for the small business deduction is not eligible for the M&P deduction. The ITA is written to ensure that the small business deduction is applied before the M&P deduction. Since both the small business deduction and the M&P apply to active business income, it is necessary to separate that part of the active business income that represents the M&P profits. This separation process is determined by extensive calculations found in the ITR.

Constraints—Taxable Income

12-149.   The legislation is written to ensure that the M&P deduction is only available on income that is actually subject to Canadian income tax. As was the case with the active business income that is eligible for the small business deduction, M&P profits that are included in net income may not find their way through to taxable income.

12-150.   This can occur when the corporation has deductions for such items as charitable donations, non-capital loss carry overs, or farm loss carry overs. For reasons that were discussed and illustrated in the discussion of the small business deduction, amounts eligible for the M&P deduction are limited by the amount of taxable income for a given year.

Constraints—Foreign Tax Credits

12-151.   As was the case with the taxable income constraint, the nature of the constraint created by deducting a multiple of foreign tax credits was explained in our discussion of the small business deduction. There is, however, one significant difference.

12-152.   In the ITA 125.1(1) formula for the M&P deduction, taxable income is reduced by a multiple of the foreign business income credit only. It is not adjusted for the foreign non-business income credit, as was the case with the ITA 125(1) formula for the small business deduction. This reflects the fact that the M&P formula contains an extra deduction from taxable income for aggregate investment income, an amount that includes foreign non-business income.

Constraints—Aggregate Investment Income

12-153.   The taxable income constraint attempts to remove active business income eligible for the small business deduction, foreign business income that is not subject to an appropriate amount of Canadian income tax, and most investment income whether earned in or outside of Canada. The objective is to set a limit on the M&P deduction where this modified taxable income figure is lower than the M&P profits that did not benefit from the small business deduction. This is accomplished by the subtraction by a CCPC of its aggregate investment income. This concept is discussed in detail in Chapter 13.

12-154. In the formula in Paragraph 12-145, note the reference to "aggregate investment income as defined in ITA 129(4)." This somewhat unusual concept of investment income is defined as follows:

Net taxable capital gains	$xxx
Property income (including foreign source)	
Interest	xxx
Rents	xxx
Royalties	xxx
Total positive amounts	$xxx
Net capital losses deducted	(xxx)
ITA 129(4) Aggregate investment income	$xxx

Note that, in contrast to the usual concept of investment income, this definition does not include most dividends. Technically only dividends that are deductible in computing a corporation's taxable income are excluded. This calculation is also included at the front of this text in "Rates, Credits, and Other Data."

Eligibility

12-155. On the surface, eligibility for the M&P deduction appears to be easily determinable. Any corporation that derives a minimum of 10% of its gross revenues from manufacturing and processing as part of its Canadian active businesses is eligible. The problem with this rule is the determination of what constitutes M&P activity.

12-156. The ITA does not define the terms "manufacturing" or "processing." However, ITA 125.1(3) provides some guidance by setting out certain types of activities that do not qualify. These include logging, farming and fishing, construction, producing industrial minerals, and processing mineral resources. Further guidance is provided in Folio S4-F14-C1, "Manufacturing and Processing."

M&P Profits Defined

12-157. We have noted that the M&P deduction is calculated by multiplying the general rate reduction percentage of 13% by "M&P profits." The determination of M&P profits is based on a fairly complex calculation that is found in ITR 5200. Given that this is largely a mechanical process and the fact that the M&P calculation no longer has an effect on the amount of federal tax payable and is not relevant to determining whether certain depreciable property qualify for the enhanced CCA as a result of the AccII or investment tax credits, we are not providing coverage of this calculation in this text.

Exercise 12-11

Subject: Amounts Eligible for Small Business and M&P Deductions

Marion Manufacturing is a CCPC throughout 2021 and has never been associated with any other company. It has net income of $462,000, which is composed of $411,000 in M&P profits (as per ITR 5200), $21,000 in foreign source business income, and net taxable capital gains of $30,000, none of which is AAII. Because of withholding on the foreign source business income, the company is entitled to a foreign tax credit of $3,150 [(15%)($21,000)].

The company's only deduction in the calculation of taxable income is donations to registered Canadian charities in the amount of $310,000. Marion anticipates large increases in taxable income in the next few years.

Determine the amount of Marion's small business deduction and M&P deduction for the year ending December 31, 2021, assuming that the company deducts all of the $310,000 of charitable donations. Assume that there are no business limit grinds for TCEC and AAII. Do you believe that deducting all of the donations is the best alternative for Marion? Explain your conclusion.

Solutions to Exercises are available in the Study Guide.

General Rate Reduction—ITA 123.4

Approach to Rate Reductions

12-158.   In considering alternative approaches to reducing the basic federal tax rate for corporations, the government has chosen to leave the basic rate of 38% unchanged. Instead of reducing the basic rate, they have created a deduction from this rate. This deduction is referred to as the "general rate reduction" percentage, and the rate is currently 13%.

12-159.   While the government wished to reduce corporate tax rates through the use of this general rate reduction, they did not want it to be available on income that was already benefitting from some other tax privilege (e.g., the small business deduction or the M&P deduction). To deal with this potential problem, the government introduced the concept of "full rate taxable income."

Full Rate Taxable Income—ITA 123.4(1)

12-160.   In defining full rate taxable income, the goal was to develop a base that did not benefit from other tax incentive provisions. In particular, the government did not want this reduction to be applied to income that was eligible for any of the following:

- The small business deduction. This deduction is only available to CCPCs.
- The M&P deduction. This deduction is available to CCPCs, public companies, and private companies that are not CCPCs.
- Refundable taxes. Refundable taxes are applicable to the aggregate investment income of CCPCs and, in some applications, to the investment income of private companies that are not Canadian controlled. Refundable taxes do not apply to public companies. While we need to consider the impact of refundable taxes on full rate taxable income at this point, detailed discussion is deferred to Chapter 13.

12-161.   The full rate taxable income definition is divided into different parts, with one applying to CCPCs and a second to other companies that are not CCPCs, such as public companies and private companies that are not CCPCs. This division recognizes that the two general categories of corporations (CCPCs versus non-CCPCs) benefit from different tax incentives.

Application to Non-CCPCs

12-162.   For these companies, the only adjustment to taxable income that is required to determine full rate taxable income is the income that is eligible for the M&P deduction. Given this, for non-CCPCs, full rate taxable income is defined as follows:

Regular taxable income	$ x,xxx
Income eligible for the M&P deduction	(xxx)
Full rate taxable income	$ x,xxx

12-163.   A simple example will serve to illustrate the relevant calculations.

EXAMPLE   For the year ending December 31, 2021, Daren Ltd., a Canadian public company, has taxable income equal to $100,000, with $40,000 of this amount eligible for the M&P deduction.

ANALYSIS   Full rate taxable income is equal to $60,000 ($100,000 - $40,000). Given this, total federal tax payable for Daren Ltd. would be calculated as follows:

Base amount of Part I tax [(38%)($100,000)]	$38,000
Federal tax abatement [(10%)($100,000)]	(10,000)
M&P deduction [(13%)($40,000)]	(5,200)
General rate reduction [(13%)($100,000 - $40,000)]	(7,800)
Federal tax payable	$15,000

12-164.   For a corporation with income consisting entirely of M&P profits, there is no general rate reduction as there is no full rate taxable income. This is illustrated by revising the example in Paragraph 12-163.

EXAMPLE—Revised   Assume that the $100,000 in taxable income of Daren Ltd. was generated solely by M&P activities.

ANALYSIS   Total federal tax payable for Daren Ltd. would be calculated as follows:

Base amount of Part I tax [(38%)($100,000)]	$38,000
Federal tax abatement [(10%)($100,000)]	(10,000)
M&P deduction [(13%)($100,000)]	(13,000)
General rate reduction [(13%)($100,000 - $100,000)]	Nil
Federal tax payable	$15,000

12-165.   This calculation illustrates the fact that the overall federal rate on income that is eligible for the M&P deduction is 15%. This is, of course, identical to the overall rate on income that is eligible for the general rate reduction, illustrating the fact that, in terms of tax payable, the M&P deduction is not advantageous at the federal level.

Exercise 12-12

Subject: Federal Tax Payable for a Public Company

For the year ending December 31, 2021, Marchand Inc., a Canadian public company, has taxable income of $320,000. Of this total, $180,000 qualifies for the M&P deduction. Calculate Marchand's federal tax payable for the year ending December 31, 2021. Include in your solution any M&P deduction available.

Solutions to Exercises are available in the Study Guide.

Application to CCPCs

12-166.   Not surprisingly, the calculation of full rate taxable income for a CCPC is somewhat more complex than it is for a public company. As we have noted, in addition to the M&P deduction, these companies may benefit from the small business deduction and the refundable tax provisions on investment income.

12-167. Full rate taxable income for a CCPC is defined as follows:

Taxable Income, reduced by:

1.   income eligible for the small business deduction;

2.   income eligible for the M&P deduction; and

3.   the corporation's aggregate investment income for the year as defined in ITA 129(4). [This is to remove income that will benefit from refundable taxes when taxable dividend distributions are made by the corporation to its shareholders. These taxes are explained in Chapter 13.]

12-168.   The definition of aggregate investment income in ITA 129(4) was briefly discussed in the coverage of the M&P deduction (see Paragraph 12-154). It includes both foreign and Canadian income from property such as interest, rents, and royalties minus losses from property. Dividends are also added except to the extent they are deductible in determining taxable income through rules such as ITA 112(1). Net taxable capital gains are also included, meaning the amount by which taxable capital gains exceed allowable capital losses and any net capital losses deducted in the year.

12-169.   A portion of the Part I tax paid by CCPCs on their aggregate investment income is refunded when taxable dividends are paid to shareholders. Because of this refund mechanism, aggregate investment income is taxed advantageously once the income is paid out as taxable dividends to individual shareholders. As a result, it does not receive the benefit of the general rate reduction.

12-170.   The following example illustrates the application of the general rate reduction for a CCPC with no investment income.

EXAMPLE   For the year ending December 31, 2021, Zaptek Ltd., a CCPC, has $200,000 in taxable income. This amount is made up entirely of active business income earned in Canada, none of which relates to M&P activity. Zaptek is associated with another company and, as per the agreement with that company, Zaptek is entitled to $100,000 of the $500,000 business limit.

ANALYSIS   The federal tax payable for Zaptek Ltd. would be calculated as follows:

Base amount of Part I tax [(38%)($200,000)]	$76,000
Federal tax abatement [(10%)($200,000)]	(20,000)
Small business deduction [(19%)($100,000)]	(19,000)
General rate reduction [(13%)($200,000 - $100,000)]	(13,000)
Federal tax payable	$24,000

12-171.   The federal tax payable of $24,000 can be verified using the general rates indicated at Paragraph 12-10. The first $100,000 of taxable income is taxed at the small business rate of 9%, or $9,000, and the next $100,000 is taxed at the general business rate of 15%, or $15,000. Together these amounts total $24,000.

Exercise 12-13

Subject: Federal Tax Payable for a CCPC

Redux Ltd. is a CCPC. For the taxation year ending December 31, 2021, the company has taxable income of $200,000, all of which is active business income. Of this amount, $145,000 is from M&P activity. As it is associated with two other corporations, its share of the business limit is $140,000. Determine the company's federal tax payable for the year ending December 31, 2021. Include in your solution any M&P deduction available.

Solutions to Exercises are available in the Study Guide.

We suggest you complete SSP 12-6, 12-7, 12-8, and 12-9 at this point.

Foreign Tax Credits for Corporations

Introduction

12-172.   The foreign tax credits that are available to individuals earning foreign business or non-business income are discussed in detail in Chapter 11. Under rules that are very similar to those applicable to individuals, corporations are also allowed to use foreign taxes paid on business and non-business income as credits against Canadian tax payable. While the rules are similar to those for individuals, there are differences that will be discussed here. IT Folio S5-F2-C1, "Foreign Tax Credit," provides the CRA's interpretations with respect to many issues concerning the determination of foreign tax credits.

Calculation of Foreign Tax Credits—ITA 126

Foreign Non-Business (Property) and Business Tax Credits

12-173.   The formula that limits the Canadian tax credit for foreign taxes paid on foreign source non-business income is as follows:

The **foreign NON-BUSINESS income tax credit** is the lesser of:

- The income or profits taxes paid in a foreign jurisdiction (for corporations, there is no 15% limit on the foreign non-business taxes paid as there is with respect to individuals)
- An amount determined by the following formula:

$$\left[\frac{\text{Foreign } \textbf{NON-BUSINESS} \text{ Income}}{\text{Adjusted Division B Income}} \right] [\text{Tax Otherwise Payable}]$$

12-174.   The meaning of "Adjusted Division B Income" and "Tax Otherwise Payable" are explained beginning at Paragraph 12-177. Both of the foreign tax credit formulae are included at the front of this text in "Rates, Credits, and Other Data."

12-175.   The formula that limits the amount of foreign business income taxes paid that can be used as a foreign tax credit is as follows:

The **foreign BUSINESS income tax credit** is the lesser of:

- The income or profits tax paid in a foreign jurisdiction
- An amount determined by the following formula:

$$\left[\frac{\text{Foreign } \textbf{BUSINESS} \text{ Income}}{\text{Adjusted Division B Income}} \right] [\text{Tax Otherwise Payable}]$$

- Tax Otherwise Payable for the year, less any foreign tax credit deducted on non-business income under ITA 126(1).

12-176.   As was the case with individuals, there is an additional factor to consider in the case of foreign business income tax credits. This is the "Tax Otherwise Payable," reduced by any foreign non-business income tax credit deducted under ITA 126(1).

Adjusted Division B Income

12-177.   The expressions "Adjusted Division B Income" and "Tax Otherwise Payable" are somewhat different for corporations than they are for individuals. The reason is that individuals use different tax rates, tax credits, and taxable income deductions than corporations. Adjusted Division B income for corporations is determined as follows:

Division B income (net income)	$x,xxx
Net capital losses deducted—ITA 111(1)(b)	(xxx)
Taxable dividends deducted under ITA 112	(xxx)
Dividends from a foreign affiliate deductible under ITA 113	(xxx)
Adjusted Division B income	$x,xxx

Tax Otherwise Payable

12-178.   The following table compares the components included in the calculation of "Tax Otherwise Payable" for foreign non-business tax credits with those used to calculate foreign business tax credits.

Tax Otherwise Payable Components	Non-Business	Business
Base amount of Part I tax (38%)	Yes	Yes
Plus: Additional refundable tax (ART) on investment income of a CCPC (see Chapter 13)	Yes	No
Minus: Federal tax abatement	Yes	No
Minus: General rate reduction (nil for non-business for CCPCs)	Yes	Yes

12-179.   The foreign tax credits are based on the Canadian income tax rate that would apply to foreign source income. The business foreign tax credit rate is 25%, determined as the 38% basic rate minus the 13% general rate reduction. We saw that this was the rate used in the foreign business tax credit component of the small business deduction calculations (see Paragraphs 12-106 to 12-108). You will note that there are no deductions allowed for M&P or the small business deduction since those deductions would not be available for foreign business income.

12-180.   For CCPCs, the "Tax Otherwise Payable" for foreign non-business income is generally 28%, calculated as the basic rate of 38% minus the 10% federal abatement. We saw in the small business deduction rules that this was the rate implied by the taxable income constraint. The foreign non-business income credit, however, also adds a 10 2/3% tax on investment income (whether foreign or Canadian sourced).

Foreign Tax Credit Carry Overs

12-181.   Unlike the situation with individuals, where the amount of foreign taxes that can be used as a credit is limited to 15% of the foreign source non-business income, the only limit for a corporation is the limit that is found in the second component of the formula. If the actual amount of foreign taxes paid is greater than this limit, there is no carry over of the excess as a tax credit. However, as was noted in Chapter 11, foreign income or profits taxes in excess of the available foreign tax credit can be deducted under ITA 20(12) in the determination of net income. Such a deduction, however, causes a recalculation of the foreign tax credit by lowering the adjusted Division B income, the foreign income, and the foreign income or profits tax that can be claimed for the foreign tax credit.

12-182.   Unlike the case with foreign non-business income taxes paid in excess of amounts used as tax credits, unused foreign business taxes paid can be carried over as a tax credit to the three preceding taxation years or the 10 subsequent taxation years to be applied only against foreign taxes of that same jurisdiction. In calculating the allowable tax credit for such carry overs, these unused amounts will be added to the foreign tax paid factor in the calculation of the foreign business income tax credit for the same foreign jurisdiction.

Exercise 12-14

Subject: Foreign Tax Credits

Internat Inc. is a Canadian public company. For the year ending December 31, 2021, it has net income of $146,000, which includes foreign business income of $20,000. The foreign jurisdiction withheld $3,000 in income and profits taxes on this income. None of the company's income involves M&P activity and, based on the federal abatement formula of ITR 402(3), 88% of the company's income is considered earned in a province. In calculating taxable income, the company deducts $30,000 in dividends received from taxable Canadian companies, a 2018 non-capital loss balance of $75,000, and a 2019 net capital loss balance of $25,000. Determine the company's Part I tax payable for the year ending December 31, 2021. Include in your answer any carry overs available at the end of the year.

Solutions to Exercises are available in the Study Guide.

We suggest you complete SSP 12-10 at this point.

Refundable Journalism Labour Tax Credit—ITA 125.6

Description

12-183.   The March 29, 2019, budget introduced three provisions designed to encourage Canadian journalism organizations.

- A 25% refundable credit for salaries and wages paid to eligible newsroom employees of a qualifying Canadian journalism organization. This credit is available for expenditures made beginning January 1, 2019.

- A non-refundable credit for individuals based on the cost of their subscriptions to digital news services. This credit was not available until 2020. This credit (ITA 118.02) is discussed in Chapter 4.

- A provision that allows some journalism organizations to register as qualified donees able to issue tax receipts for donations. These provisions were not applicable until 2020 (ITA 149.1(1)).

12-184.   The 25% credit is capped at $55,000 for each eligible newsroom employee, providing a maximum credit of $13,750 [(25%)($$55,000)] for each employee. The base for the credit will be reduced by any financial assistance received during the year from any level of government.

12-185.   It appears that, even though journalism organizations that qualify as registered donees do not pay income taxes, they will be eligible for this refundable credit.

Definitions—ITA 125.6

12-186.   As usual, the application of this credit requires an understanding of some technical definitions. These are as follows:

Qualifying Canadian Journalism Organization   To qualify, the organization must meet the following conditions:

- It must be primarily engaged in the production of written news content.
- It must not be carrying on a broadcasting operation.

- It does not receive any amount from the Canada Periodical Fund and
  - if it is a public corporation, its shares must be listed on a designated stock exchange in Canada; or
  - if it is not publicly traded, at least 75% of its shares must be owned by Canadian citizens or a publicly traded qualifying journalism organization.

Eligible Newsroom Employee   This means an individual who:

- is employed by a qualifying Canadian journalism organization;
- works a minimum of 26 hours per week throughout the portion of the taxation year in which the individual is employed;
- is employed for a minimum period of 40 consecutive weeks; and
- spends at least 75% of his or her time engaged in the production of news content, including researching, collecting information, verifying facts, photographing, writing, editing, designing, and otherwise preparing content.

Key Terms

A full glossary with definitions is provided at the end of the Study Guide.

Active Business	Grind
Active Business Income	Loss Carry Back
Adjusted Active Business Income	Loss Carry Forward
Adjusted Aggregate Investment Income (AAII)	Manufacturing and Processing Profits
Allowable Business Investment Loss (ABIL)	Deduction (M&P Deduction)
Allowable Capital Loss	Net Business Income
Annual Business Limit	Net Capital Loss
Associated Corporations	Non-Capital Loss
Business Income	Ordering Rule
Business Investment Loss	Permanent Establishment
Canadian Controlled Private Corporation	Personal Services Business
Carry Over	Preferred Shares
CCPC	Private Corporation
Common Shares	Professional Corporation
Corporation	Property Income
Designated Stock Exchange	Public Corporation
Disposition	Qualifying Canadian Journalism
Eligible Newsroom Employee	Organization
Federal Tax Abatement	Refundable Journalism Labour Tax Credit
Foreign Tax Credit	Small Business Deduction
Full Rate Taxable Income	Specified Investment Business
GAAP	Stop Loss Rules
General Rate Reduction	Taxable Capital Employed in Canada (TCEC)
	Term Preferred Shares

References

For more detailed study of the material in this chapter, we refer you to the following:

ITA 89(1)	Definitions (Canadian, Private and Public Corporations)
ITA 110	Deductions Permitted
ITA 110.1	Donation Deduction for Corporations
ITA 111	Losses Deductible
ITA 112	Deduction of Taxable Dividends Received by Corporations Resident in Canada
ITA 113	Deduction in Respect of Dividend Received from Foreign Affiliate
ITA 123	Basic Part I Rate for Corporations (38%)
ITA 123.3	Additional Refundable Tax on CCPC's Investment Income (10 2/3%)

ITA 123.4	General Deduction (13%)
ITA 124	Federal Abatement (10%)
ITA 125	Small Business Deduction (19%)
ITA 125.1	Manufacturing and Processing Profits Deductions (13%)

S4-F15-C1	Manufacturing and Processing
S5-F2-C1	Foreign Tax Credit

IT-67R3	Taxable Dividends from Corporations Resident in Canada
IT-73R6	The Small Business Deduction
IT-177R2	Permanent Establishment of a Corporation in a Province (Consolidated)
IT-189R2	Corporations Used by Practising Members of Professions
IT-206R	Separate Businesses
IT-232R3	Losses—Their Deductibility in the Loss Year or in Other Years
IT-391R	Status of Corporations
IT-458R2	Canadian Controlled Private Corporation

Self-Study Problems (SSPs)

Self-Study Problems (SSPs) provide practice in problem solving. Within the chapters, we have indicated where it would be appropriate to stop and work on each SSP. The problems can be downloaded by chapter from MyLab Accounting. Solutions are available in the Study Guide. Select problems can also be completed directly in MyLab and auto-graded.

Assignment Problems

Solutions to Assignment Problems (APs) are available to instructors only.

AP 12-1   (Corporate Taxable Income)

The income statement that has been prepared by Margo Ltd.'s accountant for the year ending December 31, 2021, is as follows:

Sales revenue		$925,000
Cost of goods sold (Note 1)		(717,000)
Gross profit		$208,000
Operating expenses:		
Salaries and wages	($40,200)	
Rents	(22,200)	
Property taxes (Note 2)	(8,800)	
Amortization expense	(35,600)	
Write-down of goodwill (Note 3)	(1,700)	
Charitable donations	(19,800)	
Legal fees (Note 5)	(2,220)	
Bad debt expense (Note 6)	(7,100)	
Warranty provision (Note 7)	(5,500)	
Social club membership fees (Note 8)	(7,210)	
Other operating expenses	(39,870)	(190,200)
Operating income		$ 17,800
Other revenues (expenses):		
Gain on sale of investments (Note 9)	$ 9,500	
Interest revenue	2,110	
Interest on late income tax instalments	(1,020)	
Investment counsellor fees	(500)	
Foreign interest income (Note 10)	1,530	
Dividends from taxable Canadian corporations	3,000	14,620
Income before taxes		$ 32,420

Notes and Other Information:

1. The calculation of cost of goods sold was based on an opening inventory of $225,000 and a closing inventory of $198,600. In addition, the closing inventory was reduced by $15,000 for a reserve for future declines in value. This is the first year the company has used an inventory reserve.

2. Property taxes include $1,200 for tax paid on vacant land. The company has held this land for five years in anticipation of relocating its head office.

3. As the result of the purchase of a business on January 15, 2021, Margo Ltd. recognized $34,000 in goodwill. As of December 31, 2021, this goodwill was found to be impaired and a goodwill impairment loss of $1,700 was recorded.

4. The maximum CCA for the current year is $79,785. This includes the appropriate write-off of the goodwill described in Item 3.

5. The legal fees are made up of $1,200 paid to appeal an income tax assessment and $1,020 paid for general corporate matters.

6. The company bases its accounting bad debt expense on the amounts acceptable for income tax purposes.

7. This is the first year that the company has deducted a provision for estimated warranties.

8. The main purpose of the social club is to provide dining and recreational facilities.

9. The gain on the sale of investments involved shares held for investment purposes with a cost of $21,000. The shares were sold for $30,500.

10. The gross foreign interest income of $1,800 was received net of $270 paid in respect of foreign income or profits tax. The company will claim this amount as a foreign tax credit rather than a foreign tax expense.

Required: Determine the minimum net income for ITA purposes and taxable income of Margo Ltd. for the year ending December 31, 2021.

AP 12-2   (Corporate Taxable Income)

Cabrera Digital is a Canadian public company. It has always used a taxation year that ends on December 31. During the year ending December 31, 2021, it had business revenues of $1,234,000 and business expenses of $962,000, resulting in business income of $272,000. The business revenues and business expenses have been determined based on the ITA and no reconciling adjustments are required. Also during 2021, it received the following dividends:

- Non-eligible dividends from a wholly owned (100%) subsidiary $23,600
- Eligible dividends from Canadian public companies   61,300

The company's only other property income was a $156,000 taxable capital gain on a sale of temporary investments. Because of this fortunate investment result, the company decides to make a $241,000 donation to a registered Canadian charity. No capital gains are anticipated in the foreseeable future.

At the beginning of the year ending December 31, 2021, the company had the following carry forward balances:

- 2019 Net capital loss $262,000
- 2015 Non-capital loss   193,000

Required: Calculate the minimum net income and taxable income for Cabrera Digital for the year ending December 31, 2021. Indicate the amount and type of any carry forward balances that are available at the end of that year.

AP 12-3   (Corporate Net and Taxable Income)

Vertin Ltd. is a Canadian public company that has always used a December 31 year end. However, as December is a very busy time for their business, it has requested a change in their taxation year end to July 31 as required by ITA 249.1(7), a date at which their business activity is at the low point for the year. The CRA has approved the request.

The change will be implemented beginning with the 2021 taxation year, resulting in a short fiscal period of January 1 to July 31, 2021. The company's income statement, prepared in accordance with generally accepted accounting principles (IFRS), for the period January 1, 2021, through July 31, 2021, is as follows:

Vertin Ltd.
Income Statement
Seven-Month Period Ending July 31, 2021

Sales (all within Canada)		$1,796,600
Cost of sales		(973,400)
Gross margin		$ 823,200
Other expenses (excluding taxes):		
Wages and salaries	($108,200)	
Administration	(194,200)	
Amortization	(97,600)	
Rent	(113,400)	
Interest expense	(13,200)	
Foreign exchange loss	(7,600)	
Travel and promotion	(86,300)	
Bad debt expense	(6,200)	
Warranty expense	(7,400)	
Charitable donations	(8,100)	
Other operating expenses	(51,200)	(693,400)
Operating income		$ 129,800
Gain on sale of investments		7,800
Income before taxes		$ 137,600

Other Information:

1. Wages and salaries includes a $28,000 bonus to Vertin Ltd.'s CEO. Because she anticipates retiring at the end of 2021, this bonus will not be paid until January 2023.

2. In determining the cost of sales, the company deducted a $23,400 reserve for inventory obsolescence.

3. The company bases its accounting bad debt expense on the amounts acceptable for income tax purposes. Amortization is on a class 1 building, class 8 furniture and fixtures, and class 10 delivery vehicles. The following information is relevant for the determination of CCA for the seven-month period ending July 31, 2021:

   Building   The January 1, 2021, UCC for the building was $872,000. During 2021, the company spent $42,000 on improved flooring in all areas of the property. The building was not a new building when it was acquired.

   Furniture and Fixtures   The January 1, 2021, UCC balance for class 8 was $285,000. During 2021, new furniture was acquired at a cost of $40,600. Old furniture with a capital cost of $28,200 was sold for $17,600.

Delivery Vehicles   On January 1, 2021, the class 10 UCC balance was $198,300. There were no additions or disposals in this class during the seven-month period ending July 31, 2021.

4. The interest expense relates to a line of credit that was used to finance seasonal fluctuations in inventory.

5. The foreign exchange loss resulted from financing costs related to the purchase of merchandise in the United Kingdom.

6. The travel and promotion expense consisted of the following items:

Business meals and entertainment	$32,400
Hotels and airfare	41,800
Golf club memberships	12,100
Total travel and promotion expense	$86,300

7. For accounting purposes, the company establishes a warranty reserve based on estimated costs. On January 1, 2021, the reserve balance was $8,200. On July 31, 2021, a new reserve was established at $7,400.

8. The accounting gain on the sale of investments is equal to the capital gain for tax purposes.

9. During the period January 1, 2021, through July 31, 2021, the company declared and paid dividends of $31,400.

10. On January 1, 2021, the company has available a $24,600 non-capital loss balance from 2019 and a $7,200 net capital loss balance from 2018.

Required: Calculate the minimum net income for ITA purposes and taxable income for Vertin Ltd. for the seven-month period ending July 31, 2021. Indicate the amount and type of any carry forwards that will be available for use in future years.

AP 12-4   (Corporate Loss Carry Forwards)

The following information relates to the operations of Notem Inc. for the taxation year ended December 31, 2021 (all amounts are based on the ITA and as a result no reconciliation is required):

Business loss	$141,800
Dividends from taxable Canadian corporations	33,500
Taxable capital gains	9,600
Allowable capital losses	4,425
Charitable donations	5,400

At the beginning of the taxation year, the company had a carry forward of unused charitable donations of $1,350 from the previous year and a net capital loss carry forward of $10,500 from 2019.

It is the policy of the company to first claim the maximum net capital loss balances prior to using any other type of carry over balance.

Required: Calculate the corporation's minimum net income and taxable income for its 2021 taxation year. Indicate any balances available for carry forward to other taxation years.

AP 12-5   (Corporate Loss Carryovers—Four Years)

Lactor Ltd. (Lactor) commenced business in 2018. The company selected a calendar-based taxation year that ends on December 31 of each year. Lactor's operations involve a dairy substitute to appeal to a growing number of children who are allergic to cow's milk. The company experienced a slow start in 2018 with small business losses but quickly reached high profits in both 2019 and 2020 only to experience debilitating losses in 2021. The company is uncertain of whether it will be able to continue into 2022. A relevant factor for the company's ability to survive is determining its income tax obligations, which depend on the ability to efficiently utilize losses it has incurred with the goal of minimizing its taxable income. The company has asked for your assistance and provided you with the following information:

	2018	2019	2020	2021
Business income (loss)	($75,000)	$38,000	$178,000	($200,000)
Net capital gains (losses)	10,000	(27,000)	(9,000)	23,000
Dividends received	11,000	21,000	33,000	42,000
Charitable donations	25,000	15,000	20,000	14,000

All of the dividends have been received from taxable Canadian corporations and are therefore deductible to Lactor through ITA 112 in determining taxable income. It is the policy of the company to minimize its net capital loss carry forward balance first, then donations second, and non-capital losses last.

Required: For each of the four years calculate and determine:

- The minimum net and taxable income, including the amount and type of any unused losses that are available to carry to other years.
- Apply any loss carry overs to the maximum extent possible to minimize taxable income in each year and then determine the loss carry over balances remaining that are available to carry to other years.
- Losses that are carried back require the completion of T2 Schedule 4 to request the carry back and do not require amending a previous year's return. Clearly indicate any previous returns that require a loss carry back request.

AP 12-6   (Corporate Loss Carry Forwards—Four Years)
Metronet Inc. is a Canadian public company with a December 31 year end. It commenced carrying on business in 2018 and has had mixed results since that time. In terms of its business income (loss), the results, determined for income tax purposes, were as follows:

	2018	2019	2020	2021
Business income (loss)	$233,500	$34,000	($163,000)	$57,000

Other Information:

1. In each of the years 2018 through 2021, Metronet receives dividends from taxable Canadian companies of $13,500.

2. In 2018, Metronet made charitable donations of $4,800, followed by a donation of $15,600 in 2019. The donations declined to $7,400 in 2020. No contributions were made in 2021.

3. In 2018, Metronet realized a capital loss of $24,600, followed by a $45,600 capital gain in 2019. In 2020, there was a capital loss of $48,400. Things improved in 2021, during which Metronet realized a $33,200 capital gain.

It is the policy of the company to maximize use of its net capital loss balances prior to using other types of carry forward amounts.

Required: For each of the four years 2018 through 2021, provide the following information:

- The minimum net income and taxable income that would be reported for Metronet Inc. Indicate the amount and type of any current-year losses that are available for carry over.
- The balances for any years to which losses are carried back.
- An analysis of the amount and type of carry overs that would be available in any of the years.

AP 12-7   (Geographical Allocation of Income)

The Sundean Company has its national headquarters in Toronto, and all senior management have their offices at this location. The company also has operations in Vancouver, Calgary, Saskatoon, and Halifax. In each of these cities, warehouse space is maintained that orders are filled from. In addition, a sales staff operates out of office space in each warehouse, taking orders throughout the province in which the warehouse is located.

For the current taxation year, the company's taxable income totalled $1,546,000, on gross revenues of $10,483,000. Also during the current year, the company had salaries and wages totalling $1,247,000. These gross revenues and expenses were distributed among the provinces where the company has operations in the following manner:

	Gross Revenues	Wages and Salaries Accrued
Alberta	$ 1,886,940	$ 261,870
British Columbia	2,306,260	274,340
Nova Scotia	1,362,790	174,580
Saskatchewan	1,257,960	99,760
Ontario	3,669,050	436,450
Total	$10,483,000	$1,247,000

Required: Calculate the amount of Sundean Company's taxable income for the current year that would be allocated to each of the five provinces. Any percentages used in the calculations should be rounded to one decimal place.

AP 12-8   (Part 1 Tax with Reduced SBD)

Deckton Ltd. is a large successful CCPC operating in multiple jurisdictions through permanent establishments in which it carries on the business of renovating residential homes. In 2021 Deckton's percentage of gross revenues and wages and salaries in each of the four jurisdictions in which they operate is as follows:

Province	Revenues	Wages	Average
Alberta	41%	48%	44.5%
British Columbia	20%	23%	21.5%
Saskatchewan	28%	22%	25.0%
U.S. Washington State	11%	7%	9.0%
Total	100%	100%	100.0%

Deckton's taxable income for 2021, which consists exclusively of active business income, is $2,447,000. Its Canadian operations account for $2,073,000 of its taxable income with the remainder of $374,000 attributable to its U.S. operations. The U.S. operations paid business and profits taxes in the amount of C$71,060.

Deckton Ltd. represents the Western Canadian operations of a corporate group composed of three companies, all of which are associated. Deckton is allocated $200,000 of the business limit of the associated group for 2021. The three companies all have taxation years ending December 31 with no short taxation years. The companies have been associated for over 10 years.

All of the gross revenues of the three associated companies are derived from arm's-length sales and there are no intercompany sales between them.

The combined adjusted aggregate investment income (AAII) of the associated group of companies is less than $50,000 in both 2020 and 2021.

The taxable capital employed in Canada (TCEC) of the associated group in 2020 was $14,125,000 and was $13,754,000 in 2021.

Assume that Deckton's foreign tax credit is equal to the foreign taxes paid of $71,060.

Required: Determine Deckton's minimum federal Part I tax payable for the year ending December 31, 2021. Show all supporting calculations.

AP 12-9 *(Corporate Tax Payable)*

For the taxation year ending December 31, 2021, Lorne Inc., a CCPC, has net income of $340,500. This is made up of $312,400 of active business income and $28,100 of taxable eligible dividends from various Canadian public companies. It has been determined that $211,300 of the active business income qualifies as manufacturing and processing profits.

During 2021, the company makes donations to registered charities totalling $31,400.

At the beginning of 2021, the company has a 2019 non-capital loss balance of $29,300. It intends to deduct all of this carry forward for 2021.

Lorne Inc. is associated with three other CCPCs. The companies have agreed that each company will claim one-quarter of the annual business limit. The combined taxable capital employed in Canada for the four associated companies is less than $10 million in both 2020 and 2021. The combined adjusted aggregate investment income of the four companies was $45,000 in 2020.

Required: Determine the minimum taxable income and Part I federal tax payable for Lorne Inc. for the year ending December 31, 2021. Show all calculations, whether or not they are necessary to the final solution. As the corporation carries on business in a province through a permanent establishment and that province provides additional M&P tax incentives, a separate calculation of the federal M&P deduction is required.

AP 12-10 *(Comprehensive Corporate Tax Payable)*

Kalex Inc, a CCPC, was incorporated in 2019 and selected a December 31 taxation year end. Kalex is a family-owned company with four equal shareholders, all of whom are siblings. The company employs in excess of 50 employees at its head office in Toronto, a further 80 employees at its manufacturing facility in Oshawa, Ontario, and a further 12 employees at its office in Syracuse, New York. The company is primarily involved in the manufacture and sale of storage shelving and pallets. You have been asked to prepare the corporate tax returns for 2021. The company provides you with its financial statements for the year ending December 31, 2021. The financial statements have been prepared using accounting standards for private enterprises (ASPE), which represents the application of generally accepted accounting principles. No attempt has been made to reconcile the net accounting income with net income for ITA purposes. Through your own observations and by asking several questions you have uncovered the following information concerning the 2021 income and expenses of Kalex:

1. Net income for accounting purposes is $2,481,986 after deducting $325,000 of current income tax expenses.

2. Other amounts either deducted or added in the determination of net income for accounting purposes are as follows:

1. Bond premium amortization applied and reduced interest expenses	$ 8,800
2. Deducted amortization expense	615,000
3. Deducted loss from employee theft (60% was recovered through insurance)	4,750
4. Deducted 10% of landscaping costs paid of $58,000	5,800
5. Deducted prepaid advertising for 24 months (covers May 1, 2021, to April 30, 2023)	37,200
6. Deducted donations to registered charities	17,400
7. Deducted 100% of meal and entertainment expenses	62,500
8. Deducted life insurance premiums for four shareholders, none of which was required by a creditor as security to obtain financing	22,000
9. Added capital dividends received from associated company	40,000
10. Deducted all of the renovation costs of adding two offices to its headquarters in Toronto	112,000
11. Deducted all of the operating costs for an automobile for the shareholder/president who uses it 40% of the time for company business	11,700
12. Deducted penalties on late income tax instalments	2,900
13. Deducted interest on late municipal tax payments	1.835
14. Added a court-ordered damage award for breach of contract. The company would have earned a profit of $37,000 had the contract been completed	33,500
15. Deducted legal expenses incurred in the breach of contract	21,000
16. Deducted annual golf club membership fees for the president to entertain customers	19,300
17. Deducted reserve for estimated warranty expenses	16,275

3. Kalex estimates it's doubtful account receivables by applying an historical percentage of 7.5% to accounts that have been outstanding for more than 30 days. At December 31, 2021, those accounts totalled $450,000, resulting in a doubtful debt expense of $33,750 [7.5% of $450,000]. After a detailed evaluation of the accounts you determine that a reasonable reserve that would be acceptable to CRA would be $28,800. The 2020 reasonable reserve claimed was $30,900—no adjustment has been made for this in 2021.

4. On January 1, 2021, Kalex had the following UCC balances:

Class 1—Toronto headquarters	$1,823,600
Class 1—Oshawa manufacturing	1,197,000
Class 8	648,000
Class 10	133,875
Class 13	119,000
Class 53	375,000

Elections were filed for each of the class 1 buildings to be eligible for additional CCA. As a result, the two buildings are in separate classes. The Oshawa building is used 100% for non-residential purposes that is manufacturing while the Toronto headquarters building is used exclusively (100%) for non-residential purposes that is not manufacturing. No capital expenditures were made for the Oshawa building, but capital renovations in the amount of $112,000 were made to the Toronto building. This amount has been deducted in the preparation of the income statement. The amount included in each class represents the capital cost of the building only and not the land.

Class 8 depreciable property represents office furniture and fixtures for the two class 1 buildings. The original cost when acquired in January 2019 was $800,000. Kalex was approached by a new business in February 2021 operating out of Niagara Falls, Ontario. The business leases refurbished office furniture and fixtures on long-term leases. After a round of negotiations and running the numbers, Kalex has decided to replace all of their class 8 property with leased property. Kalex signed a five-year contract at $4,000 monthly. In exchange, Kalex will receive $700,000 for all of its class 8 property. Kalex correctly expensed the lease payments in 2021.

The class 10 property is composed of three two-seater delivery vans with extra storage capacity. Each of the three vans cost $75,000. After hearing of the tax incentives for zero-emission vehicles and the expanding network of charging stations, the company decided to trade in the three existing vans for three zero-emission vans that cost $95,000 each. The vans were purchased on July 2, 2021. The company received $105,000 as a trade-in allowance for the three existing vans.

The company acquired a 2021 Tesla Model S in early January 2021 for $130,000. The car is used exclusively by the company president. It is estimated that the car is used by the president 40% of the time for company business.

Midway through 2019 the company realized that the Oshawa facility lacked the necessary storage space to accommodate its expanding inventory. They reached out to a local developer who agreed to lease the company a warehouse that had sat empty for a few years. A five-year lease was signed with a renewal option for an additional five years. The lease provides that Kalex can make any improvements or renovations it considers necessary but that no payment will be made by the lessor at the end of the lease as compensation for those improvements. The company spent $140,000 on modifications in 2019 and another $150,000 in July 2021. Assume that the expenditures are categorized as class 13.

In March 2021 Kalex acquired a client list from a local competitor who was on the verge of closing its doors. The company paid $80,000 for the client list.

In May 2021 the company acquired new manufacturing machinery that would double its output at the Oshawa facility. The equipment cost $900,000.

Company policy is to claim the maximum CCA it is entitled to in each year.

5. When the company began operations in early 2019 it acquired a vacant lot not far from the Oshawa facility for $150,000. The plan was to eventually build a warehouse, but the company opted to lease a warehouse instead. The company, as part of the leasing arrangement, agreed to sell the land to the lessor for $460,000. The arrangements required the purchaser to pay $175,000 on the closing date, February 1, 2021, with the remainder paid in three equal instalments of $100,000 each plus interest at 6% on January 31, 2022, 2023, and 2024. Kalex did not carry a mortgage on the vacant land but did incur municipal property taxes from the day it acquired the land to the day of sale in the amount of $11,700. No income was earned from the vacant land throughout its ownership, and as a result the municipal property taxes have not been deducted for tax purposes. Selling costs of the land were $8,300. The only adjustment made by the company for this transaction was the addition of an accounting gain of $290,000. The capital gain and accounting gain are determined in the exact same manner and are identical.

6. In late 2019 Kalex acquired a 25% shareholding of Jennco Ltd., an arm's-length "small business corporation" for $125,000. Kalex had plans to eventually acquire a controlling interest and combine the two companies, but larger competitive companies moved in, taking over the market and the share value began to decline rapidly. Kalex managed to sell the shares to an arm's-length investor for $10,000 three months before the company declared bankruptcy. Selling costs were $1,600. Kalex deducted an accounting loss on the shares of $116,600. Jennco never paid any dividends while Kalex owned the shares.

7. The portion of Kalex's taxable income that is considered to be earned in Canada using the formula in section 400 of the ITR is 83.6%.

8. The U.S. business operations resulted in net profits of C$410,000. Kalex paid U.S. taxes on those profits of C$77,900. The income statement, however, only adds that portion of the U.S. profits in excess of the U.S. taxes, or $332,100 [$410,000 – $77,900].

9. Kalex has no non-capital losses but experienced a net capital loss of $52,000 in 2020 on the sale of share investments.

10. Kalex's active business income in 2021 is $1,815,000, $1,288,000 of which represents its Canadian manufacturing and processing profits eligible for the M&P credit.

11. Kalex has been associated with one other CCPC since its incorporation in 2019. Both companies have a December 31 taxation year end and have shared the small business limit equally and will continue to do so for 2021. The taxable capital employed in Canada of the associated group in 2020 was $11.0 million and is $12.2 million in 2021. In addition, the adjusted aggregate investment income of the associated group in 2020 was $77,500 and is $92,300 in 2021.

Required:

A. Calculate the minimum net income for ITA purposes for Kalex for 2021 with a reconciliation that begins with net accounting income before taxes of $2,481,986. Make all necessary adjustments, including CCA for each class of property together with the UCC balance as of January 1, 2022. Show all supporting calculations.

B. Calculate the minimum taxable income for Kalex for 2021. Indicate the amount and type of any carry overs that are available at the end of the year.

C. Calculate the minimum federal Part I tax payable for Kalex for 2021. The province of Ontario is one of three provinces and one territory in Canada (Quebec, Saskatchewan, and Yukon are the others) that provides a reduced tax rate for M&P activity. The determination of the M&P credits in those jurisdictions uses the federal calculations, and as a result a separate calculation of the federal M&P deduction is required.

D. Assume (1) that the foreign tax credit for foreign business income is equal to the foreign taxes withheld of $77,900 and (2) that the additional refundable tax (ART) is equal to 10 2/3% of aggregate investment income of $16,500.

CHAPTER 13

Taxation of Corporate Investment Income

Learning Objectives

After completing Chapter 13, you should be able to:

1. Explain the goal of integration in the design of the Canadian taxation of investment and describe the four steps that are required to analyze the integrated flow of that investment income when taxable dividends are paid to individual shareholders (Paragraph [P hereafter] 13-1 to 13-11).

2. Explain the difference between eligible and non-eligible dividends, their purpose in terms of integration, and how to calculate their after-tax returns (P 13-12 to 13-19).

3. Demonstrate how the dividend gross up and tax credit procedures work to implement integration with respect to business income (P 13-20 to 13-26).

4. List the components of aggregate investment income as it is defined in ITA 129(4) and describe the basic concept of refundable taxes (P 13-27 to 13-36).

5. Calculate the additional refundable tax (ART) on the investment income of a CCPC (P 13-37 to 13-40). Note that additional information is provided in the appendix at the end of the chapter concerning the interaction of the ART with foreign tax credits.

6. Explain the Part I refundable tax concept and calculate Part I refundable tax on the investment income of a CCPC (P 13-41 to 13-53).

7. Explain the Part IV refundable concept and apply the provisions related to portfolio dividends (P 13-54 to 13-65).

8. Explain and apply the connected corporation Part IV concept (P 13-66 to 13-68).

9. Explain how Part IV applies when there are connected corporations and the general analysis to determine the circumstances under which Part IV applies (P 13-69 to 13-75).

10. Explain the eligible dividend designation concept and explain and calculate the GRIP of a CCPC (P 13-76 to 13-85).

11. Explain the relevance of the LRIP concept for corporations that are not CCPCs and apply the general provision (P 13-86 to 13-89).

12. Explain the purpose of Part III.1 and calculate the Part III.1 tax on excessive eligible dividend designations (EEDD) (P 13-90 to 13-98).

13. Explain in terms of integration why the RDTOH system was changed (P 13-99 to 13-104).

14. Calculate the Part I refundable tax (P 13-105 to 13-114).

15. Calculate the balance in the eligible and non-eligible RDTOH accounts (P 13-115 to 13-118).
16. Calculate the dividend refund on the payment of eligible and non-eligible dividends (P 13-119 to 13-122).
17. Describe the economic impact of the new RDTOH system and any tax planning considerations (P 13-123 to 13-137).
18. Briefly describe the systematic approach when dealing with the taxation of corporations (P 13-138 to 13-139).
19. Review a simple corporate income tax return completed using the ProFile T2 tax preparation software program.

Introduction

13-1.   In Chapter 12 our focus was on corporate taxation of business income with an emphasis on the small business deduction and a secondary emphasis on the M&P deduction, the general rate reduction, and foreign tax credits. In this chapter we will continue coverage of corporate taxation, turning our attention to the taxation of corporate investment income.

13-2.   The taxation of corporate investment income requires an understanding of integration as a number of concepts come together to ensure that corporations, particularly Canadian controlled private corporations (CCPCs), are not used to own investments the income of which would be subject to low corporate income tax rates as opposed to much higher income tax rates had the investments been owned by individuals. As a result of this concern, additional corporate income taxes are imposed on corporate investment income to discourage the use of corporations for this purpose.

13-3.   There are two specific income taxes that target corporate investment income. The first is ITA 123.3, which adds 10 2/3% of "aggregate investment income" (AII) under Part I. This tax is referred to as the additional refundable tax, or ART. Once the ART is added, the federal corporate tax on investment income becomes 38 2/3% [38% basic- 10% federal abatement + 10 2/3% ART]. Provincial corporate tax on investment income can add anywhere from an additional 8% to 16%, resulting in a combined rate of between 46 2/3% and 54 2/3%. AII includes all types of investment income, whether Canadian or foreign sourced, such as rents, royalties, interest, and net taxable capital gains (after the deduction of net capital losses). AII, however, does not include taxable dividends that would entitle the corporate recipient to a taxable income deduction under ITA 112(1), as these dividends are intended to be tax free under Part I when they are paid between Canadian corporations. The second corporate investment tax is a Part IV tax of 38 1/3% that is imposed on taxable dividends that entitle the corporate recipient to a taxable income deduction under ITA 112(1).

13-4.   The two corporate investment taxes are unique in that they are completely refundable to the corporation when taxable dividends are paid by it to shareholders. All of the Part IV tax is potentially refundable to the dividend payer, but Part IV tax may be payable by the recipient where the recipient is a corporation. The ART is also refundable plus an additional 20%, meaning that of the 38 2/3% federal tax, 30 2/3% is refundable. The remaining 8% is a permanent federal corporate income tax. As in the case with Part IV tax, taxable dividends that result in a refund of the 30 2/3% to the dividend payer may result in a Part IV liability by the dividend recipient where that recipient is a corporate shareholder. Full recovery of refundable taxes by the dividend payer that do not create refundable taxes to the dividend recipient requires a sufficiently large dividend (equal to the amount upon which the refundable taxes were initially charged) to shareholders that are individuals.

13-5.   The system in place to ensure the integrity and accuracy of this system is premised on the idea of integration. The purpose of integration is to recognize that, for example, if an individual taxpayer in a 48% federal/provincial income tax bracket earns $100 of interest income, $48 of income tax should be paid leaving the individual with $52. If, however, the individual owns all of the shares of a CCPC that owns the investments that pay the $100 there will be corporate income tax, and the payment of the after-tax cash as taxable dividends to the individual shareholder will result in additional income tax, the result of which is to leave the individual with the same $52 in cash. In other words, in the first situation the individual would pay $48 in income tax, but in the CCPC situation both the individual and corporation together pay the $48.

13-6.   These factors, taken together, add considerable complexity to the taxation of corporate investment income. The analysis requires (1) identifying the relevant investment income, (2) applying the appropriate Part I and IV taxes, (3) tracking the refundable portion of the taxes (referred to as refundable dividend tax on hand, or RDTOH), and (4) determining the portion of refundable taxes once a corporation has paid taxable dividends to its shareholders (referred to as a dividend refund). The third and fourth steps also require an understanding of eligible and non-eligible dividends, which were discussed in Chapter 7. All of these issues will be discussed in this chapter.

Integration

The Basic Concept

The Goal

13-7.   An individual taxpayer with a source of business or property income can carry on the business as a sole proprietor and own investments personally. If this approach is used, the individual would be personally liable for any income taxes on business profits and investment income.

Alternatively, the individual can incorporate both sources of income by first incorporating a company. Cash can be injected into the company through loans or as equity capital (through the purchase of shares from the company), or the company can borrow on its own account with the guarantee of shareholders if necessary. The company can then use the funds to purchase investments or business assets. The individual could also sell investments and business assets to the company. Regardless of the method used, the effect is that the company owns investments and carries on its own business. The only property owned by the individual would be shares of the newly created company. If this approach is used, there will be two levels of income tax. The income will be subject to corporate taxes as it is earned, and individual income tax will then be payable by the individual when the corporation pays taxable dividends to that individual shareholder.

13-8.   As depicted in Figure 13-1, the tax policy goal of integration, once all after-tax corporate income has been distributed as taxable dividends, is to ensure that the use of a corporation results in the same amount of income tax that would have occurred had the individual not incorporated the sources of income.

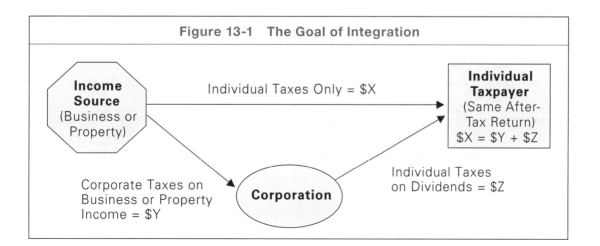

Figure 13-1   The Goal of Integration

Integration Procedures

13-9.   From the point of view of individual taxpayers, the dividend gross up and dividend tax credit mechanism is the primary tool used in building a system that integrates corporate and individual income taxes.

13-10.   As discussed in Chapter 7, the basic idea underlying the dividend gross up and dividend tax credit mechanism is that the taxable dividends received by an individual will be grossed up by a specific percentage to reflect the amount of pre-tax income earned by the corporation. This will be accompanied by a credit against tax payable that is designed to compensate the individual for the taxes that were paid by the corporation on that income. A simple example, using hypothetical rates, will serve to illustrate the fundamentals of this approach.

> **EXAMPLE**   Marion Fleury has a business that earns $100,000 of income each year. If she carries on the business as a sole proprietorship instead of a corporation she will be subject to income tax at her marginal rate of 51%.
>
> Alternatively, if she incorporates the business, the corporation will be subject to income tax at a rate of 20%.
>
> When the after-tax income of the corporation is distributed as taxable dividends, it will be subject to a gross up of 25%. The combined federal/provincial dividend tax credit in the province where Marion resides is equal to the amount of the gross up.
>
> **ANALYSIS**   If the business is carried on by Marion and not incorporated, Marion's after-tax retention would be as follows:

Pre-tax income	$100,000
Personal taxes at 51%	(51,000)
After-tax retention	$ 49,000

If, alternatively, the business is incorporated, the result would be as follows:

Corporate income before taxes	$100,000
Corporate taxes at 20%	(20,000)
After-tax income and maximum dividend payable	$ 80,000

If the maximum taxable dividend is paid by the corporation and a gross up of 25% is applied to this amount, the result would be as follows:

Dividends received	$ 80,000
Gross up [(25%)($80,000)]	20,000
Taxable dividends = Pre-tax corporate income	$100,000

As the amount of the gross up is equal to the corporate income taxes paid, adding the gross up results in taxable dividends equal to the corporate income before tax.

Based on this amount, Marion's tax payable would be calculated as follows:

Taxable dividends (after gross up)	$100,000
Marion's tax rate	51%
Tax payable before dividend tax credit	$ 51,000
Dividend tax credit (equal to gross up)	(20,000)
Marion's tax payable	$ 31,000

Based on the preceding calculation of tax payable, Marion's after-tax retention would be calculated as follows:

Dividends received	$ 80,000
Tax payable	(31,000)
After-tax retention—Use of corporation	$ 49,000

13-11.   You will note that this is exactly the same $49,000 of after-tax retention that would result from Marion receiving the $100,000 in income directly and being taxed on it at 51%. This means that, in this example, the gross up and tax credit procedures have produced perfect integration. That is, Marion has retained exactly the same amount of after-tax income, without regard to whether the business is carried on by her or by a corporation owned by her. In this instance the $51,000 of income taxes payable have been split between Marion ($31,000) and her company ($20,000).

> **AN IMPORTANT NOTE   An understanding of the dividend gross up and tax credit mechanism is essential to the material that follows in this chapter and Chapters 14, 15, and 16. If you do not fully understand these concepts, you should review the material on dividends that is found in Chapter 7.**

Eligible vs. Non-Eligible Dividends

The Problem

13-12.   The preceding example illustrates the fact that, given the appropriate combination of corporate tax rate, gross up percentage, and dividend tax credit rate, the dividend gross up and tax credit can provide perfect integration. In attempting to implement a system that provides for integration, all of the provinces use the federal gross up rates. However, there are significant variations in effective corporate tax rates, both because of the type of income earned by the corporation and the different rates applied at the provincial level. This means that there is no possibility that any single combination of gross up and tax credit rates could consistently provide integration for all corporations.

13-13.   For many years, the government ignored this issue, applying a single gross up rate and a single dividend tax credit rate without regard to the differences in the underlying corporate income tax rates. While it would not have been practical to have an array of gross up and credit rates that would reflect all of the different corporate tax rates, it was recognized that the single rate approach was not proving effective in providing for integration. In particular, the single rate that was being used was unfair to public companies that were subject to much higher rates than those applicable to CCPCs earning active business income.

13-14.   In response to this problem, a dual system of rates was developed. The two-rate system was based on a split between dividends paid out of income that was taxed at full corporate rates and dividends paid out of income that benefitted from the small business deduction or refundable taxes. The former were referred to as eligible dividends, with the latter being referred to as non-eligible dividends. In general terms, most of the dividends paid by public companies will be designated as eligible. In contrast, most of the dividends paid by CCPCs will not be designated as eligible and, as a result, will be non-eligible.

Eligible Dividends

13-15.   You may recall from Chapter 7 that ITA 89(1) defines eligible dividends as any taxable dividend that is designated as such by the company paying the dividend (designation procedures are covered in detail later in this chapter). Dividends that are designated as eligible dividends paid to individual shareholders are grossed up by 38% and are entitled to a federal dividend tax credit equal to 6/11 of the 38% gross up. As was discussed in Chapter 7, the application of these rates will result in individual shareholders receiving these dividends being taxed at a more favourable tax rate than would be the case if the dividends were non-eligible. The reason for this is that it is generally only corporate business income that is taxed at high corporate income tax rates that can qualify as eligible dividends. This means that because the corporation pays a greater share of the income tax paid, integration then requires that the individual will pay less. Globally, however, the income tax result should be the same. The perception, however, is that eligible dividends are favoured because the effective individual income tax rate is lower than non-eligible dividends.

13-16.   With the exception of capital dividends which are tax free, all types of taxable dividends may be designated as eligible dividends. This includes cash dividends, stock dividends, dividends in kind, and the various types of deemed dividends that will be introduced in Chapter 14 (e.g., ITA 84(3) dividends on redemption of shares).

Non-Eligible Dividends

13-17.   It is common to refer to dividends that have not been designated as eligible as non-eligible dividends, and this is the term we use. (Unfortunately, the term used in income tax returns is "other than eligible" dividends, which can cause confusion.) For 2021, non-eligible dividends received by individual taxpayers are grossed up by 15% and receive a federal dividend tax credit of 9/13 of the 15% gross up.

13-18.   Any taxable dividends that have not been designated as eligible will automatically be considered a non-eligible dividend. This includes cash dividends, stock dividends, dividends in kind, and the various types of deemed dividends that are discussed in Chapter 14. Note, however, that because capital dividends are not taxable dividends, they do not qualify for either the dividend gross up procedure or the tax credit procedure. In addition, corporate shareholders are not subject to the gross up and are not entitled to a dividend tax credit on any taxable dividends paid to them.

Importance

13-19.   The distinction between eligible and non-eligible dividends is extremely important to an individual shareholder. The reasons for this are as follows:

Effective Tax Rates   For an individual in the highest federal income tax bracket of 33%, the effective tax rates on non-eligible dividends can be over 14 percentage points higher than the rate on eligible dividends. Note, however, that the size of this difference varies considerably from province to province, ranging from less than two percentage points in Newfoundland to over 14 percentage points in New Brunswick.

Tax-Free Dividends   As we will discuss in Chapter 15, an individual with no other source of income can receive a substantial amount of dividends without paying any taxes as a result of the personal tax credit of $13,808 for 2021 plus the dividend tax credit. For a single individual receiving non-eligible dividends, the actual amount that can be received tax free is approximately $29,000. In contrast, this same individual can receive a little over $53,000 in actual eligible dividends. This is of great importance when a source of income is being split with low-income family members. Keep in mind, however, that these results are potentially subject to the tax on split income (TOSI), which was discussed in Chapter 11.

Rates Required for Integration

Corporate Tax Rates and Provincial Dividend Tax Credits

13-20.   In Chapter 7 we demonstrated that, for perfect integration, certain assumptions were required with respect to both the combined federal/provincial corporate income tax rate and the combined federal/provincial dividend tax credit. As noted in that chapter, those assumptions are as follows:

Corporate Federal/Provincial Tax Rate For integration to work perfectly, the corporate rate must be such that the dividend gross up percent must restore the after-tax corporate amount to the pre-corporate tax amount. The relevant rates are as follows:

- For eligible dividends that have a 38% gross up, the required rate is 27.54%. For example, $10,000 of corporate income would result in corporate taxes of $2,754 and an after-tax amount of $7,246 ($10,000 - $2,754). When the $7,246 is grossed up by 38%, the result is the original $10,000 [($7,246)(1.38)] of pre-tax corporate income.

- For non-eligible dividends that have a 15% gross up, the required rate is 13.04%. For example, $10,000 of corporate income would result in corporate taxes of $1,304 and an after-tax amount of $8,696 ($10,000 - $1,304). When the $8,696 is grossed up by 15%, the result is the original $10,000 [($8,696)(1.15)] of pre-tax corporate income.

If provincial dividend tax credits are set at the level required for perfect integration, combined corporate tax rates that exceed 27.54% (for eligible dividends) and 13.04% (for non-eligible dividends) will result in excessive corporate income tax. This is referred to as underintegration, where the integration falls short.

Provincial Dividend Tax Credit The achievement of perfect integration requires that the combined dividend tax credit equal the combined income taxes paid by the corporation. If the required corporate tax rates match what is required for perfect integration the gross up will equal the corporate income taxes paid. Putting these two facts together leads to the conclusion that the combined dividend tax credit must be equal to the gross up of dividends received. The required rates are as follows:

- For eligible dividends, the federal dividend tax credit is equal to 6/11 of the gross up. This means that, for the combined credit to equal the gross up, the provincial tax credit must equal 5/11 of the gross up.

- For non-eligible dividends, the federal dividend tax credit is equal to 9/13 of the gross up. This means that, for the combined credit to equal the gross up, the provincial credit must be equal to 4/13 of the gross up.

If the corporate tax rate is at the level required for integration, provincial dividend tax credits below these rates will result in underintegration, meaning that the dividend tax credit is insufficient to provide an offset to individual shareholders. The result is that the income taxes of both the individual and corporation will exceed that of the individual had the income not been incorporated. These required tax and dividend credit rates are summarized in Figure 13-2.

Figure 13-2
Corporate Rates and Dividend Tax Credits Required for Integration

Type of Dividends	Required Corporate Combined Tax Rate	Required Provincial Dividend Tax Credit
Eligible (38% Gross Up)	27.54%	5/11
Non-Eligible (15% Gross Up)	13.04%	4/13

Actual vs. Required Corporate Tax Rates

13-21.   It is important to be aware of how closely actual corporate tax rates compare to the rates required to implement integration. The following general comments are relevant:

Eligible Dividends   For eligible dividends, integration requires a combined federal/provincial corporate tax rate of 27.54%. As most eligible dividends will be paid by public companies, the relevant rate is the one that applies to these companies. In 2021 the combined rates for such companies currently range from 23% to 31%. As these rates are fairly close to the required 27.54%, integration is working reasonably well, with modest amounts of over- or underintegration in specific provinces.

Non-Eligible Dividends   For non-eligible dividends, integration requires a federal/provincial tax rate on corporations of 13.04%. The situation here is more complex in that the source of such dividends may be either the income of CCPCs that have benefitted from the small business deduction or the investment income of such companies.

To the extent that the non-eligible dividends reflect income that has benefitted from the small business deduction, the appropriate combined federal/provincial rates range from 9% to 13%. As was the case with eligible dividends, these rates are close to the required 13.04%, suggesting that integration is working fairly well here.

There is a problem, however, when the source of the non-eligible dividends is investment income earned by CCPCs. As we shall discover in this chapter, the combined federal/provincial rates on this type of income range from 46 2/3% to 54 2/3%. Once the refund of 30 2/3% is factored in the net corporate income tax would be in the range of 16% to 23%, which is purposefully excessive to discourage earning investment income through corporations in Canada. While there is some limited tax deferral in British Columbia, Ontario, and Quebec because of high individual income tax rates that exceed the corporate investment income rates, the overall tax cost remains high due to corporate rates in excess of the 13.04% perfect integration rate.

13-22.   For both types of dividends, the preceding analysis makes it clear that the effectiveness of integration is dependent on the province in which the corporation is subject to corporate income tax.

Actual vs. Required Dividend Tax Credits

13-23.   Also of importance is the relationship between actual provincial dividend tax credit rates and those that are required for perfect integration. The following general comments are relevant here:

Eligible Dividends   For eligible dividends, the federal credit of 6/11 represents $20.73 of a $38 gross up on $100 of eligible dividends. This means that the provincial credit required for perfect integration must equal 5/11 of $38, or $17.27 of a $100 eligible dividend, which is 17.27% of the actual dividend. In 2021 the provincial dividend tax credits ranged from $7.45 in Newfoundland to $19.32 in New Brunswick. Only New Brunswick exceeds the 17.27% rate. As a result, there will generally be underintegration with respect to eligible dividends. In terms of gross up percentages, the provincial dividend tax credit would have to represent 45.5% of the gross up [(5/11)(100)].

Non-Eligible Dividends   Applying the same logic for non-eligible dividends, the federal credit of 9/13 represents $10.38 of a $15 gross up on $100 of non-eligible dividends. This means that the provincial credit required for perfect integration must equal 4/13 of $15, or $4.61 of a $100 non-eligible dividend for perfect integration. In 2021 the provincial dividend tax credits range from $0.77 in Yukon to $6.90 in the Northwest Territories. Only Quebec and the Northwest Territories equal or exceed the required 4.61% rate of actual dividends. As a result, there will generally be underintegration with respect to non-eligible dividends. In terms of gross up percentages, the provincial dividend tax credit would have to represent 30.8% of the gross up [(4/13)(100)].

13-24.   In summary, combined corporate tax rates and the dividend tax credits interact to determine whether perfect integration is being achieved. As is the case with corporate tax rates, variations in the dividend tax credit rates make it clear that the effectiveness of integration is highly dependent on the province in which individual shareholders reside.

Exercise 13-1

Subject: Integration (Non-Eligible Dividends)

Jan Teason carries on a business as a sole proprietor. She estimates the business will generate income of $100,000 during the taxation year ending December 31, 2021. If she incorporates the business, all of the income would be eligible for the small business deduction and any taxable dividends paid will be non-eligible. In the province where she resides, such corporate income is subject to a combined federal/provincial income tax rate of 15%. Ms. Teason has other sources of income and, as a result, any additional income she receives will be subject to a combined federal/provincial income tax rate of 45%. In her province, the provincial dividend tax credit on non-eligible dividends is equal to 30% of the 15% gross up. Would Ms. Teason save any income tax if she were to incorporate her business? Explain your result.

Exercise 13-2

Subject: Integration (Eligible Dividends)

John Horst carries on a business as a sole proprietor. He estimates the business will generate income of $100,000 during the taxation year ending December 31, 2021. John is contemplating incorporating a new company to carry on his business. John controls another corporation that would be associated with the new corporation. Therefore, none of this income would be eligible for the small business deduction and any taxable dividends paid would be designated as eligible. In the province where he resides, this corporate income would be taxed at a combined federal/provincial rate of 30%. John has other sources of income and, as a result, any additional income he receives will be subject to a combined federal/provincial income tax rate of 42%. The relevant provincial dividend tax credit on eligible dividends is 28% of the gross up. Would John save any income tax if he were to incorporate his business? Explain your result.

Solutions to Exercises are available in the Study Guide.

We suggest you complete SSP 13-1 at this point.

Alternative Calculations for Dividend Tax Credits

13-25.   Note that while federal legislation calculates the dividend tax credit as a fraction of the gross up, many reporting services express the dividend tax credit as a percentage of actual dividends received, or a percentage of the grossed up amount of the dividends.

13-26.   Because our focus is largely on federal legislation, we will generally present dividend tax credits as a fraction or a percentage of the gross up. However, if needed, it is quite simple to convert different approaches to a uniform base. For example, if an eligible dividend of $100 is paid, the federal dividend tax credit of $20.73 can be calculated as:

- 6/11 or 54.55% of the $38 [(38%)($100)] gross up (which is our standard approach)
- 20.73% of the $100 in dividends received [(6/11)($38) divided by 100]
- 15.02% of the $138 of grossed up dividends [(6/11)($38) divided by 138]

Refundable Taxes on Investment Income

Meaning of aggregate investment income—ITA 129(4)

Regular Meaning

13-27.   In the following material on refundable taxes, we will be using the term aggregate investment income. The purpose of the aggregate investment income concept is to determine the types of income that are subject to the initial high rate of Part I income tax on investment income so that the refundable portion of the tax of 30 2/3% can then be identified. This term is defined in ITA 129(4) and has a very specific definition. You may recall that we briefly discussed this definition in Chapter 12. It is also included at the front of this text in "Rates, Credits, and Other Data." It is provided again here for your convenience.

ITA 129(4) Aggregate Investment Income

Net taxable capital gains	$xxx
Interest	xxx
Rents	xxx
Royalties	xxx
Total positive amounts	$xxx
Net capital loss carry overs deducted during the year	(xxx)
ITA 129(4) aggregate investment income	$xxx

13-28.   Note the differences between aggregate investment income and what we normally think of as property or investment income. Unlike property or investment income, this concept includes net taxable capital gains for the current year, which is taxable capital gains minus allowable capital losses reduced by net capital losses deducted in the year. Net capital losses are only deductible to the extent of the net taxable capital gains.

13-29.   Another difference between aggregate investment income and property or investment income is that it excludes any dividends that would be entitled to a taxable income deduction such as ITA 112(1), which is available for dividends received between taxable Canadian corporations. This reflects the fact that dividends between such corporations are not subject to Part I tax and therefore there would be no Part I taxes on such dividends to refund.

13-30.   Finally, there are a few additional points to be aware of. The first is that the definition does not differentiate between Canadian and foreign sources. This means that both Canadian and foreign amounts are to be included. The second is that any losses from property reduce the aggregate investment income. If, for example, in 2021 a corporation had interest of $5,000 and a rental property loss of $1,700, then aggregate investment income for the year would be $3,300. If, however, the rental loss was from a business, then the loss would not reduce the aggregate investment income.

Basic Concepts

The Problem

13-31.   As shown in Figure 13-3, when income is first earned by a corporation and then distributed to individual shareholders as taxable dividends there are two levels of income tax—one by the corporation that has earned the income and a second by the individual shareholders when taxable dividends are paid by the corporation with after-tax earnings. If we assume that the corporate tax rate on the investment income of a CCPC is 52% and the individual shareholder is taxed at a combined rate of 39% on non-eligible dividends received, the overall rate of taxation on investment income flowed through a corporation would be 70.7% [52% + (1 - 52%)(39%)].

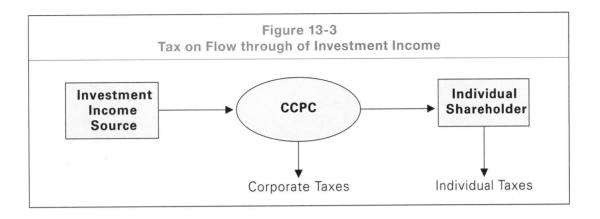

Figure 13-3
Tax on Flow through of Investment Income

13-32. This is significantly higher than the maximum federal/provincial tax rate on Canadian individuals of 54% (Nova Scotia). Such a large difference is clearly not consistent with the concept of integration. The refundable tax mechanism is designed to ensure the attainment of an appropriate result.

The Refundable Tax Solution

13-33. The most obvious solution to this problem would be to lower the rate of corporate tax on investment income of a CCPC. For example, if the corporate rate was lowered to 22%, then the overall rate would be 52.4% [22% + (1 - 22%)(39%)]. This would be within the range of acceptable rates for individuals in the highest income tax brackets.

13-34. That type of solution, however, would be counterproductive in terms of lost tax revenue to the federal and provincial governments since individuals in high tax brackets could then incorporate their investments, pay a low rate of corporate income tax, and simply leave the funds in the corporation providing an indefinite tax deferral. Using the previous numbers, $10,000 of investment income would, at a 22% corporate tax rate, result in $2,200 of corporate income tax with $7,800 remaining in the corporation to reinvest. Had the individual not incorporated, at a 54% marginal tax rate $5,400 of income tax would have been paid leaving only $4,600 to reinvest. There would be little incentive to have the corporation pay the $7,800 to the individual shareholder as a taxable dividend. In the interim, $3,200 [$5,400- $3,200] in income taxes would have been deferred.

13-35. Given the opportunity for tax deferral it is not surprising that a different solution to the problem was adopted. The solution effectively requires a corporation to prepay taxes at a high rate that significantly reduces or eliminates altogether any tax deferral advantage. This is the justification for high corporate income tax rates on investment income of private companies. Once taxable dividends are actually paid to individual shareholders, then the refundable part of the taxes can be returned to the corporation since the individuals would then be required to pay their share of the income tax on that investment income. In other words, any deferral opportunity would end with the taxable dividend payment to individual shareholders.

13-36. The success of this refundable tax system on investment income of private corporations, particularly CCPCs, can be seen in the tax deferral effect for the 2020 taxation year. Incorporating investment income in Canada results in few opportunities. The highest potential tax deferral on $1,000 of investment income is $34 for Ontario, however the overall tax cost once taxable dividends would be paid is $44. There is not a single province or territory in which incorporating investment income would save any income taxes.

Refundable Part I Tax on Investment Income

Additional Refundable Tax on Investment Income (ART)—ITA 123.3

Basic Calculations

13-37.   In Paragraph 13-6 we set out an analysis that first begins with identifying the relevant investment income then applying the investment taxes under either Part I or Part IV. The final steps in determining the refundable taxes (RDTOH) and the taxes that are refundable on the payment of taxable dividends (dividend refund) are discussed later in this chapter.

13-38.   The relevant investment income for purposes of the ART that adds 10 2/3% to the Part I tax of a CCPC is aggregate investment income, which was described in Paragraph 13-27. The ART is determined under ITA 123.3 (the definition is available at the front of this text in "Rates, Credits, and Other Data"). The ART is equal to 10 2/3% of the lesser of:

- the corporation's aggregate investment income for the year; or

- the amount, if any, by which the corporation's taxable income for the year exceeds the amount upon which the small business deduction is calculated.

13-39.   The taxable income component of the ART recognizes that corporate taxable income deductions such as deductions for charitable donations or non-capital loss carry overs are considered to be effectively applied against aggregate investment income before any amount eligible for the small business deduction. For example, assume that a CCPC has taxable income of $100,000, which is made up of aggregate investment income of $40,000 and $60,000 of active business income, all of which qualifies for the small business deduction. If the CCPC decides to claim a non-capital loss of $30,000, then taxable income would be revised to $70,000. The small business deduction remains unchanged. The amount of ART would be the lesser of aggregate investment income of $40,000 and the amount by which taxable income of $70,000 exceeds $60,000 or $10,000. The impact is that the $70,000 of taxable income is considered made up of $60,000 of active business income and $10,000 of aggregate investment income that is actually subject to income tax. This approach also ensures that the ART will not be inappropriately applied to active business income.

13-40.   As a final point there are complications associated with the interaction of the ART, small business deduction, and the general rate reduction in terms of how foreign tax credits are calculated. We have provided detail in the appendix at the end of this chapter for those who are interested.

Exercise 13-3

Subject: ART

Zircon Inc. is a CCPC with a December 31 year end. Zircon has never been associated with any other company. For the 2021 taxation year, its net income is equal to $281,000. This is made up of active business income of $198,000, portfolio dividends from taxable Canadian corporations of $22,000, interest income on long-term investments of $15,000, and taxable capital gains on the disposition of capital assets used in the active business of $46,000.

The company has a 2018 net capital loss balance of $26,000 and a 2019 non-capital loss balance of $23,000. The company intends to deduct both of these balances in the 2021 taxation year. In 2020, the corporation's adjusted aggregate investment income was $13,000, and its taxable capital employed in Canada was $6 million.

Determine Zircon's taxable income and its ART on aggregate investment income for the 2021 taxation year.

Solutions to Exercises are available in the Study Guide.

Refundable Part I Tax Basics

13-41.   In Paragraph 3-6 we described the basic process of handling investment income earned by private corporations that are CCPCs. We briefly described the ART, which together with other Part I tax resulted in a federal tax rate of 38 2/3%. Of that amount, 30 2/3% of the Part I tax is refundable with the result that the net federal corporate tax is only 8%. However, provincial taxes on investment income add another 8% to 16% for a combined potential of 16% to 24%.

13-42.   If integration for corporate investment income, specifically aggregate investment income, worked perfectly the net corporate tax (after the refund) plus the tax that would be payable on a taxable dividend distribution to an individual shareholder would equal the income tax that an individual would pay had they not incorporated the investments. Unfortunately this is not the case for Part I tax for a number of reasons.

13-43.   For perfect Part I integration to work for investment income (other than taxable dividends), the corporate tax rate, the amount of refundable taxes, and the amount eligible for a dividend refund on the payment of taxable dividends would require coordination with the non-eligible dividend gross up and dividend tax credits provided by the provinces and territories. As we have discussed, this is not the case in 2021. Given the punitive nature of corporate investment taxes, there will be a tax cost to incorporating such income.

13-44.   The main difficulties are that a combined rate of approximately 46.35% would be required. We have seen that the actual combined corporate investment tax rates in Canada range from 46 2/3% to 54 2/3%, all of which are above the required perfect integration rate. Secondly, the Part I refundable tax equals a flat rate 30 2/3%, whereas the dividend refund is based on 38 1/3% of taxable dividends paid. This dividend refund rate matches the Part IV tax and therefore provides perfect integration with respect to Part IV tax but not Part I tax.

Concepts Illustrated

13-45.   Taxable dividends paid from investment income that is eligible for refundable Part I tax can only be paid as non-eligible dividends. This is because the federal tax rate is low once refundable taxes are considered. For integration to work perfectly on non-eligible dividend payments, the overall corporate tax rate has to equal 13.04% as previously discussed; however, as we have seen the combined tax rate is actually in the 16% to 24% range. In order to give you a better understanding of how the concepts associated with the refund of Part I tax work, we will use an example based on a pre-dividend refund tax rate that will provide a 13.04% tax rate after the refund has contributed to the total dividend. While we will not go through the calculation of this rate, the required rate is 46.375%, which would include the 10 2/3% ART.

13-46.   With the initial corporate tax rate at 46.375%, a refund is necessary to reduce the rate to the required 13.04%. The dividend refund rate specified in ITA 129(1) is 38 1/3% of taxable dividends paid. The after-tax income together with the dividend refund will fund the dividend payment. As we will discuss later, this refund is limited to the balance in the corporation's RDTOH account.

13-47.   The following example involving perfect integration will illustrate the rates we have just presented:

> **EXAMPLE**   Ms. Banardi has investments that result in interest income of $100,000 per year. You have been asked to advise her as to whether there would be any income tax advantages to incorporating the investments in a CCPC. Ms. Banardi is personally subject to a combined federal/provincial tax rate of 49%. The dividend tax credit on non-eligible dividends in her province of residence is equal to 4/13 of the gross up. The CCPC would be subject to a combined federal/provincial income tax rate of 46.375% on investment income, which includes the ART.

13-48.   The calculations that follow compare the after-tax income retention of incorporating versus not incorporating the investments:

After-Tax Retention—Use of a Corporation

Corporate investment income	$100,000
Corporate tax at 46.376%	(46,375)
After-tax income	$ 53,625
Dividend refund (see analysis)	33,335
Non-eligible dividends paid to Ms. Banardi	$ 86,960

ANALYSIS   In this case, the numbers are determined by first calculating the taxable dividend required that when grossed up by 15% equals $100,000. This is calculated as $86,960 [($100,000)(1.00/1.15)]. The next step is to determine the dividend refund if a taxable dividend of $86,960 were paid. The refund would be $33,335 [(38 1/3%) ($86,960)]. The next step is to determine the after-tax corporate income of $53,625 [$86,960 - $33,335]. Finally, the income tax can now be determined as $46,375 [$100,000 - $53,625], which equals 46.375%. We have ignored rounding errors.

Note that, at this point, the total corporate tax paid is equal to $13,040 ($100,000 - $86,960). This reflects the 13.04% rate ($13,040 ÷ $100,000) that is required for perfect integration.

The assumption that all after-tax income will be paid out as taxable dividends is not consistent with the real-world approach in which the amount of the dividend is determined by a variety of factors (e.g., availability of cash or alternative investment opportunities) and very rarely, if ever, equals the after-tax income plus the dividend refund.

Calculation of the after-tax amounts retained is as follows:

Non-eligible dividends received	$ 86,960
Gross up of 15%	13,040
Additional personal income	$100,000
Personal marginal tax rate	49%
Tax payable before dividend tax credit	$ 49,000
Dividend tax credit [(9/13 + 4/13)]	(13,040)
Personal tax payable with corporation	$ 35,960

Non-eligible dividends received	$ 86,960
Personal tax payable	(35,960)
After-tax cash retained with corporation	$ 51,000

After-Tax Retention—No Corporation

Investment income—Direct receipt	$100,000
Personal tax at 49%	(49,000)
After-tax cash retained without corporation	$ 51,000

13-49.   While this example provides equal amounts of after-tax cash, it is not a realistic example. All of the combined federal/provincial rates on the investment income of CCPCs are higher than the 46.375% rate used in our example. In addition, as we shall see in the next section of this chapter, the amount of the refund is limited by the balance in the RDTOH. We have not taken that into consideration in this example. If we had, the dividend refund in this example would be limited to $30,677 [(30 2/3%)($100,000)].

Use of Other Rates in Refundable Part I Tax Example

13-50.   In this example, we will use a more realistic corporate tax rate of 54 2/3%. This will illustrate that, when realistic corporate tax rates are used, incorporating investments in a CCPC will result in a greater tax cost than owning the investments personally.

> **EXAMPLE**   Mr. Leoni has investments that earn interest income of $100,000 per year. He has over $250,000 in other income and is therefore subject to a combined federal/ provincial tax rate of 51% on any additional income. The provincial dividend tax credit for non-eligible dividends is equal to 4/13 of the gross up. Mr. Leoni is considering incorporating these investments in a CCPC. The combined federal/provincial corporate income tax rate on investment income is 54 2/3%, which includes the ART [federal (38% - 10% + 10 2/3%) + provincial 16%].

13-51.   The calculations comparing the after-tax investment income if the investments are incorporated versus continuing to own them personally are as follows:

After-Tax Retention—Use of a Corporation

Corporate investment income	$100,000
Corporate tax at 54 2/3%	(54,667)
After-tax income	$ 45,333
Dividend refund [($45,333 ÷ .61667) - $45,333]	28,180
Non-eligible dividends paid to Mr. Leoni	$ 73,513
Non-eligible dividends received	$ 73,513
Gross up of 15%	11,027
Grossed up dividends	$ 84,540
Personal tax rate	51%
Tax payable before dividend tax credit	$ 43,115
Dividend tax credit [(9/13 + 4/13)($11,027)]	(11,027)
Personal tax payable with corporation	$ 32,088
Non-eligible dividends received	$ 73,513
Personal tax payable	(32,088)
After-tax cash retained with corporation	$ 41,425

After-Tax Retention—Without a Corporation

Investment income—Direct receipt	$100,000
Personal tax at 51%	(51,000)
After-tax cash retained without corporation	$ 49,000

Note that the dividend refund is calculated based on a dividend refund rate of 38 1/3%. The after-tax amount of $45,333, therefore, represents 61 2/3% of a taxable dividend that will add 38 1/3% as a refund. The result is that the taxable dividend required is calculated as [($45,333) divided by (1 - .38333)], which can be expressed as $45,333 divided by 0.61667. The result would be $73,513. The result is after-tax cash of $45,333 plus a refund of $28,180 [($73,533) (38 1/3%)].

13-52.   There are two things that should be noted here. First, when a 54 2/3% corporate tax rate is used, the taxes of $54,667 at the corporate level are significantly higher than the $51,000 that would have been paid if Mr. Leoni had owned the investments. In other words, there are no tax deferral opportunities to incorporating the investments.

13-53.   Second, there is a tax cost of incorporating the investments. Mr. Leoni has $7,575 ($49,000 - $41,425) less after-tax cash as compared to the amount he would have retained had he not incorporated the investments. While this difference is particularly large when a 54 2/3% corporate tax rate is used, the basic result would be the same when any of the other available corporate tax rates are used. As a result, using a corporation in Canada in 2021 will always result in a tax cost. We would add that, based on information available for 2020, the tax cost of earning investment income through a CCPC ranged from 2.1% to 8.4% depending on the province or territory. Based on these percentages, the tax cost of the preceding example would range from $2,100 to $8,400.

Exercise 13-4

Subject: Incorporating Investment income

Ms. Shelly Nicastro has investments that earn interest income of $100,000 per year. Due to high employment income, any additional income she receives will be subject to a combined federal/provincial income tax rate of 51%. She is considering incorporating these investments in a CCPC. The combined federal/provincial income tax rate on investment income would be 52%. The dividend tax credit for non-eligible dividends in her province is equal to 30% of the gross up. Any dividends paid by the CCPC out of investment income will be non-eligible. Advise her as to whether there would be any tax savings as a result of incorporating the investments.

Solutions to Exercises are available in the Study Guide.

Refundable Part IV Tax Basics

13-54.   In Paragraph 3-6 we described the basic process of handling investment income earned by private corporations, particularly those that are CCPCs. We noted that the corporate tax rates are set at very high levels to discourage individuals from using a corporation's low income tax rates to defer income tax that would have been required had the various investment sources not been incorporated. We also added that there are two types of refundable taxes—one under Part I and a second under Part IV. Both sets of rules apply to private corporations, but Part I refundable taxes apply to CCPCs whereas Part IV refundable taxes apply to both CCPCs and non-CCPCs that are private corporations.

13-55.   We have discussed the Part I refundable taxes that relate to aggregate investment income, noting that such income does not include taxable dividends that would be tax free to a corporation under Part I as a result of the taxable income deduction under ITA 112(1). This appears to leave another investment savings opportunity that individuals could use to save income tax.

EXAMPLE   Xeniya resides in Alberta and earns significant employment income. Any additional income she would receive would be subjected to the highest combined federal/provincial income tax rates. She has recently purchased investments in Canadian public companies that are expected to pay eligible dividends to her of $10,000 in 2021. The actual highest tax rate on eligible dividends in Alberta in 2021 is 34.31%. This tax rate considers the dividend gross up and dividend tax credits in Alberta. She is considering incorporating the investments in public company shares to a CCPC that would be wholly owned by her.

ANALYSIS   If Xeniya receives the eligible dividends of $10,000 she will pay income tax of $3,431 [(34.31%)($10,000)]. If, however, she were to incorporate a CCPC such that the CCPC received the eligible dividends there would be no Part I tax. The effect on the CCPC for 2021 would be as follows:

Net income	$10,000
Less: Taxable dividends—ITA 112(1)	(10,000)
Taxable income	$ Nil
Corporate Part I tax payable	$ Nil

13-56.   The result of incorporating the investment in shares that pay taxable dividends is clearly significant as all Part I tax would be avoided at least until the CCPC paid the amount out as a taxable dividend to Xeniya. Since that decision is Xeniya's, as the controlling shareholder, the $80,000 in funds could be retained by the CCPC indefinitely.

13-57.   In our discussion of refundable Part I tax we mentioned that the reasoning for the high level of Part I income tax on aggregate investment income was to discourage the practice of using CCPCs to defer income tax. This same reasoning applies to taxable dividends, although it is handled somewhat differently.

13-58.   The purpose of the Part IV tax is the same as the Part I refundable tax, which is to charge a refundable tax at rates high enough to discourage individuals from using corporations to earn investment income that are taxable dividends on share investments, which are commonly referred to as portfolio dividends. This concept is designed to target investment income of individuals. In very general terms, portfolio dividends are meant to refer to dividends paid on an investment in shares that give the shareholder no influence over the decision making of a corporation. The legislation, which we will discuss in this chapter, uses a 10% benchmark to make this distinction. There is a presumption that if an individual owns 10% or less of the voting shares of a corporation and 10% or less of the value of all of a corporation's shares there is no influence and therefore any dividends paid are true investments or portfolio dividends.

13-59.   The Part IV tax applies to private companies (CCPCs and non-CCPCs) as well as closely held public companies that the legislation refers to as "subject companies." Initially, Part IV only applied to private corporations, but some tax planners used closely held public companies to circumvent Part IV. The government response was to add the concept of a subject corporation, which is defined in ITA 186(3) as follows:

> **Subject Corporation**   means a corporation (other than a private corporation) resident in Canada and controlled, whether because of a beneficial interest in one or more trusts or otherwise, by or for the benefit of an individual (other than a trust) or a related group of individuals (other than trusts).

> In this chapter, any subsequent references to private corporations should be considered to include subject corporations.

13-60.   The Part IV rate in 2021 is fixed at 38 1/3% on taxable dividends received that are eligible for the ITA 112(1) taxable income deduction. We would add that there is no provincial tax equivalent to Part IV, which is purely a federal income tax concept. The Part IV tax is refundable at the same rate of 38 1/3% when the private corporation that has received the dividend pays a taxable dividend to its shareholder(s).

13-61.   In the example in Paragraph 13-55, while there would be no Part I tax on the taxable dividend received by Xeniya's corporation there would be Part IV tax of $3,833, which exceeds the income tax she would have paid of $3,431 by $402. As a result, there is no deferral advantage of incorporating the investments. If Xeniya's company paid the $10,000 as a taxable dividend to Xeniya it would be entitled to a dividend refund of $3,833, or 38 1/3% of $10,000. Using the previous calculations, the requisite taxable dividend would be $10,000 calculated as the after-tax cash in the CCPC of $6,167 divided by 0.61667. In the example, it is clearly not in Xeniya's interest to incorporate the investments in these public company shares.

13-62.   While the Part IV tax allows for perfect integration because the Part IV tax rate of 38 1/3% is equal to the dividend refund rate of 38 1/3%, there are additional complications that must be considered. The complications centre on integration and the role of the taxable dividend deduction of ITA 112(1).

13-63.   Integration requires two levels of income tax—one by the corporation that first earns income and the second by individuals when taxable dividends are received by them. In a standard situation where a business has been incorporated and individuals own the shares of that corporation, the only taxpayers are the corporation and the individuals. When the corporation earns income it will pay income tax. When the after-tax income is paid as a taxable dividend to the individual shareholders the second level of income tax is paid and integration is complete.

13-64.   This standard integration model differs, however, when there are additional intermediary corporations, which is quite common in practice. If an individual owns all of the shares of a CCPC (X Co) that, in turn, owns all of the shares of a second CCPC (Y Co) we have the makings of an intermediary corporate structure. If Y Co carries on a business and X Co acts as an investment holding company or parent company to Y Co, then the integration concept must be adjusted. When Y Co earns income the first level of income tax is paid. When Y Co pays a taxable dividend to X Co there should be no additional income tax under Part I because integration looks to individuals and not corporations for the second level of income tax. Since taxable dividends received by X Co are required to be included in X Co's income, ITA 112(1) is used to ensure the dividend income does not make it through to taxable income. When X Co pays a taxable dividend to its individual shareholders, then the second level of income tax will be paid under the integration concept and integration is once again complete.

13-65.   If we return to the example in Paragraph 13-55 and add a second CCPC, such that Xeniya owns all of the shares of X Co and X Co owns all of the shares of Y Co, we can see how integration causes a modification to be made to Part IV tax.

EXAMPLE   Assume that the public company share investments have been incorporated and are owned by Y Co. Y Co receives $10,000 of eligible dividends on the share investments. Y Co then pays a taxable dividend of $10,000 to X Co.

ANALYSIS   As in the previous example, X Co pays no Part I tax on the $10,000 dividend received because of the ITA 112(1) deduction. X Co, however, is subject to Part IV tax of $3,833 because it has received portfolio dividends on share investments. When X Co pays a taxable dividend to Y Co it will be entitled to a dividend refund of $3,833, with the result that its net income tax liability is nil [Part IV $3,833- dividend refund $3,833]. When Y Co receives a $10,000 taxable dividend from X Co there is no Part I tax because of the ITA 112(1) taxable income deduction, but the question is whether Part IV tax should apply. The taxable dividends received by X Co are not portfolio dividends, suggesting that Part IV tax should not apply. However, if Part IV tax does not apply in this situation then individuals could avoid Part IV tax altogether by simply adding a second CCPC such as Y Co and having the first company pay a dividend to the second company to recover its Part IV tax.

THE SOLUTION   To ensure the appropriate result that Part IV tax should be primarily directed at portfolio dividends, Part IV introduces the concept of connected corporations, which establishes the 10% benchmark referred to in Paragraph 13-58. The connected corporations concept is discussed in the following section.

THE RESULT   When taxable dividends are received by a private corporation such as a CCPC or a subject corporation, Part IV tax applies as follows:

1. Portfolio Dividends: Part IV tax applies at a rate of 38 1/3% to the taxable dividends received

2. Dividends between connected corporations: Only if the company paying the dividend receives a dividend refund for the taxation year in which the dividend was paid. Part IV tax to the corporate dividend recipient equals the dividend refund of the connected corporation that paid the dividends. This amount is apportioned if there are taxable dividends paid to other shareholders during the year.

Connected Corporations—ITA 186(2), (4), & (7)

13-66.   In terms of Part IV tax, the distinction between a portfolio dividend that is considered a true investment and something else is critical to the application of Part IV. Portfolio dividends received by private companies are automatically subject to Part IV tax, whereas non-portfolio dividends are only subject to Part IV tax if the corporation that paid the taxable dividend receives a dividend refund for that same year. The 10% shareholding test that allows dividends to be separated between portfolio dividends and non-portfolio dividends is established through the definition of a "connected corporation." There are taxable dividends from corporations that are not connected (portfolio dividends) and those from connected corporations (non-portfolio dividends). Corporations are connected (ITA 186(4)) if either of the two following conditions are met:

- One corporation controls the other corporation. For this purpose, control is defined in ITA 186(2) to mean one of three possibilities: (1) One corporation owns more than 50% of the voting shares of the other, (2) persons who are non-arm's length with a corporation own more than 50% of the voting shares of the other corporation, or (3) one corporation together with non-arm's-length persons own more than 50% of the voting shares of the other corporation.

- A corporation owns shares in the other corporation that account for more than 10% of the voting shares and more than 10% of the FMV of all of the issued shares of that corporation.

13-67.   Given the definition of a connected corporation, the 10% shareholding test is generally used to determine whether the dividends received are portfolio dividends or dividends from a connected corporation (i.e., non-portfolio dividends).

EXAMPLE   A dividend is received on an investment made by a private company in 500 shares of a large publicly traded company that has 15 million shares outstanding.

ANALYSIS   The corporations would not be connected since (1) the private company does not control the public company and (2) the more than 10% shareholding test would not be met. As a consequence, the dividends would be considered portfolio dividends paid by corporations that are not connected and Part IV tax would automatically apply.

13-68.   Figure 13-4 illustrates a corporate structure where the shares of Opco are owned by three different holding companies (Holdco 1, 2, & 3), each wholly owned by one individual. You and your spouse are related and therefore non-arm's length. As a result, Holdco 1 and 2 are also related and non-arm's length. Assume that Opco has issued only one class of shares. All three Holdco's are connected to Opco as follows:

Holdco 1 and Opco   Holdco 1 is connected to Opco as it meets both situations: (1) It controls Opco because it owns more than 50% of Opco's voting shares. Note that when a corporation has issued only one class of shares, all of those shares are considered voting shares. (2) Holdco 1 is also connected by the 10% shareholding test because

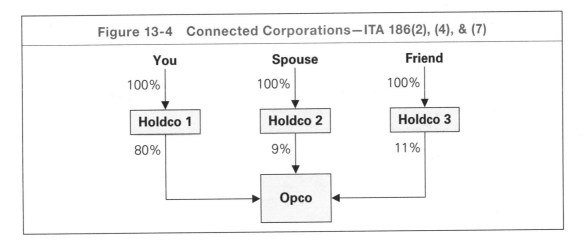

Figure 13-4   Connected Corporations—ITA 186(2), (4), & (7)

it owns shares that account for more than 10% of the voting shares and the shares it owns represents more than 10% of the FMV of all of the shares that Opco has issued.

Holdco 2 and Opco   Holdco 2 does not meet the more than 10% shareholding test and therefore must rely on whether it controls Opco. Control means one of three circumstances: (1) Holdco 2 owns more than 50% of the Opco voting shares, (2) a non-arm's-length person owns more than 50% of Opco's voting shares, or (3) that Holdco 2 together with other non-arm's-length persons owns more than 50% of Opco's voting shares. Holdco 2 would meet either of point 2 or 3, meaning that Holdco 2 is considered to control Opco, causing the corporations to be connected.

Holdco 3 and Opco   Holdco 3 is not non-arm's length with other Opco shareholders and must rely on its own shareholding in Opco to determine whether it is connected. Holdco 3 does not own more than 50% of Opco's voting shares, therefore Opco is not controlled by Holdco 3. However, Holdco 3 does meet the 10% shareholding test, which causes it to be connected with Opco.

TIP: The connected corporation definition is important for other areas of the ITA and not just Part IV. As a result, knowledge of this concept is important, as will be discussed in Chapter 16.

Part IV Analysis Flowchart

13-69.   Figure 13-5 illustrates the Part IV analysis required for a private corporation. If the taxable dividend received is a portfolio dividend, meaning that the corporations are not connected, a "No" answer to the second flowchart box that begins "Does the private corporation ..." will lead to the conclusion at the bottom of the flowchart that Part IV tax applies.

13-70.   If however the second flowchart box is answered "Yes," then the two corporations would be connected and a further analysis is required that depends on whether the corporation that paid the taxable dividends received a dividend refund for the year in which the dividend was paid. If the answer is yes, Part IV tax applies, and if the answer is no, then Part IV tax does not apply.

Example #1—Connected Corporation Dividends

13-71.   In the following paragraphs we will look at two examples of the application of refundable taxes under both Part I and IV.

EXAMPLE   Eastern Inc. owns all of the shares of Western Ltd. Both are private companies that are CCPCs with December 31 taxation year ends. During the current year, Western has income of $100,000, made up entirely of interest and taxable capital gains. Assume that the combined federal/provincial tax rate for both companies is 50 2/3%. Western pays out all of its after-tax income in dividends to Eastern Inc. This situation is illustrated in Figure 13-6.

ANALYSIS   The first point to note is that Western will only be subject to Part I refundable taxes because all of its investment income is aggregate investment income and not taxable dividends. The receipt of a taxable dividend by Eastern, however, would result in Part IV refundable taxes.

On receipt of the $100,000 of investment income, Western would pay Part I taxes of $50,667 [($100,000)(50 2/3%)]. However, when the remaining $49,333 is paid out in dividends, a dividend refund of $30,667 (38 1/3% of the $80,000 total dividend) becomes available, resulting in a total taxable dividend that can be paid to Eastern of $80,000 as shown in the following calculation:

Investment income of Western	$100,000
Corporate tax at 50 2/3%	(50,667)
Income before dividends	$ 49,333
Dividend refund [($49,333 ÷ .61667) - $49,333]	30,667
Taxable dividends paid to Eastern	$ 80,000

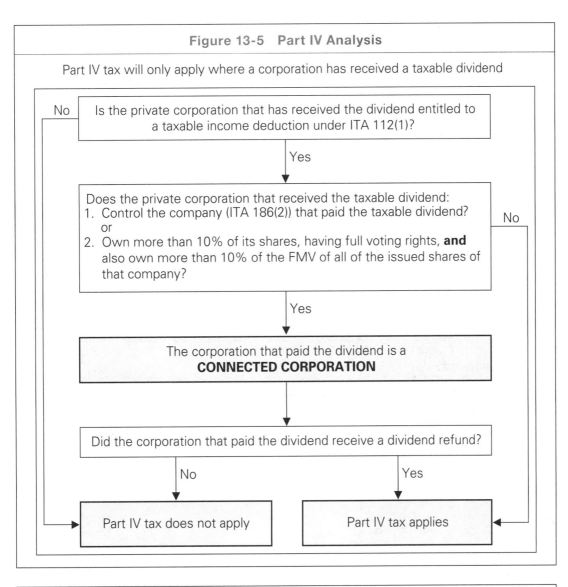

Figure 13-5   Part IV Analysis

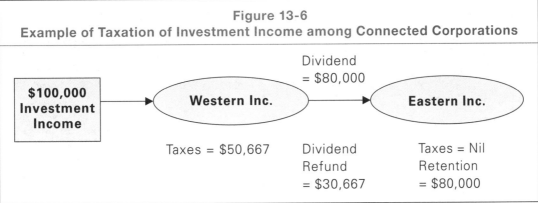

Figure 13-6
Example of Taxation of Investment Income among Connected Corporations

You will note that once the Part I refundable taxes are taken into consideration the remaining income tax is only 20% [50 2/3% - 30 2/3%]. This is reflected in the dividend that can be paid by Western to Eastern.

The taxable dividends received by Eastern will not result in any Part I tax as a result of the ITA 112(1) taxable income deduction. However, since Eastern and Western are connected corporations, the taxable dividends received are not considered portfolio dividends, meaning that Part IV tax will only apply to the extent that Western received a dividend refund for the year. Since Western was entitled to a dividend refund of $30,667, that same amount becomes a Part IV liability to Eastern. Had Eastern owned less than 100% of the shares its Part IV liability would have been equal to a proportion of Western's dividend refund based on the proportion of taxable dividends it received in the year. If, for example, Eastern owned 90% of the shares of Western and received 90% of the taxable dividends paid by Western, its Part IV liability would have been $27,600 [(90%)($30,667)].

The impact of this corporate structure is that the Part I refundable taxes of $30,667 are simply passed from one connected corporation to the other until taxable dividends are paid out to the individual shareholders of Eastern. In the example, Western incurs a high tax rate that includes $30,667 of refundable tax, and while it recovers that tax when it pays an $80,000 taxable dividend to Eastern, it is Eastern that becomes liable for that same amount.

Western has $100,000 in investment income and pays maximum dividends of $80,000 to Eastern. When the Part IV tax is taken into consideration, the tax consequences for the two companies are as follows:

Investment income received by Western	$100,000
Corporate tax at 50 2/3%	(50,667)
Income before dividends	$ 49,333
Dividend refund [($49,333 ÷ .61667) - $49,333]	**30,667**
Dividends paid to Eastern	$ 80,000
Taxable dividends received from Western	$ 80,000
Part IV tax payable by Western	**(30,667)**
Income retained by Eastern	$ 49,333

13-72. If Eastern decides to distribute the retained income to its individual shareholders, the results would be as follows:

Income retained by Eastern	$49,333
Dividend refund [($49,333 ÷ .61667) - $49,333]	**30,667**
Taxable dividend to individual shareholders	$80,000

Example #2—Connected Corporation Dividends

13-73. In many cases, a CCPC will be earning both investment income and active business income. This will result in a situation, unlike the previous example, where only some part of the dividends paid by the corporation will be eligible for a dividend refund and the remainder will not. In this type of situation, the Part IV tax will not be equal to 38 1/3% of taxable dividends received. The following example will clarify this point.

EXAMPLE Lower Ltd. declares and pays a taxable dividend of $45,000 to its shareholders. Lower Ltd. has only one class of shares. As a result of paying this dividend, the company receives a dividend refund equal to its RDTOH account balance at the end of the year of $9,000. Upper Inc. owns 60% of the outstanding shares of Lower Ltd. and receives $27,000 of the $45,000 of taxable dividends paid by Lower Ltd.

ANALYSIS In this case, the dividend refund would normally be $17,250 [(38 1/3%)($45,000)], however the refund is restricted to the RDTOH balance of the corporation at the end of its taxation year in which the taxable dividends were paid. Since the RDTOH account is only $9,000, that is the maximum refund for the year. If you follow the flowchart in Figure 13-5 in terms of Upper Inc., it has received a taxable dividend that is not subject to Part I tax because of the taxable income deduction of ITA 112(1).

Since Upper owns more than 50% of the voting shares and also meets the 10% shareholding test, the companies are connected. Finally, since Lower Ltd. received a dividend refund, Part IV tax applies to Upper Inc. to the extent of its 60% shareholding in Lower Ltd. Upper Inc.'s Part IV liability is therefore $5,400 [(60%)($9,000)].

Exercise 13-5

Subject: Part IV Tax

Opal Ltd., a CCPC, received the following amounts of dividends during its taxation year ending December 31, 2021:

Taxable dividends—Portfolio investments	$14,000
Taxable dividends from Emerald Inc. [(100%)($41,500)]	41,500
Taxable dividends from Ruby Inc. [(30%)($60,000)]	18,000

Opal Ltd. owns 100% of the voting shares of Emerald Inc. and 30% of the voting shares of Ruby Inc. The FMV of the Ruby Inc. shares owned by Opal Ltd. is equal to 30% of the FMV of all of the issued shares of Ruby Inc. As a result of paying the $60,000 taxable dividend, Ruby Inc. received a dividend refund of $15,000. Emerald Inc. did not receive any dividend refund in the year.

Determine the amount of Opal Ltd's. Part IV tax liability as a result of receiving these dividends.

Solutions to Exercises are available in the Study Guide.

Other Part IV Tax Considerations

13-74.   The preceding material has covered the fundamentals of Part IV tax where taxable dividends are received by private corporations. It is important to be aware of the intercorporate dividends that are not subject to Part IV tax. First, aside from certain foreign dividends, it is only taxable dividends paid by taxable Canadian corporations that are potentially subject to Part IV tax. This is because it is only these taxable dividends that entitle the private corporate recipient of the dividend to a taxable income deduction under ITA 112(1). In addition, the dividends must be taxable dividends and not tax-free capital dividends. Capital dividends are discussed in Chapter 14. Finally, taxable dividends paid by a connected corporation are only subject to Part IV tax if the corporation that paid the dividend was entitled to a dividend refund for the year in which it paid the dividend.

13-75.   A second point is that ITA 186(1)(c) and (d) allow a corporation to use 38 1/3% of loss carry overs that are non-capital losses and farm losses to reduce any Part IV tax. Non-capital and farm loss carry overs used in this manner reduce the loss balances that can then be applied to other years (ITA 111(3)(a)(ii)). If, for example, a CCPC had a Part IV liability of $9,200 and a non-capital loss balance from an earlier year of $60,000 it could eliminate the liability by claiming $24,000 of that non-capital loss. The Part IV reduction would be $9,200 [($24,000)(38 1/3%)]. The non-capital loss balance would be $36,000 [$60,000 - $24,000]. Since Part IV tax is refundable, this option is not recommended unless the non-capital loss or farm loss carry overs are on the verge of expiring.

Designation of Eligible Dividends

Basic Concepts

13-76.   We have previously discussed the importance of the distinction between eligible and non-eligible dividends. Eligible dividends are taxed to individuals at rates that are lower than rates that apply to non-eligible dividends. As a result, there is understandably a preference for eligible dividends among tax planners.

Designation of Eligible Dividends

13-77.   ITA 89(14) sets out the rules required to designate a taxable dividend as an eligible dividend. The provision requires that written notification be provided to every person or partnership to which a dividend is paid that the dividend or a portion of it is eligible. The notification must be made before or at the time the dividend is paid. Acceptable notification depends on whether a corporation is private or public but would include notification by letter, email, indication on a cheque stub, on a corporate website or shareholder publication. ITA 89(14.1) allows a late filed designation as long as it is made within three years from the date the dividend was paid and the minister of Revenue considers it just and equitable to allow the late designation.

13-78.   Eligible dividends are sourced to income of a corporation that has been subject to high corporate income tax rates whereas non-eligible dividends are sourced to income taxed at low tax rates. The two most important sources of income that are responsible for low tax rate income are income that has benefitted from the small business deduction and income that is subject to refundable Part I tax. Both types of low tax rate income are restricted to CCPCs. This is why taxable dividends paid by a CCPC are generally non-eligible dividends and why taxable dividends paid by other corporations (e.g., public corporations and private corporations that do not qualify as CCPCs) are generally paid as eligible dividends.

13-79.   We have previously pointed out that both types of dividends are essential parts of integration. Where a corporation pays a greater share of integrated income tax because its income is subject to high corporate tax rates, individuals will logically pay a smaller portion than would be the case were the income sourced to low corporate tax rates.

13-80.   These general observations establish a presumption that CCPCs pay non-eligible dividends and that other corporations pay eligible dividends. While this is generally true in practice there are situations where CCPCs can pay eligible dividends and situations where other corporations can pay non-eligible dividends. This reflects the fact that:

- some CCPCs may have a portion of their income taxed at full rates (e.g., active business income in excess of the annual business limit), and

- other corporations may have a portion of their income taxed at favourable rates (e.g., a CCPC that goes public with a retained earnings balance that contains amounts that benefitted from the small business deduction).

13-81.   To deal with the problem that runs contrary to the general presumption, a system is required to (1) track high rate income of a CCPC to determine whether they can pay eligible dividends and (2) track low rate income of other corporations to determine if the existence of low rate income compromises the ability to pay eligible dividends. In simplified terms, the system that has been developed is as follows:

CCPCs   To identify and track high rate income, CCPCs have a notional account referred to as a general rate income pool (GRIP). The balance in this account at the end of the taxation year of a CCPC represents the taxable dividends that can be designated as eligible dividends by that CCPC.

Other Corporations   While there are many specialty types of corporations recognized in the ITA, in general our discussion of other corporations will be restricted to public companies and private companies that are not CCPCs. As mentioned, the presumption is that these companies pay eligible dividends. However, to track components of their income that have been taxed at low rates, a notional account referred to as a low rate income pool (LRIP) is used. These other corporations are not permitted to pay eligible dividends until the LRIP balance is reduced to nil. Note that there is a timing difference between the GRIP and the LRIP. CCPCs are permitted to pay eligible dividends based on the GRIP balance on the last day of their taxation year. Other corporations, however, must determine the LRIP immediately prior to an actual dividend payment, which can occur at any time in the year.

CCPCs—The General Rate Income Pool (GRIP)—ITA 89(1)

13-82.   The GRIP is a notional account specifically designed to track amounts of a CCPC's income that qualify as a basis for paying eligible dividends. The GRIP is unique to a CCPC. As noted, the default treatment for taxable dividends paid by a CCPC is to treat them as non-eligible. However, to the extent that there is a balance in the GRIP account at the end of the year dividends can be designated as eligible.

13-83.   The GRIP is defined in ITA 89(1). It is a complex and lengthy definition that consists of numerous components, some of which are common and some not so common. For example there are components that relate to the impact of amalgamations, wind-ups, and situations where other corporations become CCPCs. The application of these latter components go beyond the scope of this text, however, and will be given no further consideration in any of our material. We have therefore modified the GRIP for our purposes to the following formula that is representative of the major GRIP components used in practice. This modified GRIP is presented at the front of this text in "Rates, Credits, and Other Data":

$$\textbf{GRIP = C + D + E - G}, \text{ where}$$

C   is the CCPC's GRIP at the end of the preceding taxation year.

D   is 72% of the CCPC's adjusted taxable income for the year.
   Adjusted taxable income equals taxable income reduced by the amount on which the small business deduction is based and the lesser of the CCPC's aggregate investment income and its taxable income for the year.

E   is the amount of eligible dividends received by the CCPC during the year.

G   is the amount of eligible dividends paid during the **preceding** year less the amount of any excessive eligible dividend designation (EEDD) made during the preceding year.

13-84.   Several comments on this formula are relevant at this point:

- The D component calculates a taxable income that is adjusted to remove income that has been subject to low corporate income tax rates. As dividends are paid out of after-tax funds, the residual income is multiplied by 72%, reflecting a notional federal/provincial tax rate of 28%. That rate is representative of high tax rate income which, in 2021, ranges from 23% in Alberta to 31% in Prince Edward Island.

- If a CCPC receives eligible dividends, the addition in E allows these dividends to retain that status.

- Note that the balance is reduced not by eligible dividends paid in the current year but by eligible dividends paid in the preceding year. The purpose of the one-year time lag is to determine what can be designated or paid out as eligible dividends for a given year, which is based on the year-end balance before deducting what can be designated for that year.

13-85.   A simple example will illustrate these provisions.

EXAMPLE   Norgrave Ltd., a CCPC, had a nil GRIP balance at the end of 2019. During 2020, the company received eligible dividends of $46,600 and designated $25,000 of its dividends paid as eligible. At the end of 2020, Norgrave has a GRIP of $46,600.

For 2021, Norgrave has taxable income of $225,000. This amount includes aggregate investment income of $55,000. In addition, the company receives eligible dividends during the year of $50,000.

In determining 2021 tax payable, the company has a small business deduction of $28,500 [(19%)($150,000)]. During 2021, Norgrave pays dividends of $40,000, with $23,000 of this amount being designated as eligible.

ANALYSIS   The 2021 ending balance in GRIP will be calculated as follows:

C—GRIP balance at end of 2020		$ 46,600
D—Taxable income	$ 225,000	
Amount eligible for the small business deduction	(150,000)	
Aggregate investment income (less than taxable income)	(55,000)	
Adjusted taxable income	$ 20,000	
Rate	72%	14,400
E—Eligible dividends received		50,000
G—Eligible dividends paid in 2020		(25,000)
GRIP at end of 2021		$ 86,000

The eligible dividends of $23,000 paid during 2021 will be deducted from the GRIP in 2022.

Exercise 13-6

Subject: GRIP Balance

Lanson Inc., a CCPC, had a GRIP balance of nil at the end of its taxation year ending December 31, 2019. During 2020, the company received eligible dividends of $35,000 and designated all of its $25,000 in taxable dividends paid as eligible. At the end of 2020, Lanson has a GRIP of $35,000.

For 2021, Lanson has taxable income of $960,000. This amount includes net taxable capital gains of $65,000, mortgage interest received of $23,000, and a 2019 net capital loss deduction of $14,000. In addition, the company receives eligible dividends during the year of $85,000. In determining 2021 tax payable, the company has a small business deduction of $42,750. During 2021, Lanson pays taxable dividends of $78,000, with $42,000 of this amount being designated as eligible. Determine the company's GRIP balance at the end of 2021.

Solutions to Exercises are available in the Study Guide.

Other Corporations—The Low Rate Income Pool (LRIP)—ITA 89(1)

13-86.   For corporations other than CCPCs (other corporations), income will generally be subject to high corporate tax rates. This means that, in general, dividends can be designated as eligible. However, in some situations these other corporations may have amounts of income that were subject to low corporate tax rates. This could include amounts of income retained by a CCPC before it became a public company, an amalgamation of a CCPC with a private company that does not qualify as a CCPC, as well as non-eligible dividends received as a result of investments in CCPCs.

13-87.   Such balances will be allocated to a notional account referred to as an LRIP. An LRIP is unique to corporations that are not CCPCs. This account, defined in ITA 89(1), is similar to the GRIP account in that it is used to track certain types of income. However, the two accounts serve different purposes:

- The GRIP account is used to track balances that can be used by a CCPC as the basis for the designation of eligible dividends. To the extent that there is a positive GRIP balance, dividends can be designated as eligible up to that amount. Note, however, that designation is at the discretion of the corporation. It is also important to recognize that eligible dividends can only be paid to residents of Canada by corporations that are also resident.

- The LRIP account is used to track balances that have been subject to low corporate tax rates. When there is a positive LRIP balance, any dividends paid by the corporation will be first considered non-eligible up to that positive balance. Stated alternatively, a corporation with a positive LRIP balance cannot designate any of its dividends as eligible until the LRIP balance is reduced to nil. This treatment is automatic with the corporation having no discretion.

13-88.   Unlike the GRIP, which is determined at the end of a taxation year of a CCPC, an LRIP is determined at a point in time that is usually determined immediately before a dividend is paid. In addition, the GRIP is increased by eligible dividends received and reduced by eligible dividends paid. An LRIP on the other hand is increased by non-eligible dividends that became payable to it and reduced by non-eligible dividends that became payable by it. The reference to "became payable" refers to the declaration of dividends irrespective of when they were received or paid. An LRIP is defined by a formula in ITA 89(1). We have shortened the LRIP formula for presentation purposes to focus on the main components. Specifically, components C, D, E, and F have been removed since they relate to specific situations, such as corporate reorganizations and complex adjustments for previous years in which the corporation was at one time a CCPC, investment company, or credit union. The modified formula is as follows:

(A + B) - (G + H), where

A   is the corporation's LRIP at the end of the preceding year.

B   is the amount of non-eligible dividends that became payable in the year from a corporation resident in Canada.

G   is the amount of non-eligible dividends that became payable by the corporation during the year.

H   is the amount of any EEDD made by the corporation during the year.

13-89.   A simple example will serve to illustrate this definition.

EXAMPLE   At the end of 2020, Ovamp Ltd. has an LRIP balance of $450,000. During 2021, the company receives non-eligible dividends from a CCPC in the amount of $225,000. During 2021, and after the receipt of the non-eligible dividends, the company pays dividends of $360,000.

ANALYSIS   Prior to the taxable dividend payment of $360,000 the corporation's LRIP balance was $675,000. As a result, none of the dividends of $360,000 can be designated as eligible. Instead they are treated as non-eligible dividends. Subsequent to that time the LRIP balance would be reduced to $315,000 [$675,000 - $360,000]. Note that the $225,000 non-eligible dividend increases the LRIP as soon as it is declared.

Part III.1 Tax—Excessive Eligible Dividend Designations (EEDD)—ITA 185.1

13-90.   A corporation, whether a CCPC or other resident corporation, can designate a taxable dividend as an eligible divided at any time. The consequences to the recipient, whether a resident individual or another resident corporation, are very favourable in terms of lower income tax rates than would be the case if the dividends were non-eligible. This raises the possibility, however, that a CCPC may have designated a dividend as eligible that exceeds its GRIP balance at year end or that other corporations have done the same when there was a positive LRIP balance at the time. These situations can arise unintentionally through errors or oversights or could be intentional. The legislation does not alter the circumstances to the recipient, meaning that the dividends remain eligible dividends to them. In any event, the effective overdesignation as eligible dividends means that the federal government would have lost tax revenues as a direct result. Part III.1 was added as a special tax to either penalize the corporations that have made excess eligible dividend designations (EEDD) or to provide a mechanism to restore the correct result.

13-91.   If the EEDD is unintentional or inadvertent, the Part III.1 tax is charged to the corporation that made the designation equal to 20% of the excessive designated amount. In these circumstances, Part III.1 provides for an elective option that will allow the corporation to avoid the 20% penalty if the excess designation is effectively reversed.

13-92.   If the CRA concludes that the EEDD was intentional and reflects an attempt to artificially manipulate either a GRIP or an LRIP account, the Part III.1 penalty tax increases to 30%. In addition, there are two other consequences:

- The penalty tax applies to the entire dividend, not just the excess or EEDD.
- No election is available to reverse the effect of the excessive designation.

13-93.   In order to appropriately track all dividend payments, any resident Canadian corporation that pays a taxable dividend (whether eligible or non-eligible) is required to file a return for the year under ITA 185.2 of Part III.1. The required return is the completion of Schedule 55 of the T2 corporate income tax return. Failure to file Schedule 55 is treated as the failure to file a return with penalties and interest being charged.

13-94.   ITA 89(1) defines EEDD differently for CCPCs as opposed to other resident corporations. These definitions will be considered separately in the following material.

EEDD for a CCPC

13-95.   If a CCPC designates an amount of eligible dividends that is in excess of its GRIP at the end of the year, it will be considered an EEDD and be subject to Part III.1 tax.

> **EXAMPLE**   At its December 31, 2020, year end, Sandem Inc., a CCPC, has a GRIP of $45,000. It paid no eligible dividends in 2020. During 2021, the company pays dividends of $100,000, of which $60,000 are designated as eligible. There are no additions to the company's GRIP during 2021.

> **ANALYSIS**   The company has an EEDD of $15,000 ($60,000 - $45,000). Provided the CRA believes that this was not intentional and was inadvertent, this amount will be subject to a Part III.1 tax of 20% on the excess of $15,000. There is also the possibility of electing to have the EEDD treated as a non-eligible dividend.

> If the CRA concludes that the EEDD was a deliberate attempt to manipulate the company's GRIP, a 30% penalty tax is charged. In addition, the 30% tax would be charged on the entire eligible amount of $60,000, not just the $15,000 EEDD amount. No elective option would be available to reverse the excessive election. We would add that the elective option is only available for a 30-month period and all of the shareholders of the corporation entitled to receive a portion of that eligible dividend must agree to effectively convert the excess portion of the eligible dividends to non-eligible dividends as if there had been no EEDD. This means that individual shareholders would be liable for additional income taxes together with interest on the additional amount owing.

EEDD for Other Corporations

13-96.   In somewhat simplified terms, an EEDD for a resident corporation that is not a CCPC is equal to the lesser of its eligible dividends paid and its LRIP at the time the dividend is paid. For example, if a non-CCPC paid an eligible dividend of $50,000 at a point in time that its LRIP was equal to $40,000, the EEDD would be $40,000. Note that, unlike the situation with EEDDs for CCPCs, where the amount is based on the end of year balance of the GRIP the EEDD for other corporations is based on the balance of the LRIP at the point in time when the eligible dividend is paid.

13-97.   A simple example will illustrate these provisions.

> **EXAMPLE**   Victor Ltd., a Canadian public company, receives $42,000 in non-eligible dividends from a CCPC on June 15, 2021. Its LRIP balance at the end of the preceding year is nil and no adjustments had been made to the account prior to the 2021 receipt of the non-eligible dividend. On September 23, 2021, Victor Ltd. pays taxable dividends of $100,000, with $30,000 of this amount being designated as eligible.

ANALYSIS As at September 23, 2021, the balance in the LRIP would be $42,000. The lesser of this amount and the eligible dividend would be $30,000 and this would be the amount of the EEDD.

This result seems somewhat counterintuitive in that a non-eligible dividend was paid in an amount sufficient to eliminate the LRIP. However, the legislation is clear that the LRIP is measured at a particular point in time and, if an eligible dividend is paid when there is a positive balance in this account, it creates an EEDD. We would note that this situation could have been avoided had the non-eligible dividend been paid before, even by one day, the payment of the eligible dividend. This situation can occur since an eligible dividend can represent part of a taxable dividend. As a result, the $100,000 taxable dividend would represent a $70,000 non-eligible dividend (because it was not designated as eligible) and an eligible dividend of $30,000.

Provided there were no further dividend transactions, the LRIP balance at the end of the year would be nil as the payment of $70,000 in non-eligible dividends would have eliminated the $42,000 balance created by the non-eligible dividends received. You may have wondered why a Canadian public company paid such a high non-eligible dividend when it appears to be under no obligation to do so. A major reason is because eligible dividends cannot be paid to non-resident shareholders. This means that any such taxable dividends would be non-eligible.

With respect to the Part III.1 tax, a tax of 20% would normally be charged on the EEDD of $30,000. However, if the CRA concludes that a deliberate attempt to manipulate the LRIP was involved, the tax rate would increase to 30%.

A Final Word on Eligible Dividends

13-98.   You should be aware that the preceding represents an overview of the provisions related to eligible dividends and their designation. The complete legislation is far more complex, dealing with a number of transitional situations, changes in a corporation's classification, as well as problems associated with corporate reorganizations. However, we feel that this version of the material is appropriate for an introductory level text in corporate taxation and provides a practical overview.

Refundable Dividend Tax on Hand (RDTOH)—ITA 129(4)

Overview—Part I and IV

13-99.   Throughout this chapter we have discussed two different types of refundable income taxes that are assessed on corporate investment income. The purpose of these refundable taxes is to discourage individuals from using private corporations to hold personal investments with the objective of subjecting the investment income to low corporate tax rates as opposed to the individual's high income tax rates. The two refundable taxes together ensure that the corporate tax rates will generally exceed that of the highest rates that apply to individuals, effectively neutralizing any income tax advantage. We can summarize the two taxes as follows:

Part I Refundable   Part I refundable taxes add 30 2/3%, resulting in a federal income tax rate of 38 2/3% (basic rate of 38% - 10% federal abatement + 10 2/3% ART). The tax applies as follows:

- Applies to aggregate investment income (Canadian or foreign sourced), which includes net taxable capital gains
- Excludes taxable dividends that entitle the corporate recipient to a taxable income deduction under ITA 112(1)
- Applies to CCPCs only

Part IV   38 1/3% is assessed as follows:

- Applies to the receipt of taxable dividends that are excluded from Part I refundable taxes
- Applies where taxable dividends represent portfolio dividends and to taxable dividends received from connected corporations but only if the connected corporate dividend payer received a dividend refund for that year
- Applies to CCPCs, private corporations that are not CCPCs, and closely held public corporations (e.g., subject corporations)

13-100.   At Paragraph 13-6 we discussed a four-step approach to dealing with the taxation of corporate investment income that comes full circle when the refundable tax is eventually refunded when taxable dividend distributions have been made to individuals. This process can be summarized as follows:

(1) Identify the Relevant Investment Income   We have seen that refundable taxes, as a rule, only apply to private corporations, whether CCPCs or not. It is important to identify the income that is investment income. In Chapter 12, in our discussion of the small business deduction and active business income, we saw that incidental investment income and investment income earned by an associated corporation in support of an active business (ITA 129(6)) were deemed not to be investment (i.e., property) income but instead were active business income. In addition, what appears to be investment income can be categorized as business income if the corporate activity of earning that income is extensive, such as a corporate business of lending money in which interest is earned.

(2) Apply Part I and IV Taxes   Once the relevant investment income has been identified, the refundable taxes under both Part I and IV can be determined.

(3) Track the Refundable Taxes (RDTOH)   Once refundable taxes under Part I and IV have been calculated a tracking mechanism is required to determine the dollar amount available to be refunded. Both refundable taxes are added to an account called a refundable dividend tax on hand account, or RDTOH. As will be discussed in this chapter, for corporate calendar-based taxation years starting from January 1, 2019, there are two separate RDTOH accounts—one for eligible dividends and one for non-eligible dividends.

(4) Determine the Dividend Refund for a Private Corporation   In our discussion of integration we saw that the refundable taxes are returned to a private corporation once the corporation pays a taxable dividend to its shareholders. If the taxable dividend is paid to a corporate shareholder that is a connected corporation the dividend-paying corporation may recover part or all of its RDTOH but the amount refunded to it may simply become a Part IV liability of any corporate shareholder that received the taxable dividend. It is only when a private corporation pays a taxable dividend to individual shareholders that the integration circle is complete.

At this point we have covered the first two steps. In this section we will complete our coverage with a discussion of steps three and four that relate to the two RDTOH accounts and the dividend refund mechanism when taxable dividends are paid by a private corporation with RDTOH account balances.

Understanding the New RDTOH System

13-101.   The 2018 federal budget introduced a change to the longstanding RDTOH concept, which was to take effect for taxation years of private corporations that began after 2018. This meant that if a private corporation, for example, had a December 31 fiscal year end, the first taxation year of the new rules would be the taxation year of January 1, 2019, to December 31, 2019. In this text our focus is on the 2021 taxation year, which would be the third year of this new RDTOH system for such private corporations. As a result, we will no longer cover the pre-2019 system.

13-102.   In brief, the change to the RDTOH resulted in taking the account and splitting it into two accounts that we will refer to as the "eligible RDTOH" and the "non-eligible RDTOH." The reason for the change can be explained as an integration mismatch that can best be illustrated with the help of the following examples.

EXAMPLE 1   A CCPC, whose shares are all owned by an individual, earns $100,000 in aggregate investment income. the CCPC has no other income. Refundable Part I tax equals $30,667 [(30 2/3%)($100,000)]. The CCPC pays a taxable dividend of $80,000, which is sufficient to refund all the refundable Part I tax [($80,000)(30 2/3%) = $30,667].

ANALYSIS 1   The CCPC is only taxed at a low rate of federal tax of 8% [38 2/3% tax on investment income-refund of 30 2/3%] on aggregate investment income. Since the income that supported the taxable dividend was sourced from low rate corporate income, integration requires that the dividend be treated as a non-eligible dividend to the individual shareholder. Integration has worked properly.

EXAMPLE 2   A private corporation, whose shares are all owned by an individual, earns $100,000 in taxable eligible dividends on portfolio investments paid by public corporations. The private corporation has no other income. Refundable Part IV tax equals $38,333 [(38 1/3%)($100,000)]. The CCPC pays a taxable dividend of $100,000, which is sufficient to refund all the refundable tax.

ANALYSIS 2   The taxable dividends received by the private corporation were initially taxed at high corporate rates when the income was earned by the public corporation. Since the income that supported the taxable dividend paid by the private corporation to its individual shareholder was sourced from high rate corporate income, integration requires that the dividend be treated as an eligible dividend to the individual shareholder. This would be identical to the treatment to the individual had the public corporation investments been personally owned. Integration has again worked as intended.

EXAMPLE 3   A CCPC, whose shares are all owned by an individual, earns $100,000 in aggregate investment income and $611,111 in active business income. The CCPC has never been associated with any other corporation. Refundable Part I tax equals $30,667 [(30 2/3%)($100,000)]. The CCPC pays a taxable dividend of $80,000, which is sufficient to refund all the refundable Part I tax [(38 1/3%)($80,000) = $30,667].

ANALYSIS 3   Under the current system a private corporation would be unable to designate an eligible dividend unless the corporation has an eligible RDTOH, which means an RDTOH account with eligible dividend components such as Part IV tax. In Example 1 the CCPC would have a non-eligible RDTOH (Part I refundable tax), whereas in Example 2 the private corporation would have an eligible RDTOH (Part IV tax). In Example 3 there would only be a non-eligible RDTOH.

In Example 3 the current system does not change the fact that the CCPC designated an eligible dividend to its individual shareholder, but the corporation cannot receive a dividend refund with respect to the payment of that dividend because there is no eligible RDTOH. If the CCPC decided not to designate the taxable dividend as eligible then the individual would receive a non-eligible dividend and the CCPC would be allowed a dividend refund of $30,667. In this latter situation the integration concept has been restored.

Practical Consideration   The most significant impact is that a CCPC with active business income above its business limit and aggregate investment income with Part I refundable tax will have the ability to designate eligible dividends because of the existence of a GRIP account but will be unable to receive a dividend refund. The preferable alternative is to pay non-eligible dividends and to recover the Part I refundable tax as a dividend refund.

13-103.   When the current system of two RDTOH accounts was first introduced a transitional rule was added to split the existing single RDTOH into two components based on the balance in the GRIP account at that time. Given that 2021 is now the third year of the current RDTOH system we will not provide any discussion of the transitional rule. With respect to the GRIP, it is important to keep in mind that, aside from the transitional rule, the GRIP is not relevant to the determination of the two new RDTOH accounts.

13-104.   We will now turn our attention to the details concerning the calculations of the Part I refundable tax, the eligible and non-eligible RDTOH accounts, and the application of the dividend refund mechanism.

Refundable Part I Tax Payable—ITA 129(4) "Non-Eligible RDTOH"

Basic Formula

13-105.   To this point we have stated that the Part I refundable tax is equal to 30 2/3% of aggregate investment income. However, as we have seen in other corporate tax calculations such as the small business deduction (Chapter 12), the base of many corporate tax calculations are not always straightforward. The cause is typically taxable income deductions, such as donations and loss carry overs, as well as the existence of foreign sourced income. These factors may impact taxable income and tax payable in general, resulting in situations where not all of the aggregate investment income may actually flow through to taxable income and be subject to corporate tax. As a result, the amount that is added to the non-refundable RDTOH account may be less than 30 2/3% of aggregate investment income. Given this, it is necessary to take the amounts of taxable income and tax payable into consideration when determining the refundable portion of Part I tax. The calculations are set out in the definition of "non-eligible RDTOH" in ITA 129(4). This definition places constraints on the refundable amount by indicating that it will be the least of the following:

- ITA 129(4)(a)(i)   An amount based on aggregate investment income
- ITA 129(4)(a)(ii)   An amount based on taxable income
- ITA 129(4)(a)(iii)   An amount based on Part I tax payable

13-106.   We will give detailed attention to each of these constraints in the paragraphs that follow.

Investment Income Constraint—ITA 129(4)(a)(i)

13-107.   The basic amount of Part I tax that should be considered refundable is the amount of aggregate investment income for the year:

ITA 129(4)(a)(i)   the amount determined by the formula

$$A - B, \text{ where}$$

A   is 30 2/3% of the corporation's aggregate investment income for the year, and

B   is the amount, if any, by which the foreign non-business income tax credit (ITA 126(1)) exceeds 8% of its foreign investment income for the year.

13-108.   Aggregate investment income is as defined in ITA 129(4) and is the sum of:

- net taxable capital gains (taxable capital gains minus allowable capital losses) for the year reduced by any net capital losses deducted during the year; and

- income from property (e.g., interest, royalties, rents) reduced by any losses from property. Taxable dividends that are deductible in computing the corporation's taxable income are excluded but are potentially subject to Part IV tax.

13-109.   If the corporation has no foreign source investment income, the ITA 129(4)(a)(i) amount is simply 30 2/3% of aggregate investment income. With respect to foreign non-business income, the underlying assumption that the Canadian tax rate on this foreign income is 38 2/3% (38% - 10% + 10 2/3%). Reflecting this assumption, the B component in the

ITA 129(4)(a)(i) formula subtracts any amount of foreign tax credit that is in excess of 8% of foreign investment income for the year.

13-110.   The basic idea here is that a foreign tax credit of 8% will reduce the Part I taxes to 30 2/3% (38 2/3% - 8% = 30 2/3%), the rate applicable to the refund. If the foreign tax credit exceeds 8% of the foreign investment income, the Canadian taxes paid would be less than the potential refund of 30 2/3%. In other words, without the 8% subtraction, the Canadian government would be providing a refund that is larger than the amount of Canadian tax paid on the foreign investment income.

EXAMPLE   A CCPC earns $50,000 in foreign investment income. Income and profits tax of 15% is paid in the foreign jurisdiction and, as a consequence, the company receives a foreign non-business tax credit of $7,500 [(15%)($50,000)].

ANALYSIS   At the assumed rate of 38 2/3%, Part I tax on this income would be $11,834 [(38 2/3%)($50,000) - $7,500]. This results in a Canadian income tax rate on this income of only 23 2/3% ($11,834 ÷ $50,000). Without some type of adjustment, the refundable taxes on this $50,000 of income would be at a rate of 30 2/3% and would equal $15,334 [(30 2/3%)($50,000)], $3,500 more than the $11,834 in Canadian Part I taxes that would be paid. This is clearly not appropriate.

To correct this situation, the excess of the foreign non-business income tax credit over 8% of the foreign investment income is subtracted from the 30 2/3% refund on the foreign investment income.

In our example, the calculations would be as follows:

30 2/3% of foreign investment income		$15,334
Deduct excess of:		
Foreign non-business tax credit	($7,500)	
Over 8% of foreign investment income		
[(8%)($50,000)]	4,000	(3,500)
ITA 129(4)(a)(i)		**$11,834**

The calculation adjustment has, in effect, reduced the amount of the refund to $11,834. As calculated at the beginning of this analysis, this is equal to the notional amount of Canadian Part I taxes paid on the foreign investment income.

Taxable Income Constraint—ITA 129(4)(a)(ii)

13-111.   The purpose of this taxable income constraint is to isolate the portion of taxable income that relates to aggregate investment income. In other words, the concern is how much of the aggregate investment income has made it through to taxable income where it is then subject to the 38 2/3% federal corporate tax rate. The calculations begin with taxable income then remove certain amounts, leaving a figure that represents the aggregate investment income that is actually subject to income tax. The determined amount may be less than aggregate investment income for the year where taxable income deductions, such as those for donations and non-capital loss carry overs, have been deducted. The design of the calculation is that taxable income deductions are effectively applied against other types of income before being applied against aggregate investment income.

This particular constraint is calculated as follows:

ITA 129(4)(a)(ii)   30 2/3% of the amount, if any, by which the corporation's taxable income for the year exceeds the total of:

A   the amount eligible for the small business deduction;
B   (100 ÷ 382/3) of the tax credit for foreign non-business income (ITA 126(1)); and
C   4 times the tax credit for foreign business income (ITA 126(2)).

13-112.   Component B is designed to remove foreign investment income that has not been subject to Part I tax because of the foreign non-business tax credit . The elimination is based on the assumption that it is taxed at a notional rate of 38 2/3% (38 2/3 ÷ 100). In similar fashion, component C is designed to remove foreign business income that is not taxed because of the foreign business income tax credit. The elimination here is based on the assumption that this type of income is taxed at a notional rate of 25%. The factor of 4 in component C is actually the result of a more complex calculation. See Chapter 12 for details of this calculation explained in the context of the small business deduction formula.

Part I Tax Payable Constraint—ITA 129(4)(a)(iii)

13-113.   A final constraint is based on Part I tax payable. A corporation may have reduced its Part I tax by certain tax credits, such as investment tax credits, foreign tax credits, or credits for scientific research and experimental development. To deal with this issue, the refundable portion of Part I tax is limited as follows:

ITA 129(4)(a)(iii)   The corporation's federal Part I tax payable for the year

Formula for Part I Tax Addition to RDTOH

13-114.   To summarize, the addition to the RDTOH for Part I tax (also available in the front of this text under "Rates, Credits, and Other Data") is the least of:

ITA 129(4)(a)(i)   30 2/3% of aggregate investment income reduced by the excess, if any, of foreign non-business income tax credits over 8% of foreign investment income. Note that our references to foreign investment income and foreign non-business income are the same.

ITA 129(4)(a)(ii)   30 2/3% of the amount, if any, by which taxable income exceeds the sum of:

- the amount eligible for the small business deduction,
- (100 ÷ 38 2/3) of the foreign non-business tax credit (ITA 126(1)), and
- 4 times the foreign business tax credit (ITA 126(2)).

ITA 129(4)(a)(iii)   Part I tax payable.

Exercise 13-7

Subject: Refundable Part I Tax

Debut Inc. is a CCPC. During the taxation year ending December 31, 2021, Debut Inc. has the following amounts of property income:

Taxable dividends from portfolio investments	$22,000
Foreign non-business income (5% foreign income tax was paid)	15,000
Taxable capital gains	19,125
Rental income	6,500
Interest income on a 10-year bond	9,200

The company's net income is $121,825. The only deductions in the calculation of taxable income are the taxable dividends on portfolio investments and a 2017 net capital loss balance of $9,000. A $9,500 small business deduction was calculated on $50,000 of active business income and a foreign non-business income tax credit of $750 served to reduce Part I tax payable. Assume that the company's Part I tax payable has been correctly calculated as $19,536. Determine the refundable amount of Part I tax for 2021.

Solutions to Exercises are available in the Study Guide.

Eligible and Non-Eligible RDTOH Accounts—ITA 129(4)

Dividend Refund Basics

13-115.   Before discussing the two RDTOH accounts there are a few basic principles to be aware of with respect to dividend refunds:

- No dividend refund can be obtained when paying eligible dividends unless there is an eligible RDTOH balance at the end of the taxation year.

- When paying non-eligible dividends a dividend refund may be obtained from both the non-eligible and eligible RDTOH account balances at the end of the taxation year. However, there is an ordering rule that requires that the non-eligible RDTOH account be accessed first with any remaining refund (once the non-eligible RDTOH has been reduced to nil) drawn from the eligible RDTOH account. This means that a corporation paying non-eligible dividends may have a dividend refund from both RDTOH accounts.

Eligible RDTOH Defined

13-116.   An Eligible RDTOH account balance at the end of a taxation year is defined at ITA 129(4). The definition is as follows:

BEGINNING BALANCE   For 2021 and subsequent years, the calculation begins with the balance in the eligible RDTOH at the end of the previous taxation year.

ADDITIONS   The following two amounts are added:

- Part IV taxes paid on eligible dividends that are portfolio dividends.

- Part IV taxes paid on eligible and non-eligible dividends from connected corporations to the extent that the dividend-paying corporation received a refund for the year from the paying corporation's eligible RDTOH. Note that a corporation can draw from its eligible RDTOH account when it pays a non-eligible dividend. See the second bullet of Paragraph 13-115.

DEDUCTION   Subtract any dividend refund claimed from the eligible RDTOH account in the previous taxation year.

Non-Eligible RDTOH Defined

13-117.   A non-eligible RDTOH account balance at the end of a taxation year is also defined at ITA 129(4) as follows:

BEGINNING BALANCE   For 2021 and subsequent years, the calculation would begin with the balance in the non-eligible RDTOH at the end of the previous taxation year.

ADDITIONS   There are amounts that are added to the non-eligible RDTOH account:

- The refundable Part I tax for the year, determined as per the calculations discussed beginning at Paragraph 13-105.

- Part IV taxes paid on non-eligible dividends that are portfolio dividends. This situation would be unusual.

- Part IV taxes paid on non-eligible dividends that are from connected corporations to the extent that such dividends included a refund from the paying corporation's non-eligible RDTOH.

DEDUCTION   Deducted from this total would be any dividend refund claimed from the non-eligible RDTOH account in the previous taxation year.

13-118.   A practical complication arises when non-eligible dividends are paid by a connected corporation with dividend refunds drawn from both eligible and non-eligible RDTOH accounts. This information would have to be communicated to the corporate recipient of the dividend in order for that company to accurately determine its own RDTOH accounts.

The Dividend Refund

Dividend Refund on Eligible Dividends—ITA 129(1)

13-119. When a CCPC pays taxable dividends in a taxation year, an amount can be designated as an eligible dividend to the extent there is a balance in the corporation's GRIP account. The refund on these eligible dividends will then be the lesser of:

- 38 1/3% of the total of all eligible dividends paid by it in the year; or
- its eligible RDTOH balance at the end of the year.

13-120. A simple example will serve to illustrate the calculations.

> **EXAMPLE** Divor Ltd. is a CCPC with a December 31 year end. On December 31, 2020, the corporation has an eligible RDTOH balance of $30,000 and a non-eligible RDTOH balance of $75,000. The company did not pay any taxable dividends in 2020. At the end of its 2021 taxation year the company has a GRIP balance of $100,000. During 2021, the corporation pays taxable dividends of $70,000, all of which are designated as eligible.

> **ANALYSIS** As the GRIP balance is $100,000, there are no issues with designating all of the $70,000 as eligible dividends. The dividend refund is equal to the lesser of:

> - $26,833 [(38 1/3%)($70,000)]; or
> - $30,000, the balance in the eligible RDTOH account at the end of 2021.

> The lesser amount would be $26,833, leaving $3,167 ($30,000 - $26,833) in the eligible RDTOH account after the dividend refund has been subtracted in 2022. There would also be a $30,000 ($100,000 - $70,000) balance in the GRIP account after the 2021 eligible dividends paid have been subtracted in 2022.

Dividend Refund on Non-Eligible Dividends—ITA 129(1)

13-121. If the amount of taxable dividends paid during the year exceeds the amount that is designated as eligible, the excess will be a non-eligible dividend. The dividend refund consists of two components—one to access the eligible RDTOH and the second to access the non-eligible RDTOH. As mentioned in Paragraph 13-115, eligible dividends can only create a dividend refund if there is a positive eligible RDTOH balance at year end. However, a non-eligible dividend can create a dividend refund with both the non-eligible and eligible RDTOH accounts as long as there are positive balances in the accounts at year end.

> **Component 1** The lesser of:

> - 38 1/3% of the total of all non-eligible dividends paid in the year; or
> - the non-eligible RDTOH balance at year end.

> **Component 2** If 38 1/3% of the non-eligible dividends paid in the year exceeds the balance in the non-eligible RDTOH, this component 2 is the lesser of:

> - the amount of the excess; or
> - any balance that remains in the eligible RDTOH after subtracting the dividend refund for the year on eligible dividends.

> If there is no excess, the second component is nil.

13-122. The following example illustrates these calculations.

> **EXAMPLE** At the end of 2021, the balance in the eligible RDTOH is $115,000, the balance in the non-eligible RDTOH is $76,667, and the GRIP balance is $115,000.

> During 2021, the company paid taxable dividends of $500,000, with $300,000 of this amount being designated as eligible and $200,000 non-eligible.

> **ANALYSIS** The dividend refund on the $300,000 of eligible dividends is $115,000. This is equal to 38 1/3% of the $300,000 of eligible dividends paid and the balance in the eligible RDTOH.

The dividend refund on the non-eligible dividends is $76,667. This is equal to 38 1/3% of the $200,000 ($500,000 - $300,000) of non-eligible dividends paid and the balance in the non-eligible RDTOH. As there is no excess of 38 1/3% of the non-eligible dividends paid over the end of year balance in the non-eligible RDTOH, component 2 is equal to nil.

Exercise 13-8

Subject: Dividend Refund

Alesia Ltd. is a CCPC with a taxation year that ends on December 31. On December 31, 2020, the balance in the eligible RDTOH was $134,167, the balance in the GRIP account was $350,000, and the balance in the non-eligible RDTOH was $95,833.

During the year ending December 31, 2021, there were no additions to either RDTOH account or to the GRIP balance. During that year, the corporation paid dividends of $600,000. Only $200,000 of these dividends were designated as eligible and the remaining $400,000 were paid as non-eligible dividends.

Determine the amount of the dividend refund on the payment of (1) the eligible dividends and (2) the non-eligible dividends.

Solutions to Exercises are available in the Study Guide.

We suggest you complete SSP 13-2, 13-3, 13-4, and 13-5 at this point.

Economic Impact of Changes

The Impact Illustrated

13-123.   We will use an example to illustrate the economic impact of these changes.

EXAMPLE   The following information relates to Sarco Inc., a CCPC with a December 31 year end:

- December 31, 2021, GRIP $1,000,000
- December 31, 2021, Eligible RDTOH   76,667
- December 31, 2021, Non-eligible RDTOH   306,667

The combined RDTOH is $383,334 ($76,667 + $306,667). To recover the full amount of refundable taxes that have been paid, a dividend of $1,000,000 must be paid ($383,334 ÷ 38 1/3%). Determine the tax consequences related to each of the following alternatives:

Alternative 1   Sarco pays a taxable eligible dividend of $1,000,000. Non-eligible dividends would be nil.

Alternative 2   Sarco pays a taxable non-eligible dividend of $1,000,000. Eligible dividends would be nil.

Alternative 3   Sarco pays a taxable eligible dividend of $200,000 and a taxable non-eligible dividend of $800,000.

ANALYSIS ALTERNATIVE 1   The maximum amount that can be designated as eligible is $1,000,000 because of the existence of a GRIP balance of the same amount at the end of the year. In this situation the GRIP balance in 2022 would be reduced to nil. The dividend refund, however, is a separate matter and a refund is only possible to the extent of the balance in the eligible RDTOH account at year end. The dividend refund will only be $76,667 calculated as the lesser of (1) 38 1/3% of eligible dividends paid of $1,000,000, or $383,333, and (2) the eligible RDTOH balance of $76,667. Sarco cannot access the non-eligible RDTOH account.

ANALYSIS ALTERNATIVE 2   Where non-eligible dividends are paid a private corporation can access both the eligible and non-eligible RDTOH accounts but the non-eligible RDTOH must be used first with any shortfall being claimed with the eligible RDTOH. Specifically, in this case the refund on the non-eligible dividends would be calculated as follows:

- **Component 1**   This amount is $306,667, the lesser of $383,333 [(38 1/3%) ($1,000,000)] and $306,667, the balance in the non-eligible RDTOH.

- **Component 2**   This amount is $76,666, the excess of 38 1/3% of the non-eligible dividends paid over the balance in the non-eligible RDTOH ($383,333 - $306,667).

This provides a total refund of $383,333 ($306,667 + $76,666), the full amount of the refundable taxes paid. Both RDTOH accounts would be reduced to nil beginning in 2022.

ANALYSIS ALTERNATIVE 3   The dividend refund on the eligible dividends would be $76,667. This amount is 38 1/3% of the $200,000 in eligible dividends paid and the balance in the eligible RDTOH. The refund on the non-eligible dividends paid would be $306,667. This amount is 38 1/3% of the $800,000 in non-eligible dividends paid and the balance in the non-eligible RDTOH. As in Alternative 2, the total refund is $383,333 (with a $1 rounding error).

SUMMARY   These results can be summarized as follows:

	Alternative 1	Alternative 2	Alternative 3
Eligible dividends paid	$1,000,000	Nil	$200,000
Non-eligible dividends paid	Nil	$1,000,000	800,000
Total dividend refund	76,667	383,333	383,333
January 1, 2022:			
GRIP balance	Nil	1,000,000	800,000
Eligible RDTOH	Nil	Nil	Nil
Non-eligible RDTOH	306,667	Nil	Nil

13-124.   The planning objectives with the two RDTOH accounts when taxable dividends are paid to individual shareholders is to (1) maximize the dividend refund and (2) minimize income taxes paid by shareholders that are individuals. Minimizing income taxes to individuals means paying out the maximum amount of eligible dividends while maximizing the dividend refund.

13-125.   If we apply these planning objectives, we can analyze the results as follows:

Alternative 1   While this is the best result in terms of lower taxes for individual shareholders because eligible dividends are taxed much more favourably than non-eligible dividends, only $76,667 of a potential $383,333 in dividend refunds was refunded. This strategy leaves $306,667 in unclaimed dividend refunds.

Alternative 2   The benefit to the all non-eligible dividend strategy is that the dividend refund is maximized at $383,333. The downside is that individual shareholders will pay additional income tax since non-eligible dividends are subject to higher income tax rates than eligible dividends.

Alternative 3   This is the preferred alternative since it (1) provides the maximum dividend refund of $383,333 and (2) optimizes the taxable dividends so that individual shareholders receive favourable treatment on the dividends paid as eligible dividends.

Conclusion   In terms of planning, one should first maximize eligible dividends to individual shareholders, meaning paying sufficient eligible dividends to obtain the maximum dividend refund based on the balance in the eligible RDTOH account at year end. Any remaining dividend refund can be maximized with non-eligible dividends.

Example of the Taxation of Corporate Investment Income

13-126.   The following example illustrates the taxation of corporate investment income to a private corporation that is a CCPC, including refundable Part I and IV taxes, the calculation of the two RDTOH accounts, and the resulting dividend refunds once taxable dividends have been paid.

EXAMPLE   Fortune Ltd. is a CCPC that has never been associated with another corporation. All of the shares of the corporation are owned by one individual. For the purposes of the federal abatement and based on the formula in ITR 402(3), 90% of the company's income is considered to have been earned in the year in a province. There were no taxable dividends paid by the company in 2020. The following information is available for the year ending December 31, 2021:

Canadian aggregate investment income	
(includes $25,000 in net taxable capital gains)	$ 100,000
Gross foreign non-business income (15% foreign income taxes)	20,000
Gross foreign business income (15% foreign income taxes)	10,000
Active business income	150,000
Portfolio dividends received	30,000
Net income	$ 310,000
Portfolio eligible dividends—ITA 112(1)	(30,000)
Net capital losses deducted—ITA 111(1)(b)	(15,000)
Taxable income	$ 265,000

2020 Taxable capital employed in Canada (TCEC)	$2,400,000
2020 Adjusted aggregate investment income	32,000
Eligible RDTOH—January 1, 2021	$ 4,600
Non-eligible RDTOH—January 1, 2021	18,400
Taxable dividends paid during 2021	60,000
GRIP—January 1, 2021	12,000

ANALYSIS   Reflecting the fact that the 2020 TCEC was less than $10 million and the 2020 adjusted aggregate investment income was less than $50,000, there would be no reduction in the business limit for the small business deduction in 2021.

The Part I tax payable would be calculated as follows:

Base amount of Part I tax [(38%)($265,000)]	$100,700
Federal tax abatement [(10%)(90%)($265,000)]	(23,850)
Small business deduction (Note 1)	(28,500)
ART (Note 2)	11,200
General rate reduction (Note 3)	(1,300)
Foreign non-business tax credit (Note 1)	(3,000)
Foreign business tax credit (Note 1)	(1,500)
Part I tax payable	$ 53,750

Note 1   In order to simplify the calculation of the small business deduction, the foreign tax credits are assumed to be equal to the amounts withheld (15%). Additional calculations would be required to support this conclusion.

The small business deduction would be equal to 19% of the least of:

1. Active business income	$150,000
2. Taxable income	$ 265,000
Deduct:	
[(100/28)($3,000 foreign non-business tax credit)]	(10,714)
[(4)($1,500 foreign business tax credit)]	(6,000)
Adjusted taxable income	$ 248,286
3. Annual business limit	$500,000

The small business deduction is $28,500 [(19%)($150,000)].

Note 2   The additional refundable tax (ART) is equal to 10 2/3% of the lesser of:

- Aggregate investment income, calculated as follows:

Canadian source investment income	$100,000
Gross foreign non-business income	20,000
Net capital loss carry forward deducted	(15,000)
Aggregate investment income	$105,000

- An amount calculated as follows:

Taxable income	$265,000
Amount eligible for the small business deduction	(150,000)
Balance	$ 115,000

This results in an ART equal to $11,200 [(10 2/3%)($105,000)].

Note 3   The general rate reduction would be calculated as follows:

Taxable income	$265,000
Amount eligible for small business deduction (Note 1)	(150,000)
Aggregate investment income	(105,000)
Full rate taxable income (= foreign business income)	$ 10,000
Rate	13%
General rate reduction	$ 1,300

13-127.   Based on the preceding information, the refundable portion of Part I tax would be the least of the following three amounts:

30 2/3% of aggregate investment income [(30 2/3%)($105,000)]		$ 32,200
Deduct excess of:		
Foreign non-business tax credit	($3,000)	
Over 8% of foreign investment income [(8%)($20,000)]	1,600	(1,400)
Amount under ITA 129(4)(a)(i)		**$ 30,800**

Taxable income		$ 265,000
Deduct:		
Amount eligible for small business deduction	($ 150,000)	
[(100 ÷ 38 2/3)($3,000 foreign non-business tax credit)]	(7,759)	
[(4)($1,500 foreign business tax credit)]	(6,000)	(163,759)
Total		$ 101,241
Rate		30 2/3%
Amount under ITA 129(4)(a)(ii)		**$ 31,048**

Amount under ITA 129(4)(a)(iii) = Part I tax payable	**$ 53,750**

The refundable portion of Part I tax is equal to $30,800, which is the least of the preceding three amounts.

13-128.   The Part IV tax would be $11,500, 38 1/3% of the $30,000 in portfolio dividends received.

13-129.   The ending balance in the eligible RDTOH would be calculated as follows:

January 1, 2021, balance	$ 4,600
Part IV tax on portfolio dividends	11,500
December 31, 2021, eligible RDTOH	$16,100

13-130.   The ending balance in the non-eligible RDTOH would be calculated as follows:

January 1, 2021, balance	$18,400
Part I refundable tax	30,800
December 31, 2021, non-eligible RDTOH	$49,200

13-131.   The ending GRIP balance would be calculated as follows:

January 1, 2020, balance	$12,000
Portfolio eligible dividends received	30,000
December 31, 2021, GRIP balance	$42,000

13-132.   Of the total dividends paid of $60,000, the amount that can be designated as eligible is limited to the GRIP balance of $42,000. The refund on these dividends is the lesser of:

- $16,100 [(38 1/3%)($42,000)]; or
- $16,100, the ending balance in the eligible RDTOH.

13-133.   If the maximum designation is made, $42,000 would be subtracted from the GRIP in 2022. Similarly, the $16,100 refund would be subtracted from the eligible RDTOH in 2022.

13-134.   With $42,000 of the dividends designated as eligible, the remaining $18,000 ($60,000 - $42,000) will be non-eligible. The dividend refund will be the lesser of:

- $6,900 [(38 1/3%)($18,000)]; or
- $49,200, the ending balance in the non-eligible RDTOH.

13-135.   The $6,900 would be subtracted from the non-eligible RDTOH in 2022.

13-136.   The total refund is $23,000 ($16,100 + $4,900). Note that this is equal to 38 1/3% of the $60,000 in total dividends paid.

13-137.   Given the receding calculations, Fortune's total federal tax payable is as follows:

Part I tax payable	$53,750
Part IV tax payable	11,500
Dividend refund	(23,000)
2021 Federal tax payable	$42,250

Working through Corporate Tax Problems

13-138.   At this point we have completed our general coverage of taxable income and tax payable for corporations. There are a great many concepts and calculations involved in this process. While we have illustrated the concepts and calculations with examples, we have not provided a comprehensive example that encompasses all corporate tax issues.

13-139.   You will find, however, that several of the Self-Study and Assignment Problems involve fairly comprehensive calculations of corporate taxable income and tax payable. Given the complexity of these problems, it is useful to have a systematic approach to dealing with this type of problem. To fill that need, we would suggest you approach the required calculations in the following order (we are assuming that only federal taxes are being calculated as this is generally the case with the problem material in this text):

- Net income for tax purposes. Depending on the problem, this may require a reconciliation of accounting income to income based on the provisions of the ITA. We refer to this as net income for tax purposes to differentiate between net income for accounting versus net income for purposes of the ITA. Ref: ITA 3

- Taxable income. Taxable income begins with net income and subtracts a number of deductions we refer to as taxable income deductions that include charitable donations, dividends from taxable Canadian corporations, and loss carry overs. Ref: ITA 2(2)

- Basic federal Part I tax payable at the 38% rate. Ref: ITA 123

- Federal tax abatement. If there is foreign business income, this may require a calculation of the amounts that are to be considered as income earned for the year in a province. Ref: ITA 124

- If the corporation is a CCPC:

  - Determine taxable capital employed in Canada (TCEC) and adjusted aggregate investment income for the previous year since both amounts may impact a corporation's business limit for purposes of the small business deduction. Ref: ITA 125(5.1)

  - Small business deduction (without consideration of the general rate reduction or the ART in the foreign income tax credit constraints). Ref: ITA 125(1)

  - Aggregate investment income, which is relevant to determining the 10 2/3% ART and determining the non-eligible RDTOH of a CCPC. Ref: ITA 129(4)

  - Additional refundable tax on investment income (ART). Note that this is an addition to Part I tax payable, not a deduction. Ref: ITA 123.3

- Manufacturing and processing profits deduction (without consideration of the general rate reduction in the foreign income tax credit constraints). Ref: ITA 125.1

- General rate reduction. Ref: ITA 123.4

- Foreign non-business income tax credit. Ref: ITA 126(1)

- Foreign business income tax credit. Ref: ITA 126(2)

- If the corporation is a CCPC:

  - Refundable portion of Part I tax. Ref: Definition of "non-eligible RDTOH," ITA 129(4)

  - The GRIP balance. Ref: ITA 89(1)

- If the corporation is a private corporation but not a CCPC:

  - Part IV tax payable. Ref: 186(1)

  - Balance in the eligible and non-eligible refundable dividend tax on hand accounts. Ref: ITA 129(4)

  - Dividend refund on eligible dividends and non-eligible dividends. Ref: ITA 129(1)

We suggest you complete SSP 13-6, 13-7, and 13-8 at this point.

Key Terms

A full glossary with definitions is provided at the end of the Study Guide.

Additional Refundable Tax (ART)	Low Rate Income Pool (LRIP)
Adjusted Aggregate Investment Income	Non-Eligible RDTOH
Aggregate Investment Income	Overintegration
Canadian Controlled Private Corporation (CCPC)	Part IV Tax
Connected Corporation	Portfolio Dividend
Dividend Gross Up	Private Corporation
Dividend Tax Credit	Public Corporation
Dividends	Refundable Dividend Tax on Hand
Eligible Dividends	(RDTOH)
Eligible RDTOH	Refundable Part I Tax
Excessive Eligible Dividend Designation (EEDD)	Subject Corporation
General Rate Income Pool (GRIP)	Underintegration
Integration	

References

For more detailed study of the material in this chapter, we refer you to the following:

ITA 82(1)	Taxable Dividends Received
ITA 89(1)	Definitions (Canadian Corporation, GRIP, LRIP, and EEDD)
ITA 123.3	Additional Refundable Tax on CCPC's Investment Income
ITA 123.4	General Rate Reduction
ITA 129(1)	Dividend Refund to Private Corporation
ITA 129(4)	Definition of Eligible and Non-Eligible Refundable Dividend Tax on Hand
ITA 129(4)	Aggregate Investment Income
ITA 185.1	Part III.1 Tax on Excessive Eligible Dividend Designations
ITA 185.2	Part III.1 Election to Treat Excessive Eligible Dividend as an Ordinary Dividend
ITA 186	Part IV Tax
IT-67R3	Taxable Dividends from Corporations Resident in Canada
IT-243R4	Dividend Refund to Private Corporations
IT-269R4	Part IV Tax on Taxable Dividends Received by a Private Corporation or a Subject Corporation
IT-391R	Status of Corporations
IT-458R2	Canadian Controlled Private Corporation

Appendix—ART and Foreign Tax Credit Calculations

13-1A.   As discussed in Chapter 12, the use of foreign taxes paid as credits against Canadian tax payable is limited by a formula that includes the "tax otherwise payable." In the case of foreign taxes paid on non-business income, the "tax otherwise payable" in the formula adds the ART that is assessed under ITA 123.3.

13-2A.   This creates a potential problem in that the calculation of the ART includes the amount eligible for the small business deduction. Since one of the factors limiting the small business deduction [ITA 125(1)(b)] is taxable income reduced by 100/28 of the foreign non-business income tax credit and 4 times the foreign business income tax credit, this could have created an insolvable circular calculation.

13-3A.   As is explained in Chapter 12, there is a similar circularity issue involving the general rate reduction under ITA 123.4. The calculation of this amount also requires knowing the amount of income that is eligible for the small business deduction.

13-4A.   To avoid both of these problems, for the purposes of calculating the small business deduction, ITA 125(1)(b)(i) permits the foreign tax credit for taxes paid on foreign non-business income to be calculated using a "tax otherwise payable" figure that does not include the ART under ITA 123.3 or the general rate reduction. ITA 125(1)(b)(ii) permits the foreign tax credit for taxes paid on foreign business income to be calculated using a "tax otherwise payable" figure that does not include the general rate reduction.

13-5A.   This means that in situations where the small business deduction, foreign tax credits, and the ART are involved, the following procedures should be used:

1.   Calculate the foreign non-business tax credit using a "tax otherwise payable" figure that excludes both ITA 123.3 (ART) and ITA 123.4 (general rate reduction). This initial version of the foreign non-business tax credit will be used only for the purpose of determining the small business deduction, with the actual credit available calculated after the ITA 123.3 and 123.4 amounts have been determined.

2.   Calculate the foreign business tax credit using a "tax otherwise payable" figure that excludes ITA 123.4 (as business income is involved, ITA 123.3 is excluded by definition). However, this credit is limited by the amount of tax otherwise payable, reduced by the foreign non-business tax credit. As a consequence, it will be necessary to calculate an initial version of this foreign business tax credit using the initial version of the foreign non-business tax credit. This initial version will be used only for the purpose of determining the small business deduction and the M&P deduction.

3.   Calculate the amount eligible for the small business deduction and M&P deduction using the numbers determined in steps 1 and 2.

4.   Using the amount eligible for the small business deduction and the M&P deduction determined in step 3, calculate the ART and the general rate reduction.

5.   Calculate the actual foreign non-business tax credit using a "tax otherwise payable" figure that includes the ART and the general rate reduction determined in step 4.

Sample Corporate Tax Return

The Chapter 13 Sample Tax Return can be found in the Study Guide.

Self-Study Problems (SSPs)

Self-Study Problems (SSPs) provide practice in problem solving. Within the chapters, we have indicated where it would be appropriate to stop and work on each SSP. The problems can be downloaded by chapter from MyLab Accounting. Solutions are available in the Study Guide. Select problems can also be completed directly in MyLab and auto-graded.

Assignment Problems

Solutions to Assignment Problems (APs) are available to instructors only.

AP 13-1   (Integration Example)
Assume the following with respect to an individual shareholder of a wholly owned CCPC:

• The corporation's only income is active business income of $340,000, all of which qualifies for the small business deduction.

- The corporation has no GRIP and therefore all of the taxable dividends it pays will be non-eligible dividends.
- The individual's marginal federal tax rate is 33% and his marginal provincial tax rate is 15%.
- The provincial dividend tax credit on non-eligible dividends is equal to 34% of the gross up.
- The combined federal and provincial corporate tax rate on business income is 12.0%.

Required: Indicate, using these assumptions, whether integration is working perfectly and whether it is beneficial to use a corporation to earn the company's active business income in this instance. Show all supporting calculations, including both the income tax comparison and after-tax return comparison of (1) the individual earning the income directly without the use of a corporation and (2) earning the income through a corporation and distributing all of the after-tax corporate income as a non-eligible dividend to the sole individual shareholder. If integration is not working properly, briefly explain why.

AP 13-2   (Part I and Part IV Refundable Taxes)

Burton Investments Ltd. is a CCPC that sells office supplies. It owns 52% of the outstanding shares of Puligny Inc. On December 15, 2021, Puligny Inc. declared and paid a dividend of $122,000, of which Burton Investments Ltd. received $63,440 (52%). None of this dividend was designated as eligible by Puligny. As a result of paying the $122,000 dividend, Puligny Inc. received a dividend refund in the amount of $12,500 from its non-eligible RDTOH.

Other 2021 income that was reported by Burton Investments consisted of the following amounts:

Taxable capital gain	$ 9,000
Eligible dividends from Bank of Montreal shares	13,480
Interest	1,150

The taxable capital gain was on the sale of land that had been used as an auxiliary parking lot but was no longer needed.

Burton's office supply business is seasonal and, as a consequence, temporary cash balances must be set aside for the purchase of inventories during the busy parts of the year. All of the $1,150 in interest was earned on such temporary cash balances.

At the beginning of 2021, the company's non-eligible RDTOH balance was $14,426. The balance in the eligible RDTOH was nil. The corporation did not have a GRIP balance on January 1, 2021.

The company's taxable income for the year ending December 31, 2021, was $62,800. No foreign income was included in this total. Assume the Part I tax payable for the year ending December 31, 2021, was correctly calculated as $12,560. Because of its association with Puligny Inc., its share of the business limit for 2021 is $40,000. Burton's active business income is more than its share of the 2021 business limit.

Burton Investments paid taxable dividends of $22,500 in 2021. It is the policy of the corporation to designate dividends as eligible only to the extent that a dividend refund will be available.

For 2020, Burton and Puligny had combined adjusted aggregate investment income of $23,000 and combined taxable capital employed in Canada of $1,600,000.

Required:

A. Determine Burton's Part I refundable tax for 2021.

B. Determine Burton's Part IV tax payable for 2021.

C. Determine the December 31, 2021, balances in Burton's eligible and non-eligible RDTOH.

D. Determine Burton's 2021 dividend refund, providing separate amounts for refunds on eligible dividends and refunds on non-eligible dividends.

AP 13-3 *(Dividend Refund)*
Case 1

Ho Trading Company is a CCPC with a December 31 year end. On December 31, 2021, it had the following balances in its accounts:

GRIP	$150,000
Eligible RDTOH	38,333
Non-eligible RDTOH	76,667

During the year, the corporation paid taxable dividends of $250,000. The corporation would like to maximize the amount of this dividend that is designated as eligible irrespective of whether it results in a dividend refund.

Determine the amounts for the corporation's 2021 dividend refund on both eligible and non-eligible dividends.

If the corporation had wanted to maximize its dividend refund while designating the maximum eligible dividend, what would the results have been?

Case 2

Amadeus Ltd. is a CCPC with a December 31 year end. On December 31, 2021, it had the following balances in its accounts:

GRIP	$400,000
Eligible RDTOH	95,833
Non-eligible RDTOH	134,167

During the year, the corporation paid taxable dividends of $500,000. It is the policy of the corporation to designate dividends as eligible only to the extent that a refund is available.

Determine the amounts for the corporation's 2021 dividend refund on eligible dividends paid and the corporation's 2021 dividend refund on non-eligible dividends paid.

AP 13-4 *(Part I and IV, Refundable Taxes, RDTOH, and GRIP)*

Rual Ltd. is a CCPC with a December 31 year end. The components of its net income are as follows:

Active business income (Note 1)	$950,225
Net taxable capital gains	112,900
Rental loss from investment property (Note 2)	(27,550)
Foreign source interest (Note 2)	45,375
Dividends (Note 3)	583,750

Note 1 The active business income amount includes manufacturing profits of $774,100. This amount qualifies for the M&P deduction. Since the company operates in a province that provides a special rate for M&P profits, the company calculates the federal M&P deduction.

Note 2 Both of the investments that generate rental income or loss and foreign source interest have been made with funds that are no longer needed in the active business operations. In addition, there are no foreign taxes required to be paid on the foreign source income as a result of an income tax treaty.

Note 3 Total dividends received in the 2021 year are made up of the following amounts:

Eligible portfolio dividends from Canadian companies	$ 142,435
Non-eligible dividends from Dual Ltd. (Note 4)	230,000
Non-eligible dividends from Fual Ltd. (Note 5)	211,315
Total dividends	$ 583,750

Note 4   Dual Ltd. is a wholly owned subsidiary of Rual Ltd. since Rual owns all of its shares. As a result, Dual is connected to Rual for the purposes of Part IV. In 2021 the payment of the dividend to Rual resulted in a dividend refund of $79,200, all of which was attributable to Dual's non-eligible RDTOH.

Note 5   Rual owns 60% of the voting shares of Fual Ltd. As a result, Fual is controlled by Rual and therefore connected to it for the purposes of Part IV. In 2021 the payment of the dividend to Rual resulted in a dividend refund of $62,700. Fual had no GRIP balance at year end, with the result that all of the dividends paid to Rual are non-eligible dividends. Fual had insufficient non-eligible RDTOH, however, and was forced to use up all of its eligible RDTOH to maximize its dividend refund. Assume that 20% of its dividend refund is attributable to its eligible RDTOH and 80% to its non-eligible RDTOH.

Additional Information

1. On December 16, 2021, Rual paid taxable dividends to its shareholders totalling $315,000. No other dividends were paid during the year. It is the policy of the company to designate dividends as eligible only to the extent that their payment will result in a dividend refund.

2. Rual has a 2017 net capital loss balance of $76,100. In addition, there is a 2019 non-capital loss balance of $40,600. Rual would like to deduct the maximum amount of these carry forward losses possible for the 2021 taxation year.

3. Rual has controlled both Dual and Fual since 2017, and as a result the three corporations are all associated in the 2021 taxation year and in the immediately preceding year. The companies have agreed that Rual will be allocated $325,000 of the small business limit for 2021, Dual $100,000, and Fual $75,000. All three corporations use a December 31 year end.

4. The combined adjusted aggregate investment income for the three associated corporations for the 2020 taxation year is $48,700 and will be $58,450 for 2021. The taxable capital employed in Canada of the three associated corporations totals $9,125,000 for the 2020 taxation year and will equal $11,660,000 for 2021.

5. At December 31, 2020, Rual had an eligible RDTOH balance of $26,875, a non-eligible RDTOH balance of $103,850, and a GRIP balance of $167,000. During 2020, Rual paid taxable dividends of $96,500, $16,500 of which were designated as eligible. As a result of paying the dividends, Rual received a dividend refund of $36,991 [(38 1/3%)($96,500)].

6. Assume for the purposes of the federal abatement that 97% of Rual's taxable income is considered to have been earned in the year in a province.

Required: Show all of the calculations used to provide the following required information, including those for which the result is nil.

For Rual Inc.'s 2021 taxation year, calculate the following items:

A. Part I tax payable

B. The refundable portion of Part I tax payable

C. Part IV tax payable

D. The balance in the GRIP account on December 31, 2021

E. The balance in both the eligible RDTOH and non-eligible RDTOH on December 31, 2021

F. The dividend refund, if any, showing separately the amount attributable to eligible dividends and the amount attributable to non-eligible dividends

G. Total federal tax payable (net of any dividend refund)

AP 13-5 (Comprehensive Corporate Tax Payable with CCA)

Oland Ltd. is a CCPC with a December 31 year end. For the year ending December 31, 2021, the income statement of the company, prepared in accordance with generally accepted accounting principles (ASPE), is as follows:

Revenues		$1,625,986
Expenses:		
Cost of goods sold	($ 776,257)	
Selling and administrative costs	(394,672)	
Amortization expense	(125,489)	
Charitable donations	(27,000)	(1,323,418)
Operating income		$ 302,568
Gain on sale of property	$ 153,600	
Loss on sale of vehicles	(55,000)	
Gain on sale of investments	11,000	
Dividends received (see Note)	123,400	233,000
Net income before taxes		$ 535,568

Note The components of the dividends received are as follows:

Eligible dividends from Canadian public companies	$ 62,300
Non-eligible dividends from 80% owned subsidiary	
(the subsidiary received a dividend refund of	
$15,000 from its non-eligible RDTOH)	48,000
Non-eligible dividends from wholly owned subsidiary	
(no dividend refund)	13,100
Total dividends received	$ 123,400

Oland is associated with both of the subsidiaries. The two subsidiaries have each been allocated $125,000 of the small business deduction's business limit. The remaining $250,000 has been allocated to Oland.

Other Information:

1. Selling and administrative costs include $22,490 in business meals and entertainment.

2. Selling and administrative costs includes interest on late income tax instalments of $1,240 and on late municipal tax payments of $625.

3. Selling and administrative costs includes bond discount amortization of $3,850.

4. During 2021, Oland Ltd. acquired a competing business at a price that included goodwill of $110,400. For accounting purposes, there is no impairment or write-down of the goodwill in 2021.

5. Selling and administrative costs include membership fees for several employees in a local golf and country club. These fees total $7,285.

6. As the company expects to issue more shares during 2021, it made a number of amendments to its articles of incorporation and included the legal costs in selling and administrative costs. These costs totalled $11,482.

7. On January 1, 2021, the company had the following UCC balances:

Class 1	$582,652
Class 8	575,267
Class 10	75,348
Class 13	88,600
Class 14.1	Nil

The class 1 balance relates to a single real property acquired in 2001 at a cost of $750,000. It is estimated that the value of the land at this time was $50,000. On February 1, 2021, this property is sold for $850,000. It is estimated that, at this time, the value of the land has increased to $80,000. In the accounting records, the carrying value of this real property was $696,400, $646,400 for the building and $50,000 for the land.

The old building is replaced on February 15, 2021, with a new building acquired at a cost of $923,000, of which $86,000 is allocated to the land. As the building is used more than 90% for non-residential purposes, it qualifies for the special 6% CCA rate. The appropriate election is made with the CRA to include this property in a separate class. No elections are made with respect to the replacement of the building.

During 2021, class 8 properties were acquired at a cost of $226,000. Class 8 properties with a capital cost of $185,000 were sold for $210,000. The class 8 properties were paintings by Canadian artists, and each was sold for an amount in excess of its capital cost. The accountant had not amortized them for accounting purposes. Class 8 contains a large number of properties at the end of 2021.

As the company has decided to lease all of its vehicles in the future, all of the class 10 properties are sold during the year. The total capital cost of these properties was $142,000 and the proceeds of disposition amounted to $43,000. The carrying value for accounting purposes was $98,000.

The class 13 balance relates to a single lease that commenced on January 1, 2016. The lease has an initial term of seven years, with two successive options to renew for three years each. At the inception of the lease, the company spent $110,000 on leasehold improvements. On January 1, 2018, an additional $44,800 was spent on further improvements.

8. It is Oland's policy to deduct maximum amounts of CCA.

9. During 2021, Oland spends $18,500 landscaping the grounds of its new building. For accounting purposes this was treated as an asset. However, the company will not amortize this balance because it believes the work has an unlimited life.

10. Investments were sold during the year for $126,000. The adjusted cost base of these investments and carrying value for accounting purposes was $115,000.

11. On January 1, 2022, Oland had the following balances:

Eligible RDTOH	$ 39,660
Non-eligible RDTOH	Nil
GRIP	$162,345

During 2020, Oland designated $12,350 of its dividends as eligible.

12. During 2021, Oland paid $42,300 in dividends. Of this total, $26,300 were designated as eligible.

13. At the beginning of 2021, Oland had a $23,000 net capital loss balance from 2018. It also had a 2018 non-capital loss balance of $36,400. The company would like to deduct as much as possible of these two carry overs during 2021.

14. All of Oland's taxable income is considered to have been earned in a province in the year.

15. It has been determined that Oland has $300,289 of active business income. Of this total, $43,000 results from manufacturing and processing activity. Because of special rates in the province in which it operates, Oland makes a separate calculation of the M&P deduction.

16. For 2020, Oland and its associated companies had combined adjusted aggregate investment income of $48,900 and taxable capital employed in Canada of $8,900,000.

Required: Show all of the calculations used to provide the following required information, including those for which the result is nil.

A. Determine Oland's minimum net income for tax purposes and taxable income for the year ending December 31, 2021. Include in your solution the January 1, 2022, UCC balance for each CCA class.

B. Determine Oland's Part I tax payable for the year ending December 31, 2021.

C. Determine the refundable portion of Oland's Part I tax payable for 2021.

D. Determine Oland's Part IV tax payable for the 2021.

E. Determine the December 31, 2021, balance in Oland's GRIP.

F. Determine the December 31, 2021, balances in Oland's eligible RDTOH and non-eligible RDTOH.

G. Determine Oland's dividend refund for 2021, separately identifying the refund related to eligible dividends and the refund related to non-eligible dividends.

H. Determine Oland's net federal tax payable for 2021.

AP 13-6   (Comprehensive Corporate Tax Payable)

Fancom Inc. is an Alberta corporation that qualifies as a CCPC. For the taxation year ending December 31, 2021, the components of its net income and taxable income are as follows:

Active business income (Note 1)	$328,000
Gross foreign business income (Note 2)	40,800
Gross foreign non-business income (Note 2)	31,200
Interest on long-term investments	49,900
Taxable capital gains (Note 3)	16,500
Eligible dividends received on portfolio investment	21,000
Net income	**$ 487,400**
Eligible dividends received	(21,000)
Charitable contributions	(86,400)
2019 Net capital loss deducted	(13,900)
2019 Non-capital loss deducted	(263,000)
Taxable income	**$ 103,100**

Note 1   As determined by the ITR, $152,000 of the active business income was manufacturing and processing profits. As these amounts are allocated to a province that has a special rate for M&P profits, the company calculates the federal M&P deduction.

Note 2   Foreign jurisdictions withheld $6,120 (15%) from the foreign business income and $7,800 (25%) from the foreign non-business income.

Note 3   The taxable capital gain of $16,500 resulted from a disposition of passive investments.

Other Information:

1. During the year ending December 31, 2021, Fancom used its existing cash resources to pay taxable dividends of $223,200. Of this total, $49,300 were designated as eligible.

2. On January 1, 2021, Fancom had the following balances:

Eligible RDTOH	$14,000
Non-eligible RDTOH	Nil
GRIP	$49,360

During 2020, Fancom designated $8,700 of its dividends as eligible.

3. For 2020, Fancom's adjusted aggregate investment income was $36,450 and its taxable capital employed in Canada was $4,652,300.

4. As determined by the ITR, 85% of Fancom's taxable income is considered to have been earned in the year in a province.

5. Assume that the foreign business and non-business tax credits are equal to the foreign taxes withheld.

Required: Show all of the calculations used to provide the following required information, including those for which the result is nil.

A. Determine Fancom's Part I tax payable for the year ending December 31, 2021.

B. Determine the refundable portion of Fancom's Part I tax payable for 2021.

C. Determine Fancom's Part IV tax payable for the 2021.

D. Determine the December 31, 2021, balance in Fancom's GRIP.

E. Determine the December 31, 2021, balances in Fancom's eligible RDTOH and non-eligible RDTOH.

F. Determine Fancom's dividend refund for 2021, separately identifying the refund related to eligible dividends and the refund related to non-eligible dividends.

AP 13-7   *(Comprehensive Corporate Tax Payable)*

Falko Ltd. is a CCPC with a December 31 year end. For its year ending December 31, 2021, its accounting net income before taxes, as determined using generally accepted accounting principles (ASPE), was $1,029,700. Relevant information for the 2021 year necessary to make the appropriate reconciliation adjustments to net income for tax purposes, taxable income, and federal taxes payable is as follows:

1. Falko's amortization expense was $494,500. Maximum deductible CCA for the year was $713,000. Company policy has always been to deduct the maximum available CCA.

2. The company's revenues included foreign source investment income of C$44,000. The amount received, however, was only C$36,080 as a result of foreign withholding income taxes of 18%, or $7,920. The company only recorded the amount received as revenue.

3. Falko sold one of its buildings that required costly renovations in favour of leasing a building. The total sales price was $1,725,000 with $500,000 allocated to the land and $1,225,000 to the building. The original cost of the land and therefore its adjusted cost base was $650,000. The capital cost and adjusted cost base of the building was $1,000,000 and its UCC at the time of sale was $885,000. For accounting purposes the carrying value of the building was $710,000. The company records accounting gains and accounting losses based on the carrying value for the building and the original cost of the land.

4. During the year, the company earned the following amounts of Canadian source investment income, all of which have been included in net income for accounting purposes:

Interest on long-term investments	$28,700
Non-eligible dividends from a 100% owned subsidiary	77,500
Eligible dividends on Bank of Nova Scotia shares	53,300

5. Falko is only associated with one company—its wholly owned subsidiary Lands Inc., after acquiring all of its shares in 2017. Lands received a dividend refund of $26,475 as a result of the dividends paid to Falko in 2021. Since Lands' non-eligible RDTOH was insufficient to recover all of the dividend refund, it was forced to partially rely on its eligible RDTOH. Lands' GRIP account balance was nil at year end, preventing it from designating any of the dividends paid to Falko as eligible. Of the dividend refund, 43% was attributable to its eligible RDTOH and 57% to its non-eligible RDTOH.

6. Company expenses for accounting purposes included (1) $39,800 spent on business meals and entertainment; (2) a write-down of inventory (for obsolescence) beyond that permitted in valuing inventory for tax purposes (the excess amount is $11,400); (3) life insurance premiums totalling $14,375 paid on the life of two of the principal shareholders; and (4) bonuses to the same two shareholders for $75,000 each. The bonuses were never paid.

7. Falko's active business income for the year was $796,400, which includes $427,000 of Canadian manufacturing profits that qualify for the M&P deduction (ITA 125.1). Since the company operates in a province that provides a special rate for M&P profits, the company calculates the federal M&P deduction every year.

8. During the year ending December 31, 2021, the company used its existing cash resources to pay taxable dividends of $285,000. It is the policy of the company to only designate dividends as eligible to the extent they generate a dividend refund.

9. At December 31, 2020, Falko had an eligible RDTOH balance of $19,446, a non-eligible RDTOH balance of $73,670, and a GRIP balance of $24,000. During 2020, Falko paid taxable dividends of $118,800, $18,800 of which were designated as eligible. As a result of paying the dividends, Falko received a dividend refund of $45,540 [(38 1/3%)($118,800)]; $7,207 of the dividend refund [($18,800)(38 1/3%)] was attributable to the eligible RDTOH and the remainder of $38,333 [($100,000)(38 1/3%)] was attributable to its non-eligible RDTOH.

10. The combined adjusted aggregate investment income for the two associated corporations for the 2020 taxation year is $47,190 and will be $62,770 for 2021. The taxable capital employed in Canada of the two associated corporations totals $6,445,000 for the 2020 taxation year and will equal $10,960,000 for 2021.

11. Falko has a 2017 non-capital loss carry forward balance of $112,000 and a 2019 net capital loss carry forward balance of $16,930. Falko's management has indicated that they wish to deduct the maximum amount of these losses possible for its 2021 taxation year.

12. Falko and its wholly owned subsidiary Lands have agreed to split the small business limit 50-50 for the 2021 taxation year.

Required: Show all of the calculations used to provide the following required information, including those for which the result is nil.

A. Calculate Falko's minimum net income for tax purposes and taxable income for the year ending December 31, 2020.

B. Assume the foreign non-business tax credit is equal to the foreign tax withheld. Calculate Falko's Part I tax payable for the year ending December 31, 2020. As the corporation operates in a province that has a reduced rate for M&P activity, a separate calculation of the federal M&P deduction is required.

C. Calculate the refundable portion of Falko's Part I tax payable for 2020

D. Calculate Falko's Part IV tax payable for the year ending December 31, 2020.

E. Determine the December 31, 2020, balance in Falko's GRIP account.

F. Determine the December 31, 2020, balances in Falko's eligible RDTOH and the non-eligible RDTOH.

G. Calculate Falko's dividend refund for the year ending December 31, 2020, showing separately the amount attributable to eligible dividends and the amount attributable to non-eligible dividends.

AP 13-8 *(Comprehensive Tax Payable)*

Industco Inc. is a CCPC. It uses a taxation year that ends on December 31. It keeps its records in accordance with generally accepted accounting principles (ASPE). For the year ending December 31, 2021, the company's condensed income statement is as follows:

Operating revenues in Canada		$ 2,937,500
Operating expenses in Canada		(1,905,000)
Operating income in Canada		$ 1,032,500
Other income items:		
Eligible portfolio dividends	$ 52,000	
Foreign non-business income (net of 15% withholding)	25,500	
Foreign business income (net of 10% withholding)	45,000	
Canadian source interest	26,000	
Gain on sale of class 8 property	225,000	373,500
Accounting income before taxes		$ 1,406,000

Other information related to operating expenses follows.

Amortization and CCA   The operating income figure was reduced by a charge for amortization of $623,000.

At the beginning of 2021, the company has a UCC balance in class 1 of $1,000,000. The only property in the class is the company's headquarters building. The company has owned this building since 2002.

In general, other property is leased. However, in February 2021, a policy change results in the acquisition of a new building at a cost of $650,000, of which $125,000 is allocated to the land on which the building is situated. The building is used 100% for non-residential purposes and is allocated to a separate class 1 after filing the appropriate election with the CRA. One-half of the non-residential use is for manufacturing and processing.

The January 1, 2021, UCC balance in class 8 was $4,200,000. During 2021, there were additions to this class in the total amount of $700,000. Also, class 8 property with a cost of $400,000 was sold for $550,000. The carrying value of these assets for accounting purposes was $325,000. There were numerous other property remaining in the class at the end of the 2021 taxation year.

At the beginning of 2021, the UCC in class 10 was $800,000, reflecting the company's fleet of trucks. As the company is changing to a policy of leasing its trucks, all of these trucks were sold during the year for $687,000. The capital cost of the trucks was $1,200,000 and their carrying value for accounting purposes was equal to the sale proceeds of $687,000.

Landscaping   The company spent $95,000 on landscaping for its main office building. This amount was recorded as an asset in the accounting records and, because the work has an unlimited life, no amortization was recorded on this asset.

Advertising   The company spent $17,000 on advertisements in *Fortune* magazine, a U.S.-based publication. Over 90% of the magazine's non-advertising content is original editorial content. The advertisements were designed to promote sales in Canadian cities located on the U.S. border.

Travel and Entertainment   Included in the travel costs deducted in 2021 was $12,000 for airline tickets and $41,400 for business meals and entertainment.

The company paid, and deducted for accounting purposes, a $2,500 initiation fee for a corporate membership in the Highland Golf and Country Club.

Taxes on Vacant Land   The company paid, and deducted, property taxes of $15,000 on vacant land that is being held for possible future expansion of its headquarters site.

Other Information

1. Industco Inc. declared and paid taxable dividends of $83,000 during 2020. It is the policy of the corporation to only designate dividends as eligible to the extent that their payment will result in a dividend refund.

2. It has been determined that 92% of Industco's taxable income is considered to have been earned in the year in a province.

3. On January 1, 2021, Industco had the following balances:

Eligible RDTOH	$ 78,000
Non-eligible RDTOH	Nil
GRIP	$298,000

4. During 2020, the company designated $64,000 of its dividends paid as eligible.

5. Industco Inc. is associated with two other CCPCs. Industco has been allocated $125,000 of the business limit for the year.

6. Assume that the foreign tax credits for the foreign non-business and foreign business income are equal to the amounts withheld.

7. Industco's Canadian active business income is equal to its net business income for ITA purposes. One-half of this Canadian active business income results from manufacturing and processing activity.

8. At the beginning of 2021, Industco has a 2019 net capital loss balance of $42,000 and a 2019 non-capital loss balance of $18,000. The company intends to deduct the maximum amount of these carry forwards during 2021.

9. For 2020, the adjusted aggregate investment income of Industco and its associated companies is $31,600 and the combined taxable capital employed in Canada was $6,420,000.

Required: Determine the following amounts. You should show all of the calculations required to provide these amounts, even when the result of the calculations is nil.

A. Industco's net income for tax purposes and taxable income for the year ending December 31, 2021. As the company's active business income is based on its net business income for tax purposes, a separate calculation of this component of net income for tax purposes is required.

B. Industco's Part I tax payable for the year ending December 31, 2021. As the company operates in a province that has a reduced tax rate for manufacturing and processing activity, a separate calculation of the federal M&P deduction is required.

C. The refundable portion of Industco's Part I tax payable for 2021.

D. Industco's Part IV tax payable for 2021.

E. Industco's GRIP balance on December 31, 2021.

F. The balances in Industco's eligible RDTOH and non-eligible RDTOH on Decembert 31, 2021.

G. Industco's dividend refund for 2021, showing separately the amount related to eligible dividends and the amount related to non-eligible dividends.

CHAPTER 14

Other Issues in Corporate Taxation

Learning Objectives

After completing Chapter 14, you should be able to:

1. Explain why the acquisition of control legislation was added to the ITA and what the rules are desined to accomplish (Paragraph [P hereafter] 14-1 to 14-10).
2. Describe the importance of a loss restriction event and explain, with a few examples, situations in which it would apply (P 14-11 to 14-14).
3. Explain the impact on an acquired corporation when its control has been acquired in terms of its year end and any impact on donation carry forward amounts and non-capital and net capital losses (P 14-15 to 14-27).
4. Describe and apply the income tax consequences to a corporation that has been subject to an acquisition of control in terms of accrued and unrealized losses on its property including elective options that may be available if there are accrued but unrealized gains (P 14-28 to 14-35).
5. Explain the purpose of the associated corporation rules (P 14-36 to 14-41).
6. Apply the associated corporation rules (P 14-42 to 14-62).
7. Explain the purpose of investment tax credits and how the rules apply when CCPCs incur qualifying capital and current expenditures (P 14-63 to 14-77).
8. Determine the refundable investment tax credits available to individuals and CCPCs (P 14-78 to 14-82).
9. Explain how the acquisition of control rules apply to investment tax credits (P 14-83 to 14-85).
10. Describe the type of distributions that a corporation can make to its shareholders (P 14-86 to 14-87).
11. Describe the parallel between financial statement accounts and income tax accounts (P 14-88 to 14-90).
12. Describe the three tax attributes of shares and explain how the tax concept of PUC is determined and how it differs from the ACB of shares (P 14-91 to 14-96).
13. Explain the purpose of a capital dividend account (CDA) and how it is calculated (P 14-97 to 14-100).

14. Describe the different types of dividends contemplated by the ITA and the impact of corporate law (P 14-101 to 14-107).
15. Describe a stock dividend, its general treatment under corporate law, and the income tax implications (P 14-108 to 14-112).
16. Explain how the payment of dividends with corporate property is treated for income tax purposes (P 14-113 to 14-117).
17. Describe the procedures necessary to elect capital dividend treatment and the income tax treatment when capital dividends are received, including the consequences of overpaying the CDA (P 14-118 to 14-123).
18. Describe the circumstances under which ITA 84(1) applies to create a deemed dividend, including any exceptions to the rule. Calculate the deemed dividend and determine the post-dividend ACB and PUC for one shareholder (P 14-124 to 14-132).
19. Describe the reporting requirements when there is a deemed dividend (P 14-133).
20. Explain the general circumstances that cause deemed dividend treatment under ITA 84(2). In addition, calculate the deemed dividend and determine the impact on the ACB and PUC of one shareholder (P 14-134 to 14-139).
21. Explain the circumstances that would result in a deemed dividend under ITA 84(3) and determine the resulting income tax consequences (P 14-140 to 14-144).
22. Explain the circumstances that cause ITA 84(4) and (4.1) to apply, including why the treatment is different. In addition, calculate the income tax consequences, including the impact on PUC and ACB of one shareholder(P 14-145 to 14-149).
23. Summarize and compare the income tax consequences of each of the five deemed dividend provisions of ITA 84 (P 14-150).

Introduction

14-1.   Chapters 12 and 13 covered the determination of taxable income and tax payable for a taxable Canadian corporation. Specifically, Chapter 12 described the reconciliation process for converting accounting income to net income for tax purposes then to taxable income. This was followed by consideration of how this taxable income is allocated to specific provinces for the purposes of the federal abatement and the determination of provincial tax payable. With respect to federal tax payable, Chapter 12 dealt with the rates applicable to corporations, the small business deduction, the M&P deduction, foreign tax credits, and the general rate reduction. The impact of taxable capital employed in Canada and adjusted aggregate investment income on the business limit for the purposes of the small business deduction were also discussed.

14-2.   After a fairly detailed discussion of the concept of integration, Chapter 13 focused on the taxation of investment income earned by CCPCs and other private corporations. A four-step process was discussed that begins with (1) identifying the relevant investment income, (2) applying refundable taxes under both Parts I and IV, (3) tracking the refundable tax through eligible and non-eligible RDTOH accounts, and finally (4) determining a corporation's dividend refund once taxable dividends are paid to shareholders.

14-3.   In presenting the material in Chapters 12 and 13, we focused on what we view as basic issues, skipping over some of the more technical considerations related to the determination of corporate taxable income and corporate tax payable. For example, we frequently mentioned associated corporations and their effect on the small business deduction, but we did not elaborate on the meaning of this concept. In this chapter we will turn our attention to these and other technical issues, providing coverage of:

- the acquisition of control rules;
- the associated corporation rules;
- investment tax credits;
- shareholders' equity concepts such as paid-up capital (PUC); and
- distributions of corporate surplus, including capital dividends and deemed dividends.

Acquisition of Control Rules

Introduction

14-4.   In previous chapters we have discussed what happens when a corporate taxpayer has losses and donations in a year that they cannot deduct because there is simply not sufficient income. The result is the creation of income tax accounts that track these balances and establish rules for how they can be claimed. Examples include loss carry overs such as non-capital and net capital losses, donations, and investment tax credits. We will refer to these balances generically as "tax preferences." These tax preferences are at the heart of the acquisition of control rules.

14-5.   As far back as the 1970s it was standard practice for a corporation to attempt to acquire tax preferences of other corporations. The practice, which continues to this day, centred on realized and unrealized losses. Realized losses were typically in the form of non-capital loss carry overs ,and unrealized losses were often represented by corporate property, often real estate inventory, that had significantly declined in value so that a sale at fair market value (FMV) would trigger a fully deductible loss. These tax planning transactions were referred to as "loss trading." There were instances of corporations advertising in local newspapers in Canada that they were looking to purchase companies with certain characteristics, such as the existence of tax loss carry overs. Once a target company had been identified it was not uncommon to set a price to purchase the shares of the company on the basis of five to ten cents on the dollar of the available tax preferences. For example, a corporation with $600,000 of non-capital losses would typically sell its shares between $30,000 [(5%)($600,000)] and $60,000 [(10%)($600,000)], depending on other factors such as the amount of corporate debt.

14-6.   When it comes to the acceptability of loss trading, the income tax planning principle established in a 1936 British decision in the case of the "Duke of Westminster" must be considered. In that case, the court stated that "taxpayers are free to arrange their affairs to minimize their income taxes." This decision has been accepted into Canadian income tax law through various Supreme Court of Canada decisions. This statement suggests that loss trading may be acceptable, but there is a caveat. The government is free to introduce legislation to block certain tax planning that is viewed as offensive. The acquisition of control (AOC) rules were introduced in 1987 to counter loss trading, and in 1988 the General Anti-Avoidance Rule (GAAR) that we discussed in Chapter 1 was introduced. As a result, today it is not uncommon for the CRA to challenge the many variations of loss trading transactions using both the AOC rules and the GAAR. At the time of writing, the Tax Court of Canada had recently ruled in favour of a corporate taxpayer in August 2020 in the loss planning case of *MMV Capital Properties Inc.* (2020 TCC 82).

14-7.   To understand the reason why loss trading is generally considered unacceptable we must first appreciate the basic income tax principle that tax preferences belong to the entity in which they were created. This means that if a corporation has a 2020 non-capital loss balance of $1 million and donation carry overs of $125,000, those tax preferences belong to that corporation and no one else. Attempts to effectively sell those loss preferences to another corporation would generally be considered offensive given this principle. We have added the word "generally" to mean that in certain cases loss trading may be acceptable, but only under strict conditions. If, for example, a corporation was in financial difficulty and had extensive non-capital losses, the AOC rules would allow the losses to be used if control of the company was acquired by another company but only if the purchaser was motivated by a genuine attempt to restore the acquired company and its business to profitability. In other words, a primary intent to purchase the losses or other tax preferences of a company with no interest in restoring the financial health of the purchased company would be considered offensive. The result of the AOC would be to deny the use of the tax preferences by any taxpayer.

Transferring Tax Preferences between Corporations

14-8.   When the control of a corporation with tax preferences is acquired, the tax preferences remain with that corporation. Accessing those tax preferences requires additional steps. These additional steps work best with a second corporation, which is usually the purchaser, but there are many structural variations. The structure chosen will depend on the planning methods required to access the tax preferences of the acquired corporation. For example, assume that Lossco is a corporation with substantial non-capital losses. Profitco is the second corporation that purchases all of the shares of Lossco, which results in an AOC. There are four general methods that can be used by Profitco to make use of the non-capital losses of Lossco:

Amalgamation   Amalgamations (discussed in Chapter 17) would result in Profitco and Lossco being merged together as one corporation. All of the property, liabilities, and tax preferences of the two companies would then be added together and be part of the one newly amalgamated company. As a result, Profitco would have indirectly accessed the non-capital losses of Lossco. (Ref: ITA 87)

Wind-Up   A wind-up (discussed in Chapter 17) would require dissolving Lossco, which means that the corporation would cease to exist. The income tax result is that all of the property, liabilities, and tax preferences of Lossco would flow through to Profitco. As a result, the non-capital losses of Lossco would have become the non-capital losses of Profitco. (Ref: ITA 88(1) & (1.1))

Business Transfer   Profitco could transfer part or all of its profitable business to Lossco on a tax-free basis (discussed in Chapter 16). As a result, by injecting business profits into Lossco the non-capital losses of Lossco would then be used to offset those profits. (Ref: ITA 85(1))

Loss Utilization Transaction   The purpose of these type of transactions is to leave Profitco and Lossco intact but create transactions that add income to Lossco while providing Profitco with a corresponding expense. If, for example, Lossco owned a building that could be used by Profitco, the building could be rented to Profitco for, say, $100,000 per year. The rental income to Lossco would not be subject to Part I income tax because Lossco would use its non-capital losses to offset the amount. The rental expense to Profitco effectively moves $100,000 of non-capital losses from Lossco to Profitco.

14-9.   The AOC rules would apply to the amalgamation, the Lossco wind-up, and the business transfer but not the loss utilization transaction, which could only be challenged by the CRA with the GAAR.

An Overview of the Acquisition of Control (AOC) Legislation

14-10.   There are numerous provisions of the ITA that regulate the operation of the AOC rules. The main rules, however, are found in ITA 111(4) through 111(5.5), 249(4), and 256(7). There are four general components of the AOC rules:

Loss Restriction Event   The AOC rules only apply if there has been a loss restriction event, which is defined in ITA 251.2(2)(a) as the acquisition of the control of a corporation by a person or a group of persons. We will refer to a loss restriction event as a simple acquisition of control or AOC

Deemed Taxation Year End   When there has been an AOC, the taxation year of the corporation whose control has been acquired is deemed to have come to an end and a new taxation year begins.

Loss Carry Overs and Other Tax Preferences Are Tainted   Any loss carry overs such as non-capital and net capital losses up to and including the deemed taxation year end become tainted, meaning there are restrictions placed on whether or not they can be used at all. This same concept applies to other tax preferences as well.

Unrealized Losses Forced Out   The acquired corporation is deemed to have disposed of any of its property that would have resulted in a loss had the property been sold for its FMV at the time of the AOC. These forced out losses affect the net income of the acquired corporation for the deemed taxation year end.

The Loss Restriction Event

14-11.   The AOC rules only apply if control of a corporation has been acquired. There are two questions that must first be answered before a determination can be made as to whether control has been acquired. The first requires an understanding of the meaning of control and the second requires determining whether an acquisition of control has taken place.

14-12.   There are three control concepts that are used in the ITA; two are legislated and one is not. The two legislated categories of control concepts are de facto control (ITA 256(5.1)) and a variety of control concepts that we refer to simply as "other control" that are scattered throughout the ITA. In Chapter 13, for example, in our discussion of Part IV tax, we noted that corporations are connected if one controls the other. For that purpose, ITA 186(2) defines control to mean that one person owns more than 50% of the voting shares but also includes situations where more than 50% of voting shares are owned by non-arm's-length persons. Using that "other control" concept would mean that a person would be considered to control a corporation even if he or she did not own any of its shares as long as a non-arm's-length person owned more than 50% of the voting shares. Neither of these two control concepts apply to the AOC rules. We will discuss the concept of de facto control later in this chapter when we look at associated corporations.

14-13.   The control concept that applies to the AOC rules is technically referred to in Latin as "de jure control," which is more commonly known as "legal control." Legal control has been defined by the Supreme Court of Canada as "owning a sufficient number of shares to elect the majority of the members of the Board of Directors." This means owning shares that entitle the shareholder to vote for members of the board of directors and not shares that are non-voting. In everyday use, common shares are usually voting shares and preferred shares are not. Note, however, that corporate law in Canada often gives limited voting rights to non-voting shares, but those rights do not impact legal control.

14-14.   The next step is to apply the legal control concept to determine if legal control has been acquired. It is important to note that the AOC rules apply to an acquisition of control and not a change in control, which can be quite different as demonstrated in the following paragraphs. The rules require that a person or a group of persons has acquired legal control. This concept leads to the following important guidelines:

One Person, One Group, or No One   The legal control concept requires that, at a point in time, either one person, one group, or no one controls a corporation. In other words, there is no such thing as multiple legal control. The analysis requires first identifying whether there is a single person who has legal control. If not, then the question is whether there is an identifiable group that has control, and if not then the conclusion is that no one has control.

Group of Persons   If there is no single person who has legal control we then turn our attention to whether there is an identifiable group of persons that has legal control. Case law requires that, in identifying a controlling group of persons, there be a connection between shareholders that goes beyond the fact that they each own shares. The objective is to determine if there exists a group that acts together with a common mind when making decisions with respect to the corporation. Family members and business associates are generally considered to possess the necessary connection, although this can be rebutted by the facts. In addition, persons who always vote the same way or that provide voting proxies to one another (voting rights) suggest that these persons are part of a group acting together. At a minimum the shareholders must at least know each other. If persons are acting in their own separate interests, then they will not be considered part of a group of persons.

Related Persons   ITA 256(7) includes a series of rules that deem no control to have been acquired when it is between persons who are related to each other.

The Before and After   Identifying whether there has been an AOC requires first identifying whether anyone has legal control before an acquisition event and who has control afterward. If there has been an identifiable person or group of persons in control afterward and that person or group of persons was not related to the controlling person or group then there is an AOC.

EXAMPLE 1   Ms. Gregorio owns all of the shares of Tower Ltd. She sells all of the shares to Mr. Jarrah. Mr. Jarrah is not related to Ms. Gregorio.

ANALYSIS 1   Prior to the purchase Ms. Gregorio controlled the company, and afterward Mr. Jarrah controls. Since the persons are not the same and are not related there has been an AOC. If they had been related there would not have been an AOC.

EXAMPLE 2   Mrs. Gregorio and her spouse own all of the shares of Tower Ltd. Mrs. Gregorio owns 75% of the shares and her spouse owns 25%. Mr. Gregorio sells his shares to Mr. Jarrah. Mr. Jarrah is not related to either Mrs. Gregorio or her spouse.

ANALYSIS 2   Prior to the purchase Mrs. Gregorio controlled the company with 75% of its shares. Afterward Mrs. Gregorio still controls with 75%. There has been no AOC. Note that Mrs. Gregorio and her spouse do not control the company as a group since she controls it by herself.

EXAMPLE 3   Mrs. Gregorio and her spouse each own 50% of the shares of Tower Ltd. Mr. Jarrah carries on a business that competes with Tower Ltd. Looking to reduce competition, he negotiates with Mrs. Gregorio and her spouse to add his business to that of the company. When the restructuring is complete, Mrs. Gregorio and her spouse together own 50% of the shares and Mr. Jarrah owns 50%. Mr. Jarrah and Mrs. Gregorio and her spouse frequently disagree on business decisions.

ANALYSIS 3   Prior to the purchase Mrs. Gregorio and her spouse control the company as a group since neither one owns more than 50% of the voting shares (sufficient to elect the majority of the members of the board of directors). After the purchase of shares by Mr. Jarrah there is no acquisition of control since no one person controls and there is no group that controls. Based on the facts, Mr. Jarrah is acting in his own interest and would therefore not be a member of a group. This would represent a situation where there has been a change in control from control by Mrs. Gregorio and her spouse to control by no one. This, however, is not an AOC.

EXAMPLE 4   The facts are identical to Example 3 except that a year later Mr. Jarrah decides that working with Mrs. Gregorio and her spouse through the company is not working. Mr. Jarrah withdraws by having the company buy back his shares in what is referred to as a share redemption. Afterward he is no longer a shareholder.

ANALYSIS 4   In this situation the withdrawal of Mr. Jarrah as a shareholder results in Mrs. Gregorio and her spouse once again in control of the company. Prior to Mr. Jarrah's departure we concluded that no one controlled the company. Afterward, control is restored to Mrs. Gregorio and her spouse who control as a group. As a result there is an AOC. This example demonstrates that one does not have to purchase shares for there to be an AOC. The test is always who controlled at one point in time and who controlled at a second point.

Deemed Year End—ITA 249(4)

14-15.   When there has been an AOC, the taxation year of the corporation whose control has been acquired is deemed to have come to an end and a new taxation year begins. The deemed taxation year end is designed to measure the tax preferences of a corporation at a point in time and then subject those preferences to restrictions with the AOC rules. This effectively draws a line up to and including the deemed year end and determines that the rules will apply as of the date of the AOC. Tax preferences that exist at the end of the deemed taxation year are not generally permitted to cross that line and be used in a subsequent taxation year. In addition, any tax preferences that occur in a taxation year after the deemed year end are not allowed to be carried back to a previous taxation year if that line will be crossed.

14-16.   If an AOC occurs prior to the corporation's normal year end, a short fiscal period will be created. For example, if the corporation's normal year end was December 31, and the AOC took place on February 1, 2021, the deemed year end would create a fiscal period of only one month (January 1, 2021, through January 31, 2021). Further, if the corporation decides to continue to use a December 31 year end, there will be a second taxation year that runs from February 1, 2021, through December 31, 2021. In effect, the corporation would have to file two 2021 tax returns. You should note that when there is a short taxation year (less than 365 days) many deductions such as CCA must be prorated (ITR 1100(3)) as well as some tax payable deductions, such as the small business deduction (ITA 125(5)(b)). In addition, a short taxation year is still a taxation year, which impacts carry over tax preferences such as non-capital and net capital losses.

14-17.   Note that ITA 249.1(7) requires a corporation that has already established a fiscal period to obtain permission from the CRA if they wish to change their year end date. ITA 249(4), however, allows an acquired corporation to change its year end when there is an AOC. No permission is required. This means that in the example in Paragraph 14-16 the corporation could have avoided a second short fiscal period by establishing January 31 as its new year end. This means that the first fiscal year after the acquisition of control would be February 1, 2021, to January 31, 2022. In practice, planned AOCs are frequently timed to match the existing fiscal period to avoid short taxation year issues.

Tainted Tax Preferences: Charitable Donations—ITA 110(1.2)

14-18.   ITA 110.1(1.2) places two restrictions on the deduction of charitable donations:

- Undeducted donations for taxation years prior to an AOC, including the deemed taxation year, are restricted or tainted and cannot cross the line to be carried forward to subsequent taxation years.

- No deduction is available for a donation made after an AOC if the gifted property was acquired prior to the acquisition date in anticipation of the AOC.

14-19.   The second bullet refers to a common planning situation that attempted to circumvent the AOC rules by waiting until the AOC had taken place to make the charitable donation. That planning was contrary to the intention of the restriction, which was to prevent the sale of tax preferences to others.

Tainted Tax Preferences: Net Capital Losses—ITA 111(4)

14-20.   ITA 111(4)(a) applies to prevent any net capital losses up to and including the deemed taxation year from being carried across the line to be claimed in a subsequent taxation year. The effect is to potentially render those net capital losses useless as they can no longer be claimed. Technically, however, the losses have not expired. The CRA earmarks such losses to alert their auditors that such losses are no longer deductible.

14-21.   ITA 111(4)(b) covers the post-AOC side of the line, clarifying that no net capital loss incurred in a taxation year ending after the deemed taxation year can be carried back to a taxation year on the other (pre-AOC) side of the line.

Tainted Tax Preferences: Non-Capital Losses—ITA 111(5)

14-22.   In Chapter 11 we discussed the composition of non-capital losses, noting that such losses were composed of losses from property, losses from business, losses from employment, and allowable business investment losses (ABILs). This distinction is important when it comes to the application of the AOC rules to non-capital losses.

14-23.   ITA 111(5)(a) and (b) do exactly the same thing as ITA 111(4)(a) and (b) with respect to non-capital losses, in that they prevent non-capital losses from crossing the line set by the deemed taxation year. There is, however, an exception but only for that part of a non-capital loss that relates to a business. In other words, one has to dissect the non-capital loss into the three corporate components of a loss from property, business, and ABIL. The part of the non-capital loss that relates to a property loss or ABIL is as severely restricted as a net capital loss, rendering that part of the loss unusable.

14-24.   The business loss portion of a non-capital loss, while tainted, may become usable if a certain condition is met. If the condition is met the business portion of a non-capital loss may be used on a restrictive basis. This means that the line mentioned can be crossed. The required condition that must be met is the following:

- After the AOC, the business that generated the non-capital losses (the "loss business") must be carried on for profit or with a reasonable expectation of profit.

14-25.   The reference to profit or a reasonable expectation of profit refers to the life cycle of a business. Businesses can generally be considered in one of three stages: (1) startup, (2) maturity, or (3) final stages to winding-up and terminating the business. In the startup stage, there is not likely any profit but there is a reasonable expectation of profit. In the maturity stage of a business there is likely both a profit and a reasonable expectation of a profit. In the final stage, however, when decisions have been made to terminate a business, there is a winding-down process as inventory is liquidated and corporate assets sold and liabilities paid. In this third stage there is no profit and no reasonable expectation of a profit, which looks to a non-existent future. This means lifting the restrictions on non-capital losses requires that the loss business be maintained and, to a degree, steps be taken to restore the health of the business. If actions are taken to wind down the business or not to do anything, then the condition to potentially allow the business portion of non-capital losses will not be met. We would add that it is the CRA's view that the condition must be met each year.

14-26.   If the loss business condition is met, then the business portion of the non-capital losses can be deducted as follows:

- To the extent of income from the loss business plus any income from another business that is virtually identical to the loss business. The legislation requires that at least 90% or more of the income from another business be the same activity of the loss business in terms of products sold or services provided. This is commonly referred to as a same or similar business concept. Both the CRA and the courts have historically applied this concept quite strictly. Not only do the products or services have to be near identical, but the nature of the business activity must also be the same. For example, a business that sells cars would not be considered similar to one that leases cars.

14-27.   A brief example can be used to illustrate these provisions.

EXAMPLE   Bostox Ltd. carries on two separate businesses, manufacturing cameras and the sale of specialty food products. During the year ending December 31, 2020, the camera business experienced a loss for income tax purposes of $5 million, while the food specialty products business had income of nil. The $5 million loss could not be carried back and, as a result, it became a 2020 non-capital loss. On January 1, 2021, the control of Bostox Ltd. is acquired by an unrelated company. During the year ending December 31, 2021, the camera business lost an additional $1 million, while the food products business had income of $7 million.

ANALYSIS   If there were no AOC, both the current 2021 business loss of $1 million and the 2020 non-capital loss of $5 million from the camera business could be applied against the income of the specialty food products business. This would have resulted in a 2021 taxable income of $1 million ($7 million profit on food products offset by a current loss of $1 million on cameras and the 2020 non-capital loss of $5 million).

Note that there is no short taxation year because the deemed taxation year would have ended December 31, 2020, which matches the existing taxation year.

However, with the AOC at the beginning of 2021, the 2020 non-capital loss is tainted and can only be applied to the extent of income from the camera business. This means that none of 2020 non-capital loss can be deducted in 2021, but the $1 million 2021 camera business loss can be netted against the $7 million food products income, resulting in a 2021 taxable income of $6 million. The $5 million 2020 non-capital loss will still be available but remains forever tainted.

Exercise 14-1

Subject: Acquisition of Control

India Inc. carries on two separate businesses, one of which sells fountain pens while the other provides professional accounting services. In its first year of operations ending on December 31, 2020, the pen business had a loss of $192,000, and the accounting business had income of $57,000, resulting in a net income of nil and a non-capital loss for the year of $135,000 [$192,000 - $57,000]. For the taxation year ending December 31, 2021, the pen business had income of $42,000, and the accounting business had income of $247,000, resulting in net income of $289,000 [$42,000 + $247,000].

Determine the minimum taxable income for 2021 assuming that (1) there was no AOC in either year and (2) there was an AOC on January 1, 2021. The company has no deductions from net income other than the 2020 non-capital loss of $135,000.

Solutions to Exercises are available in the Study Guide.

Unrealized Losses Forced Out

14-28. When the AOC rules apply they result in restricted access to tax preferences of an acquired corporation. These tax preferences take two forms. The first is existing tax accounts such as various loss carry forwards like net capital and non-capital losses. The second is unrealized losses on existing corporate property. If the AOC rules were restricted to realized losses and other tax preferences, there would be unequal treatment and therefore unfairness where one corporation had realized losses and a second only had unrealized losses.

EXAMPLE Two corporations, both with December 31 year ends, experience an AOC at the same time. The first corporation has a $100,000 net capital loss at the time of the AOC. The second corporation has no net capital losses at the time of the AOC but owns land that is non-depreciable capital property. The adjusted cost base (ACB) of the land is $450,000 and the FMV is $250,000. The second company will sell the land in the first taxation year after the AOC.

ANALYSIS As we have seen, the first corporation's net capital loss would be tainted by ITA 111(4) such that it could not be used in a taxation year ending after the AOC. If there were no rules to deal with unrealized losses, the second corporation would not be affected by the AOC. The second company could simply sell the land in the first year after the AOC and realize a $200,000 capital loss [ACB $450,000 - POD $250,000], which would become an allowable capital loss of $100,000 [(50%)($200,000)]. The allowable capital loss would then become a net capital loss of $100,000 assuming there were no taxable capital gains in the year the land was sold. Since the net capital loss would have materialized after the AOC it would not be tainted.

The Legislative Solution To address the concern over unrealized losses, the ITA contains a number of provisions that effectively ask whether the sale of any corporate property at FMV would result in some kind of loss. If the answer is yes, then all of those properties are deemed to have been disposed of at FMV and immediately reacquired at that same FMV. The purpose of these provisions are to force out the unrealized losses in the deemed taxation year caused by the AOC. In addition, the deemed reacquisition is designed to reset the tax cost such as ACB to the FMV. You will note that, as a rule, there are no specific provisions to force out unrealized losses on inventory. The reason for this is that the inventory valuation rule in ITA 10 requires that inventories be valued at the lower of cost or FMV at year end. Therefore, any declines in inventory value are already required to be recognized each year, so there is no need to add specific rules in the AOC legislation.

Applying The Legislation   Returning to our example, the land would be deemed to have been disposed of for the FMV of $250,000. The result is that there is a $100,000 net capital loss for the deemed year end that is now subject to tainting as discussed earlier. In addition, the ACB of the land has decreased from $450,000 to $250,000. The impact is that this legislation ensures that the two corporations in our example are treated the same.

Unrealized Loss Provisions

14-29.   There are further provisions that force out unrealized losses by category of property for income tax purposes. We have summarized the more common of these rules below:

Non-Depreciable Capital Property   ITA 111(4)(c) and (d) together apply to non-depreciable capital property such as investment-type property or land if the ACB of that property exceeds its FMV. The difference (the unrealized loss) is treated as a capital loss, and that same difference is used to reduce the ACB of the property. If there are no capital gains to offset the capital loss, a net capital loss will occur in the deemed taxation year that will be tainted, as discussed.

Depreciable Property   ITA 111(5.1) applies to force out any terminal losses on a class of depreciable property. The provision asks if there would be a terminal loss if every property in a class were sold for its FMV. If the answer is yes, then the provision applies to deem all of the properties of that class to have been disposed of for FMV. The result is the recognition of a terminal loss that will be either a business loss or a property loss depending on what the class of depreciable property was used for. Unlike the case with non-depreciable capital property, there are no reductions in the capital cost of individual depreciable property; rather, the adjustment for the terminal loss is made by way of deemed CCA to the UCC.

EXAMPLE   A corporations that experienced an AOC had class 8 depreciable property. The capital cost was $40,000, the UCC of the class was $27,000 (CCA previously claimed was $13,000), and the FMV was $10,000.

ANALYSIS   A sale of the property at FMV would have resulted in a terminal loss of $17,000 [UCC $27,000 - $10,000 (lesser of capital cost of $40,000 and the deemed POD (FMV) of $10,000)]. As a result, ITA 111(5.1) applies to cause a terminal loss of $17,000 to be deducted in the deemed taxation year end. In the following taxation year the UCC will be reduced by the terminal loss, which is treated as deemed CCA. The result is that the UCC is equal to the FMV at the time of the AOC of $10,000 calculated as capital cost of $40,000 - CCA of $30,000 (CCA initially claimed of $13,000 + deemed CCA of $17,000). You will note that the capital cost and ACB remains unchanged at $40,000.

Accounts Receivable   The ITA provides businesses with an option to claim a deduction for doubtful debts under ITA 20(1)(l) where the ability to collect accounts receivables is in question. If there was an AOC it would generally be in the interests of all parties to limit losses to the extent possible, which would serve to limit any loss restrictions. One strategy could be choosing not to claim a doubtful debt reserve in the deemed taxation year end and instead claiming the deduction in the following year, thus avoiding any AOC effect. ITA 111(5.3) is designed to address this situation. The provision requires that the acquired corporation claim the maximum doubtful debt reserve and that it be treated as a bad debt expense (ITA 20(1)(p)). This means that there would be no reserve add back in the next year and an establishment of a new reserve, as would be the case if it were treated as a doubtful debt deduction. The result is that the unrealized loss on the accounts receivables are recognized in the deemed year end.

Exercise 14-2

Subject: Unrealized Losses Forced Out

On November 15, 2021, Parkat Ltd., acquires control of Sparkat Ltd. Parkat and Sparkat are unrelated persons prior to the acquisition of control. On November 14, Sparkat Ltd. owns the following properties:

- Land with an ACB of $293,000 and a FMV of $215,000

- Class 8 depreciable property with a capital cost of $416,000, a UCC balance of $276,000, and a FMV of $184,000

Indicate the income tax consequences of an AOC on the above properties for Sparkat Ltd. for its deemed taxation year ending November 14, 2021.

Solutions to Exercises are available in the Study Guide.

Unrealized Gains Election—ITA 111(4)(e)

14-30.   The requirement that unrealized losses on depreciable or non-depreciable capital property be forced out in the deemed taxation year as a result of an AOC is particularly onerous in that the resulting losses may no longer be usable in a subsequent year. In recognition of this potential hardship and to restore a semblance of fairness there is an elective option that allows the acquired corporation to trigger unrealized capital gains and recapture. This option allows a corporation to offset any unrealized losses that the corporation is forced to recognize, as previously discussed, and may lessen the AOC impact overall with respect to tax preferences, such as loss carry overs that become tainted. The elective option only applies to capital property with unrealized capital gains or unrealized recapture.

14-31.   For non-depreciable capital property the election allows all or a part of the unrealized capital gain to be recognized. The election provides for a deemed disposition at an amount anywhere between the ACB and the FMV. If, for example, a corporation owned investments that are capital property with an ACB of $40,000 and a FMV of $50,000, the elective range is between $40,000 and $50,000. If the corporation only requires $6,000 of capital gains to offset unrealized capital losses, then the corporation would elect a deemed disposition of $46,000, which would also become the new ACB of the investments.

14-32.   The rules for depreciable property are somewhat more complicated, however, depending on whether a disposition at FMV would result in a capital gain and recapture or recapture only. The following examples will help clarify this issue.

EXAMPLE 1   A corporation owns one class 10 property. The capital cost and ACB are both $18,000, the UCC is $5,000, and the FMV is $25,000.

ANALYSIS 1   A disposition of the property at FMV would result in a capital gain of $7,000 [POD $25,000 - ACB $18,000] and recapture of $13,000 [UCC of $5,000 less $18,000 (the lesser of capital cost of $18,000 and the deemed POD of $25,000)]. ITA 111(4)(e) allows an elective range between the ACB of $18,000 and the FMV of $25,000. This means that any part of the unrealized capital gain can be triggered, however all of the recapture must be included. If the corporation elects to trigger part of the capital gain, only one-half of that difference will be eligible for CCA (ITA 13(7)(f)) after the AOC. This rule is identical to ITA 13(7)(e), which applies when there is a purchase of depreciable property between non-arm's-length persons. If the election was made for $25,000 the result would be a capital gain of $7,000, recapture of $13,000, and the capital cost of the deemed reacquired property would be $21,500 [$18,000 + (1/2)(the $7,000 realized capital gain)]. The ACB of the property for capital gains purposes would be $25,000.

EXAMPLE 2   A corporation owns one class 10 property. The capital cost and ACB are both $18,000, the UCC is $5,000, and the FMV is $15,000.

ANALYSIS 2   In this case a sale of the property at FMV of $15,000 would only result in recapture and no capital gain as the FMV does not exceed the ACB. The recapture would be $10,000 [UCC of $5,000 less $15,000 (the lesser of capital cost of $18,000 and the deemed POD of $15,000)]. ITA 111(4)(e) allows an elective range between the ACB and FMV when there is an unrealized capital gain, but when the FMV is below the ACB, as in this case, there is no range and the only elected amount allowed is the FMV. Using these numbers an election would have to be made at $15,000, resulting in $10,000 of recapture, as indicated. Since the elected amount of $15,000 is less than the capital cost of $18,000, the corporation is deemed to have reacquired the property for CCA purposes only at $18,000, and the $3,000 difference is treated as deemed CCA. The recapture resets the UCC for the next taxation year at nil, then adds the deemed cost of $18,000 and subtracts the $3,000 of deemed CCA, leaving UCC of $15,000, which is equal to the FMV of $15,000.

Summary — ITA 111(4)(e)

14-33.   The elective rules effectively apply to three types of capital property as follows:

Non-Depreciable Capital Property   An election is available to trigger unrealized capital gains. The elective range is between the ACB and the FMV. The new ACB equals the elected amount.

Depreciable Property (with unrealized capital gains)   The elective amount is the same range as for as non-depreciable capital property. All of the recapture must be included and the capital cost for CCA purposes afterward is the original capital cost plus one-half of the capital gain triggered as a result of the election.

Depreciable Property (no unrealized capital gains)   The elective amount is the FMV of the property only. All of the recapture may not be realized, and as a result the deemed capital cost afterward is equal to the original capital cost with any difference between the FMV and the original capital cost treated as deemed CCA.

14-34.   If the acquired corporation has net capital losses and there are non-depreciable capital properties with accrued gains, this election is clearly desirable in that it will generate capital gains, which can be used to offset the net capital losses that would become unusable as a result of the AOC. The situation is less clear cut when the gains are on depreciable property. While the deemed disposition will create capital gains, it will also result in recapture of previously claimed CCA. This may or may not be a desirable situation.

Example

14-35.   The following example will illustrate the effect of an ITA 111(4)(e) election.

EXAMPLE   Burkey Ltd. has a December 31 year end. On June 1, 2021, a new and previously unrelated investor acquires control of the company. While its basic operations have been profitable for many years, the company has a net capital loss balance of $200,000. The company has a deemed taxation year ending May 31, 2021. On that date the company owns non-depreciable capital property with a FMV of $800,000 and an ACB of $500,000. Its class 8 depreciable property has a FMV of $1,200,000, a capital cost of $1,100,000, and the UCC is $600,000.

ANALYSIS   The ITA 111(4)(e) election is clearly desirable with respect to the non-depreciable capital property. It would allow a maximum amount of taxable capital gains of $150,000 [(1/2)(POD $800,000 - ACB $500,000)]. This taxable capital gain could be applied to reduce the net capital loss balance to $50,000.

Using the maximum ITA 111(4)(e) elective amount will result in a taxable capital gain of $50,000 [(1/2)(POD $1,200,000 - ACB $1,100,000)], which is sufficient to absorb the remaining net capital loss amount of $50,000. However, the election will also result in recapture of $500,000 (UCC $600,000 - $1,100,000 (the lesser of capital cost of $1,100,000 and deemed POD of $1,200,000)). Depending on whether there were other losses, it may be advisable not to elect on the depreciable property given the potential added income tax liability as a result of the recapture. One mitigating factor would be that the election would result in an increased capital cost of $1,150,000 [$1,100,000 + (one-half of the capital gain of $100,000)] and therefore larger CCA claims in subsequent taxation years. Note that neither the accelerated investment incentive (AccII) nor the half-year rule would apply to the deemed reacquisition.

Exercise 14-3

Subject: Elective Option on an AOC

Means Ltd. has a December 31 year end. On May 1, 2021, all of the company's shares are acquired by an unrelated person. For the period January 1, 2021, through April 30, 2021, the company has a business loss of $45,000 and has a 2019 net capital loss balance of $110,000. In addition, the company owns the following properties at April 30. 2021:

Type of Capital Property	Adjusted Cost Base/ Capital Cost	UCC	Fair Market Value
Non-depreciable	$500,000	N/A	$650,000
Depreciable	400,000	350,000	500,000

Advise the company with respect to the most appropriate elections to be made to minimize the impact of the AOC. Explain your results.

Solutions to Exercises are available in the Study Guide.

We suggest you complete SSP 14-1 and 14-2 at this point.

Associated Corporations—ITA 256

Overview

14-36.   In Chapter 12 we discussed the small business deduction, which provides a Canadian controlled private corporation (CCPC) with up to $95,000 in federal income tax savings [(19%) ($500,000 maximum business limit)]. The purpose of the small business deduction from a tax policy perspective is to provide small to medium-sized Canadian businesses with additional after-tax funds to grow their business, which fuels the economy and results in increased employment opportunities for Canadians. The Department of Finance tax expenditure report for 2021 estimates that the tax cost of providing the small business deduction for 2022 will cost

Canadian taxpayers a little over $6 billion. It is therefore important, from a government perspective, that this incentive be properly targeted.

14-37.   The tax policy that underscores the small business deduction is designed to ensure that (1) there should be no more than one business limit of $500,000 for a business and (2) that each economic unit should be entitled to only one business limit. A reference to an economic unit means that the same person or group of persons controls two or more CCPCs.

14-38.   Incentives such as the small business deduction are, by their nature, prone to tax planning designed to increase or multiply the income tax savings. If, for example, Mrs. Doyle carries on a single business that expects to earn $500,000 of active business income each year it is in her interest to incorporate that business in a CCPC that she will control because the small business deduction would be available. If the business doubled in size and expected to earn $1 million in active business income, the CCPC would only be entitled to the small business deduction on half of that income. Could she double up on the small business deduction with a little tax planning? She could create a new CCPC and move half of the business to that CCPC so that each CCPC would only earn $500,000 in active business income.

14-39.   There are many ways to restructure the business of a CCPC that is motivated by multiplying access to the small business deduction, but such planning seems to run counter to the tax policy objectives mentioned in Paragraph 14-37. Attempts to circumvent the "one small business deduction for one business" policy have been met with new legislation that restricts what can be claimed as a small business deduction. These relatively new rules are found in the specified corporate income and specified partnership rules in ITA 125. These rules were not covered in Chapter 12 due to their complexity. In addition, there has always existed a special anti-avoidance rule designed to challenge the basis for splitting a single business among two or more CCPCs that will be discussed briefly in this section of the text (ITA 256(2.1)).

14-40.   The ability to potentially claim multiple small business deductions is premised on having more than one CCPC. Historically, therefore, the emphasis has been on the second policy objective mentioned, which is that the two or more CCPCs are controlled by the same economic unit. If, in our example, Mrs. Doyle, incorporated a second CCPC and transferred half of the business to it the two CCPCs would both be controlled by her, which would restrict the ability to claim the small business deduction, limiting the two CCPCs to one $500,000 business limit that they could then agree to share. The concept that achieves this result and tests whether one economic unit controls two or more CCPCs is the associated corporations concept, which is the subject of this section.

14-41.   While the associated corporation rules were specifically designed to deal with multiplication of the small business deduction, the concept has expanded over the years to apply to other areas of the ITA, specifically investment tax credits and scientific research and experimental development expenditures (SRED), which will also be discussed to some degree in this chapter. Our focus, however, will centre on the small business deduction.

Basic Concepts

14-42.   There are three different control concepts (legal, de facto, and other) applied in the ITA, but their use varies depending on which specific provision of the ITA is being considered. In Paragraph 14-13 we saw an example of the distinction noting that the AOC rules only applied legal control, which is a control concept applied uniformly throughout the ITA whenever the word "control" or variations of it are used. De facto and other control concepts are generally restricted to anti-avoidance provisions and other provisions to minimize the opportunity that the rules could be circumvented.

14-43.   The associated corporation rules are anti-avoidance in nature and have historically been modified on an ongoing basis to address structural tax planning attempts to avoid its application. As a result, the rules sometimes seem to lack coherence and appear to be restricted to very specific situations when, in fact, the rules are quite broad. At first glance there only appear to be five situations in which the associated corporation rules could apply. These situations are numbered as the five paragraphs of ITA 256(1)(a), (b), (c), (d), and (e), which we will discuss. We will refer to these five paragraphs as the general rules.

14-44.   All three concepts of control apply when considering whether corporations are associated. The ITA uses the expression "controlled, directly or indirectly in any manner whatever" to refer to both legal and de facto control. Rules in ITA 256 add a series of "other control" concepts.

14-45.   The second thing to be aware of is that the general rules make reference to "related persons" and "related groups of persons," which must be clarified.

14-46.   The following basic concepts are important to understand in order to obtain a practical understanding of the associated corporation rules:

Related Persons   We will restrict our discussion of related persons to individuals (ITA 251(2)(a)). Individuals are related to each other if they are family. This means parents, grandparents, children whether adopted or not, and siblings. The main exceptions are that an individual is not considered to be related to their aunts, uncles, nieces, nephews, and cousins under the definition used in the Act. In addition, in-law to in-law relationships are not considered to be related. This means that if an individual is married or in a common-law partnership for income tax purposes, members of his family, such as parents or brothers or sisters, would not be considered to be related to the parents, brothers, or sisters of the spouse or common-law partner. The individual would, however, be related to spouses or common-law partners of her siblings as well as any individual family member of her spouse or common-law partner.

Related Group of Persons   A related group of persons is defined in ITA 251(4) as a group in which each member is related to every other member.

Legal Control   Legal control has been defined by the Supreme Court of Canada as "owning a sufficient number of shares to elect the majority of the members of the Board of Directors." This means owning shares that entitle the shareholder to vote for members of the board of directors and not shares that are non-voting. In everyday use, common shares are usually voting shares and preferred shares are not. Corporate law in Canada often gives limited voting rights to non-voting shares, but those rights do not impact legal control.

De Facto Control   De facto control, or control in fact, is a legislated control concept (ITA 256(5.1)) that looks past controlling shareholders to others to determine if, based on the facts, there are persons that possess influence over the corporation that if exercised would mean they have the ability to factually control the company and therefore its decisions. The CRA generally applies this concept looking to what it describes as "economic, contractual or moral" influence over a corporation's affairs. Examples would include economic dependence on others, such as where a CCPC only has one client; lack of independence, such as where there are shared premises, common operational control, and other common factors; family connections; and reliance on the skills and expertise of others that are critical to the success of the corporation.

In one situation considered by the courts, a father created a new CCPC, transferred part of the main business carried on in another CCPC, and had his adult son acquire all of the shares of the new CCPC. While the son had legal control of the second CCPC his father was considered to have de facto control as the business would not have survived without the father's expertise. The facts had shown that the son, because of lack of experience, relied solely on his father for all corporate decisions. The result was that the father was considered to control both CCPCs, with the result they were associated corporations. Had the father been found not to have control of the second CCPC the two corporations would not have been associated even though they were legally controlled by related individuals.

Other Control—Group Control   In our brief discussion of legal control by a group of persons it was explained that there is no group control if a company is legally controlled by a single person. Also, if there is no single person who controls the corporation, establishing group control will require evidence that the members of the group are acting together, referred to as acting in concert. This means identifying an actual controlling group. If there is no acting in concert, then no one is considered to have legal control. ITA 256(1.2)(a) and (b) establish an extended version of control that modifies these group concepts. This extended control concept effectively means that if the same two or more persons are shareholders in two corporations, those two or more persons are a group regardless of who actually controls the corporation.

EXAMPLE 1   Shareholder A, B, C, D, and E are all unrelated to each other and each own 20% of the only issued shares of First Co. Shareholders C, D, E, F, and G are also unrelated to each other and each own 20% of the only issued shares of Second Co. None of the shareholders act in concert with each other and no one possesses any influence over either corporation. The two companies would be associated if it can be shown that they are controlled by the same person or same group of persons.

ANALYSIS 1   Given the limited facts, (1) there is no legal control because no one person can be identified as having legal control, which in this case would require owning more than 50% of the voting shares, and there is no group control because there is no one acting in concert with others. (2) There is no evidence of influence by anyone, meaning there is also no de facto control. We have just eliminated two of the three types of control that can apply to associated corporations. The "other control" concept, however, allows us to pick and choose and assemble our own group. Since C, D, and E are shareholders of each corporation, we can consider them as a group of persons. As well, since this group of C, D, and E owns 60% of the shares, which is more than 50% of the voting shares of each corporation, the two companies would be associated.

EXAMPLE 2   Same situation as Example 1, except that shareholder C owns 60% of the shares of First Co. and A, B, D, and E own 10% each. In Second Co., shareholder D owns 60% of the shares and A, B, C, and E own 10% each.

ANALYSIS 2   The conclusion is the same as in Example 1. However, since C, D, and E are all shareholders of both companies and their combined shareholdings exceed 50% in both companies, we again conclude that the corporation is controlled by the same group of persons. The fact that one shareholder has legal control does not change this outcome since we are applying a different control concept than legal control to reach this conclusion.

Other Control—FMV Control   Another "other control" concept looks to the FMV of shares (ITA 256(1.2)(c)). If a person or group of persons owns shares that account for more than 50% of the FMV of all of a corporation's issued and outstanding shares or more than 50% of the FMV of all of the issued and outstanding common shares, then that person or group of persons will be considered to control the corporation. If that same person controls a second corporation or is part of a group of persons that controls that second corporation, then both corporations would be associated. A special rule in ITA 256(1.6) treats any shares that are similar to debt as debt for purposes of this valuation control concept. Shares that are considered to be similar to debt and excluded from this special rule are shares that participate in profits, or shares where the dividends are restricted to a fixed rate in a manner similar to interest and the amount that can be received from the corporation is limited to the share investment. In practice these characteristics are often found in fixed value, limited life preferred shares. ITA 256(1.1) defines these shares as "specified shares."

EXAMPLE   Shareholder A owns all of the Class A common shares of a CCPC and a second unrelated person owns all of the Class B shares. The Class B shares allow the shareholder to elect the majority of the members of the board of directors but only represent 35% of the FMV of the company. Who controls the company for purposes of the associated corporation rules?

ANALYSIS   The Class B shareholder has legal control of the company since the shares are sufficient to elect the majority of the board of directors. Shareholder A is considered to have control as "other control" because her shares account for more than 50% of the FMV of all of the corporation's issued and outstanding shares. In effect, this means that there are two controlling persons for the associated corporation rules. Multiple control is not uncommon.

Deemed Share Ownership—Minor Children   While not a control concept per se, this rule may deem a person to own additional shares that may then result in him having control. In this case, ITA 256(1.3) applies to deem a parent who owns shares in one corporation to own shares of a second corporation if they are owned by a child of that parent who is under the age of 18. This rule is designed to prevent parents from avoiding association by having their shares owned by a minor child.

Deemed Share Ownership—Share Options   While also not a control concept, this rule deems a person who has rights to acquire shares in a corporation to have exercised that right and actually own the shares that would have been acquired when determining whether corporations are associated. If the right is only exercisable upon death, permanent disability, or bankruptcy, the rule does not apply. This rule also requires that every shareholder's options be deemed to have taken place, meaning that if the rights are proportional among all shareholders this provision will generally not change anything.

Deemed Share Ownership—Tiered Corporations   Another associated corporation provision deems a shareholder of one corporation to own shares of a second corporation owned by the first company based on proportional FMV of the shares of the first company (ITA 256(1.2)(d)).

EXAMPLE 1   Shareholder A owns 90% of the only shares issued by Holdco, a CCPC. Holdco owns 40% of the shares of an operating company that is also a CCPC that we will call Opco. Shareholder A also owns 15% of the shares of Opco personally.

ANALYSIS 1   Shareholder A is deemed to own 36% of the Opco shares as a result of her share ownership in Holdco [(90%)(40%)]. When that 36% is added to the 15% A already owns, A is considered to own 51% of the Opco shares. As a result, since A controls both Holdco and Opco the two companies would be associated. A would also be considered to have direct legal control of Opco. The legal control of Holdco means A controls the 40% block of shares Holdco owns in Opco. When added to the 15% Opco shares A owns personally, she would control 55% of the voting control of Opco.

EXAMPLE 2   Shareholder A owns 45% of the only shares issued by Holdco, a CCPC. Holdco owns 40% of the shares of an operating company that is a CCPC that we will call Opco. A also owns 33% of the shares of Opco personally.

ANALYSIS 2   A is deemed to own 18% of the Opco shares as a result of the share ownership in Holdco [(45%)(40%)]. When this is added to his 33% share ownership, he owns 51% of its voting shares. Using the FMV control concept, A owns more than 50% of the value of the issued and outstanding shares of Opco and is therefore considered to control Opco. In this second example, A would not have legal control of Opco because A does not have legal control of Holdco.

Examples—Associated Corporation Rules

14-47.   With an understanding of the three control concepts and many other rules such as deemed share ownership, it is time to look at the general rules used in determining if corporations are associated. These rules are contained in the five paragraphs of ITA 256(1). Each of the paragraphs describe a specific structural relationship that must be met for association to occur.

14-48.   The first of these paragraphs reads as follows:

ITA 256(1)(a)   one of the corporations controlled, directly or indirectly in any manner whatever, the other.

14-49.   This type of association is illustrated in Figure 14-1, in which A Company owns 75% of the issued and outstanding voting shares of B Company and therefore controls it. A Company and B Company are therefore associated because of ITA 256(1)(a). We would add that as long as there is legal control between each company represented by more than 50% of the voting shares the companies would be associated. If we altered Figure 14-1 to change the shareholding to 51% and added a third company (C Company), of which B Company owned 51%, all three companies would be associated. In that case A Company would control both B and C Company, and B Company would control C Company. Control is separately measured between each company.

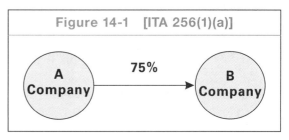

Figure 14-1   [ITA 256(1)(a)]

14-50.   The second paragraph in ITA 256(1) reads as follows:

ITA 256(1)(b)   both of the corporations were controlled, directly or indirectly in any manner whatever, by the same person or group of persons.

This type of association is illustrated in Figure 14-2. In this situation, Mr. A has a controlling interest in both A Company and B Company. As a consequence, these two companies are associated because of ITA 256(1)(b), in that they are both controlled by the same person.

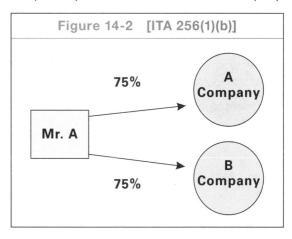

Figure 14-2   [ITA 256(1)(b)]

14-51.   The third paragraph in ITA 256(1) reads as follows:

ITA 256(1)(c)   each of the corporations was controlled, directly or indirectly in any manner whatever, by a person and the person who so controlled one of the corporations was related to the person who so controlled the other and either of those persons owned, in respect of each corporation, not less than 25% of the issued shares of any class, other than a specified class, of the capital stock thereof.

14-52.   ITA 256(1)(c) requires a precise situation with the following conditions:

• Both corporations are controlled by one person;
• The persons who control each corporation are related to each other; and
• One of those two persons own at least 25% of any class of shares in the other corporation.

14-53.   This type of association is illustrated in Figure 14-3. Mr. A controls A Company with ownership of 100% of its shares, and Mrs. A controls B Company with 70% of its shares. Mr. A and Mrs. B are spouses and therefore related to each other. Finally,

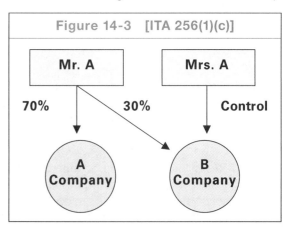

Figure 14-3   [ITA 256(1)(c)]

Mr. A owns 25% or more of a class of shares of Company B with his 30% ownership in Company B shares. The two companies are therefore associated by ITA 256(1)(c). Note that if the shares of Company B owned by Mr. A were preferred shares that had characteristics of debt, the shares would be considered shares of a "specified class" and ignored (ITA 256(1.1)). In that case the two companies would not have been associated because the 25% cross-ownership of shares would not have been met. This same notion applies to all of the 25% cross-ownership tests that are found in ITA 256(1)(c), (d), and (e).

14-54.   The fourth paragraph of ITA 256(1) reads as follows:

ITA 256(1)(d)   one of the corporations was controlled, directly or indirectly in any manner whatever, by a person and that person was related to each member of a group of persons that so controlled the other corporation, and that person owned, in respect of the other corporation, not less than 25% of the issued shares of any class, other than a specified class, of the capital stock thereof.

14-55.   Once again we have another precise situation that requires meeting very specific conditions as follows:

- One of the corporations is controlled by one person and the second corporation is controlled by a group of persons. The group of persons does not have to be a related group;
- The one person who controls one of the two corporations must be related to each member of a group of persons that controls the other corporation; and
- The single person who controlled one of the corporations must own at least 25% of any class of shares in the other corporation.

14-56.   This type of association is illustrated in Figure 14-4. In this situation, Mr. A controls A Company with a controlling interest of 80%, and a group of persons comprising Mr. A's spouse and brother have a controlling interest in the other corporation. In addition, Mr. A is related to both his spouse and his brother. Finally, Mr. A owns at least 25% of the shares of any class of the other corporation. As a result, the two corporations are associated because of ITA 256(1)(d).

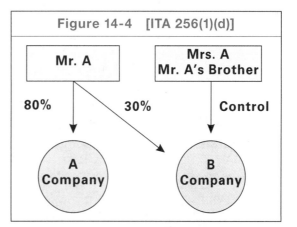

Figure 14-4   [ITA 256(1)(d)]

14-57.   The final paragraph in ITA 256(1) reads as follows:

ITA 256(1)(e)   each of the corporations was controlled, directly or indirectly in any manner whatever, by a related group and each of the members of one of the related groups was related to all of the members of the other related group, and one or more persons who were members of both related groups, either alone or together, owned, in respect of each corporation, not less than 25% of the issued shares of any class, other than a specified class, of the capital stock thereof.

14-58.   ITA 256(1)(e) requires another precise situation with the following conditions:

- Both corporations are controlled by a related group;
- Each member of one of the related groups is related to all of the members of the other related group; and
- A person or persons who are members of both related groups owns at least 25% of any class of shares of both corporations.

14-59.   We have assumed that Mr. A, as a member of both groups, owns at least 25% of the shares of each company. In addition, Mrs. B is the sister of Mrs. A. In this case both companies are controlled by related groups and all of the members of one related group are related to the members of the other related group. Note that Mr. A and Mr. B are related through their marital or common-law partner connection to Mrs. A and Mrs. B, who are sisters.

14-60. This type of association can be illustrated by the situation in Figure 14-5. Mr. and Mrs. A are a related group that controls A Company, and Mr. A, Mrs. A, along with Mr. and Mrs. B are a related group that control B Company. Mrs. B is Mrs. A's sister, and therefore each member of one related group is related to all of the members of the other related group. Mr. and Mrs. A are related to themselves as well as to Mr. and Mrs. B. Finally, Mr. and Mrs. A, who are members of both related groups, own a controlling interest in A Company and 40% of B Company. This fact

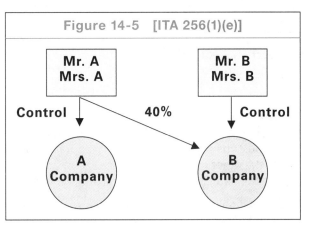

Figure 14-5   [ITA 256(1)(e)]

meets the final criteria as one or more persons who are members of both related groups owns at least 25% of a class of shares of each corporation. As a result, the two corporations are associated.

Deemed Association

14-61.   We complete the associated corporation coverage with two additional rules that deem corporations to be associated where no other association rules would apply. The two situations are described as follows:

ITA 256(2) Association through a Third Corporation   In situations where two corporations would not otherwise be associated, ITA 256(2) deems the corporations to be associated if they are both associated with the same third corporation. ITA 256(2)(b)(ii) allows the third corporation to file an election in which it can break the rule under ITA256(2). This election allows the first two companies to claim a business limit of up to $500,000 while the third corporation has a business limit of nil.

ANALYSIS—B Company & C Company   The two corporations are associated as a result of ITA 256(1)(b) because Mrs. B has legal control over both corporations with sufficient shares for her to be able to elect the majority of the board of directors of both corporations.

ANALYSIS—A Company & C Company   The two corporations are associated as a result of ITA 256(1)(c) because one person controls each corporation and the person that controls A Company (Mr. A) is related to the person that controls C Company (Mrs. A). In addition, Mr. A owns at least 25% of the shares of C Company.

ANALYSIS—A Company & B Company   None of the five paragraphs in ITA 256(1) apply to associate these two corporations. The closest match is ITA 256(1)(c), which fails because neither Mr. A nor Mrs. A passes the 25% cross-ownership test. As a result, ITA 256(1) does not apply. However, ITA 256(2) applies to deem the two corporations to be associated because they are both separately associated with a third corporation (C Company). We have illustrated the application of this deeming rule in Figure 14-6 (we will assume that all three corporations are CCPCs). There is an option, however, that would allow C Company to elect to break the deemed association between A and B Company. The price is that C Company agrees to accept a nil business limit. Interestingly, both A Company and B Company continue to be separately associated with C Company as a result of ITA 256(1). This means that while each of A and B Company have a $500,000 business limit, it may be reduced as a result of any taxable capital employed in Canada and adjusted aggregate investment income in C Company.

14-62.   The last deemed association rule is a true anti-avoidance provision found in ITA 256(2.1). The rule examines the "main reasons" behind separating a business into two or more

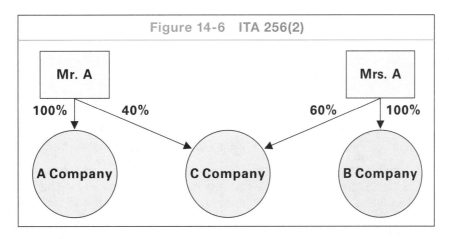

Figure 14-6   ITA 256(2)

corporations. If the main reasons behind such a structure are found to be tax motivated, such as by multiplying access to the small business deduction, the corporations will be deemed to be associated. Surprisingly, there have been many successful challenges based on arguments that the reasons behind the structuring had little or nothing to do with tax savings and instead was primarily motivated by family issues, creditor proofing, or estate planning.

Exercise 14-4

Subject: Associated Companies

The Top Company owns 65% of the shares of Middle Company as well as 10% of the shares of Bottom Company. Middle Company owns 35% of the shares of Bottom Company. Mr. Top, who owns all of the shares of Top Company, also owns 5% of the shares of Bottom Company and has options in Bottom Company shares that would, if exercised, increase his ownership by another 10%. Mr. Top's 12-year-old son owns 15% of the Bottom Company shares. Indicate whether the three corporations are associated, specifically (1) Top and Middle, (2) Top and Bottom, and (3) Middle and Bottom. Explain the reasons for your conclusions.

Solutions to Exercises are available in the Study Guide.

We suggest you complete SSP 14-3 and 14-4 at this point.

Investment Tax Credits—ITA 127(5)

Background

14-63.   In terms of directing economic incentives to specific regions or types of activities, the ITA is used extensively to deliver these incentives. Investment tax credits are a very effective tax policy tool. They can be used to provide reductions in income tax that are specifically targeted, for example to scientific research and experimental development (SRED) and can be structured to provide a refund for those taxpayers in need who have no tax payable.

14-64.   Despite their advantages in terms of targeting benefits, the use of investment tax credits has declined over the last decade. At one time, they were available on a large variety of assets used in many types of businesses through most regions of Canada. Over many years the legislation has been scaled back considerably, restricting availability to specific targeted areas and only to certain types of property and expenditures. In this section, our discussion will centre on some of the remaining common uses, such as credits for salaries of eligible apprentices, current expenditures for SRED, and for the cost of certain property referred to as "qualified property."

Overview

14-65.   Investment tax credits are tax incentives that are available to Canadian taxpayers who are earning business income or who are involved in SRED. With some exceptions, they are available on the same terms for corporations as they are for individuals.

14-66.   In general terms, the rules for investment tax credits, which are contained in ITA 127(5) through ITA 127.1(4), allow a taxpayer to claim a specified percentage of the cost of certain types of expenditures and subtract this amount from his federal tax payable. The investment tax credits provide for a direct reduction in the amount of tax that is payable on a dollar-for-dollar basis.

14-67.   As a result of ITA 13(7.1)(e), when capital expenditures are involved such as the purchase of depreciable property, the amount of the investment tax credit claimed is subtracted from the capital cost of the property so that only the net capital cost is recognized for CCA purposes. The legislation requires that the subtraction occur in the taxation year following the year in which the investment tax credit is claimed. ITA 13(7.1) also indirectly causes a reduction in the ACB of depreciable property, which is defined as its capital cost (ITA 54). The ACB of non-depreciable capital property is also reduced by the amount of any investment tax credit claimed in the preceding year as a result of ITA 53(2)(k).

14-68.   The capital cost of depreciable and non-depreciable property must also be reduced by any government assistance received or receivable for the property, such as grants, subsidies, or forgivable loans as a result of ITA 13(7.1)(f). However, this reduction in the capital cost is made in the year in which the assistance is received or the year in which the taxpayer becomes entitled to receive the amount. The entitlement is usually determined when the taxpayer has been notified by the governmental authority that the assistance has been approved.

14-69.   When a taxpayer receives non-government assistance in respect of depreciable property, the assistance is generally required to be included in income under ITA 12(1)(x) when received. An elective option exists under ITA 13(7.4) that allows the taxpayer to choose to reduce the capital cost of the depreciable property instead. A similar option is available for non-depreciable capital property with an election under ITA 53(2.1).

14-70.   When a taxpayer earns investment tax credits for current expenditures, the amount of the investment tax credit claimed is generally required to be included in income in the following taxation year as a result of ITA 12(1)(t).

14-71.   The income tax treatment of investment tax credits and other financial assistance, whether governmental or non-governmental, recognizes that a taxpayer receives amounts that offset the cost of the expenditures. As a result, only that part of the cost actually paid by the taxpayer should be recognized for income tax purposes. This is the basis for reducing the cost of property by the investment tax credit claimed. If property is not acquired but current expenditures are made, the investment tax credit claimed effectively represents a contribution toward those expenses. This is recognized by requiring a taxpayer to include the investment tax credit in income, which then offsets a portion of those expenses.

14-72.   In effect, the economics of the mechanics of investment tax credits results in an increase in after-tax cash equal to the investment tax credit claimed (which equals the tax reduction) minus the corporation's tax rate on that amount. If, for example, a corporation with a tax rate of 15% was entitled to claim an investment tax credit of $10,000 on current expenditures but was required to include that same amount in income, the cash savings would be $8,500 [$10,000 reduction in income tax - income tax of $1,500 as a result of including the $10,000 in income]. The reduction in capital cost with respect to depreciable property reduces future CCA claims, spreading the income tax impact over more than one year.

Eligible Expenditures

14-73.   The following represents a list of some of the more common expenditures eligible to a corporation with respect to investment tax credits:

Salaries and Wages of an Eligible Apprentice   An eligible apprentice is defined in ITA 127(9) and can be described as follows:

> **Eligible apprentice**   means an individual who is employed in Canada in a prescribed trade (a trade currently listed as a "Red Seal Trade") in the first two years of their apprenticeship contract. This contract must be registered with a federal, provincial, or territorial government under an apprenticeship program designed to certify or license individuals in the trade. Qualifying trades include electricians, plumbers, welders, carpenters, various mechanics, hair stylists, pipe fitters, and many more. The credit is calculated on eligible salary and wages in the first 24 months of the contract. The annual limit is 10% of the first $20,000. If the contract runs from January 1 of year 1 to December 31 of year 2, the maximum investment tax credit would be $4,000 [(10%)(2 years)($40,000)]. If, however, the contract runs from July 1 of year 1 to June 30 of year 3, there would be three years of limits that could total $6,000 in investment tax credits. This has been confirmed by the CRA.

Qualified Property   ITA 127(9) defines "qualified property" with further elaboration provided in ITR 4600 and 4601. Qualified property must be new property acquired primarily for use in Canada, and it must be available for use in specified activities. These activities include manufacturing and processing, logging, farming or fishing, and storing grain.

Qualified SRED Expenditures   These expenditures include current expenditures for basic or applied research and for the development of new products and processes. Capital SRED expenditures do not qualify. The rules related to SRED expenditures are extremely complex and the application of these rules goes beyond the scope of this introductory text. As a result, we provide limited coverage of this topic and do not include coverage of what qualifies or does not qualify as SRED expenditures.

Rates
General

14-74.   Current rates for the investment tax credits that we have described are as follows:

Type of Expenditure	Rate
Salaries and wages of eligible apprentices	
(annual limit is $20,000 of eligible salaries and wages for each apprentice)	10%
Qualified property	
In Atlantic provinces and Gaspe Peninsula	10%
Prescribed offshore regions (East Coast)	10%
Rest of Canada	Nil
SRED	
Incurred by any taxpayer	15%
Incurred by CCPCs (see Paragraph 14-75)	35%

Exercise 14-5

Subject: Investment Tax Credits

During 2021, Colus Inc. pays salaries to five eligible apprentices in the year totalling $125,000 ($25,000 per apprentice). In addition, the company purchases $3,000,000 in class 8 property, which is qualified property to be used in the Atlantic provinces. Describe the 2021 and 2022 income tax consequences associated with making these expenditures and claiming all of the related investment tax credits for the year. Include in your solution the CCA for 2021 and 2022.

Solutions to Exercises are available in the Study Guide.

Special Rate on SRED Expenditures for CCPCs

14-75.   The standard investment tax credit rate for SRED expenditures is 15%. ITA 127(10.1), however, adds an additional 20% for corporations that are CCPCs, increasing the overall rate to 35%. The 35% rate is only available to the extent of a CCPCs "expenditure limit," which is equal to a maximum of $3 million of qualifying current SRED expenditures.

14-76.   The expenditure limit is reduced as a result of ITA 127(10.2) if the preceding year's taxable capital employed in Canada was greater than $10 million. If the CCPC was associated with any other corporation, it is the taxable capital employed in Canada of all of the associated corporations for their combined taxation years that ended in the preceding calendar year. The expenditure limit reduction is determined as follows:

Annual expenditure limit = [$3,000,000][($40,000,000 − **A**) ÷ $40,000,000]

where **A** is

(a) nil if combined taxable capital employed in Canada for the corporation and any associated corporations is less than $10 million for taxation years ending in the previous calendar year.

(b) in any other case, the lesser of $40 million and the amount by which the combined taxable capital employed in Canada for the corporation and any associated corporations exceeds $10 million for taxation years ending in the preceding calendar year.

14-77.   If a CCPC and its associated companies have previous-year combined taxable capital employed in Canada of less than $10 million, the expenditure limit will be $3 million. If the associated group of corporations has taxable capital employed in Canada for the preceding year over $10 million but less than $50 million the limit will be reduced by $3 for every $40 of the excess. It will be completely eliminated when the taxable capital employed in Canada for the preceding year reaches $50 million, as shown in the following calculation:

$$[\$3 \text{ Million}] \left[\frac{\$40 \text{ Million} - (\$50 \text{ Million} - \$10 \text{ Million})}{\$40 \text{ Million}} \right] = \text{Nil}$$

Exercise 14-6

Subject: SRED Expenditure Limit

Anfax is a CCPC that has a calendar-based taxation year ending December 31. It has never been associated with another corporation. Its taxable capital employed in Canada is $12,500,000 for 2020 and $11,500,000 for 2021. Determine Anfax's expenditure limit for 2021.

Solutions to Exercises are available in the Study Guide.

Refundable Investment Tax Credits—ITA 127.1

General Rules—40% Refund

14-78.   A problem with most tax credits is that, in general, they have value only when the taxpayer has an income tax liability to apply the credit against. To deal with this problem, some tax credits are "refundable." What this means is that, when a taxpayer is entitled to a tax credit and does not have sufficient tax payable to use it in full, the government will refund all or part of the unused amount. We have encountered this type of situation previously for individuals with respect to the refundable medical expense supplement tax credit (see Chapter 4). Refundable credits generally recognize the need of a taxpayer for much needed cash. This is particularly the case for CCPCs carrying out extensive research activities that require continuous injections of cash to continue the research.

14-79.   A refund of investment tax credits is generally available up to 40% of the investment tax credits earned by a taxpayer, provided the taxpayer is:

- an individual;
- a "qualifying corporation," which is a CCPC with taxable income in the previous year (before any loss carry backs) that together with the taxable income of all associated corporations does not exceed what is referred to as the qualifying income limit. The qualifying income limit is $500,000 that will be reduced if taxable capital employed in Canada of all associated corporations exceeds $10 million; or
- a trust where each beneficiary is an individual or a qualifying corporation.

14-80.   This means that if an individual had $1,000,000 in SRED current expenditures, the individual would be eligible for a $150,000 [(15%)($1,000,000)] investment tax credit. If the individual did not have sufficient tax payable in the current year or the three previous years to use this credit, there would be a refund (payment) of up to $60,000 [(40%)($150,000)]. The investment tax credit balance, after the refund claim, would be $90,000.

Additional Refund—100% Refund

14-81.   In the case of a qualifying corporation, additional amounts are refundable. To the extent that current SRED expenditures are eligible for the 35% investment tax credit, the resulting credit is eligible for a 100% refund. This means that a qualifying corporation that spends $3,000,000 on current SRED expenditures is eligible for a refund payment of up to $1,050,000 [(35%)($3,000,000)].

14-82.   The 100% refund is only available on the first $3,000,000 of expenditures that qualify for the 35% investment tax credit. We would remind you that capital expenditures do not qualify for SRED investment tax credits.

Carry Overs of Investment Tax Credits

14-83.   Under the definition of investment tax credit in ITA 127(9), unused investment tax credits may be carried back for up to 3 years and forward for 20 years. A taxpayer is required to claim all other available tax credits before calculating and claiming the investment tax credit for the year. Also, a taxpayer must reduce, to the fullest extent possible, federal tax payable for the current year before using investment tax credits to reduce previous years' federal tax payable.

Exercise 14-7

Subject: Refundable Investment Tax Credits

Sci-Tech Inc. is a CCPC that has incurred a number of expenditures that qualify for investment tax credits. They have invested $123,000 in qualified property in Nova Scotia. In addition, they have $1,200,000 in current SRED expenditures. The company for the previous taxation year has taxable income of $176,000 and taxable capital employed in Canada of $6,000,000. The company has no tax payable for the current year or the three previous years.

Determine the amount of the refundable investment tax credit that Sci-Tech will receive as a result of the expenditures made in the year and any available carry forwards. Include in your answer any other related income tax consequences.

Solutions to Exercises are available in the Study Guide.

We suggest you complete SSP 14-5 at this point.

Effect of AOC and Investment Tax Credits

14-84.   The rules for acquisitions of control (AOC) restrict tax preferences of an acquired corporation. Similar to the treatment of loss carry overs in an AOC situation, investment tax credit carry overs are also tax preferences that may be limited in an AOC.

14-85.   The restrictions, found in ITA 127(9.1) and (9.2), apply in a manner identical to that of the treatment of non-capital losses. When a corporation with investment tax credit balances is acquired, there is a deemed year end, as previously discussed. The general rule is that any investment tax credits up to and including that deemed year end cannot be applied to subsequent taxation years nor can investment tax credits earned after that deemed taxation year be carried back to that deemed year and prior taxation years. There is an exception, however, that allows the acquired corporation to cross that deemed taxation year line if the investment tax credits relate to the same business in which the expenditures were made. The investment tax credits can also be applied to tax payable with respect to a similar business.

Corporate Distribution Principles

Overview

14-86.   In the remainder of this chapter, corporate distributions to shareholders and the related income tax consequences will be considered. Distributions by corporations to shareholders can take many forms, as indicated in Figure 14-7. The most important of these are as follows:

- **Remuneration**   These distributions include salary, wages, bonuses, and benefits such as stock options and other taxable benefits where the shareholder is an employee. The ITA treats an individual who is a member of the board of directors of a corporation as an employee.

- **Shareholder Loans**   Corporate distributions may be temporary in the form of shareholder loans, a topic discussed in Chapter 15.

- **Return of Capital (PUC)**   Corporations can make distributions of corporate capital that is paid-up capital, or PUC, for income tax purposes.

- **Interest, Rent, etc.**   Since a corporation is a separate legal entity it can transact with other legal persons such as individual shareholders. Shareholders can make loans to a corporation or rent property they own to the corporation. The corporation in turn would make payments of rent and interest.

- **Dividends**   One of the most common corporate distributions are dividends, which can be paid in a variety of ways with cash, shares of the issuing corporation, and other corporate property.

- **Other**   Corporate distributions may include other arrangements. For example, a corporation could enter into a management services arrangement with shareholders to provide management services. Shareholders would receive management fees that would be categorized as business income.

- **Shareholder Benefits**   The characterization of corporate distributions is important. All of the various distributions mentioned in this paragraph are defined in terms of their legal nature. For example, remuneration cannot be paid to an individual who is not an employee. Loans to shareholders and contractual arrangements to rent shareholder property or to provide management services require a legal understanding and relationship that is best set out in terms of a written agreement prior to any actual distribution to ensure there is no misunderstanding as to the nature of the distribution. Corporate distributions are not defined in terms of accounting entries unless those entries reflect the legal nature of the distributions. Failure to follow this approach leads to the circle at the bottom of Figure 14-7, which is the worst-case scenario in terms of income tax consequences. The distribution is treated as a shareholder benefit under ITA 15(1), which means no deduction to the corporation and full taxation to the shareholder, often with gross negligence penalties (discussed in Chapter 2) that can increase the income tax by 50%. Shareholder benefits will also be discussed in Chapter 15.

14-87. In the remainder of this Chapter, our focus will be on corporate distributions that are dividends and a return of capital referred to as a return of PUC.

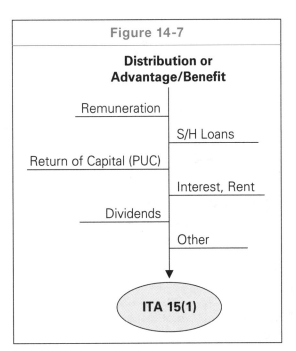

Figure 14-7

Tax Basis Equity Concepts

Overview

14-88. In order to fully comprehend corporate distributions in the form of a return of PUC and dividends, some understanding of the tax basis components of shareholders' equity is required.

14-89. A very simple situation involving a new corporation will illustrate the basic concepts. During the initial year, the following events take place: the purchase of shares by a single individual shareholder who incorporated the company, the realization of a capital gain, and the recording of after-tax profits for the year. The initial focus will be on the basic accounting entries and the corporate balance sheet for illustrative purposes only.

EXAMPLE

Transaction #1: Initial purchase of shares for $100 recorded as

Cash	100	
Share capital		100

Transaction #2: Purchase of a capital asset

Asset	100	
Cash		100

Transaction #3: Sale of the capital asset (capital gain)

Cash	300	
Asset		100
Gain on sale		200

Transaction #4: Recording of after-tax profit for the year

Asset	800	
Retained earnings		800

Balance sheet at year end

Cash	$ 300	Liabilities	$ Nil
Other assets	800	Share capital	100
		Retained earnings	1,000
Total	$1,100		$1,100

There are three income tax components that make up the share capital and retained earnings with respect to private corporations. They are paid-up capital (PUC), the capital dividend account (CDA), and earned surplus or retained earnings (R/E). The balance of these components for this example corporation, each of which could be distributed to the individual shareholder, is as follows;

PUC $100 can be distributed tax free (ITA 84)

CDA   100 can be distributed tax free (ITA 83(2))

R/E   900 can be distributed as a taxable dividend (ITA 89(1))

Total $1,100

14-90.   The example illustrates the importance of identifying different income tax equity components since some can be distributed tax free while others cannot. It is also important to recognize that while accounting principles and concepts are important to accountants in the preparation of annual financial statements, their relevance to income tax is extremely limited. The ITA either establishes its own distinctive terminology or relies on other law and the terminology used by that other law. Figure 14-8 compares the accounting terminology used in a balance sheet with comparable concepts used for income tax purposes. The figure also adds the income tax consequences of distributions from a particular income tax account. The three most common of these accounts are PUC, the CDA, and earnings in general.

Corporate Shares and the ITA

14-91.   In this chapter and many of the remaining chapters a solid understanding of income tax concepts and their application to share transactions is essential. There are three important points with respect to shares that must be kept in mind when determining the income tax consequences of transactions involving shares:

1.   **Fair Market Value (FMV)**   The FMV of a share is important to fully appreciate the application of share-based rollover transactions, certain anti-avoidance transactions, and the consequences when shares are reacquired by the issuing corporation. The FMV of shares generally depends on the characteristics of a share, including its rights. Voting common shares, for example, are entitled to participate in corporate profits and in any asset distributions

Figure 14-8

Balance Sheet	ITA Accounts	Distribution
Share capital (shares)	Paid-up capital (PUC)	Tax free
Contributed surplus	No special status	Note 1
Retained earnings	Pre-72 CSOH CDA Note 3 Earnings	Wind-up Note 2 Tax Free Taxable

Note 1 Can in certain limited cases be converted to PUC then distributed tax free [ITA (84(1)(c.1) to (c.3))]; otherwise, distributions would be required to be included in income.

Note 2 CSOH means "capital surplus on hand," which is defined at ITA 88(2.1). Can be accessed tax free but requires a corporate wind-up under ITA 88(2) to do so. Unlikely to see in practice today.

Note 3 CDA means "capital dividend account," defined at ITA 89(1). These dividends can be distributed tax free through ITA 83(2).

when a corporation is dissolved or wound up. As a result, valuing these types of shares are difficult since the FMV could change daily with profits and losses and changes in the value of a company's assets. In addition, market expectations will also be influential.

Fixed value preferred shares, on the other hand, are much easier to value since they are generally redeemable at the option of the shareholder or retractable at the option of the issuing corporation at either a fixed amount or an amount determined by formula. For example, the FMV of preferred shares redeemable for $100,000 would generally be $100,000 plus any unpaid declared dividends or cumulative dividends that have not yet been declared. The words "redeemable" and "retractable" both refer to the issuing corporation buying back the shares from the shareholders. Redeemable means that the shareholder can initiate the buyback, and retractable means that the buyback option is at the discretion of the corporation.

2. **Adjusted Cost Base (ACB)**   The ACB of non-depreciable capital property, such as corporate shares, is defined in ITA 54 as cost plus adjustments under ITA 53(1) minus any adjustments made under ITA 53(2). If the ITA 53(2) adjustments are large enough they may create what is referred to as a negative ACB. In that case the negative amount is treated as a capital gain when it occurs and resets the ACB to nil. If there are no ITA adjustments the ACB is the cost to the shareholder of acquiring the shares. Where the same shares have been purchased in multiple transactions at different costs, then ITA 47 (discussed in Chapter 8) requires a weighted averaging to determine the ACB per share.

Shares can be purchased directly from the issuing corporation or from others. The cost of shares is equal to the FMV of the consideration given up to acquire the shares. Consideration means the value or FMV of what has been given up to pay for the shares, which is generally cash plus the FMV of any other property given up. If, for example, an individual purchases shares for $5,000 cash plus land valued at $7,000, then the cost of the shares would be $12,000. Using the land to purchase shares would also be considered to be a disposition of that land, which could lead to a capital gain or a capital loss.

3. **Paid-Up Capital (PUC)**   PUC is the final tax-related share attribute to be aware of and is arguably the most important since it can be returned to shareholders tax free. In very general terms, PUC means the consideration received by the issuing corporation when the shares were first issued. There are three separate versions of this share equity concept: one for accounting purposes, one for corporate law purposes, and one for income tax purposes. The three versions of share equity are summarized as follows:

- Accounting principles and standards: Handbook section 3240 contains the general accounting rules for reporting what is generally referred to as "share capital."
- Corporate law: In Canada, each province and territory has its own corporate law, as does the federal government. As a result there are 14 different general corporate law statutes in Canada (one federal, ten provincial, and three territorial). Each statute contains rules on how to handle and calculate what is generally referred to as "stated capital." The federal *Canada Business Corporations Act* (CBCA), for example, includes some of the main rules when shares are issued in section 26 of that Act. We will refer to equity capital determined under corporate law generically as "legal capital" to avoid any confusion.
- The ITA: ITA 89(1) defines PUC as an amount first determined outside of the ITA. Once that initial amount is determined the ITA contains a number of PUC adjustments that may either increase or decrease PUC. Shares of a corporation are generally categorized as a class of shares. There can be various classes of shares, for example Class A common shares or Class C preferred shares. Classes of shares are generally divided based on different features and characteristics. ITA 89(1) defines PUC in terms of PUC per share, PUC per class of shares, and the total PUC of a corporation. All three concepts are used throughout the ITA, although the two most important ones used in this chapter and the ITA are the PUC per share and the PUC of a class of shares.

Calculating PUC and the ACB of Shares

14-92.   In Paragraph 14-91 we mentioned that ITA 89(1) states that the starting point for determining PUC is found outside of the ITA. That starting point is corporate law and not accounting. This means that we can describe PUC as follows:

Legal capital—Corporate law		XXX
Add/subtract: PUC adjustments—ITA 89(1)	XXX	
PUC—Defined in ITA 89(1)	XXX	

As a general rule, PUC, legal capital, and share capital will not always be the same. However, the share capital amount indicated on a corporate balance sheet will be the same as PUC if (1) the original shareholders have not changed; (2) there have been no rollovers (discussed in Chapters 16 and 17); (3) no new shares have been issued, including stock options; and (4) there have been no related party transactions involving shares. From a practical point of view, relying on a corporate balance sheet to determine PUC is not a good idea and can result in using PUC amounts that are inaccurate, leading to unforeseen tax consequences including penalties and interest.

14-93.   It is the relevant corporate law applicable to a corporation that is the starting point in determining PUC. The relevant corporate law is the jurisdiction under which the corporation is incorporated. If, for example, a corporation was incorporated in Alberta it would be subject to the *Alberta Business Corporations Act*, and if it was incorporated federally it would be subject to the CBCA. In terms of legal capital, the CBCA contains the following general provisions:

CBCA 26(1) Stated capital account—A corporation shall maintain a separate stated capital account for each class and series of shares it issues.

CBCA 26(2) Entries in stated capital account—A corporation shall add to the appropriate stated capital account the full amount of any consideration it receives for any shares it issues.

CBCA 26(2) refers to the "full consideration," which means the full FMV of the consideration given. CBCA 25 clarifies that share consideration must be in the form of cash or property. This means that shares must be fully paid. Owing an amount to a corporation for its shares is not allowed. In such a case the shares cannot legally be issued. In addition, a corporation is not allowed to add to its legal capital an amount in excess of the FMV of the consideration received for the shares, but in certain circumstances the corporation is permitted to add a lesser amount. As you can see, working with corporate shares requires a basic understanding of corporate law, which dictates what is allowed and what is not permissible.

14-94.   There remains one final PUC concern. ITA 89(1) requires that the PUC of each share be determined on a weighted average basis for each class of shares. Therefore, if Mrs. Finley acquires 100 Class A common shares of a federally incorporated CCPC for $1,000, her ACB would equal her cost of $1,000, or $10 for each share. CBCA 26(2) would require that full amount received of $1,000 be added to the class of shares by the company. ITA 89(1) then determines the per share PUC as $1,000 divided by 100 shares, or $10 each. At this point the ACB and PUC to Mrs. Finley would both be $10, as would the FMV. The PUC would be determined as follows:

Legal capital—CBCA 26(2)	$1,000
Add/subtract: PUC adjustments	Nil
PUC	$1,000

14-95.   Subsequently, a second individual, Mr. Liu, purchased 100 shares of the same class of common shares one year later for $3,000 because the value of the company had increased. Mr. Liu's ACB would be $30 per share, which is his cost. The PUC of the shares, however, is only $20 per share, calculated as $4,000 added to the legal capital ($1,000 by Mrs. Finley and

$3,000 by Mr. Liu) divided by 200 issued shares. The results to the two shareholders would be as follows:

Shareholder	ACB	PUC	FMV
Mrs. Finley	$10	$20	$30
Mr. Liu	$30	$20	$30

14-96. If Mr. Liu or Mrs. Finley subsequently sold their shares to another person for, say, $75 per share, the ACB to the new shareholder would be $75 but the PUC would not change since nothing has been added to the legal capital of the corporation. This leads to a general conclusion that ACB is determined as the cost to a particular shareholder but PUC is determined at the corporate level, meaning that it does not change unless the corporation is involved in the share transaction. A sale between Mr. Liu or Mrs. Finley and another person does not involve the corporation, therefore PUC does not change.

Exercise 14-8

Subject: Calculating PUC and ACB

Halide Ltd. has one authorized class of shares. The company issued its first 100,000 shares at a price of $1.10 each. Two years later, an additional 50,000 shares were issued for $1.35 per share. During the current year, a further 30,000 shares were issued for $1.82 per share. One of the individual investors in the company acquired 2,400 shares of the first group of shares issued and an additional 3,850 shares from the most recent issue. Determine, for that individual investor, the ACB and PUC per share.

Solutions to Exercises are available in the Study Guide.

Capital Dividend Account (CDA)—ITA 89(1)

Overview

14-97. In this text we have discussed numerous tax accounts that track various amounts for specific purposes; the GRIP, for example, was used to track high-rate income of a CCPC for the purposes of determining whether eligible dividends could be designated, and the RDTOH accounts tracked refundable taxes for the purposes of determining a private corporation's dividend refund. In Figure 14-8 there is a reference to pre-72 CSOH, which is an account that tracked corporation's capital gains and losses on property that had accrued prior to 1972 and that were realized after 1971. The reason for that particular account was that capital gains and losses were not taxable at all before 1972. The account tracked those tax-free amounts so that a corporation could then make a tax-free distribution of those amounts to its shareholders. While the CSOH account still exists it is no longer common.

14-98. The CDA, which accumulates tax-free amounts such as the tax-free half of a capital gain, is an important account as a private corporation can declare and pay a capital dividend to its shareholders up to the balance in its CDA account. This dividend will be received tax free by a Canadian resident shareholder. While a number of different amounts can be included in the CDA, the reason for its use can best be understood in the context of capital gains.

> **EXAMPLE** During 2018, Uval Ltd. acquires land at a cost of $150,000. During 2021, the land is sold for $190,000, resulting in a capital gain of $40,000 ($190,000 - $150,000).
>
> **ANALYSIS** There is a taxable capital gain of $20,000 [(1/2)(capital gain of $40,000)]. The remaining $20,000, however, is still being held by the corporation. The CDA adds that $20,000 non-taxable portion to the CDA so that it can maintain the tax-free status in the hands of its shareholders when distributed as a dividend.

14-99.   Unlike many tax accounts that only define balances at a corporation's year end, the CDA is determined at any point in time during a year. This allows corporations the flexibility to declare a capital dividend at any time of the year. As a result, in practice it is not unusual for a private corporation to declare a capital dividend immediately after a transaction in which there has been a significant capital gain. A CDA is only available to private corporations, without regard to whether they are CCPCs. In addition, capital dividends are only tax free to resident Canadians; therefore, it is important that capital dividends not be paid to non-residents.

Calculating the CDA

14-100.   A CDA is defined in ITA 89(1) and includes many components. Some of the more common components are as follows:

Capital Dividends Received   Capital dividends received from other private corporations are added to the CDA. This preserves the tax-free status of non-taxable amounts that move from one private corporation to another.

Capital Gains   The non-taxable portion of realized capital gains are accumulated in the CDA account, with this balance being reduced by the non-deductible portion of realized capital losses, which would include business investment losses. The wording of the definition begins with the capital gain then subtracts the portion of that capital gain that was taxable. Because of this, all of the capital gain on the donation of publicly traded shares that have been gifted to a registered Canadian charity would be included in the CDA since no part of the gain was taxable. Note that the fact that a capital loss is not deducted in a particular taxation year or becomes a net capital loss is irrelevant to the CDA for that year. The CDA automatically considers the non-deductible portion, whether deducted or not, in the year the loss is realized.

Note that this capital gain component of the CDA cannot be negative and reduce the amount of the other CDA components, such as capital dividends received.

EXAMPLE   In 2016, a resident private corporation realizes a capital loss of $15,000, the non-deductible portion of which is $7,500. In 2018, the corporation realizes a capital gain of $10,000, the non-taxable portion of which is $5,000. In 2021, the corporation receives a capital dividend of $1,000.

ANALYSIS   The capital gains component of the CDA is nil even though technically it would appear to be a negative amount of $2,500 ($5,000 non-taxable part of capital gains minus $7,500 non-deductible portion of the capital loss). The overall balance in the CDA, however, is $1,000 (the capital dividend received + a nil capital gain component). The capital gain component would only add to the CDA once it becomes a positive amount.

Life Insurance Proceeds   Life insurance proceeds received by a private corporation are added to the CDA, net of the adjusted cost basis of the policy. This treatment is provided where the corporation is the owner of the policy (i.e., the policyholder) and entitled to the proceeds on the death of an individual. This situation is quite common and provides a corporation with sufficient tax-free funds to buy out the deceased shareholder's estate. Life insurance proceeds are almost always tax free, and by adding the amount to the CDA a mechanism is provided that allows the corporation to return that amount to shareholders on a tax-free basis as a capital dividend. Note that any insurance premiums paid by a corporation in these circumstances would not be deductible.

Capital Dividends Paid   The account is reduced by capital dividends paid. As will be discussed in Paragraph 14-118, an election is required under ITA 83(2) to be entitled to pay a capital dividend.

Exercise 14-9

Subject: Capital Dividend Account

The following transactions involve the Knerd Corporation's CDA. The company has a December 31 year end.

- In 2019, land with an ACB of $86,000 was sold for cash of $108,000.

- In 2020, the company received a capital dividend of $8,200.

- On July 15, 2021, the company sold a business. The sale included goodwill of $43,000. The goodwill had not been purchased but had been developed internally. On January 1, 2021, the company's class 14.1 UCC balance was nil.

- In August 2021 the company realized an allowable business investment loss (ABIL) of $12,000.

- On October 31, 2021, the company paid an ITA 83(2) capital dividend of $16,000. The appropriate election was made.

Determine the balance in the capital dividend account on November 1, 2021.

Solutions to Exercises are available in the Study Guide.

We suggest you complete SSP 14-6 and 14-7 at this point.

Corporate Distributions

Introduction

14-101.   A corporation can make distributions in many forms for income tax purposes, as we have seen. PUC can be returned tax free, and dividends can also be paid tax free in the form of capital dividends. Both dividend distributions and a return of capital, or PUC, however, may be subject to restrictions by the relevant corporate law. For instance, CBCA 42 does not permit corporations to declare and pay dividends if it is reasonable to conclude that by doing so the corporation would be unable to pay its liabilities as they become due. A similar rule applies in CBCA 38 with respect to the ability of a corporation to reduce and pay its legal capital or PUC. The takeaway from this is that the ability to make corporate distributions is not always straightforward and is often subject to legal constraints such as corporate law and even contractual obligations. For example, a corporation that has borrowed heavily from a financial institution may be prevented from paying dividends or returning PUC to shareholders as a condition of the financing. These practical considerations must always be taken into consideration.

14-102.   In terms of dividend distributions it is important to understand the meaning of a dividend since the ITA makes a distinction between actual and deemed dividends. A dividend is legally defined in Canada as any distribution by a corporation of its income or capital gains made pro rata among its shareholders. Corporate law permits dividends to be paid in many forms, such as a stock dividend where shareholders receive additional shares in payment of a dividend. From an accounting perspective a stock dividend is handled as a capitalization of a corporation's retained earnings or earned surplus. A stock dividend, however, is arguably not a dividend since there is no actual distribution of corporate earnings in any form. The ITA, however, contains a brief dividend definition in ITA 248(1) that clarifies that any references to a dividend in the ITA is considered to include a stock dividend. This ITA definition, however, does not actually define a dividend, which requires relying on its legal meaning.

14-103.   In order to discuss issues related to the payment of dividends we will assume that there are no legal or contractual obstacles to the payment of dividends of any kind or the return of PUC (referred to as a return of capital).

14-104.   Actual dividends can be paid in three general forms: as cash, shares of the corporation (i.e., a stock dividend), or property of the corporation (referred to as a dividend in kind). In addition to these various types of actual dividends, other distributions, events, or transactions may result in what the ITA refers to as deemed dividends, meaning there will be income tax consequences to shareholders that are similar in most respects to the income tax treatment as if an actual dividend had been received. The main deemed dividend provisions are as follows:

ITA 84(1) deemed dividend on an increase in PUC

ITA 84(2) deemed dividend on the winding-up of a corporation or the reorganization of its business

ITA 84(3) deemed dividend on redemption, acquisition, or cancellation of shares

ITA 84(4) and (4.1) deemed dividend on a reduction of PUC

14-105.   The ITA, as a rule, treats all dividends the same whether they are actual dividends or deemed dividends. Actual dividends are paid by a corporation and received by a shareholder, The actual dividends may be classified as capital dividends or taxable dividends that are eligible or non-eligible dividends. Canadian resident individuals gross up taxable dividends and claim dividend tax credits. Corporate shareholders are not subject to Part I tax on taxable dividends because of the taxable income deduction of ITA 112(1) but may be subject to Part IV tax, as discussed in Chapter 13. In addition, the corporation paying the dividend may be entitled to a dividend refund when taxable dividends are paid to any shareholders.

14-106.   Deemed dividends may not actually result in the receipt of anything or may result in the receipt of something that is not an actual dividend, part of which may be a return of PUC. The deemed dividend rules identify a specific amount as the dividend. That amount is then deemed to have been received by the shareholder as a dividend and to have been paid by the corporation as a dividend.

14-107.   In the following paragraphs we will begin with actual dividends. Cash dividends were previously discussed in Chapter 7 and therefore we will not repeat that coverage at this point. We will focus our attention on actual dividends that are stock dividends and dividends in kind since their income tax treatment is somewhat different than cash dividends.

Stock Dividends

14-108.   From an accounting perspective, a stock dividend is a pro rata distribution of newly issued shares to existing shareholders of a corporation, normally accompanied by a capitalization of retained earnings or earned surplus equal to the FMV of the shares issued. Stock dividends are not technically dividends but are considered as dividends for income tax purposes and generally for corporate law purposes. Some corporate law jurisdictions, however, allow flexibility in determining the dollar amount of the stock dividend. The result is that the declared stock dividend is not required to match the FMV of the shares issued as a stock dividend. This has created shares commonly referred to as high-low shares, which mean shares with a high FMV but negligible PUC. These shares have historically been used in tax planning that the CRA generally views as offensive. There are a few anti-avoidance provisions in the ITA (e.g., ITA 15(1.1)) that specifically target stock dividends, limiting their use in certain tax planning situations.

14-109.   CBCA 43(2) is typical of most corporate law in Canada and provides rules that apply when a stock dividend is declared by a federally incorporated company. CBCA 43(2) reads as follows:

CBCA 43(2) Adjustment of stated capital account—If shares of a corporation are issued in payment of a dividend, the declared amount of the dividend stated as an amount of money shall be added to the stated capital account maintained or to be maintained for the shares of the class or series issued in payment of the dividend.

14-110.   CBCA 43(2) clarifies that the amount of the dividend declared by a corporation's board of directors determines the amount that is added to the legal capital (i.e., stated capital) for the class of shares that are paid as a stock dividend. At Paragraph 14-92 we described the calculation of PUC as beginning with the legal capital. In this case the increase in the legal capital as a result of the stock dividend equals the increase in the PUC. Since PUC is a tax-free concept, any increase in PUC should not be permitted for income tax purposes unless the amount has been included in income. This is precisely what the ITA requires. The definition of the word "amount" identifies the dollar amount of a stock dividend that is required to be included in income as follows:

ITA 248(1)(c) ... the "amount" of any stock dividend is the amount by which the paid-up capital of the corporation that paid the dividend is increased by reason of the payment of the dividend.

> **EXAMPLE**   Jessica Rabin is the only owner of Class A common shares of Fergis Ltd., a federally incorporated company. She owns 800 of the Class A common shares, which she acquired from another shareholder several years earlier for $32,000 ($40 per share). The PUC per share at that time was $12. On January 1, 2021, the board of directors declares a stock dividend of 10%, and as a result Ms. Rabin received 80 additional shares [(10%)(800)]. The PUC increases by $7.50 for each stock dividend share as a result of the stock dividend. No election is filed to treat the dividend as a capital dividend, and no designation is made to treat the dividends as eligible.
>
> **ANALYSIS—Fergis Ltd.**   The legal capital of the corporation is increased by $7.50 per stock dividend share issued, which is equal to the increase in the PUC. As a result, Ms. Rabin would be considered to have received a non-eligible dividend equal to $6,000 [($7.50 PUC increase)(80 stock dividend shares)]. The dividend would be grossed up by 15% to $6,900 [(115%)($6,000)] and she would be entitled to a dividend tax credit equal to $623 [($900 gross up)(9/13)].
>
> At this point the PUC of Ms. Rabin's shares is equal to $10,200 [(800 shares)($12) + (80 shares)($7.50)], or $12.05 each [($10,200 ÷ 880 shares)].
>
> There remains one problem, however. She paid $40 per share but has been taxed on an additional $7.50 per stock dividend share or an additional $600 of value, which is reflected in the PUC but not the ACB. To remedy this potential double tax issue, ITA 52(3)(a) considers the cost of the 80 stock dividend shares to be the same $600 stock dividend amount. As a result the ACB of Ms. Rabin's 880 shares is equal to $32,600 [(800 shares)($40) + (80 shares)($7.50)] or $40.75 per share [($32,600 ÷ 880 shares)]. In summary, the PUC of each share is $12.05 and the ACB is $40.75 as a result of the stock dividend.

14-111.   The stock dividend rules create an unfortunate situation for taxpayers, however. An individual receiving stock dividends will be taxed on a dividend even though no cash is received to assist in the payment of those taxes. This approach to the taxation of stock dividends serves to significantly discourage their use in Canada, particularly in the case of large publicly traded companies.

14-112.   As noted, however, it is possible for a company to issue stock dividend shares with a PUC that is less than the FMV of the shares. When this is the case, the cash flow issue is significantly reduced.

Exercise 14-10

Subject: Stock Dividends

On June 30, 2021, the shareholders' equity section of the balance sheet of Sturgis Inc. is as follows:

Common stock (23,400 shares outstanding)	$351,000
Retained earnings	462,000
Total shareholders' equity	$813,000

On this date, the company declares a 5% stock dividend. This dividend is not elected as a capital dividend nor is it designated as eligible. At this time, the shares are trading at $25 per share (i.e., FMV). The company increases its legal capital by the FMV of the stock dividend shares issued. Assume that the balance sheet share capital amount of $351,000 is equal to the legal capital and therefore PUC of the outstanding shares. Sturgis only has one class of shares.

Jean Tessier is holding 1,000 of the Sturgis shares, which he acquired several years earlier at a cost of $18 per share. Determine the effect of this transaction on Jean's 2021 net income and 2021 federal income tax payable. In addition, determine the ACB and PUC per share of his shares subsequent to the payment of the stock dividend.

Solutions to Exercises are available in the Study Guide.

Dividends in Kind

14-113.   While somewhat unusual, corporations do sometimes declare dividends that are payable in property other than cash or the corporation's own shares, and corporate law allows dividend payments to be made with property. In the case of large public companies an example of this might be a situation in which a corporation has a major holding of another corporation's shares and wishes to dispose of them. If the block is large, sale on the open market could significantly depress the sale price. A possible alternative is to distribute the shares on a pro rata basis to the corporation's existing shareholders.

14-114.   In a private corporate setting it is much more common. Shareholders may wish to own certain corporate property, and the distribution of that property by way of a dividend facilitates the change in ownership with a minimal cost. Although the amount of the dividend is equal to the FMV of the property distributed, the shareholder cost is equal to the income taxes payable on the dividend in kind, reducing the cost to the shareholder of receiving the property. These types of transactions are regularly targeted by the CRA to ensure that the transactions have taken place at FMV.

14-115.   Another common example of a dividend in kind is where a corporation is dissolved or wound up and corporate property is distributed as part of the wind-up process. This is discussed further in Chapter 17.

14-116.   A dividend in kind is a dividend received by a shareholder and paid by the corporation based on the FMV of the corporate property used to pay the dividend. The dividend can be elected as a capital dividend or designated as an eligible dividend.

14-117.   With respect to the corporate property, dividends in kind are regulated by ITA 52(2), which deems the cost of the corporate property acquired by the shareholder as a result of the dividend to be equal to its FMV. From the corporate perspective the corporation is deemed to have received proceeds for the disposition also equal to that same FMV. Depending on the type of property, this could result in busines income, a capital gain, capital loss, recapture, or terminal loss for the corporation.

EXAMPLE   Hold Ltd., a private corporation, owns shares in Bold Inc. These shares have an ACB of $800,000 and a FMV of $3,500,000. Hold Ltd. decides to distribute the Bold Inc. shares as a dividend in kind to its shareholders, all of whom are individuals.

ANALYSIS   The income tax consequences of this dividend are as follows:

- Based on deemed proceeds of $3,500,000, Hold Ltd. will have a taxable capital gain of $1,350,000 [(1/2)(POD $3,500,000 - ACB $800,000)].

- Hold Ltd. will have declared a dividend of $3,500,000.

- The individual shareholders will have received a taxable dividend of $3,500,000, subject to either the eligible or non-eligible dividend gross up and an entitlement to a dividend tax credit.

- The cost and therefore ACB of the Bold Inc. shares acquired by the shareholders will be the proportion of the FMV of $3,500,000 received by each of them.

- The capital gain to the corporation of $1,350,000 results in an increase in the CDA by the same amount. This cannot be used to elect capital dividend treatment for the dividend in kind, however, since the CDA addition only occurs after a capital gain has been realized.

Exercise 14-11

Subject: Dividends in Kind

Sandrine Cloutier owns 15% of the 500,000 outstanding shares of Cloutier Ltd. Cloutier Ltd. only has one class of shares. Cloutier Ltd. owns 150,000 shares of Botan Inc. The Botan Inc. shares were acquired by Cloutier Ltd. at a cost of $42 per share and have a current FMV of $51 per share. On June 30, 2021, Cloutier Ltd. declares a dividend involving the distribution of all of the Botan shares on a pro rata basis to its existing shareholders. No election is made to treat the dividend as a capital dividend and no designation is made to treat the dividend as eligible.

Determine the income tax consequences to the company on the payment of this dividend. In addition, determine the income tax consequences to Sandrine Cloutier with respect to her 2021 net income and federal income tax payable.

Solutions to Exercises are available in the Study Guide.

Capital Dividends under ITA 83(2)

14-118.   As we have previously indicated, the balance in the CDA reflects amounts that can be distributed as a dividend on a tax-free basis to shareholders of a private corporation. However, this tax-free status does not happen automatically but requires a formalized election. The election is made under the authority of ITA 83(2) and requires using a prescribed form (T2054), submitting a certified copy of the board of director resolution authorizing and declaring the dividend, and the completion of the corporate income tax T2 schedule (T2SCH89) showing the computation of the CDA immediately before the dividend was declared.

14-119.   The ITA 83(2) capital dividend election must generally be made before the dividend is declared and must be made on the full amount of the dividend. A capital dividend would be invalid if it claimed part of a dividend as a capital dividend. If a corporation wished to pay a capital dividend and a taxable dividend, it would need to declare two separate dividends.

14-120.   A timely filed election has two immediate income tax consequences. The first is that the corporation is deemed to have paid a capital dividend on the full amount of the dividend. The second is that no part of the dividend is included in the income of any shareholder who has received the dividend. If a corporation has declared a dividend, elected capital dividend treatment, and subsequently learns that the CDA was less than the full amount of the dividend there are initially tax consequences to the corporation only. Shareholders who have received the dividend continue to treat it as a capital dividend even though the CDA was insufficient to cover all of the dividend. Note that there are no ACB adjustments made to shares on which a capital dividend has been received.

14-121.   An election may be late filed up to 30 months after the declaration of the dividend (ITA 83(3)) on payment of a penalty. The maximum penalty is $500 per year (ITA 83(4)).

14-122.   If an election is made that results in the payment of a capital dividend in excess of the balance in the CDA, the corporation is liable to a penalty tax under Part III equal to 60% of the excess. The corporation can elect, within 30 months, to avoid the penalty tax with another election that effectively reverses the Part III tax by allocating the excess among the shareholders who received any part of the dividend and treating that excess part as a taxable dividend. This election requires concurrence among all shareholders who have received any part of the dividend. The consequences must be carefully considered since interest will be charged on any additional income taxes from the time the dividend was originally received.

14-123.   An excess election can occur inadvertently. For example, it is not uncommon for a CRA audit to revise amounts such as capital gains after a capital dividend election has been made. If the reassessed amounts reduce the CDA prior to a capital dividend election, the result will be an excess that is subject to Part III tax. There are many complexities associated with capital dividends, many of which are discussed at length in CRA Folio S3-F2-C1, "Capital Dividends."

ITA 84(1) Deemed Dividends—Increase In PUC

General Rules

14-124.   Since PUC is a function of corporate law's legal capital, taxpayers could receive income tax advantages by simply having a corporation increase its legal capital. Corporate law allows corporations to increase legal capital (1) by transferring amounts from surplus accounts to legal capital accounts; (2) by issuing shares as payment for acquiring property, paying for services, or for retiring corporate debt; (3) when paying a stock dividend; and (4) by transferring legal capital from one class of shares to another. In each situation the PUC of some shares will increase, and as a result the ability of shareholders to remove funds tax free from the corporation increases.

14-125.   ITA 84(1) is designed to address increases in PUC by treating the increase as a deemed dividend. There are, however, more than a few exceptions. One of the main exceptions is to ignore any part of a PUC increase that is matched by an increase in the FMV of a corporation's net assets (e.g., increase in assets or decrease in liabilities). If, for example, an individual purchased $10,000 of shares from the issuing corporation, the legal capital and therefore the PUC of the corporation's shares would increase by that same $10,000. ITA 84(1) would initially seem to apply because the PUC of the corporation has increased, but since the increase is matched by an increase in net assets of the same $10,000 there would be no deemed dividend.

14-126.   As an alternative, consider a situation where the individual acquiring shares pays the corporation for the shares with land. If the legal stated capital was increased by $10,000 and it was subsequently determined that the FMV of the land was only $7,000, ITA 84(1) would deem there to be a dividend equal to the $3,000 shortfall, meaning that the $10,000 increase in PUC exceeded the FMV increase in its net assets of $7,000 by $3,000.

14-127.   In the second example the dividend is deemed to have been paid on the class of shares rather than to the particular person who paid for their shares with land, resulting in the ITA 84(1) deemed dividend. This is because PUC of a class is averaged with the result that all shareholders of that class benefit. If there were other shareholders of that same class immediately after the transaction they would be subject to the deemed dividend based on the proportional number of shares they owned of that class.

14-128.   Another common example of this type of deemed dividend would involve situations where a corporation issues shares in settlement of a debt where the amount owing is less than the FMV of the shares issued as payment.

EXAMPLE   A corporation issues shares with legal capital and therefore PUC of $500,000 to a creditor in settlement of $450,000 that is owed to the creditor.

ANALYSIS   This transaction would result in an ITA 84(1) deemed dividend of $50,000 ($500,000 - $450,000) since the net assets of the corporation only increased by $450,000 as a result of the reduction of liabilities.

14-129.   Since a portion of the value of a shareholder's shares are taxed as a deemed dividend, an ACB adjustment is required to ensure that the deemed dividend portion is not taxed a second time if the shares are sold. As a result, the deemed dividend is added to the ACB of shares of each shareholder equal to the proportional deemed dividend included in his or her income. The ACB adjustment is added by ITA 53(1)(b).

14-130.   In our example, when the creditor accepted shares for the repayment of the debt the cost of the shares equals the FMV of what the creditor gave up, which was a right to receive the amount owed of $450,000. Therefore, the cost of the shares is $450,000. The ACB adjustment of $50,000 (assuming there are no other shareholders of that class of shares) increases the ACB to $500,000, which is the FMV. At this point the tax characteristics of the shares (e.g., FMV, ACB, and PUC) are all $500,000.

14-131.   The following example further considers the deemed dividend and ACB impact:

EXAMPLE   Lantin Inc. is authorized to issue one class of shares. The company has 250,000 shares outstanding at the beginning of the current year. These shares were all issued for $12 each, resulting in legal capital and therefore PUC of $3,000,000. Jeanne Moreau owns 10%, or 25,000, of these shares, which she acquired at the time of their issue for $12 each.

During the current year, the company issues 50,000 new shares with an FMV of $750,000 ($15 per share) in order to settle a debt of $675,000.

Shortly after the 50,000 new shares were issued, Ms. Moreau sells her 25,000 shares for $450,000 ($18 per share).

ANALYSIS   The ITA 84(1) deemed dividend will be calculated as follows:

PUC of new shares [(50,000)($15)]	$750,000
Increase in net assets (debt reduction)	(675,000)
ITA 84(1) Deemed dividend	$ 75,000

The deemed dividend would be allocated to all of the outstanding shares in the amount of $0.25 ($75,000 ÷ 300,000) per share. In the absence of a capital dividend election this would be a taxable dividend, subject to either the eligible or non-eligible dividend gross up and dividend tax credit.

With respect to Ms. Moreau's holding, the $0.25 per share dividend would increase her per share ACB to $12.25 ($12.00 + $0.25). Given this, the income tax consequences of the sale by her would be calculated as follows:

POD [(25,000)($18)]	$450,000
ACB [(25,000)($12.25)]	(306,250)
Capital gain	$143,750
Inclusion rate	1/2
Taxable capital gain	$ 71,875

Exercise 14-12

Subject: ITA 84(1) Deemed Dividends

At the beginning of the current year, Unilev Inc. has 126,000 shares of common stock issued and outstanding. The shares were originally issued at $10.50 per share, or $1,323,000 in total, with all of this amount added to legal capital and therefore PUC. During the current year, a creditor holding $450,000 of the company's debt agrees to accept 40,000 newly issued common shares of the company in exchange for complete settlement of the debt. The shares were valued at $12.70 per share at the time of the repayment.

Subsequent to the repayment, Mr. Uni, who had purchased 5,000 Unilev Inc. shares at the time of their original issue, sells all of the shares for $13.42 per share.

Describe the income tax consequence(s) to all of the shareholders of Unilev Inc. as a result of the repayment of debt for common shares. In addition, describe the income tax consequences to Mr. Uni resulting from the sale of his Unilev Inc. shares.

Solutions to Exercises are available in the Study Guide.

Excluded Transactions

14-132.   There are a number of transactions involving increases in PUC that are specifically excluded from the ITA 84(1) deemed dividend treatment. The most important of these are as follows:

- **Stock Dividends**   Stock dividends result in situations where PUC is increased without a corresponding increase in a corporation's net assets; however, since the PUC increase is the dividend for income tax purposes as previously discussed, an exception is provided to ensure the amount is not taxed twice.

- **Shifts between Classes**   When the PUC of one class of shares is decreased and, at the same time, the PUC of a different class is increased by a corresponding amount, ITA 84(1) does not apply. This exception recognizes that PUC can shift in the normal course of events, particularly in the course of reorganizations of a corporation's capital. It is noteworthy that the CRA will challenge purposeful shifts of PUC, particularly where the shift results or will potentially result in a reduction of income taxes.

- **Conversion of Contributed Surplus**   In situations where the consideration received for shares issued is in excess of the amount added to PUC, for tax purposes a contributed surplus balance is considered to have been created. This contributed surplus balance can generally be converted to PUC, without that increase in PUC being treated as a deemed dividend under ITA 84(1). Such situations typically occur in certain corporate law jurisdictions, such as BC and Nova Scotia, where par value shares have generally been permitted. Only the amount up to the par value amount is added to legal capital with any excess added to these surplus accounts.

A Word on Reporting Deemed Dividends

14-133.   Deemed dividends, particularly those under ITA 84(1), arise as a result of action taken by a company's board of directors. Shareholders who have benefitted receive nothing as a result. How are shareholders to know that a transaction has occurred that increases their net income? While corporate law contains many provisions requiring ongoing communication with shareholders, including a variety of notifications, the income tax consequences of a particular deemed dividend event may escape notice. The ITA, however, provides legislative direction. Specifically, ITR 201(1) requires corporations that have paid dividends or have taken any action that has resulted in a deemed dividend to file an information return to the CRA and those impacted. The information return is a T5 information slip. This requirement provides the necessary safeguards within the income tax system to ensure accurate reporting. Failure to file the necessary information return results in penalties and interest charges. The reporting applies to all other deemed dividend provisions discussed in this chapter as well as to actual dividends.

ITA 84(2) Deemed Dividends—Reorganization

14-134.   Corporate law provides that legal capital (PUC) can be returned to shareholders to the extent it is no longer needed by the corporation. For example, a corporation is able to reduce its stated capital for any purpose as long as the amounts paid to shareholders do not result in the corporation being unable to meet its liabilities as they become due. This return of capital could occur where a part of a corporation's business is being discontinued, a business is being wound up altogether, or the business is being reorganized.

14-135.   ITA 84(2) is written to accommodate these situations and to specifically ensure that any payment made to shareholders on the reduction of PUC be split into a tax-free return of PUC with any part of the payment in excess of PUC treated as a dividend. The relevant words of ITA 84(2) read in part as follows:

ITA 84(2)—Where funds or property of a corporation resident in Canada have ... been distributed ... to the shareholder of any class of shares ... on the winding-up, discontinuance or reorganization of its business ... the corporation shall be deemed to have paid ... a dividend ...

14-136.   ITA 84(2) applies to a reduction of PUC as a result of the reorganization of a corporation's business. Interestingly, the winding-up of a corporation's business can also occur if the corporation itself is wound up (i.e., dissolved). As a result there are two aspects to this deemed dividend rule. It applies to a business reorganization where the corporation continues to carry on its business in some modified form and also to a situation where the corporation comes to an end. This distinction is important since the termination of a corporation's existence results in the disposition of the shares of a shareholder (e.g., shares of a corporation can only exist if the corporation exists). On the other hand, if a shareholder has received a return of PUC and the corporation continues to exist, then there is no disposition of shares. The termination of a corporation's existence is referred to as the winding-up of a corporation and is covered in Chapter 17. Our focus here is on a corporation that has made a distribution of PUC to its shareholders on the reorganization of its business and continues to carry on business.

14-137.   The deemed dividend is determined for each class of shares and is equal to the FMV of the property distributed (including cash) to shareholders of that class less the amount by which the PUC of that class has been reduced. The deemed dividend is then allocated based on the number of shares each shareholder owns of that class.

14-138.   To illustrate these provisions, consider the following:

EXAMPLE   A corporation has decided to discontinue part of its business that is carried on in certain provinces, and as a result the board of directors has agreed to a return of PUC. Class B common shareholders will receive proportional payments of cash of $1,200,000. The PUC of the Class B common shares is $150,000, which will be reduced by $100,000 to $50,000. Ms. Sylvain owns 20% of the Class B common shares. The current PUC of the Class B shares is $150,000. Ms. Sylvain's ACB is $75,000.

ANALYSIS   The analysis of the $1,200,000 distribution would be as follows:

Cash distributed	$1,200,000
PUC reduction	(100,000)
ITA 84(2) Deemed dividend	$1,100,000
Deemed dividend to Ms. Sylvain [(20%)($1,100,000)]	$ 220,000

Without a capital dividend election and a designation as an eligible dividend the deemed dividend would be non-eligible.

14-139.   In practice we would have calculated the income tax consequences of the return of PUC to Ms. Sylvain as 20% of the cash distributed or $240,000 minus 20% of the PUC of $20,000 with a deemed dividend of $220,000 representing the difference. Adjustments would need to be made to the tax characteristics of Ms. Sylvain's shares to be in a position to determine any subsequent income tax implications with respect to her shares. After the distribution the PUC of her shares is equal to [(20% × $150,000) - $20,000], or $10,000. Since she has effectively recovered part of her cost as a return of PUC, the ACB of her shares must also be reduced by the PUC reduction under ITA 53(2)(a)(ii). As a result, the ACB of her shares is $55,000 [$75,000 - $20,000].

Exercise 14-13

Subject: ITA 84(2) Deemed Dividends

A corporation that is a CCPC recently closed down one of its manufacturing facilities that was no longer profitable. The corporation no longer requires the capital that supported that part of the business and has decided to make a payment to shareholders of their only class of issued shares as a partial return of PUC. The corporation has cash of $2,350,000 available for distribution to its only shareholder. The corporation was established 20 years earlier when the sole shareholder acquired the shares directly from the corporation for $250,000. This amount is both the PUC and the ACB of the shares. The payment results in the reduction of the PUC by $180,000. What are the income tax consequences of distributing the $2,350,000 to the corporation's only shareholder, including the PUC and ACB of the shares afterward?

Solutions to Exercises are available in the Study Guide.

ITA 84(3) Deemed Dividends—Share Redemption

14-140.   ITA 84(3) applies when a corporation redeems its own shares. The relevant words of ITA 84(3) are "a corporation resident in Canada has redeemed, acquired or cancelled ... any of the shares of any class of its capital stock." The three words "redeemed," "acquired," or "cancelled" are mentionned because corporate law in Canada applies different rules when a corporation is taking some action to eliminate its shares. The three words are necessary to ensure that the redemption provision applies regardless of where in Canada the corporation was incorporated. We will use the word "redeem" to refer to all three types of corporate law transactions.

14-141.   Unlike ITA 84(1) and (2), which calculate a deemed dividend on a class of shares and then proportionally allocates that deemed dividend to shareholders of the class on the basis of the number of shares they own, ITA 84(3) focuses on each shareholder separately as if the shareholder owned shares of a class separate from all other shareholders.

14-142.   Also unlike ITA 84(1) and (2), when shares are redeemed the shares are disposed of. ITA 248(1) contains a lengthy definition of a "disposition," which includes a transaction where a share is redeemed, acquired, or cancelled (ITA 248(1)(b)(i)). This means that in addition to a potential deemed dividend, proceeds of disposition and ACB must be determined to calculate whether there is a capital gain or a capital loss as a result of the redemption.

14-143.   In effect, share redemptions result in two income tax consequences: (1) a potential deemed dividend and (2) a potential capital gain or capital loss. In our earlier discussion of share characteristics it was mentioned that there are three share attributes that must always be kept in mind. Those attributes are the FMV, PUC, and ACB of each share. When shares are redeemed, the FMV refers to the "redemption amount," which represents the FMV of the shares at the time of redemption.

14-144. The mechanics of determining the income tax consequences of a share redemption begin with ITA 84(3), which first treats the payment by the corporation (the redemption amount) minus the PUC of the redeemed shares as a deemed dividend. The second step requires calculating the consequences of the disposition, which begins with modified proceeds of disposition, which is equal to the redemption amount minus the deemed dividend (before any gross up). The modified proceeds of disposition are then measured against the ACB of the shares to determine whether there is a capital gain or capital loss.

> **EXAMPLE** Mr. Jonas owns all of the preferred shares of Jonas Ltd. The PUC of the shares is $75,000 and the ACB to Mr. Jonas is $25,000. The shares are all redeemed by the corporation for $200,000.
>
> **ANALYSIS** The analysis of this transaction is as follows:
>
> | | |
> |---|---|
> | Cash distributed—Redemption amount | $200,000 |
> | PUC of shares redeemed | (75,000) |
> | ITA 84(3) Deemed dividend | $125,000 |
>
> Absent a capital dividend election or a designation to treat the dividends as eligible, the deemed dividend would be non-eligible.
>
> The capital gain on the disposition would be calculated as follows:
>
> | | |
> |---|---|
> | Redemption amount | $200,000 |
> | Less: ITA 84(3) Deemed dividend | (125,000) |
> | ITA 54 modified POD | $ 75,000 |
> | ACB | (25,000) |
> | Capital gain | $ 50,000 |
> | Inclusion rate | 1/2 |
> | Taxable capital gain | $ 25,000 |

TIP: There is a quick way to determine the tax consequences of a share redemption that focuses on the three share attributes of FMV, PUC, and ACB. The difference between the FMV and PUC is the deemed dividend, and the difference between the PUC and ACB is a capital gain, if positive, or a capital loss, if negative. This can be tested with the preceding example: FMV - PUC = $200,000 - $75,000 = $125,000 deemed dividend. PUC - ACB = $75,000 - $25,000 = $50,000 capital gain. Since the shareholder received $200,000 and the ACB of the shares is $25,000, the difference of $175,000 should equal the deemed dividend (before gross up) plus the capital gain. In the example these two amounts equal $175,000.

Modified Example: What would the results have been if the ACB had been $110,000?

Modified solution: The deemed dividend would remain $125,000 but there would be a capital loss of $35,000. If we consider the capital loss as a negative, the total would be $90,000 (deemed dividend of $125,000 - capital loss of $35,000), which is the difference between the redemption amount (FMV) and the ACB. Note that if the shareholder continued to own shares in the company and controlled the company, the capital loss would be disallowed and the capital loss amount of $35,000 would be added to the ACB of the other shares owned by the shareholder (Ref: ITA 40(3/6)). This is discussed further in Chapter 16.

Exercise 14-14

Subject: ITA 84(3) Deemed Dividends

When first incorporated, Tandy Ltd. issued 233,000 common shares in return for $1,922,250 in cash ($8.25 per share). All of the shares were issued to Ms. Jessica Tandy, the founder and incorporator of the company. A few years ago Ms. Tandy sold 15,000 of her shares to her brother for $7.90 per share. Because of ongoing difficulties between the two siblings, Ms. Tandy has arranged for Tandy Ltd. to redeem all of her brother's shares at their current FMV of $11.75 per share. Any dividends resulting from the redemption will be non-eligible. Determine the income tax consequences of this redemption to Ms. Tandy and her brother.

Solutions to Exercises are available in the Study Guide.

ITA 84(4) & (4.1) Deemed Dividends — Return of PUC

14-145.   ITA 84(4) is similar to ITA 84(2) in that it allows a return of PUC to be made to shareholders. Where the FMV of the distribution exceeds the reduction in PUC of a class of shares, the excess is deemed to be a dividend that is then allocated proportionally among shareholders of that class of shares based on the number of shares owned. This treatment ensures that PUC can be returned tax free but that any excess will be included in income as a dividend.

14-146.   ITA 84(2), however, only applies on a reorganization of a business of the corporation but can also apply when the corporation is wound up, resulting in a disposition of shares. ITA 84(4) applies to any other returns of PUC not covered by ITA 84(2). This means that it applies on a standard return of PUC not initiated by any reorganization of its business or on the winding-up of the company. Any reduction of PUC that occurs to which ITA 84(4) applies results in the same ACB reduction under ITA 53(2)(a)(ii) that would apply to ITA 84(2) where the corporation is not wound up.

> **EXAMPLE**   Jong Ltd., a CCPC, has shares with a PUC of $5,000,000. As it has accumulated excess cash, it will distribute $1,000,000 to its shareholders. In order to limit the income tax consequences of this distribution, the PUC of the shares will be reduced by $700,000.
>
> **ANALYSIS**   Under ITA 84(4), $700,000 of the total distribution will be a tax-free distribution of PUC. The remaining $300,000 is treated as a deemed dividend, which can be elected as a capital dividend, designated as an eligible dividend, or left as a non-eligible dividend. The ACB of the shares would be reduced by the PUC reduction of $700,000 as a result of ITA 53(2)(a)(ii).

14-147.   ITA 84(4.1) contains a special rule that applies only to public corporations. The rule, at first glance, appears to be an exception to the rule that PUC can be returned to shareholders tax free. ITA 84(4.1) reads that any distributions on the reduction of PUC to its shareholders will be considered a deemed dividend unless the reduction is a redemption of shares, a part of a reorganization of the corporation's business to which ITA 84(2) applies, or is a reorganization of its capital to which ITA 86 applies (discussed in Chapter 17). There are a few other exceptions that go beyond an introductory text that will not be discussed.

14-148.   The reason why ITA 84(4.1) treats a distribution of PUC by a public company as a deemed dividend is because before 1978 public companies were permitted to transfer certain tax accounts to PUC that today can only be paid to shareholders as taxable dividends. As a result, it was generally considered inappropriate to allow public companies to make tax-free distributions of PUC. Because of the ITA 84(2) exception it has become standard tax planning for public corporations to claim that their PUC distributions are based on a reorganization of their business and therefore these amounts should be distributed tax free under that provision. The CRA has provided many favourable income tax rulings in support of this planning.

14-149.   With respect to the example in Paragraph 14-146, this means that if Jong Ltd. were a public company, the entire $1,000,000 distribution would be considered a deemed dividend as a result of ITA 84(4.1). As the $1,000,000 amount will be subject to tax, the ACB of the shares will not be reduced as a result of the distribution. Remember that the ACB adjustments for descreases in PUC only occur to the extent that the PUC distribution was treated as a dividend.

ITA 84 Deemed Dividends—Summary

14-150.   Figure 14-9 summarizes the five deemed dividend provisions of ITA 84(1), (2), (3), (4), and (4.1). The figure identifies whether a particular deemed dividend is subject to an ACB adjustment, including the ITA reference where applicable, and whether there would be a disposition of shares in respect of the transaction to which the deemed dividend provision applies.

Exercise 14-15

Subject: ITA 84(4) Deemed Dividends

Mr. Jondo owns all of the outstanding shares of Jondo Ltd., a CCPC. The shares have a PUC of $450,000 and an ACB of $625,000. Because it has accumulated excess cash, Jondo Ltd. agrees to make a distribution on a reduction of its PUC. The corporation pays $330,000, accompanied by a PUC reduction of $225,000. What are the income tax consequences of this distribution to Mr. Jondo?

Solutions to Exercises are available in the Study Guide.

We suggest you complete SSP 14-8 at this point.

Figure 14-9   Deemed Dividends

ITA	ACB Adjustment*	Disposition
84(1) Increase in PUC	53(1)(b)	No disposition
84(2) Reorganization of business	53(2)(a)(ii) if no disposition	POD reduced by deemed dividend if there is a disposition
84(3) Redemption of shares	N/A	POD reduced by deemed dividend
84(4) Return of PUC	53(2)(a)(ii)	No disposition
84(4.1) Return of PUC treated as dividend	N/A	No disposition
*ACB adjustment = PUC increase or decrease		

Key Terms

A full glossary with definitions is provided at the end of the Study Guide.

Acquisition of Control	Investment Tax Credit
Business Limit	Paid-Up Capital
Apprenticeship Job Creation Tax Credit	Preferred Shares
Associated Corporations	PUC
Capital Dividend	Qualified Property
Capital Dividend Account (CDA)	Qualifying Corporation
CCPC	Redemption of Shares
Common Shares	Refundable Investment Tax Credit
Contributed Capital	Related Persons
Control	Retained Earnings
Corporation	Scientific Research and
Deemed Dividends	Experimental Development (SRED)
Deemed Disposition	Shareholders' Equity
Dividends	Specified Class ITA 256(1.1)
Dividends in Kind	Stock Dividend
Earned Surplus	Taxable Capital Employed in Canada
Group of Persons	

References

For more detailed study of the material in this chapter, we refer you to the following:

ITA 52(2)	Cost of Property Received as Dividend in Kind
ITA 52(3)	Cost of Stock Dividends
ITA 82(1)	Taxable Dividends Received
ITA 83(2)	Capital Dividend
ITA 84	Deemed Dividend
ITA 127(5) to	
127.1(4)	Investment Tax Credits
ITA 249(4)	Year End on Acquisition of Control
ITA 251	Arm's Length
ITA 252	Related Persons
ITA 256	Associated Corporations
ITR 4600	Investment Tax Credit—Qualified Property
ITR 4601	Investment Tax Credit—Qualified Transportation Equipment
ITR 4602	Certified Property
IC 78-4R3	Investment Tax Credit Rates
S1-F5-C1	Related Persons and Dealing at Arm's Length
S3-F2-C1	Capital Dividends
IT-64R4	Corporations: Association and Control (Consolidated)
IT-463R2	Paid-Up Capital

Self-Study Problems (SSPs)

Self-Study Problems (SSPs) provide practice in problem solving. Within the chapters, we have indicated where it would be appropriate to stop and work on each SSP. The problems can be downloaded by chapter from MyLab Accounting. Solutions are available in the Study Guide. Select problems can also be completed directly in MyLab and auto-graded.

Assignment Problems

Solutions to Assignment Problems (APs) are available to instructors only.

AP 14-1   (Acquisition of Control Rules—Losses)

For many years, Janice Virtue had been a professor of business ethics in the Faculty of Business at a major Canadian university. In 2019, while continuing to teach one section of business ethics, she incorporated Virtue Ltd. (VL), a CCPC, in order to market her numerous publications and online courses involving the application of ethical principles to business situations.

While the company experienced a net operating loss of $128,000 in the fiscal period ending December 31, 2019, VL experienced rapidly increasing sales during 2020. Because Janice believed the improvement was indicative of the success to come, VL moved to larger prem-ises that were purchased for $423,000. Of this total, $100,000 related to the land with the remaining $323,000 allocated to the building. Because the building was to be used exclu-sively for non-residential purposes, the necessary election was made with the CRA to allo-cate the building to a separate class 1. In selling the previous premises in 2020, VL realized an allowable capital loss on the land of $36,000. The building was sold at amount equal to the UCC.

The net income of VL for the year ending December 31, 2020, after deducting CCA on the class 1 building, was $16,000. VL realized no capital gains during the year.

In May 2021, Janice decided that it was time to see the world and retire early. Given these cir-cumstances, Janice decides to sell her VL shares. She finds an unrelated corporate buyer who is willing to acquire the shares on June 1, 2021. This buyer is a large publicly traded Canadian company. VL properties include the copyrights to all of her publications. The corporate buyer believes its marketing team will be able to return the company to profitability within a relatively short period of time.

As this acquisition of control resulted in a deemed year end, VL prepared an income statement for the period January 1, 2020, through May 31, 2021. A business loss of $34,000 is reported for the taxation year ending May 31, 2021, as a result of the acquisition of control. There were, however, no further capital losses.

On May 31, 2021, the values of VL's properties were as follows:

Property	Cost	UCC	FMV
Temporary investments	$ 32,000	N/A	$ 7,000
Accounts receivable	123,000	N/A	110,000
Land	100,000	N/A	115,000
Building	323,000	$313,310	352,000
Equipment	46,000	33,120	5,000
Vehicles (class 10)	36,000	21,420	25,000
Copyrights	Nil	Nil	42,000

VL will make all possible elections to minimize any net capital and non-capital loss balances.

Shortly after taking over VL, the corporate buyer decided that some of the extra space in VL's facilities could be used for manufacturing electronic reading devices. VL's income (loss) from the two separate businesses for the period June 1 through December 31, 2021, and for the 2022 taxation year were as follows:

Business	June 1 to Dec. 31, 2021	2022
Electronic reading devices	$123,000	($ 26,000)
Publications (loss business)	(53,000)	185,000

Required:

A. Determine the amount of the non-capital losses and net capital losses that will be tainted as a result of the acquisition of control.

B. Indicate the maximum amount of the non-capital loss carry forward that can be claimed for the taxation year June 1 through December 31, 2021.

C. Indicate the maximum amount of the non-capital loss remaining that can be claimed for the 2022 taxation year.

AP 14-2   (Acquisition of Control Rules)

Boudin Inc. was incorporated 10 years ago in New Brunswick. On incorporation, all of the shares were issued to Andre Boudin. The company carried on a business of distributing health food products throughout the Maritime provinces. The company has always used a December 31 year end.

The company operated successfully for a number of years. However, late in 2018, increased competition resulted in a steep decline in the sales of Boudin Inc.

Because of this the company reported a business loss of $42,000 in 2019 and $123,000 in 2020. In addition, the company realized an allowable capital loss of $32,000 in 2020 as a result of the disposition of some temporary investments. There were no capital gains realized in 2020.

In early 2021, seeing no real hope for a return to profitable operations, Mr. Boudin begins a search for a buyer for his company's shares. On May 1, 2021, all of the shares are sold to Healthy Bites Ltd., a manufacturer of health food products. This company hopes to be able to reverse the fortunes of Boudin Inc. Mr. Boudin is not related to the individuals who control Healthy Bites Ltd.

For the short taxation year of January 1, 2021, to April 30, 2021, resulting from the acquisition of control, Boudin Inc. reported a business loss of $48,000. The reported business loss includes a write-down of inventories to their fair market values as required by ITA 10(1) on April 30, 2021, and a deduction for doubtful receivables, determined as a result of the application of ITA 111(5.3).

On April 30, 2021, Boudin Inc. owned the following properties with the following values:

Asset	Cost	UCC	FMV
Long-term investments*	$ 47,000	N/A	$ 82,000
Land	207,000	N/A	305,000
Building	465,000	$360,000	485,000
Equipment	350,000	190,000	150,000

*Healthy Bites intends to sell these investments as soon as possible.

Required:

A. Indicate any non-capital and net capital loss balances that are tainted as a result of the acquisition of control. Assume the company will elect to trigger any eligible capital gains or recapture using FMV as the elected amount for property with accrued but unrealized gains (ITA 111(4)(e)).

B. If Healthy Bites Ltd. decides to only use the election(s) required to offset non-capital and net capital losses that would become tainted as a result of the acquisition of control, indicate the properties on which the elections should be made and the amounts that should be elected.

C. Advise Healthy Bites Ltd. as to the recommended course of action (Part A or B).

AP 14-3   (Associated Corporations)

The following situations are **independent** of each other. All of the corporations involved are CCPCs and have only one authorized class of shares.

A. Circle Ltd. owns 51% of the shares of Loop Ltd., which in turn owns 51% of the shares of Ring Ltd.

B. Gerald Stone owns 75% of the shares of Rock Ltd. and 85% of the shares of Boulder Ltd.

C. The percentage share ownership of Jukebox Ltd. and Vending Ltd. are as follows:

	Jukebox	**Vending**
Jewel Cunningham	35.0	45.0
Roger Takahashi	15.0	15.0
Kari Fisher	5.0	8.0
Ming Chen	45.0	—
Kelly Clerkson	—	32.0
Total	100.0	100.0

None of the individuals are related to each other.

D. Rainer Gosling owns 100% of the shares of Fowl Ltd. Beatrice Owlet, Rainer's sister, owns 100% of the shares of Capon Ltd. Rainer, Beatrice, and their mother and father each own 25% of the shares of Pullet Ltd.

E. Ryan McLain owns 62% of the shares of McLain Ltd. and 40% of the shares of Chatelaine Ltd. McLain Ltd. owns 18% of the shares of Chatelaine Ltd.

F. Melissa Andrews owns 75% of the shares of Andrews Ltd. and 25% of the shares of Statler Ltd. Jeremy Statler, Melissa's brother, owns 75% of the shares of Statler Ltd. and 25% of the shares of Andrews Ltd.

Required: For each of the preceding situations, indicate whether the corporations are associated and explain your conclusion with reference to the *ITA*. In order to assist you in answering this question, we have provided you with the content of ITA 256(1).

ITA 256(1) Associated corporations—For the purposes of this Act, one corporation is associated with another in a taxation year if, at any time in the year,

(a) one of the corporations controlled, directly or indirectly in any manner whatever, the other;

(b) both of the corporations were controlled, directly or indirectly in any manner whatever, by the same person or group of persons;

(c) each of the corporations was controlled, directly or indirectly in any manner whatever, by a person and the person who so controlled one of the corporations was related to the person who so controlled the other, and either of those persons owned, in respect of each corporation, not less than 25 percent of the issued shares of any class, other than a specified class, of the capital stock thereof;

(d) one of the corporations was controlled, directly or indirectly in any manner whatever, by a person and that person was related to each member of a group of persons that so controlled the other corporation, and that person owned, in respect of the other corporation, not less than 25 percent of the issued shares of any class, other than a specified class, of the capital stock thereof; or

(e) each of the corporations was controlled, directly or indirectly in any manner whatever, by a related group and each of the members of one of the related groups was related to all of the members of the other related group, and one or more persons who were members of both related groups, either alone or together, owned, in respect of each corporation, not less than 25 percent of the issued shares of any class, other than a specified class, of the capital stock thereof.

AP 14-4   *(Associated Companies)*

Each of the following is an **independent** case involving the ownership of voting shares of CCPCs. All of the corporations have taxation years that end on December 31 and have only one authorized class of shares.

A. Mr. Bond owns 55% of Sarnen Inc. Sarnen Inc. owns 40% of Barxo Ltd. Mr. Bond also owns 14% of Hax Ltd., which in turn owns 54% of the shares of Barxo Ltd. Mr. Bond's 10-year-old daughter owns 6% of the shares of Barxo Ltd.

B. Mr. Jones, Mr. Knight, and Mr. Long are three unrelated individuals.

    - Mr. Jones owns 50% of the shares of Anix Inc. and 25% of the shares of Brex Ltd.
    - Mr. Knight owns 50% of the shares of Brex Ltd.
    - Mr. Long owns 50% of the shares of Anix Inc. and 25% of the shares of Brex Ltd.

C. Sam Scully owns 60% of Scully Inc. His sister, Susan Wilson, owns 80% of Wilson Ltd. and 30% of Scully Inc. Sam Scully also owns 10% of Wilson Ltd.

D. Joan and Sarah Lartch are sisters. Joan owns 100% of the shares of JL Inc. and 31% of the shares of Meadow Ltd. Her sister Sarah owns 60% of the shares of SL Inc., with the remaining 40% of the shares held by her mother. Sarah also owns 39% of the shares of Meadow Ltd. The remaining shares of Meadow Ltd. are held by an unrelated party.

E. John and May Carp each own 30% of the shares of Jomay Inc. Serge and Beth Carp each own 45% of the shares of Besa Ltd. John and Serge Carp are brothers. Beth Carp owns 40% of the shares of Jomay Inc. and May Carp owns 10% of the shares of Besa Ltd.

Required: For each of the preceding cases, determine whether the corporations are associated. Support your conclusions with references to specific provisions of ITA 256. In order to assist you in answering this question, we have provided you with the content of ITA 256(1).

> **ITA 256(1) Associated corporations**—For the purposes of this Act, one corporation is associated with another in a taxation year if, at any time in the year,
>
> (a) one of the corporations controlled, directly or indirectly in any manner whatever, the other;
> (b) both of the corporations were controlled, directly or indirectly in any manner whatever, by the same person or group of persons;
> (c) each of the corporations was controlled, directly or indirectly in any manner whatever, by a person and the person who so controlled one of the corporations was related to the person who so controlled the other, and either of those persons owned, in respect of each corporation, not less than 25 percent of the issued shares of any class, other than a specified class, of the capital stock thereof;
> (d) one of the corporations was controlled, directly or indirectly in any manner whatever, by a person and that person was related to each member of a group of persons that so controlled the other corporation, and that person owned, in respect of the other corporation, not less than 25 percent of the issued shares of any class, other than a specified class, of the capital stock thereof; or
> (e) each of the corporations was controlled, directly or indirectly in any manner whatever, by a related group and each of the members of one of the related groups was related to all of the members of the other related group, and one or more persons who were members of both related groups, either alone or together, owned, in respect of each corporation, not less than 25 percent of the issued shares of any class, other than a specified class, of the capital stock thereof.

AP 14-5   *(Investment Tax Credits)*
Case A

In 2021, Gypsy Ltd., a CCPC with a December 31 taxation year end, hired 18 eligible apprentices—six were hired at the beginning of January, six more August 1, and the remaining six November 1. Each of the apprentices began with an annual salary of $45,000, all of which qualified for the apprenticeship tax credit. Based on the hiring dates, the first group of six each earned $45,000 for the year while the second group each earned $18,750 and the third group each earned $7,500. The total amount paid to these individuals in 2021 is $427,500.

Gypsy Ltd. also acquired new class 53 machinery for $640,000 on November 27, 2021. This equipment is to be used in New Brunswick. The machinery was delivered to the company site in early December and was put into use immediately. The machinery is qualified property for investment tax credit purposes.

Required: Describe the 2021 and 2022 income tax consequences of the salary and wages to apprentices and the acquisition of the class 53 machinery. Specifically, determine whether the amounts qualify for any investment tax credit and, if so, the amount of that tax credit and the 2022 implications of claiming any available tax credit in 2021. Assume that the company will claim the maximum CCA possible on the class 53 machinery in 2021, that the opening UCC in class 53 for 2021 is nil, that no additions will be made to the class in 2022, and that the company will have sufficient Part 1 tax payable to fully use any investment tax credits in 2021.

Case B
Taurus Ltd., a CCPC with a December 31 taxation year end, has been conducting scientific research and experimental development (SRED), which qualifies for additional federal investment tax credit incentives based on its "SRED expenditure limit." Taurus has never been associated with another corporation since its incorporation in 2015. The company has provided the following information for its 2020 and 2021 taxation years:

	2020	2021
Taxable income	$ 735,000	$ 850,000
Taxable capital employed in Canada	16,900,000	21,440,000

Required: Determine Taurus's SRED expenditure limit for its 2021 taxation year.

Case C
Libra Ltd. is a CCPC with a December 31 taxation year end. The company was incorporated in 2018 and has conducted scientific research and experimental development (SRED) since its incorporation. The company has only realized non-capital losses in each year from 2018 up to and including the 2021 taxation year. As a result, its taxable income for 2020 and 2021 is nil. The company has never applied any non-capital losses. As a result of its nil taxable income the company has no tax payable for the 2020 and 2021 taxation years.

Because of the potential success of its SRED efforts the company has received and continues to receive considerable funding in the form of share capital and long-term financing. As a result, the TCEC of the company was $21,350,000 in 2020 and $24,730,000 in 2021. The company is not associated with any other corporation.

During 2021, the company acquired the following property and incurred the following SRED expenditures that qualify for investment tax credits:

- $220,000 for the purchase of qualified property to be used in New Brunswick

- $3,110,000 in current expenditures for SRED

- $1,890,000 in capital expenditures for SRED

Required: Determine the maximum amount of refundable investment tax credits that Libra Ltd. will be entitled to receive. In addition, determine the amount of any investment tax credit carry forwards and how they could be applied. Finally, identify any other related income tax consequences that occur as a result of the refund.

AP 14-6   (Capital Dividend Account)

Since its incorporation in 2010, Park Inc. has qualified as a CCPC. During the period since incorporation until December 31, 2021, the company has had the following transactions that might involve the capital dividend account:

1. In 2012, the company sold depreciable property with an ACB of $225,000. It was the last property in its class and the balance in the class at the time of the sale was $129,600. The proceeds from the sale were $275,000. No additional property was purchased in 2012.

2. In 2014, the company received a capital dividend of $46,000.

3. In 2015, the company received life insurance proceeds, net of the adjusted cost basis of the policy, in the amount of $27,500.

4. In 2016, the company paid a capital dividend of $38,000 and eligible dividends of $19,000. The required election and designation was made.

5. In 2016, the company sold a parcel of land for $100,000. The ACB of this land was $145,000.

6. In January 2021, Park acquired all of the shares of a small business corporation at a cost of $850,000. Park had intended to merge the two corporations together, but before this could take place the company received an unsolicited offer to purchase the shares for $965,000. Finding this offer too attractive to resist, it was accepted and the shares were sold on October 1, 2021 for $965,000.

7. In 2021, the company received a capital dividend of $17,800. They paid a capital dividend of $21,600 and eligible dividends of $8,000. The required election and designation was made.

Required: Determine the balance in the company's capital dividend account as of December 31, 2021.

AP 14-7   (Corporate Surplus Distributions)

Grado Ltd. is a CCPC with a December 31 taxation year end. The company was incorporated in 2012. All of the existing shareholders are individuals. The company's condensed balance sheet, prepared in accordance with generally accepted accounting principles (ASPE), as of December 31, 2020, is as follows:

Total assets		$858,000
Current liabilities		$122,000
Long-term liabilities		384,000
Shareholders' equity:		
700 preferred Class A (paid-up capital)	$ 14,000	
1,000 common shares (paid-up capital)	87,000	
Retained earnings	251,000	352,000
Total equities		$858,000

Required: Determine the income tax consequences of each of the following **independent** transactions. Income tax consequences are considered to include the amount of taxable dividends, the dividend tax credit, any taxable capital gains and allowable capital losses, and any changes to the ACB of the relevant property and the paid-up capital (PUC) of a class of shares. Any dividends paid or deemed to be paid by Grado Ltd. would be non-eligible.

A. (i)   Mr. McDuff holds $200,000 of the currently outstanding long-term liabilities. The debt does not allow Mr. McDuff the right to convert to shares, but in an effort to restructure the company made a proposal to Mr. McDuff to convert to preferred shares, which he has accepted. Given the favourable terms and conditions, it is estimated that the value of the debt is $230,000. Grado will create a new class of preferred shares (Class B) that will be used to make the conversion. Grado will issue 500 Class B preferred shares that are redeemable at the option of the holder for $460 each. Assume that the PUC of the Class B preferred shares increased by $230,000 as a result of the conversion.

   (ii) Using the same facts described in A(i), explain what would have happened had Grado not created a new class of preferred shares to make the conversion with the debtholder but instead issued $230,000 of existing Class A preferred shares. Assume that 2,300 of additional Class A shares would be issued on the conversion.

B. The company declared and distributed a 15% stock dividend on the common shares. The PUC of the common shares increased by $35,000 with a corresponding reduction in retained earnings.

C. Mr. William Bristle owns 25% of the common shares, which he acquired in 2014 for $60 each. In April 2021 the company announced that there would be a distribution to all common shareholders following the shutdown of one of its operations. A payment of $68,000 was made shortly thereafter, with $57,000 of that distribution considered a partial return of capital (i.e., PUC). In early December 2021 Mr. Bristle decided to sell all of his common shares to an arm's-length individual who agreed to pay him $100 per share.

D. (i) Mrs. Wiebe owns 100 of the common shares. She purchased the shares for $18 a share in 2013. The company redeems these shares for $90 per share in June 2021.

   (ii) Mrs. Wilbury purchased 200 of the Class A preferred shares for $36. The company redeemed all of her shares in September 2021 for $25 per share. Assume that she owns no other shares in Grado and has no capital gains in 2021.

Tax Software Assignment Problem

Tax Software AP 14-1

RadionFaux Industries Ltd. (RIL) is a Canadian controlled private corporation located at 123 ABC Street in Ottawa, Ontario, K4E 1A1. Its Ontario corporation tax account number is 1234567. Its phone number is (613) 111-1111. It was incorporated on February 24, 1990, in Ottawa.

(The government's Crown copyright no longer permits us to use fabricated business numbers in software problems. To reduce the number of ProFile's error messages because of this, enter NR (for not registered) in the Business Number field.)

The company has 1,000 shares of common stock issued and outstanding, all of which are owned by Ms. Margaret Ottawa (SIN 527-000-301).

Ms. Ottawa, the president and director of the company, is the person who should be contacted with respect to matters concerning the company's books and records. She is the authorized person as well as the signing officer.

RIL is a retailer of pet supplies. All of its sales occur within Canada. It has net assets of $235,000 on December 31, 2020. This includes a few investments that Ms. Ottawa inherited from her father two years earlier.

RIL owns all of the 500 common shares of OttawaFaux Inc., which holds most of the investments Ms. Ottawa inherited from her father. The common shares have a book value of $1,200,000. OttawaFaux Inc. has the same location and phone number as RadionFaux Industries Ltd. OttawaFaux Inc. has a December 31 fiscal year end. Enter NR (for not registered) in the Business Number field for OttawaFaux Inc.

OttawaFaux Inc. is also involved in earning active business income through the breeding and sale of championship dogs. It has total assets of $2,000,000 and total revenues for 2020 of

$200,000. Its taxable capital employed in Canada was $350,000 as at December 31, 2019, and $365,000 as at December 31, 2020.

The following information applied to RIL:

Taxable capital employed in Canada—2019	$328,000
Taxable capital employed in Canada—2020	411,000
Total assets as at December 31, 2020	750,000
Non-eligible RDTOH as at December 31, 2019	5,200
Eligible RDTOH as at December 31, 2019	Nil
Dividends declared and paid during 2019	Nil
GRIP balance as at December 31, 2019	11,750
Capital dividend account as at December 31, 2019	6,000

RIL does not use International Financial Reporting Standards (IFRS). For the taxation year ending December 31, 2020, RIL's income statement, before any deduction for income taxes, was as follows:

Sales revenues	$ 580,000
Interest on long-term debt	27,500
Interest received on foreign bank account (Note 1)	18,000
Eligible dividends on Royal Bank shares	17,500
Non-eligible dividends from OttawaFaux Inc. (Note 2)	42,000
Gain on sale of shares (Note 3)	27,000
Total revenues	$ 712,000
Cost of goods sold	$ 208,000
Amortization expense	122,000
Other operating expenses	147,000
Total expenses (excluding taxes)	$ 477,000
Net income (before taxes)	$ 235,000

Note 1   This interest is net of $2,000 in taxes withheld in Ireland.

Note 2   As a result of paying this $42,000 in dividends to RIL, OttawaFaux Inc. received a dividend refund of $14,000 from its non-eligible RDTOH.

Note 3   On March 23, 2020, RIL sold 2,700 shares of Canadian Imperial Bank of Commerce. The common shares had cost $118,800 on June 6, 2017, and were sold for net proceeds of $145,800.

Other Information:

1. Expenses include a deduction for charitable donations to the Ottawa Civic Hospital in the amount of $5,000.

2. RIL's expenses include penalties of $3,500 resulting from a judgment in the Tax Court of Canada.

3. RIL reimbursed Ms. Ottawa $34,000 for business meals and entertainment for clients and suppliers during the year.

4. During the year, RIL incurred $20,000 in landscaping costs. For accounting purposes these are being treated as a capital expenditure, to be amortized using the straight-line method over 10 years. The related amortization is included in the amortization expense of $122,000 shown on the income statement.

5. The opening UCC balances were $246,000 for class 1, $135,000 for class 8, and $90,000 for class 10. The only disposition during the year was the sale of a delivery truck. The truck had cost $35,000 and was sold for its carrying value of $12,000. The only acquisition was an arm's-length purchase of $52,000 in office furniture on April 1, 2020.

6. During 2020, RIL paid taxable dividends of $92,000. Of these dividends, $25,000 were designated as eligible. On September 1, 2020, RIL also elects to pay the maximum capital dividend allowable.

7. RIL allocates $60,000 of the annual business limit to OttawaFaux Inc. This is $5,000 more than OttawaFaux Inc. can use in 2020, but RIL cannot use the excess.

8. RIL paid quarterly income tax instalments of $8,000 each on the 20th of March, June, September, and December during 2020.

9. RIL has a website describing the products it carries, but no income is generated from the website.

10. Assume that the adjusted aggregate investment income (AAII) of both companies is nil at the end of the 2019 year.

Required: Prepare the federal corporate tax return for RIL for the 2020 taxation year using the ProFile T2 corporate software program. Determine the eligible and non-eligible RDTOH and comment on whether the designation of $25,000 of eligible dividends was a good idea. If not, indicate the designation that you would have made. On the ProFile schedule titled "Info," the Filing question "Complete return from GIFI?" is answered Yes by default; click No. Ignore the GIFI requirements except as follows:

On GIFI Schedule 125:

- Input the total revenues less the gain on sale of shares ($685,000) on the line "Total Sales of Goods and Services" (Code 8000).

- Choose "Realized gains/losses on sale of investments" (Code 8211) from the drop-down menu under Code 8089 and input the gain on sale of shares.

- Choose "Purchases/cost of materials" (Code 8320) from the drop-down menu under Cost of Sales and input the cost of goods sold.

- Choose "Amortization of tangible assets" (Code 8670) from the drop-down menu under Operating Expenses and input the amortization expense.

- Choose "Other expenses" (Code 9270) from the drop-down menu under Operating Expenses and Other Operating Expenses.

On GIFI Schedule 100:

- Input the net income figure of $235,000 as "Cash and deposits" (Code 1000) in order to make the total assets equal to the total liabilities and equity.

Although this will not properly complete the GIFI statements, it will eliminate the warning messages that would otherwise be generated when the net income figure and amortization expense are input on Schedule 1. These GIFI entries will have no effect on the calculations in the tax return.

In addition, to prevent audit warnings, S141, "Notes Checklist," has to be completed. Assume there are no notes to the financial statements and answer "No" to any other relevant questions. Click "review engagement" in Part 2.

Corporate Taxation and Management Decisions

Learning Objectives

After completing Chapter 15, you should be able to:

1. Explain how a corporation can be used to reduce income tax, defer income tax, and facilitate income splitting (Paragraph [P hereafter] 15-1 to 15-11).
2. Describe other non-tax advantages and disadvantages of incorporation (P 15-12 and 15-13).
3. Use various individual and corporate income tax rates to determine post-tax retention of an individual where sources of income have been incorporated with after-tax corporate distributions made to individual shareholders (P 15-14 to 15-26).
4. Calculate the amount of tax reduction and tax deferral that is available when sources of income are incorporated within a public corporation (P 15-27 to 15-35).
5. Calculate the amount of tax reduction and tax deferral that is available through the use of a CCPC earning active business income (P 15-36 to 15-41).
6. Explain why bonusing down is contemplated and the advantages to individual shareholders of a CCPC eligible for the small business deduction (P 15-42 to 15-46).
7. Calculate the amount of tax reduction and tax deferral that is available through the use of a CCPC earning investment income other than dividends (P 15-47 to 15-49).
8. Calculate the amount of tax reduction and tax deferral that is available through the use of a CCPC earning dividend income (P 15-50 to 15-54).
9. Summarize the tax reduction and tax deferral conclusions available through the use of various types of corporations earning different types of income (P 15-55 to 15-57).
10. Identify the impact of provincial income taxes on the decision to incorporate (P 15-58 to 15-74).
11. Explain why significant amounts of taxable dividends can be received tax free by individuals with no other sources of income (P 15-75 to 15-86).
12. Describe and calculate the benefits that can be achieved by using a corporation for income splitting purposes (P 15-87 to 15-88).
13. Describe how shareholder benefits are determined and explain the income tax consequences (P 15-89 to 15-103).
14. Describe the purpose of the shareholder loan rules, how they apply, and the exceptions (P 15-104 to 15-124).

15. Explain the income tax principles of management compensation in the context of a closely held CCPC (P 15-125 to 15-129).
16. Describe the basic trade-off between the payment of salary and the payment of dividends (P 15-130 to 15-135).
17. Calculate the appropriate choice between salary and dividends, taking into consideration factors other than federal income tax savings (P 15-136 to 15-158).
18. Optimize the salary/dividend mix when all tax credits are not used or there is a limited amount of cash in the corporation (P 15-159 to 15-174).
19. Summarize the various non-tax factors that must be taken into consideration in making salary vs. dividend decisions (P 15-175 to 15-176).

The Decision to Incorporate

Basic Tax Considerations

Deferral and Reduction

15-1.   One of the more important decisions facing the owner of a business is deciding whether or not the business should be incorporated. There are, of course, a number of non-tax considerations involved in this decision, and these factors will be reviewed in this chapter. At this point, however, we are concerned with the influence of corporate taxation on this decision.

15-2.   The decision to incorporate, from both a legal and a tax point of view, has the immediate effect of separating the business from its owners. This is an extremely important consideration. Property of a business, whether cash, inventory, vehicles, real estate, and any other property of the corporation belongs to the legal entity that is the corporation and not the previous individual owners who carried on the business as sole proprietors. The previous individual business owners will generally own an interest in the corporation through ownership of its shares. This means that shareholders who continue to treat the assets of the incorporated business as their own may suffer serious income tax consequences.

15-3.   Shareholders can transact with their own corporation and may indirectly participate in the profits through the receipt of dividends, salaries, and other forms of compensation. The system of integration means that, in order for incorporated business income to be made available to the owner, it must go through two levels of taxation. First, the corporation is subject to income tax on its business profits. Then, when any after-tax profits are distributed by way of taxable dividends to individual shareholders, the second level of income tax will be payable on the amounts received.

15-4.   This dual system of taxation may or may not be advantageous to the individual(s) who carry on the business personally. In terms of income tax advantages that can result from incorporating business, there are two important benchmarks:

Tax Reduction   In some situations, the total income taxes that would be paid at the combined corporate and individual level will be less when the business is incorporated than would be the case if the individual had not incorporated the business.

Tax Deferral   There are two levels of income tax when business income is earned by a corporation. The initial corporate income tax rate on business income is generally quite low, particularly if the corporation is a Canadian controlled private corporation (CCPC) earning active business income and entitled to the small business deduction. Combined federal/provincial income tax rates can be as low as 9% and no higher than 14% on such income. The income tax rates on business income of the largest corporations rarely exceed 30%. These tax rates are significantly lower than the comparable high tax rates on individuals, which can exceed 50%. The result is that the incorporation of a business almost always creates a level of tax deferral. The amount of tax that can be deferred is calculated as the difference between the initial corporate income tax and what the individual would have paid had the same amount and type of income been earned personally. If the individual shareholder does not require all of the available after-tax corporate profits, then they can be left in the corporation, resulting in a postponement or deferral of the second level of individual taxation. Income such as investment income, capital gains, and taxable dividends subject to Part IV tax does not result in any deferral due to higher corporate tax rates that apply to these types of income.

15-5. In general terms, individuals in the highest income tax brackets will always experience tax deferral with respect to business profits when a business is incorporated since corporate income tax rates on business income are always substantially lower than the highest individual tax rates. In terms of tax reduction, however, there are few instances in which using a corporation will result in small amounts of tax savings. The few situations where there are potential tax savings are limited to income eligible for the small business deduction and manufacturing by small private corporations and depend on the province.

15-6. In summary, there is a high probability of tax deferral and a lower probability of tax savings once all after-tax corporate business profits have been distributed to individual shareholders as taxable dividends. The actual outcome, however, is dependent on the type of corporation (CCPCs vs. non-CCPCs), the type of business income (active business, non-active business, or manufacturing), and which provincial tax rates apply to the corporation and to the individual shareholders. This means that there is no one answer to the question of whether the incorporation of a business is or is not advantageous. Because of this, we will devote a major section of this chapter to examining the various possible combinations of types of income and types of corporations to provide you with a general understanding of tax reduction and tax deferral.

Using Imperfections in the Integration System

15-7. We have previously noted that perfect integration is premised on the assumption of a specific corporate income tax rate and a specific provincial dividend tax credit rate. Figure 13-2 describes the requisite perfect integration corporate rates as 27.54% for eligible dividends together with a provincial dividend tax credit rate of 5/11, or 45.5%. The rates for non-eligible dividends require a combined corporate rate of 13.04% and a provincial dividend tax credit of 4/13, or 30.8%. Even at the federal level, actual corporate tax rates vary from the tax rates required. As a result, perfect integration is the exception, with imperfect integration being the rule.

15-8. In addition, there are significant variations in the corporate income tax rates at the provincial level as well as variations in the dividend gross up and dividend tax credit rates. An alignment of these components is essential to achieving perfect integration. This means that the combined federal/provincial components in any given province will not produce perfect integration. On the contrary, the integration system can more accurately be described as imperfect, producing results that may favour incorporation because the integration system overcompensates individual shareholders (referred to as overintegration) or the system falls short, making incorporation much more costly (referred to as underintegration). Identifying favourable imperfections or overintegrated provinces can not only influence the decision to incorporate but can influence where the corporation should be located. These issues are discussed in this chapter.

Income Splitting

15-9. Even in situations where the use of a corporation neither reduces nor defers significant amounts of income tax for an individual, incorporation may be attractive to a family or other related group of individuals. In a typical family situation, it is fairly common to find some individuals with income subject to the highest income tax rates with others having little to no income tax subject to the lowest income tax rates.

15-10. In Chapter 1, we discussed the income splitting advantages of using a corporation. Salaries can be paid to family members and shares can be issued to them that pay discretionary amounts of dividends. The effect is to redirect business profits that would have been included in the income of individuals taxed at the highest tax rates among low-income family members. The implementation of successful income splitting strategies can result in significant permanent tax savings when compared to the personal income taxes that would have been paid by the high-income-earning individuals.

15-11.   These income splitting strategies, however, are subject to a few obstacles. Salaries to family members must be supportable and consistent with the level of experience, skills, and expertise provided. The income tax consequences of failing to adequately support salaries to family members, particularly those related to controlling shareholders, can be severe. In addition, establishing a corporate share structure with family members owning shares for the purposes of receiving dividends and realizing future capital gains that may be eligible for the capital gains deduction can result in adverse income tax consequences if not properly structured. Family members who have made no or little contribution to the business risk being subjected to the TOSI (the tax on split income rules discussed in Chapter 11) that apply the highest income tax rates to taxable dividend payments. In other words, while there are income tax benefits to an incorporation that go beyond tax reduction and tax deferral, caution must be exercised to navigate the many rules of the ITA designed to neutralize such planning. Such planning is subject to considerable scrutiny by the CRA.

Other Advantages and Disadvantages

Advantages

15-12.   There are many tax and non-tax advantages associated with the use of a corporation. Some of the more common are as follows:

Limited Liability   Because a corporation is a separate legal entity, the shareholders' liability to creditors is generally limited to the amount they have invested directly as legal capital. That is, creditors of the corporation can look only to the assets of the corporation for satisfaction of their claims. However, for smaller corporations, obtaining significant amounts of financing will almost always require the owners to provide personal guarantees, making this advantage somewhat illusory for this type of company. Note, however, that limited liability may still be important for a smaller corporation if it is exposed to significant product or environmental claims.

Capital Gains Deduction   Individuals who dispose of the shares of a qualified small business corporation are eligible to claim the capital gains deduction ($892,218 for 2021). To qualify, a business must be a CCPC with substantially all of the fair market value (FMV) of its assets (at least 90%) used in an active business carried on primarily in Canada (at least 50%) at the time of disposition. In addition, no one other than the seller or related persons can, as a rule, have owned the shares during the 24 months preceding the sale. During this 24-month period, more than 50% of the FMV of the assets must have been used in an active business carried on primarily in Canada. For a more complete discussion of this provision, see Chapter 11. The TOSI rules generally do not apply to capital gains eligible for the capital gains deduction, so a properly structured corporation may allow for multiple family members to access the capital gains deduction.

Flexibility on Timing, Type, and Distribution of Income   In the case of a corporation with a single individual shareholder, there is considerable flexibility given that the individual controls the company and makes all decisions on behalf of the company in the role of owner/manager. The individual can direct the corporation as to the amount, type, and timing of compensation (e.g., salary vs. dividends). In addition, the individual can transact with the company to borrow money from the corporation, lend money to the corporation, rent or sell property to or from the corporation, and so on.

Business Succession and Estate Planning   A corporation can be used to pass future benefits of a business to the next generation of family on a tax-free basis. It is important that the planning be properly structured to achieve the appropriate result (see Chapters 17 and 19).

Disadvantages

15-13.   Disadvantages that are normally associated with incorporation include the following:

Use of Losses   An individual who carries on a business as a sole proprietor can claim business losses against any other source of income, including employment and property income. If the business is carried on by a corporation, however, such losses belong to the corporation and are only available to that corporation against past or future corporate income. Losses are generally experienced in the first few startup years until the business is firmly established and revenues become stable. Because of this fact, general tax advice to individuals starting a business is not to incorporate while business losses are being experienced. This ensures that the individual can personally take advantage of any business losses in the first few years.

Tax Credits   A corporation is not eligible for personal tax credits, such as the basic personal, tuition fee, age, pension, and disability tax credits. This can be mitigated by ensuring that the corporation pays sufficient salaries to shareholders to fully use tax credits available to individual shareholders.

Charitable Donations   Charitable donations provide the basis for a tax credit for individuals, largely at 29% or 33% at the federal level. In contrast, they are a taxable income deduction for a corporation. In general, largely due to low corporate tax rates, this deduction will not be as valuable as the tax credit that an individual would receive for donations. As a rule it is generally preferable for donations to be made by individual shareholders.

Additional Maintenance Costs   The legal, accounting, and other costs associated with maintaining a corporation and its business will generally be higher for a corporation than for an individual (the cost of filing a corporate tax return on an annual basis, annual fees, costs of separate corporate filings under corporate law, etc.).

Winding-Up and Dissolution of a Corporation and Its Business   The complications associated with the dissolution of a corporation and the winding-up of its business will be significantly greater than would be the case with a business carried on as a sole proprietorship. In addition, there are income tax consequences of dissolving a company that are likely to result in an increased income tax liability. This topic is discussed in Chapter 17.

We suggest you complete SSP 15-1 and 15-2 at this point.

Tax Reduction and Deferral

Approach

15-14.   Whether the use of a corporation will result in a reduction or deferral of income taxes will depend on the type of income being earned as well as the income tax classification of the corporation. In this section, we will examine this issue by using a basic example to consider this issue in the following situations:

- A public corporation

- A CCPC earning active business income that is eligible for the small business deduction, and business and property income that is not eligible for the small business deduction

- A CCPC earning investment income (net taxable capital gains and other property income, excluding dividends)

- A CCPC in receipt of both eligible and non-eligible dividends

15-15.   These cases should serve to provide you with an understanding of the ability of a corporation to provide either tax reduction or tax deferral for an individual taxpayer applying current corporate income tax rates.

15-16.   To assist you in understanding this material (which is covered in detail in Chapter 13), we remind you that eligible dividends include:

- designated dividends paid by CCPCs with a positive GRIP balance at the end of a taxation year in which the dividend is paid; and

- designated dividends paid by non-CCPCs that do not have an LRIP balance immediately before the payment of a dividend.

Basic Example

Data on the Individual Taxpayer
15-17.   In order to consider the various results that can be achieved by incorporating a source of income, we will use a simple example in which an individual, Mr. Renaud, has $100,000 in income that he can choose to receive directly or indirectly through a corporation in which he will be the sole shareholder. We will assume that Mr. Renaud has other sources of income and that any additional income will be subject to a federal tax rate of 33% (amounts over $216,511 for 2021). He will have no unused personal tax credits.

15-18.   To illustrate the effects of incorporating different types of income, several cases will be presented with varying assumptions as to the source of this income and the tax status of the corporation. However, before turning to these cases, we will give consideration to the various personal and corporate tax rates that will be used.

Personal Tax Rates and Tax Payable
15-19.   In these examples, we will assume that Mr. Renaud resides in a province where the maximum provincial tax rate on individuals is 18%. As all of Mr. Renaud's additional income will be subject to this maximum rate, his combined federal/provincial marginal rate will be 51% (33% + 18%). The 18% provincial rate that we are using is representative of the 2021 personal tax rates for all provinces and territories.

15-20.   This 51% personal rate applies to the direct receipt of income by Mr. Renaud. This means that, if he receives $100,000 in additional income, taxes of $51,000 will be paid leaving him with $49,000.

15-21.   If the additional income is first earned by a corporation, the situation becomes more complex. Corporate income tax must first be paid, leaving the after-tax part of the additional income available for distribution to Mr. Renaud as a taxable dividend. When received, the taxable dividend would be grossed up, increasing net and taxable income. In addition, Mr. Renaud would be entitled to a dividend tax credit to apply against tax payable. The taxability of the dividends will depend on whether the dividends are non-eligible (e.g., paid by a CCPC out of income that has benefitted from the small business deduction) or eligible (e.g., paid by a non-CCPC out of income subject to the highest corporate income tax rates, which is generally business income not eligible for the small business deduction):

Non-Eligible Dividends   These dividends are grossed up by 15% and benefit from a federal dividend tax credit of 9/13 of the gross up. We will assume that Mr. Renaud resides in a province where the dividend tax credit on non-eligible dividends is 20% of the dividend gross up. The non-eligible dividend tax credit rate used is representative of average rates in provinces and territories in 2021.

Eligible Dividends   These dividends are grossed up by 38% and benefit from a federal dividend tax credit of 6/11 of the gross up. We will assume that Mr. Renaud lives in a province where the dividend tax credit on eligible dividends is 36% of the dividend gross up. The eligible dividend tax credit rate used is also representative of average rates in provinces and territories in 2021.

15-22.   Using these gross up and tax credit amounts, the rates applicable to Mr. Renaud on eligible and non-eligible dividends can be calculated as follows:

Personal tax on dividends	**Non-Eligible Dividends**	**Eligible Dividends**
Provincial dividend tax credit	20.0%	36.0%
Dividends received	100.0%	100.0%
Gross up	15.0%	38.0%
Taxable dividends	115.0%	138.0%
Times the combined federal/provincial tax rate	51.0%	51.0%
Equals: Combined federal/provincial tax rate on dividends received	58.7%	70.4%
Less: Dividend tax credit [(9/13 + 20%)(15%)]	(13.4%)	
Less: Dividend tax credit [(6/11 + 36%)(38%)]		(34.4%)
Effective personal tax rate on dividends received	45.3%	36.0%

15-23.   For use in our examples, we will round the non-eligible rate to 45%. For eligible dividends, we will use 36%.

Corporate Tax Rates

15-24.   In making the required calculations, we will use the corporate federal tax rates that apply for 2021. With respect to provincial rates, we will use 2.5% for income eligible for the small business deduction and 13.5% for other types of corporate income. Both of these are representative of average rates in provinces and territories in 2021. When these provincial rates are added to the corresponding federal rates, the combined rates are 11.5% (9% + 2.5%) for income eligible for the small business deduction and 28.5% (15% + 13.5%) for other corporate income. The following table provides the rates that will be used in our examples:

General Part I tax rate	38%
Federal tax abatement	10%
General rate reduction (GRR)	13%
Refundable tax on investment income of a CCPC (ART)	10 2/3%
Federal small business deduction	19%
Provincial tax rates	
Income eligible for federal small business deduction	2.5%
Income not eligible for federal small business deduction	13.5%
Refundable portion of Part I tax on investment income	30 2/3%
Refundable Part IV tax	38 1/3%

15-25.   Note that the general rate reduction does not apply to corporate income that benefits from either the small business deduction or the manufacturing and process (M&P) deduction. In addition, it does not apply to aggregate investment income of a CCPC, which adds an additional refundable tax on aggregate investment income of 10 2/3% (see Chapter 13).

15-26.   We will apply this basic information to a number of different situations in order to examine the question of whether the incorporation of a source of income that will generate $100,000 in additional income will serve to either reduce or defer taxes with respect to an individual shareholder.

Public Corporation

M&P Deduction

15-27.   Both the M&P deduction and the GRR apply the same rate reduction of 13%. Only one of the two tax rate reductions can be applied to the same income. As a result, the effective federal tax rate for a corporation will not change regardless of which one is used. For simplicity, therefore, we will not give separate attention to situations where a public corporation is earning income that is eligible for the M&P deduction.

General Results

15-28.   For all practical purposes a public corporation would not be incorporated by a single individual for only $100,000 of income. However, this case does serve to illustrate a simplified calculation of corporate income tax. The same tax calculation that would apply to a public company would also apply to a CCPC with respect to active business income not eligible for the small business deduction.

15-29.   Taxable dividends paid by non-CCPCs, such as a public corporation, will generally be designated as eligible. While a public company could have an LRIP that prevents designation of eligible dividends in favour of non-eligible dividends, this is an uncommon occurrence that does not warrant further consideration. The more common eligible dividend illustration is set out in the following calculations:

Public corporation

Federal tax [(38%)($100,000)]	$38,000
Federal tax abatement [(10%)($100,000)]	(10,000)
General rate reduction [(13%)($100,000)]	(13,000)
Federal tax payable	$15,000
Provincial tax payable [(13.5%)($100,000)]	13,500
Corporate tax payable	$28,500
Corporate business income	$100,000
Corporate tax payable	(28,500)
Maximum eligible dividend payable	$ 71,500
Personal tax on eligible dividends [(36%)($71,500)]	(25,740)
Income retained by the individual	$ 45,760
After-tax retention—With corporation	$ 45,760
After-tax retention—Without corporation	(49,000)
Advantage (disadvantage) with corporation	($ 3,240)

Analysis

15-30.   If the $100,000 had been received directly, $49,000 [($100,000)(1 - .51)] would be retained as opposed to $45,760 that is retained when the $100,000 is earned by a public corporation with a post-tax eligible dividend distribution of $71,500. Based on the facts, the individual is better to receive the additional income directly.

15-31.   However, there is a deferral of income tax. Corporate taxes were only $28,500, significantly less than the $51,000 that would have been payable had the individual received the income directly. There is some question as to whether this deferral would justify the eventual payment of an additional $3,240 in income tax.

15-32.   From another practical perspective, the issue of tax deferral versus an eventual tax reduction is moot in the case of a public corporation since individual shareholders will have little to no say regarding decisions to pay dividends. On the other hand, private corporations, particularly those with a sole shareholder, are a different matter altogether since the corporate decision to pay dividends is effectively made by the sole shareholder acting on behalf of the corporation.

Integration and Eligible Dividends

15-33.   The preceding example is based on a public corporation designating and paying eligible dividends. The income tax policy objective of the ability of a corporation to pay favourably taxed eligible dividends is in recognition that the corporation is paying a larger amount of the income tax than would be the case for non-eligible dividends. Unfortunately, while the eligible dividend concept has moved much closer to perfect integration for public corporations than was the case before taxable dividends were separated into eligible and non-eligible dividends, perfect integration remains elusive.

15-34.   Perfect integration with respect to eligible dividends requires a notional corporate income tax rate of 27.54% (see Figure 13-2). As the combined federal/provincial corporate income tax rates for 2021 range from 25% to 31%, corporate tax rates are not the main problem.

15-35.   The problem is with the dividend tax credit rates. Effective integration requires the combined federal/provincial tax credit to be equal to the gross up. This means that, given the federal rate of 6/11, the provincial dividend tax credit would have to be 5/11, or 45.5% of the gross up. In actual fact, in 2021 only New Brunswick provides a dividend tax credit above the required rate.

Exercise 15-1

Subject: Eligible Dividends and Integration

Ms. Jennifer Ashley is the sole shareholder of a number of successful associated CCPCs. For 2021, she has sources of income that would result in her being subject to a combined federal/provincial income tax rate of 45% on any additional income. She resides in a province where the provincial dividend tax credit on eligible dividends is equal to 47.1% of the gross up and 31.0% of the gross up for non-eligible dividends. Ms. Ashley has commenced a new business that is anticipated to generate business profits of $100,000 during the coming year. If she were to receive the income directly as a result of carrying on the business as a sole proprietor she would retain $55,000 [($100,000)(1 - 45%)] after taxes. If she incorporates the business within a newly incorporated CCPC no business limit would be allocated since all of the business limit is required by the other associated CCPCs. As a result, the combined income tax rate of the new CCPC would be 26.5% [federal 15% (38% basic rate - 10% abatement - 13% GRR) + 11.5%]. She has asked for your advice as to whether she should incorporate the new business or carry it on as a sole proprietor. Provide your recommendation.

Solutions to Exercises are available in the Study Guide.

CCPC—Active Business Income

General Results

15-36.   A CCPC can be subject to two different tax rates on its active business income. A low rate is available on up to $500,000 of income that is eligible for the small business deduction, with a higher tax rate on income that is not eligible for the small business deduction. At the federal level the 19% small business deduction is replaced with the GRR of 13% when active business income is not eligible for the small business deduction. The result is a range for federal income tax rates on business income at the corporate level of between 9% and 13%, a difference of up to 6%. With respect to the provinces, there is a similar dual rate system. The provincial difference averages 10%, meaning that the combined differences between active business income eligible for the small business deduction and the same income that is not eligible for the small business deduction can increase the combined tax rate by 16% on average. In addition, we will have to take into consideration the fact that dividends that have been paid out of income that has benefitted from the small business deduction cannot be designated as eligible dividends and therefore attract a higher level of personal income tax. This higher level of personal tax is balanced by lower corporate taxes.

15-37.   We will continue to use the Mr. Renaud example from Paragraph 15-17 to illustrate the income tax consequences of applying these two rates. While using the basic data from this example, we will consider two different cases:

Case One   In Case One, we will assume that the corporate income is eligible for the small business deduction. This means that dividends that are received by Mr. Renaud will be non-eligible and subject to tax at an effective rate of 45% (see Paragraph 15-24).

Case Two   In Case Two, we will assume that none of the corporate income is eligible for the small business deduction because of business limit allocations to associated corporations. The dividends that are received by Mr. Renaud can be designated as eligible and are subject to tax at an effective rate of 36%. The results in this case are identical to those for a public corporation (see Paragraph 15-29).

Active business income of CCPC	Case One SBD Deduction	Case Two No SBD
Federal tax [(38%)($100,000)]	$ 38,000	$ 38,000
Federal tax abatement [(10%)($100,000)]	(10,000)	(10,000)
Small business deduction [(19%)($100,000)]	(19,000)	N/A
General rate reduction [(13%)($100,000)]	N/A	(13,000)
Federal tax payable	$ 9,000	$ 15,000
Provincial tax payable:		
At 2.5%	2,500	N/A
At 13.5%	N/A	13,500
Corporate tax payable	$ 11,500	$ 28,500
Corporate business income	$100,000	$100,000
Corporate tax payable	(11,500)	(28,500)
Maximum dividend payable	$ 88,500	$ 71,500
Personal tax at 45% (non-eligible)	(39,825)	N/A
Personal tax at 36% (eligible)	N/A	(25,740)
Income retained by the individual	$ 48,675	$ 45,760
After-tax retention—With corporation	$ 48,675	$ 45,760
After-tax retention—Without corporation	(49,000)	(49,000)
Advantage (disadvantage) with corporation	($ 325)	($ 3,240)

Analysis

15-38.   The preceding table shows that there is a small additional tax cost of $325 that results from incorporating the business, even when the business income is eligible for the small business deduction. In the absence of the small business deduction, the corporate choice results in a much larger disadvantage of $3,240. This result is identical to that of the analysis of the public corporation situation (see Paragraph 15-29).

15-39.   In both cases the use of a corporation results in considerable tax deferral. In the small business deduction case the corporate income taxes are only $11,500, as compared to $51,000 when the business is not incorporated. When this significant amount of deferral is combined with the small tax disadvantage associated with this alternative, using the corporate route when the small business deduction is available seems advantageous, particularly if the business is expanding and requires additional capital.

15-40.   The situation is less clear when the small business deduction is not available. As corporate income taxes are only $28,500, well below the $51,000 that would be paid were the business not incorporated, there is, once again, significant deferral. However, the price is future payment of an additional $3,240 in income tax when the income is distributed by the corporation as a taxable dividend. If Mr. Renaud is in a position to leave the funds in the corporation for some length of time, then the time value of money would begin to reduce the impact.

15-41.   A further point related to tax deferral is sometimes overlooked. Any post-tax income that is left in the corporation should not be left idle. If it is not needed in the business, it should be invested to earn investment income. Excess cash not needed in support of a corporation's business is not considered as an active business asset nor is the income earned considered active business income. This can have a number of income tax consequences, including impacting the ability to claim an allowable business investment loss (ABIL), the ability to claim a capital gains deduction on the disposition of corporate shares, and a potential reduction in what may be claimed by a CCPC as the small business deduction. In addition, investment income is taxed at corporate rates that often exceed the highest tax rates charged to individuals. In effect, the ITA discourages corporations from accumulating investments and earning investment income. However, in our analysis of various situations in which investment income is earned by a CCPC we will consider the additional income taxes charged and look at whether incorporating investments is beneficial in terms of tax reduction and tax deferral.

Exercise 15-2

Subject: Incorporation of Active Business Income

Keith Slater carries on a business as a sole proprietor. He anticipates business profits of $126,000 for the taxation year ending December 31, 2021, all of which would be eligible for the small business deduction. He has employment income in excess of $300,000, which places him in the highest income tax bracket with respect to any additional income. The provincial tax rate would be 16% and the federal rate 33%. The provincial dividend tax credit is equal to 27% of the dividend gross up for non-eligible dividends. The provincial corporate income tax rate on income eligible for the small business deduction is 3% and 12% on other corporate income. Mr. Slater has asked for your advice as to whether he should incorporate his business. Advise him with respect to any tax deferral that could be available on income left in the corporation and on any tax savings that would be available if the corporation distributed its post-tax earnings as taxable dividends.

Solutions to Exericises are available in the Study Guide.

"Bonusing Down" Active Business Income

15-42.   A traditional tax planning technique for CCPCs that have active business income in excess of their business limit is to "bonus down." Bonusing down means that an extra expense is used to reduce taxable income to an amount that is fully eligible for the small business deduction. If, for example, a CCPC with no associated corporations were to have business profits from an active business of $600,000, only $500,000 would qualify for the small business deduction. The $100,000 excess amount would be subject to the high corporate tax rates as a result. However, if the business were to declare a bonus to the principal shareholder of $100,000, then business profits and net and taxable income would be reduced to $500,000, meaning all of the taxable income would benefit from the small business deduction and none of the corporate income would be subject to high corporate income tax rates.

15-43.   A bonusing strategy involves minimizing corporate income tax while deferring individual income tax to the extent possible. If, for example (using the same numbers mentioned in the preceding paragraph), a bonus of $100,000 is declared for the taxation year of a CCPC ending December 31, 2021, the corporation will have incurred an expense while the intended individual would only be required to include the bonus as employment income when received. This strategy leads to bonuses only being paid in the following calendar year to further defer personal income tax. ITA 78(4), which requires that the bonus be paid within 180 days of the taxation year of the CCPC, would have to be carefully observed. If the bonus is unpaid on the 180th day (June 29, 2022), the CCPC would lose its bonus expense for the 2021 taxation year, defeating the bonusing down strategy objectives.

15-44.   There are other concerns with respect to a bonusing down strategy. ITA 67, for example, reads that an expense will be disallowed if it is considered unreasonable in the circumstances. ITA 67 is clearly not a concern if the bonus is considered reasonable, which leads us to question what would be required to consider a bonus of $100,000 reasonable. The case law generally looks to the services provided by an employee that justify a bonus. Performance-based criteria could justify a bonus of a certain amount depending on the circumstances. For example, an employee could have a contract with the employer that provides for a specified dollar amount or percentage of sales or some other relevant indicator. This would support a bonus. A flat-rate bonus is much more difficult to justify and should always be supportable by contract to the extent possible or some other measurable criteria or industry standard at a minimum.

15-45.   The nature of the relationship between the corporate employer and the bonus recipient is also important. It is unlikely that the CRA would question bonuses to executives of a public corporation. On the other hand, bonuses paid by a CCPC with a sole shareholder or where all shareholders were members of the same family have an increased likelihood of coming under close scrutiny. The difference is the level of control over the decision to declare and pay a bonus. Executives of a public corporation likely have very little say as to bonuses, whereas CCPCs controlled by individuals—particularly related individuals—have tremendous flexibility to generally do as they please. The income tax implications of having all or a part of a bonus considered unreasonable is that the corporation would lose part or all of its expense but the employee would be required to include the full amount of the bonus in her income as employment income when received.

15-46.   Throughout the text we have referred to the importance of being aware of the provisions of the ITA and how they are interpreted, particularly by the CRA. However, we have also noted many instances (e.g., taxable employment benefits) where the CRA has granted administrative concessions or adopted administrative positions favourable to taxpayers. The CRA has longstanding administrative positions with respect to shareholder/manager remuneration through bonuses and other similar amounts (see ITTN #22 and #30). In brief, the CRA first recognizes that sole proprietors often incorporate their businesses for many genuine reasons and that the reasonableness of bonuses to them should not be challenged where they were, because of their efforts, responsible for the business profits. This typically would occur where an individual began the business and through his ongoing efforts is fully active in the business on a daily basis and ultimately responsible for the success of the business. The CRA position is that they will not challenge the reasonableness of bonuses in these circumstances where the strategy is used to reduce taxable income to an amount fully eligible for the small business deduction. In other words, the CRA effectively endorses a bonusing down strategy. It is important to be aware, however, that the CRA has made it clear that this concession does not apply to bonuses paid to family members who are generally inactive in the business and who have not made considerable contributions toward its success.

CCPC—Investment Income Other Than Dividends

15-47.   As was discussed in Chapter 13, the aggregate investment income of a CCPC is taxed at full corporate rates. Neither the small business deduction nor the general rate reduction is available to offset these rates on that income. In addition, there is an additional refundable tax under ITA 123.3 (the ART) equal to 10 2/3% of aggregate investment income. The result is that the tax rate to CCPCs on such income is 38 2/3% [38% basic rate- 10% abatement + 10 2/3% ART], 30 2/3% of which is refundable through the dividend refund and non-eligible RDTOH system discussed in Chapter 13.

15-48.   Continuing our Mr. Renaud example from Paragraph 15-17, if Mr. Renaud incorporates the investments his after-tax retention on $100,000 of investment income received by a CCPC, compared to the direct receipt of investment income, would be as follows:

Investment income of CCPC

Federal tax [(38%)($100,000)]	$ 38,000
Additional refundable tax [(10 2/3%)($100,000)]	10,667
Federal tax abatement [(10%)($100,000)]	(10,000)
Federal tax payable	$ 38,667
Provincial tax payable [(13.5%)($100,000)]	13,500
Corporate tax payable	$ 52,167
Non-eligible RDTOH balance [(30 2/3%)($100,000)]	$ 30,667
Corporate investment income	$100,000
Corporate tax payable	(52,167)
Net corporate income before dividend refund	$ 47,833
Dividend refund (see Note)	29,734
Maximum dividend payable	$ 77,567
Personal tax on non-eligible dividends at 45%	(34,905)
Income retained by the individual	$ 42,662
After-tax retention—With corporation	$ 42,662
After-tax retention—Without corporation	(49,000)
Advantage (disadvantage) with corporation	($ 6,338)

Note   The dividend refund is the lesser of the balance in the non-eligible RDTOH account ($30,667) and 38 1/3% of taxable dividends paid. The available cash of $47,833 would support a dividend of $77,567 ($47,833 ÷ .61667), which includes a potential dividend refund of $29,734 [(38 1/3%)($77,567)]. This is less than the balance in the non-eligible RDTOH, so a dividend refund of $29,734 is available, which leaves a non-eligible RDTOH balance of $933.

15-49.   As the corporate taxes of $52,167 exceed the $51,000 that would be paid on direct receipt of the $100,000, there is no tax deferral with the use of a corporation. When this fact is combined with the $6,338 reduction in after-tax retention, incorporating the investments would not be recommended.

Exercise 15-3

Subject: Incorporation of Interest Income

David Slater has investments that he anticipates will earn interest income of $126,000 for the year ending December 31, 2021. He has employment income in excess of $300,000, which means that any additional income will be subject to maximum personal tax rates in his province of residence of 18% plus federal tax at 33%. The provincial dividend tax credit is equal to 27% of the dividend gross up for non-eligible dividends. The corporate tax rate is 3% on income eligible for the small business deduction and 12% on any other corporate income. Mr. Slater has asked for your advice as to whether he should incorporate the investments to a CCPC in which he would be the sole shareholder. Advise him with respect to any tax deferral that would be available on post-tax income left in the corporation and on any potential tax savings if all of the post-tax corporate income were distributed as taxable dividends.

Solutions to Exercises are available in the Study Guide.

We suggest you complete SSP 15-3 at this point.

CCPC—Dividend Income

Possible Sources of Dividend Income

15-50.   A CCPC can only designate dividends as eligible to the extent that it has a balance in its GRIP. Taxable dividends that are eligible dividends increase the GRIP of a CCPC and therefore enable the company to designate taxable dividends as eligible. In general, taxable dividends received by a CCPC will be subject to Part IV tax. The exception is if the taxable dividend is received from a connected company that did not claim a dividend refund for the taxation year in which the dividend was paid. Taxable dividend income effects for a CCPC can be summarized as follows:

Eligible Dividends   Any portfolio taxable dividends received that are designated eligible will be added to the CCPC's GRIP balance and will also increase the eligible RDTOH. If a CCPC receives a non-eligible dividend from a connected company that entitles the connected company to a dividend refund there will be an addition to the eligible RDTOH of the recipient company to the extent that the dividend refund is attributable to the eligible RDTOH of the connected company. This latter point recognizes that a CCPC can obtain a dividend refund on the payment of non-eligible dividends from both the non-eligible RDTOH and the eligible RDTOH account.

Portfolio Dividends   These dividends will be subject to Part IV tax regardless of whether they are eligible or non-eligible.

Connected Company Dividends   These dividends can be eligible or non-eligible and may be subject to Part IV tax depending on the following:

- If a dividend refund results from the dividend payment, the dividends will be subject to Part IV tax. The fact that there is a dividend refund means that the connected company had an RDTOH account that requires investment income sources.

- If no dividend refund results from the dividend payment, the dividends will not be subject to Part IV tax. The fact that there is no dividend refund means that the connected company either did not have an RDTOH account balance at the end of a given taxation year and therefore had no investment income or instead had only business income that may or may not have been eligible for the small business deduction.

Analysis

15-51.   Continuing with the Mr. Renaud example from Paragraph 15-17, Mr. Renaud would pay income taxes on:

- eligible dividends received at an effective rate of 36%; his after-tax retention on the direct receipt of $100,000 of these dividends would be $64,000 [($100,000)(1 - .36)]; and

- non-eligible dividends received at a rate of 45%; his after-tax retention on the direct receipt of $100,000 of these dividends would be $55,000 [($100,000)(1 - .45)].

A comparison of this retention with the after-tax results from using a corporation, assuming the connected company paid non-eligible dividends, would be as follows:

Dividend income of CCPC	Eligible Portfolio Dividends	Non-Eligible Portfolio Dividends	Connected with Refund	Connected No Refund
Corporate dividend income	$100,000	$100,000	$100,000	$100,000
Part IV tax payable at 38 1/3%	(38,333)	(38,333)	(38,333)	N/A
Net corporate income before dividend refund	$ 61,667	$ 61,667	$ 61,667	$100,000
Dividend refund at 38 1/3%	38,333	38,333	38,333	N/A
Maximum dividend payable	$100,000	$100,000	$100,000	$100,000
Personal tax on:				
Eligible dividends at 36%	(36,000)			
Non-eligible dividends At 45%	N/A·	(45,000)	(45,000)	(45,000)
Income retained by individual	$ 64,000	$ 55,000	$ 55,000	$ 55,000
After-tax retention:				
With corporation	$ 64,000	$ 55,000	$ 55,000	$ 55,000
Without corporation	(64,000)	(55,000)	(55,000)	(55,000)
Advantage (disadvantage)	Nil	Nil	Nil	Nil

15-52.   In all cases, the taxable dividends paid to an individual investor total the full $100,000 that was received by the corporation. As a result, the total tax payable on dividends is the same whether the investment is held personally or within a corporation.

15-53.   The Part IV tax does, however, influence the conclusions on tax deferral. If eligible dividends are paid and are subject to Part IV tax, this 38 1/3% tax is higher than the 36% effective tax rate on eligible dividends received by Mr. Renaud, resulting in a deferral of $2,333. Alternatively, if non-eligible dividends are paid, the Part IV tax rate of 38 1/3% is less than the 45% effective tax rate that applies to these dividends, and the deferral advantage is eliminated. As a result, there is a deferral advantage with respect to non-eligible dividends of $2,333 in this case and a disadvantage of $6,667 with respect to eligible dividends.

15-54.   The situation is different in the absence of Part IV tax. While at first glance this appears to be a significant deferral advantage, the situation can generally only occur where after-tax business income of one corporation is paid as a taxable dividend to a second corporation. In this situation the tax policy of integration is that there will be no further income tax until there is a taxable dividend distribution to individual shareholders. The tax deferral advantage remains as the difference between incorporating a business versus the business being carried on by an individual.

Conclusions on Tax Reductions and Deferrals

15-55.   The results from the preceding cases can be summarized as follows:

	Corporate Taxes before Dividend Refund	After-Tax Retention on Flow Through
Public corporation ($100,000 of income) (Paragraph 15-29):	$28,500	$45,760
CCPC ($100,000 of active business income) (Paragraph 15-37):		
Eligible for SBD	$11,500	$48,675
Not eligible for SBD	28,500	45,760
CCPC ($100,000 of interest income):		
Investment income (Paragraph 15-50)	$52,167	$42,662
CCPC ($100,000 of dividend income) (Paragraph 15-53):		
Eligible portfolio dividends	$38,333	$64,000
Non-eligible portfolio dividends	38,333	55,000
Connected with refund	38,333	55,000
Connected no refund	Nil	55,000

15-56.   The conclusions reached can be summarized as follows:

Tax Reduction Available   As illustrated previously, Mr. Renaud is subject to taxes on the direct receipt of income, other than dividends, at a rate of 51%, while his effective tax rate on the direct receipt of dividends is 36% (eligible) or 45% (non-eligible). This means that his after-tax retention resulting from the direct receipt of income would be:

- $49,000 on $100,000 of business or interest income
- $64,000 on $100,000 of eligible dividend income
- $55,000 on $100,000 of non-eligible dividend income

Comparing these amounts to those in the preceding table, there is no case where there is a reduction in taxes through the use of a corporation to earn investment income. The least unfavourable scenario is where a CCPC is earning active business income. In this case, the tax cost of $325 is relatively small. This is consistent with our earlier comment that the ITA discourages CCPCs from owning investments and earning investment-type income.

When a public company is involved, the use of a corporation results in the payment of $3,240 more taxes and correspondingly less retention ($45,760 vs. $49,000). The same $3,240 shortfall results when a CCPC is earning active business income that is not eligible for the small business deduction. The situation is even worse for investment income earned by a CCPC. The shortfall here is $6,338 ($42,662 vs. $49,000).

In the case of dividend income received by a CCPC, the after-tax results are the same whether the income is received directly or the source of the income is incorporated.

Tax Deferral Available   Tax deferral occurs when corporate income is subject to income tax rates that are less than those that would have been payable had the source of the income not been incorporated. Without incorporating a CCPC Mr. Renaud would have paid the following amounts in income tax:

- $51,000 on $100,000 of business or interest income
- $36,000 on $100,000 of eligible dividend income
- $45,000 on $100,000 of non-eligible dividend income

Comparing these amounts to the corporate income tax amounts in the preceding table, we find that there is tax deferral in some, but not all, cases.

There is tax deferral in the case of public companies, with corporate income taxes on business or interest income of only $28,500.

The worst-case scenario is when a CCPC earns interest income. Corporate income taxes are $52,167, as compared to $51,000 of personal income tax without a corporation.

In the cases where Part IV tax applies, the $38,333 that would be payable, is larger than the $36,000 that would have been payable with respect to eligible dividends, but smaller than the $45,000 that would be paid in respect of non-eligible dividends.

The most significant amounts of deferral occur when a CCPC earns active business income eligible for the small business deduction. In the case of income eligible for the small business deduction, corporate income taxes were only $11,500, $39,500 less than the $51,000 that would have been payable had the business not been incorporated.

Even if a CCPC has active business income that is not eligible for the small business deduction, corporate income taxes were only $28,500, $22,500 less than the $51,000 that would have been payable had the business not been incorporated.

15-57. The above conclusions are based on assumed provincial personal and corporate tax rates as outlined previously. While the rates we have used are within the range of current actual rates, the use of other rates will produce different results. As these differences can be important, we will give some attention to this issue in the next section of this chapter.

Exercise 15-4

Subject: Incorporation of Interest and Dividend Income

One of your clients has asked for your advice on whether there would be any income tax advantages to incorporating three personal investments. The three investments include shares and bonds that are expected to earn the following amounts of investment income in 2021:

Eligible dividends on portfolio share investments	$46,000
Non-Eligible dividends from shares of a 100% owned corporation (a dividend refund of $29,000 will be received by the dividend payor)	87,000
Interest income on bonds	32,000

Your client is in the highest marginal tax bracket as a result of other sources of income. In addition, the client requires all of the income from these investments. The personal provincial income tax rate on this additional income will be 18%. The provincial dividend tax credit is 5/11 of the dividend gross up for eligible dividends and 4/13 of the dividend gross up for non-eligible dividends. The new corporation will be subject to a provincial tax rate of 2.5% on income eligible for the small business deduction and 12% on any other corporate income. The corporation will make the maximum eligible dividend designation possible. Provide the requested advice, supported by calculations, and explain your conclusions.

Exercise 15-5

Subject: Incorporation of Capital Gains

One of your clients has asked your advice on whether she should incorporate investments she owns to a new corporation that would be a CCPC. She would be the sole shareholder. She advises you that while the investments will not earn any investment income in the near future, they are expected to increase in value by $92,000. She wonders if it would be preferable that a future capital gain of $92,000 be realized by a corporation with after-tax funds distributed to her as dividends. The alternative is to realize the capital gain personally. Any capital gain would not be eligible for the capital gains deduction.

For the year ending December 31, 2021, your client has employment income in excess of $250,000 meaning that any additional income will be subject to the highest personal provincial rate of 16% and the highest federal income tax rate of 33%. If the investments are incorporated she will require all of the after-tax capital gains for personal purposes, requiring that all funds be distributed to her as dividends. The corporation will be subject to a provincial tax rate of 3.5% on income eligible for the small business deduction and 12% on any other corporate income. The provincial dividend tax credit is equal to 4/13 of the dividend gross up for non-eligible dividends and 5/11 for eligible dividends.

Provide the requested advice, including an explanation of your conclusions.

Solutions to Exercises are available in the Study Guide.

We suggest you complete SSP 15-4 at this point.

Provincial Taxes and Integration

Introduction

15-58. We have presented a number of different cases dealing with the question of whether it is better, both in terms of tax reduction and tax deferral, for an individual to receive income directly or, alternatively, to incorporate the source of income. In doing so, we have given consideration to both the type of income and the income tax classification of the corporation, particularly whether the corporation is a CCPC and therefore eligible for the small business deduction.

15-59. The conclusions that we reached were presented in Paragraph 15-56. We found that, while there were several cases in which the use of a corporation provided some degree of tax deferral, there were no scenarios that provided for an overall reduction in income taxes.

15-60. To this point the examples we have presented have focused on provincial tax rates that are representative of average provincial tax rates for 2021. With 10 provinces and 3 territories, several different types of income, and various corporate, individual, and dividend tax credit rates to consider, there are literally hundreds of possible combinations. Given this, our goal will be to help you understand how changes in provincial rates will act to influence the decision on whether the use of a corporation is beneficial in terms of tax deferral and tax reduction.

Tax Deferral

15-61. The use of a corporation to provide tax deferral is relatively straightforward. If the combined federal/provincial corporate tax rate on a specific type of income is less than the combined personal federal/provincial tax rate on the same income the use of a corporation will provide tax deferral. Some 2021 examples of this are as follows:

Alberta CCPC Earning Active Business Income   The combined federal/provincial tax rate on the active business income of a CCPC subject to Alberta corporate tax rates is 11%. An individual resident in Alberta is subject to a maximum combined federal/ provincial rate on business income of 48%. In this case, the use of a corporation would provide considerable deferral.

Manitoba CCPC Earning Investment Income   The combined federal/provincial tax rate on investment income of a CCPC subject to Manitoba corporate rates is 50.7%. An individual resident in Manitoba is subject to a maximum combined federal/provincial rate on investment income of 50.4%. In this case, the use of a corporation would provide no deferral.

British Columbia Public Corporation (or income tax on the active business income of a CCPC in excess of $500,000)   The combined federal/provincial tax rate would be 27%. An individual resident in British Columbia is subject to a maximum combined federal/provincial rate of 53.5%. In this case, the use of a corporation would again provide considerable deferral.

15-62.   Tax deferral is simply one of many factors to consider when determining whether the use of a corporation is warranted in a given situation. If the needs of shareholders require that all after-tax corporate income be distributed, then tax deferral becomes irrelevant since its value in the analysis is dependent on some or all of the after-tax corporate income being retained by the corporation for other purposes. In summary, it is the many tax and non-tax factors that must be carefully considered rather than reliance on a single factor such as tax deferral.

Tax Reduction

Introduction

15-63.   The question of whether the use of a corporation can reduce income taxes overall is somewhat more complex than a tax deferral analysis. A tax reduction analysis requires looking to the following three factors:

1.   The combined federal/provincial tax rate on individuals

2.   The combined federal/provincial tax rate on corporations

3.   The combined federal/provincial dividend tax credit

15-64.   One of the most important elements in the analysis is the relationship between the combined corporate income tax rates and the combined dividend tax credit. The dividend tax credits are designed to compensate an individual for the corporate income taxes that have been paid by the corporation. If the combined dividend tax credit exceeds the combined corporate taxes paid, the use of a corporation will result in an overall tax reduction. However, if the dividend tax credits fall short of compensating for corporate taxes then there will be no overall tax reduction with the use of a corporation.

Provincial Rates on Individuals

15-65.   Maximum combined federal/provincial income tax rates on individuals range from a low of 44.5% in Nunavut to a high of 54% in Nova Scotia. Note, however, that variations in the combined rate influence both the after-tax amount retained by an individual whether earned with or without the use of a corporation. The reason for this is based on integration, the goal of which is to equate the after-tax income of an individual with the after-tax income where a corporation is used. If an individual is in a high tax bracket, after-tax income will be low as compared to individuals in a low tax bracket. This feature does not change simply because a corporation is used.

15-66.   For any specific combination of corporate tax rates and dividend tax credit rates, the personal income tax rates applicable to individuals will not affect whether the use of a corporation will reduce income taxes. While the amount of the advantage or disadvantage associated with the use of a corporation will vary with the tax rate on individuals, the conclusion on the ability of a corporation to reduce taxes will not. This is illustrated by the following example.

EXAMPLE   A CCPC has $100,000 of active business income that will be taxed at a combined federal/provincial rate of 11.5% (9.0% + 2.5%). The provincial dividend tax credit on non-eligible dividends is equal to 4/13 of the gross up. We will consider two cases, the first based on the assumption that Niko Parma is taxed at a combined federal/provincial rate of 48% (33% federal + 15% provincial), the second based on the assumption that Nela Parma is taxed at a combined federal/provincial rate of 54% (33% federal + 21% provincial).

ANALYSIS   If the individuals earned $100,000 personally, Niko's after-tax retention would be $52,000 [($100,000)(1 - .48)] and Nela's would be $46,000 [($100,000)(1 - .54)]. The after-tax retention if the income is flowed through a corporation would be as follows:

Comparison—Rates for individuals	Niko (48%)	Nela (54%)
Corporate income	$100,000	$100,000
Corporate taxes at 11.5%	(11,500)	(11,500)
Funds available for dividends	$ 88,500	$ 88,500
Non-eligible dividends received	$ 88,500	$ 88,500
Gross up (15%)	13,275	13,275
Taxable dividends	$101,775	$101,775
Individual tax rate	48%	54%
Taxes before dividend tax credit	$ 48,852	$ 54,959
Dividend tax credit (equal to gross up)	(13,275)	(13,275)
Individual taxes	$ 35,577	$ 41,684
Dividends received	$ 88,500	$ 88,500
Individual taxes	(35,577)	(41,684)
After-tax retention with corporation	$ 52,923	$ 46,816
After-tax retention with corporation	$ 52,923	$ 46,816
After-tax retention without corporation	(52,000)	(46,000)
Advantage with corporation	$ 923	$ 816

15-67.   Despite using individual tax rates that vary significantly, the result is the same for both Niko and Nela. The use of a corporation provides tax reduction for both individuals. The determination that there is tax reduction in this case has nothing to do with the individual income tax rates but everything to do with the corporate tax rate and dividend tax credit rate.

Provincial Dividend Tax Credit and Provincial Corporate Tax Rates
15-68.   As can be seen in the preceding example, the relevant factors that determine whether the use of a corporation will provide tax reduction is the relationship between the combined corporate federal and provincial taxes and the combined federal/provincial dividend tax credit. As the federal components of these factors are the same for each province and territory, it is the provincial rates that become the determining factor.

15-69.   The following integration observations are noteworthy:

Favourable to Incorporation   If the combined federal/provincial dividend tax credit exceeds the combined corporate income taxes, the use of a corporation will reduce taxes and provide a higher level of after-tax retention because the tax credits overcompensate for corporate income tax. This is referred to as overintegration.

Unfavourable to Incorporation   If the combined federal/provincial dividend tax credit is less than the combined corporate income taxes, the use of a corporation will fail to reduce overall income tax because the dividend tax credit undercompensates for corporate income tax. This is referred to as underintegration.

Examples—Effects of Provincial Rates on Integration

Data

15-70.   The range of rates in the provinces and territories for provincial corporate income tax and provincial dividend tax credit rates are as follows:

Corporate Tax Rates   The provincial rates for public companies (which would also apply to the active business income of a CCPC that is not eligible for the small business deduction) range from 8% to 16%. When these are combined with the federal rate of 15% (38% basic - 10% abatement - 13% GRR), the combined rates range from 23% to 31%.

The provincial rates for CCPCs earning income eligible for the small business deduction range from 0% to 3.2%. When these are combined with the federal rate of 9% (38% basic - 10% abatement - 19% SBD), the combined rates range from 9% to 12.2%.

Dividend Tax Credit Rates   The provincial rates for eligible dividends range from 19.6% of the gross up to 50.8% of the gross up. When combined with the federal rate of 6/11 (54.5%) of the gross up, the combined rates range from 74.1% of the gross up to 105.3% of the gross up.

The provincial rates on non-eligible dividends range from 5.1% of the gross up to 46%. When combined with the federal rate of 9/13 (69.2%) of the gross up, the combined rates range from 74.3% to 115.2% of the gross up.

15-71.   The following two examples illustrate the effects of provincial corporate tax rates and provincial dividend tax credit rates on the after-tax retention for individuals. They both use the following information:

EXAMPLE   The company has $100,000 in business income. The individual shareholders will be subject to a combined federal/provincial income tax rate of 45% on any additional income. If the $100,000 of income is earned by such an individual, $55,000 [($100,000) (1 - .45)] will be retained.

Public Company Paying Eligible Dividends

15-72.   Dealing first with public companies that are paying eligible dividends, we will consider the following three alternative cases:

Perfect Integration   For a public company paying eligible dividends, perfect integration occurs when the combined federal/provincial tax rate on corporations is 27.536% and the dividend tax credit is equal to one·(6/11 + 5/11).

Worst Case   Here we will use a combination of the highest corporate tax rate (31%) and the lowest dividend tax credit rate (74.1%).

Best Case   Here we will use a combination of the lowest corporate tax rate (23%) and the highest dividend tax credit rate (105.3%).

ANALYSIS   If the source of the income is incorporated, the after-tax retention under the three cases described would be as follows:

Public company eligible dividends	Perfect Integration	Worst Case (31%/74.1%)	Best Case (23%/105.3%)
Corporate income	$100,000	$100,000	$100,000
Corporate taxes:			
At 27.536%	(27,536)		
At 31% (worst)		(31,000)	
At 23% (best)			(23,000)
Available for dividends	$ 72,464	$ 69,000	$ 77,000
Eligible dividends received	$ 72,464	$ 69,000	$ 77,000
Gross up (38%)	27,536	26,220	29,260
Taxable dividends	$100,000	$ 95,220	$106,260
Individual tax rate	45%	45%	45%
Taxes before dividend tax credit	$ 45,000	$ 42,849	$ 47,817
Dividend tax credit:			
[($27,536)(1)]	(27,536)		
[($26,220)(74.1%)] (worst)		(19,429)	
[($29,260)(105.3%)] (best)	N/A		(30,811)
Individual taxes	$ 17,464	$ 23,420	$ 17,006
Eligible dividends received	$ 72,464	$ 69,000	$ 77,000
Individual taxes	(17,464)	(23,420)	(17,006)
After-tax retention with corporation	$ 55,000	$ 45,580	$ 59,994
After-tax retention with corporation	$ 55,000	$ 45,580	$ 59,994
Direct receipt after-tax retention	(55,000)	(55,000)	(55,000)
Advantage (disadvantage)	Nil	($ 9,420)	$ 4,994

ANALYSIS—Continued   This example clearly illustrates the influence of varying provincial rates for corporate income tax and dividend tax credits. The results range from a $9,420 reduction in after-tax retention with the use of a corporation to a $4,994 increase in after-tax retention with the use of a corporation. Considering that only $100,000 of income was involved, this represents a significant difference in the results with the use of a corporation.

CCPC Paying Non-Eligible Dividends

15-73.   This example calculates the after-tax retention of non-eligible dividends paid by a CCPC. We will consider the following three alternative cases:

Perfect Integration   Perfect integration for a CCPC occurs when the combined federal/provincial income tax rate is 13.043% and the dividend tax credit is equal to one (9/13 + 4/13).

Worst Case   Here we will use a combination of the highest corporate tax rate (12.2%) and the lowest dividend tax credit rate (74.3%).

Best Case   Here we will use a combination of the lowest corporate tax rate (9%) and the highest dividend tax credit rate (115.2%).

CCPC—Non-eligible dividends	Perfect Integration	Worst Case (12.2%/74.3%)	Best Case (9%/115.2%)
Corporate income	$100,000	$100,000	$100,000
Corporate taxes:			
At 13.043%	(13,043)		
At 12.2% (worst)		(12,200)	
At 9% (best)			(9,000)
Available for dividends	$ 86,957	$ 87,800	$ 91,000
Non-eligible dividends received	$ 86,957	$ 87,800	$ 91,000
Gross up (15%)	13,043	13,170	13,650
Taxable dividends	$100,000	$100,970	$104,650
Individual tax rate	45%	45%	45%
Taxes before dividend tax credit	$ 45,000	$ 45,437	$ 47,093
Dividend tax credit:			
[($13,043)(1)]	(13,043)		
[($13,170)(74.3%)] (worst)		(9,785)	
[($13,650)(115.2%)] (best)	N/A		(15,725)
Individual taxes	$ 31,957	$ 35,652	$ 31,368
Non-eligible dividends received	$ 86,957	$ 87,800	$ 91,000
Individual taxes	(31,957)	(35,652)	(31,368)
After-tax retention with corporation	$ 55,000	$ 52,148	$ 59,632
After-tax retention with corporation	$ 55,000	$ 52,148	$ 59,632
Direct receipt after-tax retention	(55,000)	(55,000)	(55,000)
Advantage (disadvantage)	Nil	($ 2,852)	$ 4,632

ANALYSIS   The results for the best and worst cases for both eligible and non-eligible dividends can be compared as follows:

Advantage (disadvantage) of using a corporation	Eligible Dividends	Non-Eligible Dividends
Worst case	($9,420)	($2,852)
Best case	4,994	$4,632

In the case of eligible dividends the results are skewed toward the disadvantage side. That is, the worst-case scenario has a larger negative result than the positive result. This suggests that, on average, the effect of provincial variations in corporate tax rates and dividend tax credits do not result in a reduction in taxes for eligible dividends. The reverse is true with respect to non-eligible dividends.

Summary: Tax Deferral and Tax Reduction

15-74.   The preceding examples illustrate that the province in which corporate tax rates are determined and the province in which the individual resides that establishes the provincial dividend tax credit rate are important factors. However, it is these rates together with the type of corporation and type of corporate income that ultimately represents the deciding factors that determine whether the use of a corporation will be advantageous in terms of both tax deferral and tax reduction.

We suggest you complete SSP 15-5 at this point.

Tax-Free Taxable Dividends

Tax Rates on Dividends

15-75.   In this chapter our general focus is on businesses that are carried on by corporations that are CCPCs. In many cases, the income will either be active business income eligible for the small business deduction or, alternatively, investment income that is highly taxed but is eligible for dividend refund treatment. While such corporations may have a GRIP balance that will allow them to designate eligible dividends, many CCPCs will have no GRIP account, with the result that taxable dividends that are paid will be non-eligible. Given this, our analysis will focus on non-eligible dividends.

15-76.   An individual subject to the highest federal tax rate of 33% and subject to a provincial income tax rate of 18% who resides in a province where the dividend tax credit is equal to 4/13 of the gross up on non-eligible dividends and 5/11 on eligible dividends will have a combined federal/provincial composite tax rate as follows:

- 43.7% on non-eligible dividends [(33% + 18%)(115%) - (9/13+ 4/13)(15%)],
- 32.4% on eligible dividends [(33% + 18%)(138%) - (6/11 + 5/11)(38%)], and
- 25.5% on capital gains [(33% + 18%)(1/2)].
- 51.0% on all other income

15-77.   The rate on non-eligible dividends is well above that applicable to eligible dividends and capital gains. However, it is well below the maximum 51% rate (33% + 18%) that would apply to most other types of income. In addition to the fact that dividends are taxed at favourable rates, the existence and structure of the dividend tax credit mechanism make the receipt of taxable dividends by low-income earners a preferable choice since a substantial amount of taxable dividends can be received by individuals without any income tax whatsoever. We will explain how that is possible in this section on tax-free taxable dividends.

Use of Tax Credits

Credits in General

15-78.   For 2021, every individual with net income of $151,978 or less has a basic personal tax credit of $13,808, which effectively ensures that individuals will not pay any federal income tax on the first $13,808 of income. If an individual had taxable income of $13,808 for 2021 the federal gross tax payable would be 15% of that amount, or $2,071. The basic personal tax credit of $13,808 is then multiplied by the same 15%, resulting in $2,071, which reduces the gross federal tax payable to nil.

15-79.   Extending this analysis, it can be said that, for most types of income, the amount of income that can be received without the payment of any federal income tax is limited to the individual's total tax credit base. That is, for every dollar of tax credit amount up to taxable income of $49,020, one dollar of income can be received without the payment of federal income tax. This changes for taxable income in excess of $49,020 because it is only the first $49,020 that is taxed at 15%, which is the same rate that applies to almost all personal tax credits. There are two general exceptions to this:

Dividends   An individual with only the basic personal credit of $2,071 [(15%)($13,808)] can receive taxable dividends that are more than double the $13,808 base for the credit. In 2021 an individual can receive $30,172 in non-eligible dividends without incurring any federal income tax. (See the calculations in Paragraph 15-84.) Note that, depending on the amount of the provincial dividend tax credit, this amount may or may not be totally free of provincial tax.

Charitable Donations   The tax credit on amounts of charitable donations over $200 is based on 29% or 33%, rather than the 15% that applies to most other personal credits. The 33% rate applies to the extent that taxable income is subject to the 33% rate.

We will only consider the credit rate of 29% in this analysis. This means that a dollar of charitable donations in excess of $200 will allow an individual in the lowest income tax bracket to receive $1.93 (29% ÷ 15%) in tax-free income. More specifically, a $1 contribution in excess of $200 is eligible for a tax credit of $0.29. This $0.29 would eliminate $0.29 of tax payable, the amount of tax that an individual in the lowest bracket would pay on $1.93 of income [(15%)($1.93) = $0.29]. This is unlikely to be an important exception in that it would be unusual for someone in the 15% federal income tax bracket to be making significant charitable donations.

Special Rules for Dividends

15-80.   How can an individual receive such a large amount of dividends without paying federal income tax? The answer lies in the dividend gross up and tax credit mechanism. For an individual in the lowest tax bracket of 15%, the increase in tax associated with one dollar of non-eligible dividends received compared to one dollar of interest income can be calculated as follows:

Tax increase per $1	Dividend	Interest
Cash received	$1.0000	$1.0000
Gross up at 15%	.1500	N/A
Taxable income	$ 1.1500	$1.0000
Federal tax payable at 15%	$ 0.1725	$ 0.1500
Federal dividend tax credit [(9/13)($0.15)]	(0.1038)	N/A
Increase in federal tax payable	$0.0687	$ 0.1500

15-81.   For each dollar of non-eligible dividends received, an individual must add a taxable dividend of $1.15 ($1 + $0.15 gross up) to taxable income. For individuals in the lowest federal tax bracket of 15%, the federal tax on this amount will be $0.1725 [($1.15)(15%)]. However, there will be a federal dividend tax credit against this tax payable equal to 9/13 of the gross up, or $0.1038 [(9/13)($0.15)]. This means that there is only a $0.0687 increase in federal tax for each one dollar increase in non-eligible dividends. This is in contrast to an increase in federal tax of $0.15 for each one dollar increase in interest income (i.e., a 15% rate of increase). As the preceding calculations demonstrate, dividend income uses up an individual's available tax credits at a much lower rate than most other types of income at a 6.87% rate.

15-82.   For example, one dollar of interest income will use up one dollar [($1.00)($.15 ÷ $.15)] of an individual's personal tax credit base of $13,808. In contrast, one dollar of non-eligible dividends received will use up only $0.458 of this base [($1.00)($.0687 ÷ $.15)]. This means that, in comparison with other types of income, a much larger amount of dividends can be received before an individual's tax credits are absorbed and income taxes will have to be paid.

15-83.   The amount of dividends that can be received tax free by an individual with no other source of income is a function of the total amount of personal tax credits available and can, in fact, become a fairly large amount.

Tax-Free Amounts for 2021

15-84.   For 2021, ignoring possible tax credits other than the basic personal and spousal credits, the amount of non-eligible dividends that can be received free of federal tax by a single individual and by an individual with a dependent spouse (or eligible dependant) with no other source of income is calculated in the table that follows. Note that, in the dependent spouse case, the grossed up amount of the dividends exceeds $49,020, the top of the 15% federal income tax bracket. This means that some of this dividend will be taxed at a higher federal rate of 20.5%.

	Single Individual	Dependent Spouse
Non-eligible dividends received	$ 30,172	$51,840
Gross up of 15%	4,526	7,776
Taxable income	$34,698	$59,616
Taxed at 15%	(34,698)	(49,020)
Taxed at 20.5%	$ Nil	$10,596
Federal tax at 15%	$ 5,205	$ 7,353
Federal tax at 20.5%	Nil	2,172
Dividend tax credit (9/13 of gross up)	(3,134)	(5,383)
Basic personal credit [(15%)($13,808)]	(2,071)	(2,071)
Spousal credit [(15%)($13,808)]	N/A	(2,071)
Federal tax payable	Nil	Nil

Note   While this is not relevant to our analysis in this section, you might wish to note that, with respect to eligible dividends, the tax-free amount for a single individual would be $63,040 and approximately $80,700 for an individual with a dependent spouse. In 2021 the alternative minimum tax (AMT) consequences generally begin once grossed up dividends exceed $53,810. This means that the tax-free taxable eligible dividends are subject to the AMT, which is fully refundable within a seven-year carry forward period.

15-85.   There may or may not be provincial tax payable on the amounts in the preceding table. A number of provincial factors would have to be considered. These include the provincial tax rates, the provincial tax brackets, the provincial personal tax credit amounts, and the provincial dividend tax credit rates. In 2021, of the ten provinces, only Ontario would permit the payment of non-eligible dividend amounts indicated above without any provincial income tax.

15-86.   The AMT is not a factor in determining the amount of non-eligible dividends that can be received on a tax-free basis. As the dividend tax credit is not available in the calculation of the AMT, the dividend gross up is deducted in the calculation of adjusted taxable income for alternative minimum tax purposes. Given this, the $40,000 basic exemption that is provided by the alternative minimum tax legislation, combined with the $13,808 basic personal tax credit (plus the $13,808 spousal credit in the dependent spouse example), would serve to eliminate the alternative minimum tax on the tax-free non-eligible dividends calculated in Paragraph 15-84. However, AMT is a consideration when large amounts of eligible dividends are involved, as indicated in the note to Paragraph 15-84.

Income Splitting

Basic Concept

15-87.   In this chapter we have focused on the use of a corporation to potentially defer and permanently reduce income taxes that would have been payable in the absence of a corporation. The availability of personal tax credits to every Canadian resident individual taxpayer, the existence of low personal income tax rates, and the potential added benefits of being able to direct high amounts of non-eligible and eligible dividends to family members with no or little income tax creates an environment in which income splitting opportunities are actively pursued given the potential income tax savings.

15-88.   While a corporation may be of considerable value in terms of income splitting opportunities with family members there are many provisions, such as the attribution rules and the TOSI that are designed specifically to prevent income splitting. While there remain some income splitting opportunities, one must exercise considerable caution in navigating the complex rules of the ITA, including proper structuring.

We suggest you complete SSP 15-6 at this point.

Shareholder Benefits—ITA 15(1)

General Overview

15-89.   In this chapter we have looked at whether there are income tax and non-tax economic advantages to incorporating a source of income such as a business and investments. If the decision is made to go ahead and incorporate a business that was previously carried on by an individual as a sole proprietor it is important for the individual to realize that the business no longer belongs to her but instead belongs to the corporation. It is essential that the individual separate her personal affairs from the business affairs of the corporation to avoid adverse income tax implications to both the individual shareholder and the corporation. At the time of writing, there have been more than 550 court cases dealing with these issues, and it remains a subject that is at the top of the CRA's tax audit list when it comes to auditing CCPCs, particularly those with one or a few shareholders who may or may not be related to each other.

15-90.   The income tax provision of concern is ITA 15(1), which is commonly referred to as a shareholder benefit rule comparable, in some respects, to ITA 6(1)(a), which contains the general rules for taxable employee benefits. ITA 15(1) applies where "a benefit is conferred by a corporation on a shareholder of the corporation." The value of that benefit is then included in the income of the shareholder as income from property for the calendar year in which the benefit is conferred unless there is a specific exclusion provided. The word "conferred" means to grant or bestow rather than "receive or enjoy," which are the words that are used for employee taxable benefits. If, for example, a corporation agrees to pay a credit card bill of a shareholder of $2,000 in December 2021 but actually pays the amount in January 2022, the benefit would have been conferred in 2021 but received in 2022.

15-91.   A benefit has been defined in the jurisprudence (i.e., case law) and generally means an economic advantage that is given the widest possible interpretation. This would extend to situations in which a shareholder uses the corporation to gain an economic advantage. In terms of a corporation, a benefit would include an appropriation, which means the action of taking something for one`s own personal use without the owner's permission. If an individual has incorporated a business along with property of the business, including bank accounts, automobiles, buildings, and so on, then all of that property belongs to the corporation and any attempt by the individual to take or make use of any corporate property would result in a benefit.

15-92.   The value of a benefit has also been considered in the jurisprudence and is generally defined as the difference between the FMV of the economic advantage obtained or received minus the FMV of any consideration given up in exchange. Not all economic advantages are benefits, however. Turn to Figure 14-7 in Chapter 14 . The figure illustrates several advantages or benefits that originate from the corporation and that may be conferred on the shareholders. If an economic benefit received by a shareholder is one of the items listed, then it is not categorized as a shareholder benefit under ITA 15(1). The following examples will help to explain the basic analytical process.

EXAMPLE 1   A corporation declares a large bonus to the sole shareholder who is responsible for the success of the corporate business.

ANALYSIS 1   It is arguable that the bonus received exceeds the value of the services given up to acquire that bonus, but nevertheless the bonus is within the CRA bonus concession and is considered remuneration (e.g., employment income). As a result, the bonus is not a shareholder benefit.

EXAMPLE 2   A corporation pays a salary of $13,808 to a 5-year-old child. The child's parents are 50-50 shareholders of the company. The child accompanies the parents a few times each week when daycare is unavailable and to spend some time with her parents who are otherwise exceptionally busy. The salary payments are made to the bank account of the parents.

ANALYSIS 2   There have been a few court cases that are near identical to this situation, particularly where the salary purportedly paid matches the basic personal credit. Based on the facts, the child is not an actual employee, therefore any salary expense would be disallowed. However, the parents as shareholders have received the amounts without providing anything in return. The result is that the amounts paid are benefits under ITA 15(1). In this case the benefit would be assessed on a 50-50 basis to match each parent's shareholding interest.

EXAMPLE 3   A corporation declares a dividend.

ANALYSIS 3   Since the amount of the dividend exceeds what the shareholder gave up in exchange for the dividend (i.e., nothing) the dividend is technically a benefit. However, it is one of the exceptions, resulting in the benefit not being categorized as a shareholder benefit.

EXAMPLE 4   A shareholder does not have a separate bank account for the corporation and instead uses a personal bank account for both personal and corporate business. All corporate sales and expenses pass through this bank account. The CRA audits the business and determines that had the bank accounts been separated there would have been $32,000 in corporate cash. The bank account balance is only $10,000.

ANALYSIS 4   It appears that the individual shareholder has drawn $22,000 of corporate cash for personal purposes and has not given anything of value in exchange. The result is a shareholder benefit of $22,000. Had the shareholder acknowledged that corporate cash was being used personally, action could have been taken to treat it at that time as salary, a bonus, dividends, or even a shareholder loan. In that case there would not have been a shareholder benefit. This action cannot be resolved after the fact.

EXAMPLE 5   A corporation has its own credit card that is used to make inventory purchases and for corporate expenses. The CRA audits the business and verifies the corporate credit card charges, noting $17,000 in personal expenses of the shareholder.

ANALYSIS 5   There is a benefit of $17,000, given that the effect of the personal charges being made through the corporation's credit card absolves the individual of having to make those payments personally. With no indication that the intention was to reimburse the company, this amount would be a shareholder benefit. In addition, if the corporation claimed that amount as business expenses the expenses would be disallowed.

EXAMPLE 6   A corporation that carries on a construction business builds an in-ground swimming pool at the home of the principal shareholder. No amounts are paid by the shareholder, nor is there any indication that the shareholder acknowledges a debt to the corporation for the pool.

ANALYSIS 6   There is a shareholder benefit. Interestingly, the value of the benefit is the FMV of what it would have cost the shareholder to acquire an in-ground pool of the same type from an arm's-length person and not the cost to the company of which the individual is a shareholder. In addition, there is a rule in ITA 69(4) that deems the corporation to have sold any inventory items used in building the pool at FMV. In addition, any other corporate costs, such as salaries of employees who spent time working on the pool, would not be deductible to the corporation.

EXAMPLE 7   A corporation in the land development business sells two parcels of fully serviceable land to the principal shareholder for their initial cost plus development costs, which total $23,000 each. The two parcels of land are identical in size and are in a favourable location in a booming new development. The shareholder sells one of the parcels of land for $150,000 the following week and decides to build a home on the other.

ANALYSIS 7   There is a shareholder benefit. Based on the facts it would seem that the FMV of each parcel of land is at least $150,000. This means that the shareholder paid

$46,000 for land valued at $300,000. The result is a shareholder benefit of $254,000 [$300,000 - $46,000]. To avoid double taxation there is an adjusted cost base (ACB) adjustment that would add the shareholder benefit amount to each parcel of land (ITA 52(1)). The result is that the ACB of each parcel is $150,000. The sale of one parcel for the same $150,000 would therefore not result in any gain.

Exercise 15-6

Subject: Shareholder Benefits

Ms. Clarke is the sole shareholder of Magna Ltd., a CCPC that carries on a business of retailing high-end portable computer devices. Ms. Clarke had carried on the business as a sole proprietor for many years and incorporated the business in 2019. The business is very profitable and employs 25 people full time. Indicate whether there may be a shareholder benefit in each of the following cases:

Case 1   The company recently paid for two dental plans for the employees. The company pays the premiums of both plans. The first plan covers all employees except for Ms. Clarke and costs the company $1,200 in annual premiums. The second plan is only available to Ms. Clarke and is much more comprehensive, with no deductible and very high coverage. Annual premiums are $15,000.

Case 2   The company recently made a large sale to a new customer in the amount of $40,000. The customer wrote a cheque to Ms. Clarke, which she deposited in her personal bank account four months ago. There is no indication that she intended to repay this amount.

Case 3   The company owns a vacation property in Florida that it purchased for public relations purposes for use by its best customers. Ms. Clarke spent six weeks at the property for free.

Case 4   The company pays the life insurance premiums for Ms. Clarke of $8,000 per year. The insurance is not required as collateral for any corporate borrowings.

Case 5   Ms. Clarke wishes to borrow a substantial amount from her bank to build her dream home. The corporation does not have the available cash to loan to her. The bank is willing to provide the necessary funds but only if her corporation guarantees the loan. This means that if she fails to make any payment the bank can take action against the company to recover any unpaid amounts.

Solutions to Exercises are available in the Study Guide.

15-93.   In summary, shareholder benefit taxation requires a four-step analysis:

Step 1   Is there a benefit? (an economic advantage)

Step 2   Has the benefit been conferred because of the individual's shareholding?

Step 3   What is the value of the benefit?

Step 4   Is the benefit excluded?

15-94.   Shareholder benefit taxation requires that the benefit be attributable to the fact that an individual is only receiving the benefit because she is a shareholder. As a rule, shareholders in a controlling position are frequently in a position to cause or direct a corporation's actions. Therefore, the focus is often on controlling shareholders or groups of shareholders with combined controlling interests. This does not mean to say that minority shareholders can avoid shareholder benefits. The facts will determine the outcome.

15-95.   Shareholders are often employees as well. When an individual wears these two hats of shareholder and employee it becomes a question of fact as to whether a particular benefit is provided because of the individual's shareholding or because of his employment. This is often referred to as shareholder capacity versus employment capacity. These issues are often resolved by examining whether non-shareholders/employees are entitled to the same benefits as a shareholder/employee. In Exercise 15-6, Case 1, the shareholder/employee was provided with an expensive high-end dental plan and the general conclusion was that the benefit was a shareholder benefit. The individual could, however, have challenged this result by demonstrating that because of her management role it is common within the industry for such managers to be entitled to high-end plans. If the argument was supported by corroborating facts, the benefit would not have been a shareholder benefit but instead an employee benefit that is excluded (e.g., premiums paid by employers for private services health plans are not taxable benefits).

15-96.   While there are many examples of shareholder benefits, some of the most common in practice are the following:

- Personal expenses (e.g., paying for personal hobby interests, legal expenses, alimony and child support, divorce settlements, travel expenses, and costs of education)
- A shareholder selling personal property at amounts in excess of FMV
- A shareholder purchasing corporate property for less than its FMV
- A corporation making improvements to shareholder property

Other Important Shareholder Benefit Issues

Automobile Benefit—ITA 15(5)

15-97.   In Chapter 3 we examined automobile benefits to employees. ITA 15(5) determines automobile benefits for shareholders. The rules apply the same standby charge calculations used for employees. While the income tax treatment to the employee or shareholder is identical, the result to the corporate employer is not. Where a corporation owns or leases an automobile and makes it available to an employee, the costs of operating that automobile, together with financing costs, leasing costs, and CCA are deductible to the corporation subject to any ITA restrictions such as the class 10.1 $30,000 CCA limitation. Automobiles made available to shareholders, however, are not considered to be used for income earning purposes and therefore no expense (including CCA) can be claimed by the corporation.

Loan Benefits—ITA 15(9)

15-98.   In Chapter 3 we also discussed low-interest or interest-free loans made by an employer to an employee, noting that the interest differential between the prescribed rate of interest and the actual rate would be included in employment income as a result of ITA 6(9) together with ITA 80.4(1). ITA 15(9) contains a similar rule that applies when a low-interest or interest-free loan is made to a shareholder. The benefit is generally determined in the same manner (ITA 80.4(2)) as employee loans and is added to the shareholder's income as income from property. ITA 80.5 applies to both employee and shareholder loans to allow the interest benefit to be treated as deductible interest if the employee or shareholder use the borrowed money to acquire a source of income such as investments.

Benefits to Family Members—ITA 15(1.4)(c)

15-99.   The shareholder benefit rules also apply where a corporation provides benefits to family members of a shareholder. In such cases, once it is determined that the benefit is a result of a shareholder capacity and that there are no exclusions, the value of the benefit is determined and added to income of the related shareholder (ITA 15(1.4)(c)) and not the family member. This acts as a form of attribution rule to prevent income splitting among family members. Automobiles provided to family members of a shareholder are also treated the same way in that the benefit is added to the income of the shareholder and not the family member. Interest-free or low-interest loan benefits are the exception and are added to the income of the family member who received the loan. ITA 15(9) deems the family member to be a shareholder for the purpose of adding the benefit to his income as income from property.

Use of Corporate Property—ITA 15(1)

15-100.   It is not uncommon for a corporation to own property that may have little connection to its business. Corporations can own apartments, cottages, condos, lodges, and homes anywhere in locations that are popular vacation spots. If shareholders personally use these corporate properties for free or little cost, placing a value on the benefit can sometimes be difficult depending on the circumstances. The jurisprudence, however, has established guidelines to assist in determining that value. The analysis is first based on the purpose for the acquisition of the property by the corporation. If the reason for acquiring the property was for business purposes, then any shareholder benefit is determined for the actual period of use of the property based on what would have been charged in an arm's-length situation. If, however, the property was acquired for the personal use of a shareholder, then the benefit is based on the availability instead of actual use. This means that a benefit will be determined for each year of availability even if the property was never actually used.

Penalties and Statute-Barred Issues—ITA 163(2) and 152(4)(a)(j)

15-101.   Chapter 2 discussed the many types of penalties imposed under the ITA, one of which is referred to as the gross negligence penalty of ITA 163(2). This penalty adds 50% of any additional income taxes charged as a result of actions by the CRA, typically an income tax audit. Depending on the circumstances, it is not uncommon for the CRA to regularly apply this penalty to unreported shareholder benefits.

15-102.   In addition, the CRA is generally limited to looking into income tax returns once three years have passed from the date of the original notice of assessment. For example, if an individual income tax return for the 2018 taxation year was filed on time and had an original notice of assessment from the CRA dated May 12, 2019, the 2018 taxation year would become statute-barred on May 12, 2022. As of that date the tax return cannot be assessed unless the CRA can show that the return includes a misrepresentation attributable to neglect, carelessness, or wilful default (ITA 152(4)(a)(i)). In general, the CRA does not reassess beyond three years, however there are exceptions. Certain kinds of shareholder benefits fall within those exceptions, resulting in the CRA routinely opening up those statute-barred years plus assessing penalties. Once interest charges are added, the total income tax bill can be substantial.

Shareholder Benefit Caution

15-103.   Our coverage of shareholder benefits and ITA 15(1) is to provide a general awareness together with some broad guidelines to assist in a general identification of instances where shareholder benefits may be a concern. As mentioned, shareholder benefits are high on the list of CRA audit activities when it comes to auditing the businesses of CCPCs. Avoiding the adverse implications of shareholder benefits begins with a realization that the individuals who carried on a business and the corporation subsequently carrying on the business are two separate legal entities. The accounts of the individual and corporation must be kept separate, and any transactions between shareholders and the corporation must be carefully documented as they occur. In the next section we will discuss shareholder loans, which also garner signification attention by the CRA.

Shareholder Loans and Indebtedness—ITA 15(2)

Overview

15-104.   Under corporate law, corporations are only permitted to distribute after-tax earnings as dividends or capital as a return of paid-up capital (PUC; discussed in Chapter 14). Rather than remove earnings by dividends, shareholders could instead simply borrow the after-tax income from their own corporations for an indefinite period of time without paying any income tax. ITA 15(2) was added to the ITA many years ago to prevent this from happening. The opening words of CRA publication IT119R4, "Debts of Shareholders and Certain Persons Connected with Shareholders," reinforces this with the following words: "The purpose of this provision is to prevent dividends from being paid out in the guise of loans or other indebtedness."

15-105.   ITA 15(2) covers many situations involving shareholders that are individuals, partnerships, and trusts. ITA 15(2) does not apply to shareholders that are resident corporations or partnerships all of the members of which are resident corporations. The reason for excluding resident corporations is once again because of integration. ITA 15(2) treats shareholder loans as a quasi-dividend in the sense that it is income from property but without the benefits of the dividend gross up and dividend tax credit mechanism to individual shareholders. In our discussion of integration we saw that dividends paid between resident corporations are not subject to Part I tax because of the ITA 112(1) taxable income deduction. It is for this reason that resident corporations are excluded from ITA 15(2). In this section we will limit our coverage to individual shareholders.

15-106.   ITA 15(2) applies when an individual shareholder or an individual related to an individual shareholder either (1) receives a loan from the corporation or (2) becomes indebted to the corporation. Unlike ITA 15(1) there is no shareholder capacity condition required for ITA 15(2) to apply. The reason for the loan or indebtedness or the capacity in which the loan is received is irrelevant at this initial stage.

15-107.   A loan means borrowing money with a promise to repay it with or without interest. Indebtedness means owing an amount to a person other than as a loan. Examples of indebtedness include the unpaid purchase price of property, unpaid rent, unpaid accounts receivable, and unpaid interest, whether or not it is interest owing on a loan. In terms of terminology, parties to a loan are referred to as a borrower and lender, whereas parties to an indebtedness are referred to as a debtor and creditor.

15-108.   In general terms, ITA 15(2) requires that the receipt of a loan or the amount owing as a result of indebtedness is required to be included in the income of the individual shareholder or an individual related to the shareholder who owes the amount for the calendar year in which the loan was received or the indebtedness occurred. While this may seem harsh, this is just the general rule, which is then subject to multiple exceptions. One exception prevents the application of ITA 15(2) if the amount owing is paid by the end of the first taxation year of the corporation after the year in which the loan was advanced. This means that the loan should never appear on two subsequent balance sheets as a shareholder loan receivable.

The Mechanics of Shareholder Loans and Indebtedness

15-109.   This shareholder loan rule has two important aspects to it. The first is that ITA 15(2) applies to the principal amount owing. If one of the many exceptions apply so that ITA 15(2) does not apply, then there is a second set of rules under ITA 80.4 that requires that an interest benefit be included in income to the extent that interest at a prescribed rate exceeds the actual interest charged on the loan or indebtedness. The two sets of rules are not allowed to overlap. ITA 80.4(3)(b) specifically prevents any interest benefit from being determined on any part of a loan or indebtedness that was required to be included in income under ITA 15(2). If a loan is required to be included in income under ITA 15(2), subsequent repayments are deductible through ITA 20(1)(j) in the year of the repayment.

In general, analyzing shareholder loans requires (1) determining whether an individual has received a loan or become indebted to a corporation in which the individual is a shareholder; (2) determining whether the specific loan exceptions of ITA 15(2.4) apply (if they do apply then there is no ITA 15(2) income); and (3) determining whether the loan has been repaid within one year of the taxation year of the corporate lender. If the loan has been fully repaid within that timeframe ITA 15(2) will not apply. If part of the loan is repaid within the timeframe then that part of the loan repaid is not subject to ITA 15(2). Any part of the loan not repaid within that timeframe is then subject to ITA 80.4, which will potentially apply depending on whether the prescribed interest rate exceeds the actual interest rate on the loan. Finally, any repayments that relate to amounts included in income under ITA 15(2) will be entitled to a deduction under ITA 20(1)(j) in the year of repayment.

EXAMPLE 1   An individual is the sole shareholder of a CCPC. The individual borrows $60,000 from the company January 1, 2021. The company has a calendar-based taxation year ending December 31. The loan is interest free and requires that it be repaid in full by June 1, 2023. Assume that none of the exceptions to ITA 15(2) apply.

ANALYSIS 1   As the loan was not repaid by December 31, 2022, $60,000 must be included in the shareholder's income for the 2021 taxation year as income from property. A deduction of $60,000 will be allowed in the 2023 taxation year for the repayment. No part of the loan would be subject to an interest benefit because the loan was included in income.

EXAMPLE 2   An individual is the sole shareholder of a CCPC with a December 31 taxation year end. The individual borrows $60,000 from the company January 1, 2021. The loan is interest free. Repayments of $30,000 are required to be made December 31, 2021, and December 31, 2022. The repayments are both within the two-year exception. Assume that the prescribed interest rate throughout the two-year period is 2%.

ANALYSIS 2   **ITA 15(2) does not apply to require the loan of** $60,000 to be included in income when received because it is repaid within two years. Since the amount of the loan is not included in income it is subject to ITA 80.4. The interest benefit is calculated as the prescribed rate of 2% applied to the balance outstanding in the year and subtracting any interest paid. Since the loan was interest free the interest benefit is $1,200 [(2%) ($60,000)] for 2021 and $600 [(2%)($30,000)] for 2022.

EXAMPLE 3   An individual is the sole shareholder of a CCPC with a December 31 taxation year end. The individual borrows $60,000 from the company on January 1, 2021. The loan is interest free. Repayments of $30,000 are required to be made December 31, 2022, and December 31, 2023. Only the first repayment is within the two-year exception. Assume that the prescribed interest rate throughout the three-year period is 2%.

ANALYSIS 3   To understand the income tax implications in this case it is necessary to split the loan into two parts. The first is a loan of $30,000 that was repaid by the end of the first taxation year after the year in which it was advanced, and the second is a $30,000 loan that was only paid at the end of 2023 and therefore was not repaid within the required timeframe. ITA 15(2) applies to the second part of the loan, meaning that $30,000 is included in income in 2021 with a deduction under ITA 20(1)(j) for the repayment in 2023. Since the first part of the loan was repaid within two years it will not be included in income under ITA 15(2). It will, however, be subject to ITA 80.4. As a result, there will be an interest benefit of $600 [(2%)($30,000)] for each year. The tax consequences can be summarized as $30,600 added to income for 2021 [ITA 15(2) $30,000 + ITA 80.4 interest benefit of $600]; a $600 interest benefit under ITA 80.4 for 2022; and a deduction of $30,000 under ITA 20(1)(j) for 2023.

The Main Exceptions

15-110.   Technically there are eight exceptions to the rule that prevents a loan or indebtedness from being included in income. We have broken seven of those exceptions into four categories of (1) loans or indebtedness that occurs in the ordinary course of business, (2) loans that are repaid within two years, (3) the minority shareholder rule, and (4) exception for specific loans. There is an exception for loans between non-residents that will not be discussed because it goes beyond the scope of an introductory course. The categories of exceptions can be described as follows:

Loans in the Ordinary Course of Business and Money Lenders — ITA 15(2.3)   If an individual owns shares in a major retailer and makes purchases using a retailer credit card, technically ITA 15(2) would apply. In addition, if an employee of the Royal Bank, for example, happens to own shares of the Royal Bank, a loan made to that employee, including a mortgage, would be caught by ITA 15(2). This exception is designed to ensure that ITA 15(2) will not apply to these everyday situations.

The Two-Year Exception—ITA 15(2.6)   ITA 15(2.6) excludes a loan or indebtedness from being included in income to the extent it is repaid within one year after the end of the taxation year of the corporation in which the loan was made or the indebtedness arose. This time period is established by first determining the last day of the taxation year of the corporation in which the loan or debt occurred then adding one full year (365 days). If, for example, a CCPC with a December 31 year end made a loan to a shareholder on January 1, 2021, the deadline for repayment to avoid ITA 15(2) would be December 31, 2022. The result is that a loan or debt can remain outstanding for a maximum of two years less one day, which is why it is generally referred to as the two-year exception. Some prefer to refer to this exception as a one-year repayment period measured from the last day of the taxation year of the corporate lender, adding that if the loan is shown on two successive balance sheets that the exception would not apply. The two approaches are interchangeable, but in this chapter and in exercises and problems we refer to the exception as the two-year limitation.

The two-year exception does not apply where the loan or debt is repaid within the two-year period if it is part of a "series of loans and repayments." The words mean that there is a connection between the repayment and a subsequent loan or debt, often referred to as kiting. If in our previous example the January 1, 2021, loan was repaid on December 31, 2022, then ITA 15(2) would not apply. However, if the same loan or debt amount were taken out on January 2, 2023, it would suggest that the individual had no real intention of actually repaying the loan but intended to establish a new two-year period. In that case the repayment would be ignored and ITA 15(2) would apply subject to the availability of other exceptions.

The Minority Shareholder Exception—ITA 15(2.4)(a)   The minority shareholder rule is designed to prevent the application of ITA 15(2) with respect to loans or indebtedness to employees who happen to own a small number of shares, which is set at less than 10% of the shares of any class irrespective of whether the shares are voting or not. In brief, the exception requires that the individual is an employee of the lender or creditor, is not related to the corporation, nor owns 10% or more of the issued shares of any class of the corporation. For the 10% share ownership test, any shares owned by related persons are considered to be owned by the employee. In addition, an employee would be related to the corporation if persons related to that individual legally control the corporation.

Specific Loan Exception—ITA 15(2.4)(b) (Housing Loans), ITA 15(2.4)(c) (Share Loans), and ITA 15(2.4)(d) (Motor Vehicle Loans)   This exception applies if a loan is specifically made to purchase a home, newly issued shares of the corporate employer, or a motor vehicle.

The housing loan exception only applies to loans made or debts arising in respect of an individual who is an employee of the lender or creditor or who is the spouse or common-law partner of an employee of the lender or creditor. A loan made to an individual who is related to an employee other than as a spouse or common-law partner is not eligible (e.g., a loan to a child or to the parent of an employee). The exception further requires that the employee or spouse/common-law partner must use the loan proceeds to acquire a dwelling for the employee or spouse's/common-law partner's habitation. Using the loan proceeds to purchase a rental property would therefore not meet this exception.

The share loan exception requires that the borrower be an employee of the lender. The borrower must use the loan to acquire previously un-issued fully paid shares of the corporate employer directly from that employer. In addition, the shares must be held for the employee's benefit. Selling the shares immediately after acquiring them would disqualify the loan for the exception.

The car loan exception applies to loans made in respect of an employee of the lender where the loan proceeds are used to enable or assist the employee to acquire a motor vehicle to be used in the performance of the employee's employment duties. The expression "motor vehicle" generally refers to all types of cars, trucks, and SUVs regardless of whether the capital cost would be restricted by class 10.1 or similar restrictions for zero-emission vehicles. There is no minimum percentage use requirement for the vehicle to qualify for this exception.

15-111.   The minority shareholder exception and each of the exceptions for specific loans requires meeting the following two additional conditions:

- The loan must be made to the individual as a result of an employment capacity and not a shareholder capacity [ITA 15(2.4)(e)].

- At the time the loan is made, bona fide arrangements must be made to repay the loan within a reasonable period of time [ITA 15(2.4)(f)].

15-112.   The first of these conditions is the employee capacity concept that was discussed in Paragraph 15-95. The employee must be prepare to demonstrate that the loan or debt had nothing to do with anyone's shareholding. This determination is always fact specific. As a rule, if an employee is eligible for loans or debt that are available to other employees who are not shareholders or who are not related to shareholders then the presumption is that the loan or debt is an employee capacity situation and falls within the exception.

15-113.   The last condition requires that there are arrangements for repayment within a reasonable period of time. At one time the CRA only accepted that this condition had been met if the terms and conditions of a loan were the same as normal commercial practice. Normal commercial practice would have required a written loan agreement, regular periodic payments, collateral security, and so on. The courts consistently overruled the CRA, clarifying that the ITA does not require any terms and conditions, adding that the only important factor is that there must be an identifiable period of time in which a loan would be repaid. The courts have ruled favourably that loan terms that simply say that the loan will be repayable within five or ten years was acceptable, but that demand loans could not meet this condition because a demand loan is technically only required to be paid when called or demanded for repayment by the corporate lender or creditor.

Running Loan Accounts vs. Specific Loans
15-114.   The CRA historically has broken down shareholder loan accounts into two categories: running loan accounts and specific loans. Specific loans represent loans for specific purposes with their own separate terms and conditions, including repayments. The CRA requires that specific loans be maintained in a separate shareholder loan account (paragraph 14 of IT119R4).

15-115.   Running loan accounts represent multiple transactions, generally for cash withdrawals and the payment of personal expenditures by a corporation on behalf of a shareholder. Each shareholder would be required to have their own shareholder loan account, including separate accounts for any specific loans. In practice this is the norm for small CCPCs with sole shareholders or with shareholders of the same family. Rather than have the corporation pay regular salary, a shareholder could withdraw cash from the corporate bank account as needed and have the corporation pay for personal expenditures, including personal loans and credit card balances. Each transaction would be reflected in the shareholder loan account, evidencing the indebtedness between the shareholder and corporation. This practice when properly applied avoids shareholder benefit issues under ITA 15(1).

15-116.   The income tax implications connected to a running loan account, however, can add complexity. If, for example, a sole shareholder withdrew cash amounts from the corporation a few times a week and had the corporation pay any personal expenses throughout the year, the number of transactions in a running loan account could number in the hundreds. Each transaction would have to be separately accounted for for purposes of applying ITA 15(2) and ITA 80.4.

If, for example, $40 was withdrawn on January 17, 2021, from the corporate bank account, petty cash, or cash register, technically one would have to track when the amount was paid since the $40 cash withdrawal caused the shareholder to become indebted to the corporation. This would have to be done for each transaction regardless of how small.

15-117.   Part of the standard practice of using a running loan account is to ensure that year-end balances are cleared out and reduced to nil or, at a minimum, within the two-year repayment limitation. This avoids the application of ITA 15(2) but leaves the imputed interest benefit under ITA 80.4 to be calculated. In the previous paragraph this would mean calculating the interest benefit on the $40 from January 17, 2021, to December 31, 2021, and repeating the calculation for each transaction during the year. CRA auditors are equipped with a special software program that calculates the annual benefit after inputting the relevant transaction numbers.

Shareholder Loan Repayments

15-118.   Shareholders can make repayments against their shareholder loan accounts in many ways. Payments can be made in cash or with property or by offsetting an amount owed by the corporation to the shareholder. If a shareholder uses personal property as repayment of a shareholder loan it is critical that the ownership of the property change from the shareholder to the corporation in the same manner as would have been the case had the property been sold to an arm's-length person. Failure to transfer ownership can result in significant income tax consequences.

15-119.   In one court case a shareholder owed a corporation $100,000 and had no cash to make payment. Failure to make the payment would have resulted in the $100,000 being included in the shareholder's income for the previous year, which would have resulted in income tax and interest. The shareholder claimed that he had transferred a boat, a car, and some land to the corporation as full payment of the shareholder loan. The court concluded that none of the property had been legally transferred, with the result that no repayment had been made. The problem was that the corporation considered the loan as being paid and the balance owing was reduced to nil. The result was that the shareholder avoided $100,000 of debt. The income tax result was that the $100,000 became a shareholder benefit taxable as a result of ITA 15(1). In effect, the shareholder loan was converted to a shareholder benefit by the failure to repay the loan on time.

15-120.   A much more practical and common way to repay a shareholder loan account is through an offset. Offsets require an amount owed by the corporation to the shareholder being applied against amounts owing by the shareholder to the corporation. The two most common methods are to either declare a dividend or a bonus at year end. Dividends are generally preferable since there are no required withholdings as is the case with bonuses that require a withholding of income tax, CPP premiums, and other payroll amounts. If, for example, a shareholder loan balance at year end is $50,000, the declaration of a dividend for that amount would offset the shareholder loan account whereas it would require $60,000 or more of a bonus since it is only the amount of the bonus after withholdings that can be used to offset the shareholder loan account.

15-121.   Individuals are only required to include bonuses and dividends in income when actually received. When bonuses and dividends owing are applied to reduce a shareholder loan account the amounts are considered received at the time of the offset and are therefore required to be included in income based on the date of the offset.

15-122.   There is one final point that requires clarification where a repayment or offset is insufficient to reduce the shareholder loan account to nil. The question is how to apply the repayment. In other words, which specific transactions have been repaid? The answer to this is important in determining whether ITA 15(2) or ITA 80.4 applies or whether any part of the repayment entitles the shareholder to a deduction under ITA 20(1)(j). The manner in which repayments are applied is found in a common-law principle referred to as the Clayton rule. This rule requires that any repayment is considered to pay the earliest transactions first (a first in, first out FIFO basis). The Clayton rule, however, is subject to an exception at the discretion of the debtor. In other words, shareholders can decide which transactions are being repaid but they must state this clearly. Failure to do so means that repayments are applied automatically on a FIFO basis.

Imputed Interest Benefit—ITA 80.4

15-123. If the principal amount of a shareholder loan or indebtedness is included in an individual shareholder's income as a result of ITA 15(2), then no imputed interest benefit can apply to that amount. However, if the loan meets one of the exceptions to ITA 15(2), then ITA 80.4(2) will apply if the loan is received because of a shareholder capacity and treated as income from property. Alternatively, if the loan is received as a result of an employment capacity the interest is determined under ITA 80.4(1) and treated as employment income.

EXAMPLE On July 1, 2021, Andros Ltd., a CCPC with a taxation year that ends on December 31, loans $100,000 to its only shareholder, George Andros. The loan is interest free, is provided because of his shareholding, and is repayable in full in January 2022. ITA 15(2) does not apply to the loan because it was repaid within the two-year limitation of December 31, 2022. ITA 80.4, however, will apply in 2021 and 2022 based on the number of days the loan is outstanding in each year. Assume the prescribed rate throughout 2021 is 2%.

ANALYSIS For 2021, Mr. Andros will be required to include an interest benefit under ITA 80.4(2) of $1,008 [(2%)($100,000)(184/365 days)]. If the loan proceeds are used to earn income, the interest benefit becomes eligible to be claimed as interest expense against the source of income to which it relates.

15-124. In the case of a home purchase loan, there is a special rule that caps the interest benefit for the first five years of the loan. This means that any interest benefit cannot exceed the prescribed rate that was in effect at the time the loan was received. If the prescribed rate decreases over the five-year period the individual enjoys the advantage of a lower interest benefit, but if the rate increases the interest remains fixed at the rate in effect when the loan was received. This rule was designed to mirror a five-year fixed rate mortgage but is only available for employee capacity loans made to purchase homes. If a housing loan was made to a shareholder in a shareholder capacity, this special rule does not apply.

Exercise 15-7

Subject: Shareholder Loans—Car Purchase

Ms. Martha Rourke is an employee of Rourke Inc., a CCPC with a December 31 taxation year in which her husband owns 70% of the outstanding shares. Ms. Rourke owns the remaining 30% of the shares. On July 1, 2021, she receives a $50,000 interest-free loan that will be used to purchase an automobile to be used in her employment duties. The loan is to be repaid in full on June 30, 2025. No repayments are required to be made before that time. Assume the prescribed rate throughout 2021 is 2%. What are the 2021 income tax implications of this loan for Ms. Rourke? Calculate any interest benefit using months instead of days.

Exercise 15-8

Subject: Shareholder Loans—Term Outstanding

On June 1, 2021, Generic Inc., a CCPC with a June 30 taxation year, loans $162,000 interest free to its controlling shareholder, Ms. Jan Fisk, for personal purposes, none of which qualify for any specific loan exception. Assume that the prescribed interest rate is 2% throughout all of 2021 and 2022. What are the tax consequences to Ms. Fisk if the loan is repaid (1) on January 1, 2022, and (2) on December 31, 2022? Calculate any interest benefit using months instead of days.

Exercise 15-9

Subject: Shareholder Loans—Home Purchase

On November, 1, 2021, Hasid Ltd., a CCPC with a December 31 taxation year, loans Mr. Aaron Hasid, the CEO and controlling shareholder of the company, $123,000 interest free in order to assist him in purchasing a principal residence (i.e., a home for his habitation). Assume that the prescribed interest rate is 2% throughout all of 2021 and 2022. The loan is to be repaid in four equal annual instalments with the first required on October 31, 2022. What are the income tax consequences of this loan to Mr. Hasid if the loan is made in an employment capacity or if it is made in a shareholder capacity? Calculate any interest benefit using months instead of days.

Solutions to Exercises are available in the Study Guide.

We suggest you complete SSP 15-7 and 15-8 at this point.

Management Compensation

General Principles

Salary as the Bench Mark

15-125.   The most obvious and straightforward way to compensate managers is to pay salaries. Provided they are reasonable, the amounts are a deductible expense to the corporation and are required to be included in the income of the recipient employee. This makes salary payments neutral in terms of income tax planning. For large publicly listed corporations, salary is the usual starting point in negotiating management compensation. However, for some high-income executives, the availability of stock option plans may be of greater importance than salary.

15-126.   Even with a public corporation, however, the income tax effects of various types of compensation should not be ignored. Any form of compensation that results in a greater deduction to a corporation than what is required to be included in the income of an employee creates potential income tax savings. In addition, any form of compensation that results in a deduction in a year prior to when the compensation is required to be included in the income of an employee creates savings in the form of tax deferral. These considerations can result in improved after-tax benefits to employees or, alternatively, a lower after-tax cost to corporate employers.

Tax Effective Alternatives

15-127.   Some common examples of compensation that can be used to defer or reduce the payment of income taxes include the following:

- **Registered Pension Plans (RPP)**   Within certain limits, a corporation can make and deduct contributions towards RPPs for employees in the year of the contribution. While these employer contributions create an economic advantage to employees and would be considered taxable employee benefits, the employer contributions represent a legislative exception to the taxable benefit rules. In effect, the contributions are immediately deductible to the employer but only become income to the employee many years later. The result is considerable tax deferral. In addition to the tax effectiveness of RPPs, the availability of such plans can promote loyalty and reduce employee turnover.

- **Deferred Profit Sharing Plans (DPSP)**   In a manner similar to RPPs, corporations can make deductible contributions to DPSPs for the benefit of employees. While such contributions also create an economic advantage and therefore fall within the taxable benefit concept, a specific legislative exception prevents the employer contributions from creating a taxable employment benefit. As a result, there is a tax deferred advantage similar to that of RPPs, which also promotes loyalty and reduces employee turnover.

- **Private Health Services Plans (PHSP)**   Premiums paid by a corporate employer for health care plans such as dental, hospital coverage, prescription, and other plans can be deducted in full by the corporation and are not considered taxable employments benefits to employees because of another legislative exception.

- **Stock Options**   Stock options provide employees with an incentive to work toward increasing the success of a corporation. When shares are acquired by an employee under the terms of a stock option plan the benefit is measured at that time and included in the income of the employee. There is an exception for employees of CCPCs who are only required to include a stock option benefit in income when the shares acquired under the terms of a stock option plan are actually sold (see Chapter 3 for details). Further, the value of stock options is enhanced because of a 50% taxable income deduction that effectively taxes the stock option benefit in a manner similar to that of capital gains. The stock option deduction has become restricted for new stock option plans granted starting July 1, 2021. The new rules apply mainly to large publicly listed corporations and are discussed in Chapter 3.

Salary vs. Dividends

15-128.   The ability to choose between salary versus dividends or some combination of the two requires an element of corporate control by a shareholder/employee. For large publicly listed corporations, there is little point in considering the tax benefits related to the salary/dividend decision. The dividend policy of public corporations is normally based on considerations that extend well beyond compensation that is provided to the management group of the company, meaning that shareholders/employees have little say in such matters.

15-129.   In CCPCs with one shareholder or a small group of related shareholders who control every aspect and decision of the corporation and its business it is a different matter altogether. Shareholders/employees are free to decide on an appropriate salary/divided mix that is largely based on income tax considerations. The choice between compensation in the form of salary or in the form of dividends, the salary vs. dividend decision, is the subject of the remainder of this chapter.

Salary vs. Dividends

Overview

15-130.   To illustrate the basic trade-off that is involved in salary vs. dividend decisions, assume that Ms. Olney owns all of the shares of a corporation that has $100,000 in income, and that she has sufficient property income from other sources to place her in the 51% federal/provincial tax bracket (33% federal rate plus 18% provincial rate).

15-131.   If the full $100,000 of corporate income is paid to Ms. Olney in the form of salary, it can be deducted by the corporation and will reduce the corporation's income to nil. This means that no Part I taxes will be paid by the corporation. However, the $100,000 will be subject to income tax at Ms. Olney's marginal income tax rate of 51%. This means that she will pay tax of $51,000 and be left with after-tax funds of $49,000.

15-132.   If no salary is paid to Ms. Olney, corporate income tax will be payable on the $100,000, and any remaining amount, after adjustments for any refundable taxes, will be paid as dividends. The dividends will be subject to personal income tax and the resulting after-tax cash flow to her can be determined. These amounts, which are dependent on the type of corporation and the type of income earned, were calculated earlier in this chapter. The results of those calculations were summarized in Paragraph 15-55. You may wish to refer to this summary as you work through the remainder of this chapter.

Analysis of the Example

15-133.   In looking at the question of whether or not to incorporate a source of income such as a business or investments, we looked at the possibilities for both tax deferral and tax reduction through the use of a corporation. In a salary vs. dividend analysis we are not concerned with deferral since distributions will be made. The question we need to answer is:

> What is the most tax effective manner in which a corporation can compensate a shareholder/employee (i.e., an owner-manager)?

15-134.   In comparing Ms. Olney's $49,000 after-tax salary with the results listed in Paragraph 15-55, in all cases incorporating a business or investments where corporate income tax was paid and post-tax earnings were distributed as taxable dividends resulted in less after-tax income. Even in the case of a CCPC earning income that is eligible for the small business deduction, the after-tax retention result was only $48,675.

15-135.   This would suggest that, in general, salary should be used. However, the previous analysis was based on a number of assumptions with respect to provincial income tax rates on individuals and corporations. In addition, other factors, such as RRSP contributions, CPP contributions, and other payroll costs, were ignored. These factors will be considered in the following material.

Other Considerations

Provincial Tax Rates and Credits

15-136.   The results that were presented in Paragraph 15-55 assumed a provincial income tax rate on individuals of 18%, a provincial dividend tax credit rate on non-eligible dividends of 20% of the gross up, and provincial tax rates on income eligible for the small business deduction of 2.5% and 13.5% on any other corporate income. While these rates are fairly representative, they can vary considerably.

15-137.   In assessing the importance of these differences, it is important to recognize that the payment of salaries is economically equivalent to carrying on a business or earning investment income without a corporation. That is, if a corporation has $100,000 in business or property income and pays this entire amount as salary, corporate net and taxable income will be nil and there will be no corporate income tax. The full amount of the income would be included in the income of the individual shareholder/employee, which is exactly what would have occurred had the source of income not been incorporated. The most significant difference is that the individual receives employment income instead of business or property income, however the salary/dividend analysis still requires an evaluation of the income tax differences between earning income with and without a corporation.

15-138.   Given this, we can discuss the effect of varying provincial income tax rates on the salary/dividend decision by drawing from conclusions reached in the analysis considered in Paragraphs 15-58 through 15-76:

Tax Rates for Individuals   In the analysis contained in Paragraphs 15-67 through 15-69, we noted that high individual income tax rates clearly made the use of a corporation more attractive from the point of view of income tax deferral. However, since the salary/dividend decision looks only to the nature of distributions, deferral is not a concern, meaning that individual income tax rates are not an important factor in the analysis. This point is illustrated with the example found in Paragraph 15-68.

Dividend Tax Credit and Corporate Tax Rates   For integration to work, the combined federal/provincial dividend tax credit must be equal to the combined federal/provincial corporate income taxes.

- **Eligible Dividends**   For eligible dividends subject to a 38% gross up, this would require a combined corporate income tax rate of 27.54% and a combined dividend tax credit equal to the gross up. This in turn would require a provincial corporate income tax rate of 12.54% [27.54 - (38 - 10 - 13)] and a provincial dividend tax credit of 5/11 of the gross up (1.0 - 6/11).

- **Non-Eligible Dividends** For non-eligible dividends (the type commonly paid by a CCPC) subject to a 15% gross up, this would require a combined federal/provincial corporate income tax rate of 13.043% and a combined dividend tax credit equal to the gross up. This requires a provincial corporate income tax rate of 4.043% [13.043 - (38 - 10 - 19)] and a provincial dividend tax credit equal to 4/13 of the gross up (1.0 - 9/13).

The examples in Paragraphs 15-74 and 15-75 illustrate the results of applying the current range of corporate income tax rates and dividend tax credit rates in all of the Canadian provinces. While these examples were designed to illustrate the advantages or disadvantages of incorporating a source of income, they can also be used to evaluate the salary/dividend decision.

These previous examples highlight the point that in situations where the combined dividend tax credits exceed the combined corporate income tax and therefore overcompensate the corporate income tax, paying dividends will be preferable to paying salary. The reverse is true where the combined dividend tax credits are less than the combined corporate income tax and therefore undercompensate for corporate income tax.

Dividend Preference—Income Splitting

15-139.   A corporation can be used for income splitting purposes by paying dividends to family members who are shareholders. In Paragraph 15-84 we noted that, in 2021, an individual with no other source of income can receive $30,172 in non-eligible dividends and $63,040 in eligible dividends without paying any federal income tax. This fact clearly favours the payment of compensation as dividend distributions to such family members.

15-140.   The preference for taxable dividend distributions to family members with no or little other income must be cautiously balanced against attribution concepts such as the TOSI. If the TOSI is found to apply the result is that the taxable dividends will be subject to the highest federal income tax rate imposed on individuals of 33%. This will negate the use of an income splitting strategy involving the payment of taxable dividends.

Dividend Benefit—CNIL Reduction

15-141.   An individual's cumulative net investment loss (CNIL) is a tax account that tracks, from 1987, certain investment expenses and investment income. If the total investment expenses exceed investment income the difference reduces an individual's ability to claim the capital gains deduction (see Chapter 11). When considering the sale of property that would result in a capital gain eligible for the capital gains deduction it is good tax planning to first reduce any CNIL account balance to the extent possible.

15-142.   Reducing the CNIL balance requires increasing investment income. Grossed up dividends are investment income for this purpose, reducing the CNIL by $1.15 for each $1.00 of non-eligible dividends and by $1.38 for each $1.00 of eligible dividends. In contrast, payments of salary do not affect the CNIL. The existence of a positive CNIL account, therefore, favours the payment of dividends over salary.

Salary Benefit—Earned Income for RRSPs and CPP

15-143.   One of the most attractive features of the Canadian income tax system is the fact that individuals can make deductible contributions to RRSPs. Not only are the contributions deductible, but any income earned within an RRSP trust as a result of invested cumulative contributions are not subject to income tax as a result of a tax exemption granted to RRSP trusts (ITA 149(1)(r)).

15-144.   The ability to make contributions to an RRSP is dependent on an individual having income that qualifies as "earned income." In addition, participation in the Canada Pension Plan (CPP) requires what is referred to as pensionable earnings. Dividends do not qualify as earned income nor do they count as pensionable earnings. Salary, however, qualifies for both RRSP and CPP purposes. As a result, if a shareholder/employee has no earned income it will be necessary for the corporation to pay salary if the individual wishes to participate in retirement plans such as RRSPs and the CPP.

15-145.   Contributing the maximum allowable amount each year to the CPP will entitle an individual to the maximum CPP pension on retirement at age 65, which for 2021 is $1,203.75 per month. The maximum CPP contributions for 2021 are based on maximum pensionable earnings of $61,600 and therefore this amount, at a minimum, should be paid as salary in 2021.

15-146.   Maximum RRSP contributions for 2021 are based on an RRSP limit of $29,210. This limit is reached with earned income of $162,278 [(18%)($162,278)= $29,210]. If a shareholder/employee has no other source of earned income, 2021 salary of at least $162,278 will be required to make the maximum RRSP contribution. The RRSP deduction room can be carried forward, but there is no equivalent carry forward for the CPP program.

Salary Benefit—Earned Income for Child Care Expenses (ITA 63)

15-147.   If an individual is in a position to deduct child care expenses, the deduction is limited to two-thirds of earned income. Salary payments would add to this limit while dividends would not. For a detailed discussion of the deductibility of child care costs, see Chapter 9.

Salary Benefit—Corporate Losses

15-148.   In a particular year, a shareholder/employee may require salary that exceeds corporate income. To the extent the salary expense creates a current-year corporate loss there will be no immediate corporate income tax savings. However, the loss would become a non-capital loss that would then be available to be applied to other years. The savings, in effect, would be deferred to the year in which the non-capital loss would be claimed. This means that, to properly evaluate the payment of salaries in this situation, consideration would have to be given to the present value of money.

Salary Cost (Possible)—Provincial Payroll Taxes

15-149.   With respect to provincial payroll taxes, five provinces and two territories assess such taxes. A summary of the various rates are as follows:

British Columbia   (Employer Health Tax) No tax on the first $500,000 of payroll (BC Remuneration). If payroll is between $500,000 and $1,500,000 the amount above $500,000 is subject to a payroll tax of 2.925%. If the payroll exceeds $1,500,000 it is all subject to a rate of 1.95%.

Ontario   (Employer Health Tax) No tax on the first $1,000,000 of payroll unless total payroll exceeds $5,000,000. Excess is taxed up to a maximum of 1.95%.

Manitoba   (Health and Post-Secondary Education Levy) No tax on the first $1.25 million of payroll. Payroll between $1.25 million and $2.5 million is taxed 4.3%. If payroll exceeds $2.5 million the rate drops to 2.15%.

Newfoundland/Labrador   (Health and Post-Secondary Education Levy) No tax on the first $1.3 million of payroll. Excess is taxed at a rate of 2%.

Quebec   (Health Services Fund) Quebec has a complex system that includes exemptions for certain employers. When applicable, the tax rate ranges from 1.25% to 4.26% of payroll.

Territories   (Payroll Tax) Nunavut and the Northwest Territories tax all payroll at a rate of 2%. This tax is paid by employees and withheld as a source deduction by employers. There is no payroll tax in Yukon.

Salary Costs—CPP and EI

15-150.   In our example from Paragraph 15-130, we ignored the fact that salaries cannot be paid without contributions being made to the CPP. In addition, some provinces charge a payroll tax on salaries and wages as described in the preceding paragraph. These additional costs can result in a significant reduction in after-tax cash.

15-151.   With respect to CPP contributions, 2021 employee contributions are 5.45% of $61,600 (maximum pensionable earnings) less a basic exemption of $3,500. This results in a maximum employee contribution for 2021 of $3,166. The employer is required to withhold and remit this contribution from salaries together with an equivalent employer contribution per employee. This brings the total CPP cost of paying salaries of $61,600 or more to $6,332 per employee split equally between the employee and the employer.

15-152.   If a shareholder/employee controls more than 40% of the voting shares of the corporation, the salary is considered excluded employment and the individual cannot claim EI benefits with respect to that income (*EI Act* 5(2)). While generally not relevant in the situations covered here, an employee's maximum EI premium for 2021 is 1.58% of $56,300 (maximum insurable earnings), with no exemption, for a total of $890. The employer must contribute 1.4 times the employee's premium (*EI Act* s. 68), an amount of $1,246. This results in a total cost of $2,136 for an employee with maximum insurable earnings in excess of $56,300.

Salary Benefit—CPP and Canada Employment Tax Credits

15-153.   While CPP contributions represent an added salary cost, the payment of these contributions provides a future benefit in the form of CPP pension income, as well as a benefit from the CPP tax credit and a CPP deduction allowed in computing net income. In 2021 the maximum CPP employee contribution of $3,166 entitles an employee to a personal tax credit of $2,876 plus a deduction in determining net income of $290.

15-154.   A further benefit of paying salary is that an employee is entitled to the Canada employment credit of $1,257 for 2021. This credit is only available if salary is paid by the corporation.

Example Extended

15-155.   Returning to our example from Paragraph 15-130, as the owner of 100% of the shares of the corporation, Ms. Olney is not eligible to participate in the EI program with respect to her employment with the company. In addition, assume the province in which she lives charges a 2% payroll tax and provides a provincial tax credit for CPP contributions at a rate of 6%. The company is a CCPC and all of its $100,000 in income is eligible for the small business deduction. Given this income and the costs associated with paying salary, the maximum salary that could be paid to Ms. Olney would be $94,935, a figure that would result in no corporate income tax payable.

Pre-tax corporate income	$100,000
Employer's CPP contribution	(3,166)
Gross salary [($100,000 - $3,166) ÷ 1.02]	(94,935)
Payroll tax [(2%)($94,935)]	(1,899)
Corporate taxable income	Nil

15-156.   If $94,935 is paid to Ms. Olney as salary, her personal income tax would be as follows:

Combined tax before credits	
[(33% + 18%)($94,935 - $290 deductible CPP)]	$48,269
Credit for employee's CPP contribution	
[(15% + 6%)($2,876)]*	(604)
Canada employment credit [(15%)($1,257)]	(189)
Personal tax payable	$ 47,476

*We have assumed that Ms. Olney has other sources of income sufficient to cause her to be subject to the maximum federal tax bracket with respect to any additional income. The other income would absorb other available tax credits and, as a consequence, only the CPP and Canada employment credits that result from the payment of the salary are included in this analysis.

15-157. With this amount of income taxes payable, Ms. Olney's after-tax retention would be calculated as follows:

Salary received	$94,935
Employee's CPP contribution—Maximum	(3,166)
Personal tax payable	(47,476)
After-tax cash retained	$44,293

15-158. This more realistic result provides considerably less cash than the $49,000 [($100,000) (1 - 0.51)] that was calculated when CPP, payroll taxes, and the Canada employment credit were ignored. While the value would not be easy to quantify, the payment of CPP does provide the owner-manager with future pension benefits. Using the numbers in Paragraph 15-55, this makes payment of salary, if these additional factors are considered, less desirable than dividends paid out of:

- income eligible for the small business deduction (retention was $48,675),
- business income ineligible for the small business deduction (retention was $45,760).

Exercise 15-10

Subject: Salary and Dividend Compensation

For the year ending December 31, 2021, Broadmoor Inc., a CCPC, has active business income before consideration of dividends or salary paid to its sole shareholder of $550,000. The company has considerable cash resources sufficient to meet any additional salaries, dividends, and related tax obligations. The company makes the maximum eligible dividend designation each year. Its only shareholder, Ms. Sarah Broad, has no income other than dividends or salary paid by the corporation and she has combined federal/provincial personal tax credits that would reduce her income tax payable by $5,000.

In her province of residence, assume:

- the corporate tax rate is 3% on income eligible for the small business deduction and 14% on all other corporate income;
- her combined federal/provincial income tax payable totals $75,000 on the first $216,511 with additional amounts of income subject to 51%;
- the provincial dividend tax credit is 30% of the gross up for both eligible and non-eligible dividends; and
- there is no payroll tax.

Determine the amount of after-tax cash that Ms. Broad will retain if (1) the maximum salary is paid by the corporation out of the available cash of $550,000 and (2) the maximum amount of eligible and non-eligible dividends are paid. Ignore the required CPP contributions and the Canada employment tax credit.

Solutions to Exercises are available in the Study Guide.

Use of Tax Credits

15-159.   Our example in this section has involved an individual with other sources of income that resulted in the application of the maximum federal income tax bracket. This amount of income would be sufficient to absorb any available tax credits. However, there may be situations where a salary vs. dividend decision is being applied to an individual with no other source of income. This would be a fairly common situation when a corporation is being used for income splitting purposes, or in a case where a corporation has limited income.

15-160.   If the individual has no other source of income and provincial income tax rates favour the use of dividends over salary, there may be a problem when it comes to using all available tax credits. We noted earlier in this chapter that dividend payments use up tax credits at a much lower rate than other types of income, such as salary. If only limited amounts of income are being distributed, the use of dividends may leave a portion of the individual's tax credits unused. When this is the case, some combination of salary and dividends may provide a better solution.

15-161.   A further complication that we have purposefully avoided is that provincial tax credits can only be applied against the provincial income tax liability, and federal tax credits can only be deducted against the federal income tax liability. As a result, it would be possible to have a situation where an individual would have to pay some federal income tax to use all of the provincial income tax credits, or alternatively, pay some provincial income tax to use all of the federal income tax credits. Given the focus in this text on federal income taxes, no further attention will be given to this issue.

15-162.   The following example illustrates the salary vs. dividend issue when the full use of available income tax credits is a consideration.

EXAMPLE   Mr. Eric Swenson is the sole shareholder of Swenson Sweets, a CCPC with a December 31 taxation year. For the 2021 taxation year the company's income before the deduction of any salary expenses to its sole shareholder is only $29,500. All of the company's income is eligible for the small business deduction. The company has sufficient cash to pay salary or dividends. Mr. Swenson has combined federal/provincial personal income tax credits that would reduce any income tax liability by $3,920.

The corporation carries on business in a province with a corporate income tax rate on income eligible for the small business deduction of 3%. The province does not charge any payroll tax. The provincial income tax rate on individuals is 10% of the first $49,020 of taxable income, with a provincial dividend tax credit on non-eligible dividends that is equal to 4/13 of the gross up. CPP contributions and the Canada employment tax credit are both ignored.

15-163.   If the full $29,500 is paid out in salary, corporate net and taxable income would be nil and there would be no corporate income tax payable. Mr. Swenson's after-tax cash retention would be as follows:

Salary received		$29,500
Personal tax payable		
Personal taxes at 25% (15% + 10%)	($7,375)	
Personal tax credits (given)	3,920	(3,455)
After-tax cash retained (all salary)		$26,045

15-164.   As dividends paid are not a deductible expense, corporate income tax must be paid prior to any dividend distribution. The combined federal/provincial tax rate would be 12% (38% - 10% - 19% + 3%), resulting in corporate taxes of $3,540 [(12%)($29,500)]. This means that the maximum dividend that can be paid will be $25,960 ($29,500 - $3,540). The after-tax retention in this case would be determined as follows:

Non-eligible dividends received	$25,960
Gross up of 15%	3,894
Taxable dividends	$29,854
Personal tax rate	25%
Personal tax payable before tax credits	$ 7,464
Personal tax credits (given)	(3,920)
Dividend tax credit [(9/13 + 4/13)($3,894)]	(3,894)
Tax payable ($350 in unused credits)	Nil

Non-eligible dividends received	$25,960
Personal taxes (see Paragraph 15-84—	
No taxes would be paid on this amount)	Nil
After-tax cash retained (all dividends)	$25,960

15-165.   While the low federal/provincial income tax rate on corporations suggests that dividends should be the best choice, the preceding results do not confirm this view. The problem is that dividend income absorbs available tax credits at a much lower rate than other types of income. The fact that the all dividend solution leaves $350 of unused tax credits suggests that a better solution might be to pay a lesser amount of dividends plus sufficient salary to absorb unused credits.

15-166.   To investigate this possibility, we need to determine the salary/dividend mix that will fully use all of Mr. Swenson's income tax credits. To begin, consider what would happen when we add a $1,000 salary payment to the all dividends case. As the salary will be fully deductible, the after-tax cost of making this payment is $880 [($1,000)(1.0 - 0.12)]. As a result, in this type of situation, where the goal is to distribute all of the available corporate income, dividends will only have to be reduced by this $880 per $1,000 of salary increase.

15-167.   The resulting increase in income taxes payable can be calculated as follows:

Increase in salary	$1,000.00
Decrease in dividends	(880.00)
Decrease in dividend gross up [(15%)($880)]	(132.00)
Decrease in taxable income	($ 12.00)
Personal tax rate	25%
Decrease in tax payable before dividend tax credit	($ 3.00)
Decrease in dividend tax credit	
= Increase in tax payable [(9/13 + 4/13)($132)]	132.00
Net increase in personal tax payable	$ 129.00

15-168.   This analysis demonstrates that each $1,000 increase in salary results in an increase in personal tax payable of $129. Alternatively, this can be stated as an increase in personal tax payable of $0.129 for every dollar of increase in salary. This means that to use Mr. Swenson's $350 in unused tax credits, he will have to receive salary of $2,713 ($350 ÷ 0.129). This results in the following amount being available for dividends:

Corporate taxable income pre-salary	$29,500
Salary	(2,713)
Corporate taxable income	$ 26,787
Corporate tax at 12%	(3,214)
Available for dividends	$23,573

15-169.   When this dividend is paid out to Mr. Swenson, his after-tax retention is as follows:

Non-eligible dividends received	$23,573
Gross up of 15%	3,536
Taxable dividends	$ 27,109
Salary	2,713
Taxable income	$29,822
Personal tax rate	25%
Personal tax payable before tax credits	$ 7,456
Personal tax credits (given)	(3,920)
Dividend tax credit [(9/13 + 4/13)($3,536)]	(3,536)
Personal tax payable (salary and dividends)	Nil

Comparison	All Salary	All Dividends	Salary and Dividends
Non-eligible dividends received	N/A	$25,960	$23,573
Salary received	$29,500	N/A	2,713
Personal tax payable	(3,455)	Nil	Nil
After-tax cash retained	$26,045	$25,960	$26,286

15-170.   As shown in the preceding calculations, this mix of salary and dividends is such that it uses all of Mr. Swenson's tax credits and leaves no income tax owing. This results in a solution that not only improves on the $25,960 that was retained in the all dividend scenario, it also improves on the $26,045 that was retained in the all salary case. It represents the optimum solution for this example where only income tax effects are considered.

Optimizing a Limited Payment of Cash

15-171.   A similar analysis could be done if the corporation had limited cash. Assume that, while the corporation in the example (Paragraph 15-162) had income of $29,500, it had only $16,000 in cash. To determine the maximum salary that can be paid (X), it is necessary to solve the following algebraic equation:

$$X = \$16,000 - [(12\%)(\$29,500 - X)]$$

$$X - 0.12X = [(\$16,000 - (12\%)(\$29,500)] = \$14,159$$

15-172.   Based on this amount of salary, the amount of after-tax cash retained would be calculated as follows:

Corporate cash before taxes	$16,000
Corporate taxes [(12%)($29,500 - $14,159)]	(1,841)
Corporate cash available for salary	$ 14,159

Salary received		$14,159
Personal tax payable:		
Personal tax on salary [(25%)(14,159)]	($3,540)	
Personal tax credits (given)	3,920	Nil
After-tax cash retained ($380 in unused credits)		$14,159

15-173.   Alternatively, if maximum dividends are paid, the amount of after-tax cash retained would be calculated as follows:

Corporate cash before taxes	$16,000
Corporate taxes [(12%)($29,500)]	(3,540)
Corporate cash available for dividends	$12,460

Non-eligible dividend received	$12,460
Personal taxes (see Paragraph 15-84—No taxes would be paid)	Nil
After-tax cash retained	$12,460

15-174.   It is clear that the salary approach results in a considerably larger after-tax retention than the dividend approach. This result would be expected given that the corporate cash was insufficient to use the personal tax credits in either approach.

Exercise 15-11

Subject: Salary vs. Dividends

For the year ending December 31, 2021, Mortell Inc., a CCPC, has income of $198,000 without consideration of any deductible salary or the distribution of taxable dividends to its sole shareholder. The company has sufficient cash to meet and salary, dividend, or income tax obligations. The company is subject to a combined federal/provincial income tax rate of 12%. Ms. Mortell, the company's only shareholder, has income from other sources of $150,000 and, under normal circumstances, does not withdraw any amounts from the corporation. However, she needs an additional $30,000 in cash for home improvements. Ms. Mortell's combined federal/provincial income tax rate on any additional income is 45%. She lives in a province where the provincial dividend tax credit is equal to 25% of the dividend gross up for non-eligible dividends. She has asked your advice as to whether the payment of salary or, alternatively, the payment of non-eligible dividends would have the lowest tax cost. Ignore the required CPP contributions and the Canada employment tax credit. Provide the advice.

Exercise 15-12

Subject: Salary vs. Dividends—Limited Corporate Cash

For the year ending December 31, 2021, Fargo Ltd. has income, before consideration of deductible salary and distribution of taxable dividends to its sole shareholder, of $21,500. The company's cash balance prior to the payment of any income taxes for the year is $18,500. The company is subject to a combined federal/provincial income tax rate of 12%. There are no payroll taxes charged in the province.

Mr. Fargo, the company's president and sole shareholder, is 71 years of age and has no other source of income (he is not eligible for OAS). He has combined federal/provincial personal tax credits that reduce income tax payable by $3,950 and lives in a province that has an individual income tax rate of 10% on the first $49,020 of taxable income. The provincial dividend tax credit is 30% of the gross up for non-eligible dividends.

Mr. Fargo would like to remove all of the cash from the corporation and has asked your advice as to whether it would be better to take it out in the form of all non-eligible dividends or all salary. As Mr. Fargo is over 70 years of age, no CPP contributions are required. Ignore the Canada employment tax credit. Provide the requested advice.

Solutions to Exericses are available in the Study Guide.

Conclusion

15-175.   The salary vs. dividend decision can be complex. Determination of the total income tax consequences of the two alternatives does not always resolve the issue. In addition to the many factors discussed, such as income splitting and bonusing down, consideration should be given to:

- the administrative costs related to withholding and remitting income tax and CPP premiums when salary is paid;
- the ability to defer personal taxation to the subsequent calendar year if the payment of salary is deferred and the corporation's year end is within 180 days of December 31;
- the effect of the gross up on dividends if the OAS clawback is relevant; and
- if the shareholder/employee is applying for a mortgage or loan, it will be more advantageous to have a history of regular salary rather than dividends

15-176.   The preceding material is not intended to provide a comprehensive approach to solving these problems on a quantitative basis. Many other subjective considerations are simply not capable of any accurate analysis but play a significant role in any final resolution. In this chapter we have set out some of the more common factors that may have a bearing on the final outcome.

We suggest you complete SSP 15-9 to 15-11 at this point.

Key Terms

A full glossary with definitions is provided at the end of the Study Guide.

Active Business Income	Low Rate Income Pool (LRIP)
Aggregate Investment Income	Manufacturing and Processing
Business Limit	Profits Deduction (M&P Deduction)
Bonusing Down	Overintegration
Canadian Controlled Private Corporation	Private Corporation
Capital Gains Deduction	Public Corporation
Charitable Donations Tax Credit	Specified Employee
Eligible Dividends	Tax Avoidance
Estate Planning	Tax Deferral
General Rate Income Pool (GRIP)	Tax Planning
Income Splitting	Taxable Benefit
Integration	TOSI (Tax on Split Income)
Limited Liability	Underintegration

References

For more detailed study of the material in this chapter, we refer you to the following:

ITA 6(1)	Amounts to Be Included as Income from Office or Employment
ITA 15(1)	Benefit Conferred on Shareholder
ITA 15(2)	Shareholder Debt
ITA 18(1)	General Limitations (on Deductions)
ITA 20(1)(j)	Repayment of Loan by Shareholder
ITA 67	General Limitation Re Expenses
ITA 80.4	Loans—Imputed Interest
ITA 80.5	Deemed Interest
ITA 82(1)	Taxable Dividends Received
ITA 121	Deduction for Taxable Dividends
ITA 123 To 125.5	Rules Applicable to Corporations
ITA 146	Registered Retirement Savings Plans
ITA 147	Deferred Profit Sharing Plans
IT-67R3	Taxable Dividends from Corporations Resident in Canada
IT-119R4	Debts of Shareholders and Certain Persons Connected with Shareholders
IT-421R2	Benefits to Individuals, Corporations, and Shareholders from Loans or Debt
IT-432R2	Benefits Conferred on Shareholders

Self-Study Problems (SSPs)

Self-Study Problems (SSPs) provide practice in problem solving. Within the chapters, we have indicated where it would be appropriate to stop and work on each SSP. The problems can be downloaded by chapter from MyLab Accounting. Solutions are available in the Study Guide. Select problems can also be completed directly in MyLab and auto-graded.

Assignment Problems

Solutions to Assignment Problems (APs) are available to instructors only.

AP 15-1   *(Advantages of Incorporation)*

Philip Caron is in his mid-fifties and is married with two teenaged children. For over 15 years he has been carrying on a welding business as a sole proprietor. Business profits are approximately $250,000 per year. In recent years, Mr. Caron has been using about half of the business profits for personal needs.

In the last five years, he has been working on a new fork lift design that can be attached to half-tonne pick-up trucks. He has a product that is selling well with few malfunctions, and he is in the process of patenting the design. As a result, the focus of the welding business is now predominantly manufacturing these specially designed fork lifts.

Some of his welding equipment is in need of replacement. In addition, he needs to acquire specialty manufacturing equipment to mass produce the fork lift. The business expansion will require substantial capital investment and external financing.

Required: Briefly discuss whether Mr. Caron should incorporate the business.

AP 15-2   *(Example of Integration)*

One of your longstanding clients, Mr. Carson Jones, has carried on a a successful business as a sole proprietor for 10 years. This business is something of a sideline for him in that he has employment and investment income of over $250,000 per year. Further, these latter sources of income are more than adequate to meet his personal needs and absorb all of his available tax credits.

Given his current level of income, any additional income will be subject to a combined federal provincial income tax rate of 53% (33% federal + 20% provincial).

He is looking for ways to reduce income taxes. One approach that he would like to consider is incorporating the business as well as some of his investments. The new corporation would be named Carjon Ltd.

He has asked for your advice and, to assist you, he has provided the following information:

Expected business profits (active business income)	$115,000
Eligible portfolio dividends	133,000
Federal corporate tax rate after federal abatement	28%
Federal small business deduction	19%
General rate reduction	13%
Provincial rate on active business income of CCPCs	2%
Provincial dividend tax credits on:	
Eligible dividends	40% of dividend gross up
Non-eligible dividends	23% of dividend gross up

Required:

A. Assume that the business and investments are not incorporated and will be included in Mr. Jones' income. Calculate Mr. Jones' personal tax payable, showing separately the income tax payable on the active business income and the eligible dividends.

B. Assume that the business and investments are incorporated within Carjon Ltd. Calculate the corporate income tax payable, after-tax income available for a dividend distribution, and personal income tax that would be payable on the dividend distribution. Assume that the maximum eligible dividend distributions are made. Your calculations should show separately the income tax payable on the active business income and any eligible or non-eligible dividends.

C. Compare the tax payable with and without the use of Carjon Ltd. and explain why the tax payable amounts are different. Advise Carson as to whether he should make the proposed transfers to a new corporation.

AP 15-3 (Incorporating Investments That Earn Interest)
As an employee of a public company, Maxine Ashley has an annual salary of $155,000.

After years of playing the provincial lottery without success Maxine wins $500,000. Since her employment income is more than adequate for her personal needs, she plans to invest all of the winnings in bonds for the year ending December 31, 2021, that will pay annual interest at a rate of 5%.

The following information is applicable to the province in which Maxine is a resident:

• The provincial provincial marginal income tax rate for Maxine is 13%.

• The provincial dividend tax credit on non-eligible dividends is 28% of the gross up.

• The provincial tax rate on investment income of CCPCs is 12%.

Maxine has no other investments.

Required: Prepare calculations that will compare the after-tax retention of the interest income on the bonds in 2021 if:

A. She owns them personally.

B. The bonds are incorporated within a CCPC in which she is the sole shareholder and which pays out all available post-tax interest as dividends.

AP 15-4   (Incorporating Investments That Pay Dividends)
As an employee of a public company, Thomas Nance has an annual salary of $300,000.

After years of playing the provincial lottery without success Thomas wins $650,000. Since his employment income is more than adequate to meet all of his personal needs, he plans to invest all of the winnings in preferred shares of a public company in January 2021. The shares pay annual eligible dividends of 6%.

The following information is applicable to the province in which Thomas is a resident:

• The provincial marginal tax rate for Thomas is 19%.

• The provincial dividend tax credit on eligible dividends is 22% of the gross up.

• The provincial tax rate on the investment income of CCPCs is 11%.

Thomas has no other investments.

Required: Prepare calculations that will compare the after-tax retention of the dividend income in 2021 if:

A. Thomas owns the shares personally.

B. The preferred shares are incorporated within a CCPC in which he is the sole shareholder and which pays out all available post-tax income as eligible dividends.

AP 15-5   (Incorporation of Investment Income)

The following information is relevant to the province in which Jason Tegue resides in 2021:

- The combined federal and provincial corporate income tax rate on the investment income of CCPCs is 50 2/3%.

- The provincial dividend tax credit on eligible dividends is equal to 40% of the dividend gross up and 30% for non-eligible dividends.

- Provincial income tax payable on an individual's first $98,040 of taxable income is $12,817. Amounts in excess of this are subject to provincial income tax at a rate of 17.4%.

Jason owns the following investments and anticipates the following Canadian source income for 2021:

	Value at 31/12/2020	Type of Income	Expected Income for 2021
Power Corp Bonds	$ 78,000	Interest	$ 8,600
Larch Company Shares	312,000	Dividends	17,400
Inbridge Inc. Shares	36,000	Capital Gains	6,200
Calgary Dominion Bank Shares	38,000	Dividends	3,600
Calgary Dominion Bank Shares		Capital Gains	2,800
Totals	$464,000	N/A	$38,600

Jason only invests in the shares and debt of large, publicly traded companies. He owns less than 1% of the shares or debt in any of these corporations. All of the dividends received were taxable dividends and were designated eligible.

In 2021, in addition to the above investment income, Jason expects to earn $92,000 of employment income. He has combined federal/provincial personal tax credits that would reduce his combined income tax payable by $3,491. The total ACB for his investments is $450,000.

Jason asks you whether there are any income tax advantages of incorporating the investments based on the expected income for 2021.

Jason's lifestyle requires him to use all available income. As a consequence, he would like you to assume that, if the investments are incorporated, the corporation will distribute all post-tax income as dividends.

Required: Provide an appropriate analysis for Jason Tegue.

AP 15-6   (Individual or Corporate Partner)

Having worked as an individual management consultant, Melissa Fox has enjoyed a great deal of success. Her effectiveness has generated a fairly long list of potential clients. Recognizing the opportunities involved in this situation, Melissa has decided to join a general partnership, Consulting Unlimited (CU).

She will be admitted to the partnership January 1, 2021, with a 25% partnership interest. She is giving consideration to either becoming a partner herself or incorporating a wholly owned CCPC that will become the partner. If the CCPC becomes the partner its business limit is specified by ITA 125 and cannot exceed 25% with respect to partnership allocations of active business income. Therefore, the business limit will be $125,000 [(25%)($500,000)]. Distributions of partnership income to her will be made based on the three following approaches:

Alternative 1 Her CCPC (the corporate partner) will pay corporate income tax on allocations of partnership income, with after-tax funds being paid to Melissa as dividends.

Alternative 2 Melissa will use a bonus down strategy to reduce the corporate income to the $125,000 amount eligible for the small business deduction.

Alternative 3 Melissa will personally become a member of the partnership and will be subject to income tax on any allocations of income.

Melissa lives in a province where the provincial income tax payable on the first $216,511 of taxable income is $22,150, with additional amounts subject to a provincial income tax rate of 18%. The provincial dividend tax credit is equal to 40% of the gross up for eligible dividends and 30% of the gross up for non-eligible dividends. Melissa's tax credits for 2021 allow her to reduce income taxes payable by $4,241.

If a CCPC is incorporated to become the partner it would be subject to a combined federal/provincial income tax rate on income eligible for the small business deduction of 12.5%. The rate on any other active business income would be 27%.

During the partnership's fiscal period ending December 31, 2021, it is expected to earn $930,000 of active business income.

Because she has no other source of income, she requires all of the share of income earned by the partnership.

Required: Calculate the after-tax retention of Melissa's share of the partnership income for each of the three approaches. Ignore CPP considerations and the Canada employment tax credit in your calculations. Which approach would you recommend? Briefly explain why this alternative is the best and any other factors she should consider.

AP 15-7 *(Shareholder Loans)*

Brewers Ltd. is a CCPC with a December 31 taxation year end. The company was incorporated in 2015 by four unrelated individuals, Jamie, Spencer, Heather, and Pablo, all of whom (with the exception of Pablo) met in university while working toward their master's of business administration (MBA). They quickly realized that their business ideas were quite similar and agreed to work together to carry on a new business together. Spencer recommended they speak with a friend of his, Pablo, who had a degree in chemical engineering. Together the four individuals came up with the idea to operate their own micro-breweries. Pablo created unique mixtures that have been used to produce very successful beers in three provinces with strong sales and brand loyalty.

In 2021 the company employs 200 people. In an effort to retain staff the company provides a generous package of benefits to its employees. Part of the benefit package includes participation in a stock option plan and the availability of interest-free loans. In 2021, 150 employees own shares in the company. The company has issued two classes of shares. Jamie, Spencer, Heather, and Pablo each own 2% of the common shares, and the employees own all of the Class A preferred shares, which are non-voting but offer a participating cumulative dividend. No single employee owns more than 1.5% of the preferred shares.

Three types of interest-free loans are offered for specific purposes once an employee has passed a probationary period of six months. Once a loan has been approved, quarterly payments are required throughout the term of the loan, although early repayments are allowed. If employment is terminated the loan must be paid in full within 30 days of termination. Interest-free loans are permitted for the following:

- **Housing Loan**   To purchase a principal residence in which the employee and his or her family will live on a continual basis. Loans for cottages and other vacation properties do not qualify. The company will advance between $50,000 and $200,000 depending on the number of years the employee has worked for the company and the nature of the employee's job—managers, for example, are entitled to larger amounts. The loan period cannot exceed 10 years.
- **Automobile Loan**   To purchase an automobile, the company will loan up to $30,000 and does not require that the automobile be used in the employee's employment. The loan period is limited to three years.
- **Vacation Loan**   Once every three years an employee who has passed his or her probationary period is entitled to a vacation loan of $12,000. Quarterly loan payments are required with a maximum loan period of 18 months.

Additional Information:

- Quarterly loan payments are made through payroll withholdings.
- The company does not permit loans to family members of employees or shareholders.
- Jamie, Spencer, Heather, and Pablo are all on the board of directors of the company and work in the daily operations in senior management positions.
- All approved loan agreements are in writing.
- The company is not in the business of lending money and, aside from employee loans, has never made loans to anyone else.
- Quarterly payments are required to be made on the first day of the fourth month following the receipt of the loan and every three months thereafter. Early payments may be made.
- Assume that the prescribed interest rate is 2% at all times.

During 2020 the company made the following loans listed in points 1 to 5 and an unusual payment in point 6:

1.   On April 1, Heather borrowed $200,000 to purchase shares in three separate public companies to increase her personal investment holdings. She has agreed to repay the loan with five annual payments of $40,000 beginning January 1, 2022. She received $18,000 of eligible dividends in December 2021 from these additional investments.

2.   Francois and Danielle Gagnon are brother and sister. They have been employed with the Quebec operations since the fall of 2020 and completed their six-month probationary period in March 2021. On June 1, 2021, they each borrowed $30,000 to purchase a new car. Danielle will use the car in her employment duties that include meeting with clients. Francois' duties do not require him to use a car for his employment. Both Francois and Danielle acquired preferred shares of the company in April 2021 under the employee stock option plan. Assume that Danielle calculates that for the period June 1 to December 31, 2021, she used her car 32% of the time for employment purposes.

3.   On September 1, Pablo borrows $350,000 from the company to assist in the finance of a new home. He has agreed to make equal annual payments of $17,500 over the next 20 years beginning September 1, 2022.

4.   Jacob Abernathy is a senior manager in the Toronto operations who has been renting an apartment since he began working for the company in 2015. Jacob has received a loan of $200,000 on May 1 that he will use to purchase a home. The loan will be for 10 years and require quarterly payments of $5,000 [$200,000 ÷ (10 years)(4 quarterly payments)]. Jacob owns preferred shares in the company, which he acquired through the company stock option plan.

5. Two employees (Safwan and Melody) have been working for the Vancouver operations since 2017. They are long-time friends and have regularly taken vacations together with their families. They each plan on requesting the maximum vacation loans, which they will use for a fall/winter 2021 and spring 2022 vacation. They each borrow $12,000 on July 1. Safwan is a shareholder as a result of the company stock option plan, but Melody is not.

6. On October 1, Spencer received $280,000 from the company that he used to build an addition to his Vancouver home. No payments have been made nor have any loan agreements been written.

With the exception of point 6, assume that all repayments have been made as scheduled.

Required: For the five loans indicated in points 1 to 5, determine the income tax consequences of each of the amounts received as loans under ITA 15(2) and ITA 20(1)(j) for the 2021, 2022, and 2023 taxation years. Only show the ITA 80.4 calculations for the 2021 and 2022 taxation years. Provide your analysis, together with any calculations, to identify specific amounts that are required to be included in the net income of the recipients together with any other income tax implications, including loan repayments.

Discuss the implications of the payment to Spencer in point 6. Did he receive a loan?

AP 15-8   (Bonusing Down)

Debee Ltd. is a CCPC with a December 31 taxation year end. The company was incorporated in New Brunswick in 2014 by its sole shareholder, Rene Debee, who lives in Saint John, New Brunswick. The company only earns income from an active business that would qualify for the small business deduction, and it has never been associated with any other corporation. The company's taxable income prior to 2021 has never exceeded its small business limit of $500,000. The company is not subject to any reduction to its small business limit attributable to either of its taxable capital employed in Canada or its adjusted aggregate investment income.

In 2019 and 2020 Rene was paid employment income from Debee of $20,000 a month, or $240,000 for each of the two years. As a result of the addition of a significant new client and resulting long-term contract, Debee estimates that its taxable income for 2021 will be $700,000, which takes into consideration the $240,000 of employment income paid to Rene. Rene's accountant has informed him that the additional $200,000 of taxable income above the $500,000 small business limit will be subject to tax at a rate of 29.0% instead of the 11.5% rate that would have applied to the first $500,000. The result is that the additional income will result in an additional $35,000 of corporate tax [($700,000 - $500,000)(0.29 - 0.115)].

Rene is not pleased with the additional corporate income tax and has asked his accountant if there is some way to reduce that amount. He adds that he is planning on building his dream home overlooking the ocean over the next few years and he will need the additional cash earned by the company as a result of the new client contract. The accountant tells him that he could "bonus down," explaining that this is an acceptable tax planning strategy. When Rene enquires further the accountant explains that the options are to (1) have the company pay him additional salary of $200,000 to reduce the taxable income to $500,000, avoiding the high level of corporate tax on income above the small business limit, or (2) have the corporation pay tax on its taxable income of $700,000 and distribute the additional $200,000 after-tax income as a dividend. Assume that the company balance in its GRIP account at the beginning of 2021 is nil.

In 2021 the following information is relevant to New Brunswick:

- The provincial tax rate on active business income (ABI) eligible for the small business deduction is 2.5% and is 14.0% on ABI in excess of the small business deduction. The federal equivalent rates are 9.0% and 15.0%, respectively.

- The highest provincial personal income tax rate is 20.3%, which applies to taxable income in excess of $162,383. The equivalent federal rate applies to taxable income in excess of $216,511 at a rate of 33.0%.

- The dividend gross up will be 38% for eligible dividends and 15% for non-eligible dividends.

- The federal dividend tax credit will be 6/11 of the gross up for eligible dividends and 9/13 of the gross up for non-eligible dividends.

- The provincial dividend tax credit will be 50.8% of the gross up for eligible dividends and 21.1% of the gross up for non-eligible dividends.

Required: As Rene's income tax consultant, advise him whether bonusing down with additional salary of $200,000 in 2021 is preferable to not bonusing down and withdrawing the additional after-tax cash as taxable dividends. Justify your conclusions with supporting calculations applying a marginal analysis that focuses on the additional $200,000 of corporate income. Add at least three other considerations that should be brought to Rene's attention that may influence his decision, and comment on any tax deferral should Rene not require the funds immediately.

AP 15-9   *(Salary vs. Dividends—Required Amount)*

Linda Cross is the sole shareholder of Cross Ltd., a CCPC incorporated in Alberta in 2011. The company taxation year end is December 31. The company business is carried on in Edmonton, Alberta, where Linda resides.

All of the income earned by Cross Ltd. is from an active business and is eligible for the small business deduction. The taxable income of the company has never exceeded its annual small business limit of $500,000, and this trend will continue into 2021. In 2021 the company will be subject to a provincial tax rate on income eligible for the small business deduction of 2.0%, which when combined with the federal rate on that same income of 9.0% will equal 11.0%.

The income of Cross Ltd. began to stabilize at the end of 2018 due to a solid customer base, and as a result Linda purchased a new home and re-evaluated her future cash needs. Working with her accountant, she decided that an annual salary of $158,000 would provide her sufficient after-tax cash to meet all of her personal needs. The company began to pay her an annual salary of $158,000 in 2019 with no plan to make any changes to that amount in 2021.

In the spring of 2021 Linda decided that it was time to put in a pool since the summers seemed to be getting warmer each year. She obtained a number of quotes and has decided on an in-ground pool that will cost her $25,000. She spoke to her accountant about the additional cash she would need and the best way to draw the funds from the company as either additional salary or dividends.

Additional Information

(i)   Assume that Linda's salary is her only income and that it also equals her taxable income.

(ii)   Cross Ltd.'s GRIP account at the beginning of 2021 is nil and no amount will be added to it in 2021.

(iii) The Alberta personal income tax rate in 2021 is 13.0% for taxable income between $157,464 and $209,952 and 14.0% for taxable income between $209,953 and $314,928.

(iv)   The federal personal income tax rate in 2021 is 29.0% for taxable income between $151,978 and $216,511 and 33.0% for taxable income in excess of $216,511.

(v)   In 2021 Alberta provides a dividend tax credit on non-eligible dividends of 16.7%, and 29.5% on eligible dividends.

Required: As Linda's accountant, determine the additional amount that would be required if Linda were to receive sufficient salary or dividends to leave her with the $25,000 cash she needs to put in an in-ground pool. Provide all supporting calculations and determine which of the two alternatives is most cost effective considering the income tax consequences to both Linda and Cross Ltd.

AP 15-10   (Salary vs. Dividends—Required Amount)

Simon Fahrquest is the sole shareholder of Dawg Ltd., a successful business that was incorporated a number of years ago. The company is a CCPC and uses a December 31 taxation year end.

Simon has never been particularly fond of people, but has always loved dogs, particularly those of mixed breed. While he has no family, he currently owns 12 dogs, none of which are purebred.

While Dawg Ltd. has always been profitable, Simon has chosen to live modestly in a dog-friendly residential property that he has owned for many years. Each year, he estimates the amount of cash that he will need for his living expenses, which vary year to year, and looks to his corporation to provide the needed cash.

Since after meeting Simon's financial needs Dawg Ltd. always has cash that isn't required for operations, it donates at least $100,000 per year to the Society for the Prevention of Cruelty to Animals (SPCA), a registered charity. The donations specify that the funds must be used for the protection, maintenance, and placement of mixed breed dogs.

For 2021, Simon estimates that he will need $50,000 in after-tax cash to meet his personal needs. He expects Dawg Ltd. will have taxable income of $350,000 before any payments to him, all of which will qualify for the small business deduction. The provincial tax rate on such income is 3%.

In Simon's province of residence, the provincial taxes on the first $49,020 of taxable income total $4,528. Additional income will be taxed at a provincial rate of 12%. Also in this province, the provincial dividend tax credit for non-eligible dividends is equal to 32% of the dividend gross up.

For the 2021 taxation year, Simon estimates that his personal tax credits will will result in a reduction in tax payable of $3,260.

Required:

A. Determine the tax cost of providing Simon with the required $50,000 in after-tax cash using only salary payments.

B. Determine the tax cost of providing Simon with the required $50,000 in after-tax cash using only dividend payments.

C. Given the information in this problem, do you believe that better results could be achieved with a combination of salary and dividends? Would your answer be different if Simon's personal tax credits totalled $10,000 instead of $3,260? Calculations are not required in answering this Part C.

D. Simon would like to increase his donations to the SPCA and has asked your advice on the most tax advantageous way to do this. What factors should be taken into consideration in the analysis?

Ignore CPP contributions and the Canada employment credit in your solution.

AP 15-11   (Salary vs. Dividends—Optimum Mix)

Robert Lorca is the only shareholder of Rolorc Ltd., a CCPC with a taxation year that ends on December 31. His only source of income is either taxable dividends or salary provided by Rolorc. For 2021, because of extensive medical costs, he has available tax credits that would reduce his tax payable by $9,500.

While Rolorc's 2021 taxable income before any salary or dividend payments is $185,000, large capital expenditures has left the company with only $89,000 in cash that is available for distribution.

Relevant information with respect to Robert's province of residence is as follows:

- In order to simplify calculations, assume that all of Robert's taxable income will be taxed at a combined federal/provincial rate of 24%.

- The provincial dividend tax credit is equal to 33% of the gross up on non-eligible dividends.

- The provincial corporate tax rate is 3% on income eligible for the small business deduction.

Required: Ignore the required CPP contributions and the Canada employment tax credit when answering Parts A to D.

A. Determine the after-tax amount of cash that Robert will retain if all of the company's cash is used to pay taxes and salary.

B. Determine the after-tax amount of cash that Robert will retain if the company pays the maximum possible dividend.

C. Can Robert improve his after-tax cash retention by using a combination of salary and dividends? Explain your conclusion.

D. If your answer to Part C is yes, determine the combination of salary and dividends that will produce the maximum after-tax cash retention for Robert. Calculate the amount of the after-tax cash retention.

CHAPTER 16

Rollovers under Section 85

Learning Objectives

After completing Chapter 16, you should be able to:

1. Describe the purpose of ITA 85(1) and the common situations in which it is used (Paragraph [P hereafter] 16-1 to 16-14).
2. Explain the general rules that are applicable to the persons participating in the rollover, including the type of property that is eligible for rollover treatment (P 16-15 to 16-22).
3. Describe the types of consideration that can be received and the importance of FMV and mismatches of value (P 16-23 to 16-29).
4. Describe the procedures required for making the election, including filing on time, when penalties could apply, and some important features of the T2057 election form (P 16-30 to 16-34).
5. Determine the acceptable range of elected amounts that can be used with respect to eligible property (P 16-35 to 16-40).
6. Apply the general rules that apply to all eligible property that determine the range of elected amounts that can be used (P 16-41 to 16-47).
7. Apply the detailed rules for determining elected amounts for eligible property that is accounts receivable, inventories, and non-depreciable capital property (P 16-48 to 16-61).
8. Describe the rules related to the transfer of non-depreciable capital property, including identifying superficial losses and their income tax consequences (P 16-62 to 16-70).
9. Explain the rules used for determining elected amounts for depreciable property, including options when depreciable properties are sold at the same time (P 16-71 to 16-75).
10. Explain the consequences to a rollover under ITA 85(1) when a sale of depreciable property to an affiliated person would result in a terminal loss (P 16-76 to 16-77).
11. Summarize the rules for determining the elected amount for all eligible property (P 16-78 and Figure 16-3).
12. Calculate the allocation of the elected amount to all consideration received on the sale of eligible property to a corporation (P 16-79 and 16-83).
13. Determine the tax cost of eligible property acquired by a corporation, including the impact of the AccII, ITA 85(5), and ITA 13(7)(e) (P 16-84 to 16-92).
14. Calculate the PUC of share consideration received, including where multiple classes of shares are issued (P 16-93 to 16-105).
15. Analyze and apply the rules of ITA 85(1) where a business carried on as a sole proprietorship is incorporated (P 16-106 to 16-120).

16. Explain the reasons for the gifting rule of ITA 85(1)(e.2), including the income tax consequences to the person responsible for the gift and the person who benefits from the gift. In addition, explain what changes in terms of the tax cost and PUC of consideration received (P 16-121 to 16-136).

17. Explain and calculate the income tax consequences when a shareholder receives too much consideration on a rollover transaction under ITA 85(1) and whether the result may be influenced by certain corporations (P 16-137 to 16-143).

18. Explain the purpose of ITA 84.1 and the standard type of tax planning to which it applies (P 16-144 to 16-148).

19. Calculate the income tax consequences when ITA 84.1 is applicable and determine the best way to minimize any income tax consequences (P 16-149 to 16-164).

20. Explain the purpose of ITA 55(2), the conditions necessary for its application, and the exceptions that limit or prevent its application (P 16-165 to 16-170).

21. Calculate the income tax consequences when ITA 55(2) applies and discuss the relevance of safe income and its impact (P 16-171 to 16-185).

Overview

16-1.   In Chapter 15 we discussed whether the incorporation of investments owned by an individual or the incorporation of a business carried on by an individual would result in any income tax savings. The analysis focused on the concept of integration, which looked to various provincial tax rates and dividend tax credits. The analysis then became a comparison of the after-tax cash available to the individual had they not incorporated versus the after-tax cash available once the income had been earned by a corporation, and the corporation distributed all of its after-tax income as dividends to the individual shareholder. In the discussion we assumed that the incorporation of investments and that of a business had taken place without any discussion of the underlying process.

16-2.   The incorporation of investments or a business of an individual first requires the creation of a corporation unless one already exists. When a corporation is incorporated under one of fourteen different corporate law jurisdictions within Canada (1 federal + 10 provincial + 3 territorial), the corporate law creates a legal entity that is given the same legal rights, powers, and privileges as a human being (see CBCA s. 15). This means that the corporation can purchase and sell property, enter into contracts, borrow money, carry on a business, and so on. This is the first step to incorporating property owned by an individual, as the process requires that property ownership change from the individual to the corporation.

16-3.   When an individual owns investments personally or carries on a business as a sole proprietor, the individual may wish to retain complete control of the corporation once the process is complete. This means that the corporation will have one sole shareholder who will be that one individual. The opportunity exists, however, to add other individuals, such as family members, as shareholders with the goal that the family may benefit from the success of the corporation as the investments increase in value and the business grows and profitability increases. While shareholders can be added at any time, it is often more convenient (and less costly) to include identifiable family members as shareholders from the beginning.

16-4.   Once a corporation has been created and the share structure and shareholders determined, the incorporation of property can take place. Assume, for example, that an individual owns investments that cost $70,000 a few years ago and that today are worth (i.e., fair market value [FMV]) $100,000. If the individual wishes to incorporate the investments and change the ownership, a sale of the investments to the corporation is required. The individual will give up the investments for payment by the corporation equal to the value of the investments. This is the essence of a legal contract.

16-5.   The sale should be undertaken in the same manner as if the investments or any other property were being sold to an arm's-length person. This is of particular concern since some might suggest that the individual and her wholly owned corporation are really one and the same since the individual makes all the decisions on behalf of the corporation. The law, however, views this quite differently, seeing two separate and distinct legal entities—the individual and the corporation. Due to the relationship between the two, some courts have commented that the level of formality required in documenting and evidencing the sale transaction should be much more thorough. As a result, in practice, it is important to be vigilant and ensure that all legal steps are taken and properly documented in support of any transaction between a controlling shareholder and the corporation.

16-6.   From an income tax perspective, there is a tax principle that the sale of any property between two legal entities must occur at FMV irrespective of whether the parties to the sale are non-arm's length or not. Continuing with our example, this would imply that the individual would sell the investments for their FMV of $100,000 and the corporation would acquire the investments at that same amount. Initially this would mean that the individual would realize a capital gain of $30,000 (POD $100,000- ACB $70,000) and the cost, or adjusted cost base (ACB), of the investments to the corporation would be $100,000. Any investment income would belong to the corporation as owner of the investments, and a subsequent sale by the company would result in either a capital gain or capital loss, depending on the value of the investments at that time.

16-7.   From the purchaser's perspective, the corporation must pay $100,000 to purchase the investments. When a new corporation is created the corporation will not have access to third-party financing, such as a bank, and the only property it will own will be cash or property provided by any person when the corporation issued its shares to that person. This likely means that the corporation has minimal cash and nothing else. This raises the question of how that corporation can then purchase investments from an individual or acquire all of the property (including goodwill) necessary to carry on a business formerly carried on by an individual as a sole proprietor. The answer is that a newly created corporation will pay for the purchase by either issuing its own shares, issuing a promissory note, or a combination of the two. A promissory note is a legal obligation, often in writing, that is a promise to pay a certain amount, with or without interest, at some specified date or on demand. In our example in Paragraph 16-4, the corporation could have paid for the investments by (1) issuing shares with legal capital of $100,000, which the company would add to its stated capital account (paid-up capital [PUC] for income tax purposes); (2) issue a promissory note for $100,000; or (3) some combination of the two, such as a $70,000 promissory note plus issuing shares with a legal capital of $30,000.

16-8.   From a legal perspective all of the pieces are in place: (1) the creation of a corporation, (2) a contract for the sale of property owned by the individual to the corporation at a price equal to the FMV of the property, and (3) as part of the contract, the payment by the corporation for the individual's property. The payment by the corporation is referred to as the "consideration" for the property acquired. For ITA purposes, consideration is broken down into two parts: share consideration and non-share consideration. Share consideration means shares of the corporate purchaser issued by the corporation as payment for the property acquired. Non-share consideration (NSC) means any other form of payment. Note that NSC is frequently referred to as "boot" among lawyers and certain other professionals. In the third alternative payment mentioned in Paragraph 16-7, there would be share consideration of $30,000 and NSC of $70,000.

16-9.   If we apply the third alternative payment that includes $30,000 in shares and $70,000 as NSC, we have all of the necessary details to determine the income tax implications of a sale of investments for $100,000 between the individual and the corporation.

   Individual (Seller)   (1) A disposition of investments for $100,000 resulting in a capital gain of $30,000 and a taxable capital gain of $15,000 [(50%)($30,000)], (2) the promissory note has an ACB of $70,000, (3) the cost and ACB of the shares would be $30,000, and (4) the PUC of the shares issued would be $30,000.

   Corporation (Purchaser)   (1) A purchase of investments for $100,000, which equals the cost and ACB of the investments and (2) an addition of $30,000 to the legal capital of the corporations' shares, which is the starting point for determining the PUC of the class of shares. From a balance sheet perspective there would be an asset of $100,000 for the investments, a liability of $70,000 for the promissory note, and share capital of $30,000.

The ITA 85 Impact

16-10.   In the investment sale example it is clear that the basic rules of the ITA together with income tax principles would appear to discourage the incorporation of any property owned by individuals. In the example, a disposition at FMV requires the individual to pay income tax on a $15,000 taxable capital gain even though the individual did not receive any additional cash as a result of the sale. ITA 85(1) is specifically designed to eliminate any immediate income tax consequences associated with the incorporation of property owned by an individual and others and therefore facilitate the incorporation of property and businesses.

16-11.   ITA 85(1) is referred to as a "rollover," which is a word not used in the ITA but consistently used in practice. The word means that the income tax consequences of a disposition of property at FMV are passed, or rolled over, from a person (i.e., the individual) to a corporation. In this chapter we will discuss the specific details of the rules of ITA 85(1) together with some other important related ITA provisions.

16-12.   There are five important objectives, listed in Figure 16-1, to keep in mind when learning about ITA 85(1). The first and most important is that ITA 85(1) overrides the general FMV rule that would result in immediate income tax consequences of incorporating property owned by an individual. The rollover provides flexibility, unlike any of the other many rollovers found within the ITA. In addition, it is an essential tool when it comes to many common types of income tax planning. Understanding the basic application of this rollover is essential to any accounting and income tax practice.

16-13.   The power of the rollover lies in its flexibility, which allows the individual and corporation to choose or "elect" the amount of the sale price within a certain range. In our example, the initial range is between the ACB of the investments of $70,000 and the FMV of the investments of $100,000. This range can be reset if NSC is between those two amount. If, for example, the corporation paid for the investments by issuing a promissory note of $83,000 and shares of $17,000, the allowable range would change to $83,000 to $100,000 because the NSC falls within the initial $70,000 to $100,000. Returning to the original consideration of $70,000 and $30,000, the income tax consequences indicated in Paragraph 16-9 would be revised as follows if $70,000 was chosen as the elected amount:

Individual (Seller)   (1) A disposition of investments for $70,000 resulting in no capital gain, (2) the promissory note has a cost and therefore an ACB of $70,000, (3) the cost and therefore the ACB of the shares would be nil, and (4) the PUC of the shares issued would also be nil.

Figure 16-1
ITA 85(1) Objectives

1.   Overrides FMV rule

2.   Determines sale POD to the individual

3.   Determines the purchase cost (tax cost) to the corporation

4.   Determines the tax cost of consideration received by the individual as payment from the corporation

5.   Determines the PUC of share consideration received by the individual as payment from the coporation

---

Corporation (Purchaser)   (1) A purchase of investments for $70,000, which equals the cost and ACB of the investments and (2) an addition of $30,000 to the legal capital of the corporation's shares, which is the starting point for determining the PUC of the class of shares and a reduction of PUC determined under the ITA of $30,000. In effect, legal capital would be $30,000 but the PUC would be nil.

An explanation as to how these amounts are determined will be provided in this chapter.

Common Uses for ITA 85(1)

16-14.   ITA 85(1) allows property to pass from an individual to a corporation without immediate income tax consequences. This defers the realization of any accrued gains or income. It is the ability to transfer property that sets the stage for certain income tax planning. The most common uses of ITA 85(1) are the following:

- The incorporation of a business
- To pass the future economic growth of a corporation to family members through what is referred to as an estate freeze
- To crystallize capital gains on shares for capital gains deduction purposes
- To insert a holding corporation
- To creditor-proof a corporation by moving property susceptible to creditor claims from one company to another
- To use the losses in one company against income in another company as long as the corporations are affiliated
- To remove property of a corporation that affects the ability of the shares to qualify for the capital gains deduction; this is referred to as a purification transaction

General Conditions — ITA 85(1)

Overview

16-15.   All rollovers contain conditions that generally serve to restrict the use of the rollover to a narrow set of circumstances. ITA 85(1), while much broader than other rollovers, provides limitations through a number of conditions that effectively narrow its application somewhat. The conditions identify acceptable purchasers and sellers to a transaction, the type of property that is eligible, the type of consideration that must be received by the seller, and the formalized election process, including timelines and penalties when filings are not made on time. Once the conditions are met the rollover sets out a number of overlapping provisions that determine the dollar amounts that can be elected and the consequences of the election to both parties.

Seller and Purchaser (Transferor and Transferee)

16-16.   The word "transferor" is used in the election form to identify the person who wishes to incorporate property owned by that person. In our investment example, that person would be the individual seller. The "transferee" is also used in the election form to identify the corporation that is purchasing the property of the transferor. The two words are not used in the ITA except sparingly in ITA 85(4). Instead the predominant words are "taxpayer," which is used to identify the seller, and "corporation" to identify the corporate purchaser. Since the words "transferor" and "transferee" are used extensively in the prescribed form T2057, we will continue to use those words throughout the remainder of the chapter. Our main focus will be on individuals incorporating property they own to a corporation that is a CCPC.

16-17.   The transferor must be a taxpayer, meaning an entity recognized or treated in the ITA as a legal entity. These include individuals, trusts, estates, or other corporation. Partnerships are not legal entities and can therefore not use ITA 85(1), but they can take advantage of a similar rollover specifically designed for partnerships, which is found in ITA 85(2).

16-18.   The transferee must be a "taxable Canadian corporation," which is defined in ITA 89(1) as a corporation that is resident in Canada, incorporated in Canada, and not exempt from Part I tax. These corporate conditions are designed to ensure that Canada can actually impose income tax on the corporation when it subsequently disposes of property acquired through a rollover under ITA 85(1).

Eligible Property—ITA 85(1.1)

16-19.   ITA 85(1) only allows property of a taxpayer to use the rollover if the property meets the definition of "eligible property." The most common types of eligible property include the following:

- Both depreciable and non-depreciable capital property, except real property (e.g., land and buildings) that is owned by non-residents
- Canadian resource property
- Foreign resource property
- Inventory, other than real property inventory
- Any property owned by a non-resident person and used in a business carried in Canada by that non-resident person

16-20.   The exclusion for real property owned by non-residents reflects the fact that this type of property is taxable Canadian property and any capital gains on a disposition would be subject to Canadian income tax. The exclusion is designed to prevent a non-resident who owns Canadian real estate from selling the property to a corporation, using ITA 85(1) to avoid any immediate income tax consequences, and subsequently selling any shares received as consideration from the corporation. The transaction can be structured so that the shares received would not be subject to Canadian income tax were they to be sold at a gain. In effect, this type of planning would open the door to allowing a non-resident to substitute one type of property (e.g., real estate) for another (e.g., shares) to avoid paying Canadian income tax. If, however, the non-resident owns real property that is used in a business in Canada the rollover can be used, but any shares received as consideration are deemed by ITA 85(1)(i) to be taxable Canadian property to ensure that Canada can subject any gain on the shares to Canadian income tax.

16-21.   The second exception is Canadian-resident-owned real property that is inventory. An example would be a land developer or a construction company that builds and sells residential homes. Any gains on the sale of properties would be fully taxable business income and not capital gains. The reason for the exception is to prevent taxpayers from converting a fully taxable business profit to a one-half taxable capital gain by again substituting the real property inventory for shares of a corporation.

16-22.   The real property inventory exception can prove to be problematic if real property of an individual is incorporated on the understanding it is capital property. If CRA were to subsequently challenge the validity of the ITA 85(1) election on the basis that the real property was inventory and therefore not eligible property, the repercussions would be considerable. The ITA 85(1) election would be invalid, and without rollover protection the real property would be considered to have been sold for FMV at fully taxable business income. The income tax liability would arise in the year of the sale, resulting in interest charges and possible penalties.

Consideration (Share and Non-Share)

16-23.   When an individual sells property to a corporation and elects with that company to use the rollover there are a few important points to keep in mind. The first is that technically ITA 85(1) applies separately to each property being sold. The second point is that the consideration paid by the corporation for each property must include shares (i.e., share consideration as opposed to NSC). The ITA does not dictate the type or quantity of shares that must be issued as payment. As a result, the position of the CRA is that a part of a share counts as consideration for each eligible property. This is important where a business is incorporated and multiple properties (including goodwill) are sold at the same time. If there are 30 different business properties being sold to the corporation, then only one share need be issued for all of the properties. If shares are not issued, then ITA 85(1) is invalid and the sale, having lost the rollover protection, occurs at FMV.

16-24. The next important point is that it is best to use shares the FMV of which is readily determinable. While ITA 85(1) refers to both common and preferred shares, in practice it is rare to see common shares used because of the difficulty in establishing their value at any point in time. Instead fixed value preferred shares are used. Fixed value preferred shares generally refer to shares that are redeemable at the option of the shareholder or retractable at the option of the corporation for a fixed dollar amount that includes any cumulative dividends.

16-25. An additional point involves the assumption of transferor liabilities by a corporation. There are a few concerns that must be addressed. The first is that if there exists a liability attached to a specific property, such as a mortgage on a home, the individual owner may be prevented from selling the property to anyone, let alone a corporation, without the consent of the creditor or lender. This would mean that an individual who declares he is transferring a property to a corporation and then receives payment from the corporation would be potentially liable to ITA 15(1) since he did not legally transfer anything to the corporation but removed value to his benefit.

16-26. A second concern about the assumption of liabilities is that it may prevent the ability to sell eligible property to a corporation without income tax consequences. If, for example, an individual owns land with a FMV of $600,000 and an ACB of $240,000 and the individual borrowed against the land a year ago, the amount owing is $500,000. ITA 85(1) would establish an initial range between $240,000 and $600,000. The assumption of the borrowing (which generally cannot be separated from the property) represents $500,000 of NSC and would reset in a range from $500,000 to $600,000. As a result, the lowest possible elected amount would be $500,000, which would result in a $260,000 capital gain. The CRA will allow assumed debt to be allocated among other properties where a taxpayer sells multiple properties to a corporation. If an individual is only willing to use ITA 85(1) if there is no income tax, then caution should be exercised where debt is assumed as a result of the sale of property.

16-27. Another point is that it is important that there be no mismatches of value. This means that when a property is sold by an individual to a corporation that the FMV of the property sold matches the FMV of the consideration (share plus NSC) paid by the corporation. If the shareholder receives FMV consideration that exceeds the FMV of the property sold, the shareholder would be subject to income tax for the excess. If, for example, an individual shareholder sold property to the corporation that was valued at $100,000 but received $160,000 in consideration from the corporation, there would be a $60,000 difference that would be required to be included in the individual's income, generally as a shareholder appropriation through ITA 15(1), which was discussed in Chapter 15.

16-28. If the individual shareholder received only $60,000 in consideration for the $100,000 property sold to the corporation, there would generally only be income tax consequences of leaving the $40,000 excess value in the company if there were other shareholders who at the time were related to the individual transferor and benefitted as a result. This issue is referred to as a "gifting problem" and will be discussed later in this chapter.

16-29. Given that mismatches in value can have serious income tax implications it is critical to attempt to manage the valuation risk. The risk can be managed through what is referred to as a "price adjustment clause" (see CRA Folio S4-F3-C1, "Price Adjustment Clauses"). A price adjustment clause (PAC) is a clause added to a written purchase and sale agreement between the individual and the corporation (transferor and transferee) that generally reads that everything was done to determine the FMV of the property sold and the consideration paid and that if the CRA subsequently discovers there is a mismatch the parties to the transaction will revise the amounts to reflect the agreed upon FMV. If this is properly done there will be no income tax consequences as a result of the FMV mismatch. In general, the CRA requires that the PAC reflects a bona fide intention to determine FMV, which is determined on a case-by-case basis. The best way to prove a bona fide intent is to hire valuators licensed to value the specific type of property. The CRA has challenged the validity of PACs on the basis that there was no true intent to determine FMV. A PAC is important when controlling shareholders of a corporation or their family members are selling property to the corporation. The CRA does not normally challenge FMV between arm's-length persons.

The Election

16-30.   The transferor and the transferee must jointly elect in prescribed form to apply ITA 85(1) to a particular disposition of property. This prescribed form is T2057 (transfers from individuals, trusts, and corporations). The due date for filing the form is the earliest of the date that the individual and corporation are required to file their annual income tax return for the taxation year in which the disposition occurred. If, for example, an individual with a June 15 filing date sells property on October 10, 2021, to a corporation with a taxation year end of August 31, the date for filing the election would be June 15, 2022, the filing date for the 2021 tax return of the individual. Since the property disposition occurred in the taxation year of the corporation, which ends August 31, 2022, the filing date for the 2022 taxation year of the corporation would have been six months later, or February 28, 2023.

16-31.   A valid election may be filed up to three years late after the filing date as long as a penalty accompanies the late election (ITA 85(7)). The maximum penalty is $100 a month to a maximum of $8,000 (ITA 85(8)). Elections may also be late filed beyond three years but only with the express permission of the CRA, which is not regularly granted (ITA 85(7.1)). In addition, if an election is filed with missing information the election will be considered invalid and treated as if it were never filed. An amended or revised election can be filed to fix the problem, but it also requires approval by the CRA with payments of the same penalties (ITA 85(7.1)).

16-32.   Common errors in completing the T2057 often relate to accountants adding all of the balance sheet assets to the form. The problem, however, is that the ITA focus is on the legal concept of property, which does not always match accounting assets. For example, while cash and prepaid amounts are valid assets for accounting purposes, neither are property for ITA 85(1) purposes. In addition, goodwill may be present but not shown as an asset on the financial statements. Since a business cannot be separated from any existing goodwill, forgetting to add goodwill to the form will create difficulties. Other common errors include overlooking the assumption of liabilities of the transferor.

16-33.   As a final point, the T2057 form contains eight general questions that require a yes or no answer. Certain responses to the questions can lead to queries by the CRA that can result in a tax audit that could deny the rollover. For example, question 1 asks if there is a written agreement in respect of the property sold to the corporation. The relevance depends on the type of property. If the property is real property, a written agreement would be expected and in many cases required to evidence the sale. Answering "no" to the question will often flag the election for queries. The second question ask whether there is a PAC. If the property sold is not easily valued, one would expect such a clause to exist within a written agreement. Again, answering "no" will increase the likelihood of queries by the CRA.

16-34.   There are many benefits associated with the availability of a rollover election under ITA 85(1), but there are also many formalities that must be respected. It is important to ensure that the property dispositions are within the rules to avoid any subsequent difficulties.

The Elected Amount

Importance

16-35.   One of the most significant features of ITA 85(1) is that it provides for the transfer of eligible property to a corporation at amounts that are jointly elected by the transferor and transferee. The ability to determine an acceptable election amount requires information, specifically the FMV of the eligible property to be sold to the corporation and its tax cost characteristics, such as cost for inventory, capital cost for depreciable property, UCC for depreciable property of a class, and ACB for non-depreciable capital property. As indicated in Figure 16-1, ITA 85(1) establishes four important amounts, all of which begin with the elected amount:

Transferor   The deemed proceeds of disposition (POD) for the eligible property sold

Transferor   The cost, ACB, or capital cost of all consideration received as payment from the corporation

Transferor   The PUC of the share consideration received as payment from the corporation

Transferee   The tax cost (e.g., cost, ACB, capital cost, and UCC) of the eligible property purchased by the corporation

Electing to Avoid Accrued Gains

16-36.   Choosing an elected amount for eligible property with accrued but unrealized gains is relatively straightforward as long as the FMV of the property and its tax cost, such as ACB, are known with certainty. As mentioned in Paragraph 16-13, the rules allow an initial elective range between the ACB and FMV of the eligible property to be sold where the property is non-depreciable capital property, such as investments and land that is not inventory. NSC, however, can reset the range if its FMV falls within that initial range. If the goal is to avoid paying any income tax on the sale of the property to a corporation, then the elected amount would be set at the ACB of the property to be sold. In addition, if an individual wished to recover cash as quickly as possible it would be recommended that they maximize the NSC (promissory note) by limiting it to that same elected amount and taking any additional consideration up to the FMV of the property sold as share consideration. A simple example will serve to illustrate this concept.

EXAMPLE   Mr. Thompson owns land that is capital property with a FMV of $330,000 and an ACB of $200,000. He wishes to sell the land to a corporation in which he is the controlling shareholder. He wants to avoid any income tax on the sale but also wants to recover cash from the company as quickly as possible, also without any income tax consequences.

ANALYSIS   The initial range of acceptable elected amounts for this property is between the ACB of $200,000 and the FMV of $330,000. If Mr. Thompson wishes to avoid any income tax on the sale of the land, a joint election will be filed under ITA 85(1) to elect the sale price as $200,000. As a result, there is no capital gain since the deemed POD of $200,000 (the elected amount) does not exceed the ACB of the same amount. This is the first part of the analysis.

The second part of the analysis relates to the consideration to be paid by the corporation for the property. To avoid mismatches of FMV (see Paragraphs 16-27 to 16-29) it is important that the FMV of the consideration match the FMV of the property sold to the corporation. In this example, this means that the corporation must provide $330,000 in consideration.

The third step is to determine the composition of the consideration to be paid by the corporation as between share and non-share consideration (NSC). If Mr. Thompson wishes to recover cash from the corporation as quickly as possible and without any income tax consequences, then NSC must be maximized. This means limiting the NSC to the elected amount and taking any difference as share consideration. In this example, this would mean that the corporation will provide a $200,000 promissory note and shares with a legal capital of $130,000.

RESULT   The result of selecting an elected amount of $200,000 with a promissory note of $200,000 and share consideration of $130,000 can be described as follows:

Transferor   The deemed POD is $200,000 to Mr. Thompson; no capital gain.

Transferor   The cost or ACB of the promissory note to Mr. Thompson is $200,000 and the ACB of the shares is nil.

Transferor   The PUC of the share consideration received as payment from the corporation is nil.

Transferee   The cost and ACB of the land to the corporation is $200,000.

If in 2022 the company pays $50,000 of the promissory note, there will be no income tax consequences to Mr. Thompson since in effect he is simply recovering part of the tax cost of $200,000. If, however, the company redeemed $50,000 of the shares, Mr. Thompson would be considered to have received a deemed dividend of $50,000 as a result of ITA 84(3), which would result in the payment of income tax. In conclusion, ITA 85(1) has been used to satisfy the objectives of the sale of the land to the corporation—no income tax on the sale and no income tax on the repayment of the promissory note. You will note that this strategy effectively allows an individual to receive cash from the corporation up to the ACB of the property sold without any income tax consequences. This is particularly effective when incorporating a business.

Electing Other Amounts

16-37.   The use of a rollover under ITA 85(1) would likely lead many to conclude that the real advantage of these rollovers is to defer any income tax on the sale of eligible property from tax-payers to a corporation. This implies that the tax cost of the property to be sold is almost always chosen as the elected amount, as illustrated in the example in Paragraph 16-36. This is not always the case, however, and is dependent on the facts, including the reason behind the use of the rollover.

16-38.   In Paragraph 16-14 we described some common uses for ITA 85(1). One of the uses is what is referred to as a "crystallization" transaction. This transaction is undertaken by an individual who wishes to use her capital gains deduction immediately for a number of reasons, including estate planning purposes. For example, assume that an individual has used the capital gains deduction extensively throughout her life. In 2021 she has $110,000 of capital gains deduction remaining. The individual owns shares that qualify for the capital gains deduction that have an ACB of $90,000 and a FMV of $490,000. The individual wishes to use her remaining capital gains deduction, which would require selling the shares. A sale to an arm's-length person for $490,000 would result in a capital gain of $400,000. The use of the capital gains deduction of $110,000 would reduce the capital gain to $290,000 with half of it, or $145,000, being subject to income tax as a taxable capital gain. The individual, however, does not really want to sell the shares in the sense that the individual no longer controls the shares.

16-39.   The strategy is to incorporate a new company and to sell those shares to the new company using ITA 85(1) to accomplish this goal. The result is an elected amount of $200,000, which results in a capital gain of $110,000 (deemed POD $200,000- ACB $90,000), which is protected with the capital gains deduction of $110,000, avoiding any income tax on the sale. The new corporation pays for the shares of the individual with shares of its own that have legal capital of $490,000. The result is that the individual now owns different shares with the same $490,000 FMV but with an ACB of $200,000 instead of $90,000. The economic effect is that the strategy has enabled the individual to own shares the ACB of which has increased because of the use of the capital gains deduction. This strategy is discussed further in this chapter under the heading "Dividend/Surplus Stripping—ITA 84.1."

16-40.   The brief illustration of a crystallization transaction was to demonstrate that the use of ITA 85(1) does not always result in an elected amount that is equal to the tax cost of eligible property sold to a corporation. Other reasons for electing excessive amounts that result in gains, recapture, or other income is the existence of net capital and non-capital losses that can be used by the transferor to offset the additional income or capital gains. In addition, the assumption of liabilities (see Paragraphs 16-25 and 16-26) may automatically result in an elected amount that exceeds the tax cost of the eligible property.

The Elected Amount—The Detailed Rules

Rules Applicable to All Eligible Property

Overview

16-41.   There are multiple provisions in ITA 85(1), but there are three principal rules that create the framework for the main objectives of this rollover, including establishing the initial range of acceptable elected amounts. These three general rules are briefly described in the following paragraphs.

Proceeds and Cost—ITA 85(1)(a)

16-42.   ITA 85(1)(a) establishes the first rule. The elected amount or deemed elected amount becomes the deemed POD to the transferor and the deemed cost of the eligible property to the corporation. The word "deemed" is used to recognize that without a rollover the POD to the seller and tax cost to the purchaser would be determined using FMV, as described in the example in Paragraph 16-9. A deemed elected amount can occur when the CRA reviews the election form T2057. If, for example, the form indicates that the elected amount is the ACB of the eligible property sold to the corporation but it is determined that the FMV of the NSC is higher than the initial elected amount, then the elected amount will change and become the new or deemed elected amount.

Non-Share Consideration (NSC) or Boot—ITA 85(1)(b)

16-43.   The term "boot" is commonly used to refer to the NSC paid by the corporation to acquire the eligible property. Common examples of NSC include cash paid by the corporation, promissory notes issued by the corporation, and the assumption of liabilities of the transferor. In our earlier examples our initial focus was on a newly created corporation that issued promissory notes as payment for eligible property given that it did not have sufficient cash to make payment.

16.44.   ITA 85(1)(b) establishes the rule that if the elected amount agreed upon is less than the FMV of the NSC that the elected amount is deemed to be equal to the FMV of that consideration. This means that if the elected amount of eligible property with accrued gains that has been chosen is equal to the tax cost of the eligible property but the FMV of NSC exceeds that amount, then the elected amount changes. We have expressed this legislative rule as resetting the accepted range where the FMV of NSC falls within that initial range.

Fair Market Value (FMV)—ITA 85(1)(c)

16-45.   The initial accepted range for ITA 85(1) purposes for eligible property with accrued gains is between the tax cost and the FMV. The FMV maximum is legislated by ITA 85(1)(c).

Summary

16-46.   These general rules apply to all eligible property sold to a corporation by a taxpayer where ITA 85(1) has been used to override the general FMV tax principle.

Ceiling (Maximum) Elected Amount   FMV of the eligible property sold to the corporation.

Floor (Minimum) Elected Amount   The lowest amount or floor that can be chosen will be equal to the greater of:
- the FMV of the NSC paid by the corporation for the eligible property; or
- the tax cost of the eligible property.

16-47.   The tax cost of eligible property is dependent on the classification of the property for income tax purposes. These differences will be discussed in the following paragraphs.

Accounts Receivable—ITA 22

16-48.   Accounts receivables are non-depreciable capital property to most businesses. When a business is sold, any gains or losses on the sale of accounts receivables are treated as capital gains or capital losses. The purchaser would not have the benefit of being able to claim any doubtful debt reserve or bad debt deduction with respect to the purchased receivables since the ITA restricts their use to the original owner of the receivables. ITA 22 is a joint elective provision between the seller and buyer of a business that treats the receivables on income account. This means that if the seller experiences a loss it would be fully deductible instead of being treated as a capital loss. The purchaser would have to include in income an amount equal to the deductible loss to the seller. In addition, the purchaser would be permitted to claim doubtful debt reserves and a bed debt deduction as if they were the original owner of the receivables.

16-49.   ITA 22 only applies if all or substantially all of the property (more than 90%) used in carrying on a business has been sold to a purchaser who will continue to carry on that business. The incorporation of a business results in the sale of all or substantially all business properties to a corporation that will continue that business. The result is that the elective option of ITA 22 is available to the individual and corporation. ITA 22 is discussed in detail in Chapter 6.

16-50.   While accounts receivable are eligible property for the purposes of ITA 85(1), both ITA 22 and ITA 85(1) cannot be used simultaneously. An election under ITA 22 precludes an election under ITA 85(1). ITA 85(1) would allow accounts receivables to be elected to be sold at their tax cost or cost amount, which is generally equal to the amount owing. A sale of receivables using the ITA 22 joint election requires a sale at FMV since the election is not a rollover provision.

Inventories and Non-Depreciable Capital Property—ITA 85(1)(c.1)

16-51.   When a business is incorporated, the seller both disposes of the business and ceases to carry on the business. When existing inventory is sold in bulk to a purchaser there is an argument that the inventory becomes a capital disposition, which would mean any income or loss would be a capital gain or a capital loss. To prevent that occurrence, ITA 23(1) clarifies that the sale of the inventory will be treated as if it were sold in the ordinary course of carrying on the business. This means that any gain or loss will be treated as contributing to business income or a business loss. This is not an elective provision and applies automatically.

16-52.   When non-depreciable capital property is sold and there is an accrued gain, the initial allowable elected range is between the ACB and the FMV of the eligible property. If the NSC is greater than the ACB and less than the FMV, the FMV of the NSC becomes the new minimum amount, resetting the range as previously discussed.

16-53.   If there is an accrued loss where the ACB of the property is greater than its FMV there is no minimum and maximum range and the elected amount must be the FMV of the eligible property. As a result, there is no advantage to using ITA 85(1) since the income tax consequences would be the same as a sale to the corporation at FMV without a rollover.

16-54.   One of the difficulties in the many rules of ITA 85(1) that determine acceptable elected amounts is that the rules work with the elected amount first chosen by a taxpayer and a corporation. The rules then measure the acceptability of the elected amounts and adjust them accordingly.

EXAMPLE   An individual sells investments to a corporation of which he is a sole shareholder. The FMV of the investments is $100, the ACB $20, and the FMV of the NSC is $80. A T2057 is filed electing an amount of $15.

ANALYSIS   Intuitively we know that the acceptable range should be between $80 and $100, therefore the elected amount of $15 is not valid. There are three provisions necessary to adjust the elected amount chosen:

ITA 85(1)(b) is the first of the three provisions necessary to fix this problem. The rule asks if the elected amount chosen in the election ($15) is less than the FMV of the NSC of $80. Clearly the answer is yes. ITA 85(1)(b) deems the elected amount to be $80 (the FMV of the NSC).

ITA 85(1)(c.1) is next since it applies to non-depreciable capital property. This rule asks whether the elected amount chosen in the election ($15) is less than the least of the FMV ($100) and tax cost ($20) of the investments. In this case the least of the FMV and tax cost of the investments is the $20 ACB. The elected amount chosen was less than that amount at $15. As a result, ITA 85(1)(c.1) deems the elected amount to be $20.

The last provision is ITA 85(1)(e.3), which applies where two rules such as ITA 85(1)(b) and (c.1) produce different results. In other words, ITA 85(1)(e.3) is a tie-breaker rule. It deems the elected amount to be the greater of (1) the FMV of the NSC, or $80, and (2) the lesser of the tax cost of the investments of $20 and the FMV of the investments of $100. The second component is therefore $20. The greater of #1 of $80 and #2 of $20 is $80, which becomes the deemed elected amount.

16-55. The above analysis serves as a valuable reminder that working through the many provisions of ITA 85(1) can, at times, be a tedious exercise and not always necessary. It is much more important to be aware of how acceptable ranges are determined for different types of eligible property whether there are accrued gains or accrued losses. This knowledge will allow proper planning in terms of choosing the optimum amount of NSC.

16-56. In summary, with respect to inventory and non-depreciable capital property the rules for determining an elected amount are (1) where there is an accrued gain the range is between the tax cost and the FMV of the eligible property but the FMV of any NSC can reset that range and (2) if there is an accrued loss then there is no acceptable range and the eligible property must be elected at its FMV only. Part of the underlying tax policy is that these rules are written to prevent taxpayers from claiming artificial gains and artificial losses.

16-57. These rules can be illustrated using the three examples that follow:

	Example 1	Example 2	Example 3
FMV of eligible property	$15,000	$10,000	$20,000
FMV of eligible property	12,000	12,000	14,000
FMV of NSC (boot)	5,000	5,000	15,000

16-58. In Example 1, the acceptable range is between $12,000 and $15,000. Since the $5,000 NSC is not between these amounts the range remains at $12,000 to $15,000. Note that the individual could have taken an additional $7,000 in NSC without changing the range.

16-59. In Example 2, there is an accrued loss, which means that the only elected amount is the FMV of $10,000. If the eligible property were inventories, the result would be a $2,000 loss, which would decrease business profits or increase a business loss. If the eligible property were non-depreciable capital property, the result would be an allowable capital loss of $1,000 [(1/2)(POD $10,000 - ACB $12,000)]. The next section of this chapter will discuss some additional income tax implications when capital losses occur.

16-60. In Example 3, applying the general concept results in an elected amount between $14,000 and $20,000, but the FMV of the NSC resets the lower $14,000 limit to $15,000, resulting in an acceptable range of $15,000 to $20,000. If this eligible property were inventory, an election at the lowest amount of $15,000 would result in additional business income of $1,000 ($15,000 - $14,000). If the election were made with respect to eligible property (i.e., non-depreciable capital property), the result will be a taxable capital gain of $500 [(1/2)($15,000 - $14,000)].

16-61. If the goal is to avoid any immediate income tax on the sale of eligible property, the elected amount for property with accrued gains must be equal to the tax cost of that eligible property. This also means making certain that the FMV of NSC does not exceed that same tax cost so as to reset the acceptable range. Achieving this result in Example 3 would require limiting the FMV of the NSC to $14,000.

Exercise 16-1

Subject: Elected Amount for Non-Depreciable Capital Property

Jean Doan carries on a business as a sole proprietor. The tax cost of the inventory is $140,000 and the FMV is $125,000. In addition, he owns land that is capital property. The ACB of the land is $110,000 and the FMV $350,000. He intends to incorporate the inventory and land within a new corporation of which he will be the sole shareholder. As payment for the sale of these properties to the corporation he wants to receive $275,000 in promissory notes and $200,000 in shares. If he uses ITA 85(1), what are possible ranges for the elected amount for the two properties? Assume he elects the lowest possible elected amount in each case. What are the income tax consequences for Mr. Doan?

Solutions to Exercises are available in the Study Guide.

Losses on Non-Depreciable Capital Property

General Rules

16-62.   The special rules described in the following material apply only to non-depreciable capital property, which is generally limited to investment-type property such as land, shares, bonds, and ownership interests in partnerships and trusts, such as mutual funds.

16-63.   When non-depreciable capital property with an accrued loss is sold, a capital loss is realized. This can occur for any type of disposition regardless of whether a rollover is used. In the second example of Paragraph 16-57, we saw that a capital loss was realized using ITA 85(1) but that same result would have occurred without the use of ITA 85(1). In other words, the rule that potentially impacts capital losses is not limited to dispositions elected under ITA 85(1).

16-64.   When a capital loss is realized there is a series of rules in the ITA, generally referred to as "stop loss" rules, that deny the capital loss to the seller. These rules, however, only apply to dispositions within an affiliated group of persons. An affiliated group would mean between spouses, common-law partners, or an individual and a corporation controlled by that individual. A sale by an individual to one of these persons is considered to have occurred within an affiliated group, essentially meaning that the individual maintains some control and benefit from the property even though she technically no longer owns the property. The expression is "affiliated persons," which is defined in ITA 251.1.

16-65.   The provision that denies the capital loss to an individual seller is ITA 40(2)(g), which reads that the capital loss of an individual, to the extent that it is a "superficial loss," is deemed to be nil. A superficial loss is defined in ITA 54 (Subdivision c, which provides the rules for capital gains and capital losses) as follows:

> **"[S]uperficial loss"** of a taxpayer means the taxpayer's loss from the disposition of a particular property where
>
> (a)   during the period that begins 30 days before and ends 30 days after the disposition, the taxpayer or a person affiliated with the taxpayer acquires a property (in this definition referred to as the "substituted property") that is, or is identical to, the particular property, and
>
> (b)   at the end of that period, the taxpayer or a person affiliated with the taxpayer owns or had a right to acquire the substituted property.

16-66.   There are two types of superficial loss rules—one for individuals and another for corporations, partnerships, and trusts. Both sets of rules deny the capital loss to the seller. Our focus, however, will be on individuals. The superficial loss rules apply to an individual if the answers to the following three questions are yes:

1. Has an individual sold non-depreciable capital property that has resulted in a capital loss?

2. Has the individual or someone affiliated with the individual acquired the same or identical property in the 61-day period that begins 30 days before the day of the sale and ends 30 days after the day of sale?

3. On the last day of the 61-day period, does the individual or someone affiliated with the individual own the same or identical property?

Turning to Example 2 of Paragraph 16-57, there is an individual selling non-depreciable capital property with an accrued loss to a controlled corporation. If we assume that the company owns the property for two years, then the answers to all three questions is yes and the capital loss is a superficial loss, which is denied to the individual. The remaining income tax consequences are discussed in the following paragraphs.

Affiliated Persons—ITA 251.1

16-67.   The expression "affiliated person" is contained in a lengthy definition found in ITA 251.1(1). Some of the more important parts of that definition are as follows:

A. An individual is affiliated to another individual only if that individual is his or her spouse or common-law partner.

B. A corporation is affiliated with:
   1. a person who controls the corporation (control means both legal and defacto control);
   2. each member of an affiliated group of persons who controls the corporation (an affiliated group is a group where each member of the group is affiliated with each other. An example would be a corporation where spouses or common-law partners each own 50% of the voting shares); and
   3. the spouse or common-law partner of a person listed in (1) or (2) (this would mean that if one spouse or common-law partner controls a corporation the other spouse or common-law partner is automatically considered to be affiliated with that company).

C. Two corporations are affiliated if:
   1. each corporation is controlled by a person, and the person by whom one corporation is controlled is affiliated with the person by whom the other corporation is controlled (this would mean that if one corporation is controlled by one spouse and a second corporation controlled by the other spouse the two corporations would be affiliated);
   2. one corporation is controlled by a person, the other corporation is controlled by a group of persons, and each member of that group is affiliated with that person; or
   3. each corporation is controlled by a group of persons, and each member of each group is affiliated with at least one member of the other group.

The Disallowed Capital Loss

16-68.   Figure 16-2 indicates the specific rules of the ITA that apply when a seller is an individual versus when the seller is a partnership, corporation, or trust.

Superficial Losses	Figure 16-2 Superficial Losses	
	Transferor Is an Individual	**Transferor Is a Partnership, Trust, or Corporation**
Three conditions Superficial loss	ITA 54 definition	ITA 40(3.3)
Result = Loss Deemed Nil	ITA 40(2)(g)(i)	ITA 40(3.4)(a)
Loss passed to affiliated person as ACB adjustment	ITA 53(1)(f)	Not applicable
Loss suspended to transferor until subsequent event	Not applicable	ITA 40(3.4)(b)

16-69.   When the seller is an individual, the disallowed capital loss follows the property and is added to the ACB as a result of ITA 53(1)(f).

EXAMPLE—Individual   Ms. Hannah Howard, the sole shareholder of HH Ltd., sells land with an ACB of $50,000 and a FMV of $40,000 to HH Ltd. An ITA 85(1) election is filed selecting the only possible elected amount of $40,000. The corporation has no plans to sell the property.

ANALYSIS   The $10,000 capital loss (POD $40,000 - ACB $50,000) is a superficial loss because of a disposition to an affiliated person (the controlled corporation) within the 61-day period where that affiliated person owns the property on the 61st day. The capital loss is disallowed to the individual as a result of ITA 40(2)(g)(i). The superficial loss of $10,000 will follow the property, which is owned by the corporation. The ACB of the property to the corporation is equal to $50,000 (initial cost of $40,000 + the ITA 53(1)(f) adjustment for the disallowed capital loss).

16-70.   If the seller is a corporation, trust, or partnership, the capital loss is a denied loss based on the same analysis discussed in Paragraph 16-66. The capital loss is deemed to be nil as a result of ITA 40(3.4)(a), however the loss does not follow the property and add to the ACB. Instead, the loss becomes suspended within the seller and can only be claimed by the seller as a capital loss based on certain future events. The events are generally designed to track the property ownership. If the property is eventually owned by a non-affiliated person, then the seller can recognize the capital loss at that future time. Two of the more common future events are the following:

- The affiliated person sells the property to a non-affiliated person;
- If the transferor is a corporation,
    - it is subject to an acquisition of control; or
    - the corporation ceases to exist in a taxable dissolution or wind-up that is subject to ITA 88(2), which is discussed in Chapter 17.

EXAMPLE—Partnership, Corporation, or Trust   HC Ltd. sells land with an ACB of $50,000 and a FMV of $40,000 to HCSub, a corporation controlled by HC Ltd. (i.e., an affiliated person). Two years later, HCSub sells the land for $35,000 to a non-affiliated person.

ANALYSIS   The $10,000 ($40,000 - $50,000) capital loss of HC Ltd. is disallowed by ITA 40(3.4)(a). However, when the land is sold two years later by HCSub for $35,000, HC Ltd. will be allowed to recognize the disallowed capital loss of $10,000 (POD $40,000 - ACB $50,000) in that later taxation year. In addition, HCSub will realize a $5,000 (POD $35,000 - ACB $40,000) capital loss at the time of sale. The $5,000 capital loss to HCSub would not be disallowed since the three conditions described in Paragraph 16-66 are not met.

Depreciable Property — ITA 85(1)(e)

General Rules

16-71.   As was the case for other property, the same principal applies to determine acceptable elected amounts where there are accrued capital gains or accrued recapture or both. In general, the elected amount range would be from the tax cost to the FMV of the depreciable property. Tax cost would generally mean the UCC of the class, however if the capital cost of a particular depreciable property is less than the UCC then the minimum elected amount becomes that capital cost. Once the range of acceptable elected amounts is identified the FMV of the NSC could again reset that range, as previously discussed.

Examples — Elected Amounts

16-72.   These rules can be illustrated with the following two examples, each involving the sale of the only depreciable property remaining in a specific capital cost allowance (CCA) class:

	Example 1	**Example 2**
FMV of the eligible property	$50,000	$18,000
UCC of class (last property in the class)	20,000	20,000
Capital cost of the eligible property	27,000	30,000
FMV of the NSC (boot)	15,000	15,000

Example 1 Analysis   In Example 1, the acceptable range of elected amounts is between $20,000 and $50,000. Since the FMV of the NSC is less than the minimum of $20,000, the range is not reset. Electing at $20,000 avoids both capital gains and recapture. In this example, $5,000 of additional NSC could have been taken without any immediate income tax consequences if the election were made at $20,000.

Example 2 Analysis   In Example 2, there are no accrued capital gains or recapture. Instead, if the depreciable property were sold at FMV there would be a terminal loss of $2,000 (UCC $20,000 - POD $18,000). Because there is an accrued terminal loss there is no acceptable range of elected amounts and, instead, the FMV of the property of $18,000 is the only option. A sale to a controlled corporation, an affiliated person, that results in a terminal loss is also subject to another stop loss rule that is discussed in the following paragraphs.

Example — Order of Disposition — ITA 85(1)(e.1)

16-73.   An additional problem arises in the case where multiple depreciable properties of the same class are sold at the same time. The issue is illustrated in the following example.

EXAMPLE   An individual carries on a business as a sole proprietor and wants to incorporate the business. There are two class 10 properties used in the business. The UCC for the class is $28,000. The capital cost and FMV of the two depreciable properties are as follows:

	Property One	**Property Two**
Capital cost	$15,000	$30,000
FMV	20,000	25,000

16-74.   If the two depreciable properties are sold at the same time, a common occurrence in the incorporation of a business carried on as a sole proprietorship, the range of acceptable elected amounts for each property uses the same UCC of $28,000. This means that the acceptable range for the first property would be between $15,000 (the least of capital cost of $15,000, FMV of $20,000, and UCC of $28,000) and $20,000 (FMV of the property). The only possibility for the second property would be $25,000 because there are no accrued gains or recapture. As a result, the minimum elected amounts for both properties would total $40,000 ($15,000 for property one and $25,000 for property two), which would create recapture of $12,000 (UCC $28,000 - $40,000 dispositions).

16-75.   ITA 85(1)(e.1) provides a resolution by allowing a taxpayer to designate the order of the sale of each depreciable property. Technically this could be resolved by selling the two properties at separate times, but this provision achieves the same result. If, for example, the taxpayer designated property one to be sold first then a sale at an elected amount of $15,000 would reduce the UCC to $13,000 for property two. The sale of property two at an elected amount of $13,000 would not result in any recapture.

Exercise 16-2

Subject: Elected Amounts for Depreciable Property

Eric Li has two depreciable properties: a class 1 building and a class 10 vehicle. The properties are to be sold to a corporation controlled by Mr. Li using ITA 85(1). Relevant information for the two properties is as follows:

	Class 1	Class 10
FMV of the eligible property	$475,000	$12,000
UCC of the class (last property in the class)	150,000	8,000
Capital cost of the eligible property	220,000	28,000
FMV of the NSC (boot)	250,000	10,000

What are the acceptable elected amounts for each property? What are the income tax consequences for Mr. Li if the minimum elected amount is chosen?

Solutions to Exercises are available in the Study Guide.

Depreciable Property—Disallowed Terminal Losses

General Rules

16-76.   In Paragraph 16-72, we noted that the terminal loss resulting from the required election on the depreciable property in Example 2 would be disallowed as a disposition to an affiliated person (i.e., a controlled corporation). More specifically, if depreciable property is sold to an affiliated person by an individual, trust, corporation, or partnership and the result of that disposition is a terminal loss, then ITA 13(21.2) applies a specific stop loss provision with the following rules:

- The rules of ITA 85(1) do not apply to that property.
- The POD are deemed to be the UCC amount, which eliminates any terminal loss.
- The purchaser's capital cost is deemed to be the seller's capital cost, with the excess that would have been treated as a terminal loss deemed to be previously deducted CCA.
- The seller is deemed to have purchased depreciable property of the same class equal to the disallowed terminal loss. The result is that the terminal loss can be deducted in part in future years as deemed CCA. If certain future events occur, such as those mentioned in Paragraph 16-70, the remaining balance can be deducted as a terminal loss by the seller in that future year.

16-77.   In Example 2 from Paragraph 16-72, the property had a capital cost of $30,000, UCC of $20,000, and a FMV of $18,000. If the property is sold to an affiliated person then ITA 13(21.2) would clarify that the rules of ITA 85(1) do not apply to the property, that the deemed POD are $20,000 instead of $18,000, eliminating the terminal loss, and the capital cost to the purchaser would be $30,000 with deemed CCA of $12,000 and a resulting UCC of $18,000. The $2,000 disallowed terminal loss will be deemed to be a depreciable property owned by the seller and available for annual CCA in the same manner as any other purchased depreciable property.

Summary of Acceptable Elected Amounts—ITA 85(1)

16-78.   Figure 16-3 provides a summary of acceptable elected amounts by classification of property.

Figure 16-3
Acceptable Elected Amounts by Type of Property

Accrued Gains/Recapture

Inventory =	Cost*	$\longrightarrow$	FMV
Non-depreciable capital property	ACB	$\longrightarrow$	FMV
Depreciable property	Tax cost**	$\longrightarrow$	FMV

*Cost = Cost for ITA 10 valuation purposes
**Lesser of UCC and capital cost of specific property
If the FMV of non-share consideration is between the range, the range will reset with a new minimum.

Accrued Losses/Terminal Losses

Inventory = FMV
Non-depreciable capital property = FMV*
Depreciable property = FMV*
*Stop loss rules may apply

We suggest you complete SSP 16-1 and 16-2 at this point.

Allocating the Elected Amount

The Tax Cost of Consideration Received

16-79.   Figure 16-1 describes the objectives of a rollover under ITA 85(1). The fourth point is to determine the tax cost of all consideration received by the seller/transferor from the purchaser/transferee as payment for a particular eligible property.

16-80.   In a sale transaction that is not altered by ITA 85(1), the FMV of the property sold generally determines the income tax consequences to each person. If, for example, an individual sells property for $100 in an arm's-length transaction and the tax cost of that property to the seller is $40, there will be a $60 gain to the seller and the purchaser's cost is the $100 paid. If the purchaser paid with consideration of $100 then that consideration would also have a tax cost of $100.

16-81.   If, however, ITA 85(1) is used, and the objective of the seller is to avoid all income tax at the time of the sale, an elected amount of $40 would be chosen. Non-share consideration would have to be limited to $40 with the remaining $60 paid by the corporate purchaser in shares of the purchaser. Since the goal was to avoid the $60 gain to the seller, it would not make sense for the cost of the consideration received by the seller as payment for the property to be more than $40. The essence of ITA 85(1) is that a transaction occurs at FMV, but for income tax purposes it is as if the sale took place at the elected amount, or $40 in our example. As a result, the purchaser corporation's cost of the property acquired is $40, the POD to the seller is $40, and the total tax cost of consideration paid by the purchaser corporation should also be $40.

16-82.   The total consideration received by the seller is equal to the elected amount. The ITA requires that the consideration be broken down into three parts: (1) non-share consideration (NSC), (2) share consideration that is preferred shares, and (3) share consideration that is common shares. The rules that allocate the elected amount among these three types of consideration are found in ITA 85(1)(f), which first allocates the elected amount to NSC up to its FMV; ITA 85(1)(g), which next applies any remaining elected amount to preferred shares also up to its FMV; and finally ITA 85(1)(h), which applies to common shares if any elected amount remains. The sequential process can be outlined as follows:

Elected amount	$xxx
Less: FMV of non-share consideration (NSC)	(xxx)
Balance to be allocated to share consideration	$xxx
Less: Preferred shares issued (maximum FMV)	(xxx)
Balance to be allocated to common shares issued	$xxx

EXAMPLE Jason Browning incorporates a business he carried on as a sole proprietor to a newly created CCPC. The FMV of all of the eligible properties equals $1,650,000. A combined elected amount of $972,000 is chosen to minimize income tax. The total FMV of consideration matches the FMV of the eligible properties sold to the corporation, avoiding any value mismatches. The FMV of the consideration received is broken down as follows:

- Promissory note for $220,000.
- Preferred shares of $345,000.
- Common shares of $1,085,000.

ANALYSIS The $972,000 elected amount would be applied to this consideration as follows:

Elected amount	$972,000
Less: FMV of NSC	(220,000)
Balance to be allocated to share consideration	$752,000
Less: Preferred shares issued (maximum FMV)	(345,000)
Balance applied to common shares issued	$ 407,000

16-83.   The result is that the ACB of the promissory note is $220,000, the ACB of the preferred shares is $345,000, and the ACB of the common shares would be $407,000. If the individual seller wanted to maximize the NSC it could have been increased to $972,000 with the remaining FMV of $678,000 ($1,650,000 - $972,000) attributable to the share consideration. In that case, since all of the elected amount would have been applied to the NSC, there would be nothing left to apply to share consideration, meaning that the FMV of the issued shares would be $678,000 but the ACB would be nil.

Exercise 16-3

Subject: Allocating the Elected Amount—Tax Cost of Consideration

Mrs. Jennifer Lee sells non-depreciable capital property that is eligible property to a corporation for its FMV of $176,000. The ACB of the property is $62,000. An ITA 85(1) election is filed with respect to the sale choosing an elected amount of $62,000. The corporation pays her $176,000 of consideration, which consists of a promissory note for $51,000, preferred shares with a FMV of $53,000, and common shares with a FMV of $72,000. Determine the ACB of each type of consideration received by Mrs. Lee.

Solutions to Exercises are available in the Study Guide.

Tax Cost of Eligible Property to the Corporate Purchaser

General Rules

16-84. With respect to eligible property purchased by the transferee corporation, the basic rules are as follows:

Non-Depreciable Capital Property and Inventories   The elected amount becomes the tax cost to the corporation.

Depreciable Property   Where the seller/transferor's capital cost exceeds the elected amount for the eligible property that is depreciable property, ITA 85(5) requires that the income tax characteristics of the property to the seller are inherited by the purchaser corporation. This concept is referred to as a "recapture preservation rule," which is common among rollover provisions. The rule ensures that in a subsequent sale of the depreciable property by the corporation there will be recapture to the same extent that the seller would have been subject to recapture had the depreciable property not been sold to the corporation. In most cases, the elected amount for depreciable property with accrued gains or recapture will be equal to the seller/transferor's UCC. ITA 85(5) requires that the difference between the capital cost and elected amount (UCC) be treated as deemed CCA. To illustrate this, consider the following depreciable property characteristics:

Capital cost	$100,000
UCC	67,000
FMV	105,000
FMV of NSC	67,000
Elected amount	67,000

Without ITA 85(5), the cost to the corporation would be $67,000. If the corporation immediately sold the property for its FMV of $105,000, there would be a capital gain of $38,000, only 50% or $19,000 of which would be taxable [(50%)(POD $105,000 - ACB $67,000)]. If the seller/transferor had not sold the property to the corporation but instead sold it at FMV to an arm's-length person without the use of ITA 85(1), there would be a $2,500 taxable capital gain [(50%)(POD$105,000 - ACB $100,000)] and recapture of $33,000 [(UCC $67,000 - lesser of POD of $105,000 and capital cost of $100,000)]. It is this latter result that the legislation imposes on the corporate purchaser when ITA 85(1) is used.

ITA 85(5) deems the capital cost to the purchaser corporation to be the same $100,000 capital cost to the seller/transferor with $33,000 deemed to have been claimed as CCA. The result is that the UCC to the purchaser corporation is $67,000, which is equal to the elected amount. Therefore, if the corporation immediately sold the depreciable property for $100,000 the income tax consequences are identical to what the seller would have experienced in an arm's-length sale without ITA 85(1).

The AccII—ITR 1104(4)

16-85.   An additional question is whether the corporate purchaser can claim accelerated CCA based on the Accelerated Investment Income (AccII) for the year of purchase or whether the half-year rule applies to limit the first year CCA to 50% of what is normally allowed. The analysis begins with determining if the AccII applies. The AccII rules (ITR 1104(4)) require meeting one of two conditions. The first is that no CCA claims were made by anyone prior to purchasing the property. The second condition requires the property was not acquired by a rollover or was not owned by a non-arm's-length person. In the example in Paragraph 16-84, none of these conditions are met, meaning that the AccII does not apply to the corporate purchaser.

The Half-Year Rule—ITR 1100(2.2)

16-86.   Having eliminated the AccII, we now turn our attention to the half-year rule. The half-year rule does not apply where the purchase was between non-arm's-length persons and that non-arm's-length person owned the property for at least one year (measured from the last day of the taxation year of the corporate purchaser) and used the property to earn income from a business or property. If the seller is non-arm's length with the corporate purchaser and owned the property for at least one year, then the half-year rule would also not apply. The result would be CCA determined without the AccII or the half-year rule.

Elected Amounts and Capital Gains on Depreciable Property—ITA 13(7)(e)

16-87.   The general objective of using ITA 85(1) is to avoid any immediate income tax consequences when incorporating eligible property. In such cases the elected amount is set at the tax cost of the eligible property sold to a corporate purchaser.

16-88.   There are, however, circumstances in which the seller/transferor may wish to realize capital gains because of the availability of losses that would absorb any potential income tax.

16-89.   This creates a potential issue with respect to depreciable property in that, under the general rules of ITA 85(1), the elected amount becomes the cost of the depreciable property to the purchaser and therefore the basis for calculating CCA. The selection of an elected amount that exceeds the capital cost of the seller/transferor and therefore the ACB of depreciable property would result in a capital gain, only one-half of which would be included in income. The following example will illustrate this problem.

> **EXAMPLE**   Jan Harding plans to sell depreciable property to a CCPC in which she is the sole shareholder. A joint election will be filed under ITA 85(1). Because of a net capital loss balance from a prior year she will elect an amount that will generate sufficient capital gains to absorb the remaining net capital loss balance. The relevant information is as follows:
>
> | | |
> |---|---:|
> | Capital cost | $ 80,000 |
> | FMV | 200,000 |
> | UCC | 75,000 |
> | Elected amount | 120,000 |
>
> **ANALYSIS**   The election at $120,000 would result in the following income:
>
> | | |
> |---|---:|
> | Recaptured CCA ($80,000 - $75,000) | $ 5,000 |
> | Taxable capital gain [(1/2)($120,000 - $80,000)] | 20,000 |
> | Total income | $25,000 |
>
> In the absence of a special rule, the cost and UCC of the depreciable property to the corporation would be $120,000. This amount would create $45,000 of additional CCA for the corporation than would have been available to the seller/transferor ($120,000 - $75,000). The price of the additional $45,000 would have been an increase in the seller/transferor's income of only $25,000.

16-90.   ITA 13(7)(e) corrects this imbalance by limiting the capital cost to the purchaser corporation for CCA purposes where the seller and purchaser are non-arm's length. The capital cost is only allowed to be increased with respect to amounts included in the income of the seller/transferor. In this case, since only $25,000 was added to the income of the seller/transferor, the capital cost to the purchaser is only $100,000 ($75,000 elected amount + $25,000). ITA 13(7)(e) expresses the amount somewhat differently as follows:

Seller/transferor's capital cost		$ 80,000
Elected amount (POD)	$120,000	
Seller/transferor's capital cost	(80,000)	
Capital gain	$ 40,000	
Taxable portion	1/2	20,000
Capital cost to corporate purchaser for CCA purposes		$100,000

Summary of Depreciable Property Rules

16-91.   If depreciable property is acquired by a corporation with the use of ITA 85(1), ITA 85(5) will apply unless the seller recognizes 100% of the recapture. In the example in Paragraph 16-89, ITA 85(5) would not apply since all of the recapture is included in the seller/transferor's income.

16-92.   If the sale of depreciable property using ITA 85(1) results in a taxable capital gain to the seller/transferor and the relationship between the seller and corporate purchaser is non-arm's length then ITA 13(7)(e) will apply to reduce the capital cost to the corporate purchaser for CCA purposes.

Share Consideration—PUC, ITA 85(2.1)

Overview

16-93.   In the ITA it is important to be able to identify at any point in time three attributes of corporate shares: FMV, ACB, and PUC. The FMV is relevant for many purposes throughout the ITA, but in ITA 85(1) it is important to avoid mismatches in value that can lead to a seller receiving consideration that is more or less than the FMV of the eligible property being sold to a corporate purchaser. It is much easier to value preferred shares than it is with respect to common shares as previously mentioned. This means that common shares are rarely used in rollover transactions.

16-94.   The ACB of a share is important to determine whether there is a capital gain or capital loss when shares are sold. ITA 85(1) establishes the ACB of share consideration based on the allocation of the elected amount that was discussed beginning with Paragraph 16-79.

16-95.   PUC is also important mainly for the fact that it can be returned to shareholders tax free (as mentioned in Chapter 14 in the discussion of deemed dividends under ITA 84). PUC, however, is potentially problematic since it begins with the determination of legal capital under corporate law. The standard corporate law provision requires that a corporation add the FMV of consideration received for the issuance of its shares to the legal capital for those shares. This means that the legal capital and therefore initial PUC will be based on FMV.

16-96.   To illustrate the problem, assume that investments with a FMV of $100 and ACB of $25 are sold to a corporation for consideration that consists only of preferred shares valued at $100. An elected amount of $25 is chosen to avoid any immediate income tax consequences. We know that the seller is deemed to have disposed of the investments for $25, the corporation is deemed to have acquired the investments for $25, and the ACB of the share consideration received by the seller is also $25. The legal capital of the share consideration, however, is $100, which represents the fact that the corporation received property (the investments) valued at $100 for the issuance of its shares. The legal capital of $100 is therefore the initial PUC. It makes little sense that PUC should reflect FMV when ITA 85(1) is using only $25. To correct this situation, ITA 85(2.1) contains a PUC reduction designed to bring the PUC amount to an acceptable amount consistent with the rollover. ITA 85(2.1), which is discussed in the following paragraphs, would result in a PUC reduction of $75 in the example, bringing the PUC to $25 (legal capital of $100- ITA 85(2.1) reduction of $75).

PUC Reduction—ITA 85(2.1)

16-97.   To further elaborate on the need for a PUC reduction, as well as the procedure for calculating the reduction, the following example is presented.

> **EXAMPLE**   A non-depreciable capital property with a FMV of $200,000 and an ACB of $150,000 is sold to a corporation. A joint election is filed under ITA 85(1) with an elected amount of $150,000. Consideration consists of a promissory note of $120,000 and shares with a legal capital of $80,000.
>
> **ANALYSIS**   The elected amount establishes the recognition of a transaction as if the sale price was $150,000. The seller is considered to have received POD of $150,000,

the corporation to have purchased the property for $150,000, and the ACB of the consideration would be $150,000, which is first applied to the NSC in the amount of $120,000 with the remaining amount of $30,000 representing the ACB of share consideration. The PUC must also be consistent with the elected amount. The tax value of all consideration must be equal to $150,000. In a manner somewhat similar to how the elected amount is allocated to the various types of consideration, for purposes of determining PUC the elected amount is first taken up with non-share consideration with any remaining amount allocated among the PUC of shares issued. Where there is only one type of share issued, as in this example, the full remaining amount becomes the PUC of the shares issued as consideration. This would mean that the PUC of the shares should be $30,000, and to arrive at that result would require a PUC reduction of $50,000.

16-98.   The PUC of $30,000 can be verified by first applying the PUC reduction as follows:

Eligible property: FMV = $200,000, ACB = $150,000

Consideration: Promissory note = $120,000

Legal capital of shares issued = $80,000

Elected amount = $150,000

Increase in legal capital		$80,000
Less excess, if any, of:		
Elected amount	($150,000)	
Less: The FMV of NSC	120,000	(30,000)
PUC reduction		$50,000
PUC of shares issued ($80,000 - $50,000)		$30,000

16-99.   The three attributes of the share consideration are now known: FMV $80,000, ACB $30,000, and PUC $30,000. If the shares are sold there would be a $50,000 capital gain, and if the shares are redeemed (ITA 84(3)) there would be a deemed dividend of $50,000 and no capital gain or capital loss. The $50,000 of income on a disposition of the shares represents the deferred gain of $50,000 on the eligible property that was avoided by using ITA 85(1) and choosing an elected amount equal to the eligible property's tax cost.

16-100.   It is worth noting that there is an element of double taxation when using rollovers such as ITA 85(1). In effect, if the corporation in the previous example were to immediately sell the eligible property purchased for $200,000, the company would realize a $50,000 capital gain. If the seller were to sell the shares for FMV of $80,000, the seller would also realize a capital gain of $50,000, which mirrors the gain on the eligible property sold. Because of this potential issue it is generally not recommended to use ITA 85(1) to buy and sell property unless the corporation will use that property for years to come. An exception would be if the gain was not subject to tax because of offsetting losses or, where the seller is an individual, the income tax on any capital gain could be avoided to some degree with the use of the capital gains deduction.

16-101.   As a rule, shares of a corporation must be owned for at least two years before the shares can qualify for the capital gains deduction. However, ITA 54.2 and ITA 110.6(14)(f) contain rules that waive that condition where an individual, carrying on an active business as a sole proprietor, incorporates the business. The result is that such individuals can incorporate and avoid immediate income tax consequences by electing minimum amounts under ITA 85(1). The individual could receive share consideration and immediately sell the shares using the capital gains deduction, which would shelter income tax on up to $892,218 of capital gains in 2021 for qualified small business corporation (QSBC) shares. The shares would still have to meet the other conditions to qualify as QSBC shares. These rules remain popular for sole proprietors who receive offers to purchase their business.

Share Consideration—Multiple Classes of Shares

16-102.   If the elected amount equals the FMV of NSC there will be no room remaining for any PUC with the result that the PUC reduction will reduce the PUC to nil. In the example in Paragraph 16-98, if the FMV of the NSC was $150,000 the PUC reduction would have been $80,000, resulting in nil PUC. Typically this occurs when incorporating a business carried on as a sole proprietorship.

16-103.   If, however, the FMV of the NSC is less than the elected amount then there is room for PUC among the shares issued on the sale of eligible property to a corporation. If multiple classes of shares are issued as consideration, the PUC reduction is prorated on the basis of the relative legal capital, which itself is generally based on the relative FMV of the shares. We would add that, in practice, issuing multiple classes of shares in a rollover under ITA 85(1) is not a common occurrence.

16-104.   The application of the ITA 85(2.1) PUC reduction, where two classes of shares are issued as share consideration, is demonstrated in the example that follows.

EXAMPLE   Joan Creek sells eligible property that is non-depreciable capital property with a FMV of $1,600,000 to a corporation she controls. An election is jointly filed under ITA 85(1). The elected amount chosen is $900,000, which is equal to the ACB of the eligible property sold. The corporation provides her with a promissory note of $600,000, redeemable preferred shares with a FMV of $250,000, and common shares with a FMV of $750,000. There are no mismatches of value since the FMV of the total consideration equals the FMV of the eligible property.

ANALYSIS   The tax cost (ACB) of the consideration received would be determined as follows:

Elected amount	$900,000
Less: FMV of NSC	(600,000)
Balance for share consideration	$300,000
Less: FMV of the preferred shares (maximum)	(250,000)
Balance applied to the common shares	$ 50,000

The PUC reduction would be calculated as follows:

Increase in legal capital		
($250,000 + $750,000)		$1,000,000
Less excess, if any, of:		
Elected amount	($900,000)	
Less: FMV of NSC	600,000	(300,000)
PUC reduction		$ 700,000

The PUC of the two classes of shares, reduced by a pro rata allocation of the $700,000 PUC reduction on the basis of their relative FMV, would be as follows:

$$\text{PUC Of Preferred Stock} \left[\$250,000 - \left(\frac{\$250,000}{\$1,000,000} \right)(\$700,000) \right] = \underline{\underline{\$75,000}}$$

$$\text{PUC Of Common Stock} \left[\$750,000 - \left(\frac{\$750,000}{\$1,000,000} \right)(\$700,000) \right] = \underline{\underline{\$225,000}}$$

16-105.   The attributes of the shares are now complete and will be required to determine any income tax implications should the shares be sold or redeemed. The FMV of the preferred shares is $250,000, the ACB $250,000, and the PUC $75,000. The FMV of the common shares is $750,000, the ACB $50,000, and the PUC $225,000.

Exercise 16-4

Subject: Transfers under Section 85—PUC Reduction

Mr. Rob McCleen sells eligible property that is non-depreciable capital property to a corporation. A joint election is filed under ITA 85(1) with respect to the property at an elected amount of $114,000. The FMV of the eligible property is $234,000 and its ACB is $114,000. The consideration provided by the corporation consists of a promissory note for $83,000, preferred shares with a FMV and legal capital of $97,000, and common shares with a FMV and legal capital of $54,000. Determine the tax cost (ACB) of all of the consideration and the PUC of the preferred and common shares.

Solutions to Exercises are available in the Study Guide.

We suggest you complete SSP 16-3 at this point.

Comprehensive Example—Section 85 Rollovers

Basic Information

16-106.   John Martin has been carrying on a business as a sole proprietor. On January 1, 2021, the tax costs (UCC, capital cost, ACB, or inventory cost) and FMV for its assets and liabilities as listed on the balance sheet prepared by his accountant are as follows:

	Tax Cost	**FMV**
Cash	$ 20,000	$ 20,000
Accounts receivable	50,000	49,000
Inventories	100,000	105,000
Prepaid expenses	10,000	10,000
Land	50,000	70,000
Building (capital cost = $150,000)	110,000	140,000
Equipment (capital cost = $70,000)	40,000	35,000
Goodwill	Nil	50,000
Total assets	$380,000	$479,000
Liabilities	$100,000	$100,000

Excluded Property

16-107.   Mr. Martin plans to incorporate his business by first incorporating a new company (the Martin Company) in which he will be the sole shareholder. He will then sell the properties used in the business, including having the company assume the $100,000 of liabilities. A joint election will be filed under ITA 85(1) to minimize the income tax consequences of incorporating the business. The following balance sheet assets will be excluded from the rollover:

Excluded Asset	**Tax Cost**	**FMV**
Cash	$ 20,000	$ 20,000
Accounts receivable	50,000	49,000
Prepaid expenses	10,000	10,000
Equipment	40,000	35,000
Total	$120,000	$114,000

16-108.   Cash and the prepaid expenses are not eligible property (ITA 85(1.1)) and therefore cannot be included in the rollover. It is recommended that Mr. Martin loan the cash to the company, which would create a credit balance in his shareholder loan account that he can withdraw tax free at any time.

16-109.   The accounts receivable are non-depreciable capital property and could participate in the rollover, however the $1,000 ($50,000 - $49,000) loss would have to be treated as a capital loss, which would be disallowed to Mr. Martin as a superficial loss by ITA 40(2)(g). The disallowed loss would then be added to the tax cost of the receivables to the company. Further, any additional bad debts incurred by the corporation would also be treated as capital losses.

16-110.   The alternative is a joint election under ITA 22. This allows the $1,000 current loss to be treated as a business deduction. While the corporation will have to include this same $1,000 in income, it will then be able to claim doubtful debt reserves and deduct the full amount of any bad debts with respect to the purchased receivables. Accounts receivables that have been the subject of an election under ITA 22 cannot be included in a rollover under ITA 85(1).

16-111.   The sale of the equipment is between affiliated persons since Mr. Martin controls the company. In addition, a sale at FMV would result in a terminal loss. As a result, ITA 13(21.2) applies to determine the income tax consequences on a sale of the equipment to the company. ITA 13(21.2) provides that the income tax consequences are not to be determined under ITA 85(1) and therefore the equipment would be excluded from the rollover. The effect of ITA 13(21.2) is to deem the POD to be equal to the UCC of the equipment, which eliminates the terminal loss to Mr. Martin. Mr. Martin, however, would be allowed to treat the $5,000 terminal loss as if it were purchased depreciable property. He would then be allowed to claim CCA on that deemed depreciable property. The corporate purchaser is deemed to retain Mr. Martin's capital cost of $70,000 with the difference between the capital cost and the FMV of $35,000 considered deemed CCA of $35,000. A terminal loss could have been allowed had the equipment been sold to a non-affiliated person.

Implementing the Election

16-112.   Mr. Martin is interested in deferring any accrued income or capital gains on properties that are not to be excluded. As a result, the minimum acceptable election range will be chosen for each eligible property to be included in the rollover to ensure that no income or capital gains arise. The one exception to this is the internally generated goodwill. The minimum elected amount cannot be nil but must be a nominal amount, as previously discussed. As a result, an elected amount of $1 has been chosen. This $1 amount represents the POD of the goodwill to Mr. Martin, which when measured against the ACB of nil results in a $1 capital gain or a taxable capital gain of $0.50. There is no impact to class 14.1 of the proprietorship since the class can only be credited with the lesser of the capital cost of nil and the POD of $1.

16-113.   Mr. Martin's total elected amount of $260,001 is determined as follows:

Tax costs of all property	$380,000
Less: Tax costs of excluded property (Paragraph 16-107)	(120,000)
Add: Nominal amount for goodwill	1
Total elected amount	$260,001

16-114.   The combined FMV of eligible property to be included in the rollover is $365,000 ($479,000 total less the $114,000 FMV of property that will not be included in the rollover). If the goal is to maximize NSC while choosing the minimum elected amounts, the total elected amount and FMV of NSC should both be $260,001. Share consideration of $104,999 ($365,000 - $260,001) would represent the difference. The $260,001 in NSC would consist of $100,000 in assumed liabilities plus new debt issued by the corporation as a promissory note of $160,001.

16-115.   The ITA 85(1) election is made on a property-by-property basis, requiring both a separate elected amount and the identification of consideration for that property that must include shares. In the schedule that follows, NSC is separately determined for each eligible property. The FMV of the consideration must equal the FMV of the specific eligible property elected under ITA 85(1). In addition, the FMV of the NSC must be no greater than the elected amount or else the acceptable range will change.

		FMV of Consideration	
	Elected Amount	**Non-Share**	**Share**
Inventories	$100,000	$100,000	$ 5,000
Land	50,000	50,000	20,000
Building (capital cost = $150,000)	110,000	110,000	30,000
Goodwill	1	1	49,999
Total assets	$260,001	$260,001	$104,999

16-116.   From the point of view of the corporation, the elected amounts would become the initial tax cost to the corporation. The ACB of the shares that were issued to Mr. Martin would be determined as follows:

Total elected amount	$260,001
Less: FMV of NSC	(260,001)
Cost of the shares	Nil

16-117.   The initial PUC of these shares would be their legal capital of $104,999. Since all of the elected amount has been taken in NSC there is no remaining room for PUC and therefore the PUC should be nil. This would require a PUC reduction of $104,999, which is confirmed by the following calculations:

Increase in legal capital		$104,999
Less excess, if any, of:		
Total elected amount	($260,001)	
Less: FMV of NSC	260,001	Nil
Reduction in PUC		$104,999
PUC of shares issued ($104,999 - $104,999)		Nil

16-118.   The three share attributes are FMV of $104,999 and PUC and ACB of nil. A sale of the shares at FMV would result in a capital gain of $104,999 while a redemption of the shares would result in a deemed dividend (ITA 84(3)) of $104,999. In other words, the deferred income and capital gains on the eligible property included in the ITA 85(1) rollover are reflected in the share consideration.

16-119.   In addition, there are two other income tax consequences to the corporate purchaser. The elected amount for the building was $110,000, which was equal to the UCC, but the capital cost was $150,000. This means that there is a potential recapture of $40,000 should the FMV of the building increase to $150,000. As a result, ITA 85(5) applies to deem the corporation's capital cost to be $150,000 and deems the company to have previously claimed CCA of $40,000. The net result of $110,000 represents the elected amount, which is equal to the UCC.

16-120.   In addition, the sale of the goodwill resulted in a taxable capital gain of $0.50. The capital cost of the goodwill to the corporate purchaser would usually be the elected amount of $1, but since the sale of the goodwill was between non-arm's-length persons (the individual and a corporation controlled by that same individual), ITA 13(7)(e) applies to restrict the corporation's capital cost for CCA purposes to $0.50. While the amount is clearly negligible, technically ITA 13(7)(e) would apply.

Exercise 16-5

Subject: ITA 85(1)—Income Tax Consequences

Ms. Jasmine Wiens has carried on the business of an alternative medicine pharmacy as a sole proprietor for a number of years. Ms. Wiens is considering incorporating her business in a corporation of which she will be the sole shareholder. The total FMV of all business properties is $1,150,000. Of this amount, internally generated goodwill accounts for $300,000 and other tangible business properties account for the remaining $850,000. The tax cost of the tangible business properties is $275,000. Business liabilities are equal to $83,000. Ms. Wiens would like to incorporate the business with the assistance of a joint election under ITA 85(1) to minimize income tax to the extent possible.

On January 20, 2021, she will sell all of the business properties to a newly created corporation for $1,150,000. The corporation will assume the existing $83,000 of business liabilities and will issue her a promissory note for $17,000. The remaining consideration will consist of redeemable preferred shares with a FMV of $125,000 and common shares with a FMV of $925,000. Any dividends paid by the corporation will be non-eligible. Determine the following:

1.   The tax cost of each type of consideration received by Ms. Wiens. Assume that it is acceptable to elect a nil amount for the goodwill.
2.   The PUC of the preferred and common shares issued as consideration.
3.   The income tax consequences to Ms. Wiens if all of the preferred shares issued as share consideration are redeemed for their FMV of $125,000.

Solutions to Exercises are available in the Study Guide.

We suggest you complete SSP 16-4 to 16-7 at this point.

Gift to a Related Person—ITA 85(1)(e.2)

General Rules

16-121.   In Paragraphs 16-27 to 16-29 the importance of matching the FMV of the eligible properties included in a rollover with the FMV of consideration received in exchange was discussed. Mismatches of FMV can cause considerable difficulty if steps are not taken to minimize the risk. Price adjustment clauses are an essential feature of rollover planning to allow the CRA to agree to reverse the consequences of mismatches of value.

16-122.   In this section of the chapter we will discuss what is referred to as "gifting" within a rollover transaction under ITA 85(1). Gifting is an attribution concept that refers to transactions the result of which is to indirectly provide related persons with an economic advantage with respect to property owned by those related persons.

EXAMPLE   A company is incorporated by a family member of an individual (i.e., a related person). The family member purchased the only common shares for $100 when the company was incorporated. The following day the individual sells land valued at $100,000 to the family member's company in exchange for consideration that consists only of redeemable preferred shares valued at $30,000. The ACB of the land is also $30,000. An election is filed under ITA 85(1) to choose an elected amount of $30,000 to avoid any income tax on the accrued gain.

ANALYSIS   In this case the individual has left $70,000 of value in the company since the company paid $30,000 for land valued at $100,000. After the sale of land the company has $100,100 of property, consisting of $100 in cash obtained from the family member on the issuance of the common shares plus land valued at $100,000. The preferred shares owned by the individual are only worth $30,000, meaning that the remaining corporate value of $70,100 is attributable to the common shares owned by the family member. As a result, the FMV of the family member's common shares have increased by $70,000, from $100 to $70,100. The reason for this increase is as a direct result of the land sale by the individual. This is a classic example of gifting in the context of a rollover under ITA 85(1).

16-123.   Gifting would not occur if an individual is the only shareholder of the company. If in the example the individual purchased $100 of common shares and then sold the land to the company for $30,000 of redeemable preferred shares the common shares owned by that individual would also have increased by $70,000. In other words, there is no gifting to a related person, and although there is a mismatch of value with respect to the sale of land there is no actual economic change since the one individual owns property (the common and preferred shares) that matches the value of the company.

16-124.   In summary, gifting will arise when a taxpayer uses ITA 85(1) in such a manner as to indirectly economically benefit related persons. As a rule this would only occur if a family member, in the case of an individual taxpayer, owns common shares of the company at the time of the rollover transaction.

16-125.   In practice, gifting typically arises because of a difference of opinion with the CRA with respect to either the FMV of the eligible property or the FMV of consideration paid by the company. A challenge by the CRA can be remedied by the existence of a valid price adjustment clause that avoids the income tax consequences of the gifting provision of ITA 85(1)(e.2), which is purposefully designed to be punitive as discussed in the following paragraphs.

16-126.   ITA 85(1)(e.2) applies if the FMV of the eligible property exceeds the greater of:

1.   the FMV of all consideration received from the corporation; and
2.   the elected amount for the eligible property

and it is reasonable to regard that excess as a gift made by the seller/transferor for the benefit of a related person. The CRA considers the condition to have been met if a related person owns common shares of the company at the time of the rollover.

16-127.   ITA 85(1)(e.2) modifies the election by increasing the initial elected amount by the amount of the gift, which is generally equal to the value left within the corporation. The revised elected amount, however, does not change the original amounts allocated to any share consideration, although the revised elected amount is considered when determining the PUC of the share consideration. In addition, there is no adjustment made to increase the ACB of the common shares owned by the related person to reflect the increase in FMV as a result of the gift.

Example

16-128.   The following example will serve to illustrate the application of ITA 85(1)(e.2).

EXAMPLE   Mr. Pohl owns a non-depreciable capital property with an ACB of $30,000 and an estimated FMV of $130,000. A new corporation is created with all of the common shares being issued to Mr. Pohl's adult son for $1,000. Mr. Pohl sells the property to the corporation for $130,000. A joint election is filed under ITA 85(1) and an elected amount of $30,000 is chosen to avoid any income tax on the accrued gain.

Consideration paid by the corporation consists of a $30,000 promissory note and preferred shares with a FMV and legal capital (initial PUC) of $100,000. Mr. Pohl filed the election on the assumption that the FMV of the property sold to the corporation is $130,000. However, on review, the CRA valuators disagree with the value and conclude that the FMV is $180,000. CRA reassesses and applies ITA 85(1)(e.2). Mr. Pohl agrees to accept the CRA valuation.

16-129.   Based on the reassessed value, the FMV of the eligible property exceeds the FMV of the consideration received as shown in the following calculation:

FMV of eligible property (reassessed value)	$180,000
Less the greater of:	
• FMV of consideration received = $130,000	
• Elected amount = $30,000	(130,000)
Excess (gift)	$ 50,000

16-130.   As Mr. Pohl's son is the only common shareholder of the new corporation, it would be reasonable to regard this $50,000 as a gift to his son since it increases the FMV of the common shares by the same amount. As a result, ITA 85(1)(e.2) would apply to this transaction and Mr. Pohl's revised elected amount of $180,000 would result in the following income tax consequences:

Revised elected amount = POD	
($30,000 initial elected amount + $50,000 gift)	$80,000
ACB	(30,000)
Capital gain	$50,000
Inclusion rate	1/2
Taxable capital gain	$25,000

16-131.   Any CRA reassessment based on the revised FMV is in respect of specific eligible property. In this example, there was only one non-depreciable capital property involved, resulting in the recognition of a capital gain. If the eligible property was depreciable property or inventory, the accrued gain could have been recapture or business income.

16-132.   In Paragraph 16-127 it was noted that the ITA 85(1)(e.2) revised elected amount does not change the ACB of the share consideration, which relies on the initial elected amount. As a result, the ACB of the preferred shares received on the sale of eligible property to the corporation would be calculated as follows:

Elected amount (initial amount)	$30,000
Less: FMV of NSC	(30,000)
ACB of the preferred shares (unchanged)	Nil

16-133.   Note, however, that the revised elected amount does apply when determining the PUC reduction.

Increase in legal capital (based on FMV)		$100,000
Less the excess, if any, of:		
Revised elected amount	($80,000)	
Less: FMV of NSC	30,000	(50,000)
PUC reduction		$ 50,000
PUC of shares ($100,000 - $50,000)		$ 50,000

16-134.   The value of the corporation is $181,000. This includes $1,000 invested by Mr. Pohl's son on the issuance of the common shares plus eligible property valued at $180,000. The corporation owes $30,000 as a promissory note to Mr. Pohl plus has issued $100,000 of redeemable preferred shares, leaving $51,000 in value all of which is attributable to the common shares. There is no adjustment to the ACB of the common shares, which remains at $1,000. This means that if the son sold the shares for FMV of $51,000 there would be a capital gain of $50,000 ($51,000 - $1,000). In effect, the $50,000 gift is immediately taxed to Mr. Pohl as the individual who entered into a transaction that caused the gift, plus the son has an accrued gain of the same amount that will be realized when the shares are sold at some future date. This punitive double tax impact is purposefully designed to discourage gifting transactions with the ITA 85(1) rollover.

16-135.   The actual and potential gains resulting from the application of ITA 85(1)(e.2) to this transaction are as follows:

Actual capital gain to Mr. Pohl on the sale	$ 50,000
Future capital gain on Mr. Pohl's preferred shares ($100,000 - nil)	100,000
Future capital gain on son's common shares ($51,000 - $1,000)	50,000
Total gain	$200,000

16-136.   If Mr. Pohl had simply sold the eligible property, the total gain would have been only $150,000 ($180,000 - $30,000). The additional $50,000 is attributable to the double tax impact of the gifting rule.

Exercise 16-6

Subject: Gift to Related Party—Section 85

Janice Bellows incorporates a new CCPC. Common shares are issued to her adult daughter for cash of $1,000. Ms. Bellows then sells investments that are eligible property to the corporation. The ACB of the investments are $50,000 and the FMV is estimated at $65,000. The corporation pays for the investments with a $50,000 promissory note and $15,000 in redeemable preferred shares. Ms. Bellows jointly elects with the company to include the investments in a rollover under ITA 85(1). An elected amount of $50,000 is chosen.

The CRA subsequently challenges the valuation of the investments, concluding that the FMV is $110,000. There is no valid price adjustment clause, and Ms. Bellows accepts the valuation by the CRA. After the reassessment, Ms. Bellows and her daughter sell their shares to arm's-length persons for their FMV.

Describe the income tax consequences of the reassessment for both Ms. Bellows and her daughter. How would the income tax consequences differ if Ms. Bellows had simply sold the investment to the corporation for $110,000?

Solutions to Exercises are available in the Study Guide.

We suggest you complete SSP 16-8 at this point.

Excess Consideration—ITA 15(1)

Introduction

16-137.   In the previous section we considered one side of mismatches of value where a taxpayer sells property to a corporation and does not take back sufficient consideration. In this section we look at the other side, where a taxpayer sells property to a corporation but takes back too much consideration.

16-138.   When a rollover under ITA 85(1) is used to minimize the income tax consequences of a sale of eligible property to a corporation, the conditions of the rollover require that the seller receive share consideration. The result is that the taxpayer either becomes a shareholder or remains a shareholder with additional shares. ITA 15(1) applies to taxpayers who are shareholders and to those who enter into transactions with a corporation in contemplation of becoming a shareholder. This means that individuals incorporating a business or other property with the assistance of ITA 85(1) will be potentially subject to ITA 15(1) if they sell property to a corporation and take back too much consideration. Since ITA 15(1) was discussed in some detail in Chapter 15, our coverage in this chapter will be limited to a standard rollover using ITA 85(1).

16-139.   The identification of mismatches of value is of course dependent on an understanding of FMV, which is sometimes anything but straightforward. Even professional valuators frequently come up with different values for the same property. In the context of ITA 15(1) and rollover transactions there are three different scenarios that require elaboration. One is when transactions take place between a corporation and shareholders (including contemplated shareholders) where (1) the corporation is newly created and owns little to no property; (2) the corporations have been in existence for some time, are profitable, and are more than able to pay their bills as they become due; and (3) insolvent companies.

16-140.   The reason for this distinction between corporations is that in many rollover transactions the goal is to defer income tax, which means limiting the elected amount to the tax costs of eligible property and taking that minimum amount as NSC. The difference between the FMV of the eligible property and the FMV of NSC for that property will be represented by share consideration. NSC is commonly paid using promissory notes; therefore consideration in rollovers involving ITA 85(1) includes both promissory notes and preferred shares that are redeemable for a fixed dollar amount.

16-141.   The FMV of promissory notes and preferred shares, however, is reflective of the FMV of the property given to a corporation. If, for example, an individual incorporates a new company and pays the corporation $10 for one common share, then the value of the corporation and that one common share is equal to $10. If the individual sells land with a FMV of $1,000 to the corporation for $5,000, the individual would appear to have received a shareholder benefit of $4,000, which represents the excessive consideration received. Since it is a new corporation, the only way that the company could pay the amount is to provide a $5,000 promissory note, or $5,000 in redeemable shares, or some combination of the two.

16-142.   The amount of a shareholder benefit under ITA 15(1) with respect to a specific transaction is equal to the FMV of consideration received less the FMV of the property given up in exchange. If we assume that the corporation provided a $5,000 promissory note and nominal share consideration, then the benefit would appear to be calculated as $5,000 consideration received less the FMV of the land of $1,000. The difficulty is that even though the promissory note states that $5,000 is owed, the reality is that the note is not worth $5,000 because the company does not currently have the ability to pay that amount given the FMV of its assets is only $1,010. In other words, the FMV of the promissory note is only $1,000, with the result that there would be no immediate benefit. The result would be the same were the corporation in existence for many years but insolvent. However, if the corporation was solvent and had no shortage of assets and access to funds, the value of the promissory note would be the full $5,000. This concept would also be equally applicable were share consideration issued instead of a promissory note. A good rule of thumb to assess FMV is to ask what amount a financial institution such as a bank would give you as collateral security for the note issued by the new company or an insolvent company. That amount would generally be representative of the FMV.

Shareholder Benefit—ITA 15(1)

16-143.   The following example illustrates a situation in which the use of ITA 85(1) results in a shareholder benefit.

EXAMPLE   In 2012 Ms. Sally Swit incorporated her business within a CCPC of which she is the sole shareholder. The company has been very successful and the current FMV of the company exceeds $1,000,000. In 2020 she sells land that is non-depreciable capital property to the corporation. The ACB of the property is $65,000, and she believes

Excess Consideration—ITA 15(1)

that the FMV is $200,000. To avoid any immediate income tax consequences she jointly elects with the company under ITA 85(1), choosing an elected amount of $65,000. She takes back a promissory note for $65,000 and a special class of preferred shares that are redeemable for $135,000.

In 2021, the CRA reassesses on the basis that the FMV of the land sold to the company was only $150,000 at the time of the sale. Ms. Swit does not challenge the reassessment since she did not have the land valued by a professional valuator.

ANALYSIS   Ms. Swit has received a shareholder benefit under ITA 15(1) calculated as follows:

FMV of consideration received	$200,000
FMV of property given in exchange	(150,000)
ITA 15(1) shareholder benefit	$ 50,000

In the original ITA 85(1) election, the elected amount was $65,000, the FMV of the promissory note was $65,000, and the FMV of the preferred shares was $135.000. The ACB of the consideration is $65,000 for the promissory note and nil for the shares. Since all of the $65,000 elected amount was received as NSC, the PUC of the preferred shares after the PUC reduction will also be nil. The income tax consequences of the initial election is therefore POD to Ms. Swit of $65,000 less an ACB of the land of $65,000, resulting in no capital gain or capital loss. The ACB of the note is $65,000 and the ACB and PUC of the preferred shares are both nil.

The reassessment does not change the elected amount. The revised capital gain calculation would be as follows:

Elected amount after reassessment		$ 65,000
ACB		(65,000)
Capital gain	$	Nil
Inclusion rate		1/2
Taxable capital gain after reassessment	$	Nil

The reassessment increases net income for 2020 by $50,000:

Initial taxable capital gain	$	Nil
Shareholder benefit		50,000
Revised taxable capital gain		Nil
Total change to net income		$50,000

The ACB of the note remains unchanged at $65,000 and the PUC of the preferred shares also remain unchanged at nil. ITA 52(1) contains an ACB adjustment where the excess consideration results in a shareholder benefit under ITA 15(1). Had the corporation known that the FMV of the land was only $150,000 it would have only issued $85,000 in share consideration instead of $135,000. Therefore, it is the additional $50,000 in shares that represents the excess consideration. As a result, the ACB of the preferred shares is increased from nil to $50,000.

ACB of the preferred shares ITA 85(1)	Nil
ITA 52(1) ACB adjustment	50,000
ACB of the preferred shares	$50,000

The revised amounts can be reconciled. When Ms. Swit sold the land to her company for $200,000 she would have recognized a gain of $135,000 since her ACB was only $65,000. Of that gain, $50,000 was included in income as a shareholder benefit, leaving

$85,000 that has yet to be included in income. The FMV of the preferred shares are $135,000 with a revised ACB of $50,000; therefore, if she sells the shares she will recognize the remaining gain of $85,000.

Exercise 16-7

Subject: Excess Consideration—ITA 85(1)

In 2020, Mr. Larry Custer sells investments to a company of which he is the sole shareholder. He incorporated the company in 2014 and it has become very successful. The company is estimated to be worth $2,000,000. The ACB of the investments is $123,000 and he believes that the FMV is $270,000. To defer any immediate income tax, Mr. Custer jointly elects with the company under ITA 85(1) for an amount of $123,000. Mr. Custer receives consideration consisting of a promissory note of $123,000 and a special class of redeemable preferred shares of $147,000. The purchase and sale agreement does not contain a price adjustment clause.

In 2021, Mr. Custer is reassessed on the basis that the FMV of the investments sold to the company was only $217,000. He accepts the reassessment without objection.

Describe the income tax consequences of the sale of the investments to the company by Mr. Custer and the results of the reassessment. Indicate the ACB of all consideration and the PUC of the preferred shares after the reassessment.

Solutions to Exercises are available in the Study Guide.

We suggest you complete SSP 16-9 at this point.

Dividend/Surplus Stripping—ITA 84.1

Overview

16-144.   In previous chapters we have discussed integration, Part IV taxes, the capital gains deduction, deemed dividends, transactions between shareholders and the corporation, and rollovers under ITA 85(1). All of these topics come together and frequently play a part when considering ITA 84.1, an anti-avoidance rule that targets attempts to remove corporate surplus (e.g., after-tax earnings) on a tax-free basis.

16-145.   If an individual shareholder had a choice as to how to characterize a distribution from a corporation in the most tax effective manner, the choices generally come down to the payment of a bonus or dividend. Bonuses, however, are subject to full income tax rates, whereas dividends, whether eligible or non-eligible, are subject to lower rates of income tax and are therefore generally preferable. Capital gains, however, are subject to tax rates that are even lower than taxable dividends and are much more preferable. Additional advantages can be claimed if the capital gain is realized on QSBC shares since the capital gain would be tax free to the extent of the capital gains deduction available. One of the goals, therefore, of putting corporate surplus in the hands of shareholders is to do so by way of capital gains—specifically capital gains eligible for the capital gains deduction.

16-146.   The difficulty with realizing capital gains on QSBC shares is that the shares have to be sold. Shareholders who wish to extract corporate surplus as tax-free capital gains eligible for the capital gains deduction are not willing to give up control of their corporations. Fortunately, the capital gains deduction is available whether shares are sold to arm's-length or non-arm's-length persons. As a result, a standard strategy emerged many years ago when the capital gains deduction was first introduced to effectively create the necessary income tax environment to extract corporate surplus tax free. ITA 84.1 applies to this standard tax planning to ensure that the removal of corporate surplus that would typically occur by way of a taxable dividend distribution is subject to income tax. The words of ITA 84.1, however, apply to many other types of transactions that sometimes have nothing to do with the extraction of corporate surplus. For example, the creation and insertion of an intermediary holding company will often result in the application of ITA 84.1.

The Standard Planning to Which ITA 84.1 Applies

16-147.   The standard planning for which ITA 84.1 was designed can be explained with the following example.

FACTS   Ms. Atwater is the sole shareholder of Water Co., a CCPC that was incorporated in 2010. The company is valued at $2,000,000 in 2021 and currently holds $900,000 in cash. The income tax attributes of Ms. Atwater's shares are that the FMV is $2,000,000 and both PUC and ACB are nominal since the shares she owns were all issued for $1. Ms. Atwater has never used her capital gains deduction and she has been advised that the shares are QSBC shares. The capital gains deduction limit for QSBC shares in 2021 is $892,218, but we will assume that it is $900,000 for purposes of this example. Ms. Atwater would like to remove the $900,000 of cash without paying any income tax. Assume that Water Co. has no RDTOH at the end of its 2021 taxation year. Note that the absence of RDTOH ensures that when a taxable dividend is paid between connected corporations there will be no Part IV tax. The following transactions are undertaken to achieve that goal.

Step 1   A new CCPC is created (Hold Co.) with all of the shares issued to Ms. Atwater for nominal consideration.

Step 2   Ms. Atwater sells all of her shares in Water Co. to Hold Co. for $2,000,000. She files a joint election with Hold Co. under ITA 85(1) and chooses an elected amount of $900,000. Hold Co. pays her $2,000,000 in consideration, which consists of a promissory note for $900,000 and $1,100,000 in redeemable preferred shares. As a result of the election, Ms. Atwater is deemed to have sold her Water Co. shares for $900,000 and Hold Co. is deemed to have purchased the Water Co. shares for $900,000, which becomes the ACB to Hold Co. The ACB of the promissory note to Ms. Atwater is $900,000 and the ACB and PUC of the preferred shares issued by Hold Co. are both nil.

Step 3   Water Co. will declare and pay a cash dividend of $900,000 to Hold Co. The taxable dividend is included in Hold Co.'s net income and deducted in determining taxable income (ITA 112(1)). As a result, there is no Part I tax with respect to the taxable dividend. There is also no Part IV tax since the two corporations are connected and Water Co. was not entitled to a dividend refund as a result of the payment of the taxable dividend to Hold Co.

Step 4   Hold Co. uses the cash received from Water Co. as a taxable dividend to pay the promissory note to Ms. Atwater.

16-148.   The end result of the tax planning is that $900,000 of Water Co.'s surplus has been removed and Ms. Atwater has $900,000 in additional cash that originated with Water Co. In addition, Ms. Atwater, when filing her 2021 income tax return, would have reported a taxable capital gain of $450,000 [(50%)(POD $900,000 - ACB nil)] and a taxable income deduction of $450,000 [(50%)($900,000)] for the capital gains deduction (ITA 110.6). While there may be some refundable alternative minimum tax, the result is that there is no permanent income tax as a result of these transactions. ITA 84.1 is designed for this exact type of planning. If this planning were acceptable, individual shareholders could remove corporate surplus without tax to the extent of their available capital gains deduction.

Applying ITA 84.1—All NSC or All Shares

16-149. We will focus on the previous example of an individual selling shares. There are three conditions that must be met for ITA 84.1 to apply:

Condition One   An individual resident in Canada sells shares of a corporation resident in Canada (the first corporation) to a second corporation.

Condition Two   The individual is non-arm's length with the second corporation at the time of the sale.

Condition Three   Immediately after the sale of the shares the two corporations are connected corporations as defined in Part IV (ITA 186(2) and (4)). Generally, this occurs if the second corporation owns more than 10% of the voting shares of the first corporation.

16-150.   Returning to the example in Paragraph 16-147, we see that all three conditions have been met. Ms. Atwater sold shares of Water Co. to Hold Co., a corporation she was non-arm's length with because she controlled the corporation and, after the share sale, Hold Co. was connected to Water Co. because it owned more than 10% of its shares.

16-151.   ITA 84.1 provides for a limit that allows an individual selling shares to take back NSC no greater than the PUC and the ACB of the shares being sold. In the example, the Water Co. shares PUC and ACB is nominal (e.g., $1). This means that she should not have taken any NSC from Hold Co. when the Water Co. shares were sold. The result is that she took $900,000 too much. ITA 84.1(1)(b) deems that amount to be a deemed dividend, which would be subject to a dividend gross up and eligible for a dividend tax credit. In addition, a deemed dividend of $900,000 under ITA 84.1 reduces the POD that she reported when filing her 2021 income tax return to nil. As a result, the initial reported capital gain of $900,000 is revised to nil (POD nil- ACB of Water shares nil). Ms. Atwater still has her capital gains deduction. The impact of ITA 84.1 is, in this case, to effectively convert her original capital gain, which would have been received tax free, to a deemed dividend, which is subject to income tax. This is considered consistent with the tax policy view that removing surplus from a corporation should be treated as a dividend and not a capital gain, particularly where the shareholder still retains overall control of the corporation.

16-152.   The deemed dividend impact of ITA 84.1 can be avoided by limiting the NSC to the PUC and ACB of the shares sold. Had Ms. Atwater taken back only preferred share consideration of $2,000,000 there would not have been any deemed dividend. ITA 84.1 also uses the same NSC limit to restrict the PUC of the preferred shares to the maximum of the PUC and ACB of the shares sold (the Water Co. shares). Since that limit in the example was nil, there can be no PUC on the preferred shares. ITA 84.1(1)(a) would provide a PUC reduction of $2,000,000, resulting in nil PUC for the preferred shares. The PUC reduction in ITA 84.1 overrides the PUC reduction under ITA 85(2.1) where the sale is included in a joint election filed under ITA 85(1).

16-153.   If the tax planning had occurred with only preferred shares being issued but retaining the elected amount of $900,000, ITA 85(1) would apply to deem the ACB of the shares to be $900,000 but the PUC, determined under ITA 84.1, would be nil. Ms. Atwater's POD would remain at $900,000 and her original filed 2021 income tax return would not be changed. She would continue to report a taxable capital gain of $450,000 and a capital gains deduction of $450,000. However, when preferred shares are chosen as consideration there is no actual removal of surplus in Water Co. as there was when only a promissory note was taken back. If Ms. Atwater wishes to access the $900,000 of cash in Water Co., she can only do so by redeeming her preferred shares. The tax attributes of the preferred shares would be FMV of $2,000,000, ACB of $900,000, and PUC of nil. If the shares were redeemed there would be a $2,000,000 deemed dividend (ITA 84(3) redemption amount of $2,000,000 minus nil PUC) and there would be a capital loss of $900,000, which would be disallowed (adjusted POD of nil after subtracting the deemed dividend minus ACB of $900,000). In other words, ITA 84.1 impacts the tax attributes of the share consideration, ensuring that any subsequent redemption will result in income taxes. While the crystallization intent is acceptable, the ability to remove corporate surplus tax free is prevented.

Dividend/Surplus Stripping—ITA 84.1

Applying ITA 84.1—Mixed Consideration

16-154.   A second example, illustrated in Figure 16-4, will serve to illustrate the application of ITA 84.1 where the consideration consists of both NSC and shares.

16-155.   Ms. Barton is the only shareholder of Barton Industries (BI), a CCPC. The company was established in 2006 when Ms. Barton acquired all of the issued common shares for $25,000. No additional shares have been issued and, as a consequence, both the ACB and PUC of the shares are $25,000. The FMV of the shares is currently $900,000. Because of her previous use of the capital gains deduction, Ms. Barton's available capital gains deduction is only $650,000. The shares of BI are QSBC shares, and the GRIP and RDTOH account balances at year end are nil.

16-156.   Ms. Barton could, of course, make use of her capital gains deduction by selling the BI shares to an arm's-length person and realizing a capital gain of $875,000 ($900,000 - $25,000), of which $225,000 would be taxable after claiming the available capital gains deduction of $650,000. However, this approach is not acceptable to her, as she would lose control of the company.

16-157.   Given these considerations, she chooses to sell the BI shares to a new company, Barton Holdings Ltd. (BHL), electing rollover treatment under ITA 85(1). She will file a joint election with BHL and will choose an elected amount of $675,000 in order to limit her capital gain to $650,000 ($675,000 - $25,000). BHL pays her with a promissory note for $675,000 and redeemable preferred shares valued at $225,000.

16-158.   ITA 84.1 will apply to the sale of BI shares to BHL by Ms. Barton because the three conditions of ITA 84.1 have been met, namely that (1) a resident individual (Ms. Barton) sold shares of a resident company (BI) to a second company (BHL), (2) Ms. Barton was non-arm's length with the second corporation (BHL) at the time of the sale because she controlled it, and (3) immediately after the sale the two corporations are connected.

16-159.   We previously mentioned that when ITA 84.1 applies it restricts the NSC to the greater of the PUC and ACB of the shares sold. Any NSC in excess of that amount will be treated as a deemed dividend and will cause the capital gain on the share sale to be reduced through a reduction in the POD. In this case, the ITA 84.1 limit is only $25,000. Since Ms. Barton received a promissory note that exceeded the $25,000 limit, the excess of $650,000 will be treated as a deemed dividend (FMV of the note of $675,000 minus the ITA 84.1 limit of $25,000). The $650,000 excess will also reduce the capital gain by $650,000 by reducing the POD of the share sale of $675,000 (the ITA 85(1) elected amount) to $25,000. Ms. Barton's capital gains deduction of $650,000 would remain available for future years.

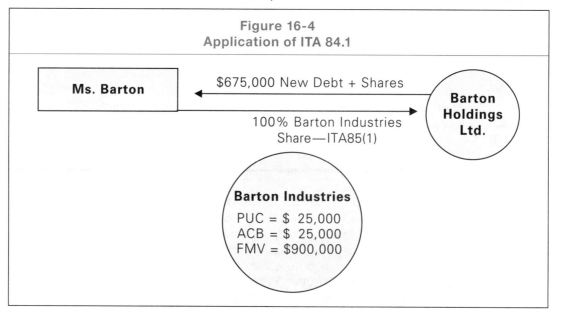

Figure 16-4
Application of ITA 84.1

Ms. Barton

$675,000 New Debt + Shares

Barton Holdings Ltd.

100% Barton Industries Share—ITA85(1)

Barton Industries
PUC = $ 25,000
ACB = $ 25,000
FMV = $900,000

16-160.   In addition, the ITA 84.1 limit of $25,000 establishes the maximum amount that can be taken in NSC and PUC. The $25,000 limit is first applied up to the FMV of NSC, and if any room remains it can be filled with PUC. Since the $25,000 is taken with the promissory note (NSC), there is no room left for PUC, which will be nil as a result of a PUC reduction.

ITA 84.1—The Calculations

16-161.   There are two main paragraphs that outline the calculations needed under ITA 84.1. ITA 84.1(1)(a) determines any PUC reduction, which can only apply when share consideration is received. ITA 84.1(1)(b) is the deemed dividend calculation, which can only apply where NSC is received. Where both share and NSC are received the rules require that ITA 84.1(1)(a) be calculated first since the PUC reduction result is needed for the ITA 84.1(1)(b) deemed dividend calculation. Since both NSC and shares are received in the example, we must first determine the PUC reduction:

Increase in legal capital of BHL shares		$ 225,000
Less excess, if any, of:		
ITA 84.1 limit (Note One)	($ 25,000)	
Over the FMV of the NSC	675,000	Nil
ITA 84.1(1)(a) PUC reduction		$225,000

> **Note One**   This amount is technically the greater of the PUC and the ACB. In this example, the two amounts are the same.

16-162.   The result, as expected, would be PUC of nil ($225,000 - $225,000). Given the PUC reduction, the deemed dividend calculation of ITA 84.1(1)(b) can now be determined:

Increase in legal capital of BHL shares		$225,000
FMV of NSC		675,000
Total		$900,000
Less the sum of:		
The greater of the PUC and ACB of Barton		
Industries shares	($ 25,000)	
PUC reduction under ITA 84.1(1)(a)	(225,000)	(250,000)
ITA 84.1(1)(b) deemed dividend (non-eligible)		$650,000

16-163.   The results from Ms. Barton's disposition of her BI shares would be as follows:

Elected POD—ITA 85(1)	$675,000
Less: ITA 84.1(1)(b) deemed dividend (see Note)	(650,000)
ITA 54 adjusted POD	$ 25,000
ACB of Barton Industries shares	(25,000)
Capital gain or capital loss	Nil

> **Note**   The definition of POD in ITA 54 requires that the POD be reduced by a deemed dividend under ITA 84.1(1). In the absence of this exclusion, the deemed dividend could be taxed a second time as a capital gain.

16-164.   Ms. Barton could have achieved the capital gain crystallization with the use of the capital gains deduction and avoided the deemed dividend under ITA 84.1, but she would have had to limit the NSC to $25,000 and taken share consideration for the difference of $875,000. In that case, the elected amount of $675,000 would have been valid for Ms. Barton and BHL, the ACB of the shares would have been $650,000, and the PUC nil (ITA 84.1(1)(a)). The capital gain

reported and capital gains deduction claimed would remain unchanged. Note that the crystallization simply means that Ms. Barton has used her $650,000 in capital gains deduction to effec-
tively increase the ACB of shares she owns. Before the transaction she owned BI shares with
an ACB of nil, and afterwards she owns BHL shares with an ACB of $650,000.

Exercise 16-8

Subject: Dividend Stripping

Ms. Sarah Cole is the sole shareholder of Cole Inc., a CCPC the shares of which qualify
as QSBC shares for the capital gains deduction. The ACB and PUC of the shares are both
$125,000 and the current FMV is $767,000. The GRIP and RDTOH account balances at
year end are nil. On February 1, 2021, Ms. Cole sells all of her Cole Inc. shares to Sarah's
Holdings Ltd. (SHL) for $767,000. As payment she receives consideration consisting of
a promissory note for $450,000 and redeemable preferred shares with a FMV and a
legal capital of $317,000. Ms. Cole owns all of the shares of SHL. In addition, she has
never claimed the capital gains deduction. What are the income tax consequences of
the share sale to SHL? Note that a rollover under ITA 85(1) is not used.

Solutions to Exercises are available in the Study Guide.

We suggest you complete SSP 16-10 at this point.

Capital Gains Stripping—ITA 55(2)

Overview

16-165.   In the discussion of ITA 84.1 it was observed that, in general, this anti-avoidance rule is
designed to prevent the income tax planning advantages of transactions that use the capital gains
deduction as a means to withdraw after-tax earnings (i.e., surplus) of a corporation without the
payment of any income tax by individual shareholders. In earlier chapters the merits of the integration process were emphasized, explaining that when a source of income is incorporated there are
two levels of income tax: corporate level tax and individual level tax when the after-tax earnings of
a corporation are distributed as taxable dividends to individual shareholders. In other words, the
purpose of rules such as ITA 84.1 is to ensure the integrity of the integration process.

16-166.   ITA 55(2) is one of the most complicated provisions found in the ITA, and this coverage
is solely for the purpose of providing a practical awareness, including explaining the purpose of
this anti-avoidance rule, its conditions and exceptions, and a few examples to put the discussion
in context. When ITA 55(2) applies it impacts a corporation that has received a dividend that is
tax free as a result of the taxable income deduction of ITA 112(1) and is generally not subject to
Part IV tax. Part or all of the dividend received is replaced with a capital gain that is subject to
Part I tax.

16-167.   ITA 55(2) is an anti-avoidance rule that also has its roots embedded within the integration process, but unlike ITA 84.1, which focuses in on the individual level of income tax, the
focus of ITA 55(2) is on corporate income tax. In brief, the tax policy concern is that a corporation
resident in Canada has sold corporate property to arm's-length persons at FMV without the payment of income tax on the accrued gain. The most egregious type of planning is demonstrated
in the following example.

EXAMPLE   An individual, Mr. Georgio, purchased land for $30,000 many years ago.
A corporate real estate developer has offered him $1,000,000. Mr. Georgio spoke to
his tax advisor about the income tax consequences of a sale. The advisor tells him that

the income tax will be approximately $250,000 due to the fact that he is in the highest income tax bracket. Mr. Georgio feels that is unfair and asks if there is something that can be done. The following tax plan is put together:

Step 1   Mr. Georgio will incorporate a new CCPC (Land Co.). The company will issue one common share to him for $1.

Step 2   Mr. Georgio will sell the land to Land Co. for $1,000,000. Land Co. will pay him with a promissory note for $30,000 and preferred shares redeemable for $970,000. A joint election will be filed under ITA 85(1) at an elected amount of $30,000. Mr. Georgio would report the sale on his income tax return as a nil capital gain (POD $30,000- ACB $30,000) and the cost of the land to the company will be $30,000. The promissory note to Mr. Georgio will have a tax cost (ACB) of $30,000 and the PUC and ACB of the preferred shares will both be nil.

Step 3   Land Co. will sell the land to the corporate developer for $1,000,000. The developer corporation will pay for the land with $1,000,000 of preferred shares. Land Co. and the corporate developer will file a joint election under ITA 85(1), choosing $30,000 as the elected amount. As a result, Land Co. has no capital gain (POD $30,000- ACB $30,000) and the corporate developer's cost of the land is $30,000. The $1,000,000 of preferred shares of the corporate developer owned by Land Co. have an ACB and PUC of $30,000 as a result of ITA 85(1). At this point the land is now in the hands of the corporate developer.

Step 4   The final step requires Land Co. receiving a $1,000,000 payment from the corporate developer. The payment is made by redeeming the corporate developer preferred shares owned by Land Co. The difference between the redemption payment of $1,000,000 and the PUC of the shares of $30,000 is a deemed dividend of $970,000 to Land Co. Since a redemption is also a disposition of shares, capital gains and capital losses must also be determined. The POD are reduced by the deemed dividend, resulting in adjusted POD of $30,000. As a result, the capital gain to Land Co. is nil (POD $30,000- ACB $30,000). Land Co. includes the $970,000 in income but is eligible for a taxable income deduction of $970,000 as a result of ITA 112(1). The result is that there is no Part I tax. Additional steps are necessary to avoid Part IV tax, which can complicate the planning and would also neutralize any tax savings since Part IV, if it applied, would equal $371,830 [(38 1/3%)($970,000)], which greatly exceeds the $250,000 personal income tax Mr. Georgio is attempting to avoid.

Conclusion   Mr. Georgio has used a corporation to sell land to a corporate developer, an arm's-length person, at FMV. In tax policy terms, Land Co. should have paid corporate income tax on a taxable capital gain of $485,000 [(50%)($970,000)], which would have exceeded 50% since capital gains are highly taxed within a corporation. While some would argue that the $1,000,000 is not in Mr. Georgio's hands (yet), the undeniable truth is that the land was sold for $1,000,000 yet there is no income tax payable by Land Co. as a result. Mr. Georgio would be able to extract the funds from Land Co. in the future through redemptions of the shares he owns in Land Co. In effect, the income tax consequences of the land sale would be within his control. This is contrary to the Canadian income tax system that operates on the realization principle that when there is a sale of property to arm's-length persons there should be an accounting for income tax at the time of the sale. It is this type of planning that is considered particularly offensive that led to ITA 55(2).

16-168.   In the example presented in Paragraph 16-167, there was an accrued gain of $970,000 on the land. ITA 85(1) was used to move the land from the individual to Land Co., then finally to the developer corporation without income tax consequences. In addition, the use of ITA 85(1) led to a payment with preferred shares with a high FMV but nil PUC and ACB. The creation of the preferred shares then allowed Land Co. to realize the $970,000 accrued gain not as a capital gain but as a taxable dividend. The taxable income deduction of ITA 112(1) then ensured that no amount would be added to taxable income, avoiding Part I income tax. The overall result is that a capital gain of $970,000 was converted to a tax-free dividend. We also saw this conversion process in the ITA 84.1 planning when a withdrawal of surplus from a corporation that would normally have been treated as a taxable dividend was effectively converted to a capital gain, which because of the capital gains deduction was tax free.

The Conditions and Exceptions—ITA 55(2)

16-169.   There are five conditions to ITA 55(2) as follows:

- The receipt of a taxable dividend by a resident corporation

- The corporation is entitled to a taxable income deduction under ITA 112(1) with respect to the dividend

- The taxable dividend is part of a series of transactions

- The purpose of the taxable dividend is to cause a significant reduction on a capital gain on the disposition of a share

- The purpose is to reduce the FMV of any share or to increase the tax cost of property owned by the corporate recipient of the taxable dividend

The last condition was added in 2015 and generally relates to certain types of tax planning that go beyond the scope of our coverage. We will therefore focus on the purpose test that looks to whether there was a significant reduction in a capital gain.

16-170.   There are five general exceptions to avoid ITA 55(2):

- **PURPOSE**   None of the purposes of the taxable dividend have anything to do with avoiding income tax on a capital gain. Acceptable planning generally includes purification transactions to ensure that the shares of a company qualify for the capital gains deduction; creditor proofing, which involves moving certain corporate property to other corporations to avoid creditor risk; and certain loss utilization planning among affiliated persons.

- **PART IV**   The taxable dividend is subject to Part IV tax that is not refunded as part of the planning.

- **SAFE INCOME**   The taxable dividend distribution is supported by corporate earnings that have already been subject to corporate income tax. The distribution by a corporation of its safe income is not considered offensive.

- **RELATED PERSONS**   The series of transactions is only between persons who are related to each other. There is much more to this particular rule that again goes beyond our coverage. This rule only applies if the taxable dividend is as a result of a share redemption transaction under either of ITA 84(2) or (3).

- **BUTTERFLY**   There is an exception for what is referred to as a butterfly reorganization, which often includes multiple intercompany taxable dividends. A butterfly reorganization generally results in a corporation distributing all of its property on a pro rata basis to its corporate shareholders as a result of a reorganization. This topic is also beyond the scope of our coverage.

Applying ITA 55(2)

16-171.   We can illustrate the application of ITA 55(2) to the example presented in Paragraph 16-167. The first step involves identifying the transactions that are part of a series of transactions, which includes pre- and post-planning transactions. In the example, the initial contact by the corporate developer would generally be considered the beginning of the series. Within the series it is important to next identify an intercorporate taxable dividend that entitles the dividend recipient to a taxable income deduction under ITA 112(1). This occurs in step 4 when, on the redemption, Land Co. is deemed to receive a taxable dividend of $970,000.

16-172.   The final condition is whether the purpose of the taxable dividend was to significantly reduce the capital gain on a share owned by the corporate recipient of the dividend. This condition looks to the preferred shares of the corporate developer that were owned by Land Co. The FMV of those shares was $1,000,000 and the ACB was $30,000, therefore an arm's-length sale of those shares at FMV would have resulted in a capital gain of $970,000. This hypothetical result is then compared to the actual capital gain that occurred as a result of the redemption. The actual capital gain on the redemption was nil because the $1,000,000 proceeds were reduced by the ITA 84(3) deemed dividend of $970,000 to $30,000, which matched the ACB. The result is that because of the taxable dividend a potential capital gain of $970,000 was reduced to nil. Historically, the CRA generally considers there to be a significant reduction if the amount is at least $50,000.

16-173.   The analysis demonstrates that ITA 55(2) would appear to apply to the $970,000 taxable dividend received by Land Co., but we can only draw that conclusion once the exceptions have been analyzed. In the example, the purpose was clearly tax motivated and the taxable dividend occurred within the tax motivated planning transactions. In addition, Part IV did not apply to the taxable dividend, the related person rule does not apply since Land Co. and the corporate developer were not related, nor were the transactions representative of a butterfly reorganization. The final exception is safe income, which requires further elaboration.

A Word on Safe Income

16-174.   In very general terms, safe income means safe income on hand, which is equal to corporate net income minus corporate income taxes and taxable dividends paid that have accumulated since the shares in question were acquired. The safe income concept is premised on the FMV of a share. In general, the FMV of a share is made up of three components consisting of the cost of the shares plus after-tax income retained in the company (safe income) plus other amounts such as unrealized appreciation on corporate property, goodwill, and market expectations. In effect, once a share is purchased its future value will be directly impacted by the corporation's success, which includes profitability and increased value in its properties (e.g., net assets).

> **EXAMPLE**   InvestCo owns all of the only issued shares of ShopCo. The ShopCo shares cost InvestCo $100,000 and, in 2021, the FMV of the shares have increased to $5,000,000. The safe income of ShopCo in 2021 has been calculated as $3,000,000. In terms of the FMV of the ShopCo shares the value can be broken down into cost of $100,000 + safe income of $3,000,000 + other of $1,900,000 representing untaxed corporate surplus or gains. If an arm's-length person approached InvestCo to purchase the shares of ShopCo for $5,000,000, InvestCo could arrange to have ShopCo pay a $3,000,000 taxable dividend to InvestCo prior to the sale. The dividend would reduce the value of the ShopCo shares to $2,000,000. InvestCo could then sell the shares to the arm's-length person and recognize a capital gain of $1,900,000. In this situation the conditions of ITA 55(2) would have been met, but the safe income exception would apply with the result that ITA 55(2) would not apply to the $3,000,000 taxable dividend. It is common tax planning practice for corporations to distribute their safe income annually as taxable dividends to corporate shareholders, which is perfectly acceptable.

Back to Applying ITA 55(2)

16-175.   Returning to our example, the question is whether the preferred shares of the corporate developer have any safe income that could reduce or eliminate the income tax consequences of ITA 55(2). The tax cost of the shares to Land Co. are $30,000, which was determined using ITA 85(1). The $970,000 difference between the $1,000,000 FMV and the tax cost of $30,000 has nothing to do with corporate earnings of the corporate developer; in fact, that difference is solely attributable to an unrealized gain of $970,000 on the underlying land. The result is that, in terms of safe income, the FMV of the preferred shares owned by Land Co. would be composed of a tax cost $30,000 + nil safe income + $970,000 of untaxed unrealized gains. As a result, none of the exceptions apply and the $970,000 taxable dividend deemed received by Land Co. on the redemption of the shares by the corporate developer are subject to ITA 55(2). If Land Co. and the corporate developer had been related, ITA 55(2) would not have applied to the taxable dividend of $970,000 on the redemption.

The Income Tax Consequences of ITA 55(2)

16-176.   If the conditions for ITA 55(2) are met and none of the exceptions apply, then very specific tax consequences apply to the corporation that received the taxable dividend. The rules are divided into three separate paragraphs. ITA 55(2)(a) applies to the dividend recipient, and either ITA 55(2)(b) or (c) applies depending on whether the dividend is a deemed dividend as a result of a redemption of shares or any other type of dividend.

> **ITA 55(2)(a)**   This provision deems a taxable dividend to which ITA 55(2) applies not to be a dividend to the dividend recipient. It is important to recognize that the corporation paying the taxable dividend is still considered to have paid a dividend. This would mean that the dividend could qualify for a dividend refund, but more importantly the dividend-paying corporation should not designate the dividend as an eligible dividend since the dividend recipient cannot add that amount to its GRIP account because ITA 55(2)(a) deems it not to be a dividend.

> **ITA 55(2)(b)**   If the taxable dividend is a deemed dividend as a result of either ITA 84(2) or (3), the capital gain part of the calculation that reduces the redemption proceeds by the deemed dividend to determine an adjusted POD is reversed to restore the capital gain.

> **ITA 55(2)(c)**   If the taxable dividend is any other type of taxable dividend, then no adjusted POD calculations are necessary. In that case, ITA 55(2)(c) simply deems the taxable dividend to be a capital gain.

Example 1—ITA 55(2)(b)

16-177.   This first example illustrates the mechanics of the dollar amounts where the taxable dividend is a deemed dividend that has occurred as a result of a redemption of shares. It is diagrammed in Figure 16-5.

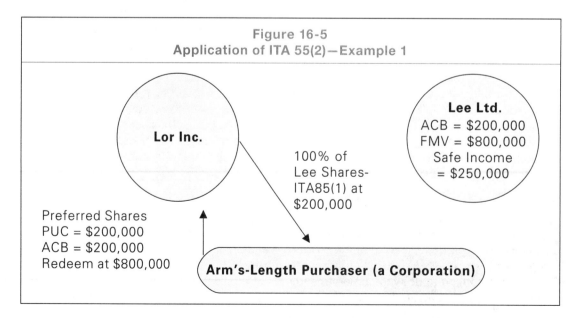

Figure 16-5
Application of ITA 55(2)—Example 1

Lor Inc.

Preferred Shares
PUC = $200,000
ACB = $200,000
Redeem at $800,000

100% of
Lee Shares-
ITA85(1) at
$200,000

Lee Ltd.
ACB = $200,000
FMV = $800,000
Safe Income
= $250,000

Arm's-Length Purchaser (a Corporation)

16-178. In this example, Lor Inc. owns all of the shares of Lee Ltd. An arm's-length corporate purchaser has offered to purchase the Lee Ltd. shares from Lor Inc. at their FMV of $800,000. Lor Inc. will sell the shares to the corporate purchaser for $800,000. The corporate purchaser will pay consideration to Lor Inc. of $800,000 in redeemable preferred shares. Lor Inc. and the purchaser corporation will file a joint election under ITA 85(1) and choose an elected amount of $200,000. As a result, there are no income tax consequences to Lor Inc. because the elected amount of $200,000 is equal to the ACB of the Lee Ltd. shares. The attributes of the preferred shares received by Lor Inc. as consideration are FMV of $800,000 and both PUC and ACB are $200,000.

16-179. The redemption of the preferred shares by the corporate purchaser has the following income tax implications to Lor Inc.:

Proceeds of redemption	$800,000
PUC	(200,000)
ITA 84(3) deemed dividend [without ITA 55(2)]	$600,000
Redemption amount	$800,000
Less: ITA 84(3) dividend	(600,000)
Adjusted POD	$200,000
ACB	(200,000)
Capital gain [without ITA 55(2)]	Nil

16-180. All of the conditions of ITA 55(2) have been met. In determining whether there was a significant reduction of a capital gain, the test is to compare the capital gain that would have arisen had Lor Inc. sold the preferred shares at their FMV of $800,000 versus the actual capital gain as a result of the redemption. In this case, the hypothetical capital gain would have been $600,000 (POD $800,000 - ACB $200,000) versus no capital when the shares were redeemed. The reduction of the capital gain attributable to the redemption, therefore, is $600,000.

16-181. The only exception that is applicable would be for the safe income, which is listed as $250,000. This means that only $350,000 of the $600,000 taxable dividend is caught by ITA 55(2). ITA 55(2)(a) deems $350,000 of the $600,000 taxable dividend not to be a dividend to Lor Inc. ITA 55(2)(b) will apply to revise the capital gain portion of the redemption calculation as follows:

Adjusted POD	
(see calculation in Paragraph 16-179)	$200,000
Adjustment—ITA 55(2)(b)	350,000
Revised POD	$550,000
ACB	(200,000)
Capital gain	$350,000

16-182. A much simpler approach would have been for Lee Ltd. to pay a safe income dividend to Lor Inc. in the amount of $250,000, which would have reduced the FMV of the Lee Ltd. shares to $550,000. A sale of the Lee Ltd. shares by Lor Inc. for $550,000 would then have resulted in a capital gain of $350,000. ITA 55(2) would not have applied to the $250,000 taxable dividend since it was all attributable to safe income.

Example 2—ITA 55(2)(c)

16-183. This second example begins with the same corporations and the same tax attributes as listed in Example 1 in Paragraph 16-179. The only difference is that Lee Ltd. borrows $600,000 from a bank (financial institution) to fund a $600,000 taxable dividend to Lor Inc. The payment of the dividend reduces the value of the Lee Ltd. shares from $800,000 to $200,000. Lor Inc. then sells the Lee Ltd. shares to the arm's-length purchaser for their FMV of $200,000, realizing no capital gain because the ACB is also $200,000. The purchaser pays down the Lee Ltd. loan of $600,000. This scenario is illustrated in Figure 16-6.

Capital Gains Stripping—ITA 55(2)

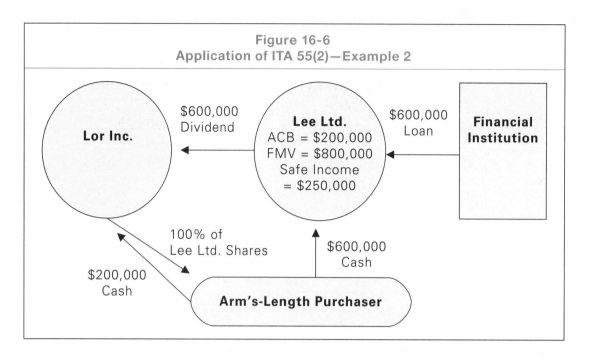

Figure 16-6
Application of ITA 55(2)—Example 2

16-184.   In effect, the purchaser has paid $800,000 for the Lee Ltd. shares as $200,000 directly to Lor Inc. and $600,000 indirectly to Lor Inc. as the bank loan that financed the $600,000 taxable dividend. All of the conditions of ITA 55(2) have been met since the $600,000 dividend caused a hypothetical capital gain of $600,000 that would have occurred without the dividend beingreduced to nil. The only exception that would apply is for the safe income. The result is that $250,000 of the taxable dividend is safe and only the remaining $350,000 is caught by ITA 55(2). That part of the dividend is deemed not to be a dividend by ITA 55(2)(a) and is deemed to be a capital gain by ITA 55(2)(c). The result is reflected in the following:

Taxable dividend received	$600,000
Dividend attributable to safe income—	
Retains its status as a dividend	(250,000)
Amount deemed by ITA 55(2)(a) not to be a dividend	
and by ITA 55(2)(c) to be a capital gain	$350,000

16-185.   As was the result in Example 1, ITA 55(2) has served to convert the portion of the dividend not paid from safe income into a capital gain, which will be taxed as a capital gain. The $250,000 portion of the dividend attributable to safe income will retain its status as a taxable dividend and is a taxable income deduction under ITA 112(1). The net income impact would be a taxable dividend of $250,000 + a taxable capital gain of $175,000 [(50%)($350,000)] for a total of $425,000. The taxable income impact would be net income of $425,000 minus the ITA 112(1) taxable income deduction of $250,000 for a net total of $175,000.

Exercise 16-9

Subject: Capital Gains Strip—ITA 55(2)

Markem Ltd. owns all of the issued common shares of Larkin Ltd. The shares of Larkin have an ACB of $75,000 and a FMV of $840,000. The safe income attributable to the Larkin Ltd. shares owned by Markem Ltd. is $225,000. Markem Ltd. has been approached by an arm's-length person (Mr. Leaner) to purchase all of the Larkin Ltd. shares. As part of the planning to implement this sale, Markem Ltd. has instructed Larkin Ltd. to borrow $750,000 from the bank, which will be used to pay a taxable dividend to Markem Ltd. prior to the sale. The shares will then be sold to Mr. Leaner for $90,000. What are the income tax consequences to Markem Ltd.?

Solutions to Exercises are available in the Study Guide.

We suggest you complete SSP 16-11 at this point.

Key Terms

A full glossary with definitions is provided at the end of the Study Guide.

Adjusted Cost Base	Non-Share Consideration
Affiliated Group of Persons	Paid-Up Capital
Affiliated Person—ITA 251.1(1)	PUC
Boot	Recapture of CCA
Capital Cost	Rollover
Capital Gains Stripping	Safe Income
Controlled—ITA 251.1(3)	Subject Corporation
Corporation	Superficial Loss—ITA 54
Depreciable Capital Property	Taxpayer
Dividend Stripping	Terminal Loss
Eligible Capital Property	Transfer
Gift	Transferee
Individual	Transferor
Non-Depreciable Capital Property	Undepreciated Capital Cost (UCC)

References

For more detailed study of the material in this chapter, we would refer you to the following:

ITA 13(21.2)	Loss on Certain Transfers
ITA 15(1)	Benefits Conferred on a Shareholder
ITA 40(2)(g)	Superficial Losses
ITA 40(3.4)	Loss on Certain Properties
ITA 54	Definitions (Proceeds of Disposition and Superficial Loss)
ITA 55(2)	Deemed Proceeds or Capital Gain
ITA 84.1	Non-Arm's-Length Sale of Shares
ITA 85	Transfer of Property to Corporation by Shareholders
ITA 89(1)	Definitions
ITA 251.1	Affiliated Persons
IC 76-19R3	Transfer of Property to a Corporation under Section 85
S4-F3-C1	Price Adjustment Clauses
IT-188R	Sale of Accounts Receivable
IT-291R3	Transfer of Property to a Corporation under Subsection 85(1)
IT-489R	Non-Arm's-Length Sale of Shares to a Corporation

Self-Study Problems (SSPs)

Self-Study Problems (SSPs) provide practice in problem solving. Within the chapters, we have indicated where it would be appropriate to stop and work on each SSP. The problems can be downloaded by chapter from MyLab Accounting. Solutions are available in the Study Guide. Select problems can also be completed directly in MyLab and auto-graded.

Assignment Problems

Solutions to Assignment Problems (APs) are available to instructors only.

AP 16-1 (Direct Sale of Real Estate vs. Incorporation of the Real Estate for Shares Followed by a Sale of the Shares)

For a number of years, Brett Manson has owned an apartment building in the city of London, Ontario. Cost information is as follows:

Acquisition cost	$1,355,000
Cost of the land	(462,000)
Capital cost of the building	$ 893,000

At the beginning of the current year, values related to the property are as follows:

FMV of property	$1,610,000
FMV of land	(574,000)
FMV of the building	$1,036,000
UCC of the building	$ 685,000

Brett incorporates a company in which he owns all of the shares and sells the land and building to the corporation for $1,610,000. The company pays for the land and building by issuing preferred shares redeemable for $1,610,000. Brett and the corporation file a joint election under ITA 85(1) to elect an amount of $462,000 for the land and $685,000 for the building.

Later in the year, Brett sells all of the preferred shares to an arm's-length individual for $1,610,000.

Required:

A. Determine the income tax consequences to Brett of the ITA 85(1) election.

B. How do these results compare with the income tax consequences of simply selling the land and building directly to the arm's-length individual for $1,610,000?

AP 16-2 (ITA 85(1)—Mini Cases)

In the following three independent cases a joint election is filed under ITA 85(1).

Case One Depreciable property with a capital cost of $130,000, a UCC balance of $59,904, and FMV of $183,400 is sold to a corporation for consideration that consists of a promissory note of $140,000, preferred shares redeemable for $22,000, and common shares with a FMV of $21,400. The depreciable property is the only property in the class.

Case Two Inventory with a tax cost of $87,000 and FMV of $120,000 is sold to a corporation for consideration that consists of a promissory note for $93,000 and preferred shares that are redeemable for $27,000. The inventory is not real property (land and buildings).

Case Three Land with an ACB of $617,000 and FMV of $823,000 is sold to a corporation for consideration that consists of a promissory note of $72,000 and preferred shares redeemeable for $751,000.

Required: For each of the three cases provide the following information:

A. The range of acceptable elected amounts.

B. Assuming that the minimum elected amount determined in Part A is chosen, determine the additional income that will be included in the income of the seller.

C. Again assuming that the minimum elected amount under Part A is chosen, determine the ACB of all consideration and the PUC of the share consideration. Your answer should indicate whether there are any mismatches of value that could result in either the application of the gifting rule (ITA 85(1)(e.2)) or a shareholder benefit (ITA 15(1)).

AP 16-3   (ACB of Consideration and PUC)

Lily Haring owns a property that is depreciable property that is the last property in its class. The capital cost is $623,000, the UCC is $229,663, and the FMV is $946,000. The depreciable property is used in a business.

Lily will sell this property to a corporation that she will control. A joint election will be filed under ITA 85(1) in which the minimum elected amount will be chosen. She is considering receiving three different consideration packages, all of which total $946,000:

> **Package One**   The company will pay her consideration consisting of a promissory note for $229,663 and preferred shares with a FMV of $716,337.

> **Package Two**   The company will pay her consideration consisting of a promissory note for $100,000, preferred shares with a FMV of $100,000, and common shares with a FMV of $746,000.

> **Package Three**   The company will pay her consideration consisting of a promissory note for $700,000 and preferred shares with a FMV of $246,000.

Required: For each of the three packages, determine:

- The minimum elected amount that Lily can choose and the amount and type of income that will result.

- The ACB of the consideration received.

- The PUC for the share consideration.

AP 16-4   (ITA 85 Sale of Depreciable Property)

Mr. Rob Banting owns a property that is depreciable property and that is the only property in the class. The capital cost of the property is $343,000, the UCC is $213,790, and the FMV is $420,000. The depreciable property is used in a business.

Mr. Banting will sell the depreciable property to a newly incorporated company in which he will own all of the shares.

Mr. Banting has a 2018 net capital loss balance of $26,000 that he wishes to use in the current year to the extent possible. To that end, he jointly elects with the company under ITA 85(1) and chooses an elected amount of $395,000.

The company pays Mr. Banting consideration consisting of a promissory note for $175,000, preferred shares with a FMV of $90,000, and common shares with a FMV of $155,000.

Required: Describe the income tax implications to both Mr. Banting and the company.

AP 16-5   (Mini Cases with Mismatches in FMV [Gift and Shareholder Benefit])

Peter Kowalski owns a rental property that was acquired years ago at a cost of $1,200,000. At the time, he estimated the value of the land to be $200,000 and the value of the building to be $1,000,000.

Peter estimates that the current FMV of the property is $1,500,000, with $300,000 attributable to the land and $1,200,000 to the building. The UCC of the building is $460,800.

Peter has decided to sell the property to a corporation. A joint election will be filed under ITA 85(1) with respect to the sale. He is considering three different scenarios.

Scenario 1   Peter sells the property to a new corporation in which he will be the sole shareholder. He has a 2019 net capital loss balance of $50,000. As he does not anticipate any capital gains in the current year he would like the sale of the rental property to generate a capital gain of $100,000, sufficient to offset the net capital loss balance. As a result, the elected amount for the land will be $300,000 and for the building $460,800. The consideration to be paid by the company will consist of a promissory note for $760,800 and preferred shares with a FMV of $739,200.

Scenario 2   Peter sells the property to a corporation of which he is the sole shareholder. The corporation has been very profitable, has no debt, and has acumulated excess cash. The elected amount for the land is $200,000 and $460,800 for the building. The consideration to be paid by the company will consist of a promissory note for $660,800 and redeemable preferred shares. The legal capital of the preferred shares will be $839,200. The preferable features of the shares result in a FMV of $939,200.

Scenario 3   Peter's daughter, Stella, incorporates a new corporation. She acquires all of the common shares for $10,000 using her own money. Peter subsequently sells the rental property to the corporation. A joint election is filed under ITA 85(1) and the elected amount chosen for the land is $200,000 and $460,800 for the building. As he would like to provide financial assistance to his daughter, in his election he claims that the FMV of the land is only $200,000, hoping that the CRA will not inquire as to the value of the land. Based on this, the company pays him consideration consisting of a promissory note for $400,000 and preferred shares with a FMV of $1,000,000.

On a review of the ITA 85(1) election, the CRA discovers the undervaluation and reassesses Peter on the basis that the FMV of the land is $300,000. Peter does not object to the reassessment.

Required: For each of the three scenarios, determine for Peter:

- The income tax consequences to him.
- The tax cost of the land and building to the corporation.
- The ACB of the share consideration.
- The PUC of the share consideration.

In your solution for Scenario 3, include the effects of the reassessment.

AP 16-6   *(ITA 85(1) with Sale/Redemption of Shares)*

Three years ago, Connie Bright purchased a commercial property consisting of land and a building at a total cost of $1,475,000, with $300,000 attributable to the land and $1,175,000 to the building. The purchase was facilitated with a $550,000 mortgage on the property.

During 2019 and 2020, the property was very profitable. Connie believes that the time is right to incorporate the property. She plans to sell the property in January 2021 to a new corporation in which she will be the sole shareholder. The relevant facts about the property at the time of the sale are as follows:

	Land	Building
FMV	$475,000	$1,300,000
Adjusted cost base/capital cost	300,000	1,175,000
UCC	N/A	1,071,365
Mortgage balance	N/A	525,000

A joint election will be filed under ITA 85(1) and an elected amount of $475,000 will be chosen for the land and $1,100,000 for the building.

The corporation will pay consideration consisting of the assumption of the $525,000 mortgage balance, a promissory note of $1,050,000, and redeemable preferred shares with a FMV of $200,000.

The new corporation does not have a balance in its GRIP account at the end of any of its taxation years.

Required:

A. What are the income tax consequences of choosing elected amounts totalling $1,575,000 ($475,000 + $1,100,000)? Your answer should identify any amounts required to be included in Connie's income as a result of the sale, as well as the tax costs of the land and building to the corporation.

B. Compute the ACB of any consideration received.

C. Compute the PUC of the share consideration.

D. What are the income tax consequences to Connie if, during 2021, she sells the preferred shares to an arm's-length person for $400,000?

E. What are the income tax consequences to Connie if, during 2021, the corporation redeems the preferred shares for $400,000?

AP 16-7   *(Transfer of Land and Building to a Corporation)*

Howard Foster has owned and operated his own professional income tax preparation and bookkeeping business as a sole proprietorship for many years. The business is quite successful and has gradually grown to the point where Howard employs over 40 individuals full time, which doubles with the addition of part-time staff to help at tax time. The business offices are located in a building in downtown Halifax that Howard purchased a few months before he began the business.

Recently, a relatively new client threatened legal action against Howard on learning that the bookkeeping services provided had not produced accurate and current books and records, resulting in a reassessment as a result of a CRA audit of the client. Howard personally worked with the client to resolve the issue but was sufficiently worried about the impact of a lawsuit that he decided to speak with his lawyer. The lawyer advised that the land and building be separated from the business to remove it from the reach of creditors should a lawsuit ever materialize. Howard agreed with the advice and a new corporation, 123789 Ltd., was incorporated in Nova Scotia. Howard will be the only shareholder and has acquired 100 common shares for $100.

Howard purchased the land and building for $4,100,000 using $775,000 of his own personal funds and financing the remainder with a mortgage of $3,325,000. Five years ago Howard spent $500,000 on major renovations to add a dozen new offices, which he financed by renegotiating the existing mortgage. The original cost of the property of $4,100,000 was split between the land, which was valued at $680,000, and the building at $3,420,000.

Howard will sell the land and building to the new company on December 9, 2021, for a total of $7,615,000, which represents the FMV of the property according to a recent valuation. The company will assume the mortgage balance. Once the property is sold, Howard and the company will enter into a rental agreement for the continued use of the property in Howard's business. Howard plans to file an election under ITA 85(1) with respect to the sale. Since Howard has realized allowable capital losses of $52,000 in 2021, he wishes to create sufficient taxable capital gains as part of the ITA 85(1) election to offset those losses.

Information relevant to the land and building is as follows:

• FMV of the land	$ 915,000
• ACB of the land	680,000
• FMV of the building	6,700,000
• Capital cost of the building	4,600,000
• UCC	2,764,600
• Mortgage balance	2,335,000

Howard wishes to get paid as quickly as possible and prefers promissory notes to shares, which can be troublesome to redeem. Since Howard is not all that familiar with ITA 85(1) he has approached you, his tax advisor, to handle the election. He initially proposes the following breakdown of how the company will pay him:

Assumption of the mortgage	$ 2,335,000
Promissory note	3,000,000
Preferred shares	2,280,000
Total sale price of the property	$ 7,615,000

Howard proposes to elect an amount of $784,000 for the land, to provide sufficient capital gains to offset his capital losses, and $4,551,000 for the building. Together these two amounts equal the assumed mortgage and promissory note.

There will be no additions to 123789 Ltd.'s GRIP in 2021.

Required:

A. Determine the income tax consequences of the sale by Howard to 123789 Ltd. if ITA 85(1) is not used.

B. Determine the income tax consequences of Howard's ITA 85(1) proposal. Your answer should include (i) the POD of the land and building, (ii) the tax cost to the company of the land and building, (iii) the tax cost of the promissory note, (iv) the tax cost (ACB) of the preferred shares, and (v) the PUC of the preferred shares. Comment on whether Howard's proposed elected amounts are within the acceptable range for ITA 85(1) purposes.

C. Using the tax values determined in Part B, what amounts would be included in Howard's net income if, during 2022, he were to (i) sell all of the preferred shares for $2,500,000 or (ii) redeem the preferred shares for $2,500,000?

D. As his tax advisor, determine the best use of ITA 85(1) that would result in no immediate income tax consequences other than a capital gain sufficient to offset his $52,000 of allowable capital losses. Your answer should include (i) the POD of the land and building, (ii) the tax cost to the company of the land and building, (iii) the tax cost of the promissory note, (iv) the tax cost (ACB) of the preferred shares, and (v) the PUC of the preferred shares. Assume that Howard wishes to maximize the amount of new debt he can receive.

E. Using the tax values determined in Part D, what amounts would be included in Howard's net income if, during 2022, the corporation redeems all of the preferred shares for $4,500,000? Include the amount of any federal dividend tax credit.

Show all supporting calculations.

Bonus Question: Howard plans to pay rent to 123789 Ltd. and continue operating the business as a sole proprietor. 123789 Ltd. will have only one employee. Is there a better way that would be much more tax effective for the business and 123789 Ltd.? Explain your answer.

Hint: This was discussed in Chapter 12 and relates to active business income.

AP 16-8　(The Incorporation of a Business and Redemption of Shares)
Ms. Martha Fleck carries on a business as a sole proprietor that operates out of leased premises. On December 31, 2020, the tax costs and FMV of property used in the business is as follows.

	Tax Cost	FMV
Accounts receivable	$132,000	$ 127,500
Inventory	261,000	312,000
Equipment (capital cost = $420,000)	351,000	475,500
Goodwill	Nil	525,000
Total	$744,000	$1,440,000
Liabilities	(142,500)	(142,500)
Net	$601,500	$1,297,500

All of the above properties of the business will be sold to Rollex Inc., a newly incorporated company. The accounts receivable will be sold using a joint election under ITA 22.

A joint election under ITA 85(1) will be filed with respect to the inventory, equipment, and goodwill. The corporation will pay consideration of $1,312,500 ($1,440,000 - $127,500), consisting of new debt of $112,500, assumption of the existing liabilities of $142,500, preferred shares with a FMV of $337,500, and common shares with a FMV of $720,000. The new corporation does not have a balance in its GRIP account in any taxation year.

Ms. Fleck wishes to incorporate her business in a manner that minimizes any income tax resulting from the sale.

Required:　Ignore the lifetime capital gains deduction in your solution.

A.　Do you agree with the decision to file an election under ITA 22 with respect to the accounts receivable? Explain your conclusion and determine the income tax consequences of this decision.

B.　Given that Ms. Fleck wishes to minimize income tax on the sale, indicate the amounts that should be elected for each of the inventory, equipment, and goodwill.

C.　Determine the ACB of all consideration received by Ms. Fleck.

D.　Determine the PUC of the share consideration.

E.　Determine the income tax consequences to Ms. Fleck if the preferred and common shares issued as consideration were redeemed in January 2021 at their FMV determined at the time of sale.

AP 16-9　(Gift to a Related Person—ITA 85(1)(e.2))
Ms. Martine Renaud has carried on a business as a sole proprietor for over 25 years. The business has been very successful and, on January 1, 2021, the tax cost and FMV of its business property and liabilities are shown below. The tax cost of the class 8 property and the building are the UCC.

	Tax Cost	FMV
Accounts receivable (no reserve taken)	$ 60,000	$ 57,000
Inventories	825,000	840,000
Depreciable property—CCA class 8 (Note One)	1,725,000	1,780,000
Land	923,000	1,450,000
Building (Note Two)	1,760,000	2,436,000
Total	$5,293,000	$6,563,000
Liabilities	(430,000)	(430,000)
Net	$4,863,000	$6,133,000

Note One   The capital cost of the properties in class 8 total $1,960,000.

Note Two   The capital cost of the building is $3,600,000.

Ms. Renaud has two daughters, Alma aged 26 and Amanda aged 28.

Ms. Renaud would like to involve her daughters in the future growth of her business. To accomplish this, in January 2021 she arranges for them to incorporate a new corporation. Each of the two daughters purchases 100 common shares for $1,000. The new corporation is named Almand Inc., and at this point the corporation balance sheet reflects $2,000 in cash and $2,000 in share capital.

On January 1, 2021, Ms. Renaud sells all of the business properties to Almand Inc. A joint election is filed under ITA 22 with respect to the accounts receivables and a joint election is filed under ITA 85(1) with respect to all of the remaining properties. The business does not have any goodwill.

The elected amount chosen under ITA 85(1) for each property is the tax cost, which, absent the accounts receivables, totals $5,233,000 ($5,293,000 - $60,000). Almand Inc. will provide consideration that consists of the assumption of the existing $430,000 in liabilities, the issuance of a promissory note of $1,570,000, and redeemable preferred shares with a FMV of $4,506,000 for a total of $6,506,000, which matches the FMV of the properties purchased absent the accounts receivables.

The CRA subsequently reviews the ITA 85(1) election and determines that the FMV of the land is $1,850,000, $400,000 more than the value claimed by Ms. Renaud in the T2057 election form. Since there was no price adjustment clause added to the purchase and sale agreement and Ms. Renaud did not obtain a professional valuation, she decides not to object to the CRA reassessment to apply the gifting rule of ITA 85(1)(e.2).

Required: Ignore the lifetime capital gains deduction in your answer.

A. Taking into consideration the effect of the reassessment, determine the income tax consequences to Ms. Renaud. Your answer should identify amounts to be included in Ms. Renaud's income as a result of the sale and the impact of the reassessment, as well as the ACB of all of the consideration and the PUC of the preferred share consideration.

B. Determine the income tax consequence to Ms. Renaud if all of her preferred shares are redeemed for $4,506,000 immediately after the reassessment.

C. Alma decides to sell her common shares of Almand Inc. shares to an arm's-length person for $275,000 immediately after the reassessment. Determine the income tax consequences of the sale to Alma.

AP 16-10   (Excess Consideration)

Moe Granite incorporated his residential construction business 15 years ago. The company, Bedrock Ltd., has been very successful and profitable to the point that it has excess cash that it has been regularly investing.

Moe and his family live in a home he purchased a few years before he was married. Moe also acquired two plots of land—one located along the lakefront of an expanding area that has grown in popularity since he purchased it and a second in an area that Moe expected would one day become a growing commercial sector given its proximity to a major city.

The family home is his only principal residence. Moe had always planned to build a luxurious home on the vacant land, but he has been so busy with the company he never had a chance to begin the construction of that lakefront home.

Moe recently sat down with his accountant, telling him about his plans and adding that he needed additional cash from the company to realize his dreams. He estimated that the construction of the lakefront home would take almost a full year given its location and would likely cost in excess of $1 million. He is unwilling to sell the current family home until the construction of the lakefront home was complete. He is also unwilling to sell the second piece of land, telling his accountant that the time was not right and he expected the value to increase substantially in the next few years.

Moe told his accountant that he was in a quandary as to how to come up with the cash he would need given he was unwilling to borrow from commercial lenders or his own company, did not want to sell his current family home or the second plot of land, or pay any additional income taxes by drawing additional salary or dividends since he was already paying tax in the highest tax bracket. Given the expanded tax on split income (TOSI), he was also unwilling to entertain any family income splitting planning with his spouse and their three minor children.

Moe's accountant told him that he had a plan that would accomplish his objectives at minimum cost. The accountant explained that Moe could sell both the current family home and the second piece of land to his company. This, explained the accountant, would keep the current home and the land "in the family" while giving him all the funds necessary to complete the lakefront construction and avoiding the payment of any additional income taxes. Moe agreed. The plan is to sell the current family home and the second piece of land to the company. ITA 85(1) will be used to defer any taxable gains on the properties. The accountant added that while ITA 85(1) is not necessary for a FMV sale of the family home since none of the gain will be taxable, he advised that the additional flexibility provided made it worthwhile to include it in the election. The sale agreements are all dated November 18, 2021. The two properties and their relevant FMV on the date of the sale are as follows:

	Tax Cost (ACB)	Fair Market Value
Principal residence	$450,000	$1,000,000
Vacant land	115,000	500,000

The FMV for each property was estimated by Moe. Assume that no professional valuation was done. There is an existing mortgage on the principal residence of $160,000.

The company will pay Moe the following amounts for each property:

Assumption of the mortgage	$ 160,000
Promissory note	840,000
Preferred shares	Nominal
Total sale price of the principal residence	$1,000,000

Note: The reference to "nominal" means $1 or other negligible amount, which you can ignore in your answer.

Assumption of the mortgage	$ Nil
Promissory note	115,000
Preferred shares	385,000
Total sale orice of the vacant land	$500,000

Total consideration for ITA 85(1) purposes is as follows:

Assumption of the mortgage	$ 160,000
Promissory note	955,000
Preferred shares	385,000
Total sale price of the principal residence and vacant land	$1,500,000

The ITA 85(1) elected amount for the principal residence will be $1,000,000 and $115,000 for the land.

Assume that in 2023, the 2021 ITA 85 election is audited and reassessed by the CRA on the basis that the FMV pf the principal residence was only $750,000 and $250,000 for the vacant land.

Required:

A. Calculate the effect on Moe's net income that will result from the ITA 85(1) election as originally filed.

B. Determine the ACB and PUC of the preferred shares and ACB of the promissory note received by Moe on the sale.

C. Determine the income tax consequences of the reassessment by the CRA. Be sure to include in your answer revisions to the ACB of the promissory notes and ACB and PUC of the preferred shares after the reassessment.

D. Could Moe have done anything different to avoid the CRA reassessment?

AP 16-11   (Dividend Stripping)

Sandrine Hoskirk incorporated her successful business 10 years ago. The corporation, Hoskirk Ltd., is a CCPC with a December 31 taxation year end. Sandrine is the only shareholder and, on incorporation, acquired 1,000 common shares for $100 each. No new shares have been issued since incorporation. As a result, the ACB and PUC of the shares are both $100 each, or $100,000 in total for the single class of shares.

The incorporated business has enjoyed great success and with eligibility for low corporate tax rates has grown considerably in value to a point that a valuation recently estimated the common shares were worth $2,770,000, or $2,770 per share.

Sandrine's only child is her 33-year-old daughter, Debra Hoskirk Stephenson, who recently gave birth to her first child. Sandrine would like to provide her daughter and her growing family with financial security and has spoken to her accountant to discuss the best way to accomplish that goal. A variety of options are discussed, but Sandrine decides on using an estate freeze transaction with a new corporation that will result in her daughter benefitting from the future increase in value of Hoskirk Ltd.

The tax plan is to first have Debra incorporate her own corporation. Debra will be the only common shareholder with her spouse and newborn child owning preferred shares. The next step is to have Sandrine sell her common shares in Hoskirk Ltd. to her daughter's corporation.

The day after Labour Day, September 7, 2021, Debra incorporated HS Ltd., a CCPC with a December 31 taxation year end. At the end of September an agreement will be drawn up that will have Sandrine sell some or all of her common shares of Hoskirk Ltd. to HS Ltd.

Sandrine has never used any of her capital gains deduction and has never realized allowable business investment losses (ABIL). In addition, she will have no cumulative net investment loss (CNIL) in 2021. The result is that she has full access to the 2021 capital gains deduction limit of $892,218, which will eliminate income tax on $446,109 in taxable capital gains [(50%) ($892,218)] with the exception of any alternative minimum tax (AMT).

Sandrine's accountant explains that by structuring the share sale using ITA 85(1) two main objectives/benefits are achieved: (i) Her capital gains deduction is immediately used, resulting in an increased ACB of any shares issued by HS Ltd. to Sandrine, which will reduce future capital gains; and (ii) any immediate income taxes are avoided. Sandrine has made it clear that she does not want to have to pay any additional income taxes as a result of these transactions.

Since HS Ltd. has no cash or other assets, it can only acquire the shares from Sandrine by issuing either interest-bearing debt (e.g., a promissory note), shares, or a combination of both. Because using ITA 85(1) requires that shares be issued as consideration and deferring tax means limiting non-share consideration, HS Ltd. will acquire Sandrine's shares for a combination of a promissory note and redeemable preferred shares.

After careful consideration, Sandrine proposes the following alternatives to her accountant:

Proposal 1:   HS Ltd. will acquire all of Sandrine's common shares of Hoskirk Ltd. for $2,770,000 with payments of a promissory note of $2,000,000 bearing interest of 3.0% and redeemable preferred shares for the balance of $770,000. ITA 85(1) will be used.

Proposal 2:   Sandrine sells just enough of her shares to HS Ltd. to use all of her capital gains deduction. Sandrine would continue to keep any remaining shares. ITA 85(1) will be used.

Assume that neither Hoskirk Ltd. nor HS Ltd. would have a positive balance in their GRIP account in any taxation year.

Required:

A. As her accountant, advise Sandrine on whether her first proposal is a good idea given her objectives. Show the results if ITA 84.1 did not apply and the results with ITA 84.1.

B. Indicate how Sandrine's first proposal could be modified to produce a better result that avoids any immediate income tax to her. Assume that Sandrine wants to maximize the non-share consideration.

C. Evaluate Sandrine's second proposal and add the necessary numbers to ensure it results in no income tax consequences.

Provide your analysis and all supporting calculations.

AP 16-12   *(Dividend Stripping)*

Daryl Foster has owned all of the shares of Foster's Fasteners Inc., a CCPC, for the last 15 years. The company carries on an active business of retailing specialty hardware items. When the company was first incorporated Daryl paid the company $780,000 for its authorized common shares, which represents the PUC and ACB as no new shares have been issued since.

The company has been very profitable, and as a result the current FMV of its shares is $6,200,000.

Daryl is nearing retirement age and he would like to extract at least $600,000 from his corporation while minimizing any income tax, if possible. He has discussed this matter with Thornton Brockton, his self-trained accountant of many years. While Thornton has never been involved in such planning he mentions that he has heard that a rollover under ITA 85(1) would allow Daryl to sell his shares to a new corporation using an elected amount that will result in a capital gain of $600,000 that would be tax free because of Daryl's available capital gains deduction of the same amount. Thornton advises Daryl that he can effectively withdraw the original cost of his shares of $780,000 plus an additional $600,000 as a capital gain without having to pay any income tax.

The plan is for Daryl to sell all of the Foster's Fasteners shares to Foster Investments, a new company in which Daryl will be the only shareholder. The elected amount for the purposes of ITA 85(1) will be $1,380,000.

The new company will pay Daryl consideration that consists of a non-interest-bearing promissory note for $1,380,000, plus Foster Investment redeemable preferred shares with a FMV of $4,820,000. Given the cash resources of Foster's Fasteners, this company's shares should be able to pay sufficient dividends to Foster Investments to allow the repayment of the promissory note within one year.

Neither of the companies have a balance in their GRIP account or in any of the RDTOH accounts in any taxation year.

Required:

A. In the absence of ITA 84.1, indicate the income tax consequences of the sale of the shares of Foster's Fasteners to Foster Investments.

B. Determine whether ITA 84.1 would apply. Assuming that ITA 84.1 is applicable, calculate any deemed dividend that would arise as a result of the share sale. In addition, indicate the net economic effect of the share sale if all of the preferred shares were redeemed for their FMV of $4,820,000.

AP 16-13   (Capital Gain Strips)

Dolteck Ltd. (Dolteck) is a company involved in commercial construction. It was incorporated in Alberta 20 years ago and has been a CCPC with a December 31 taxation year end ever since. Dolteck was authorized to issue multiple classes of shares, but the only shares it issued were common shares, which were issued on incorporation to its sole corporate shareholder, Holdteck Ltd. (Holdteck), which is also a CCPC incorporated in Alberta with a December 31 taxation year end. Holdteck's role is as a strict holding company offering administrative, financing, managerial, and other support services to Dolteck for which it charges an annual fee based on the level of services provided.

The shares of Dolteck owned by Holdteck were acquired three years after its incorporation for $900,000, which currently remains the ACB. The PUC of the Dolteck shares is only $100,000.

A large, arm's-length, publicly listed construction company, Giant Co., with a track record of buying up small competitors recently approached Holdteck with an offer to purchase all of the Dolteck shares for $7,000,000. The offer has been accepted with a closing date of December 31, 2021. Safe income on hand attributable to the common shares of Dolteck owned by Holdteck is $2,200,000.

Assume that Dolteck will not have any balance in its eligible RDTOH, non-eligible RDTOH, or GRIP account at any time. In addition, assume that the provincial tax rate on investment income, including taxable capital gains, is 12.0%.

Required: Indicate the tax consequences of each of the following independent situations, specifically indicating whether ITA 55(2) applies, supported with explanations. Also comment on the application of Part IV, RDTOH, corporate tax rates, and the capital dividend account. Show all supporting calculations.

A. Holdteck sells all of the Dolteck shares to Giant Co. for $7,000,000.

B. Holdteck sells all of the Dolteck shares to Giant Co. for $4,800,000 after Dolteck declares and pays a safe income dividend of $2,200,000 to Holdteck. Assume that Dolteck has sufficient cash to pay the dividend in full.

C. Assume that Dolteck has no cash or borrowing power to raise additional cash to pay any dividends. Giant Co. loans Dolteck $6,100,000 on December 28, 2021. On December 29, 2021, Dolteck declares and pays a dividend to Holdteck of $6,100,000. On December 30, 2021, Holdteck sells all of its common shares in Dolteck to Giant Co. for $900,000.

D. Using ITA 85(1), Holdteck sells all of the common shares it owns in Dolteck to Giant Co. The elected amount will be $900,000 and Holdteck will receive $7,000,000 of a newly created class of retractable preferred shares of Giant Co. The Giant Co. shares will be redeemed in early January 2022 for cash of $7,000,000. Ignore any Part IV implications in this case.

CHAPTER 17

Other Corporate Rollovers and Sale of a Corporate Business

Learning Objectives

After completing Chapter 17, you should be able to:

1. Explain the purpose and tax policy reasons why certain corporate-based rollovers are permitted (Paragraph [P hereafter] 17-1 to 17-5).
2. Explain the purpose of ITA 85.1, the basic situation in which it applies, situations in which it does not apply, and the income tax consequences of its application (P 17-6 to 17-17).
3. Explain the purpose of ITA 86, how it applies, and some of the most common practical uses for it (P 17-18 to 17-21).
4. Explain the basic functions of the application of ITA 86 to a standard estate freeze (P 17-22).
5. Describe the conditions that must be met to use the ITA 86 rollover, including characteristics of preferred shares received on the exchange (P 17-23 to 17-25).
6. Apply the tax calculations required of ITA 86 and explain how to avoid any immediate income tax consequences (P 17-26 to 17-35).
7. Explain the circumstances that lead to the gifting rule and determine the income tax consequences when gifting applies (P 17-36 to 17-47).
8. Explain the different tax planning considerations in share exchange reorganizations between ITA 85 and ITA 86, including how these rules can be used in key employee estate freezes (P 17-48 to 17-53).
9. Explain the nature of an amalgamation and the role of corporate law (P 17-54 to 17-58).
10. Explain the purpose of ITA 87, specifically what it is expressly designed to accomplish and its effect on shareholders of predecessor corporations (P 17-59 to 17-64).
11. Describe some of the advantages and disadvantages of an amalgamation and some of the practical reasons why it is used (P 17-65 to 17-69).
12. Explain the nature of the winding-up of a corporation, the wind-up process, and the role of corporate law (P 17-70 to 17-72).
13. Describe the three types of wind-up situations contemplated by the ITA (P 17-73 to 17-74).
14. Explain the impact of ITA 88(1) to both the subsidiary and the parent company, including the treatment of subsidiary losses once the wind-up is complete (P 17-75 and 17-79).
15. Explain the purpose of the bump and when and how it applies (P 17-80 to 17-85).

16. Describe the legal and income tax difference between an amalgamation and a subsidiary dissolution, including any preferences for one over the other (P 17-86 to 17-91).
17. Describe the common situations in which ITA 88(2) is used and the income tax consequences when it applies (P 17-92 to 17-95).
18. Apply the income tax consequences when a corporation is dissolved, including final corporate distributions to shareholders (P 17-96 to 17-104).
19. Describe the income tax consequences when a corporation is involuntarily dissolved without the knowledge of the shareholders (P 17-105 to 17-108).
20. Explain the rollover rule of ITA 51, including the conditions that cause it to apply and the income tax consequences of its application (P 17-109 to 17-115).
21. Explain the purpose of ITA 51.1 (P 17-116).
22. Briefly explain how the gifting rule applies in a rollover under ITA 51 (P 17-117).
23. Compare the differences between selling the shares of a corporation versus selling its assets, including the advantages and disadvantages of each to the purchaser and seller (P 17-118 to 17-123).
24. Explain the meaning of a restrictive covenant, its purpose, and the income tax consequences to both the payor and recipient (P 17-124 to 17-129).
25. Describe the income tax consequences and process when a corporation sells its assets and distributes all of its property in the course of winding-up (P 17-130 to 17-134).
26. Describe the income tax consequences of selling a corporation by selling its shares and some tax planning considerations that may minimize income tax to shareholders (P 17-135 to 17-137).
27. Apply the ITA provisions and analyze the results when comparing a sale of corporate assets versus a sale of shares (P 17-138 to 17-149).

Introduction

17-1.   One of the cornerstone income tax principles that we have discussed throughout the text is the realization principle that recognizes that transactions between taxpayers are applied on the basis of fair market value (FMV). This ensures that any gain or loss is recognized at the time of each transaction for income tax purposes. There are, however, a number of circumstances in which recognizing transactions on the basis of FMV is counterproductive, particularly where the transactions are undertaken as part of a reorganization. For example, we saw in Chapter 16 that sole proprietors who wish to incorporate their business would face serious obstacles if the ITA viewed the movement of business property to a corporation at FMV. To facilitate the incorporation, ITA 85 was added to allow the movement of business property from individuals to corporations at tax costs, avoiding any immediate income tax consequences. Chapter 18 will discuss additional rollover rules that allow taxpayers to form partnerships on a rollover basis and to incorporate the business of a partnership on a rollover basis.

17-2.   The underlying tax policy of rollovers is to generally recognize that the income tax system should remain neutral when taxpayers undertake to reorganize their businesses, which is assumed to be in the best interests of all parties, including the tax authorities. The best way to achieve this policy objective is to ensure that no additional income tax liability is created as a result of a reorganization.

17-3.   Since reorganizations of businesses typically involve corporations, the majority of reorganizational-based rollover rules apply with a focus on corporate issues, such as corporate shares and debt as well as corporate property and corporate tax accounts such as the capital dividend account (CDA), GRIP, RDTOH, and so on. The extent of the rollover rules, however, is dependent on the nature of the underlying reorganization.

17-4.   In this chapter we will turn our attention to other corporate reorganization-based rollovers that address corporate takeovers through share exchanges (ITA 85.1), transactions to facilitate estate freezes where corporate interests are passed on to the next generation of family members

(ITA 86), where synergistic results are achieved through the amalgamation of two or more corporations (ITA 87), and where wholly owned subsidiaries are dissolved or wound up into a parent company (ITA 88(1)).

17-5. Reorganizational-based rollovers presume that the underlying business continues in some form. Where a corporation is dissolved, in circumstances other than the winding-up into a parent company, the related transactions are not eligible for rollover treatment (ITA 88(2)). This situation often involves selling off or liquidating the corporation's business, paying off creditors, and distributing any remaining property to its shareholders. The income tax consequences of this type of corporate dissolution will also be discussed in this chapter.

Share-for-Share Exchanges—ITA 85.1

Background

17-6. ITA 85.1 is designed to facilitate share-for-share transactions where shareholders (referred to as the "vendors") exchange shares of one taxable Canadian corporation (referred to as the "acquired corporation") for shares of a second corporation that is a Canadian corporation (referred to as the "purchaser corporation") in the course of an arm's-length sale of the shares of the acquired corporation.

17-7. ITA 85.1 is typically used in large public company takeovers where the purchaser corporation does not have the liquidity to purchase the shares of another corporation outright. Instead, the purchasing company acquires the outstanding shares using its own shares as payment.

> **EXAMPLE** PurchaseCo, a large publicly listed taxable Canadian corporation, wishes to take over TargetCo, another publicly listed taxable Canadian corporation. TargetCo has thousands of resident Canadian shareholders and its shares are estimated to be worth $500 million. PurchaseCo is estimated to be worth $2 billion. PurchaseCo does not have the available cash to purchase the shares of TargetCo and instead approaches TargetCo with an offer that is eventually accepted by the TargetCo shareholders. TargetCo shareholders sell their shares to PurchaseCo for FMV, receiving PurchaseCo shares as consideration.

> **IMPACT** In the absence of a rollover, each TargetCo shareholder would be considered to have sold their shares for FMV proceeds, resulting in capital gains or capital losses. Resident Canadian individual shareholders would not be able to use the capital gains deduction because TargetCo is a public corporation. Subsequent to the takeover, PurchaseCo would own all of the shares of TargetCo and the previous TargetCo shareholders would become shareholders of PurchaseCo. In other words, the TargetCo shareholders would still have an interest in TargetCo but indirectly through PurchaseCo. PurchaseCo would have achieved its takeover objective while avoiding any liquidity concerns.

ITA 85.1 in Practice

17-8. The previous example describes a common use of ITA 85.1 consistent with its purpose. In practice, however, takeover transactions can be quite complex, involving many non-tax issues such as corporate law and other regulatory concerns. ITA 85.1, however, provides a simple and effective income tax mechanism for avoiding any income tax consequences and neutralizing the income tax concerns. ITA 85.1, however, is not the only rollover means of facilitating takeover transactions.

17-9. ITA 85(1) also provides a rollover with much greater flexibility in that it allows shareholders to recover the cost of their shares in non-share consideration (e.g., cash or promissory notes). The administrative difficulty with ITA 85(1), however, is that a separate election would be required for each shareholder. This would require what is referred to as a bulk ITA 85(1) election where thousands of elections are filed in connection with a particular takeover. ITA 85.1 is designed to avoid that eventuality by providing an automatic rollover that does not require the filing of an election. The downside is that ITA 85.1 does not have the flexibility provided by ITA 85(1). In practice, however, it is not uncommon for takeovers to include a number of options to shareholders such as (1) filing an election under ITA 85(1), (2) relying on the automatic application of ITA 85.1, or (3) a combination of the two. Consideration packages often include a combination of shares and a certain amount of cash to encourage shareholders to participate in the takeover. This allows shareholders to choose an option that is in their best interests.

The ITA 85.1 Coverage

17-10.   Our coverage will focus on the takeover of a corporation with one sole shareholder. While we realize that ITA 85.1 would not generally apply in this situation, it provides an opportunity to focus on and illustrate the income tax consequences of the application of ITA 85.1. The income tax consequences would have been the same had the individual been one of thousands of shareholders of the company that was subject to a takeover bid.

General Rules

17-11.   The general rules for this rollover apply automatically as long as the conditions of ITA 85.1 are met. The general scenario involves resident Canadian shareholders (the vendors) who sell shares (referred to as the "exchanged shares") of a Canadian resident corporation (the acquired corporation) to another Canadian resident corporation (the purchaser corporation) for shares of that second corporation. Since we are dealing with share transactions, the income tax questions that must be answered are (1) What are the POD to the vendor shareholders? (2) What is the adjusted cost base (ACB) and paid-up capital (PUC) of the purchaser shares received by the vendors as payment? and (3) What is the cost of the exchanged shares to the purchaser corporation? These three questions are answered by the legislation as follows:

ITA 85.1(1)(a)   The vendor is deemed to have:

    (i)   disposed of the exchanged shares for POD equal to their ACB (Question 1).

    (ii) acquired the shares of the purchaser corporation at a cost equal to the ACB to the vendor of the exchanged shares immediately before the exchange (Question 2).

ITA 85.1(1)(b)   The cost to the purchaser of each of the acquired shares is deemed to be the lesser of: (Question 3)

    (i)   its FMV immediately before the exchange, or

    (ii) its PUC immediately before the exchange.

ITA 85.1(2.1)   The PUC of the purchaser shares that have been issued to the vendor is limited to the PUC of the shares given up by the vendor. This latter rule is designed to ensure that overall PUC cannot increase as a result of the takeover. (Question 2) If overall PUC were allowed to increase there would be income tax consequences as a result of the takeover.

17-12.   ITA 85.1(1)(b) establishes the cost of the exchanged shares to the purchaser corporation as the lesser of FMV and PUC. If, for example, the purchaser issues $500 of its shares for an acquired share with a FMV of $500, an ACB of $400, and a PUC of $100, the cost and therefore ACB to the purchaser corporation of that acquired share will be $100. Arguably, if the vendor shareholder used ITA 85.1 the POD would be $400 and the cost of the purchaser share would also be $400. It would be logical to allow the purchaser a cost of the acquired share at the same $400. In effect, the purchaser loses $300 of tax cost, being the difference between the $400 ACB of the share to the vendor and the purchaser's deemed cost of $100. Tax practitioners refer to this issue as a detriment to the use of ITA 85.1. Our understanding is that the reason for ITA 85.1(1)(b) is that it would be administratively improbable for the purchaser corporation to identify the ACB of the shares of thousands of vendors, therefore PUC was used instead given it is much more readily determinable.

Additional Conditions for the Application of ITA 85.1

17-13.   Even though the general conditions of ITA 85.1(1) have been met, ITA 85.1(2) adds the following additional conditions that prevents access to this automatic rollover:

ITA 85.1(2)(a)   The vendor and purchaser corporation must be dealing with each other at arm's length.

ITA85.1(2)(b)   The vendor, or persons non-arm's length, cannot control the purchaser corporation immediately after the exchange or own more than 50% of the FMV of the outstanding shares of the purchaser corporation. This condition is designed to prevent reverse takeovers.

ITA 85.1(2)(c)   The vendor and purchaser corporation cannot have filed an election under ITA 85(1) with respect to the exchanged shares. This rule gives priority to rollovers under ITA 85(1).

ITA 85.1(2)(d)   The vendor must not have received any non-share consideration (NSC) on the exchange. This condition means that only newly issued purchaser corporation shares can be used as payment for the exchanged shares.

17-14.   The condition under ITA 85.1(2)(d) also includes an option that allows a vendor to exchange some shares for shares of the purchaser corporation that would be entitled to the rollover and also to sell other exchanged shares to the purchaser corporation for cash or other NSC. This means that vendors can use the rollover for some shares and FMV for other shares. This is referred to as an "allocation of consideration" and is discussed in detail in paragraph 1.7 of Folio S4-F5-C1 "Share-for-Share Exchange."

Example

17-15.   The following example will serve to illustrate the basic application of ITA 85.1:

EXAMPLE   Ms. Cowper is the sole shareholder of Cowper Inc., owning a total of 1,000 shares with a PUC and ACB of $10,000. The FMV of the Cowper Inc. shares are $125,000.

Mega Holdings Ltd. acquires all of the Cowper Inc. shares in exchange for 5,000 of its newly issued common shares, which are currently trading at $25 per share, resulting in a total FMV of $125,000.

ANALYSIS   The information in the example is presented graphically in Figure 17-1.

Figure 17-1
ITA 85.1 Example

1,000 Cowper Inc. Shares
PUC = ACB = $10,000
FMV = $125,000

Mega Holdings Ltd.

Ms. Cowper

5,000 Mega Holdings Shares
at $25 Per Share
FMV = $125,000

In the absence of ITA 85.1, Ms. Cowper would have a capital gain of $115,000 (POD $125,000 - ACB $10,000). The results of the rollover under ITA 85.1 are as follows:

- Ms. Cowper is deemed to have received POD of $10,000, which is equal to the ACB of the Cowper Inc. shares. This means that there is no capital gain on the disposition (deemed POD $10,000 - ACB $10,000). [ITA 85.1(1)(a)(i)]

- Ms. Cowper is deemed to have acquired the common shares of Mega Holdings Ltd. at a cost equal to the ACB of the Cowper Inc. shares, or $10,000. [ITA 85.1(1)(a)(ii)]

- The ACB of the Cowper shares acquired by Mega Holdings Ltd. is deemed to be equal to $10,000, the lesser of their FMV of $125,000 and their PUC of $10,000 [ITA 85.1(1)(b)]. This limit applies even in situations where the vendor opted to forgo the rollover under ITA 85.1 by including the gain in income (see Paragraph 17-16).

- The PUC of the Mega Holdings Ltd. shares that have been issued to Ms. Cowper is limited to the $10,000 PUC of the Cowper shares that have been given up. This is accomplished through a PUC reduction of $115,000 under ITA 85.1(2.1) that is determined as the difference between the $125,000 of legal capital and the PUC of the exchanged shares of $10,000. The PUC of the common shares issued by Mega Holdings Ltd. would equal $10,000 [legal capital of $125,000 - PUC reduction of $115,000].

Opting Out of ITA 85.1

17-16.   ITA 85.1(1)(a) provides an all-or-nothing elective option that allows vendors to include the capital gain or capital loss in their income tax return for the year in which the exchange takes place. Including any part of that gain or loss in an income tax return forfeits the rollover treatment for that vendor. This does not affect the deemed cost of the exchanged shares to the purchaser corporation. In the example, Ms. Cowper could have opted out of the rollover by including the taxable capital gain of $57,500 [(1/2)($125,000 - $10,000)] in her income tax return. In this case the cost and therefore ACB of the shares of the purchaser corporation to Ms. Cowper would be equal to their FMV of $125,000.

17-17.   If Ms. Cowper wished to recognize only part of the capital gain the elective option would not be available, however other acceptable methods to achieve that result would include (1) filing an election with the purchaser corporation under ITA 85 or (2) structuring the exchange using ITA 85.1 to allocate the proceeds such that part of her shares would be exchanged for cash resulting in the recognition of part of the total capital gain and exchanging the remaining shares for purchaser corporation shares, which would use the rollover. The shares sold for cash would be excluded from the rollover.

Exercise 17-1

Subject: Share-for-Share Exchange

Ms. Aly Alee is the sole shareholder of Aayee Ltd., a CCPC. The ACB and PUC of the shares are $450,000 and the estimated FMV is $2,450,000. The shares of her company are acquired by a large publicly traded company, Global Outreach Inc., in exchange for 50,000 newly issued shares. At the time of the exchange the Global Outreach Inc. shares are trading at $49 per share. Indicate the income tax consequences of this share-for-share exchange to both Ms. Alee and Global Outreach Inc.

Solutions to Exercises are available in the Study Guide.

We suggest you complete SSP 17-1 and 17-2 at this point.

Share Exchange in a Capital Reorganization—ITA 86

Application of ITA 86(1)

Overview

17-18.   The ITA refers to two general types of reorganizations: a reorganization of the business of a corporation (ITA 84(2)) and a reorganization of its capital (ITA 86). The limited case law that has referred to a reorganization of corporate capital considers it to mean a change or alteration in capital (shares) in a manner such that substantially the same persons will continue on as shareholders once the reorganization process has been completed.

17-19.   Under corporate law in Canada, a corporation can add or delete different classes of shares, modify existing shares, change share privileges (non-voting to voting), and so on. These changes must generally first be approved by either a shareholder or director vote and then must be approved by the governing corporate law authority in the jurisdiction where the company was incorporated. Upon approval, amended articles of incorporation or similar documentation is issued evidencing the new corporate capital structure. The CRA generally requires amended articles of incorporation or supplementary letters patent to substantiate that the capital of a corporation has changed and that therefore a capital reorganization has taken place.

17-20.   While there are numerous tax and non-tax reasons for reorganizing corporate capital, two of the most common for income tax purposes are for estate freezes and what is referred to as dividend sprinkling.

> **DIVIDEND SPRINKLING**   GenCo was incorporated in 2019 and was authorized to issue one class of shares. There are three equal individual shareholders. Each individual owns 100 of the 300 outstanding common shares. The tremendous success of the company by 2021 and the different level of involvement in the company business of each of the shareholders has led to disputes about having to share dividends. It is decided to reorganize the shares into different classes so that dividends can be separately determined for each shareholder. Corporate law requires that shareholders who own the same class of shares be treated the same, therefore it is not legally possible to vary dividends among the three shareholders if they all own shares of the same class.

> **THE PROCESS**   All three shareholders agree to add different classes of shares. Approval is then obtained by the provincial corporate authority where the company was incorporated and amended articles of incorporation are issued authorizing the addition of three new classes of shares—common shares Class B, C, and D. The original common shares become Class A. Each individual shareholder exchanges all of their previous shares for a new class of common shares so that each of the shareholders own separate classes once the capital reorganization has been completed. At that point the corporation is able to vary the dividends it pays to each shareholder.

> **THE INCOME TAX CONSEQUENCES**   From an income tax perspective the previous common shares of each shareholder are reacquired by the issuing corporation with payment made by issuing new and different shares. This transaction falls under the rules of ITA 84(3), which applies when the issuing corporation acquires, redeems, or cancels its own shares. Share redemption-type transactions result in two income tax consequences, one as a potential deemed dividend and a second as a capital gain or capital loss. At this point we recommend reviewing the Chapter 14 coverage for ITA 84(3).

17-21.   The purpose of ITA 86 is to provide rollover treatment to avoid any income tax consequences as a result of these redemption-type transactions. The availability of this rollover requires that a shareholder give up all of the shares of a particular class (referred to as the "old shares") and receive in exchange, as consideration, shares of different classes (referred to as the "new shares"). The rules allow the shareholder to receive non-share consideration (NSC) as well but caution must be exercised to limit the NSC to the lesser of the PUC and the ACB of the old shares. Taking back NSC in excess of that limit will result in income tax consequences. In practice, most ITA 86 transactions are undertaken on a pure share-for-share exchange basis to avoid any potential income tax consequences, particularly where there is some uncertainty concerning the ACB or PUC of the old shares.

Use in Estate Freeze

17-22.   One of the most common applications of ITA 86(1) is in an estate freeze, where an owner/manager of a corporate business wishes to pass on the future economic growth of the corporate business to family members. If a parent of a million dollar company were to have the company issue shares to family members for $10 that gave them 50% of the common shares of the company, there would be income tax consequences to the parent and the family members since they would have effectively received $500,000 in share value for $10 in non-arm's-length circumstances. Avoiding this result requires matching the FMV of the shares to the payment for those shares. This is accomplished through an estate freeze.

> **EXAMPLE**   A parent owns all of the outstanding common shares of a corporation. There is a considerable unrealized gain on the shares as their FMV exceeds their ACB and PUC. If the parent continues to own the shares any future economic growth in the corporation would accrue to the parent.

> **THE PLAN**   In a manner similar to that of the dividend sprinkling scenario, the capital of the corporation will be reorganized to add new classes of shares, particularly preferred shares. The parent will then exchange all of his common shares for fixed value preferred shares that equal the FMV of the common shares given up. In other words, all of the value of the company will be attributable to these preferred shares. This is generally referred to as freezing the value at a point in time, which is where the expression "estate freeze" originates. With all of the value of the company locked in to the preferred shares, the family members can then acquire common shares at nominal amounts. A family member who acquires one common share for $1 would have a match in FMV since the common share is only worth $1 at the time the share would be issued.

> If the parent wishes to retain control of the corporation there are a number of options, such as (1) attaching voting rights to the preferred shares, (2) having the parent acquire more than half of the newly issued common shares, or (3) setting up a family trust to own the common shares with the parent controlling the trust as a trustee with the family members as beneficiaries.

Qualifying for Rollover Treatment under ITA 86

General Conditions

17-23.   For the provisions of ITA 86 to apply, several conditions must be met.

Shares Must be Disposed of to the Issuing Corporation   First, the shares must be disposed of only to the corporation that issued the shares, which is the basis for ITA 84(3).

Shares Must be Capital Property   Second, the shares must be capital property to the shareholder. Traders or dealers in shares would be excluded since they would be considered to be carrying on a business of buying and selling shares.

All Shares Owned of a Class   A third condition is that the shareholder must dispose of all of the shares owned of a particular class. The rollover is on a shareholder by shareholder basis, meaning that whether other shareholders of the same class dispose of their shares is irrelevant. If a shareholder did not want the rollover to apply, this could be achieved by keeping one of the shares.

Reorganization of Capital   A fourth condition that was previously discussed is that the transactions are part of a reorganization of capital.

Transferor Must Receive Shares   A final condition is that the shareholder must receive shares of the issuing corporation. NSC can also be received.

Establishing FMV for Preferred Shares

17-24.   An estate freeze requires the ability to fix the FMV of shares at a point in time. Aside from professional valuation issues, the ability to fix the value of common shares is difficult because the value fluctuates with the value of the company since common shares, by their nature, are entitled to the earnings of a company by way of dividends and to the net assets of the company on dissolution, the FMV of which are constantly changing. In Chapter 16, when discussing rollovers under ITA 85, it was mentioned that mismatches of FMV can lead to many income tax issues. The difficulties with FMV, however, can be resolved with preferred shares that allow a fixed value to be set, instilling relative certainty to the tax planning.

17-25.   The CRA has been quite vocal concerning preferred share attributes that are necessary to establish a set FMV. The preferred share attributes that the CRA wishes to see are as follows:

- The preferred shares must be redeemable at the option of the shareholder. This means that the shareholder reserves the right to be able to require the corporation to redeem the shares. This right, however, is subject to corporate law solvency restrictions.

- The preferred shares should be entitled to a dividend at a reasonable rate. Without a reasonable dividend entitlement the shares could not hold their value. This would be roughly equivalent to comparing the FMV of a loan receivable without interest to one that charges interest at the going market rate. There is no CRA requirement, however, that the dividend entitlement be cumulative.

- The corporation must guarantee that dividends will not be paid on any other class of shares if the payment would result in the corporation having insufficient funds to redeem the preferred shares.

- Preferred share dividends must become cumulative if the value of the corporation falls below the redemption value of the preferred shares or if the corporation is otherwise unable to redeem the shares.

- The preferred shares may or may not have full voting rights. However, they should have voting rights with respect to any matter regarding the preferred shares. This would prevent others from altering preferred share rights and privileges without the consent of the preferred shareholders, which could potentially reduce the FMV of the shares.

- The preferred shares should have preference on liquidation of the corporation. While the very nature of preferred shares tends to guarantee preference, the CRA requires additional assurance of this preferential treatment.

The Income Tax Calculations

General Rules

17-26.   ITA 86(1) determines the specific amounts that are necessary to rewrite the income tax consequences of the redemption of the old shares for the new shares. This ensures that there are no deemed dividends or capital gains/losses and that the redemption benefits fully from rollover treatment. There may, however, be income tax consequences in two situations where (1) the FMV of the NSC exceeds either the ACB or PUC of the old shares, or (2) there is a FMV mismatch that results in a gift to a related person. The main calculation components are as follows:

Non-Share Consideration (NSC)   ITA 86(1)(a) sets the cost of the NSC as equal to its FMV

Cost of New Shares   ITA 86(1)(b) sets the cost of the new shares as equal to the ACB of the old shares less the FMV of the NSC. The first two steps of ITA 86(1)(a) and (b) take the ACB of the old shares and allocate it first to the NSC with any remainder allocated to the new shares. If there is no NSC then the ACB of the old shares becomes the ACB of the new shares.

Proceeds of Redemption for Old Shares   The first step in a redemption calculation is to determine whether there is a deemed dividend. A deemed dividend is equal to the difference between the "amount paid" and the PUC of the shares being redeemed. The "amount paid" equals the FMV of any NSC plus the PUC of any new shares issued by the corporation (ITA 84(5)(d)). The PUC of the new shares is determined after applying a PUC reduction under ITA 86(2.1).

Proceeds of Disposition (POD) for Old Shares   The second part of a redemption is calculating whether there is a capital gain or a capital loss on the disposition of the old shares. For this purpose, ITA 86(1)(c) sets the POD as being equal to the total of the amounts determined under ITA 86(1)(a) and (b).

PUC Reduction Calculation—ITA 86(2.1)

17-27.   A PUC reduction may be required with respect to the issuance of the new shares. The reduction is calculated as follows:

Increase in legal capital of new shares		$xxx
Less the excess, if any, of:		
PUC of old shares	($xxx)	
Less: FMV of NSC	xxx	(xxx)
ITA 86(2.1)(a) PUC reduction		$xxx

17-28.   The PUC reduction formula is designed to pass the PUC of the old shares to the new shares except to the extent that NSC has been taken. If the FMV of the NSC is equal to or greater than the PUC of the old shares, the PUC of the new shares (after the reduction) will be nil. If the FMV of the NSC exceeds the PUC of the old shares there will be income tax consequences as a result of the redemption caused by the share exchange. If there is no NSC then the PUC of the old shares becomes the PUC of the new shares.

17-29.   The PUC reduction is applied on a class by class basis. If more than one class of shares has been issued to the shareholder in the exchange, the PUC reduction will be prorated among each class of shares on the basis of the relative FMV of each class. In practice, however, estate freeze transactions rarely result in the issuance of more than one class of shares.

Example Using ITA 86(1) in an Estate Freeze

Basic Data

17-30.   The following example will serve to illustrate the ITA 86(1) calculations. The example is illustrated graphically in Figure 17-2.

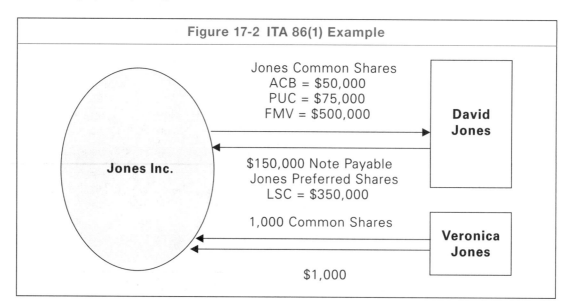

Figure 17-2 ITA 86(1) Example

EXAMPLE Mr. David Jones owns all of the outstanding common shares of Jones Inc. The ACB of the shares are $50,000, the PUC is $75,000, and the current FMV is $500,000.

Mr. Jones would like to have any future economic growth in the corporation accrue to his daughter, Ms. Veronica Jones. Veronica is 30 years old and has been actively and substantially involved in the business for over five years. The corporation undergoes a reorganization of capital and obtains approval to amend the articles of incorporation to add different classes of shares. The corporation then reacquires all of the common shares of Mr. Jones and, as consideration, issues a $150,000 promissory note and preferred shares that are redeemable at the option of Mr. Jones for $350,000. The legal capital and FMV of the newly issued preferred shares are both $350,000. Common shares are then purchased by Veronica Jones for $1,000. Subsequent to these transactions Veronica is the only common shareholder.

ITA 86(1) Components

17-31.   Before the income tax consequences of the redemption can be calculated we first need to determine the ACB of the NSC and the ACB and PUC of the preferred shares. Each of the three component is determined as follows:

Cost of NSC = FMV (note payable)		$150,000
ACB of old shares		$ 50,000
Less: FMV of NSC		(150,000)
ACB of preferred shares (new shares)		Nil
Legal capital of preferred shares		$350,000
Less The excess, if any, of:		
PUC of the old shares	($ 75,000)	
Less: FMV of NSC	150,000	Nil
ITA 86(2.1) PUC reduction		$350,000
Legal capital of preferred shares		$350,000
Less: PUC reduction		(350,000)
PUC of preferred shares (new shares)		Nil

The Income Tax Consequences

17-32.   The income tax effect of the redemption can now be calculated as follows:

PUC of preferred shares (new shares)	Nil
Plus: FMV of NSC	$150,000
Proceeds of redemption—ITA 84(5)(d)	$150,000
PUC of old shares	(75,000)
ITA 84(3) deemed dividend	$ 75,000
ACB of preferred shares (new shares)	Nil
Plus: FMV of NSC	$150,000
POD—ITA 86(1)(c)	$150,000
Less: ITA 84(3) deemed dividend	(75,000)
Adjusted POD	$ 75,000
Less: ACB of old shares	(50,000)
Capital gain	$ 25,000
Inclusion rate	1/2
Taxable capital gain	$ 12,500

Economic Analysis

17-33.   The tax attributes of the common shares owned by Veronica are all $1,000 (FMV, ACB, and PUC). However, if the corporation prospers, all future increases in value will increase the FMV of the common shares and therefore will accrue to her. In other words, by exchanging his common shares for fixed value non-growth preferred shares, Mr. Jones has frozen the value of his interest in Jones Inc. at $500,000 and passed any future growth in the company to his daughter.

17-34.   In reviewing this example, Mr. Jones' initial unrealized gain was $450,000 (FMV $500,000 - ACB $50,000). As a result of the share exchange he has realized $100,000 ($75,000 dividend + $25,000 capital gain) of this economic gain. The remaining $350,000 is built into the preferred shares that have a FMV of $350,000 and a PUC and ACB that are both nil. If he redeems the shares there would be a $350,000 deemed dividend, and if he sells the shares there would be a $350,000 capital gain.

17-35.   The example demonstrates the risks associated with taking NSC. As long as the FMV of the NSC does not exceed either of the PUC or ACB of the old shares, then any deemed dividend or capital gain can be avoided. In this case, had the NSC been limited to $50,000 there would not have been any income tax consequences leading to an immediate income tax liability. In practice, capital reorganization transactions to which ITA 86 applies are almost always done without NSC.

Exercise 17-2

Subject: Exchange of Shares in a Capital Reorganization (ACB = PUC = NSC)

Mr. Sam Samson is the sole shareholder of Samdoo Ltd., a Canadian controlled private corporation (CCPC) that is authorized to issue only one class of shares (common shares). The ACB and PUC of the common shares are both $1,000,000 and the current FMV is $2,300,000. The balance in the GRIP account at year end is expected to be nil. The company will obtain approval to add new classes of shares. Mr. Samson will exchange all of his common shares for consideration consisting of cash of $1,000,000 and fixed value preferred shares that are redeemable at the option of Mr. Samson for $1,300,000. Determine the ACB and PUC of the redeemable preferred shares. Determine the amount and type of any income that will result from this transaction.

Exercise 17-3

Subject: Exchange of Shares in a Capital Reorganization (ACB > PUC, PUC = NSC)

Mr. Sam Samson is the sole shareholder of Samdoo Ltd., a CCPC that is authorized to issue only one class of shares. The ACB of the shares is $1,250,000, the PUC $1,000,000, and the FMV $2,300,000. The balance in the GRIP account at year end is expected to be nil. The company will obtain approval to add new classes of shares. Mr. Samson will exchange all of his Samdoo Ltd. common shares for consideration consisting of cash of $1,000,000 and fixed value preferred shares that are redeemable for $1,300,000. Determine the ACB and PUC of the redeemable preferred shares. Determine the amount and type of any income that will result from this transaction.

Exercise 17-4

Subject: Exchange of Shares in a Capital Reorganization (ACB > NSC > PUC)

Mr. Sam Samson is the sole shareholder of Samdoo Ltd., a CCPC that is authorized to issue only one class of shares. The ACB of the shares is $1,250,000, the PUC $1,000,000, and the FMV $2,300,000. The balance in the GRIP account at year end is expected to be nil.

The company will obtain approval to add new classes of shares. Mr. Samson will exchange all of his Samdoo Ltd. common shares for consideration consisting of cash of $1,200,000 and fixed value preferred shares that are redeemable for $1,100,000. Determine the ACB and PUC of the redeemable preferred shares. Determine the amount and type of any income that will result from this transaction.

Solutions to Exercises are available in the Study Guide.

We suggest your complete SSP 17-3 at this point.

Gifting to a Related Person—ITA 86(2)

Overview

17-36.   ITA 86(2) contains a rule designed to prevent an individual taxpayer, in the course of a reorganization of capital, from conferring a benefit on a related person. This gifting rule applies when a shareholder exchanges shares for new shares and non-share consideration the total value of which is less than the exchanged shares. In effect, the shareholder has not been fully compensated for the exchanged shares, and the result is that the value left behind adds to the value of shares owned by related persons. As a result, related persons indirectly receive a benefit. A benefit would generally require that a related person owns common shares.

17-37.   Technically there must be an intent to undertake the exchange transaction in such a way as to purposefully leave value behind that will benefit related persons. The CRA, however, assumes purposeful intent when the valuation difference is material. The nature of an estate freeze typically involves bringing in family members as common shareholders; therefore, the CRA will scrutinize these transactions to ensure that any valuation is supportable. Valuation risk can be reduced through the use of a valid price adjustment clause, as discussed in Chapter 16.

17-38.   The legislative design of the gifting rules is to penalize the person responsible for the gift. The ITA will add the value of the gift (referred to in ITA 86 as the "gift portion") to POD, resulting in immediate capital gain consequences to the gifting person. The recipient of the gift, however, is left with common shares with an increased FMV without the benefit of an increase to the ACB of the shares. The long-term result is that the amount of the gift is immediately taxed to the gifting person rather than being deferred if there had been no gift. In addition, the same gain is subject to be taxed a second time to the recipient of the gift when the recipient subsequently sells or otherwise disposes of her shares. This double tax result is intentionally punitive as a means of discouraging indirect gifts through share exchanges.

The Calculations

17-39.   In situations where the gifting rule applies, ITA 86(2) modifies the ACB of the new shares and the POD of the old shares to add the gift portion. The following modifications are made to the share exchange rules where there is a gift:

Proceeds of Disposition (POD)   Under ITA 86(2)(c), the POD for the old shares will be equal to the lesser of:

- the FMV of the NSC *plus the gift portion*; or
- the FMV of the old shares.

This compares to the POD under ITA 86(1)(c), which is equal to the cost of the new shares plus the FMV of NSC.

Capital Losses   Under ITA 86(2)(d), any capital loss resulting from the disposition of the old shares will be deemed to be nil.

Cost of New Shares   Under ITA 86(2)(e), the cost to the taxpayer of the new shares will be equal to:

- the ACB of the old shares; less
- the sum of the FMV of the NSC *plus the gift portion.*

This compares to a cost for the new shares under ITA 86(1)(b), which was equal to the ACB of the old shares less the FMV of any NSC. The only difference is the additional cost reduction for the gift portion.

17-40.   To illustrate the detailed calculations, we will modify the example in Paragraph 17-30 by decreasing the amount of consideration received to create a $100,000 gift. The revised example is as follows.

EXAMPLE   Mr. David Jones owns all of the outstanding common shares of Jones Inc. The ACB of the shares are $50,000, the PUC is $75,000, and the current FMV is $500,000.

Mr. Jones would like to have any future economic growth in the corporation accrue to his daughter, Ms. Veronica Jones. Veronica is 30 years old and has been actively and substantially involved in the business for over five years. The corporation undergoes a reorganization of capital and obtains approval to amend the articles of incorporation to add different classes of shares. The corporation then reacquires all of the common shares of Mr. Jones and, as consideration, issues a $150,000 promissory note and preferred shares that are redeemable at the option of Mr. Jones for $250,000. Common shares are then purchased by Veronica Jones for $1,000. Subsequent to these transactions Veronica is the only common shareholder.

Calculation of the Gift Portion

17-41.   The gift portion is determined as follows:

FMV of the old shares		$500,000
Less FMV of total consideration:		
NSC	($150,000)	
Preferred shares	(250,000)	(400,000)
Gift portion		$100,000

17-42.   Since Mr. Jones' daughter, a related person, is the only common shareholder, the $100,000 gift portion would increase the FMV of her common shares, resulting in the application of ITA 86(2).

PUC Reduction

17-43.   The PUC reduction and PUC of the preferred shares is calculated as follows:

Cost of NSC (promissory note)		$150,000
Legal capital of preferred shares (new shares)		$250,000
Less the excess, if any, of:		
PUC of the common shares (old shares)	($ 75,000)	
Less: FMV of NSC	150,000	Nil
ITA 86(2.1)(a) PUC reduction		$250,000
Legal capital of preferred shares (new shares)		$250,000
ITA 86(2.1)(a) PUC reduction		(250,000)
PUC of preferred shares (new shares)		Nil

Other Calculations

17-44.   The remaining calculations that would be required under ITA 86(2) are as follows:

ACB of the common shares (old shares)		$ 50,000
Less:		
FMV of NSC	($150,000)	
Gift portion (See Paragraph 17-41)	(100,000)	(250,000)
ACB of preferred shares (new shares)		Nil

PUC of preferred shares	Nil
Plus: FMV of NSC	$150,000
Proceeds of redemption—ITA 84(5)(d)	$150,000
PUC of common shares (old shares)	(75,000)
ITA 84(3) deemed dividend	$ 75,000

POD—ITA 86(2)(c)—Lesser of:	
• FMV of common shares (old shares) = $ 500,000	
• FMV of NSC plus the gift portion ($150,000 + $100,000) = $250,000	$250,000
Less: ITA 84(3) deemed dividend	(75,000)
Adjusted POD—ITA 54	$175,000
ACB of common shares (old shares)	(50,000)
Capital gain	$125,000
Inclusion rate	1/2
Taxable capital gain	$ 62,500

17-45.   At the time of the reorganization, the potential gain on David's shares was $450,000 (FMV $500,000 - ACB $50,000). In the original version of this example (Paragraph 17-30), a gain of $100,000 was recognized (deemed dividend $75,000 + capital gain $25,000) at the time of the reorganization, leaving $350,000 of the gain deferred until David's preferred shares are redeemed or sold (the FMV of the preferred shares was $350,000, with both PUC and ACB equal to nil).

17-46.   In this modified version of the example, the gain that is recognized at the time of the reorganization is $200,000 ($75,000 + $125,000), $100,000 larger than in the original version of the example. This reflects the fact that the gift portion of $100,000 was added to the POD by ITA 86(2)(c), increasing the capital gain by $100,000. The total $450,000 gain, however, is unchanged. While the current recognized gain is increased to $200,000, the deferred amount is reduced to $250,000 (the FMV of the preferred shares is $250,000, with both ACB and PUC of nil). While the gift portion was immediately included in income it could have been deferred with proper planning.

17-47.   ITA 86(2) does, however, involve a punitive element to his daughter, Veronica. The FMV of the common shares issued to Veronica are equal to $101,000, the $1,000 she paid plus the $100,000 gift. If she were to sell the common shares immediately she would realize a capital gain that duplicates the additional capital gain to Mr. Jones.

Exercise 17-5

Subject: Gift to a Related Person—ITA 86(2)

Janrev Inc. is a CCPC that is authorized to issue only one class of shares. The FMV of all of the shares is $1,600,000 and the PUC is $250,000. Ms. Jan Reviser owns 80% of the shares, which she acquired from the corporation for $200,000. The remaining 20% of the shares are owned by her 19-year-old daughter and were also acquired directly from the corporation for $50,000. At the end of April 2021 the corporation receives approval to amend the articles of incorporation to add a new class of preferred shares. At the beginning of May 2021, Ms. Reviser exchanges all of her common shares for cash of $300,000 and fixed value preferred shares that are redeemable for $800,000. The company balance in its GRIP account at year end is expected to be equal to nil. Indicate the amount and type of any income that will result from the share exchange.

Solutions to Exercises are available in the Study Guide.

ITA 86(1) vs. ITA 85(1)—Tax Planning Considerations

General Comments

17-48.   Capital reorganizations and share exchanges can occur on a rollover basis under ITA 85 or ITA 86. ITA 86(3) gives priority to ITA 85, which is elective. Therefore, if an indivdual chooses to exchange shares as part of a capital reorganization through an election under ITA 85(1), then ITA 86 becomes unavailable.

17-49.   As a rule, both ITA 85 and 86 are similar in many respects as both allow non-share consideration and both provide a gifting rule with similar consequences. ITA 85, however, is much more flexible in terms of selecting an elected amount whereas such flexibility does not exist with ITA 86. A significant feature of ITA 85 is that an election is required that notifies the CRA that shareholder transactions have taken place. ITA 86 is automatic with no election required. While an election adds to the compliance and administrative costs, the filing times for the elections are very flexible with minimum penalties for late filing. In addition, late filing extensions are often available. In general terms, elections can be filed up to three years late without any required justification as long as the applicable penalties are paid. Elections can be filed after the three-year general deadline (along with the penalties), but the CRA's approval is required. If the purpose of the late filing beyond three years is an attempt to retroactively fix a tax planning concern then the CRA will deny the request to late file.

17-50.   In general, an awareness of the two rollover rules, including their similarities and differences, is important to ensuring the optimum income tax results in specific circumstances. For example, those who rely on ITA 86 may be in a position to remedy an error in tax attributes, such as ACB and PUC, with an election under ITA 85(1) that can be filed up to three years late.

Use in Key Employee Successions

17-51.   In addition to its use in estate freezes, an exchange of shares can be effective when arranging for gradual succession to a key employee (referred to as a "key man estate freeze"). For example, consider a situation where an employee has little personal equity but has a good work record with the company, excellent owner/manager potential, and has contributed significantly to the ongoing success of the corporate business. The mechanics of this type of freeze are identical to those with family members with the exception that specifically identified employees are the focus rather than family.

17-52.   An ITA 86(1) reorganization could be used to convert common shares owned by the existing owner/manager shareholder into preferred shares. The employee could then acquire common shares from the corporation at minimal cost. The original owner/manager shareholder could continue to be involved in the business throughout the period of succession.

17-53.   Eventually, the original owner/manager shareholder could recover the value of her freeze shares through redemption, sale to the key employee, or a combination of the two.

We suggest you complete SSP 17-4 and 17-5 at this point.

Amalgamations—ITA 87

Amalgamations and Corporate Law

17-54.   In Canada, it is corporate law that allows the recognition of an amalgamated corporation, which is simply considered to be a continuation of each of the participating corporations referred to as amalgamating corporations. In general, Canadian corporations (those incorporated in Canada) are not allowed to amalgamate unless they are governed by the same corporate law. This means that if a corporation incorporated under Alberta corporate law wanted to amalgamate with a federally incorporated company under the *Canada Business Corporations Act* (CBCA) an amalgamation would not be possible. The solution to this initial problem is what is referred to as a "continuance," which simply allows one of the two amalgamating corporations to change its jurisdiction for corporate law purposes. In our example, the Alberta corporation could seek a continuance to be subject to the CBCA, or the federally incorporated company could seek a continuance under Alberta corporate law, or both could change to a different corporate law jurisdiction such as Ontario. In any case, the goal would be that all amalgamating corporations would then be governed by the same corporate law and an amalgamation could then take place. The corporate law process also requires obtaining permission to leave the first corporate law jurisdiction (i.e., a discontinuance).

17-55.   Corporate law also draws a distinction between what are referred to as long form and short form amalgamations. Long form amalgamations are amalgamations between two or more corporations that are not related, such as corporations controlled by unrelated persons. Short form amalgamations, on the other hand, are between corporations that are related or under common control, such as a parent corporation and a subsidiary or two subsidiaries of the same corporation. Under corporate law, the level of formality required is much more extensive for long form as opposed to short form amalgamations. The ITA generally provides favourable treatment where amalgamating corporations are related but less favourable treatment where the corporations are unrelated. This is discussed further in the following paragraphs.

17-56.   Corporate law also plays a role in many other circumstances, such as requiring that the directors sign off that their company is solvent (able to meet its obligations as they become due). Corporate law contains many safeguards that restrict the ability of a corporation experiencing financial difficulty from participating in an amalgamation, including obtaining approval from creditors and hearing and carefully considering any dissents by shareholders of either amalgamating company. In addition, amalgamation agreements are required to provide the details of the amalgamation, and either shareholder or director approval may be required depending on whether the amalgamation is a short form or a long form.

17-57.   At this stage you may wonder why it is necessary to discuss any of these corporate law concepts. The fact is that when the ITA refers to amalgamated corporations it is only referring to amalgamations that have passed all of the legal obstacles and formalities necessary to establish an amalgamated corporation, which the ITA refers to as a "new corporation." On the completion of the legal process, the governing corporate authority will issue a "certificate of amalgamation" that evidences the existence of the amalgamated corporation as of a specific date.

17-58.   The CRA receives notification from the provinces and territories that certain corporate actions have been approved, including changing the share structure, winding-up, or amalgamating. The CRA can readily identify a corporation as an amalgamated company by the business number used, which adds "1" to the business number for each amalgamation. If, for example, an amalgamated corporation has previously gone through three previous amalgamations, the business number will show the number "4" at the end of its business number (the original assigned ending numbers are "001" plus "3" for each amalgamation).

Amalgamations and the ITA

17-59.   ITA 87 provides the rules that effectively allow rollover treatment where there is a statutorily approved amalgamation under corporate law among amalgamating corporations each of which is a taxable Canadian corporation. The rules of ITA 87 address the following four issues:

- **PROPERTY:** All of the property of each amalgamating corporation (referred to by the ITA as "predecessor corporations") becomes property of the amalgamated corporation (referred to by the ITA as the "new corporation") (ITA 87(1)(a)). The only exception to this rule is for intercompany amounts such as receivables. In other words, if one of two predecessor corporations has accounts receivables from the other amalgamating company, the receivables cannot flow through the amalgamated corporation. These intercompany accounts are resolved prior to the amalgamation.

- **LIABILITIES:** All of the liabilities of each predecessor flow through to become liabilities of the new corporation (ITA 87(1)(b)). Intercompany liabilities are not permitted to flow through to the new corporation. Again, these intercompany accounts are resolved prior to the amalgamation.

- **TAX ACCOUNTS:** The income tax accounts of each predecessor, such as loss carry over balances, CDA accounts, GRIP, RDTOH (both eligible and non-eligible), and others, flow through to become the tax accounts of the new corporation. There are dozens of provisions that flow these amounts through, almost all of which are found in ITA 87(2). See Paragraph 17-63 for some specific examples with ITA references.

- **SHAREHOLDERS:** As a rule, the shareholders of predecessors either receive shares of the new corporation in exchange for their predecessor shares or the predecessor shares are deemed to be shares of the new corporation for shareholders of a parent predecessor that amalgamates with a wholly owned subsidiary. In such cases the ITA treats the shareholders of predecessor corporations as having disposed of their predecessor shares. Rollover rules establish the ACB and PUC of the new shares and are designed to avoid any immediate income tax consequences as long as a shareholder does not receive any NSC or leaves value in the new corporation that creates a gift to a person related to that shareholder (ITA 87(1)(c), 87(3) and 87(4)).

17-60. In our discussion of different types of corporate-based rollovers, such as ITA 85 or 86, there is an actual disposition of property. In those cases the ITA simply sets the POD and tax costs to ensure that there are no immediate income tax liabilities, which then facilitates the transactions. Amalgamations, however, apply a different concept altogether since the corporate law treats the predecessors as continuing to exist, albeit in a different form. In support of this continuation notion, ITA 87(1) uses the word "becomes" when discussing the movement of property and liabilities from predecessors to the new corporation and is very methodical in ensuring that the tax costs of all underlying property also flows through on the amalgamation. In other words, this flow-through concept is necessary since there are no dispositions of any predecessor property and liabilities that occur, which differs from other types of corporate transactions. The end result is that the income tax consequences of an amalgamation are equivalent to adding the properties and liabilities (at tax costs with the exception of intercompany accounts) of each predecessor corporation plus all income tax accounts.

17-61. One of the most important basic amalgamation rules is ITA 87(2)(a), which applies a taxation year concept as if the predecessor corporations come to an end and the newly amalgamated corporation is created as a brand new corporation. If, for example, A Co., which has a taxation year ending December 31, and B Co., which has a taxation year ending August 31, amalgamate to form AB Co. on October 10, 2021, ITA 87(2)(a) applies to deem the taxation years of each of A Co. and B Co. to have ended immediately before that time. As a result, A Co. would have a 2021 taxation year from January 1, 2021, to October 9, 2021, and B Co. would have two 2021 taxation years, the regular taxation year ending August 31, 2021, and a second short taxation year from September 1, 2021, to October 9, 2021. In addition, as a new corporation, AB Co. would be free to choose its own taxation year end as long as it is no more than 53 weeks from October 10, 2021, which is day one of its first taxation year.

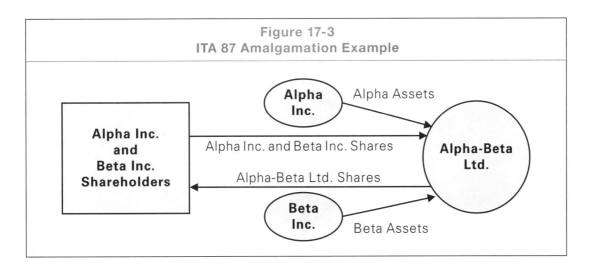

Figure 17-3
ITA 87 Amalgamation Example

17-62.   Figure 17-3 provides a graphic display of a basic amalgamation. Alpha Inc. and Beta Inc. combine the two companies into an amalgamated corporation identified as Alpha-Beta Ltd. The shareholders of the two predecessors exchange their shares of each predecessor for newly issued shares of Alpha-Beta Ltd. As long as the shareholders receive no NSC on the exchange and the FMV of their predecessor shares matches the FMV of the amalgamated company shares there will be no income tax consequences to the shareholders and the share exchange will occur on a rollover basis at the ACB of the predecessor shares. The new corporation shares will be equal to the ACB of the predecessor shares (ITA 87(4)). In addition. the PUC of the issued shares of the new corporation will be equal to the combined PUC of the shares of the predecessor corporations (ITA 87(3)). The PUC result is achieved through PUC reductions to the new corporation shares. The reality of ITA 87 and many other corporate-based rollovers is that the ACB and PUC attributes of predecessor shares become the ACB and PUC of the shares of the new corporation received in exchange on the amalgamation.

17-63.   With respect to property, reserves, loss carry forwards, and other tax accounts of the predecessor companies, ITA 87 provides flow-through treatment as follows:

Select Flow-through Provisions—ITA 87(2)

Item	Rollover Effect
Inventories—ITA 87(2)(b)	At cost
Depreciable property—ITA 87(2)(d)	At UCC
Non-depreciable capital property—ITA 87(2)(e)	At ACB
Reserves—ITA 87(2)(g)	Flowed through
Non-capital losses—ITA 87(2.1)	Flowed through
Net capital losses—ITA 87(2.1)	Flowed through
Restricted farm losses—ITA 87(2.1)	Flowed through
General rate income pool (GRIP)—ITA 87(2)(vv)	Flowed through
Low rate income pool (LRIP)—ITA 87(2)(ww)	Flowed through
Capital dividend account (CDA) (see Note 1)—ITA 87(2)(z.1)	Flowed through
RDTOH (see Note 1)—ITA 87(2)(aa)	Flowed through

Note 1   The amalgamated company is treated as a public company if, prior to the amalgamation, any of the predecessor companies were a public company (ITA 87(2)(ii)). If this is the case, the amalgamated company will no longer have access to any capital dividend accounts or refundable dividend tax on hand (RDTOH) accounts of the predecessor companies.

Predecessor Shareholders—ITA 87(4)

17-64.   The shareholders of the predecessor corporations are deemed to have received POD equal to the ACB of the their predecessor shares, and they are deemed to acquire the shares of the new corporation at the same amount. Qualifying for this rollover treatment requires that a shareholder meet the following conditions:

- The shareholders must not receive any NSC in the new company.
- The predecessor shares must be capital property to the shareholder.
- The share exchange on the amalgamation must not result in a gift to a related person.

Amalgamation Concerns

17-65.   As a rule, the provisions of ITA 87 are designed to facilitate amalgamations among Canadian corporations by allowing a combination of rollover treatment to predecessor shareholders and the ability to combine tax accounts of each predecessor corporation within the new corporation so that no tax accounts are lost. There are, however, situations that could result in income tax consequences to shareholders of predecessor corporations and the loss of the benefits of tax accounts.

17-66.   Many of the adverse income tax implications relate to whether there is an acquisition of control (AOC), which was discussed in Chapter 14. ITA 256(7)(b) contemplates an AOC on an amalgamation where the predecessor corporations were not related companies and, after the amalgamation, the shareholders of one of the predecessors own more than 50% of the voting shares of the new corporation. In effect there is no likelihood of an AOC in a short form amalgamation but a strong likelihood when there is a long form amalgamation. The most severe income tax implications are that the tax accounts that have flowed through from a predecessor whose control has been acquired as a result of the amalgamation are tainted. This means that the new corporation may be unable to use those tax accounts, specifically loss carry overs.

17-67.   Other concerns that arise on an amalgamation include the following:

- **GOODWILL:** Since there are no actual dispositions of property and liabilities of predecessor corporations as a result of an amalgamation, there can be no re-evaluation to increase costs to FMV or recognize property such as goodwill.

- **PREDECESSOR LIABILITIES:** If one predecessor has acquired liabilities of another predecessor in advance of the amalgamation, the likelihood of income tax consequences to the second predecessor increases. The reason for this is that any debt between amalgamating corporations is deemed to have been settled with a payment equal to the creditor's cost. If, for example, Credit Co. purchased a $1,000,000 debt of Borrow Co. for $700,000, on the amalgamation Borrow Co. would be deemed to have paid an amount equal to Credit Co.'s cost of the debt of $700,000. As a result, Credit Co. would have no tax implications since it received an amount equal to its cost. Borrow Co., on the other hand, would effectively have avoided having to repay $300,000 on a deemed basis. The result is that there is a forgiveness of debt of $300,000 to Borrow Co. immediately prior to the amalgamation. This creates income tax implications to Borrow Co., such as reducing its loss carry overs on a dollar for dollar basis;

- **REORGANIZATION COSTS:** Reorganization costs incurred on amalgamations are generally non-deductible capital expenditures, however they are generally included in class 14.1 as long as the reorganization was undertaken for the purpose of earning income from a business. Most amalgamation expenses should qualify.

- **SHIFTING OF PUC:** If the post-amalgamation PUC has shifted so that some shareholders of predecessor corporations have more or less than prior to the amalgamation, the CRA will likely question this shift, particularly where it potentially results in a reduction of income tax in the short term or long term. The CRA will consider applying the General Anti-Avoidance Rule (GAAR) in this case.

Amalgamations—Tax Planning Considerations

17-68.   There are numerous reasons for an amalgamation, including combining with a competitor to reduce competition, eliminating inactive companies, consolidating internal financing where separate corporations were used for financing, and in takeover strategies. Some of the main income tax advantages associated with an amalgamation include the following:

- The amalgamation could result in the use of loss carry over balances that a specific predecessor corporation(s) might not have been able to use because of insufficient income. The success of this benefit is dependent on avoiding the acquisition of control rules. This strategy is effective where the predecessor corporations are related prior to the amalgamation.

- Bringing together a profitable and an unprofitable corporation may allow for faster write-offs of depreciable property (through CCA) than would otherwise be possible by an unprofitable predecessor corporation. However, there are disadvantages with respect to depreciable property of any predecessor that has been subject to an acquisition of control as a result of the amalgamation.

- The amalgamation may provide for an increase in the amount of the manufacturing and processing profits tax deduction.

- The amalgamation could facilitate a change of taxation year end, since ITA 87(2)(a) deems the amalgamated corporation to be a new company. The CRA has stated, however, that amalgamating with a shell corporation expressly for the purpose of changing a taxation year end will be challenged where the CRA would have denied the request for a change of a taxation year.

17-69.   The timing of an amalgamation can be an important tax planning issue. As the amalgamation transaction results in a deemed year end, the company may have a short fiscal year for purposes of calculating CCA. In addition, outstanding reserves may have to be brought into income sooner, and the short fiscal period will count as a full year in the eligible loss carry forward years.

Exercise 17-6

Subject: ITA 87 Amalgamations

During its 2020 taxation year ending December 31, Downer Ltd. has a non-capital loss of $93,000 and a net capital loss of $150,000. Neither loss can be carried back. On January 1, 2021, the company is amalgamated with Upton Inc., an unrelated company that also uses a December 31 taxation year end. The new corporation is named Amalgo Inc. and it will choose to use a December 31 taxation year end. The terms of the amalgamation give 20,000 Amalgo Inc. shares to the Downer Ltd. shareholders and 150,000 Amalgo Inc. shares to the Upton Inc. shareholders. Amalgo Inc. was established with only one class of shares. For its first year ending December 31, 2021, Amalgo Inc. has net income of $1,200,000, including over $300,000 in taxable capital gains. Will Amalgo Inc. be able to claim any of the loss carry overs that were flowed through from Downer Ltd. for its 2021 taxation year? Explain your conclusion.

Solutions to Exercises are available in the Study Guide.

Winding-Up a 90% Owned Subsidiary—ITA 88(1)

Wind-Ups and Dissolutions—Corporate Law

17-70.   Both the creation of a corporation (incorporation) and the termination of its existence (dissolution) are functions of corporate law. A corporation can generally be dissolved in one of three circumstances: by a court order, by a resolution of its shareholders, or by the director of the corporate law authority for failing to comply with corporate law requirements, such as the payment of annual fees and certain annual reporting. In effect, dissolutions of a corporation fall into two broad categories: The dissolution can be voluntary, as is the case where a majority of shareholders vote in favour to dissolve the corporation, or involuntary, where other persons, specifically a judge of a provincial court or the director of the corporate law authority, dissolve the corporation. The most common types of dissolutions are voluntary.

17-71.   Corporate law refers to both the dissolution and the winding-up of a corporation, which are two different parts of the same process. In the winding-up process there is a beginning, the process itself, and an end. The winding-up process can be as short as a day or two where the subsidiary has no debt and simply acts as an investment holding company, or it can be as long as a few years depending on whether it has employees, outstanding contracts, extensive property, and liabilities.

17-72.   An awareness of the corporate law is important to understanding how the ITA applies to voluntary wind-ups and dissolutions. A summary of the process follows:

The Beginning Corporate law requires that the process generally be initiated by a corporate resolution that, at a minimum, requires that a shareholder vote in favour of a dissolution be made by shareholders who account for more than 50% of the voting shares of the corporation. This can vary depending on the specific province or territory. The shareholder resolution and other documents are then sent to the corporate law authority for permission to proceed with the wind-up. When the permission is granted, the winding-up process can then begin. For purposes of the ITA, the CRA views the process as beginning at the time there is a shareholder resolution authorizing the winding-up and dissolution of the corporation.

The Winding-Up Process Once corporate law permission has been obtained, the winding-up process gets underway. Corporate law requires that the corporation cease all normal business activity, notify creditors, dispose of all of the corporate property, settle any liabilities, and distribute any remaining residue to shareholders based on their priority entitlements (preferred shareholders are generally restricted to what they can receive as opposed to common shareholders).

The End—The Dissolution Once the corporation has complied with all aspects of the winding-up process, documents are submitted to the corporate law authority to ensure that all necessary steps have been followed and any disputes with creditors or shareholders (particularly minority shareholders) have been resolved. If any unresolved issues remain, and specifically if creditors, shareholders, or other interested parties decide to pursue legal action, then the corporation will generally not be permitted to dissolve. However, if all conditions have been met then the corporate law authority will issue a certificate of dissolution that evidences the end, and therefore the last day, of the corporation's existence. The CRA has an administrative concession that allows corporations that have not been formally dissolved to the benefits of the ITA 88(1) rollover where the only reason for the delay in the winding-up process is because of outstanding litigation (see Paragraphs 4 and 5 of IT-126R2, "Meaning of 'Winding Up.'")

Wind-Ups and Dissolution—The ITA

17-73.   The ITA follows the winding-up process applied under corporate law. The winding-up process is critical to the ITA 88(1) rollover treatment because it is only property distributed to the parent corporation during the winding-up process that is eligible for the rollover. The ITA, however, uses different expressions and words than used under corporate law. For example, the beginning of the winding-up process is referred to as the commencement of the wind-up or a time immediately before the winding-up. The winding-up process itself is referred to by the expressions "in the course of the winding up" or "on the winding up." Finally, the date of the dissolution is referred to in the ITA as the time at which a corporation has been "wound up."

17-74. The ITA contemplates the following three different wind-up situations:

ITA 88(1) This provision provides for a voluntary winding-up and dissolution of a taxable Canadian corporation to its parent corporation that is also a taxable Canadian corporation on a tax-free rollover basis. The rollover treatment only applies to distributions by the subsidiary to the parent company if the parent company owns at least 90% of each class of shares issued by the subsidiary. In addition, if there are any minority shareholders of the subsidiary the parent company must be arm's length with all of them. Any distributions made during the winding-up process to minority shareholders are not eligible for rollover treatment. When the conditions of ITA 88(1) are met the rollover applies automatically without any requirement to file an election form with the CRA.

ITA 88(2) This provision refers to wind-ups and dissolutions other than those to which ITA 88(1) applies. The types of situations to which ITA 88(2) apply include distributions to minority shareholders in the wind-up of a subsidiary to its parent under ITA 88(1), the voluntary dissolution of a corporation when it goes out of business (corporate law generally refers to these as liquidations), and the involuntary dissolution of a corporation that is dissolved by the corporate law authority for failing to comply with corporate law requirements, such as annual fees and reporting.

ITA 88(3) This provision applies to Canadian shareholders of foreign affiliates. It applies where the foreign affiliate dissolves and, in the process, distributes shares of another foreign affiliate to the Canadian shareholder as consideration. Limited coverage of foreign affiliates can be found in Chapter 20.

Voluntary Wind-Ups and Dissolution—ITA 88(1)

17-75. The reasons for voluntarily winding up a subsidiary into a parent corporation through ITA 88(1) are identical in many respects to the reasons for amalgamating corporations. The income tax rules must address the same issues that arise when corporations amalgamate, namely (1) the property of the subsidiary that is disposed of to the parent, (2) liabilities assumed by the parent, (3) the tax accounts of the subsidiary, and (4) the shares of the subsidiary owned by the parent. A summary of each of these four issues follows:

- **PROPERTY:** ITA 88(1)(a) applies to deem any property of the subsidiary that is disposed of to the parent in the course of the winding-up process to have been disposed of by the subsidiary at its cost amount, which is a defined term in ITA 248(1) essentially meaning the tax cost of the property. Additional rules are added, such as ITA 88(1)(f), which is designed to pass the tax attributes of depreciable property of the subsidiary to the parent. ITA 88(1)(c) determines the tax cost of the distributed property to the parent, which begins with the same amounts determined as POD to the subsidiary under ITA 88(1)(a). In summary, these rules provide rollover treatment by considering subsidiary property to be distributed at its tax cost and for the parent to acquire the property for the same amount.

- **LIABILITIES:** Where the parent assumes the debt obligations (e.g., liabilities) of the subsidiary to others, ITA 87(7) together with ITA 88(1)(e.2) ensure that there are no income tax consequences to the parent or the subsidiary as a result. This can be important since a corporation that is no longer indebted to specific creditors or lenders can experience income tax consequences as a result, which are referred to as the debt forgiveness rules. In addition, ITA 80.01(4) applies to ensure rollover treatment where there is intercompany debt between the parent and subsidiary. The rules, however, can create income tax consequences if the debt did not originate between the parent and the subsidiary.

- **TAX ACCOUNTS:** ITA 88(1)(e.2) contains a linking rule that uses the tax account flow-through concept that applies to amalgamations and revises select wording to ensure that it applies equally to wind-ups and dissolutions between a parent and a subsidiary where the conditions of ITA 88(1) are met. The result is that the tax accounts of the subsidiary flow through to the parent.

- **PARENT SHAREHOLDER:** When a corporation is dissolved its shares are legally cancelled, which is considered a disposition for income tax purposes. Technically ITA 84(2) applies redemption-type deemed dividend rules when the subsidiary is dissolved because the business of the subsidiary is wound up. This would mean calculating deemed dividends and capital gains or capital losses, which would be dependent on the amounts received by the subsidiary shareholders on the dissolution of the subsidiary. ITA 88(1)(d.1), however, deems that ITA 84(2) cannot apply to the parent company. ITA 84(2), however, still applies to any other subsidiary minority shareholders. ITA 88(1)(b) applies to the parent and determines the POD of the subsidiary shares. In almost all cases, ITA 88(1)(b) will deem the parent to have disposed of the subsidiary shares for POD equal to the ACB, therefore avoiding any capital gain or capital loss. Circumstances where capital gains can occur are discussed in Paragraph 17-86.

17-76.   The combination of a parent and subsidiary, whether by an amalgamation or through the dissolution of the subsidiary, are economic equivalents and, as a result, the income tax treatment is similar. When the winding-up process begins there are two separate corporations—the parent and the subsidiary—each with their own property, liabilities, tax accounts, and shareholders. Once the wind-up process is complete the only company remaining is the parent, which owns the property of the subsidiary, the debt obligations of the subsidiary, and the subsidiary tax accounts. This compares with an amalgamation of a parent and subsidiary where at law the two corporations merge to form one corporate entity that is considered a continuation of each of the predecessors. The amalgamated corporation owns all of the property, liabilities, and tax accounts of the predecessor corporations within one corporation.

17-77.   In the discussion of amalgamations we noted that there is a specific taxation year rule in ITA 87(2)(a) that treats amalgamating predecessor corporations as if they came to an end and the amalgamated new corporation as a newly incorporated company. The result was that the predecessors' taxation year ends and the new corporation was free to choose any taxation year end. This is the case even when a parent and subsidiary combine together through an amalgamation. When a parent and subsidiary combine by dissolving the subsidiary, in terms of the taxation year impact, the subsidiary experiences a final taxation year end that is the date of the dissolution. The parent corporation experiences no change whatsoever in its taxation year.

Subsidiary Losses—ITA 88(1.1) & 88(1.2)

17-78.   Whether a combination of a parent and subsidiary occurs by way of an amalgamation or a dissolution of a subsidiary does not change the fact that the tax accounts of the subsidiary flow through to the new corporation in an amalgamation or the parent company in a subsidiary dissolution. There is, however, one notable difference. On an amalgamation, any subsidiary loss carry overs are immediately available to the new corporation for its first taxation year subject, of course, to any restrictions on their use by the acquisition of control rules. However, under ITA 88(1.1), loss carry overs are only available to the parent corporation for its first taxation year that begins after the date that the wind-up process began. In effect, there is a potential delay for up to one year depending on the taxation year of the parent and the date the winding-up process began.

> **EXAMPLE**   If a parent's taxation year begins on February 1 and the winding-up process began on February 15, 2021, the loss carry overs of the subsidiary that were flowed through to the parent will not be available to the parent until its next taxation year that starts after February 15, 2021. In this case, it would be the parent's taxation year beginning February 1, 2022.

17-79.   For purposes of determining the expiry of loss carry overs, subsidiary loss carry overs are deemed to be loss carry overs of the parent based on the taxation year end of the subsidiary in which the loss carry over arose. If the parent and subsidiary use the same taxation year end, the subsidiary loss carry overs will become parent loss carry overs for the same taxation year. Where the taxation year ends are different, then the subsidiary losses are deemed to have occurred in the parent's taxation year that includes the last day of the subsidiary's taxation year end.

EXAMPLE   A parent has a June 30 taxation year end and the subsidiary a September 30 taxation year end. The winding-up process commences on August 15, 2021, and is completed with the dissolution of the subsidiary on August 31, 2021. The subsidiary has a 2016 non-capital loss for the taxation year that ended August 31, 2016.

ANALYSIS   Since August 31, 2016, falls in the 2017 taxation year of the parent (July 1, 2016, to June 30, 2017), the loss will be deemed to be a 2017 non-capital loss of the parent. This implies that the loss would then expire June 30, 2037. However, ITA 88(1.1)(b) limits the carry forward period to the period that would have been available to the subsidiary if it had not been wound up. This means that, in actual fact, the 2017 non-capital loss expires on June 30, 2036. If the subsidiary experienced any short taxation years after the realization of the 2016 non-capital loss they will also be factored in and reduce the expiry period.

Exercise 17-7

Subject: Losses in a Winding-Up

Park Inc. has a September 30 taxation year end, while its 100% owned subsidiary, Side Ltd., has an October 31 taxation year end. The process to wind up Side Ltd. begins on June 1, 2021, and ends with the issuance of a certificate of dissolution dated June 30, 2021. Side Ltd. has a 2018 non-capital loss balance of $50,000 for its taxation year ending June 30, 2018. What is the earliest taxation year in which this non-capital loss can be claimed by Park Inc.? When would the 2018 non-capital loss expire?

Solutions to Exercises are available in the Study Guide.

The Bump—ITA 88(1)(c) & 88(1)(d)

17-80.   Parent and subsidiary corporations can combine through the dissolution of the subsidiary to which ITA 88(1) applies. In that case the parent corporation must own at least 90% of each class of shares. The combination can also occur by way of an amalgamation referred to as a vertical short form amalgamation, which is contemplated by ITA 87(11). In this latter case, however, the amalgamation can only qualify if the parent corporation owns 100% of the issued shares of the subsidiary.

17-81.   The ITA treats the parent/subsidiary combinations, whether by dissolution or amalgamation, in a similar manner given that the economic result is the same. Therefore, the rollover rules are essentially the same with respect to property, liabilities, tax accounts, and shares. There is, however, another common income tax feature shared by both types of reorganizations that is referred to as "the bump." In brief, the bump allows the parent company or the amalgamated company (i.e., the "new corporation") to increase the tax cost of non-depreciable capital property acquired by it on the reorganization.

17-82.   The bump can be illustrated with the following basic example:

EXAMPLE   SubCo is a taxable Canadian corporation that acquired land 10 years earlier for $300,000. The plan was to build residential homes on the land in anticipation of anticipated growth in the area. Unfortunately, the company was unable to obtain city approval for their plans and the land has sat idle since. The land is the only property owned by the corporation. In addition, the company has no debt. The SubCo shareholders are all individuals. The shareholders are approached by a large construction company (ParentCo) that wishes to acquire the land. The company offers $2,000,000 for the land but the offer is turned down. The SubCo shareholders agree, however, to sell their shares for $2,000,000. As a result, ParentCo acquires the shares of Subco for $2,000,000. ParentCo plans to dissolve SubCo immediately to effectively move the land to it. ITA 88(1) applies to the dissolution of SubCo.

ANALYSIS   ITA 88(1)(a) deems the land distributed to ParentCo by SubCo to have been disposed of by SubCo for POD equal to its tax cost (cost amount) of $300,000, and ITA 88(1)(c) deems ParentCo to have acquired the land for the same $300,000 amount. ParentCo is deemed by ITA 88(1)(b) to have disposed of the SubCo shares for its ACB to ParentCo of $2,000,000. The result is that there are no income tax consequences to either SubCo or ParentCo. The same results would have applied had ParentCo and SubCo amalgamated.

THE PROBLEM   While there are no immediate income tax consequences as a result of the subsidiary dissolution (or amalgamation for that matter), there is an inherent underlying tax concern. ParentCo paid $2,000,000 for the shares of SubCo and received in exchange on the dissolution land with an ACB of only $300,000. This would imply that if ParentCo immediately sold the land for $2,000,000 there would be a gain of $1,700,000 even though it is only recovering its investment. In practice, this is referred to as a loss of tax basis, meaning that ParentCo has lost $1,700,000 in tax cost.

THE SOLUTION = THE BUMP   To address this inequity the ITA adds what is referred to as the bump to ITA 88(1)(c) and (d). The bump is an addition to the parent corporation's cost of eligible property acquired as a result of a subsidiary dissolution or an amalgamation. Eligible property generally means non-depreciable capital property such as land and investments. The bump rules can be extremely complicated depending on the circumstances, but the basic concept is relatively straightforward. The effect of the bump is to allow the tax cost of certain property acquired by the parent on the dissolution or amalgamation to be increased to its FMV in recognition of the high tax cost of the subsidiary shares. In this case, the bump calculations begin with the ACB to the parent of the subsidiary shares ($2,000,000) and then subtracts what is referred to as the "net tax value" (NTV) of the subsidiary. The NTV is equal to the total tax cost of all subsidiary property immediately before the winding-up process minus any amounts owing (liabilities) immediately before the wind-up process. In our example, the NTV would be $300,000 (ACB of the land $300,000 - nil liabilities). The maximum bump is then determined as the difference between the ACB of the subsidiary shares ($2,000,000) and the NTV ($300,000). Therefore, the bump is $1,700,000. The maximum bump can be designated by the parent to non-depreciable capital property only and cannot add an amount that results in the property exceeding its FMV. In the example, since the FMV of the land is $2,000,000 the full bump of $1,700,000 can be added to the ACB. The result is that the ACB of the land to the parent is the original ACB of $300,000 plus a bump of $1,700,000 for a total of $2,000,000.

17-83.   The specific ITA details of the bump calculations are explained in the following para-graphs. The amount of the bump is limited by the two following amounts:

1.   The maximum amount of the bump is found in ITA 88(1)(d)(i) and (i.1). This amount is the excess of the ACB of the subsidiary shares owned by the parent minus the sum of:

   - the tax costs of the subsidiary's property minus the amount of any debt owing at the time of the winding-up (the "NTV"); and

   - any dividends paid by the subsidiary to the parent (including capital dividends).

2.   ITA 88(1)(d)(ii) restricts the amount of the bump that can be applied to specific eligible property to an amount up to the FMV of the property at the time the parent acquired control of the subsidiary. This limitation means that if a parent company acquired control of a subsidiary in 2005 when the FMV of eligible property was $100,000 and a wind-up occurred in 2021 when the FMV of the eligible property was $900,000, the FMV for purposes of applying the bump would be the $100,000 amount.

17-84.   The following example will further illustrate the detailed calculations:

EXAMPLE   On December 31, 2011, ParentCo acquires 100% of the shares of SubCo for $5,000,000. At that time, the only non-depreciable capital property owned by SubCo was land with a FMV of $2,000,000 and a tax cost of $1,000,000. Between December 31, 2011, and December 31, 2021, SubCo pays dividends of $150,000 to ParentCo. On December 31, 2021, when the tax costs of SubCo's property total $4,200,000, SubCo is wound up. ITA 88(1) applies to the dissolution of SubCo.

ANALYSIS   The bump that can be applied to the land is the lesser of the two amounts described in Paragraph 17-83:

ACB of SubCo shares		$5,000,000
Tax costs of SubCo property on the winding-up	($4,200,000)	
Dividends paid to ParentCo by SubCo	(150,000)	(4,350,000)
Maximum bump		$ 650,000

FMV of the land when SubCo was acquired by ParentCo	$2,000,000
Less: ACB of the land	(1,000,000)
Maximum bump that can be applied to the land	$1,000,000

17-85.   In this situation, the bump to the land is restricted to the lower amount of $650,000. As a result, the subsidiary is deemed to have disposed of the land for $1,000,000 with no capital gain or capital loss (ITA 88(1)(a)). However, the parent is deemed to have acquired the land for $1,650,000 (tax cost to the subsidiary of $1,000,000 + a bump of $650,000).

Exercise 17-8

Subject: Winding-Up of a Subsidiary—ITA 88(1)

On January 1, 2017, Procul Ltd. acquired 100% of the outstanding shares of Lorne Inc. at a cost of $1,200,000. At that time the only non-depreciable capital property was land that was originally acquired in 2013 for $140,000. The FMV of the land when Procul acquired control in 2017 was $270,000. The FMV of the land when Lorne was dissolved in 2021 was $450,000.

On December 31, 2021, Lorne Inc. is wound up. ITA 88(1) applies to the dissolution. Lorne Inc. did not pay any dividends to Procul Ltd. at any time. On December 31, 2021, the condensed balance sheet of Lorne Inc. is as follows:

Cash	$ 120,000
Land—At cost (purchased in 2013)	140,000
Depreciable property—UCC (purchased in 2013)	240,000
Total assets	$500,000

Liabilities	$ 75,000
Shareholders' equity	425,000
Total equities	$500,000

Determine the tax cost of property acquired by Procul Ltd. from Lorne Inc. during the winding-up process.

Solutions to Exercises are available in the Study Guide.

Disposition of Subsidiary Shares—ITA 88(1)(b)

17-86.   Paragraph 17-75 mentioned that in almost all cases when a subsidiary is wound up (ITA 88(1)) or a parent/subsidiary amalgamation occurs (ITA 87(11)) the subsidiary shares are deemed to have been disposed of for POD equal to their ACB resulting in no income tax consequences (ITA 88(1)(b)). ITA 88(1)(b), however, sets the POD at the greater of (1) the ACB of the subsidiary shares or (2) the lesser of the PUC of the subsidiary shares and the NTV. Since PUC is generally the smallest amount (less than ACB and NTV), the result would be a disposition at POD equal to the ACB and no income tax consequences. There are, however, situations where the PUC of subsidiary shares can exceed the ACB. When this occurs the PUC would become the POD, resulting in a capital gain. The calculations make it impossible for there to be a capital loss.

> **EXAMPLE**   Prawn Ltd. owns 100% of the shares of Shrimp Inc. The ACB of the shares is $4,000,000. This subsidiary is wound up and the provisions of ITA 88(1) apply. At the time of the wind-up, the NTV is $4,800,000 and the PUC $4,500,000.

> **ANALYSIS**   Given these facts, ITA 88(1)(b) applies to deem POD of the subsidiary shares to be $4,500,000, which is the greater of (1) the ACB of $4,000,000 and (2) the lesser of the PUC of $4,500,000 and the NTV of $4,800,000. As a result, the POD are deemed to be $4,500,000 and there is a capital gain of $500,000 (POD $4,500,000 - ACB $4,000,000).

> **TAX PLANNING**   In the example there is a simple solution to eliminating the capital gain of $500,000. The subsidiary could authorize a return of PUC of $500,000 to its shareholders. Since returns of PUC are generally tax free, this would resolve the problem and result in a revised amount of $4,000,000 under ITA 88(1)(b). In 2018 the CRA was asked whether such planning was acceptable. They responded that when the PUC of subsidiary shares exceeds the ACB, the intent of the wind-up and parent/subsidiary amalgamation rules is to treat that difference as a capital gain; therefore, attempts to eliminate that gain with such planning would be viewed as potentially offensive and subject to challenge under the General Anti-Avoidance Rule (GAAR).

Tax Planning Considerations—Amalgamation vs. Winding-Up

17-87.   Figure 17-4 contains a comparison of some of the income tax differences of combining a parent and subsidiary company by way of an amalgamation under ITA 87(11) versus a dissolution of the subsidiary under ITA 88(1).

17-88.   While the income tax differences are negligible to some degree, other non-tax differences are much more significant in practice. These differences relate to the legal nature of an amalgamation versus a dissolution. In an amalgamation, the predecessor corporations do not legally cease to exist as opposed to a dissolution of a subsidiary where the corporation legally comes to an end. This core difference leads to a preference for amalgamations. For example, when a corporation ceases to exist and its property is distributed by its legal representatives to persons such as creditors, shareholders, and others, there is a concern by the CRA that any GST/HST and income tax liabilities will become uncollectible. To ensure that these tax liabilities are prioritized, the ITA contains a couple of provisions to allow the CRA to pursue legal representatives (ITA 159) who have been responsible for distributing corporate property that could have been used to settle tax liabilities and to also pursue anyone who has received such property (ITA 160).

17-89.   Legal representatives can avoid this unpleasant situation by following "clearance certificate" procedures (ITA 159(2) and IC82-6R12, "Clearance Certificates"), which involves notifying the CRA. Once the CRA determines any tax liabilities and these amounts are provided for, then the CRA will issue a clearance certificate that absolves legal representatives of any responsibility for distributions of corporate property that jeopardize the CRA's ability to collect tax. Corporate clearance certificate procedures are only necessary when a corporation is to be dissolved. Since an amalgamation does not involve the dissolution of predecessor corporations, the clearance certificate process does not apply.

	Figure 17-4	
	Comparison of Amalgamation under ITA 87(11) and Winding-Up under ITA 88(1)	
Factor	**Vertical Short Form Amalgamation—ITA 87(11)**	**Winding-Up of 90% Owned Subsidiary—ITA 88(1)**
Property	Tax costs of property of predecessor corporations flow through to the amalgamated company	Tax costs of subsidiary property flow through to the parent
The bump	Requires that the parent own all of the subsidiary's shares	Requires that the parent own at least 90% of each class of shares of the subsidiary plus be arm's length with all minority shareholders
Capital cost allowances (CCA)	CCA claim available to predecessors in their deemed final year end and to the amalgamated company in its deemed first year	No CCA claim by subsidiary in year of dissolution since there can be no depreciable property at year end; parent can claim CCA in the year depreciable property is distributed to it by the subsidiary
Loss carry forwards	Flowed through to the amalgamated corporation and can be used immediately subject to any acquisition of control restrictions	The same as for amalgamation except that the parent can only claim any losses for its first taxation year starting after the commencement of the wind-up
Taxation year	Deemed year end before amalgamation for predecessors and parent can choose any taxation year for its first taxation year	The taxation year end of the parent is unchanged; the subsidiary has a final taxation year end based on the date of dissolution

17-90.   When a subsidiary corporation has no employees, owns little property other than shares in other corporations, has no liabilities, and no or little business, then amalgamating or dissolving the company would be a simple and inexpensive endeavour. If, however, a subsidiary has employees and may have to deal with unions, conducts extensive business including multiple short- and long-term contracts, leases property including real property, has extensive debt and extensive properties, then the difference between dissolution and amalgamation becomes critical, particularly if the business combination must occur quickly. The dissolution of such a company would require negotiating with unions, changing legal titles for property owned (possibly having to pay provincial transfer taxes), negotiations with creditors who could block the dissolution, renegotiating all contracts with others, and so on. You can readily see that the costs and time involved to resolve these issues clearly favours amalgamations, which avoids much of these issues.

17-91.   In summary, the decision to restructure using amalgamations or wind-ups comes down to the specific facts and circumstances, including tight timelines. The provisions of the ITA are designed to minimize any differences given that the economics of amalgamations versus wind-ups are virtually the same. The ITA therefore abides by a longstanding principle that the ITA should minimize its impact on how business is conducted or structured. The real differences in practice often are decided on the basis of non-tax considerations given the similar income tax treatment.

We suggest you complete SSP 17-6 at this point.

Winding-Up a Canadian Corporation—ITA 88(2)

Overview

17-92.   ITA 88(2), as briefly described in Paragraph 17-74, applies where a Canadian corporation is dissolved in a situation other than an ITA 88(1) wind-up. Since ITA 88(1) only applies where a taxable Canadian corporation is wound up into its parent corporation in very specific circumstances, ITA 88(2) would apply to all other corporate dissolutions. The two most common types of dissolutions are (1) when a corporation is terminating its business by selling all of its property, paying its debts (including any tax liabilities), and distributing any excess to its shareholders; and (2) where corporations controlled by individuals fail to comply with corporate law requirements with the result that the corporation is dissolved. The first type of dissolution is voluntary and the second involuntary.

17-93.   Unlike ITA 88(1) that provides rollover treatment with respect to property distributed to the parent by the subsidiary in the course of a winding-up, ITA 88(2) provides no rollover treatment whatsoever and is generally referred to as a taxable dissolution throughout the winding-up process. Our focus will be on voluntary dissolutions where the corporate business is being liquidated. We will also provide brief coverage of the consequences of an involuntary dissolution where the inaction of individual shareholders to abide by corporate law requirements has led to the dissolution of the corporation. See Paragraph 17-105

Income Tax Consequences—ITA 69(5), 84(2), & 88(2)

17-94.   When a decision has been made to terminate the business of a corporation there is a finality that, in tax policy terms, requires there to be a final accounting for both income tax and GST/HST purposes. Once the process is initiated by a shareholder resolution the normal business activity ends and the corporation is in liquidation mode, where inventory and other property are sold off with creditors being paid. During this process the corporation tracks its profits and losses, capital gains, and capital losses as if it were business as usual. The corporation will continue to file corporate income tax returns for regular taxation years that end during the winding-up process with a final income tax return required for the last taxation year that ends with the dissolution of the corporation.

17-95.   When the winding-up process nears its conclusion, and distributions are made by the corporation to its shareholders in settlement of their rights as shareholders, the following three main income tax rules apply:

Corporate Property Distributions to Shareholders—ITA 69(5)   When a corporation makes a distribution of corporate property (other than cash) to a shareholder as part of the wind-up process, ITA 69(5)(a) deems the corporation to have received POD for that property equal to its FMV. ITA 69(5)(b) deems the cost of the property to the recipient shareholder to also be the same FMV.

Shares Cancelled on Distributions of Corporate Property—ITA 84(2)   When a corporation is dissolved (i.e., wound up) its shares can no longer legally exist and are cancelled. The legal cancellation of shares is considered a disposition for income tax purposes. There are two steps to the income tax consequences: (1) ITA 84(2) deems the shareholder to have received a dividend to the extent that the FMV of amounts received by a shareholder as settlement on the cancellation of the shares exceeds the PUC of those shares, and (2) a capital gain or capital loss is then determined as the difference between the adjusted POD (FMV of amounts received less the ITA 84(2) deemed dividend) and the ACB of the shares.

Special Rules for Certain Tax Accounts—ITA 88(2)   ITA 88(2) serves two main functions. The first is that it addresses timing issues to allow a corporation to adjust its capital dividend account (CDA) and certain other accounts (pre-1972 capital surplus on hand [CSOH]) that provide tax-free distribution treatment to shareholders. These adjustments allow a shareholder to benefit from the accounts even though technically they were not available when corporate distributions were made that resulted in the cancellation of the shares. The second function is to establish an ordering rule for purposes of the deemed dividend determined under ITA 84(2). The rules provide that the first part of the deemed dividend is made up of the CDA (requires an election), the second part is made up of the 1972 CSOH, and any remaining balance is considered a taxable dividend. None of our examples or problem material will refer to the 1972 CSOH as it is beyond the scope of an introductory text.

Example

Basic Information

17-96. The income tax consequences of a voluntary dissolution of a corporation and the liquidation of its business is illustrated in the following example. Assume that the wind-up occurs on the last day of the 2021 taxation year to avoid any short taxation year issues.

EXAMPLE The Marker Company, a CCPC with a December 31 taxation year end, was incorporated 20 years ago. On December 15, 2021, the following balance sheet, based on tax costs, has been prepared in contemplation of liquidating the business and dissolving the company:

The Marker Company
Balance Sheet
As at December 15, 2021 (Tax Cost ("cost amount" ITA 248(1))

Accounts receivable	$ 12,000
Non-eligible RDTOH	8,000
Land (Note One)	250,000
Building—UCC (Note Two)	195,000
Total	$465,000

Liabilities	Nil
Common shares (Note Three)	$ 10,000
Retained earnings (Note Three)	455,000
Total	$465,000

Note One The FMV of the land is $300,000.

Note Two The capital cost of the building was $320,000 and the FMV is $350,000.

Note Three The PUC and ACB of the common shares are both $10,000.

The CDA balance determined in accordance with ITA 88(2) is $75,000. There is no pre-72 CSOH and the GRIP account at all times is nil.

All of the corporate property is sold for their FMV of $662,000 (accounts receivables $12,000 + land $300,000 + building $350,000). The company has no income for the 2021 taxation year other than as a result of the disposition of its property. The provincial corporate income tax rates are 2.5% on income eligible for the small business deduction and 14% on other corporate income.

Cash Available for Distribution to Shareholders

17-97. The sale of the corporate property would result in the following income to the company:

Property	Proceeds	Taxable Capital Gain	Active Business Income
Accounts receivable	$ 12,000	Nil	Nil
Land	300,000	$25,000	Nil
Building	350,000	15,000	$125,000
Totals	$662,000	$40,000	$125,000

The income tax payable on Marker's taxable income of $165,000 ($40,000 + $125,000) would be calculated as follows:

Federal income tax on active business income [(38% - 10% - 19%)($125,000)]	$11,250
Federal income tax on investment income [(38% - 10% + 10 2/3%)($40,000)]	15,467
Part I tax payable	$26,717
Provincial income tax on active business income [(2.5%)($125,000)]	3,125
Provincial income tax on investment income [(14%)($40,000)]	5,600
Total corporate income tax payable	$35,442

17-98.   The only 2021 addition to an RDTOH balance would be the refundable portion of Part I tax payable, which would be added to the non-eligible RDTOH account. The amount to be added would be the least of:

- 30 2/3% of investment income [(30 2/3%)($40,000)] $12,267

- 30 2/3% of taxable income, less amount eligible for the small business deduction [(30 2/3%)($165,000 - $125,000)] $12,267

- Part I tax payable $26,717

17-99.   The non-eligible RDTOH balance would equal:

Opening balance	$ 8,000
Add: Part I refundable tax	12,267
Non-eligible RDTOH	$20,267

17-100.   The after0tax amount of cash that is available for distribution to shareholders is calculated as follows:

Sale proceeds	$662,000
Corporate tax payable	(35,442)
Dividend refund from non-eligible RDTOH*	20,267
Available for distribution	$646,825

*Given the amount of the sale proceeds of $662,000, the balance in the non-eligible RDTOH is sufficient to result in a full refund.

Distribution to Shareholders

17-101.   The CDA can be distributed to the shareholders as a tax-free capital dividend with the appropriate election under ITA 83(2). The CDA balance is determined as:

Opening balance	$ 75,000
Add: Capital gain on land	25,000
Add: Capital gain on the building	15,000
CDA balance available—ITA 88(2)	$115,000

17-102.   In the absence of a GRIP account, all of the dividends would be non-eligible. The non-eligible taxable dividend component of the total distribution to the shareholders is determined as follows:

Total distribution	$646,825
Less: PUC	(10,000)
ITA 84(2) deemed dividend	$636,825
Less: CDA—ITA 88(2)(b)	(115,000)
Taxable non-eligible dividend	$521,825

17-103.   The taxable non-eligible dividend will be grossed up to $600,099 [(115%)($521,825)]. The dividend will generate a federal dividend tax credit of $54,190 [(9/13)(15%)($521,825)] that will be applied to reduce federal income tax payable.

17-104.   The capital gain consequences of the cancellation of the shares as a result of the dissolution of the corporation is determined as follows:

Total distribution to shareholders	$ 646,825
Less: ITA 84(2) deemed dividend	(636,825)
Adjusted POD—ITA 54 ("POD")	$ 10,000
ACB of shares	(10,000)
Capital gain	Nil

Exercise 17-9

Subject: Liquidation of a Corporate Business and Dissolution of the Corporation—ITA 88(2)

Windown Inc. is a CCPC. After the liquidation sale of its property and settling all of its liabilities, including all income tax and GST/HST, the company is left with cash of $865,000. The PUC and ACB of the company shares are both $88,000. Subsequent to the liquidation of the business the combined eligible and non-eligible RDTOH accounts total $47,000. The CDA balance is $26,000 and the GRIP balance is nil. Determine the income tax consequences to the shareholders if maximum distributions are made on June 1, 2021. Assume that all appropriate elections and designations are made to minimize income tax payable by the shareholders.

Solutions to Exercises are available in the Study Guide.

We suggest you complete SSP 17-7 at this point.

Involuntary Dissolution by Corporate Law authority

17-105.   The right to incorporate a company comes with obligations, including filing annual information returns and payingyingying small fees. Many of these requirements can be fulfilled online. Failure to abide by these requirements, however, can result in the director of the corporate authority dissolving a corporation. CBCA 212(1), for example, sets out rules that allow the director of the *Canada Business Corporations Act* to dissolve a corporation if there are delays exceeding one year of fulfilling annual corporate law requirements. A further 120 days is provided upon notification to allow additional time for the matter to be resolved. If these notifications are ignored it is then up to the director to take the necessary action. It is not unusual for some provincial jurisdictions to do nothing, but the possibility remains that action may legally be taken to dissolve a corporation. Many years ago the corporate law authority in Ontario had amassed a list of thousands of corporations that were in default of reporting and other obligations. The province decided to take action to dissolve all of these corporations in one year. The result caused considerable income tax issues for the shareholders of the dissolved companies as well as the CRA who was notified of the corporate action.

17-106.   The CRA began a campaign of tracking down the shareholders of the dissolved corporations to advise them of the income tax consequences. It took the CRA more than a few years to contact everyone involved. In many cases the individual shareholders pleaded that they were unaware that the corporation no longer existed. Many individuals had incorporated their individual businesses carried on as sole proprietors, with many continuing to file corporate income tax returns and GST/HST returns long after the dissolution. For those individuals, the income tax and GST/HST reassessments were a serious matter.

17-107.   When the corporations were dissolved, ITA 69(5), 84(2) and 88(2) automatically applied. This meant that all of the corporate property became property of the shareholders and the shares owned were legally cancelled. ITA 69(5) would have deemed the corporation to have effectively sold all of its property, creating business income for inventories, capital gains, recapture or terminal losses on depreciable property, and capital gains and capital losses on non-depreciable capital property. The first step of the reassessment was to determine the additional corporate income for the company's final taxation year based on the date of the dissolution. Second, the FMV of all corporate property that became the property of the former individual shareholder was used to calculate a deemed dividend under ITA 84(2) and a potential capital gain or capital loss. Finally, the businesses continued to be carried on but not by a corporation. The result was that the business was carried on as a sole proprietorship or as a partnership personally by the former individual shareholders. The individuals were personally reassessed for this business income at high individual tax rates instead of the low rates for CCPCs. In addition, the GST/HST responsibilities became personal responsibilities of the individual.

17-108.   The impact of failing to maintain the necessary corporate law requirements can therefore be quite costly. Individuals ignore them at their peril. Fortunately, in most provinces and territories there is a corporate law process to repair the damage and reverse the negative income tax implications. The corporate law process is referred to as a "revival" (see CBCA 209). Many formalities are required to effectively restore the corporation's existence, but the wording of the corporate law will determine whether one's income tax and GST/HST problems disappear. If the corporate law is a retroactive restoration, then the income tax and GST/HST reassessments will be withdrawn. However, if the corporate law restoration rule is not retroactive, then the tax reassessments will remain.

Convertible Properties—ITA 51

Overview

17-109.   ITA 51 applies to two situations, both of which are with the same corporation. The first, ITA 51(1)(a), applies where a shareholder of a corporation exchanges shares of one class for shares of a different class. Second, ITA 51(1)(b) applies where a taxpayer who holds debt of the corporation that is a bond, debenture, or note receivable exchanges that debt for shares. In the second situation the debt must contain a legal right that allows the debtholder to make the exchange. ITA 51(1) refers to the properties (shares or debt) being exchanged as "convertible property."

17-110.   ITA 51 is a rollover rule that allows the exchange to take place without any income tax consequences as long as there is no NSC received on the exchange. This rollover is automatic and does not require the filing of an election. However, since share-for-share exchanges with the same corporation can occur on a rollover basis as a result of ITA 51, 86, and 85 there are a few ordering rules (ITA 51(4) and 86(3)) that deny the rollover under ITA 51 if either ITA 85 or 86 applied to the share-for-share exchange. The effect of the rules is that priority first goes to ITA 85 then to ITA 86 and finally to ITA 51.

17-111.   The ITA 51 rollover is unique in that if the conditions are met ITA 51(1)(c) deems the exchange not to have been a disposition of any property. This avoids many of the complexities of the ITA, including capital gain or capital loss calculations.

17-112.   When shares are acquired as a result of the exchange the tax attributes must be established, specifically the ACB and PUC of the shares. ITA 51(1)(d) deems the ACB of the shares to equal the ACB of the convertible property; therefore, if a note receivable of $26,000 is exchanged for shares, the ACB of those shares will also be $26,000.

17-113.   If the exchange is a share-for-share exchange then there is a PUC reduction rule under ITA 51(3) that is designed to ensure that the PUC of the shares issued on the exchange have the same PUC as the convertible property shares. Therefore, if the PUC of the convertible property shares was $19,000 but the legal capital, and therefore PUC, of the shares issued on the exchange is $50,000, ITA 51(3) will calculate a $31,000 PUC reduction that will reset the PUC of the issued shares to $19,000 to match the convertible property shares. This ensures that no deemed dividend is created as a result of the exchange. In summary, the tax attributes of the issued shares inherit the tax attributes of the convertible property shares.

17-114.   In practical terms, this rollover is designed to accommodate the conversion of certain debt into shares of the same corporation and shares into other shares of the same corporation.

> **EXAMPLE**   An individual acquires $10,000 of convertible bonds directly from the corporation. The bonds are convertible at the option of the holder into 500 shares of the issuing company's Class D common shares. The individual exercises the conversion feature when the Class D common shares are trading at $22 per share.

> **ANALYSIS**   In the absence of ITA 51, the conversion of the bonds would be a disposition with the following income tax results:

POD [(50)($22)]	$11,000
Less: ACB	(10,000)
Capital gain	$ 1,000

17-115.   If ITA 51 applies, the exchange is deemed not to be a disposition (ITA 51(1)(c)) and the cost, and therefore ACB, of the shares are deemed to be equal to the ACB of the bonds of $10,000 (ITA 51(1)(d)). The legal capital of the shares and therefore the PUC of the issued shares would generally be equal to the amount owing of $10,000 as a result of corporate law. Once the rules of ITA 51 apply, the tax attributes of the issued shares would be an ACB and PUC of $10,000 and FMV of $11,000.

Other Exchange Considerations—ITA 51.1 & ITA 51(2) Gifting

17-116.   ITA 51 allows convertible debt and shares to be exchanged for shares of the same company on a rollover basis. ITA 51.1 allows the same debtholders (bond, debenture, or note) to exchange their debt for other debt of the same corporation on a rollover basis as long as the debt provides a legal right to make the exchange. ITA 51.1 also requires that the amount owing remain unchanged. ITA 51.1 is designed to assist corporations restructuring their debt for multiple purposes, including to revise the payment period or lower the interest costs.

17-117.   Share-for-share exchanges, whether eligible for rollover treatment under ITA 85 or ITA 86, provide an opportunity for an individual to shift value and therefore indirectly benefit family members (related persons) by receiving shares that are worth less than the shares exchanged. The conferral of these benefits generally requires the related person to be a common shareholder of the same company. The ITA sets out gifting provisions that are designed to penalize the individual responsible for making the gift with additional immediate income tax consequences that could have been deferred. In addition, the rules also result in the gift amount being subject to income tax a second time when the related person disposes of the shares. ITA 51(2) also provides for a gifting rule that is identical in many respects to the gifting rule in ITA 86(2).

Sale of an Incorporated Business

17-118.   Selling a business of a corporation can be accomplished in one of two ways. Either the business assets (property) are sold individually to multiple purchasers or to one buyer. The difference is that when selling a business in its entirety one can consider goodwill, which attaches to the business as a whole. An alternative to selling business assets is to simply sell all of the shares of the corporation. Our discussion will focus on the sale of all business assets to one purchaser and the sale of all of the shares to one purchaser.

17-119.   As a rule, resident Canadian purchasers of a Canadian business prefer to purchase assets rather than shares. The main reason is that the purchase price can be allocated among all of the business assets based on their FMV. This FMV recognition provides for higher tax costs and ultimately results in larger deductions, such as CCA. The purchaser can also decide to be selective in the assets purchased and not purchase everything. Sellers, on the other hand, prefer to sell shares since, in general, the only income will be a capital gain on the shares that may allow individual shareholders to offset any capital gains with the capital gains deduction.

17-120.   Purchasers are reluctant to purchase shares for many reasons, including that the corporation is left intact with assets that have tax costs below their FMV. The result is smaller income tax deductions and ultimately higher levels of capital gains and other income such as recapture. In addition, the purchase of shares between arm's-length persons frequently results in an acquisition of control with adverse consequences depending on the corporate tax accounts and plans for the corporate business. Finally, the purchase of shares requires a greater level of due diligence since there may be undisclosed liabilities, including potential income tax and GST/HST liabilities, that may have to be provided for. These latter situations often result in holding back, and releasing over time, portions of the sale price as protection for the purchaser in case liabilities subsequently emerge. Purchase and sale agreements for shares frequently involve the addition of indemnity clauses to provide for a wide variety of contingencies.

17-121.   Sellers/shareholders are reluctant to sell assets because it creates increased income in the corporation and therefore additional corporate income tax. In addition, the provinces may charge land transfer taxes and other fees. Indirect payment to shareholders is made through redemptions and dissolutions that result in the distribution of corporate after-tax cash. These distributions are treated as deemed dividends, which are subject to higher tax rates than taxable capital gains even without considering the impact of the capital gains deduction. The impact of higher tax rates on taxable dividends can be mitigated somewhat if the dividends result in dividend refunds to the corporation.

17-122.   When it comes to deciding the best course of action compromises are often necessary given that sellers prefer to sell shares and purchasers prefer to purchase assets. An analysis is required to determine the best alternative. Often the compromise is in the selling price for shares. Sellers are often willing to accept a lower price for shares than for the sale of assets based on a comparison of after-tax cash flows for each alternative.

17-123.   There are many complexities associated with such transactions and our coverage is intended to provide the basic elements of the analysis. In our discussion we will assume that both the purchaser and seller are not compelled to buy or sell and therefore both parties have equal say in the ultimate decision.

Restrictive Covenants—ITA 56.4

Overview

17-124.   When a purchaser acquires a business there are many concerns, including that the seller may set up a competing business alone or with others, provide consultation to competitors, attempt to recruit existing employees central to the business, or steal away existing customers. These concerns are frequently addressed by way of restrictive covenants (or non-compete payments), which are designed to protect the purchaser from such action and to provide a basis for pursuing legal action should the seller(s) breach the purchase and sale contract that includes such covenants.

17-125.   These covenants may require actual payments by the purchaser to the seller(s) to compensate them for forgoing their right to take any of these actions. In effect, these covenants are written into the agreements and provide that, for a stipulated amount, the recipient will agree not to pursue certain specific activity often within a selective geographical region and for a specified period of time.

General Rules

17-126.   In the past there was considerable controversy as to how these payments would be handled for income tax purposes. ITA 56.4 was added to the ITA to clarify the income tax treatment and in certain circumstances provide flexibility in the form of elective options. The rules, unfortunately, can be quite complex but the basic default rule is ITA 56.4(2) requires that any amount received or receivable in a taxation year be included in the recipient's income as "other income." Alternatively, if no amount is paid there are generally no income tax consequences unless it is determined, through ITA 68, that part of the proceeds for the sale does in fact relate to the restrictive covenant. The CRA confirmed that if an agreement states that $1 will be paid for the restrictive covenant to ensure it is an enforceable contract, that amount will not be consideration as consideration for the purposes of applying the rules of ITA 56.4. In summary, ITA 56.4 will only apply where actual payments are made to those forgoing certain rights.

17-127.   ITA 56.4(3) provides a number of exceptions to the general rule. A brief explanation of the main exceptions follows.

ITA 56.4(3)(a) — Employment Income   If an employee quits or retires, a non-compete payment may be made to attempt to restrict the employee from accepting employment with a competitor or other action that could jeopardize the success of the business. In such cases the payment is treated as employment income to the recipient and as an employment expense to the payor.

ITA 56.4(3)(b) — Class 14.1   If the nature of the payment is attributable to property that would be included in class 14.1, such as goodwill, then the payor and recipient may file a joint election to treat the payment to the payor as a purchase of class 14.1 depreciable property and a disposition of a class 14.1 property by the recipient.

From the point of view of the payor, this is an unfavourable treatment. Instead of being a fully deductible expense, the payment is added to class 14.1 where it will only be deductible on a 5% declining balance basis.

However, from the point of view of the recipient, this treatment is preferable to a full income inclusion under ITA 56.4(2) since the amount will generally be treated as a taxable capital gain, particularly if it relates to goodwill that was internally generated since the ACB would be nil.

ITA 56.4(3)(c) — Sale of an Eligible Interest   An eligible interest includes an interest in shares in a corporation that carries on business. If the payment can be considered as additional consideration for the sale of shares, then an election can be filed by both the purchaser and seller to treat the payment as additional sales proceeds for the shares. In this case the purchaser's cost will be increased and the sellers' POD will also be increased, resulting in an additional capital gain or lower capital loss. There are many rules surrounding this particular exception that can result in the payment being divided into two parts: share proceeds and a regular payment that would be subject to the general rule of ITA 56.4(2). The result to the recipient could therefore be part income and part capital gain.

17-128.   If the default rule of ITA 56.4(2) applies it only describes the income tax treatment to the recipient of any payment and not the payor. The elections under ITA 56.4(3)(b) and (c), however, describe the tax consequences to both recipient and payor. The CRA confirmed that the treatment of the payor under the default rule is determined by applying general tax principles.

17-129.   The first exception, treatment of the restrictive covenant payment as employment income, is not generally relevant to the purchase and sale of a corporate business. However, the other two exceptions are very significant when a business is being sold, so it will be given further attention in our discussion of the alternative ways in which a business can be sold.

Sale of the Business

Overview

17-130.   The sale of a corporate business is motivated by multiple factors in regard to both the purchaser and seller. The implication is that the purchaser acquires the business along with all of its assets and liabilities for the purpose of continuing that business independently or merging it with the purchaser's business. In either case the purchase of the whole of a business will include any goodwill that has been created with respect to that business.

17-131.   From a practical income tax perspective the sale of a corporate business means the sale of each corporate asset and the resolution or settlement of all corporate liabilities, including any additional income tax and GST/HST liabilities that are created as the result of the sale of all of the assets.

17-132.   In broad terms, determining the outcome of the sale of assets first requires calculating the income or loss that arises as a result of each individual asset sale. This would include business income or loss on the sale of inventory and capital gains, capital losses, recapture, and terminal losses on the sale of other corporate assets, including goodwill. Once the income or loss has been determined, then the corporate income tax liability can be calculated, including determining whether the company may be entitled to a dividend refund to offset some or all of the income tax liability. At this stage the corporation should be able to determine any excess cash remaining after the payment of all liabilities. The first stage deals exclusively with corporate income tax.

17-133.   The second major aspect is determining the residual amount that is available to be distributed to the shareholders as a liquidating-type dividend on the dissolution of the company that was discussed in the ITA 88(2) coverage. The second stage generally involves personal income tax considerations where the shareholders are individuals. These two broad steps of (1) selling all the assets and paying all liabilities and (2) the final distributions to shareholders provide the necessary after-tax information that can be used to compare the income tax consequences to determine which alternative is preferable.

Income Tax Considerations on the Sale of Corporate Property (Assets)

17-134.   In the first stage of selling all of the corporate properties (e.g., assets), an understanding of the income tax consequences is necessary. The income tax consequences are summarized as follows:

Cash   In most circumstances, cash is either used to pay liabilities or to make final distributions to shareholders when the corporation is dissolved. There are no income tax consequences associated with cash unless it is foreign currency.

Accounts Receivable   In the absence of any special election, the sale of accounts receivable will generally be treated as a capital transaction. This means that any difference between the amount owing and the sale price will be treated as a capital gain or capital loss.

However, ITA 22 provides for a joint election to effectively treat the sale of accounts receivables as on income account. This allows the purchaser to treat any difference between the amount paid for the receivables and the amount actually collected as a bad debt expense and allows the seller to claim any loss as an expense. The loss claimed by the seller is required to be included in the income of the purchaser. ITA 22 is discussed in detail in Chapter 6.

Inventory   Even when inventory is sold as part of the sale of a business, any difference between the sales price and the vendor's tax cost will be treated as either business income or loss (ITA 23).

Prepayments   Prepayments represent expenses incurred in a year that relate to a subsequent year. The result is that they would have been deductible in the future year had the corporate business continued into that year (ITA 18(9)). While they are recognized as assets for accounting purposes, they are not considered property for income tax purposes. If a purchaser compensates the seller for these expenses, the purchaser assumes the entitlements represented by the expenses such as prepaid rent. Any reimbursements made to the seller have no income tax consequences since they represent recovery of an expenditure that was not deductible.

Non-Depreciable Capital Property   The most common types of non-depreciable capital property are land and investments. The sale of this type of property results in either a capital gain or a capital loss. Part of any capital gain may be claimed as a capital gains reserve where part of the sale price is not due until a subsequent year (ITA 40(1)(a)). Such reserves may not be practical, however, where the objective is to dissolve the company as quickly as possible.

Depreciable Property   The sale of depreciable property can result in recapture, a terminal loss, or some combination of recapture and a capital gain. In general terms, a capital gain occurs where the sale price exceeds the ACB of the property. ACB of depreciable property is generally the capital cost. If the sale price is less than the ACB there can be no capital loss since the ITA accounts for any loss in value of depreciable property as eventual terminal losses. Both recapture and terminal losses are part of the income or loss from a business where they were used in a business, whereas capital gains on the same depreciable property are treated differently as investment income.

Goodwill   Goodwill represents the difference between the FMV of a corporation and the FMV of its identifiable net assets (assets minus liabilities). Any amounts identified as attributable to goodwill will be treated as POD of depreciable property class 14.1. If the goodwill was not purchased and has been generated internally throughout the life of the corporate business the capital cost and ACB will be nil. As a result, a sale will create a capital gain. If the goodwill had been previously purchased then the normal CCA/UCC rules of capital gain, recapture, and terminal losses will apply.

Sale of Shares

Overview & Tax Planning Considerations

17-135.   In terms of accounting, legal, and tax considerations, the sale of shares is the simplest way to sell a corporate business and is generally the method preferred by shareholders. The sale results in a capital gain or capital loss equal to the difference between the sale price and the total of the ACB and selling costs.

17-136.   In preparing for the sale of shares, a corporation will often take certain preparatory steps to reduce any taxable capital gain and to ensure that the shares of the corporation qualify for the capital gains deduction. Reducing the capital gain on the sale of shares generally requires withdrawing value from the corporation prior to the share sale. Specific pre-sale planning includes the following:

CDA (ITA 83(2))   Paying out any balance in the capital dividend account (CDA) to resident shareholders (see Chapter 14). Non-resident shareholders cannot withdraw capital dividends tax free because of a withholding tax charged under Part XIII (see Chapter 20).

Dividend Refunds   Declaring taxable dividends to generate dividend refunds where a private corporation has RDTOH accounts (eligible or non-eligible). The net tax rate of the difference between the individual personal tax rate on the taxable dividend and the recovery of either 30 2/3% or 38 1/3% that represents refundable taxes that have accumulated in RDTOH produces rates significantly lower than capital gain rates. Dividend refunds and RDTOH are discussed in Chapter 13.

Safe Income Dividends (ITA 55(2))   Individual shareholders can incorporate holding companies to own their shares and then have these holding corporations pay intercorporate dividends that are tax free (ITA 112(1)). Avoiding the conversion of the intercorporate dividends to capital gains under ITA 55(2) requires limiting intercorporate dividends to the safe income. ITA 55(2) is discussed in Chapter 16.

Purifications (ITA 110.6) QSBC Shares   One of the most significant advantages of selling shares is the fact that the capital gains deduction could offset a large portion of the taxable capital gain and reduce personal income tax. Planning is required to ensure that the shares qualify for the deduction. One of the most important conditions is that at the time of the sale of shares that 90% or more of the FMV of the corporation's assets are attributable to an active business carried on in Canada. If this condition is not met then the capital gains deduction will not be available on the sale of those shares. Planning referred to as purification involves moving assets that fail to qualify out of the corporation in advance of the sale so that the 90% test is met. The capital gains deduction is discussed in Chapter 11.

17-137.   Each of the tax planning steps is designed to remove value from the corporation for the benefit of shareholders on a tax-free or low tax cost that is less than the tax rate on capital gains. The planning also ensures that each individual shareholder will be able to access the capital gains deduction to the maximum extent possible.

Example

17-138.   To illustrate the sale of an incorporated business, we will use the following example.

EXAMPLE   Mr. O'Leary owns all of the outstanding shares of O'Leary Ltd., a CCPC with a December 31 taxation year end. Mr. O'Leary has reached retirement age and wishes to dispose of the business. He has received an offer to buy the shares for $180,000 or, alternatively, to sell all of the corporate assets for $200,000. All of the liabilities of the business have been settled in advance of the sale.

Both the ACB and PUC of Mr. O'Leary's shares are $50,000. The provincial income tax rate on business income eligible for the small business deduction is 2.5%. The provincial income tax rate on all other income is 14%. The corporation has no balance in its RDTOH accounts, its CDA, or its GRIP account. Mr. O'Leary is subject to a combined personal federal/provincial income tax rate of 46% on non-dividend income and 31% on non-eligible dividends.

The tax costs and FMV by type of corporate asset are as follows:

Asset	Cost	FMV
Accounts teceivable	$ 15,000	$ 15,000
Inventory	55,000	60,000
Land	20,000	40,000
Equipment (UCC = $45,000)	95,000	60,000
Goodwill	Nil	25,000
Total	$185,000	$200,000

Sale of Shares for $180,000

17-139.   With respect to the sale of shares, the income tax consequences are as follows:

POD	$180,000
Less: ACB	(50,000)
Capital gain	$130,000
Inclusion rate	1/2
Taxable capital gain (Mr. O'Leary)	$ 65,000

17-140.   The after-tax results for Mr. O'Leary are as follows:

Proceeds received	$180,000
Income tax payable [(46%))($65,000)]	(29,900)
Cash retained	$150,100

17-141.   While this might be the result, it is likely that the shares of O'Leary Ltd. qualify for the capital gains deduction resulting in Mr. O'Leary retaining the entire $180,000. Alternative minimum tax (AMT) might apply with the use of the capital gains deduction, although the AMT is recoverable. AMT is discussed in Chapter 11.

Sale of Assets for $200,000

17-142.   The income tax consequences resulting from selling the assets are as follows:

Account		Income
Inventories ($60,000 - $55,000)		$ 5,000
Equipment—Recaptured CCA ($60,000 - $45,000)		15,000
Active business income		$20,000
Taxable capital gains		
Land [(1/2)($40,000 - $20,000)]	$10,000	
Goodwill [(1/2)($25,000)]	12,500	22,500
Corporate taxable income		$42,500

17-143.   The resulting corporate income tax would be calculated as follows:

Federal income tax on:	
Active business income [(38% - 10% - 19%)($20,000)]	$ 1,800
Investment income [(38% - 10% + 10 2/3%)($22,500)]	8,700
Part I tax	$10,500
Provincial income tax on active business income [(2.5%)($20,000)]	500
Provincial income tax on investment income [(14%)($22,500)]	3,150
Total corporate income tax	$14,150

17-144.   The GRIP and RDTOH balances at the beginning of the year are both nil. This means that the only amount available for a dividend refund would be the addition to the non-eligible RDTOH for the refundable portion of the Part I tax. This amount would be the least of:

- 30 2/3% of investment income [(30 2/3%)($22,500)] $ 6,900

- 30 2/3% of taxable income less the amount eligible for the
  small business deduction [(30 2/3%)($42,500 - $20,000)] $ 6,900

- Part I tax $10,500

17-145.   The CDA balance would be determined as follows:

Non-taxable portion of capital gain on:	
Land [(1/2)($20,000)]	$10,000
Goodwill [(1/2)($25,000)]	12,500
Capital dividend account (CDA)	$22,500

17-146.   Given the preceding analysis of the sale of the corporate assets, the net cash retained by Mr. O'Leary after the distribution of corporate assets can be calculated as follows:

POD—Sale of assets	$200,000
Corporate income tax (before dividend refund)	(14,150)
Dividend refund (Note)	6,900
Funds available for distribution	$192,750
Less: PUC	(50,000)
ITA 84(2) deemed dividend	$142,750
CDA (ITA 83(2) election required)	(22,500)
Taxable dividend	$120,250
Income tax rate (on non-eligible dividends)	31%
Personal income tax	$ 37,278

Note Technically, the dividend refund is the lesser of the $6,900 balance in the non-eligible RDTOH account and 38 1/3% of taxable dividends paid. The shareholder dividend distribution is more than sufficient to result in a full refund of the RDTOH balance of $6,900.

17-147. There would be no capital gain or capital loss on the disposition of the shares, as shown in the following:

Total distribution	$192,750
Less: ITA 84(2) deemed dividend	(142,750)
Adjusted POD	$ 50,000
Less: ACB	(50,000)
Capital gain/loss	Nil

17-148.   Based on the preceding calculations, Mr. O'Leary's after-tax retention from the sale of assets would be determined as follows:

Amount distributed	$192,750
Less: Personal income tax	(37,278)
Cash retained	$155,472

17-149.   The cash retention from the sale of assets of $155,472 exceeds the cash retention from the share sale of $150,100 by $5,175. However, the sale of shares would be much more favourable if the capital gains deduction were available since the after-tax retention would rise to $180,000.

We suggest you complete SSP 17-8 at this point.

Key Terms

A full glossary with definitions is provided at the end of the Study Guide.

Adjusted Cost Base (ACB)	Parent Company
Amalgamation	Proceeds of Disposition (POD)
Business Combination	Qualified Small Business Corporation Share
Canadian Corporation	Recapture of CCA
Capital Gains Deduction	Redemption of Shares
Convertible Property	Reorganization of Capital (ITA 86)
Corporation	Restrictive Covenant
Disposition	Rollover
Exchange of Shares in a Reorganization (ITA 86)	Share-for-Share Exchange (ITA 85.1)
Gift	Small Business Corporation
Goodwill	Subsidiary
Legal Capital	Taxable Canadian Corporation
Merger	Terminal Loss
Non-Share Consideration (NSC)	Vertical Amalgamation
Paid-Up Capital (PUC)	Winding-Up of a 90% Owned Subsidiary
	Winding-Up of a Canadian Corporation

References

For more detailed study of the material in this chapter, we refer you to the following:

ITA 22	Sale of Accounts Receivable
ITA 23	Sale of Inventory
ITA 51	Convertible Property
ITA 51.1	Conversion of Debt Obligation
ITA 54	Definitions (POD)
ITA 84(2)	Distribution on Winding-Up, etc.
ITA 84(3)	Redemption of Shares
ITA 84(5)	Amount Distributed or Paid
ITA 85	Transfer of Property to Corporation by Shareholders
ITA 85.1	Share-for-Share Exchange
ITA 86	Exchange of Shares by a Shareholder in Course of Reorganization of Capital
ITA 87	Amalgamations
ITA 88(1)	Winding-Up a 90% Owned Subsidiary
ITA 88(2)	Winding-Up a Canadian Corporation
ITA 110.6	Capital Gains Deduction
S4-F3-C1	Price Adjustment Clause
S4-F5-C1	Share-for-Share Exchange
S4-F7-C1	Amalgamations of Canadian Corporations
IT-115R2	Fractional Interest in Shares
IT-126R2	Meaning of "Winding-Up"
IT-140R3	Buy-Sell Agreements
IT-142R3	Settlement of Debts on the Winding-Up of a Corporation
IT-146R4	Shares Entitling Shareholders to Choose Taxable or Capital Dividends
IT-149R4	Winding-Up Dividend
IT-188R	Sale of Accounts Receivable
IT-243R4	Dividend Refund to Private Corporations
IT-287R2	Sale of Inventory
IT-302R3	Losses of a Corporation—The Effect That Acquisitions of Control, Amalgamations, and Windings-Up Have on Their Deductibility—After January 15, 1987
IT-444R	Corporations—Involuntary Dissolutions

Self-Study Problems (SSPs)

Self-Study Problems (SSPs) provide practice in problem solving. Within the chapters, we have indicated where it would be appropriate to stop and work on each SSP. The problems can be downloaded by chapter from MyLab Accounting. Solutions are available in the Study Guide. Select problems can also be completed directly in MyLab and auto-graded.

Assignment Problems

Solutions to Assignment Problems (APs) are available to instructors only.

AP 17-1   (ITA 85.1 Share-for-Share Exchange after ITA 85(1) Rollover)

In 2013, Sandy O'Brien began to carry on a business, Sandy's Frames, as a sole proprietor. The business specialized in providing frames for high-end paintings and drawings.

In 2016 business profits had increased to the point where Mr. O'Brien no longer needed all of the income for living expenses and as a result he decided to incorporate the business.

His accountant advised that he could avoid any immediate income tax on the incorporation of the business with a joint election under ITA 85(1). In preparation of the sale of the business properties to a new corporation scheduled to take place in early January 2017, the following amounts were determined for the business properties:

Tax costs	$1,820,000
FMV	$3,140,000

Frames Ltd. was incorporated on January 6, 2017, with Mr. O'Brien as the sole shareholder. All of the business properties were sold for the FMV of $3,140,000 a few days later. A joint election was filed under ITA 85(1) (T2057) and a combined elected amount of $1,820,000 was chosen as the elected amount to defer any income tax. The consideration paid by the company included a promissory note for $900,000, $920,000 of redeemable preferred shares, and 6,950 common shares with a FMV of $1,320,000. No other shares have been issued since that time.

Over the next few years, the business continued to expand and prosper and, on January 1, 2021, he receives an offer from Conglomerate Inc., a large public company, to purchase all of the common shares for $1,970,000. Conglomerate Inc. will pay for the common shares by issuing a separate class of its own shares valued at $1,970,000.

In addition, subsequent to the share exchange, Mr. O'Brien's preferred shares will be redeemed for $920,000. The GRIP and RDTOH balances of Frames Ltd. are both nil at all times. Mr. O'Brien is arm's length with Conglomerate Inc. at all times.

While Mr. O'Brien has been very successful with his business, he has personally made a number of poor real estate investment decisions. As a consequence, he has a 2019 net capital loss balance of $420,000.

The shares of Frames Ltd. do not qualify for the capital gains deduction.

Required:

A. Determine the income tax consequences of (1) the redemption of the preferred shares and (2) the exchange of shares with Conglomerate Inc.. Your answer should contemplate both the application of ITA 85.1 and a decision to opt out.

B. Determine the cost and therefore the ACB of the Frames Ltd. common shares to Conglomerate Inc.

C. Advise Mr. O'Brien as to planning alternatives to use his 2019 net capital loss balance in conjunction with the share exchange.

AP 17-2   (ITA 85(1) and ITA 86(1) Share Exchange)

Homer Parsons began carrying on a retail business as a sole proprietor in 2014. This business, registered as Parsons' Paranormal Services, provides services related to helping individuals track down their ancestry.

Homer quickly gained a reputation for success and, by 2017, he has expanded and opened several locations throughout the city. As a result, the business is producing income far in excess of his current needs. His accountant advises him that the timing is right to incorporate the business. Homer's concerns about having to pay additional income tax on selling his business to a newly created corporation are resolved when he learns that a special election under ITA 85(1) can be filed, the effect of which will be to avoid any income tax on the sale.

On January 6, 2017, the tax costs of the business properties total $1,986,000 and FMV $2,950,000. The new corporation, Parsons Paranormal Inc. (PPI), is incorporated by Homer on January 4, 2017. On January 7, 2017, all of the business properties are sold to PPI for $2,950,000 with an elected amount for income tax purposes of $1,986,000 to defer any income on the sale. The corporation pays for the purchase of the business by issuing a promissory note for $1,500,000 and common shares with a FMV of $1,450,000. PPI will select a calendar-based taxation year (January 1 to December 31).

The business continues to be successful such that by January 1, 2021, the FMV of the company has grown to $8,450,000 and the underlying tax costs of business properties total $7,347,000.

Homer has an adult child, Orpheus, who has been active in the business from the beginning. He has demonstrated superior research skills, which have resulted in ancestral research that far surpasses the competition. As Homer now has sufficient resources to retire comfortably, he would like to transfer the future economic growth of the company to Orpheus.

To achieve this goal Homer will pursue an estate freeze in which he will exchange his common shares in PPI for $5,000,000 in cash plus $3,450,000 of redeemable preferred shares. Subsequent to the exchange, PPI will issue 200 common shares to Orpheus for $20,000.

The GRIP and RDTOH balances are nil in all relevant years.

Required:

A. Determine the income tax consequences to Homer as a result of the estate freeze. Your answer should also include the ACB and PUC of the preferred freeze shares.

B. Determine the income tax consequences to Homer if all of his preferred freeze shares are subsequently redeemed for $3,450,000.

AP 17-3 *(ITA 86 Capital Reorganization with Gift)*

Lartex Inc. was incorporated in 2012 to carry on the business of producing cutting-edge sports clothing. On incorporation the company issued 20,000 common shares for $50 per share with 15,000 issued to Ms. Lara Text and the remaining 5,000 issued to Mr. Bentley Rolls. The two individuals are not related.

In 2016, Mr. Rolls dies suddenly. Lara acquires the 5,000 shares that were purchased by Mr. Rolls from his estate for $90 each. In order to finance the company's expanding business, the company issues an additional 5,000 shares to Ms. Text for $90 each. At this point all of the 25,000 issued common shares are owned by Ms. Text.

Ms. Text has a son, Lance Text, whose dream is to make Lartex a household name. Starting in 2017, he seeks out the most challenging and rigorous courses in the business program at a local university. During the following two years he excels in all of the courses, especially the income tax courses, which he considers the most interesting and rewarding. To encourage him in his studies Lara gifts Lance 2,500 shares of Lartex Inc. The FMV of the shares at the time of the gift is $100 each.

On January 1, 2021, the FMV of the Lartex Inc. shares has increased to $120 each. Lance has become increasingly active in the company business and Lara feels it is time to benefit him with the future economic growth in the company. Lara speaks with her accountant who advises undertaking an estate freeze structured to benefit from the rollover under ITA 86.

In order to implement the estate freeze the corporation applies to amend its capital to allow it to issue a new class of redeemable preferred shares. The corporate law authority approves the amended articles of incorporation to add a new class of shares. Lara then exchanges her 22,500 common shares of Lartex Inc. for a $500,000 promissory note and $2,000,000 of redeemable preferred shares. The only remaining common shares subsequent to the freeze will be the 2,500 shares owned by Lance. The company GRIP balance is nil throughout all relevant years.

Required:

A. Determine the immediate income tax consequences of the estate freeze transaction to Lara Text, including the following:

- The amount of any gift that Lara has made to Lance
- The PUC of the preferred freeze shares
- The ACB of the preferred freeze shares
- The amount of any deemed dividends arising on the exchange
- Any capital gain or capital loss resulting from the exchange of the common shares

B. Describe the income tax impact of the freeze transaction to Lance.

C. Determine the tax income consequences to Lara if her preferred freeze shares are redeemed for $2,000,000. Ignore the capital gains deduction.

AP 17-4   *(ITA 86(1) and 86(2))*

Squire Ltd. is a successful CCPC that was incorporated in Manitoba in 1986 by its sole shareholder and incorporator, Mr. Larry Squire. Squire Ltd. uses a December 31 taxation year end. The company was initially authorized to issue an unlimited number of two classes of common shares (Class A and B). Mr. Squire acquired 1,000 of the Class A common shares for $10.00 each, or $10,000, for that class of common shares. Mr. Squire initially financed the company with a combination of bank financing (which he had to give a personal guarantee) and an interest-free shareholder loan.

In 2017 on the advice of his accountant, Mr. Squire undertook a crystallization transaction to use $290,000 of his capital gains deduction to recognize the increasing value of the company. The result of this acceptable tax planning was that Mr. Squire gave up all of his Class A common shares for Class B common shares. The 1,000 Class B common shares now owned by Mr. Squire have a PUC of $10.00 per share ($10,000 for the class of shares) and an ACB of $300 per share. By mid-2021 the value of the company has increased to the point that the FMV of the Class B common shares is $930 per share for a total FMV of $930,000.

Mr. Squire wishes to retire and pass on the incorporated business to his only daughter, Amanda, who has worked alongside him since 2002 and is well versed in all aspects of the company business. He has spoken to his accountant about a business succession plan that will pass control of the company to Amanda with the least tax cost possible while allowing him to gradually remove the $930,000 value of his shares over the next five years. He has advised his accountant that he wishes to maximize any non-share consideration such as promissory notes. Mr. Squire advises that the company currently needs all of its existing cash for working capital purposes but will generate excess cash later in 2021 and subsequent years that will be sufficient to pay him out.

The shares of Squire Ltd. do not meet all of the conditions to qualify as QSBC shares, and therefore the capital gains deduction is not a consideration in the succession planning. In addition, the company balance at year end in its GRIP account is expected to be nil and remain so into the foreseeable future.

As the accountant for Mr. Squire and the company you recommend a business succession plan that will result in an estate freeze share exchange under ITA 86 that would (1) require amending the articles of incorporate to add a new class of fixed value preferred shares that will be exchanged for all of Mr. Squire's Class B common shares, (2) maximize the NSC (e.g., a promissory note) received by Mr. Squire on the share exchange without income tax implications, (3) allow Amanda to acquire Class A common shares at a minimal cost, and (4) allow Mr. Squire to receive his investment value of $930,000 over the next five years through a combination of preferred share redemptions and payments on any promissory note. Assume that Amanda acquired 100 Class A common shares for $10 each, or $1,000 in total, once the estate freeze was completed.

Required:

A. If it were not for rollovers such as ITA 86, what would the income tax consequences have been had Squire Ltd. redeemed all of Mr. Squire's Class B shares?

B. Determine both the maximum amount of NSC and the FMV of the preferred shares that Mr. Squire can take back on the share exchange without triggering any income tax consequences.

C. Determine the ACB and PUC of the preferred shares received by Mr. Squire on the share exchange.

D. Determine both the proceeds of redemption and proceeds of disposition as a result of Mr. Squire giving up his Class B common shares on the share exchange.

E. Determine whether the ITA 86 share exchange avoided any income tax consequences such as capital gains, capital losses, and deemed dividends using the numbers from Part D above.

F. Calculate the income tax consequences to Mr. Squire if he were to redeem all of the preferred shares received on the exchange in 2022 for their FMV.

G. Assume that in 2022 the CRA decides to review the ITA 86 exchange and determines that the FMV of the Class B common shares owned by Mr. Squire was $1,500,000. Determine the same income tax implications as determined in Parts B to F above to both Mr. Squire and his daughter.

AP 17-5   (ITA 87 vs. ITA 88(1))

Hubble Inc. owns 100% of the shares of Palomar Ltd. Hubble has decided to combine with its subsidiary. It has asked for your advice on whether the combination should proceed by way of an amalgamation to which ITA 87 will apply or a dissolution of the subsidiary to which ITA 88(1) would apply.

Information in respect of property of Palomar Ltd. immediately prior to the combination is as follows:

Property	Original Cost	Tax Cost	FMV
Equipment (tax cost = UCC)	$ 11,000	$ 3,300	$ 700
Land (tax cost = ACB)	154,000	154,000	192,000
Goodwill (tax cost = ACB)	Nil	Nil	22,000

There are no liabilities and no net capital or non-capital losses.

Hubble acquired control of Palomar several years ago, paying $231,000 for all of the shares. At that time, the FMV of the equipment was $11,000, the FMV of the land was $209,000, and the FMV of the goodwill was $1,000.

Palomar has paid $5,000 in dividends to Hubble Inc. since acquiring all of its shares.

Required: Outline what the income tax consequences would be if:

A. Palomar was amalgamated into Hubble Inc. using ITA 87.

B. Palomar was rolled into Hubble Inc. using a ITA 88(1) winding-up.

AP 17-6   (ITA 88(1) Winding-Up—The Bump)

In 2017, Acme Ltd. purchased all of the outstanding shares of Cross Industries Ltd. for $1,400,000. The total tax cost of the property of Cross Industries Ltd. at the time of the acquisition was $1,250,000 and included a piece of land that was being held as a location for a possible second manufacturing facility. This land had been acquired in 2013 for $640,000 and, at the time Acme acquired the Cross shares, the FMV was $705,000.

Acme believes that the operations of Cross Industries have become so integrated with its own that it makes sense to combine the two corporations. As a consequence, they are considering the possibility of dissolving Cross Industries Ltd. ITA 88(1) would apply to the dissolution.

On January 17, 2021, the total tax costs of the property of Cross Industries is $1,270,000.

The company continues to own the land for the same purpose, and the FMV has since increased to $790,000.

Acme Ltd. has received $20,000 in dividends from Cross Industries since it acquired its control in 2017.

Required: Determine the maximum bump available to Acme Ltd. and how much of the bump can be applied to the land of Cross Industries received by Acme on the winding-up.

AP 17-7   (Winding-Up a Corporation)

Hoxey Ltd. is a CCPC with a December 31 taxation year end that was incorporated in Saskatchewan in 1998 by its incorporator/founder and sole shareholder, Spencer Richmond. Spencer was somewhat of a child protégé, quickly becoming conversant in computer technology at an early age, including writing advanced computer code. He quickly developed, created, and produced some of the first online video games that still remain popular. In an attempt to come up with new gaming ideas to deal with ever-increasing competition, Spencer suffered a heart attack in September 2021 and has decided to dissolve the business, wind-up the company, and enjoy life rather than working all the time. Spencer is not interested in selling his shares to anyone or selling the rights to the business to any one purchaser.

Spencer has spoken to his long-time accountant about an exit strategy. Since he has never married or lived common law there is no one to continue the business. He explains that he simply wants to sell it all and move on with his life. The accountant explains that the plan will be to have the company sell all of its assets, pay any outstanding liabilities (including any income tax), and distribute the remaining cash to Spencer.

Spencer's accountant has prepared the following information to assist Spencer in determining how much he will have remaining once the company makes its final distribution to him. The assets will all be sold in the first half of December 2021 at the FMVs indicated on the statement of net assets shown below. The company is formally dissolved and wound up on December 31, 2021. Assume that net active business income from ongoing operations throughout 2021 is $410,000 and that taxable capital gains are $62,700 without considering the effect of the sale of the company assets. The company did not receive any dividends on any of its investments and therefore was not liable to any Part IV taxes.

Hoxey Ltd.
Statement of Net Assets
At December 15, 2021

	Tax Cost	FMV
Accounts receivable	$ 121,000	$ 89,000
Public Co. investments	774,000	1,125,000
Private Co. investment	946,000	381,000
Inventory	697,000	510,000
Office building (class 1)	2,458,000	6,000,000
Office building land	725,000	1,000,000
Office furniture (class 8)	300,720	380,000
Computers (class 50)	54,675	28,000
Total assets	$6,076,395	$9,513,000
Liabilities	(217,400)	(217,400)
Net assets	$5,858,995	$9,295,600

Based on tax costs, the components of the net asset tax cost balance sheet are as follows:

PUC	$ 1,000
Capital dividend account (CDA)	10,000
Income retained (surplus)	5,847,995
Total net asset balance	$5,858,995

Other Information:

1. The tax costs shown for each of class 1, 8, and 50 are the undepreciated capital cost (UCC) as of January 1, 2021.

2. The capital cost of the building is $3,800,000, the office furniture $537,000, and the computers $600,000.

3. Since all of the depreciable properties are sold prior to the final company taxation year end as a result of the dissolution on December 31, 2021, no CCA can be claimed for 2021.

4. The investment in a private company is for an arm's-length CCPC that qualifies as a small business corporation.

5. The ACB of the common shares is $501,000 as a result of a capital gains crystallization transaction a few years earlier.

6. On January 1, 2021, the company has a balance in its GRIP account of $74,500.

7. The provincial corporate tax rate on income that qualifies for the small business deduction is 2% and is 12% on all other income, including investment income and capital gains.

8. The January 1, 2021, balance in the company's eligible RDTOH is $76,700, while the balance in the non-eligible RDTOH is $194,500

9. Assume that the CDA balance of $10,000 has already been adjusted for the $62,700 of taxable capital gains realized in the year prior to the sale of all of the company's assets.

10. The company has no non-capital losses but has a 2019 net capital loss balance of $71,000 at the beginning of 2021.

11. No dividends were paid during the previous two years.

12. Assume that there are no reductions to the small business limit for adjusted aggregate investment income or taxable capital employed in Canada.

13. No ITA 22 election was filed for the transfer of the accounts receivables.

Required:

A. Calculate the amount that will be available for distribution to Spencer after the sale of all of the company's assets. This will require calculating the company's net and taxable income, federal and provincial income taxes payable, RDTOH account balances including any eligible and non-eligible dividend refund(s), the CDA, and the GRIP balance. Show all supporting calculations.

B. Determine the eligible and non-eligible dividend and capital gain components of the distribution to Spencer that will accrue as a result of the winding-up of Hoxey Ltd. Ignore the possibility that Spencer might be subject to the alternative minimum tax. Assume that all appropriate elections, designations, and filings will be made on a timely basis to minimize his personal income taxes.

C. Determine Spencer's net personal income tax on the taxable dividends received after considering federal and provincial dividend tax credits. Assume that (1) Spencer is subject to the highest federal rate of 33% and the highest Saskatchewan rate of 14.5% and (2) that the provincial dividend tax credit on eligible dividends equals 40% of the gross up and is equal to 26% of the gross up on non-eligible dividends.

Assignment Problems

AP 17-8   *(Sale of Assets vs. Shares)*

Naimo Ltd. is a CCPC that was incorporated in British Columbia in 2007 by its incorporator and sole shareholder, Mr. Roger Naimo. The company's taxation year end is December 31. Naimo Ltd. operates a successful restaurant on Vancouver Island that includes catering. Roger had first opened the restaurant as a sole proprietor in 1998. His accountant convinced him in late 2006 that it was time to incorporate, which led to the creation of the company in early 2007. The business and all of its assets and liabilities were transferred to the company using the rollover rule of ITA 85(1). Roger acquired 100 common shares for $15,000 at the time of incorporation. No other shares have been issued since.

In recent years there has been an acceleration in new residential and commercial construction followed by a proliferation of new restaurants and plenty of competition. Roger has been approached by two different investors—one proposes to acquire all of the shares of the corporation for $800,000 and the second to acquire all of the assets, including assuming any outstanding liabilities, for a net payment of $953,800. If the assets are sold, Roger plans on winding up the company after paying off any outstanding corporate taxes and distributing any remaining cash to him.

Roger has decided to sell and move somewhere else where it is a little quieter. He has asked his accountant for advice on which offer he should accept. The accountant has prepared the following statement dated December 1, 2021, which contains a list of assets and liabilities, their tax costs, and FMV as of that date determined by a local business valuator. The FMVs will serve as the basis for the asset sale and assumption of corporate liabilities. If there is a sale of shares the transaction will close on December 31, 2021. If Roger decides on a sale of assets all sales and assumption of liabilities will be concluded by December 18, 2021, with the company being formally dissolved December 31, 2021.

Naimo Ltd. has never owned investments and therefore has no investment income. All of its income is from an active business, which has never exceeded its small business limit. There are no associated companies and, in 2020, its adjusted aggregate investment income was nil and its taxable capital employed in Canada was less than $1 million. Assume that its net active business income for 2021 prior to the sale of shares or assets is $284,000.

Naimo Ltd.
Statement of Net Assets
At December 1, 2021

	Tax Costs	FMV
Accounts receivable	$ 22,700	$ 19,000
Inventory	46,500	57,700
Restaurant building	284,000	755,000
Restaurant building land	134,000	217,000
Kitchen equipment	34,100	62,900
Kitchen utensils	Nil	5,200
Delivery van	1,800	17,000
Goodwill	Nil	220,000
Total assets	$ 523,100	$1,353,800
Accounts payable	(94,100)	(94,100)
Mortgage payable	(306,000)	(306,000)
Net assets	$ 123,000	$ 953,700

Based on tax costs, the components of the net asset tax cost balance are as follows:

PUC	$ 15,000
Capital dividend account (CDA)	Nil
Income retained (surplus)	108,000
Total net asset balance	$123,000

Other Information:

A. The tax costs shown for each of the restaurant building, the kitchen equipment, kitchen utensils, and the delivery van are the undepreciated capital cost (UCC) as of January 1, 2021.

B. The capital cost of the building is $466,000, the kitchen equipment $115,000, the kitchen utensils $16,300, and the delivery van $44,000.

C. If the assets are sold no CCA can be claimed in 2021 since the company will have no depreciable assets on hand on the last day of its final taxation year as a result of the dissolution on December 31, 2021.

D. The shares of the company qualify for the capital gains deduction. Roger's available capital gains deduction immediately prior to a sale of shares or assets is $116,472, and his cumulative net investment loss account is nil.

E. The ACB and PUC of the common shares are both $15,000.

F. On January 1, 2021, the company has a nil balance in its GRIP account.

G. The provincial corporate tax rate on income that qualifies for the small business deduction is 2% and is 12% on all other income, including investment income and capital gains.

H. The company has nil balances at January 1, 2021, in both its eligible and non-eligible RDTOH.

I. The company's CDA balance at the time of a sale of shares or assets is nil.

J. The company has a 2019 non-capital loss balance of $49,600 and no net capital losses.

K. No dividends were paid during the previous two years.

L. The 2021 provincial dividend tax credit rate on non-eligible dividends is 15% of the gross up and 36.3% of the gross up for eligible dividends.

M. Assume that any income received by Roger as dividends and capital gains will be subject to the highest federal personal tax rate of 33% and that the BC rate is 20.5%.

N. Assume that on a sale of assets no ITA 22 election will be filed for the accounts receivables since the amounts are not considered significant enough.

Required:

1. Determine which of the two offers Roger should accept in terms of maximizing his after-tax cash retention. For the sale of assets you will have to calculate the company's net and taxable income, federal and provincial income taxes payable, RDTOH account balances including any eligible and non-eligible dividend refund(s), the CDA, and the GRIP balance. You will also have to determine the eligible and non-eligible dividend and capital gain components of the distribution to Roger as a result of the winding-up of Naimo Ltd. Ignore any alternative minimum tax implications and assume that all appropriate elections, designations, and filings will be made on a timely basis to minimize personal income taxes. On the sale of shares, consider that Roger will maximize the use of his capital gains deduction.

2. What non-tax advantages and disadvantages should you, as Roger's accountant, communicate to him that may influence his ultimate decision.

AP 17-9   (Sale of Assets vs. Shares)
Mr. Nathan Naper is the president and only shareholder of Nepean Ltd., a CCPC. The company's taxation year end is December 31. Mr. Naper incorporated the company 15 years ago. The ACB and the PUC of the shares are both $265,000. No other shares have ever been issued.

Mr. Naper is considering selling the corporation and, in order to better evaluate this possibility, he has prepared a special statement of assets. In this special statement, comparative disclosure is provided for the accounting values, the tax costs for income tax purposes, and the FMVs. This statement is as follows:

Nepean Ltd.
Statement of Assets
As at January 1, 2021

	Accounting Carrying Value	Tax Cost	FMV
Cash	$ 54,500	$ 54,500	$ 54,500
Accounts receivable	406,000	406,000	372,250
Inventories	869,750	869,750	976,000
Land	201,500	201,500	405,000
Building (Note One)	538,000	469,250	2,061,000
Equipment (Note Two)	434,000	294,000	171,250
Goodwill	Nil	Nil	811,000
Totals	$2,503,750	$2,295,000	$4,851,000

Note One   The building was constructed on the land for a total cost of $1,281,000.

Note Two   The equipment had a cost of $807,500.

At the same time that this statement of assets was prepared, a similar statement of equities was drawn up. This latter statement contained the following accounting carrying values and income tax costs:

	Accounting Carrying Value	Tax Cost
Current liabilities	$ 697,000	$ 697,000
Loan from shareholder	137,500	137,500
Future income tax liability	542,000	N/A
Common shares	265,000	265,000
Capital dividend account (CDA)	N/A	164,500
Other income retained	N/A	1,031,000
Retained earnings	862,250	N/A
Totals	$2,503,750	$2,295,000

In addition to the information included in the preceding statements, the following other information about the company is available:

- The company has a 2019 non-capital loss balance of $83,000.
- The company has a 2019 net capital loss balance of $129,650.
- Nepean Ltd. is subject to a provincial tax rate of 3% on income that qualifies for the federal small business deduction and 14% on other income.
- On December 31, 2020, the company has no balance in either its RDTOH account or its GRIP account.
- The shares of Nepean Ltd. do not qualify for the capital gains deduction.

Mr. Naper has received two offers for his company, and he plans to accept one of them on January 2, 2021. The first offer involves a cash payment of $3,508,000 in return for all of the shares. Alternatively, another investor has expressed a willingness to acquire all of the assets, including goodwill, at a price equal to their combined FMV. This investor would assume all of the liabilities of the corporation and has agreed to file an ITA 22 election with respect to the accounts receivable. If the assets are sold, it is Mr. Naper's intention to dissolve the corporation subsequent to the final distributions.

Mr. Naper will have over $300,000 in other sources of income and, as a consequence, any additional income will be subject to a federal income tax rate of 33% and a provincial income tax rate of 18%. He lives in a province where the provincial dividend tax credit on eligible dividends is 5/11 of the gross up and on non-eligible dividends is equal to 4/13 of the gross up.

Required: Determine which of the two offers Mr. Naper should accept. Ignore the possibility that Mr. Naper might be subject to the alternative minimum tax (AMT). Assume that appropriate elections or designations will be made on a timely basis to minimize any personal income taxes.

CHAPTER 18

Partnerships

Learning Objectives

After completing Chapter 18, you should be able to:

1. Explain the basic approach to the taxation of partnerships (Paragraph [P hereafter] 18-1 to 18-6).
2. Describe, for income tax purposes, the meaning of a partnership and the common-law features necessary to establish the existence of a partnership (P 18-7 to 18-12).
3. Identify the three types of partnerships used in Canada and their differences (P 18-13 to 18-20).
4. Describe the difference between partnerships and co-ownership, joint ventures, and syndicates (P 18-21 to 18-31).
5. Explain the basic rules set out in ITA 96(1) that are used in the determination of partnership income and the impact on members of partnerships (P 18-32 to 18-47).
6. Reconcile accounting business income to business income for income tax purposes (P 18-48 to 18-49).
7. Explain the allocation of other types of income from a partnership to partners, specifically capital gains, dividends, foreign source income, and charitable donations (P 18-50 to 18-56).
8. Explain the concept of a partnership interest and its relevance (P 18-57 to 18-60).
9. Determine the income tax consequences when a partner is admitted to a partnership (P 18-61 to 18-69).
10. Calculate the ACB of a partnership interest on the first and last day of a fiscal period (P 18-70 to 18-77).
11. Explain what is meant by a negative ACB, when it applies, and its consequences (P 18-78 to 18-80).
12. Determine the income tax consequences when a partner disposes of his or her partnership interest (P 18-81 to 18-82).
13. Explain the meaning of a limited partner for income tax purposes (P 18-83 to 18-85).
14. Explain the at-risk concept and determine the at-risk amount and limited partnership losses (P 18-86 to 18-94).
15. Explain the meaning of a Canadian partnership and its relevance (P 18-95 to 18-97).

16. Explain and apply the basic default rules of the ITA when property is sold between partners and a partnership (P 18-98 to 18-100).
17. Explain the purpose and basic application of the rollover under ITA 97(2) (P 18-101 to 18-103).
18. Explain the purpose and basic application of the rollover under ITA 98(5) & 98(6) (P 18-104 to 18-108).
19. Explain how the ITA accommodates the incorporation of a partnership on a rollover basis (P 18-109 to 18-116).

Introduction

Taxable Entities in Canada

18-1.   The ITA is applicable to individuals (human beings), corporations, and trusts in the sense that they each file annual income tax returns (T1, T2, or T3). In the case of individuals and corporations, these taxpayers have a separate legal existence. Partnerships do not have a legal existence separate from the partners unless a partner happens to be another partnership. *The ITA, however, does not recognize partnerships as a separate taxable entity.*

18-2.   The ITA recognizes that a partnership is relevant in determining the income tax consequences to its members (i.e., partners) since partnership income or loss is allocated between its members and therefore has an impact on the income tax liability of those members. As a result, the ITA deems a partnership to be a person resident in Canada but not a taxpayer. The distinction is important in that only taxpayers are required to file income tax returns. The ITA goes one step further and clarifies that partnerships are only considered persons for the purpose of calculating the income or loss of its members. The reason for this is to ensure that the rules of the ITA that apply to determining income or loss apply equally to partnerships as they would to other taxpayers such as human beings, corporations, and trusts.

18-3.   In general terms, a partnership is treated as a flow-through entity. Rather than require each partner to separately calculate income or loss from each source of the partnership's income, the rules of the ITA require that the partnership itself determine income or loss in the same manner as taxable entities. Once the income or loss is determined it can be allocated to partners that are individuals, trusts, or corporations based on the amounts agreed to in a partnership agreement or in equal proportions in the absence of a partnership agreement. This process is illustrated in Figure 18-1.

18-4.   While partnerships are not taxable entities under the ITA, they are considered reportable entities for GST/HST purposes (see Chapter 21). This means that a partnership must file a GST/HST return, pay any GST/HST owing, or may be entitled to receive a GST/HST refund.

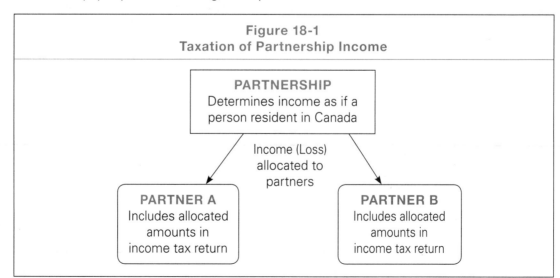

Figure 18-1
Taxation of Partnership Income

PARTNERSHIP
Determines income as if a person resident in Canada

Income (Loss) allocated to partners

PARTNER A
Includes allocated amounts in income tax return

PARTNER B
Includes allocated amounts in income tax return

Chapter Coverage

18-5.   In this chapter we will examine the income taxation of partnerships. We will begin by defining partnerships. This will be followed by a discussion of the different types of partnerships in Canada, as well as other similar income/loss sharing relationships such as co-ownerships, joint ventures, and syndicates. Our focus will then shift to the rules for determining partnership income or loss and the process of allocating that income/loss and other amounts among the partners.

18-6.   Other topics that will be discussed include:

- the adjust cost base (ACB) of a partnership interest;
- admitting new partners and retiring existing partners;
- limited partnerships, limited partnership losses, and the at-risk rules;
- property transfers between partners and the partnership; and
- the reorganization of a partnership as a new partnership, as a corporation, and as a sole proprietorship.

Partnership Defined

The Importance of Defining a Partnership

18-7.   The general rules for determining the income tax consequences for partnerships and their members are found in Subdivision j of Division B of Part I of the ITA, ITA 96 through 103. However, since these rules apply specifically to partnerships, we must first determine if the relationship is in fact a partnership. This requires understanding the legal definition of a partnership.

18-8.   The importance of this definition is that it allows us to differentiate a partnership from other similar types of organizations such as syndicates, joint ventures, and co-ownership arrangements. This is necessary since the income and loss calculations for partnerships differ significantly from those other relationships.

Basic Partnership Elements

18-9.   There is no definition of a "partnership" in the ITA. There are, however, a few definitions of certain partnership expressions found in the ITA. For example, ITA 102(1) defines a "Canadian Partnership" and ITA 197(1) defines a "SIFT Partnership." However, these specialized definitions presume that a partnership already exists. When the ITA does not define a specific word or expression the general rules of interpretation require that the word generally be given its legal meaning if such a meaning exists, otherwise the meaning in everyday usage or some other meaning may apply. In the case of partnerships, each common-law province (all provinces except Quebec) have provincial partnership legislation that provides a consistent definition based on jurisprudence that is more than a hundred years old. The province of Quebec defines a partnership in a similar manner but the meaning applies a civil law concept rather than a common-law concept (see paragraph 1.18 of IT Folio S4-F16-C1, "What Is a Partnership?").

18-10.   General guidance on defining a partnership is provided in IT Folio S4-F16-C1, "What Is a Partnership?" This folio notes that "whether a partnership exists is a matter of fact and law." It then proceeds to discuss provincial law dealing with this issue, as well as several Canadian Supreme Court of Canada decisions. There are three basic elements in defining a partnership:

1   There must be a relationship that exists between two or more persons.
2.   These persons must be carrying on a business in common.
3.   There must be a profit motive to the carrying on of a business.

18-11.   The difficulty with defining a relationship as a partnership is that it requires an intent on the part of the participants to work together for the common purpose of carrying on a business with a profit motive. That intent can never be proven with any certainty as it would require the ability to read the minds of those participants. As a result, it is common to look to facts one would expect to see if the relationship is a true partnership. In the Supreme Court of Canada decision in *Backman* (2001 SCC 10), the court listed several relevant factors that, while not determinative, would be viewed as providing evidence of the existence of a partnership:

- The contribution by the parties of money, property, effort, knowledge, skill to a common undertaking
- A joint property interest in the subject matter of the adventure
- The sharing of profits and losses
- A mutual right of control or management
- Financial statements prepared as a partnership
- Bank accounts in the name of the partnership
- Correspondence with third parties as a partnership

18-12.   The presence of a valid partnership agreement would also serve to support the view that a partnership exists. Such agreements will usually include provisions that deal with many issues, including the following:

- The initial and ongoing partner contributions and ownership percentage of each partner
- The responsibilities of each partner and the division of work between the partners
- How income and drawings will be allocated and how much compensation is to be paid
- Signing authority on the partnership bank accounts and required approval for purchases
- Procedures for bringing in new partners
- Procedures to deal with the withdrawal or death of a partner or the sale of the business

Types of Partnerships

General Partnerships

18-13.   A general partnership is one in which all of the partners are general partners. As defined in the "*Guide for the T5013 Partnership Information Return*" (T4068):

> A **general partner** is a partner whose personal liability for the debts and obligations of the partnership are not limited.

18-14.   Provincial partnership law provides additional guidance on the rights, duties, and obligations of general partners. These include the following:

- Each partner is considered to act on behalf of the partnership, which means that the actions of each partner are generally binding on the other partners.
- Partners are jointly and severally liable for partnership debt and wrongful acts of other partners. This means that a partner can be liable, together with all other partners, for unpaid partnership debt and wrongful acts of other partners.
- Property contributed to the partnership or acquired with partnership funds is considered partnership property and is to be held exclusively for partnership use.
- Partners are entitled to share equally in profits and losses, unless there is an agreement to the contrary.
- Partners are not entitled to remuneration (salary or wages) or to interest on capital contributions. As is explained later in this chapter, any remuneration or interest on capital is treated as an income allocation and is not deductible to the partnership.

18-15.   When the term "partnership" is used without a qualifying adjective, the reference is normally to a general partnership.

Limited Partnerships

18-16.   A limited partnership is a partnership with at least one general partner (i.e., a partner whose liability is unrestricted) and one or more limited partners. General partnership interests are often held through corporations to limit the liability of its shareholders. To be considered a limited partnership, the partnership has to be registered with the appropriate provincial authority. For example, section 3 of the *Ontario Limited Partnership Act*, section 52 of the *Alberta Partnership Act*, and section 51 of the *B.C. Partnership Act* all require a formalized declaration process to establish a limited partnership. In the absence of such registration, the partnership will not benefit from limited partnership protection and it will be considered a general partnership.

18-17.   A limited partner has the same rights, duties, and obligations as a general partner with one important difference: A limited partner is only liable for partnership debt and wrongful or negligent actions of other partners to the extent of the limited partner's actual and promised contributions to the partnership.

> **EXAMPLE**   A limited partner contributes $1,000 and agrees to contribute a further $2,000 within a certain period of time. That partner will be potentially liable for up to $3,000 of claims against the partnership.

18-18.   A limited partner will also forfeit limited liability protection, and therefore become liable in the same manner as a general partner, if the limited partner participates in the management of the partnership.

Limited Liability Partnerships (LLP)

18-19.   This form of partnership is only available to certain types of professionals as specified in provincial legislation. For example, in Ontario, only lawyers and chartered professional accountants are currently permitted to form such partnerships. In contrast, Alberta extends the LLP legislation to include several other types of professionals.

18-20.   Unlike members of limited partnerships, members of limited liability partnerships are personally liable for most types of partnership debt. There is, however, an important exception: Members of limited liability partnerships are not personally liable for obligations arising from the wrongful or negligent actions of:

- their professional partners; or
- the employees, agents, or representatives of the partnership who are conducting partnership business.

We suggest you complete SSP 18-1 at this point.

Co-Ownership, Joint Ventures, and Syndicates

Introduction

18-21.   Co-ownership, joint ventures, and syndicates are specific types of arrangements that contain features common to partnerships. For example, each of these organizational structures requires two or more persons. This common feature is but one of several that may make it difficult to determine whether a specific arrangement is, in fact, a partnership or, alternatively, a different type of arrangement. The clarification of the nature of a particular relationship is key to the ability to apply the income tax law.

Co-Ownership

18-22.   Two or more persons co-own property when they share a right of ownership in the property. For income tax purposes, the most important consideration is that profits and losses are shared in partnerships but are typically accounted for individually by joint or co-owners.

18-23.   Two common forms of co-ownership are joint tenancy and tenancy in common. A joint tenancy is a form of property ownership where two or more joint tenants have ownership and possession of the same property. Individual interests are identical and the property cannot be sold or mortgaged without the consent of the other joint tenant(s). Spouses commonly own their principal residence and other properties in joint tenancy.

18-24.   In a tenancy in common arrangement, tenants can sell or mortgage their interests without the consent of other tenants in common. An example of a situation where a tenancy in common might be used would be the ownership of a vacation property by siblings. Each co-owner would be considered to own an interest in property equal to their proportionate ownership interest.

Joint Ventures

Defined

18-25.   Joint ventures are not defined taxable entities under the ITA. Further, such arrangements are not governed by provincial legislation, although they are recognized legal relationships by the courts. However, both the ITA and the ETA mention joint ventures, implicitly recognizing their existence.

18-26.   The similarity of partnerships and joint ventures led the CRA to make the following statement in 1988:

> Unlike partnerships, the concept of joint venture is not recognized by statute (i.e., provincial legislation). Although the Canadian courts have, in certain cases, recognized joint venture as being a business relationship that is distinct from partnership, in our experience, many so-called joint ventures are in fact partnerships … The CRA would rely on provincial partnership law in making such a determination.

18-27.   This means that, even if participants in a joint venture call the arrangement a joint venture or if agreements are written up that refer to the relationship as a joint venture, if it contains the three basic partnership elements it will be considered a partnership for income tax purposes and treated accordingly.

18-28.   Factors that have been used to distinguish joint ventures from partnerships include the following:

- Co-venturers contractually do not have the power to bind other co-venturers.
- Co-venturers retain ownership of property contributed to the undertaking.
- Co-venturers are not jointly and severally liable for debt of the undertaking.
- Co-venturers share gross revenues, not profits.
- While partnerships may be formed for the same purpose as a joint venture, they are usually of longer duration and involve more than a single undertaking.

Income Tax Treatment of Joint Ventures

18-29.   If an arrangement is considered to be a joint venture rather than a partnership, there will be no separate calculation and allocation of income at the organization level. The participants will individually include the gross income earned and deduct any expenses they have incurred based on their own taxation year. CCA can be claimed on any depreciable property used in the undertaking by a particular joint venturer. No separate fiscal period is provided for a joint venture as it is with a partnership.

Syndicates

18-30.   A syndicate is generally defined as a group of persons who have agreed to pool their resources for some common purpose. Because a syndicate is not a legal entity but a legal relationship, a reference to an interest in a syndicate usually means the property of each syndicate member used in the undertaking. The courts have traditionally reserved the name "syndicate" for specialized projects that are financial in nature. An example of a syndicate would be an association of insurance companies who combine forces to underwrite substantial high-risk insurance policies.

18-31.   There are no specific income tax rules that apply to syndicates. This means that, if there are any activities of the syndicate that result in income, each syndicate member would include in income any amounts to which they are entitled under any agreement.

We suggest you complete SSP 18-2 at this point.

Partnership Income, Losses, and Tax Credits

Introduction

18-32.   The goal of partnership taxation is to apply the income tax consequences of partnership income, losses, and tax credits to the persons who are its partners. To implement this, a two-stage process is involved:

Stage 1   Determine, at the partnership level, the various components of partnership income. This requires separate calculations for business income, property income, taxable capital gains, and allowable capital losses. For most partnerships, the most important component will be business income. Technically a partnership cannot exist solely for investment purposes or capital gains purposes as the legal definition of a partnership requires that a business be carried on.

Stage 2   Allocate the amounts that were determined in Stage 1 to the members of the partnership on the basis of the partnership agreement or equally in the absence of a partnership agreement.

18-33.   In determining the business income, we generally begin with the partnership's accounting figure for business income. The normal procedure is to then reconcile or convert the accounting income to that acceptable for income tax purposes. This reconciliation process is similar to that used to determine business income for individuals and corporations (see Chapters 6 and 12). There are, however, some additional adjustments that are unique to the calculation of business income for partnerships.

18-34.   Following the determination of the amount of business income to be allocated to partners, separate calculations are carried out for amounts of property income, taxable capital gains, and allowable capital losses that will be allocated to the members of the partnership. It is important to note that, in this allocation process, the various types of income retain their tax characteristics. That is, a partnership capital gain is treated as a capital gain to the partner to whom it is allocated. This would mean that if a partnership realized a capital gain that would be eligible for the capital gains deduction, it remains eligible for the deduction to the extent that part or all of that capital gain is allocated to partners who are individuals.

18-35.   While it would be possible to calculate net income for a partnership, which combines various sources of income, it would be meaningless to do so since all that is required in the allocation process is that each type of partnership income or loss be separately determined. In effect, the partnership income/loss allocations stop short of determining net and taxable income because those amounts are only relevant to individuals, corporations, and trusts that are required to file annual income tax returns.

Applicable Concepts

Taxation Year

18-36.   ITA 96(1) sets out the general rules that apply with respect to determining the income of a person who is a member of a partnership. ITA 96(1)(a) requires that partnership income must be calculated as if the partnership was a separate person resident in Canada. This first rule allows income or losses to be determined at the partnership level. ITA 96(1)(b) sets the measurement period for calculating income or loss as if the taxation year of the partnership were its "fiscal period." The ITA 249.1(1) definition of "fiscal period" requires the partnership to use a calendar-based fiscal period (January 1 to December 31) if any member of the partnership is an individual or a professional corporation. In effect, this means that, if all of the members of a partnership are corporations (other than professional corporations), the partnership is free to select any fiscal period.

18-37.   ITA 249.1(4) provides an exception to the fiscal period rules that are described in the preceding paragraph. If the following conditions are met, the partnership can elect to use a non-calendar-based fiscal period:

- All of the members of the partnership are individuals.
- An election is filed with the CRA using a prescribed form (T1139) prior to the end of the partnership's first fiscal year. The complications associated with making this election are discussed in Chapter 6 on business income.

> **EXAMPLE**   ABC Partnership has five corporate partners, two of which are professional corporations, and one partner who is an individual. The new partnership wishes to select a March 31 fiscal period.

> **ANALYSIS**   The partnership must use a December 31 fiscal period. The presence of both an individual and professional corporations as partners prevents the use of a non-calendar fiscal period under the ITA 249.1(1) definition. Similarly, the presence of corporations prevents the election of a non-calendar fiscal period under ITA 249.1(4).

18-38.   The CRA has been concerned with the ability of a corporate member of a partnership to defer taxes because it has a different year end from the partnership. Consider a partnership that has a fiscal period ending on January 31, 2021, and a corporate member with a December 31, 2021, year end. The corporation would not have to include the partnership income earned during the year ending January 31, 2021, until it files its income tax return for its taxation year ending December 31, 2021, despite the fact that most of that income was earned in the corporation's taxation year ending December 31, 2020. In effect, this provides an 11-month deferral of income.

18-39.   To address this concern, special rules apply to situations where a partnership has a fiscal period that ends after the taxation year end of a corporation that has a significant interest (more than 10%) in that partnership. A significant interest means more than 10% of the income or loss of the partnership or an entitlement to more than 10% of the net assets of the partnership were it to dissolve (ITA 34.2)(1)). For this purpose, the share of any related and affiliated partners must also be added.

18-40.   The rules (ITA 34.3) would require income adjustments similar to those required for "additional business income," which is covered in Chapter 6.

18-41.   In the example from Paragraph 18-37, the legislation requires the corporate partner to include 334/365 of the partnership income for its fiscal year ending January 31, 2021, in its income for its taxation year ending December 31, 2020. This effectively represents the partnership income for the period February 1, 2020, to December 31, 2020. This accrual would be deducted in the following taxation year ending December 31, 2021, with a new accrual added for 334/365 of the partnership income for the fiscal period ending January 31, 2022.

Partnership Property

18-42.   In general, partners legally have an ownership interest in partnership property in co-ownership. While the partnership cannot own property since it is not a legal entity, partnership law recognizes that property brought into the partnership or acquired by the partnership is "partnership property." This creates a problem for income tax purposes because the partnership income tax rules require that the partnership determine its income or loss as if it were a separate person.

18-43.   If the partnership does not own partnership property, then gains and losses from the disposition of such property would not be considered those of the partnership. In addition, the partnership would not be able to claim CCA. ITA 96(1)(c) resolves this problem with an assumption that the partnership, for income tax purposes, is considered to own partnership property. In addition, ITR 1102(1a) applies to deem an ownership interest of a member of a partnership in partnership property that is depreciable property not to be property of that partner. This latter rule means that only the partnership can claim CCA with respect to partnership property that is depreciable property.

Retention of Income Characteristics

18-44.   Partnerships are flow-through vehicles, meaning that the nature of the capital gain, capital loss, and income or loss from any source flows through to the partners to the extent of their share of that income. If, for example, a partnership earns dividend income, capital gains, or realizes a business loss, these same amounts would be received as dividend income, capital gains, or business losses to the partners to the extent of their share of that income (ITA 96(1)(c), (f) & (g)).

EXAMPLE   Partnership Deux, a general partnership, has two equal partners. Aside from its business income, Deux earns $50,000 of interest income and realizes a $20,000 capital gain. None of this amount is withdrawn by the two partners. Corporation Dos has two equal shareholders. It also earns $50,000 of interest income and realizes a $20,000 capital gain. The corporation does not pay out any of this amount as dividends.

ANALYSIS—Partnership   For Partnership Deux, each partner is considered to have received $25,000 [(1/2)($50,000)] of interest income and to have realized a $5,000 taxable capital gain [($20,000)(1/2)(1/2)]. These amounts are income of the partners despite the fact that none of it has been withdrawn from the partnership (see the next section on "Accrual Basis").

ANALYSIS—Corporation   In the case of Corporation Dos, no amount will be included in the income of shareholders until the corporate income is distributed to them. The income will be subject to corporate income tax on the basis of its nature (e.g., capital gains, business, or property income). When it is distributed to the shareholders, it will not retain its nature as capital gains, business, or property income but will be treated as dividend income.

18-45.   In addition to retaining its nature, the location of each source of income is also retained (ITA 96(1)(f) & (g)). If, for example, a partnership earns dividends on shares of U.S. corporations, the income will retain its nature as foreign source dividends. The proportion of any foreign income or profits tax paid by the partnership is considered to have been paid by the partners to the extent of their share of the related foreign income. As a result, the partners can claim any related foreign tax credits. (See paragraph 1.39 of IT Folio S5-F2-C1, "Foreign Tax Credit").

Accrual Basis

18-46.   The partnership must calculate its business income on an accrual basis in the same manner as any other taxpayer that carries on a business unless the cash basis is permitted, which is generally restricted to farming or fishing businesses by ITA 28. The allocation of partnership business income is added to the income of a partner based on the taxation year in which the partnership fiscal period ends. The addition to income occurs regardless of whether the allocated income has actually been received.

18-47.   Withdrawal made by a partner does not affect allocated income but will have an impact on the interest that the partner has in the partnership, which is referred to as a "partnership interest." An interest in a partnership is considered property for income tax purposes and is similar in many ways to other investments, such as shares of a corporation or an interest in a mutual fund that is a trust.

Exercise 18-1

Subject: Partnership Income—Accrual Basis

During the year ending December 31, 2021, PQR Partnership has business income of $55,000, capital gains of $40,000, and receives eligible dividends of $10,000. Norm Peters has an interest in the partnership that entitles him to 50% of each type of income or gain of the partnership. During 2021, Norm withdraws $30,000 from the partnership. Determine the income tax consequences for Norm for the 2021 taxation year.

Solutions to Exercises are available in the Study Guide.

Calculating the Amounts to Be Allocated

Business Income

18-48.   For most partnerships, the major source of income to be allocated is the partnership's income from carrying on a business. Every partner is also considered to be carrying on the business of the partnership irrespective of their role in the business. The most important step in determining the business income of a partnership for income tax purposes is the reconciliation process that begins with the accounting net income. Various adjustments are made to that accounting net income to conform to the provisions of the ITA. The major adjustments in this process are described below.

Salaries or Wages to Partners (Add Back)   Partnership agreements often provide that partners be paid salaries or wages to recognize the time they devote to the partnership business. Salaries and wages to partners are not deductible for income tax purposes since they represent a distribution of partnership profits and are not a valid expense. Since a partner carries on the partnership business, the payment of a salary would be the same as employing and paying oneself a salary. As a result, a sole proprietor or a member of a partnership cannot pay himself a salary and claim a business expense. This would be different if an individual owned all of the shares of a corporation that carried on a business. As a separate legal entity, the corporation could employ the shareholder and pay him a salary.

If salaries or wages to partners have been deducted in determining accounting net business income, the amounts deducted must be reversed by adding back the amount deducted. If the partnership agreement provides for salary or wage entitlements for specific partners, the specified amounts will be used in the ultimate determination of how business profits will be shared.

As previously mentioned, any amounts withdrawn from the partnership that are intended to be a substitute for salary or wages do not impact the income of the partner.

Interest on Partner Capital Contributions (Add Back)   The preceding analysis of the treatment of partner salaries also applies where the partnership pays interest on capital contributions made to the partnership by partners. Any interest payments would not be eligible for an interest expense using the same logic that the result would be comparable to paying interest to oneself. Payments of interest on capital contributions are considered to represent a distribution of business profits and are a factor in the business profit allocation process only and not the determination of business income or loss.

If interest payments on partner capital contributions have been deducted in the determination of the accounting-based business income, they must also be reversed by adding the expense amount back in the reconciliation process. If the specified amounts are withdrawn, the withdrawal does not affect the partner's net income.

EXAMPLE—Salaries and Interest on Capital Contributions   Bob and Ray are partners who share the business profits of their partnership equally after a provision has been made for salaries and Ray's interest on his capital contributions. For the year ending December 31, 2021, the income statement of the partnership, prepared in accordance with ASPE, is as follows:

Revenues		$135,000
Expenses:		
Cost of sales	($45,000)	
Salary to Bob	(30,000)	
Salary to Ray	(10,000)	
Interest on Ray's capital contributions	(11,000)	
Other expenses	(10,000)	(106,000)
Accounting net income		$ 29,000

ANALYSIS   For income tax purposes, the business income of the Bob and Ray Partnership would be calculated as follows:

Accounting income	$29,000
Add:	
Salaries to Bob and Ray ($30,000 + $10,000)	40,000
Interest on capital contributions	11,000
Business income (profits)	$80,000
Allocations for salaries and interest on	
capital contributions ($40,000 + $11,000)	(51,000)
Residual business income (to be shared equally)	$29,000

This amount would be allocated to the two partners as follows:

	Bob	**Ray**
Priority allocation for salaries	$30,000	$10,000
Priority allocation for interest	N/A	11,000
Allocation of residual on equal basis		
[(50%)($29,000)]	14,500	14,500
Total business income allocation	$44,500	$35,500

Despite the fact that the partnership agreement may refer to salaries or wages or for interest on capital for the partners, from a legal point of view they are allocations of business profits or losses. Since salaries and wages cannot be legally paid to partners, payroll procedures (e.g., information reporting (T4), source deductions for CPP and EI) are not required.

Drawings (Add Back)   Drawings by partners are not deductible business expenses in the determination of any type of partnership income. If drawings have been claimed in the determination of accounting-based net income they must be reversed by adding them back in the reconciliation process.

Dividend Income (Deduct)   Dividends received will be included in a partnership's accounting net income. These amounts are allocated to partners as a separate source of income. Given this, dividends must be separated from other sources of income. If dividends received have been included in business income they must be deducted in the reconciliation process.

Charitable Donations (Add Back)   These amounts are normally deducted in the determination of a partnership's accounting net income. Since donations are not a valid business expense they must also be reversed by adding them back in the reconciliation process to determine business income or loss for purposes of the ITA.

Donations made by a partnership that otherwise qualify as charitable donations are flowed to the partners based on the partnership agreement. Corporations are entitled to a deduction in arriving at taxable income, whereas individuals are entitled to a non-refundable credit against federal tax payable. Donations, and the related credit or deduction, are only allocated to those partners who are partners on the last day of the partnership's year end. Partnership donations are allocated to partners who are individuals as a result of ITA 118.1(8) and to corporations as a result of ITA 110.1(4).

Personal Expenditures (Add Back)   In some situations, a partnership may pay personal expenses of one or more partners. While these amounts may be deducted as an expense for accounting purposes, they are not deductible to the partnership in determining its business income. To the extent that these amounts have been deducted in the determination of accounting net income, they will have to be added back in the reconciliation process. These expenses typically are the equivalent of drawings by a partnership and do not impact a partner's income.

Business Transactions with Partners (No Adjustment)   While this may not be consistent with basic legal principles and partnership law, administrative practice of the CRA does not restrict the ability of partners to enter into legitimate business transactions with their partnerships. Examples include loans between partners and the partnership and the renting of a partner's property to the partnership. As long as the transactions are on regular commercial terms, such transactions will be treated for income tax purposes in the same manner as transactions with persons who are not partners.

In general, such transactions will not require any adjustment of the accounting net income to arrive at the partnership's business income or loss.

Capital Cost Allowance   CCA can be deducted by the partnership with respect to partnership property. Other depreciable property rules, such as the half-year rule, the Accelerated Investment Incentive (AccII), the available-for-use rules, and rental property restrictions, are also applicable when determining the amount of CCA that a partnership can claim.

It is not uncommon in partnership financial statements for the amortization deducted to be based on the CCA amounts used for income tax purposes. If this is the case, no reconciliation adjustments would be necessary. However, when the accounting amortization is different than the available CCA the reconciliation process requires reversing the accounting amortization by adding it back and deducting the appropriate CCA.

Amounts Related to Dispositions of Capital Property   Accounting net income will include 100% of the accounting gains and losses on dispositions of depreciable and non-depreciable capital property. These amounts must be added back (losses) or deducted (gains) in the reconciliation process.

As net taxable capital gains will be separately allocated to the partners, these amounts are not included in the calculation of the business income of the partnership.

Dispositions of depreciable property can also result in recapture of CCA or terminal losses. If recapture occurs, it will be added in the reconciliation process, whereas terminal losses will be deducted. The terminal losses and recapture may be a component of either business or property income depending upon their use.

Reserves   The use of reserves is discussed in both Chapter 6 (e.g., reserve for doubtful debts) and Chapter 8 (e.g., capital gains reserve). These reserves are claimed by the partnership in exactly the same manner as individuals, corporations, and trusts.

In general, accounting reserves that have been deducted are added back in the reconciliation process and any applicable income tax reserves are deducted.

18-49.   Figure 18-2 provides a list of the more common adjustments that arise in the reconciliation process of converting the accounting net income of a partnership to business income for purposes of the ITA.

Capital Gains and Capital Losses
18-50.   Capital gains and capital losses are allocated to the members of the partnership and included in their income in the same manner as would be the case had they been realized personally. One-half of the net capital gains will be included in net income for income tax purposes. The lifetime capital gains deduction may be available, and some capital losses may qualify as business investment losses. If the partner is a private corporation, there will be an addition to the capital dividend account.

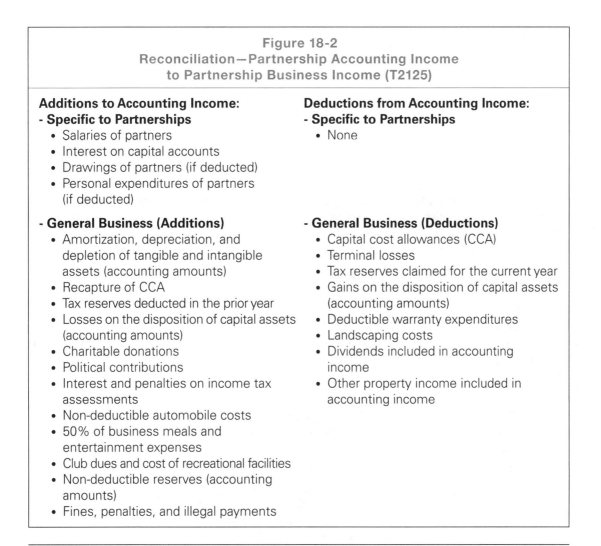

Figure 18-2
Reconciliation—Partnership Accounting Income
to Partnership Business Income (T2125)

Additions to Accounting Income:
- Specific to Partnerships
- Salaries of partners
- Interest on capital accounts
- Drawings of partners (if deducted)
- Personal expenditures of partners (if deducted)

- General Business (Additions)
- Amortization, depreciation, and depletion of tangible and intangible assets (accounting amounts)
- Recapture of CCA
- Tax reserves deducted in the prior year
- Losses on the disposition of capital assets (accounting amounts)
- Charitable donations
- Political contributions
- Interest and penalties on income tax assessments
- Non-deductible automobile costs
- 50% of business meals and entertainment expenses
- Club dues and cost of recreational facilities
- Non-deductible reserves (accounting amounts)
- Fines, penalties, and illegal payments

Deductions from Accounting Income:
- Specific to Partnerships
- None

- General Business (Deductions)
- Capital cost allowances (CCA)
- Terminal losses
- Tax reserves claimed for the current year
- Gains on the disposition of capital assets (accounting amounts)
- Deductible warranty expenditures
- Landscaping costs
- Dividends included in accounting income
- Other property income included in accounting income

Exercise 18-2

Subject: Partnership Business Income

The JL Partnership has two partners. Partner J, because he is actively managing the partnership, receives an annual salary of $45,000. Because Partner L has contributed most of the capital for the business, he receives an interest allocation of $22,000. The partnership agreement provides that any residual profits remaining after the salary and interest, plus all other allocations, be split 60% to J and 40% to L. The salary and interest amounts have been deducted in the determination of accounting net income and were withdrawn by the partners during the year.

During the fiscal period ending December 31, 2021, the partnership's accounting net income is $262,000. Other relevant information is as follows:

- The accountant deducted amortization of $26,000. Maximum CCA available is $42,000.
- Accounting net income includes a deduction for charitable donations of $2,500.
- Accounting net income includes a gain on the sale of land of $24,000.

Determine the amount of partnership business income to be allocated to Partner J and Partner L for the year ending December 31, 2021.

Solutions to Exercises are available in the Study Guide.

Dividend Income

18-51.   Dividends received by a partnership are separated in the determination of the partnership's income. When they are allocated to the members of the partnership to be included in their income, they retain their character as eligible, non-eligible, or capital dividends. Their treatment subsequent to allocation will depend on the type of partner (e.g., an individual, trust, or corporation) involved and the nature of the dividend:

- Partners who are individuals must gross up the dividends by either 38% (for eligible dividends) or 15% (for non-eligible dividends). The dividends are then eligible for dividend tax credits.
- Dividends allocated to corporate partners will not be grossed up. All of the allocated amount will be included in the corporation's net income. If the dividends are taxable dividends and received from taxable Canadian corporations, they are eligible for a taxable income deduction (ITA 112(1)).
- Capital dividends received by the partnership are allocated as capital dividends to both individual and corporate partners, retaining their tax-free nature.

Foreign Source Income

18-52.   Foreign source income received by a partnership will be allocated to the partners as either business or property income. The full amount of any allocated amounts will be converted to Canadian currency and included in the net income of the partners. Any foreign income and profits taxes will also be allocated to the partners for purposes of claiming foreign tax credits.

Exercise 18-3

Subject: Partnership Income Allocations

The ST Partnership has two partners who share all types of income equally. Partner S and T are both individuals. The partnership's accounting net income for the fiscal period ending December 31, 2021, is $146,000. No salaries or interest payments to partners were made in the year. However, the $146,000 includes $12,000 in eligible dividends as well as a $31,000 gain on the sale of unused land. Amortization expense deducted equals the maximum available CCA. Determine the amounts that will be included in the net income of Partner S and Partner T for the year ending December 31, 2021.

Solutions to Exercises are available in the Study Guide.

Allocations of Tax Credits

18-53.   Partnership income and expenditures could give rise to the following tax credits:

- Dividend income—This tax credit is available if the partner is an individual.
- Charitable donations—This tax credit is available if the partner is an individual.
- Foreign source income—This tax credit is available to all partners if foreign income or profits tax was paid.

Exercise 18-4

Subject: Allocations to Partners—Tax Credits

For the year ending December 31, 2021, the MN Partnership has correctly computed its business income to be $141,000. The partnership agreement provides equal allocations of all partnership income and expenditures. Partner M and N are both individuals and neither partner is subject to the 33% federal income tax rate in 2021.

In the business income reconciliation process the accountant added back $3,500 in charitable donations and deducted $4,200 in eligible dividends. The partners made no personal charitable donations. Determine the amount of any tax credits that are available to the partners as a result of partnership allocations for the fiscal period ending December 31, 2021.

Solutions to Exercises are available in the Study Guide.

Methods of Allocation

18-54.   Partnership income must be allocated on a source-by-source basis. While a partnership agreement might simply state that all types of income will be allocated on the same basis, there is nothing to prevent different allocations for different sources. For example, business income could be allocated on an equal basis, with a significant portion of capital gains being allocated to one specific partner, particularly if the partner contributed that property to the partnership.

18-55.   There are many ways in which the members of a partnership may agree to allocate income or losses. These allocations may be fixed, variable, or a combination of fixed and variable elements. Factors such as the value of services provided to the partnership (a salary component), capital contributions (an interest component), and amounts of risk assumed (personal assets at risk) may be taken into consideration. Alternatively, allocations may be based on fixed ratios determined by the partners or, in the absence of some other agreement, the equal allocation that automatically applies under partnership law.

18-56.   In general, the CRA will accept any income allocation agreement that is reasonable. It is possible, however, that the agreement could be constructed in a manner that would reduce or postpone income taxes (e.g., an example of this would be the allocation of all partnership losses to partners subject to high income tax rates). In addition, an allocation could be used for income splitting purposes (e.g., allocation of large amounts of partnership income to a low-income spouse on a basis that is not consistent with his or her contribution of services or capital). In either of these circumstances, the CRA can apply one of the two anti-avoidance rules in ITA 103(1) or (1.1) that target unreasonable allocations, allowing the CRA to reassess on the basis of what is reasonable in the circumstances.

We suggest you complete SSP 18-3 and 18-4 at this point.

The Partnership Interest

The Concept

18-57.   A person who is a member of a partnership has the right to participate in profits and losses of the partnership and the right to an interest in partnership property, usually on the dissolution of the partnership. Such rights, collectively referred to as a partnership interest, constitute property for income tax purposes much in the same manner as a share of capital stock of a corporation.

18-58.   A partnership interest is generally considered a non-depreciable capital property that is held for the purpose of earning business or property income and, as a consequence, a disposition of a partnership interest will usually result in a capital gain or loss.

18-59.   In many cases, a partnership interest is acquired when a partnership is formed. Each member of the new partnership will acquire an interest, usually through a contribution to the partnership that is specified in the partnership agreement.

18-60.   Alternatively, a partnership interest can be acquired from an existing partnership. This type of transaction can take two forms:

- The interest can be acquired directly from a current partner or partners by purchasing their interest.

- The interest can be acquired directly from the partnership.

Acquiring a Partnership Interest

New Partnership

18-61.   For founding members of a new partnership, establishment of the cost and ACB of the partnership interest is very straightforward. For each of the partners, the cost and there-fore the ACB of their interest will simply be the fair market value (FMV) of the property con-tributed to the partnership in exchange for the interest.

Admission to Existing Partnership

18-62.   From a legal point of view, a partnership ceases to exist whenever the composition of partners changes and a new partnership is established. This is based on the fact that a partner-ship, at law, is a relationship among its members, so if the members change then the previous relationship ends and a new one is created. This legal principle cannot be overridden by a clause in a partnership agreement that declares the partnership continues to exist when new partners are admitted or existing partners retire.

18-63.   The provisions of the ITA are written to accommodate this legal principle. ITA 98(1) and (3), for example, set out rules when a partnership ceases to exist because of a change in the composi-tion of the partners. The rules, however, allow a partnership to be considered to continue to exist until such time as the partnership is truly dissolved and all partnership property has been distributed to its partners. Other rules, such as ITA 98(6), apply to consider the partnership to continue if an existing partner retires and the remaining partners continue carrying on the business of the partner-ship. As a result, the ITA essentially ensures that there are few income tax consequences when the composition of partners change and the partnership continues on with business as usual.

18-64.   In those cases where a partnership interest is purchased directly from an existing part-ner, the income tax consequences are near identical to purchasing other types of investments from arm's-length persons. If a person becomes a partner by acquiring another partner's inter-est, the cost of the partnership interest will equal the purchase price. For example, if Mr. Davis acquires the one-third interest of Mr. Allan for $90,000, then both the cost and ACB to Mr. Davis and the proceeds of disposition (POD) to Mr. Allan would be $90,000.

18-65.   The situation becomes a bit more complex when the partnership interest is acquired from more than one partner.

> **EXAMPLE**   An existing partnership has three equal partners, each of whom has made a capital contribution of $16,000. They would like to bring in a new equal partner, with each partner then having a 25% interest in the partnership. The new partner, Mr. Zheng, agrees to pay $30,000 to each of the existing partners for one-quarter of their one-third interest. Note that by selling one-quarter of their one-third interest, each partner has disposed of 25% of their interest, which is considered a partial disposition (ITA 43(1)).

> **ANALYSIS**   Mr. Zheng would have a cost and therefore an ACB of $90,000, which is equal to the FMV of the consideration given up for the 25% partnership interest.

> Each of the original partners would have a capital gain calculated as follows:

POD for each partner	$30,000
ACB of part interest [(25%)($16,000)]	(4,000)
Capital gain for each partner	$26,000

18-66. The capital accounts of the partnership for accounting purposes and the partners' ACB will be determined as follows:

	Partner 1	Partner 2	Partner 3	Mr. Zheng
Capital before admitting Mr. Zheng	$16,000	$16,000	$16,000	Nil
Adjustment for admission of Mr. Zheng	(4,000)	(4,000)	(4,000)	$12,000
Ending capital accounts (accounting)	$12,000	$12,000	$12,000	$12,000
ACB of partnership interest (income tax)	$12,000	$12,000	$12,000	$90,000

18-67. Note that, while the capital accounts for accounting purposes of the original three partners are equal to their ACB, this is not the case for Mr. Zheng. The admission of Mr. Zheng results in a reallocation of the partners' capital accounts for accounting purposes, but these amounts are not relevant for income tax purposes.

18-68. To this point, we have only considered situations where a partnership interest is acquired directly from existing partners. A partnership interest can also be acquired by making a payment/contribution to the partnership. However, if a person is admitted as a new partner and any initial contributions by that new partner are removed immediately by another partner the CRA will likely view these two transactions as one and treat the circumstances as if the other partner sold her partnership interest to the new partner.

18-69. Returning to the example in Paragraph 18-65, if Mr. Zheng had paid the $90,000 directly to the partnership, there would be no income tax consequences for the existing partners since there was no disposition of any part of their interest. Economically, their interest has been diluted from 33.3% to 25% but there is no actual disposition by any of them. This is similar to a shareholder's equity interest being diluted when new shareholders acquire newly issued shares. The ACB of the existing partners' interest would remain unchanged at $16,000. The cost of Mr. Zheng's interest would also remain unchanged at $90,000 for both income tax and accounting purposes.

Exercise 18-5

Subject: Admission of a Partner

Alan and Balan are equal partners in the Alban Partnership. On September 1, 2021, Alan and Balan's partnership capital account balances for accounting purposes are $48,000 each. This also happens to equal to the ACB of their partnership interests. As the result of paying $40,000 to each of Alan and Balan, Caitlan is admitted as an equal partner (1/3 interest) on September 1, 2021. Calculate the income tax consequences to Alan and Balan as a result of the new partner being admitted. In addition, determine the accounting balances for each of the partner's capital accounts after the admission of Caitlan, as well as the ACB for each partner.

Solutions to Exercises are available in the Study Guide.

Adjusted Cost Base (ACB)—Partnership Interest

Basic Concept

18-70. A partnership interest is non-depreciable capital property. The ACB of a capital property is defined in ITA 54 as cost plus adjustments under ITA 53(1)(e) minus adjustments under ITA 53(2)(c).

18-71. In the preceding section, we illustrated how the cost of a partnership interest would be determined at the time a partnership interest is acquired. Subsequent to its acquisition, the partnership interest is determined by starting with the ACB of the preceding year and making certain adjustments. The most common adjustments are for:

- current-year income or loss allocations;
- current-year drawings; and
- current-year capital contributions.

18-72.   There are, however, many other possible adjustments, and some of these will be covered in this section. It is critical to note the importance of making these adjustments. If these adjustments were not made, any capital gain or capital loss on a subsequent disposition of the partnership interest would result in these amounts becoming part of the gain or loss on the sale.

> **EXAMPLE**   John Port acquires his partnership interest for $100,000. At a later point in time, he makes an additional capital contribution of $20,000. Subsequent to making this additional contribution, he sells his interest for $150,000.

> **ANALYSIS**   John will add the $20,000 capital contribution to his ACB, resulting in a balance of $120,000 ($100,000 + $20,000). Given this, the capital gain on the disposition of the interest will be $30,000 (POD $150,000 - ACB $120,000). If the adjustment had not been made, the gain would have been $50,000 ($150,000 - $100,000).

Timing of ACB Adjustments

18-73.   There are two general timing rules that apply to ACB adjustments. The first are those adjustments that are made at the time of the particular transaction. The two most common examples of this are capital contributions and drawings.

18-74.   The second timing rule applies specific adjustments based on the fiscal period of the partnership. In these cases the ACB adjustment is not made until the first day of the next fiscal period. Allocations of income, loss, or expenditures that qualify for tax credits (e.g., donations) fall into this category.

ACB Adjustments for Income Allocations

18-75.   Allocations of income for a fiscal period of a partnership are reflected in the ACB beginning with the next fiscal period. However, there are additional factors that must be considered that depend on the type of income being allocated. The following explanations will elaborate on these additional factors:

> **Business Income**   Allocations of business income must be made after a reconciliation from accounting business income to business income for income tax purposes. The ACB adjustment for allocated business income or loss does not occur until the first day of the following fiscal period.

> > **EXAMPLE**   Tom and Theresa begin the Double T Partnership in January 2021 with a calendar-based fiscal period. They each contribute $1,000 to the partnership. During 2021, the partnership earns $21,000 in gross business revenue. The only expenses incurred are $6,000 in business meals and entertainment.

> > **ANALYSIS**   Accounting net income would be $15,000 ($21,000 - $6,000). However, business income for income tax purposes would be $18,000, the $15,000 of accounting net income plus $3,000 reconciliation for the non-deductible one-half of the expenses for business meals and entertainment (ITA 67.1). This means that each partner would be allocated $9,000 [(1/2)($18,000)] in business income, and each partnership interest would be increased by the same amount. The allocated business income of $9,000 would be included in the partners' 2021 net income, however the adjustment to the ACB would not be made until January 1, 2022.

> **Capital Gains and Capital Losses**   These amounts will generally be allocated to the partners on the basis of the partnership agreement. Once these amounts are allocated, the taxable or allowable amounts (one-half) will be included in the partner's net income for the taxation year in which the fiscal period of the partnership ends.

Despite the fact that only one-half of capital gains and capital losses are recognized for income tax purposes, the adjustment to the ACB of partnership interests is for the full amount and also occurs on the first day of the following fiscal period. Including the full amount of the capital gain or capital loss ensures that the non-taxable one-half of the gain or loss will retain its tax-free status if the partnership interest is sold.

EXAMPLE Weekday Partnership has four equal individual partners and a calendar-based fiscal period. Each partner contributed $1,950 when the partnership began on May 1, 2021. Weekday used the initial contributions of $7,800 to acquire two parcels of land. Both parcels were capital property and were sold in December 2021. The sale of parcel A resulted in a capital gain of $5,300, and the sale of parcel B resulted in a capital loss of $700. There were no other transactions during the 2021 fiscal period.

ANALYSIS The total capital gain for each partner is $1,150 [(1/4)($5,300 − $700)]. Each partner would be required to add $575 [(1/2)($1,150)] to their net income for 2021. However, the ACB adjustment will add the full amount of $1,150. The ACB of each partnership interest would be calculated as follows:

ACB—May 1, 2021, to December 31, 2021		$1,950
Net capital gain allocated:		
Capital gain [(1/4)($5,300)]	$1,325	
Capital loss [(1/4)($700)]	(175)	1,150
ACB of partnership interest—January 1, 2022		$3,100

Dividends As previously discussed, taxable dividends earned by a partnership retain their nature (i.e., eligible, non-eligible, or capital) when they are allocated to the partners. In calculating the ACB of a partnership interest, a partner's share of both capital dividends and taxable dividends received is added to the ACB of the partnership interest on the first day of the following fiscal period.

EXAMPLE Fred and Barney are equal partners in Stone-Works Partnership that began operations January 1, 2021. The partnership uses a calendar-based fiscal period. Each partner initially contributed $5,000. The only income received by the partnership was $13,000 of eligible dividends and $4,200 of capital dividends. No amounts were withdrawn from the partnership in 2021.

ANALYSIS Each partner is allocated one-half of the taxable dividends of $13,000. Each taxable eligible dividend would be subject to a 38% gross up. As a result, $8,970 [(50%)($13,000)(138%)] would be added to the 2021 net income of each individual partner. Each partner would also be eligible for a federal dividend tax credit of $1,347 [(50%)($13,000)(38%)(6/11)], which would be applied to reduce federal tax payable for 2021. The capital dividends are not required to be included in net income (ITA 83(2)). The ACB of Fred and Barney's interest would be as follows:

ACB—January 1, 2021, to December 31, 2021	$ 5,000
Allocation of taxable dividends [(50%)($13,000)]	6,500
Allocation of capital dividends [(50%)($4,200)]	2,100
ACB of partnership interest—January 1, 2022	$13,600

Two things should be noted in this calculation. First, for purposes of calculating the ACB of the partnership interests, the gross up is not added. Second, the dividends do not adjust the ACB until the first day of the following fiscal period of the partnership.

ACB Adjustments—Capital Contributions and Drawings

18-76.   These adjustments require little in the way of explanation:

- Any additional capital contributions are added to the ACB of a partnership interest.
- Drawings of capital or profits reduce the ACB of the partnership interest.

  Note that the ITA draws a line between capital contributions and loans by a partner to the partnership. Capital contributions add to the ACB of a partnership interest but loans do not.

  EXAMPLE   The ACB of Mr. Allan's partnership interest is $20,450 on January 1, 2021. In March 2021, he contributes $8,200 to the partnership as a capital contribution and makes withdrawals of $2,000 in each of May, August, and November 2021.

  ANALYSIS   The ACB of Mr. Allan's partnership interest after the November 2021 withdrawal is calculated as follows:

ACB—January 1, 2021	$20,450
Capital contributions—March 2021	8,200
Drawings—May, August, and November 2021 [($2,000)(3)]	(6,000)
ACB—November 30, 2021	$22,650

ACB Adjustments—Charitable Donations

18-77.   Charitable donations made by a partnership in a particular fiscal period are considered donated or contributed by each partner based on their share of the eligible amount of a gift. The eligible amount of a gift is reduced by any advantage received with respect to that gift (see Chapter 4). As it is the partners who enjoy the benefits of the gifts (i.e., the deductions or tax credits), such amounts reduce the ACB of the partnership interest. The ACB adjustment does not occur until the first day of the following fiscal period.

  EXAMPLE   During the fiscal period ending December 31, 2021, the eligible amounts of gifts made by the partnership equalled $7,500. The three partners, who are all individuals, have agreed to share the eligible amount of the gifts equally. All donations are eligible for the charitable donations tax credit.

  ANALYSIS   Each of the three partners would be entitled to allocations of $2,500 toward the calculation of their individual charitable donations tax credit for 2021. As a consequence of this allocation, the ACB of each of their partnership interests would be reduced by $2,500. As we have noted, this reduction does not occur until January 1, 2022.

Negative ACB—ITA 40(3) & 53(1)(a)

18-78.   In general, if the ACB reductions determined under ITA 53(2)(c) exceed the cost and positive adjustments under ITA 53(1)(e) a potential problem exists, which is commonly referred to as a "negative ACB," although technically a negative ACB is not possible. When this happens the negative portion is considered the equivalent of a capital gain and, as a result of ITA 40(3), it must be included in net income when it occurs. When this applies, an ACB adjustment follows under ITA 53(1)(a) to immediately restore the ACB to nil to ensure the same amount is not subject to income tax a second time. The ACB adjustment is not made under ITA 53(1)(e) since it is generic in nature and not limited to partnership interests. If, for example, a shareholder experiences a return of capital that creates a negative ACB the shareholder would be considered to have realized a capital gain at that time.

18-79.   A potential negative ACB can be a common occurrence since partners draw amounts from a partnership throughout the course of a year as an equivalent to salary for living expenses. Because of this problem, the ITA *exempts active* general partners from this rule. Limited partners and inactive general partners are, however, subject to the negative ACB and will be required to include the amount in their net income as a capital gain.

  EXAMPLE   During 2021, in anticipation of the 2021 allocation of partnership income, an active general partner draws $42,000 from the partnership. For 2021, the partners' share of partnership income is $45,000. On January 1, 2021, the ACB of the partnership interest is $25,000.

ANALYSIS   On December 31, 2021, the ACB of the partnership interest would be nil and there would be an excess of drawings over the January 1, 2021, ACB of $17,000 ($25,000 - $42,000). In the absence of a special provision for partnership interests, $8,500 [(1/2)($17,000)] would have to be taken into the partner's income as a taxable capital gain. However, because of the exemption for active general partners, this will not be the case. Note that, on January 1, 2022, the ACB of this interest would be $28,000 ($25,000 - $42,000 + $45,000).

18-80.   When the disposition results from a deemed disposition at death, there are rollover provisions that allow the ACB characteristics of the deceased to become the ACB characteristics where the partnership interest is bequeathed to a spouse or common-law partner or a trust in favour of a spouse or common-law partner (ITA 70(6)(d.1)). As a result, a negative ACB can move from one person to another in these circumstances.

Exercise 18-6

Subject: ACB of Partnership Interest

On January 1, 2021, Raymond and Robert form the RR Partnership. The partnership has a December 31 fiscal period. The partnership agreement provides Robert with a 40% share of profits and losses. Robert initially contributes $12,500 and makes a further contribution of $7,200 on June 10, 2021. He withdraws $4,000 on October 31, 2021. RR Partnership has the following sources of income for 2021:

Capital gain on corporate shares	$11,600
Eligible dividends received from Canadian corporations	3,100
Business income	46,700

Determine the ACB of Robert's partnership interest on December 31, 2021, and at January 1, 2022. In addition, determine the amount that would be included in Robert's 2021 net income as a consequence of his interest in the RR Partnership.

Solutions to Exercises are available in the Study Guide.

Disposition of a Partnership Interest

Sale to an Arm's-Length Person

18-81.   If a partnership interest is sold to an arm's-length person, the income tax consequences are straightforward. The ACB of the partnership interest is subtracted from the POD resulting from its sale. The result will be either a taxable capital gain or an allowable capital loss for the taxation year of the partner in which the last day of the fiscal period of the partnership falls.

Withdrawal from Partnership

18-82.   When a partner withdraws from a partnership she disposes of her partnership interest. The withdrawal can occur in many different ways, including a distribution of partnership property to the partner by the partnership or by having one or more of the other partners purchase the interest of the withdrawing partner.

EXAMPLE   The QST Partnership has three partners who share all income amounts on an equal basis. The ACB of their partnership interests are as follows:

Partner Q	$250,000
Partner S	250,000
Partner T	250,000

Partner T has decided to retire and will withdraw from the partnership. Partners Q and S will each purchase half of the interest for $175,000.

ANALYSIS   Partner T will realize a taxable capital gain of $50,000 [(1/2)($175,000 + $175,000 - $250,000)]. There will no immediate income tax consequences to either partners Q or S. However, the cost and therefore the ACB of each of their interests will be increased to $425,000, the original $250,000 plus the additional purchase price of $175,000.

Assuming that the partnership property is not revalued, the accounting capital accounts for the interests of each of the remaining partners will be $375,000 [$250,000 + (1/2) ($250,000)].

We suggest you complete SSP 18-5 and 18-6 at this point.

Limited Partnerships and Limited Partners

Definitions

Limited Partner—ITA 96(2.4)

18-83.   A limited partnership is one that has at least one limited partner and one general partner. Most provincial partnership legislation defines a limited partner as one whose liability for the debts of the partnership is limited to the amount of his actual and promised contributions and who is not permitted to participate in the management of the limited partnership. A partner whose liability is limited under partnership law is considered a limited partner for income tax purposes (ITA 96(2.4)(a)).

18-84.   While the term "limited partner" generally refers to a partner who is relieved of general responsibility for amounts in excess of his capital contribution, the definition in ITA 96(2.4) also includes partners whose risk and liability are limited by certain contractual arrangements (ITA 96(2.2)(d)). Examples include:

- guarantees that someone will acquire his partnership interest regardless of its FMV;
- provisions indicating that amounts a partner has agreed to contribute to the partnership may never have to be paid; and
- provisions that guarantee that the partner will be reimbursed for any partnership losses, usually by the general partner.

18-85.   Members of a limited liability partnership do not fall within the definition of a limited partner (ITA 96(2.4)(a)). They have limited responsibility for certain types of liabilities (e.g., liabilities arising as the result of negligent action by their professional partners). However, they continue to have unlimited liability for other partnership obligations.

At-Risk Rules—ITA 96(2.2)

Overview

18-86.   Historically, limited partnerships have been used to fund high-risk ventures that benefit from generous income tax incentives. Examples include Canadian films, Canadian mining and exploration, scientific research and experimental development (SRED), certain real estate, and construction.

18-87.   General partners entice investors with limited liability protection, combined with the advantages of significant flow through of deductible losses and other tax incentives. The general partners usually do not share in the deductions, receiving their compensation through fees that are charged to the limited partners for managing the partnership.

18-88.   The at-risk rules were introduced to restrict the ability of certain investors in partnerships, typically limited partners, to benefit from income tax deductions or tax credits that exceed the amount they stand to lose on their investment. In simplified terms, the at-risk rules work to ensure that $30,000 of tax deductions are not available to a limited partner who has less than $30,000 at risk.

The At-Risk Amount (ARA)—ITA 96(2.2)

18-89.   The ARA sets the annual limit on the amount of tax preferences and incentives that may flow through to limited partners. Specifically, the ITA provides restrictions on the allocation to limited partners of SRED credits, resource expenditures, investment tax credits, non-farming business losses, and property losses. Under ITA 96(2.2), the ARA is calculated at the end of a partnership's fiscal period as follows:

ACB of the partnership interest		$xxx
Share of partnership income (but not losses) for the current fiscal period		
(equals the ACB income adjustment that would normally be made		
on the first day of the following fiscal period)		xxx
Subtotal		$xxx
Less:		
Amounts owing to the partnership	($xxx)	
Other amounts intended to reduce the investment risk	(xxx)	(xxx)
ARA		$xxx

18-90.   The addition of the share of partnership income (not losses) is intended to ensure that current-year income allocations, which will not be added to the ACB of the partnership interest until the following fiscal year, are taken into consideration at the end of the current year. The amount that is added is the same income allocation that will be added to the ACB.

18-91.   The ARA is reduced by two amounts. The first represents the outstanding balance of any amount owing by the partner to the partnership with respect to the purchase of the partnership interest. This amount is subtracted since it is reflected in the ACB of the partnership interest. Prior to an actual payment, it is not really at risk. Often the amount owing represents non-recourse financing, which means if the amount is unpaid no legal action can be taken against the personal property of the limited partner to recover the amount.

18-92.   The second amount relates to financial incentives designed to reduce the investment risk or exposure to the limited partner. An example of this would be a promise by the general partner to acquire the partnership interest at an amount in excess of the FMV of the partnership interest at a future time at the option of the limited partner. These optional buyouts are often conditional and require the limited partner to remain a partner for a certain period of time.

Limited Partnership Losses (LPL)—ITA 96(2.1)

18-93.   The at-risk rules limit the ability of a limited partner to claim certain types of losses. The rules do not directly affect farm losses and capital losses since these losses carry their own restrictions. Farm losses during the current year may be limited by the restricted farm loss rules and, in addition, any carry over of such restricted farm losses can only be applied against farming income. Similarly, current-year allowable capital losses are only deductible to the extent of current-year taxable capital gains.

18-94.   ITA 96(2.1) indicates that a partner's share of losses, other than those associated with farming or the disposition of non-depreciable capital property, can only be deducted to the extent of the at-risk amount (ARA). Any excess is referred to as the "limited partnership loss" (LPL). An LPL is a loss balance that can be carried forward indefinitely and can only be claimed against future income from the partnership or future increases of the ARA from the same partnership. LPLs cannot be carried back.

    EXAMPLE   On January 1, 2021, Jenny Johnson acquires a 10% limited partnership interest in Tax-Time, a partnership that provides income tax preparation services. This interest cost her $15,000, with $6,000 paid in cash and the balance of $9,000 payable in 36 months, without interest. For its fiscal period ending December 31, 2021, Tax-Time has a $22,000 capital gain and an $111,000 business loss. Jenny is allocated 10% of each of these amounts.

ANALYSIS   As a 10% limited partner, Jenny is allocated a portion of the business loss equal to $11,100. However, her ARA restricts the business loss that she can claim. Her ARA is calculated as follows:

ACB of the partnership interest		$15,000
Share of partnership income [(10%)($22,000 capital gain)]		2,200
Subtotal		$17,200
Less:		
Amount owed to the partnership	($9,000)	
Other amounts intended to reduce the investment risk	Nil	(9,000)
ARA—December 31, 2021		$ 8,200

For 2021, Jenny will be able to deduct only $8,200 of the partnership loss of $11,100 allocated to her. Her 2021 LPL would be $2,900 ($11,100 - $8,200). Jenny will be able to deduct the 2021 LPL in 2022 or subsequent years if her ARA increases. This may occur if she makes additional contributions, is allocated additional income from the partnership, or pays down the amount owing to the partnership. There are several more adjustments to the ACB of a limited partner's partnership interest that are beyond the scope of our coverage.

Exercise 18-7

Subject: Limited Partnership Loss

During 2021, Stuart Jones acquires an interest in a limited partnership for $200,000. An initial $50,000 is paid immediately, with the $150,000 balance payable in eight years. The general partner has agreed to acquire Stuart's interest at any subsequent date, returning his $50,000 payment and assuming responsibility for the $150,000 payable. For 2021, the limited partnership allocates non-farming business losses of $75,000 to Stuart. How much of this loss can Stuart deduct for 2021? Indicate the amount of his 2021 LPL.

Solutions to Exercises are available in the Study Guide.

We suggest you complete SSP 18-7 at this point.

Dispositions of Property to and from a Partnership

Canadian Partnership—ITA 102(1)

18-95.   Since the ITA treats partners as separate and distinct from the partnership, property dispositions between the partners and the partnership may have income tax consequences. Such consequences are generally dependent on the purpose of the disposition and whether the partnership meets the ITA 102(1) definition of a "Canadian partnership":

ITA 102(1)   In this subdivision, "Canadian partnership" means a partnership all of the members of which were, at any time in respect of which the expression is relevant, resident in Canada.

18-96.   Whether the partnership is a general, limited, or limited liability partnership is irrelevant to the determination of its status as a Canadian partnership. In addition, the definition does not require that the partnership be formed in Canada. For example, a U.S.-based partnership with all Canadian resident members would qualify.

18-97.   If the partnership qualifies as a Canadian partnership the ITA contains partnership roll-over provisions that provide for tax deferral in certain situations. However, where a partnership rollover is not available with respect to dispositions of property between partners and a partnership, then default rules will apply that will deem the dispositions to occur at FMV (ITA 97(2) and ITA 98(1)).

Dispositions with No Rollover Provision

Dispositions from Partners to the Partnership—ITA 97(1)
18-98.   If a person disposes of property to a partnership of which the person is already a member, or to a partnership of which they will become a member as a result of a disposition of property to the partnership, then ITA 97(1) deems the person to have disposed of the property at FMV and the partnership to have acquired the property at the same amount. This provision recognizes that purchases and sales of property from a partner to a partnership are to be treated as FMV transactions.

18-99.   If the disposition of property is to acquire a partnership interest or to make a capital contribution, then the FMV of the property becomes a part of the ACB of the partner's partnership interest. This rule is a default rule that applies regardless of whether the partnership qualifies as a Canadian partnership.

> **EXAMPLE**   Diane Jefferson is a member of CG Partnership. She is required to make an additional capital contribution to the partnership and decides to make the contribution by contributing non-depreciable capital property she had purchased for $10,000. At the time of the contribution the FMV of the property was $24,000.
>
> **ANALYSIS**   Diane will be considered to have disposed of the property for proceeds of $24,000. This will result in a $7,000 [(1/2)(POD $24,000 - ACB $10,000)] taxable capital gain. Diane will also be considered to have made a $24,000 capital contribution that will increase the ACB of her partnership interest by the same amount. The partnership will be considered to have purchased the property from Diane for $24,000.

Exercise 18-8

Subject: Dispositions of Property from a Partner to a Partnership (No Rollover)

Charles Woodward is one of four equal partners in LIU Partnership (LIU). During the current year, Charles contributes land to the partnership. Charles does not use a rollover provision to make the transfer. Charles acquired the land for $33,000 and, at the time of the contribution, the FMV is $100,000. Describe the income tax consequences to Charles and LIU in the following three situations:

A.   No consideration is received from LIU.
B.   Charles receives $25,000 in cash from LIU on the disposition of the land.
C.   Charles receives $112,000 in cash from LIU on the disposition of the land.

Solutions to Exercises are available in the Study Guide.

Dispositions from a Partnership to Partners—ITA 98(2)
18-100.   If a partnership disposes of property to a partner, ITA 98(2) deems the partnership to have disposed of the property at FMV and the partner to have acquired the property for the

same amount. There is no requirement that the partner remain a partner after the disposition and the rule (a default rule) applies regardless of whether the partnership qualifies as a Canadian partnership. This provision is typically used when a partnership is dissolved or when partial distributions of partnership property are made in an ongoing partnership.

EXAMPLE   Bill Davis is a 40% partner in the FV Partnership. The partnership owns land that has an ACB of $2,900 and disposes of it to Bill in June 2021 for no consideration. The FMV of the land at that time is $10,000.

ANALYSIS   The partnership is considered to have disposed of the land for its FMV of $10,000, resulting in a capital gain of $7,100 (POD $10,000 - ACB $2,900). Bill's share of this gain is $2,840 [(40%)($7,100)]. This amount will be allocated to Bill and, as a consequence, he will report a taxable capital gain of $1,420 [(1/2)($2,840)] in his 2021 net income. Bill will also be considered to have acquired the land for $10,000 and to have made a withdrawal from the partnership of $10,000. The ACB of his partnership interest will be reduced by the $10,000 withdrawal and increased by the $2,840 allocation of the capital gain.

Exercise 18-9

Subject: Disposition of Property from a Partnership to Partners

Darlene is one of five equal partners in the DG Partnership. During its 2021 fiscal period, which ends December 31, DG equally distributes some of its investments to each of the five partners. The FMV of the investments at the time is $94,000 and the ACB is $39,000. Darlene receives one-fifth (20%) of the investments. At the time of the property distribution the ACB of Darlene's partnership interest is $30,000. What are the income tax consequences to DG and Darlene with respect to the distribution? Your answer should include Darlene's ACB of the investments and the ACB of her partnership interest on both December 31, 2021, and on January 1, 2022.

Solutions to Exercises are available in the Study Guide.

Common Partnership Rollovers

Disposition from Partners to a Partnership—ITA 97(2)

18-101.   If a person disposes of property to a Canadian partnership and all members of that partnership jointly elect, then the property may be disposed of on a rollover basis. This means that the proceeds for the property disposition can be set at tax costs instead of at FMV. This rule applies both to persons who are existing partners as well as to persons who become partners by contributing property to the partnership.

18-102.   ITA 97(2) applies a bridging concept to modify the ITA 85(1) rollover such that it applies to partners selling property to their partnership. The word "partnership" is substituted for "corporation," the words "members of the partnership" are substitutes for "shareholders," and the reference to "share consideration" becomes a reference to "an interest in a partnership." With these substitutions the rules of ITA 85(1) are deemed to apply to these partnership situations. There are, however, some differences in how the rules apply to partnerships. The more notable of these differences are as follows:

- Real property inventory can be sold to a partnership, but not to a corporation.

- When there is a mismatch of value in favour of the corporation where there is a related shareholder who economically benefits, the rules of ITA 85(1)(e.2) apply a gifting concept that effectively taxes the shareholder who caused the gift. In the case of a partnership, the gift portion is considered an additional capital contribution and would be added to the ACB of the partnership interest. In other words, the negative consequences associated with gifting between corporations and their shareholders does not apply between a partner and a partnership. This would also be the case if a shareholder took excess consideration that resulted in a shareholder benefit under ITA 15(1). In a partnership setting, the excess consideration would be considered drawings that would reduce the ACB of the partnership interest.

18-103.   Differences between the elected amount for the property sold and the consideration other than a partnership interest affect the ACB of the partnership interest in the same manner as the non-share consideration (NSC) impacts the ACB of shares received as consideration when ITA 85(1) applies to shareholders.

EXAMPLE   Janice Donovan will join the On-Off Partnership that provides interior lighting products. She plans to make an initial capital contribution of land with an ACB of $100,000 and a FMV of $250,000. She elects to sell the land to the partnership at an elected amount of $160,000. The existing members agree and a joint election is filed authorizing the rollover at $160,000. Janice has a choice between three different packages of consideration:

A.   No cash
B.   Cash of $100,000
C.   Cash of $160,000

ANALYSIS   The range of elected amounts would be between the tax cost (ACB) of the property of $100,000 and its FMV of $250,000. Cash consideration would reset the range. In this case, the third alternative that would result in $160,000 of cash consideration would have reset the range from $160,000 to $250,000, therefore the $160,000 elected amount is acceptable for all three packages of consideration. The relevant amounts for the three cases are as follows:

Case	ACB of Partnership Interest	Capital Gain
No cash	$160,000	$60,000
Cash of $100,000	$ 60,000	60,000
Cash of $160,000	Nil	60,000

Exercise 18-10

Subject: Transfers from Partners to Partnerships (With Rollover)

Samantha Floren is one of three equal partners in the SFL Partnership. During the current year, Samantha contributes land to the partnership as a capital contribution. She had acquired the land several years ago for $156,000. At the time of the contribution, the FMV of the land is $263,000. She would like to use any available rollover provision to minimize income tax on the disposition of the land to the partnership. What are the income tax consequences of the contribution assuming that an election is filed under ITA 97(2) to minimize any income tax?

Solutions to Exercises are available in the Study Guide.

Partnership Property Transferred to a New Partnership — ITA 98(6)

18-104.   As mentioned in Paragraphs 18-62 and 18-63, a partnership may cease to exist in a number of situations, such as when the composition of the partners change for any reason. The rules of the ITA, however, generally prevent any adverse income tax implications as long as partnership property has not actually been distributed to members of a partnership as a result.

18-105.   ITA 98(6) is one example that applies where a partnership has ceased to exist because a member dies or retires. The result would be a new partnership with members who were members of the old partnership. In such cases the rule applies a continuation concept that applies as long as all of the partnership property continues to be used in the new partnership. A continuation concept avoids the complexity associated with actual dispositions of property that require deemed elected amounts to avoid adverse income tax implications.

18-106.   Many years ago there was a concern that ITA 98(6) could not apply where partnership property was distributed to the retiring partner since the rule suggested that all of the partnership property had to be used in the new partnership. The CRA took the view that "all of the partnership property" meant the partnership property remaining after the settlement with the retiring partner or her estate where a partner had died.

Partnership Property Used in a Sole Proprietorship—ITA 98(5)

18-107.   This rollover, provided for in ITA 98(5), applies automatically where a Canadian partnership ceases to exist because one of two partners retires, dies, or otherwise withdraws and the remaining partner carries on the partnership business as a sole proprietor within three months of the partnership ceasing to exist. This rollover treatment is only provided to the ex-partner who becomes a sole proprietor with respect to any partnership property distributed to the sole proprietor that is used in carrying on the previous partnership business. In general, the rule ensures that there are no income tax consequences associated with the disposition of that proprietor's partnership interest. The rollover is not available to the other partner, and as a result dispositions of the partners' partnership interest and dispositions of partnership property by the partnership to that partner will occur at FMV.

18-108.   The purpose of ITA 98(5) is to permit the partner who will carry on the partnership business as a sole proprietor to avoid any income tax implications when the partnership ceases to exist because there are no longer two partners. There is, however, an exception to avoiding income tax implications in situations where the tax cost of partnership property received by the proprietor exceeds the ACB of his partnership interest. In this case, there will be a capital gain. Alternatively, if the ACB of the proprietor's partnership interest exceeds the tax cost of partnership property received by the proprietor, the rules allow the tax cost of non-depreciable capital property to be increased to reflect this difference (ITA 98(5)(c)).

Incorporating a Partnership—ITA 85(2) & (3)

18-109.   The decision to incorporate a partnership generally arises when a partnership that has realized losses in its initial years becomes profitable. Prior to that time, the use of a partnership allows the partners to personally use the partnership losses to offset their income from other sources and therefore to reduce income tax. Once the partnership has become profitable, corporate status may be preferred because of the availability of the small business deduction, the substantial deferral of income taxes on income retained in the corporation, or the desire to potentially split income with other related persons subject to the TOSI and other attribution concerns.

18-110.   In Chapter 16 we discussed the rollover available in ITA 85(1) that facilitates the incorporation of a sole proprietorship by permitting sales of business properties to a corporation to take place at tax costs. There is a similar rollover available for the incorporation of a partnership, but it requires a two-step process that uses two rollovers, ITA 85(2) and ITA 85(3). Under ITA 85(2), eligible partnership property is first sold to a taxable Canadian corporation for either shares or a combination of shares and non-share consideration (NSC). ITA 85(2) requires a joint election (T2058) by the corporation and all members of the partnership. Elected amounts are then determined using the same rules of ITA 85(1) to avoid any income tax implications. The partnership is not required to be a Canadian partnership, however capital property owned by the partnership that is real property is only eligible for the election if the partnership is a Canadian partnership.

18-111.   At the completion of the first ITA 85(2) step, the corporation is carrying on the business previously carried on by the partnership and the partnership has become a shareholder of that same corporation. The partners' interest in the partnership is unchanged.

18-112.   The second step involves ITA 85(3), which provides for the winding-up and dissolution of the partnership. The partnership must follow the necessary legal formalities for winding-up the partnership, including the settlement of partnership liabilities and potential de-registration within the province in which the partnership was formed. In the wind-up process the partnership interests come to an end and are settled by distributions of property from the partnership. These events result in (1) the disposition of partnership property by the partnership to the partners in settlement of partnership interests, (2) the disposition of the partnership interests by the partners, and (3) the acquisition of partnership property by the soon-to-be former partners. In the absence of a rollover, these transactions would all take place at FMV, resulting in potential income tax consequences.

18-113.   ITA 85(3) rollover treatment does not require an election and is automatically applied as long as the following conditions are met:

- The partnership must have disposed of property to a taxable Canadian corporation under ITA 85(2).

- The partnership must be wound up within 60 days of the disposition of its property to the corporation.

- Immediately before the partnership is wound up, the only property it holds is money or property received from the corporation as a result of ITA 85(2).

18-114.   On the wind-up of the partnership, a partner receives NSC and shares of the corporation owned by the partnership. The ACB of the partnership interest is then allocated to the NSC and shares in a manner similar to that of ITA 85(1). The allocations begin with the FMV of the NSC. If that amount is less than the ACB of the partnership interest, then the remaining ACB is allocated as the tax cost of any preferred and common shares as a result of ITA 85(3). The PUC of the share consideration is determined under the regular rules of ITA 85(1) as a result of ITA 85(2). If the FMV of NSC happens to exceed the ACB of the partnership interest, the excess amount will be a capital gain. In that case the ACB of the share consideration received by the partners on the wind-up would be nil.

18-115.   The rollover rules of ITA 85(2) and 85(3) are designed to provide a tax-free means of incorporating a partnership. However, income tax consequences may arise in two particular instances. First, ITA 85(2) only applies to "eligible property" as defined in ITA 85(1.1). The major item that would not be included in this definition would be an inventory of real property (i.e., real property held for sale rather than use). If such non-eligible property is sold by a partnership to a corporation, the sale will occur at FMV, resulting in the usual income tax consequences.

18-116.   A second situation in which the incorporation of a partnership may result in income tax consequences was discussed in Paragraph 18-114, when the FMV of NSC received by a partner on the winding-up of the partnership exceeds the ACB of the partnership interest.

> **EXAMPLE**   Daniel and Christine are equal partners in Flag Partnership. The recent success of the business has led to a decision to incorporate. The only property owned by the partnership is an inventory of flags with a tax cost of $50,000. The FMV of the inventory is $200,000. The ACB of each partner's partnership interest is $34,000. The inventory is sold to the corporation for $200,000 and an election under ITA 85(2) is filed selecting an elected amount of $50,000. The corporation issues common shares with a FMV of $200,000 as consideration for the flag inventory.

> **ANALYSIS**   The Flag Partnership will be deemed to have disposed of the inventory for $50,000 and the corporation will be considered to have acquired the inventory for $50,000. The ACB and PUC of the share consideration will both be $50,000. At this point, the Flag Partnership owns shares of the corporation and the corporation owns the inventory.

> When the Flag Partnership winds-up and distributes the common shares it owns to Daniel and Christine, the following income tax consequences will arise:

> - The Flag Partnership will be considered to have disposed of the shares for their tax cost of $50,000, resulting in no tax consequences (ITA 85(3)(h)).

- Each partner will be considered to have acquired the shares for an amount equal to the ACB of his or her partnership interest ($34,000) (ITA 85(3)(f)).

- Each partner will be considered to have disposed of his or her partnership interest for proceeds equal to the ACB of the shares acquired from the partnership ($34,000). As a result, there is no capital gain or loss (POD $34,000- ACB $34,000) (ITA 85(3)(g)) to either partner on the disposition of his or her partnership interests.

We suggest you complete SSP 18-8 at this point.

Key Terms

A full glossary with definitions is provided at the end of the Study Guide.

At-Risk Amount (ARA)	Limited Liability Partnership
At-Risk Rules	Limited Partner
Canadian Partnership	Limited Partnership
Co-ownership	Limited Partnership Loss (LPL)
Deeming Rule	"Negative" ACB
General Partner	Partner
General Partnership	Partnership
Joint Tenancy	Partnership Interest
Joint Venture	Syndicates
Limited Liability	Tenancy in Common

References

For more detailed study of the material in this chapter, we refer you to the following:

ITA 40(3)	Negative ACB
ITA 53(1)(e)	Addition to Cost Base of an Interest in a Partnership
ITA 53(2)(c)	Deduction from Cost Base of an Interest in a Partnership
ITA 85(2)	Transfer of Property to Corporation from Partnership
ITA 85(3)	Where Partnership Wound Up
ITA 96	General Rules (Partnerships and Their Members)
ITA 97	Contribution of Property to Partnership
ITA 98	Disposition of Partnership Property
ITA 99	Fiscal Period of Terminated Partnership
ITA 100	Disposition of an Interest in a Partnership
ITA 102	Definition of "Canadian Partnership"
ITA 103	Agreement to Share Income
S4-F16-C1	What Is a Partnership?
IT-81R	Partnerships—Income of Non-Resident Partners
IT-231R2	Partnerships—Partners Not Dealing at Arm's Length
IT-242R	Retired Partners
IT-278R2	Death of a Partner or of a Retired Partner
IT-378R	Winding-Up of a Partnership
IT-413R	Election by Members of a Partnership under Subsection 97(2)
IT-457R	Election by Professionals to Exclude Work-in-Progress from Income
IT-471R	Merger of Partnerships
T4068	Guide for the T5013 Partnership Information Return

Self-Study Problems (SSPs)

Self-Study Problems (SSPs) provide practice in problem solving. Within the chapters, we have indicated where it would be appropriate to stop and work on each SSP. The problems can be downloaded by chapter from MyLab Accounting. Solutions are available in the Study Guide. Select problems can also be completed directly in MyLab and auto-graded.

Assignment Problems

Solutions to Assignment Problems (APs) are available to instructors only.

AP 18-1   (Existence of a Partnership)

Sam and Sarah Block are spouses residing east of Ottawa, Ontario. They have been married for 15 years and have three children ages 6, 8, and 11. Sarah was an elementary school teacher before she met Sam and decided just before the birth of their first child that she would leave her teaching position, become a stay-at-home mom, and devote herself full time to the care of her children.

Sam has been a police officer with the Ottawa Police Service for the last 17 years and recently passed all of the tests to become a detective—a lifelong ambition. Unfortunately, his role as a detective often results in irregular hours. With Sam being away on assignments and the children all in school, Sarah has found herself with a lot of time on her hands. To occupy her time she enrolled in pottery classes and discovered a creative side she believed she could turn into a profitable business. Upon graduation Sarah spoke with Sam about converting a small building behind their home into a pottery shop. A contractor was hired in May 2020 and three weeks later the conversion was complete.

Sarah purchased the necessary equipment and materials to begin creating her specialized pieces of vases, planters, bowls, and so on. Sarah hired a specialty firm to help develop a website and obtained an agreement from Pottery-Is-Us Inc., a national retailer, to display her pieces for sale. While sales were initially slow, an interview with a national magazine and a local news network in August 2021 have resulted in an increased demand for her pieces from both inside and outside of the country. The increased demand has resulted in Sarah having to hire two graduates from the local pottery trade school. Sarah personally interviewed over 20 candidates for the positions before carefully making her decision.

Sarah was proficient in using accounting software to create books and records but did not possess the skills necessary to deal with the preparation of financial statements and the filing of tax returns, so she hired a local accountant.

Using a December 31 fiscal year end for the business, the accountant determined that the business suffered a loss for income tax purposes of $87,300 for 2020 and another loss of $126,100 in 2021. The accountant explained that the losses were not unexpected given the accelerated CCA incentives and the fact that such businesses usually did not begin to make profits until the third or fourth year. The accountant added that projections indicated there would be a profit in excess of $60,000 in 2022.

In early 2021, on learning that Sarah's business had generated losses in 2020 and, at that time, anticipated losses for 2021, Sam had asked whether he could use some of the losses against his own income to obtain an income tax refund. The accountant explained that it would only be possible if the business were considered a partnership, with Sam being considered a partner, and then a portion of the losses could be allocated to him to use against his employment income. The accountant explained that as a sole proprietorship Sarah would be unable to use any of the losses in 2020 or 2021, since she had no other income to apply it against. The accountant explained that the losses would be considered non-capital losses, which could be applied to future years.

In support of an argument that there was a partnership of which Sam was a member they told the accountant that they had registered the business in Ontario under the name "Sarah and Sam's Pottery" and that Sam had provided financing for the business plus co-signed lines of credit. Sam added that their home and the building used for the business were jointly owned by the two of them and that he participated in the business on occasion. The accountant agreed to file Sam and Sarah's income tax return on the basis that the business was a partnership and that Sam was a partner. After discussions with the accountant it was agreed that Sam would be entitled to an 80% interest and Sarah 20%.

Additional Information:

- Sam and Sarah have always had one joint bank account in which Sam's salary and Sarah's monthly child benefits have been deposited. The joint account is used for all family expenditures. Sarah deposited all pottery sales in this same account in 2020 and 2021, but on the advice of her accountant she plans to open a separate bank account for the business in 2022.

- All payments to the business are only made out to Sarah, although invoices are in the same of "Sarah and Sam's Pottery."

- Sarah obtained a credit card in her own name that she uses exclusively for the pottery business. Monthly payments are made from the family joint bank account.

- When the business began in 2020, Sam loaned Sarah $40,000 interest free from funds he had received as an inheritance when his mother passed away. Sam had deposited his inheritance in an investment account under his name. These funds were used to convert their backyard building. There is no written loan agreement between them. Sarah has been making monthly payments to Sam from the business sales, which Sam has been re-depositing to his investment account.

- When the business began, Sarah needed additional financing for working capital to acquire the necessary equipment and materials and pay ongoing expenses. Sarah obtained a commercial bank loan and a line of credit with a local bank. The bank, however, was unwilling to authorize the financing without Sam's signature since Sarah did not have any income of her own at the time. Sam co-signed the bank documents.

- Sarah communicates directly with suppliers, retailers, and makes all decisions concerning the development of new products and obtaining new customers, although she asks Sam for his advice on occasion.

- When at home, Sam assists Sarah by answering the odd phone call and relaying messages to her. He also picks up supplies for her when she is too busy to do it herself and has taken on a bigger responsibility of watching the children when his schedule permits. Sam recently convinced Sarah to donate some of her pieces for a charitable auction for the Ottawa Police Foundation.

- Sarah and her employees signed up for advanced pottery classes in December 2021 that involve woodworking and ceramics. She was able to finance this education without anyone's involvement (including Sam's) given increased sales.

- There is no written partnership agreement.

Required:

A. Do you agree with the decision to file Sam and Sarah's income tax returns on the basis that the pottery business is a partnership? Explain the reasons for your decision.

B. Assuming that a partnership does exist, do you believe that the 80-20 split is justified? Could the CRA challenge the 80-20 split between Sam and Sarah? Explain the reasons for your decision.

C. Had there been a written partnership agreement, would it have supported the existence of a partnership?

AP 18-2   *(Existence of a Partnership)*

Mr. Poliacik joined Mr. Ewing's practice by entering into a business association with Mr. Ewing. They operated under the name "Ewing/Poliacik." Mr. Poliacik made no capital contribution on joining.

Both individuals were lawyers. Mr. Poliacik's specialty was litigation. Mr. Ewing was involved in non-litigation matters.

An agreement was signed, but it never referred to the individuals as partners or the association as a partnership. When asked why they did not refer to themselves as partners, Mr. Poliacik stated that they did not know each other well enough to accept the risks of partnership. The agreement stated that all fees billed by each individual belonged to that individual.

Both individuals agreed to open a combined general and trust bank account. Both individuals had signing authority on the general account, although Mr. Poliacik's authority was limited to client disbursements only. Mr. Ewing had sole signing authority on the trust account. The accounts did not indicate that they were registered to a partnership.

Mr. Poliacik's fees were to be split based on a graduated scale. The first $100,000 was to be split 50-50, then 60-40 on the next $25,000, 80-20 on the next $25,000, and 90-10 thereafter. The larger percentage went to Mr. Poliacik. In addition, Mr. Poliacik was entitled to 10% of fees billed by Mr. Ewing to clients introduced by Mr. Poliacik.

Mr. Ewing agreed to be 100% liable for office expenses and bookkeeping services. Mr. Poliacik's share of the office operating expenses was $62,500 in the first year. This amount would be adjusted in the future as the expenses increased. Mr. Poliacik was not entitled to the 10% finder's fee from Mr. Ewing until his share of the annual expenses had been paid.

Mr. Poliacik was responsible for making his own CPP contributions and maintaining professional insurance. He will register for GST/HST as an individual, and his personal income tax return will not include a separate calculation of partnership income.

The combined business was not registered for GST/HST purposes. There were no filings with the law society indicating that Mr. Poliacik and Mr. Ewing were partners.

Required: Determine whether the business association is a partnership.

AP 18-3   *(Partnership vs. Joint Venture)*

Chantale Bergeron is a real estate agent who had always dreamed of becoming a real estate developer. In 2018, she received a substantial inheritance and purchased land with the intention of developing a number of residential lots. She paid $1,200,000 for the land, which she had secretly learned from contacts would soon be adjacent to a new highway exit.

As Chantale had spent her inheritance purchasing the land and had no track record in the development business, she had difficulty finding financing for the required $700,000 in site servicing costs. She finally located a developer, Elise Ltd., who was willing to provide the required $700,000 on an interest-free basis in return for 40% of the profit from the future sale of the lots.

By December 31, 2021, it was estimated that the FMV of the land had increased to $2,000,000 because of the opening of the highway exit. During 2022, the sites were developed, with the servicing costs coming in at the estimated $700,000. All of the lots are sold prior to December 31, 2022, for total proceeds of $3,700,000.

> **Case A**   On December 31, 2021, Chantale and Elise Ltd. enter into a joint venture agreement. Chantale sells the land to Elise Ltd. on condition that the profits on eventual sales be split as agreed. At the end of 2022, Elise Ltd. provides Chantale with 60% of the profits resulting from the development and sale of the lots.

Case B   On December 31, 2021, Chantale and Elise Ltd. form a partnership to develop the lots. Chantale contributes the land to the partnership on a rollover basis under ITA 97(2). The partnership agreement specifies that Chantale is entitled to all of the deferred gain on the land transfer at December 31, 2021, as well as 60% of the profits resulting from the sale of the lots.

Required: Calculate the amount that will be added to Chantale's 2021 and 2022 net income for Case A and Case B and compare the results.

AP 18-4   *(Partnership Income Allocation)*

Saul and Samuel Brock are brothers and CPAs with significant experience in income tax. Until 2021, they have worked separately. However, they have decided that working together would produce synergies that would increase their total income. Given this, as of January 1, 2021, they form the Brock and Brock Partnership. The partnership will use a calendar-based fiscal period (January 1 to December 31).

Saul will be entitled to a salary of $72,000 per year, while Samuel's salary will be $48,000. In addition, Samuel will receive interest at 6% on his average capital balance for the year. The salary and interest allocations were withdrawn by each of them prior to December 31, 2021.

The components of their partnership agreement dealing with income allocation are as follows:

Business Income   After the allocation of priority amounts for salaries and interest on capital contributions, any remaining business income will be shared 60% to Saul and 40% to Samuel.

Capital Gains   As Samuel has contributed the majority of capital to the partnership, he will be entitled to all capital gains that are realized by the partnership.

Dividends   Any dividends received by the partnership will be shared equally.

For the fiscal period ending December 31, 2021, the financial statements prepared by their accountants using Accounting Standards for Private Enterprises (ASPE) show business income of $649,522. Other relevant information is as follows:

- Salaries to Saul and Samuel of $120,000 ($72,000 + $48,000) were deducted.

- Interest on Samuel's capital contribution of $4,800 was deducted.

- Business meals of $18,976 were deducted.

- Amortization expense of $31,632 was deducted.

- Charitable contributions of $4,520 were deducted.

Other Information

1. The brothers intend to deduct maximum CCA of $38,597 for 2021.

2. The partnership realized $16,164 in capital gains in 2021.

3. The partnership received $10,462 in eligible dividends during 2021.

4. The charitable contributions will be allocated equally between the two brothers.

Required:

A. Determine the amount of partnership income required to be included in the 2021 net income of each brother.

B. Identify the amount of any federal income tax credits that each of the two brothers would be entitled to as a result of allocations made by the partnership for 2021.

AP 18-5   (Partnership Income and ACB)

On January 1, 2021, a partnership is formed between two lawyers who have, for a number of years, practised individually. Each partner initially contributes $70,000.

During 2021, each partner is paid a salary of $125,000, as well as interest on their opening capital balances at an annual rate of 5%. These amounts are all withdrawn during the year. Any business income that remains after priority allocations for salaries and interest will be shared equally by the two partners.

For the fiscal period ending December 31, 2021, the bookkeeper has prepared the following financial statements for the partnership. No amortization expense was deducted in preparing these statements.

Settlements Unlimited
Balance Sheet
As at December 31, 2021

Cash	$ 45,189
Accounts receivable	186,485
Work-in-progress	232,814
Furniture and fixtures	56,581
Computer hardware (cost)	17,608
Computer applications software (cost)	13,440
Total assets	$ 552,117

Accounts payable	$ 109,872
Initial partner capital	140,000
Income for the fiscal period	302,245
Total liabilities and equity	$ 552,117

Settlements Unlimited
Income Statement
For the fiscal period ending December 31, 2021

Revenues	$682,946
Meals and entertainment	$ 23,334
Office supplies	12,382
Partners' salaries	250,000
Interest on capital contributions [(5%)($140,000)]	7,000
Rent	46,440
Non-partner salaries	41,545
Total expenses	$ 380,701
Income for the fiscal period (accounting amounts)	$302,245

The work-in-progress (WIP) represents work done by the lawyers at their standard charge rate that has not been billed to clients at year end. Reported revenues of $682,946 accurately reflect the amount of WIP required to be included in net income for purposes of the ITA.

Required:

A. The lawyers have come to you to determine the minimum amount they must include in their net income for 2021 as business income from the partnership.

B. Determine the ACB of each partner's partnership interest at December 31, 2021, and January 1, 2022.

Your answers should ignore any GST/HST and PST considerations.

AP 18-6   (Partnership Income and Sale of a Partnership Interest)

Michael Masterson and Martin Minton were competitors providing heating and cooling products and services within the same geographical region near Edmonton, Alberta. An influx of workers to the nearby oil fields brought in increased competition, causing Michael and Martin to agree to join forces by forming a general partnership registered as the Double M Partnership. They have both contributed all of their business assets, including vehicles, tools, and equipment, which have become partnership property. In addition, capital cash contributions were required to provide the partnership with much needed working capital.

The general partnership was established on November 12, 2020, after signing a formalized written partnership agreement. The agreement required an initial cash contribution from each partner of $125,000, which was made in December 2020. The agreement further provides that each partner can draw up to a maximum of $10,000 per month to meet personal needs and expenditures beginning January 1, 2021. Profit and loss allocations will be determined at the end of each year based on a formula that considers the number of hours worked and fees invoiced. Any capital gains or capital losses realized will be allocated on a 50-50 basis unless the gain or loss is connected to a contribution of property to the partnership by a specific partner, in which case all of the gain or loss will be allocated to that partner. In addition, any investment income or capital gains/losses realized on investments acquired by the partnership with surplus cash will be allocated equally. Finally, any charitable donations made by the partnership will also be allocated equally.

The partnership operates through leased business premises where the employees and partners carry out the day-to-day management and administration of the business. The partnership uses a calendar-based fiscal period.

The partnership's 2021 income statement, prepared in accordance with ASPE, is as follows:

Income Statement
Double M Partnership
Year Ending December 31, 2021

Revenues		$991,600
Operating expenses:		
Lease of business premises	($84,000)	
Inventory and supplies	(275,000)	
Amortization expense (Note 1)	(31,300)	
General office costs	(27,000)	
Meals and entertainment	(19,100)	
Charitable donations	(10,000)	
Interest on partner loan	(7,000)	
Vehicle operating costs	(41,000)	
Partner home office costs	(30,000)	
Office salaries	(88,600)	(613,000)
Operating income		$378,600
Other income:		
Capital gains (Note 2)	$22,200	
Non-eligible dividends received from private company investment	13,000	35,200
Net accounting income		$413,800

Note 1   Maximum CCA for 2021 is $17,400.

Note 2   In 2021 the partnership realized a capital gain of $13,300 from partnership property contributed by Martin and a second capital gain of $8,900 from the sale of some of the share investments made by the partership. None of the capital gains would qualify for the capital gains deduction.

During 2021, Michael's only income was from the partnership and his only federal tax credit, other than those allocated from or attributable to the partnership, is the basic personal credit.

On January 1, 2022, Michael sells his interest in the partnership to an arm's-length individual for $875,000. Selling costs related to the sale are $7,400. Assume that the ACB of his partnership interest on January 1, 2021, is $222,160.

Additional Information:

A. At December 31, 2021, the partnership accountant determines that Michael worked more hours and invoiced more than Martin. The result is that Michael will be allocated 58.7% of any business income or loss while Martin will be allocated the remaining 41.3%.

B. In February 2021, the partnership used some surplus cash to acquire share investments in a large private corporation that manufactures the type of furnaces the partnership installs and services. The partnership received $13,000 in non-eligible dividends and $4,200 in capital dividends from that investment in December 2021.

C. Both Martin and Michael have offices in their homes to prepare and accumulate monthly paperwork before bringing the documents and summaries to their business premises. The business premises have sufficient office space, but the two partners prefer to prepare some business documentation in their homes. The partnership pays them each $1,250 per month for the use of that office space, and those amounts are deducted by the partnership in determining its business income. Neither of the partners would qualify to deduct home expenses because of the limitations of ITA 18(12).

D. In late December 2020, Michael and Martin met with their accountant to discuss working capital requirements. The accountant advised that they could use an additional $200,000. Michael agreed to loan that amount to the partnership at 3.5% interest, which is paid monthly. There is a written loan agreement that only requires the monthly payment of interest with no principal payments until January 2023.

E. Neither Michael nor Martin made any capital contributions to the partnership in 2021.

F. Each of Michael and Martin withdrew the maximum monthly amount of $10,000 in every month of 2021.

G. The partnership made a donation of $10,000 to the local food bank in May 2021. The food bank is a registered charitable organization for federal income tax purposes.

Required:

1. Determine Michael's 2021 net income and federal income tax payable.

2. Determine the income tax consequences of the sale of Michael's partnership interest in 2022. You will have to provide a detailed breakdown of the ACB of his partnership interest, beginning with the January 1, 2021, balance of $222,160. Show all supporting calculations.

AP 18-7   (Withdrawal of a Partner)
Tammy, Loretta, and Crystal formed a partnership on January 1, 2019. The partnership is organized to provide a variety of consulting services to a broad range of clients. Each partner makes an initial capital contribution of $270,000. The partners agree to use a calendar-based fiscal period.

The partnership agreement contains the following provisions:

1. Both business income and charitable contributions will be shared equally by the three partners.

2. Any capital gains realized by the partnership will be allocated on a 50-50 basis to Crystal and Loretta.

3. All of the eligible dividends received by the partnership will be allocated to Tammy.

Assignment Problems

During the the three-year period January 1, 2019, through December 31, 2021, the partnership operates successfully. The following information relates to that period:

- The partnership earned business income of $315,000.

- Amounts not included in business income were the following:

  - The partnership received eligible dividends totalling $6,300.

  - The partnership realized a $24,800 capital gain.

  - The partnership made charitable donations of $9,900, all of which were made in 2021.

- Withdrawals from the partnership were as follows:

  - Tammy—$149,000

  - Crystal—$306,000

  - Loretta—$72,000

- Additional capital was required to expand the operations of the office and, as a consequence, each partner contributed an additional $104,000 in cash.

Near the end of 2021, after a number of heated arguments between Tammy and Crystal, Loretta decides to withdraw from the partnership effective January 1, 2022. After some negotiations, each of the other partners agree to pay her $210,000 in cash for one-half of her interest in the partnership, a total of $420,000. The payments are made on February 1, 2022. The partnership has business income of $27,600 during January 2022.

Loretta incurred legal and accounting fees in connection with the sale of her partnership interest totalling $2,300.

Required:

A. Calculate the ACB of Loretta's partnership interest as at January 1, 2022.

B. Determine the amount of Loretta's gain or loss on the sale of her partnership interest. Explain how this amount, and any other amounts related to the partnership, will affect her net income for 2022.

C. Indicate how the ACB of each remaining partner's interest will be affected by the withdrawal of Loretta from the partnership.

AP 18-8 (Limited Partnerships—ACB, At-Risk Amount (ARA), and Limited Partnership Losses (LPL))

In mid-December 2020, Rebecca Richardson is approached by her investment advisor with an opportunity to invest in a lucrative limited partnership that will be created in early January 2021. Rebecca has always been willing to invest in somewhat riskier ventures, and she is intrigued by this particular opportunity. After a careful review and discussions with her advisors she agrees to participate and acquires 12.0 limited partnership units of the Junction Enterprises LP that will be created under the *Limited Partnership Act* of Manitoba. The limited partnership fiscal year end will be December 31, and only 400 units will be issued and sold. Each unit will entitle the limited partner unitholder to one-quarter of 1% of any income or loss of the limited partnership.

The terms of the limited partnership offer and agreement require a minimum purchase of two units with a maximum of twelve units for newly admitted limited partners. The per-unit purchase price will be $24,000 and will require a cash down payment of 10% by each unitholder with the remaining amount financed by the general partner at 6.75% annual interest. On the last business day of December 2021, 2022, and 2023, one-third of the principal amount of the financing must be repaid. Finally, each unitholder is personally responsible to pay an annual administration fee to the general partner based on the number of units held.

In addition, to encourage unitholders to remain with the limited partnership for at least three years, the general partner agrees to repurchase all of a limited partners' units at 8% of the purchase price if this option is chosen within the 2021 calendar year; 16% for 2022; and 24% for 2023 and subsequent years.

Rebecca purchases the maximum 12 limited partnership units on January 18, 2021, at $24,000 each for a total price of $288,000. This number of units entitles her to 3.0% [(12 units)(.0025)] of any income or losses of Junction Enterprises LP. She pays 10% of the purchase price of $28,800 and finances the remaining amount of $259,200 through the required financing provided by the general partner.

Junction Enterprises LP earns the following income and realizes the following losses:

- 2021 business loss of $2,000,000 and eligible dividends of $118,000

- 2022 business loss of $4,400,000 and eligible dividends of $104,000

- 2023 business loss of $1,700,000 and eligible dividends of $129,000

Assume that Rebecca will remain a limited partner until 2025. Also assume that she has sufficient other sources of income to fully use any deductible losses allocated to her by the limited partnership, including any deductible limited partnership loss carry overs.

Required: For each of 2021, 2022, and 2023, calculate the following amounts related to Rebecca's limited partnership interest in Junction Enterprises LP:

- The ACB at the beginning of each year

- The ARA at the end of each year

- The limited partnership income or loss for each year

- The deductible annual partnership loss and LPL for each year

- The limited partnership loss carry forward balance at the end of each year

In addition, calculate the ACB of the partnership interest at January 1, 2024.

AP 18-9 *(Incorporating a Partnership)*

The Jones, Haggard, and Twitty Partnership was formed several years ago by Conway Jones, George Haggard, and Merle Twitty. To establish the partnership, each of the individuals invested $450,000 in cash. They prepared a standard partnership agreement providing that all income and losses would be shared equally. The partnership uses a calendar-based fiscal period.

On January 1, 2021, the ACB of the three partners are as follows:

Conway Jones	$ 880,000
George Haggard	698,000
Merle Twitty	567,000
Total	$2,145,000

The tax cost of all partnership property totals $2,145,000, the same amount as the combined ACBs of the three partners. On January 2, 2021, all of the partnership property is sold to a corporation on a rollover basis as a result of an election filed (T2058) under ITA 85(2). The elected amounts equal the tax costs.

An appraisal establishes that the FMV of the partnership is $2,925,000. Based on this amount the corporation pays the purchase price using the following consideration:

Cash	$ 900,000
Preferred shares (FMV)	675,000
Common shares (FMV)	1,350,000
Total consideration	$2,925,000

The partnership will be liquidated within 60 days of the ITA 85(2) rollover, and property received from the corporation by the partnership will be distributed to the three partners in settlement of the partnership interests. ITA 85(3) will apply to dissolve the partnership. Each partner will receive consideration on the partnership dissolution:

	Jones	Haggard	Twitty	Total
Cash	$ 465,000	$283,000	$152,000	$ 900,000
Preferred shares	225,000	225,000	225,000	675,000
Common shares	450,000	450,000	450,000	1,350,000
Total	$1,140,000	$958,000	$827,000	$2,925,000

Required:

A. Determine the ACB of the share consideration assets received by the partners on the dissolution of the partnership.

B. Calculate the income tax consequence of the disposition of the partnership interest for each partner.

AP 18-10   *(Additional Business Income)*

Note   This problem involves knowledge of "additional business income" when the election of a non-calendar fiscal period is made. This material is covered in Chapter 6 of the text.

On April 1, 2019, Craig Cardinal and Don Kvill formed a partnership to carry on a business of providing flying lessons on small aircraft. They elected to use a March 31 fiscal period, to coincide with the end of the winter aircraft maintenance program and the beginning of the summer training schedule. The two partners share equally in the profits and losses of the partnership.

In the partnership income calculation for their 2020 tax returns, the "additional business income" was calculated to be $42,200. During the year ending March 31, 2021, partnership income totalled $64,000 and the partners withdrew $26,000 each.

From April 1, 2021, to March 31, 2022, the partnership earned income of $58,000 and the partners withdrew $20,000 each.

Required: Determine the minimum amount of partnership income that Craig Cardinal and Don Kvill will have to include in their net income for 2021 and 2022.

CHAPTER 19

Trusts and Estate Planning

Learning Objectives

After completing Chapter 19, you should be able to:

1. Explain the basic concepts of trusts from an income tax and legal perspective (Paragraph [P hereafter] 19-1 to 19-15).
2. Explain the difference between a trust and an estate, including the concept of a GRE (P 19-16 to 19-20).
3. Describe what is required to establish a trust (P 19-21 to 19-23).
4. Describe the tax return filing requirement for trusts and when taxes owing must be paid and whether instalments are required (P 19-24 to 19-25).
5. List the major non-tax reasons for using trusts (P 19-26).
6. Describe the different classifications and types of trusts (P 19-27 to 19-46).
7. Explain the basic model for the taxation of trusts (P 19-47 and 19-49).
8. Describe the type of situations that allow rollovers for contributions of property to a trust (P 19-50 to 19-61).
9. Describe the circumstances in which the ITA allows trust property to be distributed tax free to beneficiaries (P 19-62 to 19-66).
10. Describe the reasons for the 21-year rule and the basic concept (P 19-67 to 19-69).
11. Describe some alternatives offered by the ITA that shift income between a trust and beneficiaries, and describe how net income and taxable income are determined for a trust and how it differs from other taxpayers (P 19-70 to 19-81).
12. Describe the treatment of income allocations to beneficiaries (P 19-82 to 19-102).
13. Explain the calculation of federal income tax payable for testamentary and inter vivos trusts (P 19-103 to 19-111).
14. Explain how the attribution rules apply to trusts and any related tax planning considerations (P 19-112 to 19-117).
15. Explain the concept of an income and capital interest in a trust and the income tax implications of each (P 19-118 to 19-123).
16. Describe the major tax planning considerations when evaluating various types of trusts such as family, spousal, and alter ego (P 19-124 to 19-135).
17. List the non-tax and tax factors that should be considered in an evaluation of an estate plan (P 19-136 to 19-138).
18. Explain the general objectives of an estate freeze (P 19-139 and 19-140).

19. Describe the estate freeze techniques that do not involve the use of a rollover (P 19-141 to 19-148).
20. Describe the use of the rollover of ITA 86(1) to implement an estate freeze involving a family trust (P 19-149 to 19-157).
21. Describe the considerations involved in choosing between a rollover under ITA 85 and 86 when implementing an estate freeze (P 19-158 to 19-159).

Introduction

19-1.   The ITA applies to individuals (human beings), corporations, and trusts in the sense that they each file annual income tax returns (T1, T2, or T3). Individuals, at law, have a separate legal existence, meaning that they can own property, enter into contracts, and so on. Corporations also have a separate legal existence, which is granted to them as a result of corporate law in Canada. The notion of a separate legal existence simplifies the application of the ITA since, as legal entities, they can legally enter into transactions that generate income that in turn results in incurring income tax obligations.

19-2.   In Chapter 18 we saw that the ITA applies to partnerships but because partnerships are not legal entities, but rather a legal relationship between the members of the partnership, specific legislation was required to address how the income or loss of a partnership would be taxed. Trusts, with the exception of trust companies, which are corporations, also fall into this non-legal category in that they are not legal entities and therefore do not have a separate legal existence. Trusts, like partnerships, are a legal relationship, but in this case between the persons responsible for its creation and management. As a result, the ITA adds a separate set of legislative rules that apply exclusively to trusts, in a manner similar to partnerships.

19-3.   The comparison between partnerships and trusts is interesting since the rules of the ITA effectively treat trusts as if they were a legal entity for all purposes, whereas partnerships are only treated as a legal entity for the purpose of computing income or loss. Both partnerships and trusts, however, are flow-through vehicles in the sense that income earned flows through to members of a partnership, fully retaining the character of the income or loss. In the case of a trust, distributions of income to trust beneficiaries also benefit from a similar flow-through concept, but it is not as comprehensive as is the case with partnerships.

19-4.   A well-rounded understanding of corporations, trusts, and partnerships is essential to determining an optimal tax planning structure, evaluating the effectiveness of acceptable tax planning alternatives, and aligning the plans with the tax objectives of individuals in the most cost-effective manner. In terms of trusts this means having a good understanding of trust basics together with how the rules of the ITA apply once a trust has been established. In recent years legislative changes have limited the usefulness of testamentary trusts (trusts that are created on the death of an individual) by limiting access to low tax rates, expanding the tax on split income (TOSI, discussed in Chapter 11) to a wider range of individuals, and adding new trust reporting rules that increase the amount of information that needs to be provided to the CRA, thus escalating the probability of a CRA audit. These and other factors must be carefully considered when deciding on the role that trusts play in any tax planning.

19-5.   In this text we have discussed various trust income tax issues as they have arisen in relation to the subjects of previous chapters. For example, in Chapter 1 we discussed how to determine the residency of a trust; in Chapter 2 the new trust reporting rules were discussed; in Chapter 7 we added the income tax consequences when distributions are made by a mutual fund trust to investors; and Chapter 10 dealt with deferred income plans such as RRSPs and TFSAs, which are all trusts. In this chapter we focus our attention on the general rules affecting the taxation of trusts and its beneficiaries with emphasis on personal trusts, which are either trusts established during an individual's lifetime or trusts that arise as a result of the death of an individual (e.g., an estate). In addition, we have added a section on the use of trusts in tax planning to demonstrate one of the more common types of planning that applies where trusts are used in an estate freeze. We discussed the use of corporations in estate freeze planning in Chapter 17.

Basic Concepts

What Is a Trust?

Legal Perspective

19-6.   From a legal perspective, a trust is a relationship that arises when a person responsible for the creation of the trust (the settlor) transfers the ownership of property to a person (a trustee) who is responsible to administer the property for the benefit of others (the beneficiaries). This relationship is depicted in Figure 19-1. It is the contractual relationship between the settlor and trustee in terms of the trust property that defines a trust. The essence of a trust is that property ownership is split between the trustee who has legal ownership (i.e., title) and the beneficiaries who possess the beneficial ownership of the property.

19-7.   The settlor is the person who transfers ownership of property that represents the trust fund. The settlor decides the purpose or objectives of the trust, and finally it is the settlor who provides the necessary authority or power to the trustee to oversee and manage the trust. In general the role of the settlor ends once the trust has been established. In practice the settlor may continue to have a role in the trust as the trustee or as a beneficiary or both. The ongoing involvement of the settlor in the trust can have adverse income tax implications, however, since the basic tax policy premise is that the settlor provides the property and steps away. The new trust reporting requirements (see Chapter 2) require that the trust disclose the settlor's ongoing involvement with the trust, particularly where the settlor has the power to exert control over the trust and override decisions of the trustee.

19-8.   The trustee is the person (individual or institution such as a trust company) that holds legal title to the trust property for the benefit of others (the beneficiaries). The trustee administers the trust under the terms of the trust documents referred to as the trust deed or indenture that set out the various powers of the trustee, including distribution of income and capital to beneficiaries. The trustee must also abide by common-law principles and other law within the particular jurisdiction, such as *Trustee Acts* that exist in many provinces. As a result the legal obligations of a trustee include (1) treating the beneficiaries equally and impartially; (2) acting personally, meaning they cannot generally delegate their responsibilities to others; and (3) keeping the beneficiaries informed, including accounting to them for the administration of the trust.

19-9.   Beneficiaries are named persons or a class of persons who have been identified as potentially benefitting from the trust property. Beneficiaries are generally not active in the affairs of the trust with their role relegated to enforcing any rights they may have to the income or capital of the trust as set out in the trust documents. The ITA refers to beneficiaries with potential entitlements to income as "income beneficiaries" with an ownership interest referred to as an "income interest." On the other hand, those beneficiaries who have a potential entitlement to the capital of the trust are referred to as "capital beneficiaries" with an ownership interest referred to as a "capital interest." Beneficiaries may have both an income and capital interest.

19-10.   While each of the three roles of settlor, trustee, and beneficiary is separate and distinct, there are generally no restrictions that prevent a person from occupying multiple roles. A common example of this would be a parent who is the settlor of a trust in favour of children, but who also serves as one of the trustees to maintain some semblance of control over the trust property. An illustration of this multiple role concept would be a cottage owned by parents who wish to ensure that their five adult children have equal access to and use of the property and perhaps a shared entitlement to rental profits when the cottage is not being used by the family.

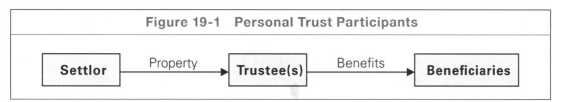

Figure 19-1   Personal Trust Participants

Settlor → Property → **Trustee(s)** → Benefits → **Beneficiaries**

The parents, as settlors, would transfer the ownership of the cottage to a trust in which the parents are also trustees. The beneficiaries would be the five adult children, and potentially the parents as well. This would mean that the parents would occupy all three trust roles.

19-11.   When a trust is created where the settlor and the trustee(s) are the same, a "declaration of trust" is required, which legally means that property owned by the parents (the cottage) is declared to be held in trust for the beneficiaries. This is the same concept that applies when minor children receive cash gifts from others that are held in bank accounts by the parents.

19-12.   Once a trust has been established it is generally difficult to vary or terminate it. This is of particular importance in the case of a trust created on the death of an individual. While the content of a will (e.g., the trust document) can be challenged by a disgruntled beneficiary and its intentions altered by a surviving spouse, this is a much more difficult process with respect to property that has become property of a trust. In addition, the ability of a settlor to change or terminate a trust implies that the trust property can be recovered, which is inconsistent with the tax policy objectives of stepping away. Adverse income tax implications can occur even if that right to change or terminate the trust is never acted upon.

Tax Perspective

19-13.   Consistent with the legal perspective of trusts, the T3 trust guide (T4013) defines a trust as a binding obligation enforceable by law when undertaken. This definition also notes that it may be created by a person (either verbally or in writing), a court order, or by a statute.

19-14.   While trusts do not have a separate legal existence and are therefore not a legal entity separate from the trustees, the ITA treats trusts as a separate taxable entity, which requires meeting and complying with the same income tax obligations as would be the case for individuals and corporations, such as filing an annual income tax return (T3). ITA 104(1) and 104(2) are responsible for this income tax treatment:

> **ITA 104(1)**   In this Act, a reference to a trust or estate (in this subdivision referred to as a "trust") ... be read to include a reference to the trustee ... having ownership and control of the trust property ...

> **ITA 104(2)**   A trust shall, for the purposes of this Act, and without affecting the liability of the trustee or legal representative for that person's own income tax, be deemed to be in respect of the trust property an individual ...

19-15.   Together these two provisions treat a trust or an estate as a trust, which in turn is treated as an individual that is represented by the trustee. Since an "individual" is defined in terms of a legal entity (i.e., a human being), the effect is that a trust is given the same status but only for income tax purposes. The ITA clarifies that the income tax obligations of the trustee for his own personal affairs are separate from his responsibility to the trust and its property. This would prevent the CRA from ceasing trust property to settle a personal tax liability of a trustee.

Trusts and Estates

19-16.   When an individual dies, her property is actually disposed of to others, such as the executor of an estate, a trust, or to certain persons who are generally determined in accordance with one's will or provincial intestate legislation in the absence of a will. The ITA alters this somewhat by deeming a disposition for income tax purposes of certain property such as capital property to have taken place while the individual was alive. In addition, the ITA establishes the proceeds of disposition (POD) at either fair market value (FMV) or a lesser amount depending on the new owner of that property. This overall treatment ensures that any income tax liability with respect to that property is legally attached to the estate of the deceased individual and sets the income tax attributes of that property to the new owner.

19-17.   In this context, an "estate" is legally defined as the sum of all of the property of a deceased individual, including legal rights, interests, and entitlements to property of any kind less any liabilities. Based on this comprehensive definition, an individual can only have one estate.

The estate will be administered by an individual or trust company named in a will to settle the estate of the deceased in accordance with the will.

19-18.   In the great majority of cases, the estate property will pass to a beneficiary or beneficiaries immediately and will not require much attention from advisors. For example, Mom dies, leaving all of her property, which consists of a savings account and a principal residence, both of which are jointly held with Dad, to Dad. There are no income tax concerns in this type of situation and therefore we do not need to devote any attention to this case.

19-19.   However, some estates are quite extensive with many different types of property. This can include shares of private and public corporations, rental properties, businesses, and foreign investments. In such cases, there may be a considerable period of time between the date on which the individual dies and the date on which all of the estate is distributed to beneficiaries. During this period, the estate is administered by an executor (the equivalent to a trustee). The estate may earn income throughout this period and, as a result, will have to file an annual income tax return to account for any income.

19-20.   As a rule, personal trusts are subject to the highest federal income tax bracket of 33% on all of its income. It is therefore generally important to ensure that trust income is distributed to beneficiaries who would then be subject to income tax at their own personal lower income tax rates. In terms of estates, however, the concept of a graduated rate estate (GRE) applies where a trust is established on the death of an individual. This GRE status provides, as one of its benefits, that graduated federal income tax rates apply for a period of three years. This means that any income is taxed federally in the same manner as individuals, beginning with the 15% federal income tax bracket.

Establishing a Trust

Three Certainties

19-21.   The use of a trust in tax planning requires that a trust be established at law at a point in time. This means ensuring that all the necessary steps have been taken consistent with the law of the particular jurisdiction. In Canada, all provinces and territories, with the exception of Quebec (which is a civil law jurisdiction), apply the common law, which sets out legal necessities to establish a trust. These necessities are referred to as the three certainties, each of which must be met to ensure the creation of a trust, which also requires an actual transfer of property ownership or a declaration of trust where the settlor and trustee are the same. The new trust reporting rules will undoubtedly lead to increased scrutiny of trusts by the CRA, particularly trusts used to split income among family members. This increases the importance of ensuring that a trust can be defended on the basis that it has been properly established.

19-22.   The three certainties can be described as follows:

Certainty of Intention   The person creating the trust must intend to create the trust and that intention must be clear to outside observers. This is usually accomplished by preparing a written document clearly establishing the trust and that the conduct of the settlor is consistent with the agreement.

Certainty of Property   The property that is to be held in the trust must be known with certainty at the time the trust is created. This is usually accomplished by clearly defining the property in the trust document.

Certainty of Beneficiaries   The persons or class of persons who will benefit from the trust property must be ascertained or be capable of being ascertained. Beneficiaries do not have to be named, but the trust must clarify who is a beneficiary and who is not. This means that persons must either be specifically identified (named as persons, such as Ms. Sally Phar) or be part of an identifiable class (e.g., my children). When a class designation is used, it must refer to a clearly identifiable group of persons. For example, designating "friends" as beneficiaries would not create an identifiable group. In summary, it must be possible to identify whether a person is or is not a beneficiary.

19-23.   Failure to meet any of the three certainties means that a trust has not been created. In addition to the three certainties there must be an actual transfer of the settlor's property to the trustee. The transfer of ownership must be final and irrevocable unless the trust document contains a revocation clause. Transfers of property must be gratuitous (e.g., no consideration is paid). Sales of property by a settlor to the trustee at FMV would therefore not be considered a valid transfer of ownership. In summary, both the three certainties and the transfer of property from the settlor to the trustee are required to establish a trust.

Exercise 19-1

Subject: Establishing a Trust

In each of the following cases, an individual is attempting to establish a trust. For each of these cases, indicate whether the attempt has been successful. Explain your conclusion.

Case A   Jack Black sends a cheque to his sister to be used for the education of her two children.

Case B   Jane Folsem transfers property ownership to a trustee, specifying that the income from the property should be distributed to her friends.

Case C   Robert Jones transfers property ownership to a trustee, specifying that the income from the property should be distributed to his children.

Case D   Suzanne Bush has signed an agreement that specifies that she will transfer her securities portfolio to a trustee, with the income to be distributed to her spouse.

Solutions to Exercises are available in the Study Guide.

Returns and Payments—Trusts

19-24.   Trusts must file income tax returns no later than 90 days after a trust's taxation year end, which is generally based on a calendar year ending December 31. In addition, any income tax owing must also be paid within 90 days of the year end. Trusts that are GREs are legislatively exempt from a requirement to pay instalments, and most other trusts are administratively exempt from making instalments.

19-25.   The CRA will, consistent with the administrative position not to require instalment payments, not apply penalties and interest to insufficient instalment payments. Other penalties and interest that apply to individuals equally apply to trusts such as those for late filing or late payment of taxes.

Non-Tax Reasons for Using Trusts

19-26.   Our coverage is principally concerned with the income tax planning uses of trusts. However, the use of trusts has many purposes that are not tax motivated. Some of these non-tax uses are as follows:

Administration of Assets   A trust can be used to separate the administration of assets from the receipt of benefits. For example, an individual with extensive investment knowledge might have assets transferred to a trust for a spouse or common-law partner on death. The objective would be to provide professional management of the investments for beneficiaries with limited knowledge of investments.

Protection from Creditors   An individual proprietor of a business might transfer ownership of business properties to a trust to protect them from claims by business creditors. However, if this transfer of ownership is made at a time when the individual is in financial difficulty and the intent was to evade creditor obligations, there are provisions in other legislation that may nullify the transfer, allowing creditors to file claims to the property in settlement of debt.

Privacy   If assets are bequeathed in a will, they will be subject to probate, the results of which are available to the public. This is not the case where assets become trust property on the death of an individual.

Avoiding Subsequent Changes in Beneficiaries   If a parent transfers ownership in property to a trust for the benefit of his minor children, then the minor children will become the ultimate beneficiaries of the property. In contrast, if, as is common, the will of a parent results in the transfer of all property to a surviving spouse or common-law partner with the intention that their children will be the ultimate beneficiaries, there is no legal obligation on the part of the surviving spouse to carry out that intention. This can be a particularly important issue if the surviving spouse remarries. In this latter situation, property of the former deceased spouse could become property of persons other than the minor children.

Classification of Trusts

Introduction

19-27.   The notion of a trust is that property is contributed by a person to another person who then holds and uses that property for the benefit of others. This concept explains why RRSPs are trusts, since an individual (the settlor) makes a gratuitous contribution that is administered by a bank (the trustee) for the ultimate benefit of the individual or a spouse or common-law partner (the beneficiary) at some future time. Similar trust arrangements are recognized throughout the ITA that provide some income tax advantage (generally that income earned in the trust is tax exempt) for disabled persons, employees under certain conditions, environmental or health issues, education, and so on. The result is that there are dozens of specific types of trusts recognized by the ITA, all with their own unique definitions and conditions.

19-28.   Trusts are also categorized using popular expressions that have no exact match in the ITA such as family trusts, which are generally viewed as trusts established during one's lifetime for the benefit of family members, and protective trusts that are often established in offshore jurisdictions to protect one's assets from all claims, including income tax.

19-29.   It is not our objective to provide comprehensive coverage of all categories of trusts. Our coverage will focus on trusts that have been established by individuals as part of a tax or estate planning scenario. This broad range of trusts, which would include family trusts, is covered under the main trust category ITA definition referred to simply as "personal trusts."

Personal Trusts

General Definition
19-30.   The *ITA* contains the following definition of a personal trust:

ITA 248(1)   Personal Trust means

(a) a graduated rate estate, or

(b) a trust in which no beneficial interest was acquired for consideration payable directly or indirectly to

  (i) the trust, or
  (ii) any person or partnership that has made a contribution to the trust by way of transfer, assignment or other disposition of property.

Figure 19-2 Classification of Personal Trusts	
Testamentary	**Inter Vivos**
Graduated rate estate Spousal or common-law partner Other beneficiaries joint	Spousal or common-law partner Alter ego Joint Spousal or common-law partner Family

19-31.   A personal trust, therefore, automatically includes GREs and a trust where no beneficiary paid to acquire her interest in the trust. A family trust would qualify as a personal trust since no beneficiary would have paid something to acquire the beneficial interest. A mutual fund trust, however, would fail to qualify as a personal trust since beneficiaries (the investors) purchase their interest either directly from the trust or from other trust investors.

19-32.   Personal trusts enjoy a number of income tax advantages not afforded to the other types of trusts. Some of the key advantages include access to the capital gains deduction, the principal residence exemption, and the ability to make a capital distribution to capital beneficiaries on a tax-free rollover basis.

Testamentary vs. Inter Vivos Trusts

19-33.   Personal trusts can be further classified based on whether they are established during one's lifetime (inter vivos) or whether they are established on the death of an individual (testamentary). Testamentary trusts are defined as follows:

> **ITA 108(1)   Testamentary Trust** in a taxation year means a trust that arose on and as a consequence of the death of an individual ...

19-34.   Inter vivos trusts are defined as follows:

> **ITA 108(1)   Inter Vivos Trust** means a trust other than a testamentary trust.

19-35.   Within each of these classifications, there are various subclassifications. In this chapter, we will describe three types of testamentary trusts and four types of inter vivos trusts. The types that we will cover are outlined in Figure 19-2.

Testamentary Trusts

Graduated Rate Estates (GREs)

19-36.   GREs are defined in ITA 248(1) as follows:

> **ITA 248(1)   graduated rate estate,** of an individual at any time, means the estate that arose on and as a consequence of the individual's death if
>
> (a)   that time is no more than 36 months after the death,
> (b)   the estate is at that time a testamentary trust,
> (c)   the individual's Social Insurance Number (or if the individual had not, before the death, been assigned a Social Insurance Number, such other information as is acceptable to the Minister) is provided in the estate's return of income under Part I for the taxation year that includes that time ...
> (d)   the estate designates itself as the graduated rate estate of the individual in its return of income under Part I for its first taxation year ... and
> (e)   no other estate designates itself as the graduated rate estate of the individual in a return of income under Part I for a taxation year ...

19-37.   The main income tax advantages of GRE status include the following:

- The ability to calculate tax payable using the graduated rates that apply to individuals, rather than having tax payable calculated at the maximum rate of 33% on income.

- The ability to use a non-calendar fiscal period.
- Classification as a personal trust without regard to the circumstances in which the beneficial interest was acquired. This means that a GRE carries with it the ability to use the tax advantages referred to in Paragraph 19-32 as well as a few others, including the ability to carry back certain losses in the first year of the GRE to the final taxation year of the deceased (ITA 164(6)).
- Exemption from the requirement to make instalment payments.
- Use of the $40,000 exemption in calculating alternative minimum tax.
- Extended periods for refunds, reassessment, and filing of objections.

19-38. The GRE definition only allows this preferential status for a maximum period of 36 months, which is generally considered sufficient time to make all distributions to beneficiaries. GRE status ends on the day it makes the final distribution as long as the distribution is made within the 36-month period. If the final distribution is not made within 36 months the trust becomes a regular testamentary trust that must use a calendar year end.

> **EXAMPLE 1**   Gary Crotty dies on November 1, 2021. His estate (all of his property at death) consists entirely of shares of public listed corporations. Under the terms of his will the ownership of the shares are immediately transferred to a trust exclusively for his spouse.

> **ANALYSIS — Example 1**   Since all of the property of the estate has been transferred to a spousal trust beneficiary, no designation can be made to treat the estate as a GRE. In effect, the estate has been fully administered and a final distribution made on the first day. Technically the estate qualifies as a GRE for one day, although there would be no benefit to designating that status as there would not have been any estate income.

> **EXAMPLE 2**   Lizabeth Jerrard dies on November 1, 2021. Her will requires that all of her estate be transferred to a spousal trust. Her estate consists of a large number of investments in real estate and CCPC shares, some of which will take considerable time to dispose of or transfer. As of December 31, 2024, the estate administration is not yet complete as some investments still remain under the administration of the executor.

> **ANALYSIS — Example 2**   The executor will be required to file an annual income tax return (T3) for any income earned. The estate can be designated as a GRE and can select a year end as late as October 31. If October 31 is selected, the first return will cover the period November 1, 2021, to October 31, 2022, and will be due 90 days later on January 29, 2023, along with any income taxes owing.

> The final taxation year end as a GRE will be for the year ending October 31, 2024, which is 36 months after the day the individual died. A new year starting November 1, 2024, will apply as a non-GRE testamentary trust ending December 31, 2024. Any income earned in that period will be subject to the maximum federal tax rate of 33%. If the trust continues after December 31, 2024, the year end will remain as December 31 in each successive year until final distributions are made, at which time the trust will have a final year end on that date.

19-39. Two additional points are relevant:

- Because GREs are included in the definition of a personal trust, a decision can be made to tax the income to the GRE at graduated rates assuming that the executor is not required to make income distributions to beneficiaries. Once the income of the GRE has been subject to income tax, the after-tax funds can be distributed to the beneficiaries as a tax-free distribution of capital.

- GRE status can be designated as long as the estate has not been fully administered and all property distributed. This means that estate property can be distributed to some beneficiaries without losing GRE status.

Spousal or Common-Law Partner Trust

19-40.   This category of trust is not specifically defined in the ITA. Rather, it is an expression used when a trust is established exclusively for a spouse or common-law partner. As shown in Figure 19-2, such trusts can either be an inter vivos trust established by a living person or, alternatively, a testamentary trust that is established when an individual dies. A spousal or common-law partner testamentary trust created by a will can never be designated as a GRE since the will brings the administration of an estate to an immediate end. In effect, an estate is not formed on the death of an individual as a result of all of the property of the estate becoming property of the trust on death.

19-41.   The benefit of qualifying as a spousal or common-law partner trust is that the ITA provides the settlor with the ability to transfer ownership of property to the trust on a rollover basis, meaning that there will be no income tax implications to the settlor. Without this ability the transfer of property ownership would occur at FMV (ITA 69(1)(b)(ii)). The relevant rollover provisions are found in ITA 73(1.01) for inter vivos trusts and in ITA 70(6) for testamentary trusts.

Other Beneficiaries

19-42.   Although listed in Figure 19-2 as a type of trust, other beneficiaries joint trusts represent testamentary trusts that are not a spousal or common-law partner trust. Common other beneficiaries would be children or other close relatives of the deceased.

Inter Vivos Trusts

Spousal or Common-Law Partner Trust

19-43.   As noted in Paragraph 19-40, spousal or common-law partner trusts can be established as testamentary trusts on the death of an individual or, alternatively, as inter vivos trusts during the lifetime of an individual.

Alter Ego Trust

19-44.   An alter ego trust is an inter vivos trust created by an individual (the settlor) who is 65 years of age or older and who is the sole beneficiary. As was the case with spousal or common-law partner trusts, if certain conditions are met the ITA *provides rollover treatment with respect to property contributed to the trust by the settlor or property distributed from the trust to the beneficiary/settlor.*

Joint Spousal or Common-Law Partner Trust

19-45.   A joint spousal or joint common-law partner trust is an inter vivos trust created by an individual who is 65 years of age or older. Similar to the alter ego trust, this type of trust is created with an individual and her spouse or common-law partner as the sole beneficiaries during their lifetimes. Also similar to alter ego trusts, if certain conditions are met the same rollover treatment is available with respect to property contributed to the trust and distributed from the trust.

Family Trust

19-46.   While the expression "family trust" is not used in the ITA, it generally refers to a trust that has been established by an individual for the benefit of family members. While a family trust could be a testamentary trust, the term is usually used in reference to an inter vivos trust. The most common goal of this type of trust is income splitting. The extension of the TOSI to include related adults has reduced some of the benefits of this type of planning.

Taxation of Trusts

Taxation Year

19-47.   With the exception of two types of trusts, the taxation year of a trust is based on the calendar year end of December 31. The first day of a taxation year begins the day the trust is established and ends on the day the trust is terminated or, in the case of an estate, final distributions to beneficiaries and others are made.

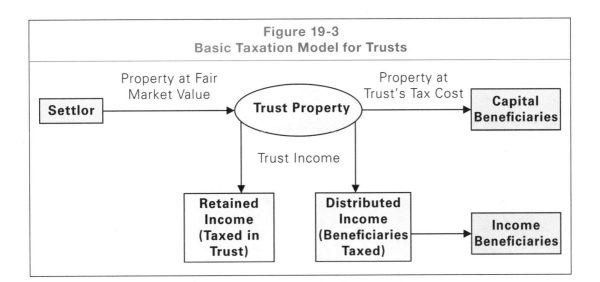

Figure 19-3
Basic Taxation Model for Trusts

19-48. The two exceptions are (1) mutual fund trusts, which have a December 15 taxation year end, and (2) GREs, which can choose any taxation year end as long as it is within one year of the day the GRE is established, which is the day an individual dies. If, for example, an individual dies August 5, 2021, the fiscal period chosen could be as late as August 4, 2022.

The Basic Taxation Model

19-49. While there are always exceptions to the rules, and many additional rules that are specific to certain types of trusts, the basic model for the taxation of trusts is as shown in Figure 19-3. There are three features to this model:

Settlor's Transfer of Property When property ownership is transferred by a settlor on the establishment of a trust, it results in a disposition of property for income tax purposes. The default FMV rule of ITA 69(1)(b) applies to deem the settlor to have received proceeds equal to FMV and that the cost to the trust is the same amount. As a result, there would be income tax implications to the settlor in terms of potential income, capital gains, recapture, or terminal losses depending on the nature of the property disposed. This default FMV rule, however, can be overridden by various rollover provisions that are discussed later in this chapter.

Transfers of Trust Property to Beneficiaries Where trust property is distributed to a capital beneficiary, ITA 107(2) provides rollover treatment allowing the proceeds of disposition to the trust and cost to the beneficiary to equal the tax cost to the trust, which avoids any immediate income tax implications to both parties. Exceptions to this general rollover provision are also discussed later in this chapter.

Income from Trust Property A trust can earn income with respect to property contributed to it and property that it has acquired. It is fundamental to the taxation of trusts that any income actually distributed by the trust to beneficiaries or income to which beneficiaries have an enforceable right or claim is deductible to the trust in determining its net income. In many situations it is common for trusts to distribute all income, reducing its taxable income and therefore tax payable to nil. This is particularly important if a trust is subject to the highest federal income tax rate of 33% while beneficiaries are subject to lower rates.

Any income that a trust does not distribute to beneficiaries or to which beneficiaries have an enforceable right will be part of the taxable income of the trust and subject to income tax. Subsequent distribution of the after-tax income is not subject to income tax to beneficiaries as it is not income to them but represents a capital distribution.

Exercise 19-2

Subject: Basic Taxation of Trusts

On January 1, 2021, Joanne March transfers ownership of investments with a FMV of $220,000 to establish an inter vivos trust for her 28-year-old daughter, Jocelyn, who will be the only beneficiary. The cost of the investments to Joanne March was $200,000. During 2021, the investments earn interest of $15,000, all of which is distributed to Jocelyn. On January 1, 2022, the investments are distributed to Jocelyn in satisfaction of her capital interest in the trust. At this time, the FMV of the investments have increased to $230,000. Jocelyn sells all of the investments for $230,000 on January 5, 2022. Joanne is not a trustee of the inter vivos trust.

Indicate the income tax consequences for Joanne, Jocelyn, and the trust in each of the 2021 and 2022 taxation years.

Solutions to Exercises are available in the Study Guide.

Rollovers to a Trust

Introduction

19-50.   The basic taxation model for trusts generally requires that contributions by a settlor to establish a trust be deemed to have been made at FMV. This default concept can discourage the use of a trust given the potential income tax implications of a disposition of property at FMV. However, there are a number of exceptions to this default FMV rule that permits a disposition at tax cost, avoiding any immediate income tax implications. This rollover treatment exists for spousal or common-law partner trusts, alter ego trusts, and joint spousal or common-law partner trusts provided certain specific conditions are met.

19-51.   In this section we turn our attention to the conditions necessary to ensure that these three special types of trusts qualify for the rollover treatment. When the trust qualifies, the proceeds to the settlor are set at the tax cost of the property contributed. Tax cost would mean the adjusted cost base (ACB) for non-depreciable capital property and the undepreciated capital cost (UCC) for depreciable property. The trust would inherit the tax cost of the property to the settlor and, in the case of depreciable property, be considered to have retained the capital cost and previously claimed capital cost allowance (CCA). In effect, the trusts steps into the shoes of the settlor with respect to the tax attributes of the property as if the property contributed had always belonged to the trust.

19-52.   We will revisit these three types of trusts in a later section on tax planning. At that point we will discuss how these trusts can be used to reduce or defer income tax.

Qualifying Spousal or Qualifying Common-Law Partner Trust

19-53.   In Chapter 9 we discussed transfers of capital property ownership between spouses and common-law partners, noting that direct transfers could be undertaken for income tax purposes on a rollover basis at the tax cost of the property to the owner. ITA 73(1.01) applies to inter vivos transfers whereas ITA 70(6) applies rollover treatment as a consequence of death.

19-54.   These two rollovers that authorize direct transfers of property ownership also apply to indirect transfers where the property becomes property of a trust in favour of a spouse or common-law partner. However, transfers to a trust must meet certain additional conditions to qualify for the rollover. In this text, we refer to spousal and common-law partner trusts that qualify for the rollover treatment because they meet the conditions of the ITA simply as qualifying spousal or qualifying common-law partner trusts.

19-55.   With respect to inter vivos spousal or common-law partner trusts, the conditions for qualifying for the rollover are as follows:

ITA 73(1.01)(c)(i)   The individual's spouse or common-law partner is entitled to receive all of the income of the trust that arises before the spouse's or common-law partner's death and no person except the spouse or common-law partner may, before the spouse's or common-law partner's death, receive or otherwise obtain the use of any of the income or capital of the trust.

19-56.   A similar provision provides the rollover conditions for testamentary spousal or common-law partner trusts:

ITA 70(6)(b)   A trust, created by the taxpayer's will, that was resident in Canada immediately after the time the property vested indefeasibly in the trust and under which

(i)   the taxpayer's spouse or common-law partner is entitled to receive all of the income of the trust that arises before the spouse's or common-law partner's death, and

(ii)   no person except the spouse or common-law partner may, before the spouse's or common-law partner's death, receive or otherwise obtain the use of any of the income or capital of the trust.

Vested indefeasibly means that the trust has the right to absolute ownership of the property. This would generally not be the case where there is a legal dispute, such as a challenge to the will or trust that blocks the transfer of property ownership until resolved.

19-57.   While these rollover provisions are, in general, a desirable way to avoid paying income taxes on transfers of ownership to a spousal or common-law partner trust, there may be circumstances where an individual would prefer a transfer at FMV. For example, if the settlor of the trust has available net capital losses or access to the capital gains deduction that could apply to capital gains on contributed property, he might wish to realize the capital gains. The result would be that there could be no or little income tax while increasing the tax cost of the properties to the trust to FMV. Fortunately, the settlor has the option of electing that the rollover not apply. In that case the transfer would be deemed to take place at FMV. For inter vivos transfers, this election is authorized under ITA 73(1) and ITA 70(6.2) for testamentary transfers. The election is made by the settlor for inter vivos transfers and by the settlor's legal representative for testamentary transfers.

Exercise 19-3

Subject: Transfer to Spousal Trust

Louise died late this year and bequeathed common share investments to a qualifying spousal trust created in her will. Louise is survived by her spouse who is to receive the shares from the trust in accordance with the terms of the trust documents three years to the day of her death. At the time of death the ACB of the shares was $60,000 and the FMV $90,000. Determine the income tax consequences of the transfer of the shares to the trust on death, including the ACB of the shares to the trust and to the surviving spouse on the subsequent distribution from the trust.

Solutions to Exercises are available in the Study Guide.

Alter Ego Trust

19-58.   An alter ego trust is an inter vivos trust created by an individual (the settlor) who is 65 years of age or older at the time the trust is settled and who is the sole beneficiary. An alter ego trust qualifies for rollover treatment if it meets the following conditions:

ITA 73(1.01)(c)(ii)   The individual is entitled to receive all of the income of the trust that arises before the individual's death and no person except the individual may, before the individual's death, receive or otherwise obtain the use of any of the income or capital of the trust.

19-59.   An individual settlor can elect out of rollover treatment, choosing instead to apply the disposition of property at FMV. However, if the election is made to avoid rollover treatment then the trust will not qualify as an alter ego trust.

Joint Spousal or Joint Common-Law Partner Trust

19-60.   A joint spousal or common-law partner trust is an inter vivos trust established by a settlor who is 65 years of age or older at the time the trust is settled. Both the settlor and a spouse or common-law partner are required to be the sole beneficiaries of the trust. To qualify for rollover treatment the following conditions must be met:

ITA 73(1.01)(c)(iii) either

(A) the individual or the individual's spouse is, in combination with the other, entitled to receive all of the income of the trust that arises before the later of the death of the individual and the death of the spouse and no other person may, before the later of those deaths, receive or otherwise obtain the use of any of the income or capital of the trust, or

(B) the individual or the individual's common-law partner is, in combination with the other, entitled to receive all of the income of the trust that arises before the later of the death of the individual and the death of the common-law partner and no other person may, before the later of those deaths, receive or otherwise obtain the use of any of the income or capital of the trust.

19-61.   An individual can elect out of the rollover, choosing to have the transfer to the trust take place at FMV.

Exercise 19-4

Subject: Transfers to Trusts

An individual owns common shares with an ACB of $1,000 and a current FMV of $1,600. Seven scenarios are presented for the transfer of the ownership of these shares by the settlor to establish a trust. For each scenario, indicate the income tax consequences to the settlor at the time of transfer, as well as the ACB of the shares to the trust.

Scenario 1:	Transfer to an inter vivos trust for an adult child
Scenario 2:	Transfer to an inter vivos trust for a minor child
Scenario 3:	Transfer to a testamentary trust for a friend
Scenario 4:	Transfer to an inter vivos qualifying spousal trust
Scenario 5:	Transfer to a testamentary qualifying spousal trust
Scenario 6:	Transfer to a joint spousal trust
Scenario 7:	Transfer to an alter ego trust

Solutions to Exercises are available in the Study Guide.

Rollovers to Capital Beneficiaries
General Rule

19-62.   As is the case with transfers of property ownership by a settlor to a trust, the distribution of property to a capital beneficiary in full or partial settlement of her capital interest in the trust is a disposition of property by the trust. However, for many trusts ITA 107(2) provides rollover treatment for these transfers. The rollover deems the proceeds to the trust and the cost to the beneficiary to equal the tax cost of the property to the trust. The tax attributes of the property are retained in the hands of the beneficiary such that for depreciable property the capital cost to the trust becomes the capital cost to the beneficiary and the CCA previously claimed by the trust is considered CCA claimed by the beneficiary. The result is that there are no tax consequences to the trust and the beneficiary inherits the tax attributes of the property to the trust.

Exceptions

19-63.   In general the realization of capital gains is avoidable where property ownership moves between spouses and common-law partners as long as no other persons can obtain any economic advantages of the property such as the ability to access any income from the property or part of a capital gain of the property. This concept applies equally when property ownership moves to a trust exclusively for the benefit of spouses or common-law partners. In terms of the ITA, Paragraphs 19-50 to 19-60 detailed the specific provisions that authorized rollover treatment. ITA 107(2) continues that rollover notion by allowing property to be distributed to capital beneficiaries in these circumstances. The economic effect is equivalent to what would have occurred had the property ownership been made directly between spouses or common-law partners rather than through a trust.

19-64.   The ITA 107(2) rollover also applies in situations where a trust is created other than for one's self (alter ego) or spouse or common-law partner. In these instances a settlor is deemed to have disposed of capital property at FMV and the trust is deemed to have acquired the property at a cost equal to that FMV. If an individual were to gift property directly to a family member, other than a spouse or common-law partner, the gift would be treated as a disposition at FMV. No further income tax consequences would arise until the family member sold the gifted property. ITA 107(2) continues this concept by allowing the family member to receive property from the trust on a rollover basis so that no further income tax implications occur with respect to that property until the family member sells that property.

19-65.   Consistent with the tax policy justification for rollover treatment, ITA 107(2) would not apply in the following cases:

- If property is transferred out of an **alter ego** trust to anyone other than the settlor

- If property is transferred out of a **joint spousal** or common-law partner trust to anyone other than the settlor or the spouse or common-law partner

- If property is transferred out of a **qualifying spousal** or common-law partner trust to anyone other than a spouse or common-law partner

19-66.   In the absence of available rollover treatment, the distribution of property by a trust to a beneficiary would take place at FMV. This will generally result in income tax implications to the trust.

We suggest you complete SSP 19-1 at this point.

21-Year Deemed Disposition Rule

19-67.   The nature of trusts is that property contributed by individuals can appreciate in value without any income tax consequences well past the lifetime of that individual. In policy terms this is generally unacceptable since it is the death of an individual that typically results in a final accounting for income tax purposes with deemed dispositions on death.

19-68.   In order to place limits on this extended deferral, ITA 104(4)(b) requires that there be a deemed disposition and reacquisition of trust capital property, land inventory, and resource properties every 21 years. The rules (1) deem there to be a disposition and (2) deem the proceeds of that disposition to be FMV, resulting in the recognition of any accrued gains on these properties. In the case of depreciable property, if the deemed proceeds are less than the capital cost, the tax attributes are retained to ensure that any potential recapture is accounted for.

19-69.   This 21-year rule generally applies only to personal trusts and does not apply to certain types of trusts such as employee benefit plans or registered education savings plans (RESPs). In addition, the rules are modified in the case of qualifying spousal or common-law partner trusts, alter ego trusts, and joint spousal or common-law partner trusts. Standard tax planning to avoid the 21-year rule is to make distributions of trust property to capital beneficiaries that would be eligible for rollover treatment under ITA 107(2) prior to the 21-year expiration period.

Other Deemed Dispositions

19-70.   Where the primary beneficiary of an alter ego, spousal, or common-law partner trust dies, or the last surviving beneficiary of a joint spousal or common-law partner trust dies, there is a deemed year end of the trust on the date of the beneficiary's death.

Net Income of a Trust

Basic Rules

19-71.   ITA 104(2) treats trusts and estates as individuals for income tax purposes, meaning that the word "individual" means human beings, trusts, and estates. This concept results in trusts and estates following the same income tax rules that apply to human beings when calculating net income and taxable income. There are, however, a few exceptions. For example, personal tax credits such as the basic personal credit, the married or common-law partner credit, the dependent credit, the disability credit, and the caregiver credit are only available to human beings and not to trusts and estates. In addition, the capital gains deduction of ITA 110.6 limits this taxable income deduction to "individuals (other than trusts)," again limiting the deduction to human beings. However, capital gains that do qualify for the capital gains deduction can be flowed through a trust to individual beneficiaries (e.g., human beings) who would then be able to use their own capital gains deduction. In the remainder of this chapter we refer to human beings as individuals and trusts and estates as trusts and estates.

19-72.   Net income includes capital gains and capital losses realized by the trust on the disposition of capital property of the trust. In addition, any eligible or non-eligible dividends that are not allocated to beneficiaries are grossed up and included in the income of the trust. The trust, in the calculation of its federal tax payable, would be eligible to claim a dividend tax credit.

19-73.   A trust can also deduct a number of different amounts in calculating its net income, some of which are as follows:

Amounts Paid or Payable to Beneficiaries   A trust can deduct amounts that are paid or payable to one or more beneficiaries. This particular deduction is usually the most significant of net income deductions to a trust. In many cases, all of the trust's income will be allocated to beneficiaries, reducing net income to nil. This important deduction will be discussed later in the chapter.

Trustee's or Executor's Fees   Any amounts paid that are related to earning trust income, or that are paid to an executor or trustee whose principal business includes the provision of such services, are deductible to the trust. Many provinces have their own trustee legislation, limiting the amount that can be legally charged by a trustee depending on the time spent and nature of the services provided.

Amounts Paid by the Trust to Others and Allocated to the Income of a Beneficiary
A trust can make payments to third parties to provide goods or services to beneficiaries. The CRA considers such amounts to be another way of paying income to beneficiaries and, as a consequence, such amounts are deductible to the trust and included in the income of the beneficiaries.

Income Allocated to a Preferred Beneficiary   Trusts can elect to allocate certain income to a preferred beneficiary while retaining the income in the trust. This election allows certain income to be subject to the lower tax rates of the beneficiary rather than higher trust tax rates. Logistically the effect of this election is that the trust deducts the requisite amount from its net and taxable income and the preferred beneficiary includes that amount in his net and taxable income. There is further discussion of this election in the next section of this chapter.

Amounts Deemed Not Paid   A trust can designate amounts to be deemed not to have been paid when, in fact, the amounts are paid or payable to beneficiaries that would entitle the trust to a deduction from net income. The logistics of this designation is that rather than deducting the income payable to beneficiaries and having the income subject to tax by the beneficiaries, the trust includes the amount in its net income. This is often done because the trust has taxable income deductions such as non-capital losses that would offset the income. The result is that the income is included in the net income of the trust but not its taxable income.

Amounts Retained for a Beneficiary under 21 Years of Age   Provided the eventual payment is not subject to any future condition, amounts that are held in trust for a beneficiary who is under age 21 at the end of the year can be deducted by the trust and therefore included in the net income of that beneficiary. Logistically this allows the trust to avoid paying income tax at high trust tax rates in favour of the low tax rates of the beneficiary.

The three rules of (1) a preferred beneficiary, (2) a minor beneficiary (under 21 years of age), and (3) the ability to allow a trust to include income to offset loss carry overs provide significant opportunities that effectively allow trust income to be subject to the lowest tax rate between the trust and certain beneficiaries. These advantages, however, are not freely available to all trusts depending instead on meeting strict conditions to ensure they are properly targeted to the future care of individuals who may require additional assistance given their individual circumstances, such as disability and physical and mental impairments. Additional commentary on each of these three advantages is included in the following sections.

Preferred Beneficiary Election

19-74.   In determining net income, a trust can normally only deduct amounts that are paid or payable to a beneficiary. One of the exceptions is if a joint election is made by a trust and a beneficiary. Under the election, the trust will deduct the amount and the beneficiary will include the amount in net income. As a result, any potential income tax liability is moved from the trust to the beneficiary.

19-75.   The preferred beneficiary election is only available if:

- the beneficiary is claiming the disability tax credit; or
- the beneficiary is 18 years of age or older, is claimed by another individual as a dependant because of a mental or physical impairment, and does not have income that exceeds the base for the beneficiary's personal tax credit (i.e., $13,808 for 2021).
- In addition, the beneficiary must be the settlor of the trust; the spouse, common-law partner, or former spouse or common-law partner of the settlor of the trust; the child, grandchild, or great grandchild of the settlor of the trust, or the child, grandchild, or great grandchild of the spouse or common-law partner of the settlor of the trust.

19-76.   The election is typically used in situations where it is desirable to use the low tax rates of a beneficiary without actually giving that individual full access to the trust funds, particularly where the funds are eventually to be used for the assistance of the individual. An example of this would be a child with an impairment with no or little income but who lacks the ability to deal responsibly with financial matters.

Amounts Deemed Not Paid

19-77.   Amounts paid or payable to a beneficiary are normally deducted by the trust in determining its net income and included in the net income of the beneficiary. However, ITA 104(13.1) permits a trust to designate all or part of its income for a year as "not to have been paid" or "not to have become payable." These words are designed to prohibit a deduction by the trust, which then ensures the amounts remain as part of the net income of the trust. They also ensure that the amount is not included in the net income of a beneficiary. As a result, the amounts are potentially subject to income tax in the trust with any after-tax amounts available for tax-free distribution to beneficiaries. This designation is only available to trusts that are resident in Canada throughout the taxation year and that are not exempt from Part I tax, such as RRSPs, TFSAs, RESPs, and so on.

19-78.   A trust cannot allocate loss carry over amounts to beneficiaries. This means that the only way an unused current-year trust loss can be used is through a carry over to another taxation year of the trust. Since many trusts are legally obliged to distribute all trust income to beneficiaries, the result is that net income would generally be nil. A solution to this problem is to designate sufficient income as having not been paid to absorb the loss carry over. This can satisfy the legal requirement to distribute the income while simultaneously creating sufficient net income in the trust to absorb the loss carry forward. There is, however, a limitation (ITA 104(13.3)) that invalidates a designation unless the taxable income of the trust is nil after the deduction of the loss carry over. This means that the designation must only add enough income so that when the trust loss carry overs are applied taxable income is nil. The purpose of the limitation is to prevent trusts from moving excess income to the trust that would be subject to low tax rates. As a rule this would only impact GREs since all other taxable trusts are subject to the highest 33% federal tax rate.

Amounts Retained for a Beneficiary under 21 Years of Age

19-79.   If benefits are actually paid to a minor beneficiary, the amounts can be deducted by the trust. However, an adult settlor may decide that it would be better for the income to be held in trust until the beneficiary reaches some specified age. The difficulty with this approach, however, would be that the income would be taxed in the trust at high tax rates. Provided the beneficiary has not reached 21 years of age prior to the end of the year and none of the income has become payable, ITA 104(18) deems amounts that are retained to have actually become payable during the year. This allows the trust to deduct the amount in determining its net income, thus avoiding high trust tax rates, and requires the beneficiary to include the amount in net income at lower tax rates.

19-80.   To qualify for this treatment, the amounts must be vested with the beneficiary before the end of the year and there cannot be any future condition that would prevent payment. "Vested" means that the funds are set aside for the beneficiary and cannot be accessed by any other person. When these amounts are eventually distributed, they will be received by the beneficiary on a tax-free basis as a capital distribution.

Taxable Income of a Trust

19-81.   Once the net income of a trust for a taxation year is determined, there are taxable income deductions such as non-capital losses, net capital losses, and farming losses from other years. The same rules that apply to individuals equally apply to trusts, such as restrictions or limitations on the carry over period in which losses can be applied and the type of income against which the losses are allowed to be applied. Trusts cannot claim certain taxable income deductions available to human beings such as the capital gains deduction, the northern residents deduction, or the stock option deduction.

Exercise 19-5

Subject: Trust Net Income and Taxable Income

During the current year, the Jordan family trust, an inter vivos trust, has business income of $220,000. Distributions of $170,000 are made to beneficiaries, and a preferred beneciary election is made to have the remaining $50,000 included in the income of a beneficiary who qualifies for the disability tax credit. This beneficiary has no other income.

The trust has a non-capital loss balance of $35,000 from a previous year. To use the loss, the trust designates an amount of $35,000 of the $170,000 paid to beneficiaries as not having been paid during the year.

Determine the trust's net income and taxable income for the current year. Explain why the trust would make the preferred beneficiary election and designate amounts paid not to have been paid.

Solutions to Exercises are available in the Study Guide.

Income Allocations to Beneficiaries

General Rules

19-82. Since a trust is treated as a separate taxable entity, any income earned by the trust will initially be included in its income subject to allocations to beneficiaries, which would represent a net income deduction to the trust and a corresponding addition to the net income of those same beneficiaries. In effect, trust income is either taxed to the trust when there are no allocations to beneficiaries, taxed to beneficiaries when all of the income of a trust is allocated to beneficiaries, or a combination of the two where there are partial allocations of trust income to beneficiaries.

19-83. Allocations of trust income can also occur on an indirect basis, such as where a trust makes payments to third parties on behalf of beneficiaries for goods or services provided to them. These amounts reduce trust net income and increase the net income of the respective beneficiaries. These payments are often made on behalf of minors and generally include personal expenses for items such as day care, tuition, and medical fees.

19-84. The ability of a trust to deduct amounts distributed to beneficiaries depends on whether the amounts were "paid or payable." While it is generally easy to determine whether an amount has been paid, questions often arise in determining whether or not an amount is payable to a beneficiary. ITA 104(24) provides that:

> ... an amount is deemed not to have become payable to a beneficiary in a taxation year unless it was paid in the year to the beneficiary or the beneficiary was entitled in the year to enforce payment of it.

19-85. Issuing a promissory note or a cheque payable to the beneficiary for the share of the trust income will usually fulfill the payable requirement. The CRA provides their views on the meaning of the word "payable" in paragraphs 4 and 5 of archived IT-286R2, "Trusts—Amount Payable," by clarifying that an amount will not be considered to be payable in any of the following circumstances:

- A beneficiary can only enforce payment of an amount of income by forcing the trustee to wind up the trust. In such a case the amount would only be considered payable when the trust is winding up.
- The beneficiary's right to income is subject to the approval of a third party. No amount is considered payable until the third-party approval has been obtained
- Payment of income is at the trustee's discretion and this provision has not been exercised.
- The beneficiary has the power to amend the trust deed and must do so to cause the income to be payable. It is the actual amendment of the trust deed that would then establish a "payable" date.

Discretionary and Non-Discretionary Powers

19-86. Both testamentary and inter vivos trusts can be set up as either discretionary or non-discretionary trusts. A discretionary trust is one in which the trustees are given the power to decide the amounts of income or capital that can be distributed to beneficiaries.

19-87. In many cases, this discretionary power will apply only to annual income distributions. However, the trust could be structured to provide discretion on both income and capital distributions, or to capital distributions only. The trustees may also be given the power to control the timing of distributions to beneficiaries.

19-88.   When discretionary trusts are used, it is important that only the amounts allocated to beneficiaries are considered to be paid or payable. If, for example, a trustee's exercise of discretion requires the approval of a third party, no amount is payable until the approval has been obtained.

19-89.   A non-discretionary trust is one in which the amounts and timing of distribution are fixed (i.e., specifically set out in the trust documents). In some cases, the trust documents may have a combination of discretionary and non-discretionary power. For example, a trustee of a spousal trust may have fixed annual income payments but allows the trustee, on a discretionary basis, to distribute the capital of the trust.

Flow-Through Provisions

General Applicability

19-90.   Income that is paid out to beneficiaries through a trust is deemed, by default, to be property income (ITA 108(5)). The property income default rule, however, is overridden for some types of income, in which case those types of income retain their character to the beneficiaries to which they are paid or payable as long as the trust designates the amount to beneficiaries, which includes reporting through the issuance of T3 slips specifically identifying the amount to each beneficiary.

19-91.   The types of income that are permitted to retain their character include net taxable capital gains, dividends from taxable Canadian corporations, capital dividends, foreign business income, and foreign non-business income. It is important to keep in mind, however, that the trust documents must allow a specific type of income to be paid out to a beneficiary in order for that beneficiary to take advantage of these character retention rules. You may also have noted that if a trust carries on a business in Canada any business income allocated to beneficiaries would be categorized as property income since there is no character retention rules that apply to Canadian source business income. This fact discourages the use of trusts to earn business income in Canada.

Dividends

19-92.   If either eligible or non-eligible dividends from taxable Canadian corporations are received by a trust and distributed in their entirety to beneficiaries of the trust, the dividends will retain their character to all beneficiaries. This means that individual beneficiaries will be required to apply the dividend gross up and be eligible for the dividend tax credit when calculating income tax payable. Corporate beneficiaries will include the dividends in net income and will be entitled to a taxable income deduction under ITA 112(1). Corporate beneficiaries may also be subject to Part IV tax with respect to dividends flowed through a trust. The trust will include the full amount of the dividends received in its income, without any gross up, and will deduct that same amount as a net income deduction where all of the dividends are paid out to beneficiaries.

19-93.   If some of the eligible or non-eligible dividends received from taxable Canadian corporations are not paid or payable to beneficiaries, then the amounts retained are subject to the gross up and included in the trust's net income. The trust would be eligible for a dividend tax credit with respect to the amounts retained when it determines its own tax payable for the year.

19-94.   Capital dividends also retain their character and are not required to be included in the income of any beneficiaries nor are they required to be included in the income of the trust if not paid or payable to beneficiaries. However, the trust must report any capital dividends paid or payable to beneficiaries since such dividends may have future income tax consequences, such as impacting the ability of beneficiaries to claim future capital losses and, for beneficiaries that are private corporations, the capital dividend account balance of that corporate beneficiary. Finally, the payment of capital dividends to non-resident beneficiaries is taxable under Part XIII (see Chapter 20).

Capital Gains

19-95.   Under trust law, capital gains that are realized in a trust are considered an addition to capital and, in the absence of a special provision in the trust agreement, would not be payable to income beneficiaries. However, the ITA treats one-half of a capital gain as a taxable amount. As a consequence, if this taxable amount is not paid out to beneficiaries, it will be included in the net income of the trust. The remaining non-taxable half of the capital gain represents an addition to the capital of the trust that can be distributed to capital beneficiaries on a tax-free basis at any time subject to any constraints set out in the trust documents.

19-96.   If the trust pays out the full amount of a capital gain, the character retention rule means that one-half of this amount will be included in the net income of the beneficiary as a taxable capital gain. The remaining one-half is tax free and is therefore not required to be included in net income.

19-97.   The ITA requires two separate designations with respect to "net taxable capital gains," which are defined in ITA 104(21.3) as total taxable capital gains minus allowable capital losses minus any net capital loss carry overs deducted in the year. ITA 104(21) allows a designation based on amounts payable to beneficiaries in accordance with the trust documents. The amounts designated are deemed to be a taxable capital gain to the beneficiary and included in net income. The designation allows the beneficiary to apply any net capital loss carry overs to offset the inclusion.

19-98.   A separate designation is required for capital gains deduction purposes under ITA 104(21.2). The designation applies a proportionate allocation based on the amounts designated under ITA 104(21), meaning that flowing through capital gains eligible for the capital gains deduction to beneficiaries that are individuals requires the two designations. It also means that a trust cannot direct all capital gains that qualify for the capital gains deduction as it pleases, since it is based on a formula approach that depends on the proportion allocated of all net taxable capital gains. If, for example, an individual beneficiary is allocated 15% of the net taxable capital gains of the trust, then that individual beneficiary can only be allocated 15% of the capital gains that qualify for the capital gains deduction.

Tax on Split Income (TOSI)

19-99.   As discussed in Chapter 11, as of 2018 individuals of any age receiving certain types of income (referred to as split income), such as taxable dividends, business income, rental income, and capital gains not eligible for the capital gains deduction, where that split income is connected to certain related persons, may be subject to the TOSI. The result of the TOSI is that the split income is subject to the highest federal income tax rate of 33%, which is the same rate that would apply to personal trusts other than GREs. The TOSI only permits the claiming of certain tax credits, such as the dividend tax credit and foreign tax credit, as they relate to the split income. While we will not repeat the TOSI coverage here, it is important to keep in mind that split income earned through a trust is equally subject to the TOSI, which means an analysis of the nature and source of the income that flows through the trust to beneficiaries and the relationship of the beneficiaries to other persons involved in activities that generated the income that would qualify as split income.

Exercise 19-6

Subject: Flow through to Beneficiaries

During 2021, the Han family trust received $100,000 of eligible dividends from Canadian public corporations and $30,000 of non-eligible dividends from a family-owned CCPC. The trust also realized a capital gain of $20,000 on the sale of investments that do not qualify for the capital gains deduction.

The only beneficiary of the trust is the family's 19-year-old son, Bryan Han. Bryan is actively engaged in the family-owned CCPC on a regular and continuous basis and, as a consequence, the TOSI would not apply to treat any income received from the trust as split income.

In 2021, $60,000 of the eligible dividends, all of the non-eligible dividends, and all of the $20,000 capital gain were paid to Bryan. The trust makes the necessary designations with respect to the dividends and the capital gain.

Indicate the income tax consequences of these transactions on the net income for both Bryan and the trust.

Solutions to Exercises are available in the Study Guide.

Business Income, CCA, Recapture, and Terminal Losses

19-100.   Under trust law, the amount of income that can be distributed to beneficiaries should be determined after providing for depreciation expense calculated using methods similar to those specified under ASPE or IFRS. While this could create a difference between a trust's accounting net income and its net income for tax purposes, this problem is resolved in most situations by setting accounting depreciation expense equal to the CCA claimed.

19-101.   Business income is calculated by the trust applying the same rules that apply to other taxpayers, such as individuals and corporations. This means that business income takes any CCA claimed, recapture, or terminal losses into consideration. Once the business income has been determined, then allocations can be made to beneficiaries. Any allocations of Canadian-sourced business income to beneficiaries is treated as property income. This categorization to beneficiaries also avoids CPP and GST/HST complications, which would generally arise were the beneficiaries considered to have earned business income.

Exercise 19-7

Subject: CCA and Recapture on Trust Property

The Husak family trust has only one beneficiary, Martin Husak, the 32-year-old son of the settlor, Dimitri Husak. The trust is an inter vivos trust and its only property is a rental property with a FMV equal to its capital cost. The trust is non-discretionary with respect to income and is required to distribute all of its income to Martin each year. During the year ending December 31, 2021, rental income before the deduction of CCA is $32,000. Maximum CCA for the year is $26,000.

The trustee has discretionary power with respect to capital and is considering selling the rental property at the end of 2021. A sale would result in recapture of $65,000. The trustee has asked you to compare the income tax consequences for both Martin and the trust if (1) the sale takes place in December 2021 and (2) the rental property is not sold.

None of the trust income would be categorized as split income to Martin; therefore, the TOSI would not apply.

Solutions to Exercises are available in the Study Guide.

Principal Residence Exemption

19-102.   Prior to 2017, a residence held in a trust that was ordinarily inhabited by a beneficiary of the trust, or by a spouse or common-law partner, former spouse or common-law partner, or a child of a beneficiary, was eligible for the principal residence exemption (see Chapter 8). This is no longer the case. For years ending after 2016, only alter ego trusts, joint spousal or common-law partner trusts, spousal or common-law partner trusts, qualified disability trusts, or a qualifying trust for a minor child will be able to claim this exemption to eliminate or reduce any capital gain resulting from the sale of a residence held in the trust and designated as a principal residence.

Tax Payable of Personal Trusts

Gross Tax Payable

19-103.   Although trusts are treated as individuals for income tax purposes, the tax rates that apply to the taxable income of a trust vary depending on whether the trust is an inter vivos trust, a non-GRE testamentary trust, or a GRE. These differences are elaborated on in this section.

Graduated Rate Estates (GREs)

19-104.   In the first trust income tax return (T3) filed subsequent to an individual's death, property of an estate that is under the administration of an executor can be designated as a GRE. GRE status can be maintained for a maximum period of 36 months from the date of the death of the individual.

19-105.   The most significant income tax advantage of a GRE designation is that, during the period in which the designation is in effect, the trust determines its income tax liability using the graduated tax rates that apply to individuals. In 2021 the federal income tax rates range from 15% on the first $49,020 of taxable income to 33% on amounts in excess of $216,511.

Inter Vivos Trusts and Non-GRE Testamentary Trusts

19-106.   With the exception of GREs, both inter vivos and non-GRE testamentary trusts are subject to a federal income tax rate of 33% on their taxable income (ITA 122(1)).

Other Tax Payable Considerations

Availability of Tax Credits

19-107.   While, in principle, trusts are to be taxed in the same manner as individuals, there are obvious differences between a trust and a human being. These differences are reflected in the fact that trusts are not eligible for many of the tax credits that are available to individuals.

19-108.   ITA 122(1.1) specifically prohibits a trust from claiming any of the credits listed under ITA 118 (personal tax credits). Further, most of the other credits listed in ITA 118.1 through 118.9 are clearly directed at individuals (e.g., a trust will not have medical expenses). However, some tax credits are available to trusts, generally on the same basis as they are available to individuals. These include the following:

- Donations and gifts (as is the case with individuals, there is a credit of 15% on the first $200 of donations and either 29% or 33% on amounts above $200)
- Dividend tax credits
- Foreign tax credits
- Investment tax credits

Alternative Minimum Tax (AMT)

19-109.   As is the case with individuals, trusts are subject to the AMT. Individuals are also eligible for the $40,000 exemption; however, with respect to trusts, only GREs are eligible for the exemption.

Tax-Free Taxable Dividends

19-110.   The notion of a tax-free taxable dividend seems contradictory, but for our purposes it refers to the ability of an individual with no other source of income to receive a certain amount of taxable dividends without the payment of any income tax. This situation occurs because of a combination of the individual's dividend tax credit and available personal tax credits. This concept was explained in Chapter 15; here we will add that this only applies when income is subject to the two lowest federal income tax rates of 15% and 20.5%, which typically apply to low-income individuals. Since both inter vivos and non-GRE testamentary trusts are taxed at 33% on all of their taxable income, these trusts cannot receive any taxable dividends on a tax-free basis.

19-111.   GREs, however, are a different matter since they are eligible for graduated rates, creating a situation where taxable dividends may be received tax free. A GRE with no other source of income can receive approximately $35,000 in eligible dividends without paying any federal income tax.

Exercise 19-8

Subject: Trust Tax on Taxable Dividends

A trust receives $100,000 in eligible dividends. This is the trust's only income for the current year. The only beneficiary of the trust is the settlor's adult son. The son's only income is from the trust, none of which is subject to the TOSI. The only available tax credits are the basic personal credit and any credits related to the allocated trust income. Ignoring any AMT implications, determine the taxable income and federal income tax payable for both the trust and beneficiary under the following alternative assumptions:

A.   The trust is a GRE and all of the dividends are distributed to the beneficiary.

B.   The trust is a GRE and none of the dividends are distributed to the beneficiary.

C.   The trust is an inter vivos trust and none of the dividends are distributed to the beneficiary.

Solutions to Exercises are available in the Study Guide.

We suggest you complete SSP 19-2, 19-3, and 19-4 at this point.

Income Attribution—Trusts

General Rules

19-112.   We introduced the income attribution rules for individuals in Chapter 9. Briefly summarized, they are as follows:

Transfer to a Spouse or Common-Law Partner   Under ITA 74.1(1), if property ownership is transferred to a spouse or common-law partner for consideration that is less than FMV, any income earned from the property while owned by that individual, as well as any capital gain resulting from a disposition of the property, will be attributed back to the transferor (i.e., the original owner) and no amount will be included in the income of that individual transferee. The same attribution rules apply regardless of what is paid as consideration where the transferor does not elect out of the ITA 73 rollover provision with the result that the property transfer occurs at the transferor's tax cost, avoiding any immediate income tax implications. In practice this occurs where property is gifted between spouses and common-law partners.

Transfer to a Related Minor   Under ITA 74.1(2), if property ownership is transferred to a related individual under the age of 18 for consideration that is less than FMV, any income earned from the property while owned by that minor individual will be attributed back to the transferor until the year the individual becomes 18 years of age. No amount will be included in the income of the minor. Capital gains on a subsequent sale of the property by the minor will not be attributed back to the transferor.

It is only income from property and capital gains that are subject to attribution, therefore if the transferred property generates business income the attribution rules will not apply to attribute that business income. The attribution rules also do not apply if the TOSI applies to the income or capital gains.

19-113.   The attribution rules are not limited to direct transfers between spouses, common-law partners, and to minor children but are equally applicable when there is an indirect transfer to spouses, common-law partners, or related minors through an inter vivos trust in which any of these individuals are beneficiaries. As was the case with direct transfers to individuals, the rules apply to any transfer of property where the consideration paid by the trust is less than the FMV of the property transferred.

19-114.   Attribution does not occur at the time property is transferred to a trust in which a spouse, common-law partner, or related minor is a beneficiary. Rather, attribution occurs when income from the property is allocated to one of these individuals. If the trust chooses to include the income in its own net income or if the income is allocated to beneficiaries other than a spouse, common-law partner, or related minor, the income will not be attributed back to the transferor. In addition, income attribution comes to an end on the death of the settlor.

Exercise 19-9

Subject: Income Attribution—Trusts

Last year, Trevor Carlisle established a family trust with the gratuitous transfer of bond investments that pay interest of $27,000 per year. The beneficiaries are Trevor's spouse, Carmen, and their two children, Mitch (16 years old) and Rhonda (22 years old). The beneficiaries' only income is from the trust. The trust is a non-discretionary trust that allocates all income and capital gains equally among the three beneficiaries. In the current year the trust earned $27,000 in interest and realized a capital gain of $6,000 on the disposition of one of the bonds.

Determine the net and taxable income of each beneficiary for the current year and determine whether there is any impact on Trevor, the settlor. How would your answer change if Trevor died on January 1 of the current year?

Ignore any potential TOSI implications.

Solutions to Exercises are available in the Study Guide.

We suggest you complete SSP 19-5 and 19-6 at this point.

Attribution to Settlor (Reversionary Trust)

19-115.   There is another attribution rule that is unique to settlors of trusts. This attribution rule applies to attribute both income and capital gains from the contributed property to the settlor if any of the conditions of ITA 75(2) are met. As a rule, avoiding the attribution rule requires that the settlor sever any connection to the contributed property. ITA 75(2) does not apply to any property that is sold at FMV to a trust.

19-116.   ITA 75(2) applies irrespective of the identity of the beneficiaries of the trust if any one of the following conditions is satisfied:

1.   The transferred property can revert to the settlor at a later point in time. In this situation, the trust is commonly referred to as a reversionary trust. This means that the settlor can recover the property contributed.

2.   The transferred property will pass to persons to be determined by the settlor at a later point in time. This requirement prevents the settlor from adding additional beneficiaries or classes of beneficiaries subsequent to the creation of the trust.

3.   The transferred property cannot be disposed of except with the settlor's consent or in accordance with the settlor's direction.

19-117.   The three conditions of ITA 75(2) can only apply if the settlor retains some level of control over the property once it has been contributed to a trust. Severing all connections to the property require that the settlor not be a beneficiary or a trustee with decision-making authority nor that existing trustees may be required to follow the settlor's wishes or instructions with respect to the contributed property. In practice if the settlor decides to be a trustee it is important that any decisions not necessarily require the settlor's approval as a trustee. This is often accomplished by having multiple unrelated trustees where decisions are made by a majority vote. If, for example, there were three trustees, decisions could be made without the approval of the settlor/trustee by the other two unrelated trustees.

Purchase or Sale of an Interest in a Trust

Income Interest

19-118.   An income interest in a trust is the right of a beneficiary to receive all or part of the trust income as determined under trust and estate law (ITA 108(3)), which would exclude capital gains. The purchaser of an income interest in a trust will have a cost equal to the FMV of the consideration paid for that interest. This cost can be deducted to the extrent of trust income that is included in the beneficiary's net income. Any portion of the cost that is not deducted against income from the trust in the current year can be carried forward for deduction against allocated trust income in subsequent years.

19-119.   From the point of view of the vendor of an income interest, the proceeds of disposition will be equal to the FMV of the consideration received. If the cost of the income interest (often nil) is different than the proceeds received, there will be a gain or loss on the disposition. The full amount of any gain is required to be included in net income and the full amount of any loss is fully deductible in determining net income. In other words, the gain or loss on the disposition of an income interest is not a capital gain or capital loss.

Capital Interest

19-120.   As defined in ITA 108(1), a capital interest means all of the rights of a beneficiary of a trust other than, in the case of a personal trust, an income interest. As the name implies, a capital interest is considered capital property and therefore any gain or loss on a disposition will be treated as a capital gain or capital loss.

19-121.   When a capital interest in a trust is purchased, the ACB is equal to the FMV of the consideration given. The ACB is reduced by future capital distributions from the trust. In general, ITA 107(2) provides for a tax-free rollover of property distributed from a trust in partial or complete settlement of the capital interest of a beneficiary. The tax cost of any property distributed as a capital distribution would reduce the ACB of the capital interest.

19-122.   If a beneficiary sells a capital interest in a trust, the proceeds of disposition will equal the FMV of the consideration received. Unless the taxpayer has purchased the capital interest the ITA deems the ACB to be nil. This means that the entire proceeds of disposition would be a capital gain. However, to determine the gain on a disposition of a capital interest in a trust resident in Canada, ITA 107(1)(a) defines the ACB to be the greater of:

• the ACB as usually determined, which is usually nil, and

• the "cost amount" to the beneficiary.

19-123.   ITA 108(1) defines the cost amount as the beneficiary's proportionate interest in the net property of the trust at their tax costs. This rule prevents beneficiaries from being taxed on the underlying tax cost of a trust's properties. In effect, beneficiaries receive credit for the tax cost of trust property as part of the ACB of their capital interest.

Exercise 19-10

Subject: Sale of a Capital Interest

The Jardhu family trust was established when a parent gratuitously transferred ownership of publicly traded shares with a cost of $120,000 and a FMV of $250,000 in settlement of the trust. The beneficiaries of the trust are the parent's two sons, Sam, aged 25, and Mehrdad, aged 27. They are both income and capital beneficiaries and have an equal interest in the income and capital of the trust.

At the beginning of the current year, Mehrdad sells his capital interest in the trust to Sam. There have been no capital distributions from the trust. At the time of the sale, the FMV of the shares is $380,000. The sale price of the capital interest is $190,000 [(1/2) ($380,000)]. Determine the income tax consequences of the sale of the capital interest to each of the two brothers.

Solutions to Exercises are available in the Study Guide.

Tax Planning

Family Trusts

19-124.   The term "family trust" is not defined in the ITA but rather is commonly used in practice to refer to a personal trust that has been established with members of the settlor's family as beneficiaries. These trusts can either be inter vivos trusts established during the settlor's lifetime or, alternatively, testamentary trusts created when the settlor dies. The provisions of these trusts often contain a non-discretionary fixed entitlement to recurring income payments to beneficiaries but may also contain a discretionary power given to trustees with respect to distributions of income or capital.

19-125.   While family trusts can be used for a variety of purposes, such as passing on a business to family members, protecting the interests of family members from future creditor claims, or allowing a parent to exercise control over certain property until children become of age, the most common tax planning objective is income splitting. In this section we will turn our attention to income splitting in the context of family trusts. It is noteworthy that the expansion of the TOSI to include adults has resulted in an additional layer of complexity that can limit effective income splitting strategies among family members.

Discretionary Family Trusts

19-126.   A family trust that is established for income splitting purposes often provides the trustee or trustees with discretionary power to minimize overall income tax by directing trust income to beneficiaries with no or little income. To ensure that all beneficiaries receive income, the trust may provide for a minimum fixed entitlement plus a discretionary entitlement allowing for larger allocations to select beneficiaries based on a number of considerations. There are many variations on this theme depedning on the wishes of the settlor.

19-127.   Discretionary family trusts often serve to allow a settlor to exercise control over family members that may either punish or reward them based on spending habits, behaviour, and other subjective criteria. It is important, however, to ensure that the level of control exercised by the settlor does not cross certain bounderies that would effectively trigger the application of the reversionary trust attribution rule of ITA 75(2), thus negating any income tax splitting benefits of the trust by having trust income included in the net income of the settlor who is often the wealthiest family member in the highest income tax bracket. As a rule the settlor should not be a trustee whose decision is instrumental to any trust decisions or a beneficiary, particularly a capital beneficiary who may be in a position to ultimately recover property contributed to the trust.

Income Splitting

19-128. If a family trust is set up properly, the potential income tax savings from income splitting can be significant. The table in Paragraph 19-129 compares the federal income tax payable on eligible dividends of $63,000 received by:

- a parent who is subject to the maximum federal income tax rate of 33%; and

- an adult daughter with no other source of income and on the assumption that no trust income will be subject to the TOSI.

19-129. The required calculations, including the impact of the AMT, are as follows:

	Parent	Daughter	AMT (Daughter)
Eligible dividends received	$63,000	$63,000	$63,000
Gross up at 38%	23,940	23,940	N/A
Taxable dividends/income	$86,940	$86,940	$63,000
Federal tax			
[(33%)($86,940)]	$28,690		
[(15%)($49,020) + (20.5%)($37,920)]		$15,127	
[(15%)($63,000 - $40,000 exemption)]			$3,450
Federal dividend tax credit			
[(6/11)($23,940)]	(13,058)	(13,058)	N/A
Basic personal credit (Note)	N/A	(2,071)	(2,071)
Federal income tax payable/AMT	$15,632	Nil	$1,379

NOTE Since the father would have other income against which he could apply his basic personal credit, it has not been taken into consideration in the preceding calculations. Personal credit = $2,071 [(15%)($13,808)].

19-130. This example is designed to use the maximum of tax-free eligible dividends that can be paid to an individual with only the basic personal tax credit. As shown in the preceding calculations, this serves to reduce the daughter's regular income tax payable to nil. However, AMT will be payable, resulting in a net tax savings through the use of a family trust in the amount of $14,253 ($15,632 - $1,379). The corresponding savings in provincial income taxes would increase this amount significantly. Note that this income tax savings would be available for each beneficiary if there were multiple beneficiaries. Of equal importance is the fact that this is not a one-time event. These income tax savings can be achieved on an annual basis as long as the beneficiaries have no other source of income. Even with other sources of income there will be income tax savings as long as the marginal income tax rate of beneficiaries is less than 33%. These results depend on ensuring that the TOSI does not apply to taxable dividends received by any low-income beneficiaries.

Exercise 19-11

Subject: Family Trusts

Sarah Block owns investments that earn annual interest of $110,000. She has other sources of income in excess of $250,000. She has two children, a daughter, Jerri, 22 years old with no income, and a son, Mark, 26 years old who is married. Marks' spouse has no income and Mark has annual rental income of $48,000.

Determine the savings in federal income tax that could be achieved if Sarah transferred the investments to a family trust with her two children as equal income beneficiaries.

The trust will be non-discretionary and will be required to distribute all of its income equally to each of the two adult children each year.

Assume that Jerri's only tax credit is the basic personal amount and that Mark's only tax credits are the basic personal amount and the spousal credit. Also assume the TOSI will not apply to any income received by either beneficiary.

Solutions to Exercises are available in the Study Guide.

Qualifying Spousal or Common-Law Partner Trusts

19-131.   A rollover of capital property to a spouse or common-law partner can be achieved without the use of a trust. Transfer of capital property ownership on a rollover basis between spouses and common-law partners during one's lifetime is provided for by ITA 73(1) and (1.01) and by ITA 70(6) in the case of transfers as a consequence of death. In effect, the use of a trust is not necessary to achieve this tax-free result. Why, then, are we concerned with qualifying spousal or common-law partner trusts? There are essentially two important reasons:

1.   A trust can provide for the appropriate management of the transferred property, particularly when property is used to carry on an active business. In many cases, the spouse or common-law partner of a settlor may have little to no experience in the management of such property and, in such situations, the trust document can ensure that professional management is used.

2.   The use of a trust can also ensure that properties are distributed in a manner consistent with the wishes of the settlor. While qualification for the income tax advantages requires that the transferred properties "vest indefeasibly" in the trust, the trust document can direct who the properties should be distributed to on the death of the spouse or common-law partner. This could ensure, for example, that the properties are ultimately distributed only to the settlor's children if the spouse or common-law partner were to remarry and have additional children.

Alter Ego Trusts

19-132.   The most commonly cited reason for using an alter ego trust is that the trust property will not be included in the settlor's estate and, as a consequence, will not be subject to probate procedures (probate is a court process that proves the authenticity and validity of a will and the appointed executors). There are a number of advantages associated with avoiding probate:

- The probate fees can be high. In Ontario, for example, they are equal to $15 or 1.5% for each $1,000 over $50,000 of the FMV of the estate with no upper limit. On a $10 million estate these fees would total $149,250 [(0.015)($10,000,000 - $50,000)], a payment that can be avoided with the use of an alter ego trust.

- The probate process can be time consuming. This can create difficulties for the management of an active business, as well as liquidity problems for the estate until probate is complete.

- When property such as real estate is held in more than one jurisdiction (e.g., Canada and the U.S.), the probate procedures must be undertaken in multiple jurisdictions.

- Once probated, a will is in the public domain, meaning that the information is available to the public. For a nominal fee, any interested individual can obtain a copy of the will.

19-133.   There are additional tax and non-tax planning considerations. For example, planning opportunities may exist to establish the residence of a trust in Canada in any one of the ten provinces or three territories. In 2021, the combined federal/provincial/territorial income tax rates on individuals vary from 44.5% in Nunavut to 54% in Nova Scotia. This 9.5% difference makes the province or territory of residence a significant tax planning issue. The CRA, as part of their arrangements with provinces and territories, has increased their review of trust residency in Canada, particularly where trusts claim residence in a low-rate province or territory.

19-134.   In terms of non-tax planning, the establishment of an alter ego trust versus a will has additional advantages in that, from a legal standpoint, it is much easier to challenge the validity of a will than it is to challenge the validity of a trust. Courts can be asked to consider moral obligations to family members in distributing property of an estate. With a trust, there is no will to challenge.

Joint Spousal or Joint Common-Law Partner Trusts

19-135.   A joint spousal or joint common-law partner trust has the same income tax characteristics as an alter ego trust. The basic difference is that these trusts are established with respect to the combined properties of both spouses or common-law partners. As a result, the tax planning advantages are largely the same as that of alter ego trusts.

Estate Planning

Non-Tax Considerations

19-136.   The subject of estate planning is complex and involves considerations that go well beyond the scope of this text. In fact, appropriate planning for a large estate will often involve lawyers, investment advisors, accountants, and tax advisors. Some of the more important non-tax considerations in planning an estate include the following:

Intent of the Testator   The foremost goal of estate planning is to ensure that the wishes of the testator (a person who has died and left a valid will) are carried out. This will involve ensuring that estate property is distributed at the appropriate times and to named beneficiaries. The will is the primary document for ensuring that the intent of the testator is fulfilled.

Preparation of a Final Will   The major document in the estate planning process is the latest or final will. It should be carefully prepared to provide detailed instructions for the disposition of property, investment decisions to be made, and the extent to which trusts will be used. An executor should be named to administer the estate, and the will should be reviewed periodically to ensure that it is current and reflects the testator's current family situation.

Preparation of a Living Will   A living will provides detailed instructions regarding investments and other personal decisions in the event of physical or mental incapacity at any point in a person's lifetime. A power of attorney is similar, except that it does not require the individual to be mentally or physically incapacitated.

Ensuring Liquidity   A plan should be established to provide for liquidity at the time of death. Major expenses such as funeral expenses and income taxes will arise early in the process. Funds needed for these payments should be available or adequate life insurance should be arranged in advance to avoid the need for emergency sales of property to raise the necessary cash.

Simplicity   While the disposition of a large estate will rarely be simple, effective estate planning should ensure that the plan can be understood by the testator and all beneficiaries of legal age. In addition, any actions that can reduce the cost and complexity of administering the estate should be considered. This might involve disposing of investments in non-public shares or repatriating property located in foreign countries that might become subject to foreign taxes.

Avoidance of Family Disputes   Unfortunately, disputes among beneficiaries are a common feature of many estate settlements. If equitable treatment of beneficiaries is a goal of the testator, efforts should be made to ensure that all beneficiaries have been treated equally. If the testator wishes to distribute property in an inequitable manner it is important that beneficiaries be advised well in advance and that a desire to make such distributions was intentional.

Expediting the Transition The settlement of an estate should be as expeditious as possible. A long, drawn-out settlement period can increase uncertainties related to the FMV of estate property, add to the complications associated with the required distribution of property, and prolong the frustration of beneficiaries.

Income Tax Considerations

19-137. In addition to the preceding non-tax considerations, estate planning must also consider various income tax factors. Fundamental tax planning goals for all taxpayers apply equally to estate planning. Briefly, these goals involve the legal and orderly arrangement of one's affairs, in advance of the time of a transaction or event, to reduce and defer income taxes.

19-138. In effective estate planning, the overriding income tax goals are to defer and minimize income tax payments. Several important issues should be considered in dealing with this objective, which include the following:

Prior to Death Planning should attempt to minimize income taxes for the individual in the years prior to death. If the individual earns income that is not required, attempts should be made to defer the payment of tax and transfer the source of the income to the ultimate beneficiaries. Gifting property directly or using a discretionary trust can assist in achieving this goal.

Year of Death Planning should attempt to minimize income taxes payable in the year of death. Deemed dispositions will occur and, in addition, amounts in certain types of deferred income plans usually must be included in the individual's final income tax return. Relief can be achieved through rollovers to a spouse or common-law partner and transfers of certain types of property (e.g., farm property) to children or grandchildren. The will can also contain instructions to ensure that the maximum RRSP contribution is made to RRSPs for a spouse or common-law partner within the appropriate deadlines.

Planning may also involve filing elective multiple income tax returns. For example, if an individual owns all of the shares of a private corporation, declaring a dividend just prior to their death, with payment following death, could provide for the filing of a rights and things return (see Chapter 11 Appendix), a procedure that would involve significant income tax savings.

Income Splitting Effective planning should allow income splitting among family members who are in lower tax brackets. This can be accomplished by the appropriate splitting of income (e.g., paying salaries and wages for services rendered) and distributing property among beneficiaries throughout one's lifetime, recognizing any limitations imposed by the TOSI.

Foreign Jurisdictions Planning should also minimize taxes that will be incurred in foreign jurisdictions. This is especially true for jurisdictions that impose significant estate taxes since such taxes are generally not eligible for foreign tax credits or deduction for Canadian income tax purposes. To the extent that it is consistent with the individual's investment plans and the residence of intended beneficiaries, the ownership of foreign property at death, or distributions to beneficiaries in foreign locations, should usually be avoided by residents of Canada. Minimizing the ownership of foreign property will also simplify the administration of an estate.

Administration Period Planning should minimize income during the administration of an estate. Discretion provided to trustees in distributing the income of an inter vivos trust may assist in achieving this goal.

Estate Freeze

Objectives of an Estate Freeze

19-139.   The objectives of an estate freeze were discussed in Chapter 17. In brief, the purpose is to fix or freeze the value of the shares of individuals of a corporation at a particular point in time through a restructuring of shares referred to as a capital reorganization. This restructuring allows family members who would generally be unable to purchase shares of an incorporated family business at FMV to do so at a nominal cost. It also provides parent shareholders with an alternative to gifting shares to family members that would involve severe income tax consequences as a result of the ITA treating gifts as dispositions at FMV. In Chapter 17 the estate freeze discussion focused on corporations and individual shareholders. In this section we expand the estate freeze discussion to include the common use of family trusts in these corporate settings but also to discuss how trusts can be used in estate planning with family members for property whether or not it is used in an active business. The beneficiaries of family trust arrangements are typically spouses, common-law partners, children, and grandchildren.

> **EXAMPLE**   Mr. Chisholm is a wealthy and successful investor and entrepreneur who has a spouse and two minor children. He owns a variety of capital properties that are earning income and appreciating in value. He has several objectives in creating an estate plan:
>
> - During the remainder of his life, Mr. Chisholm would like to transfer property that is the source of all or part of his income to a group of individuals and charities who will ultimately be the beneficiaries of his estate.
>
> - Mr. Chisholm would like to freeze the value of his properties to allow future appreciation to accrue to the benefit of family members.
>
> - All of Mr. Chisholm's properties have appreciated in value and he wishes to avoid any immediate income tax consequences that would result from a disposition.
>
> - Mr. Chisholm does not want any increase in value of his properties that has accrued to the benefit of family members to be realized until a time subsequent to his death.
>
> - Mr. Chisholm wants to retain the right to the current FMV of his properties at the time of the estate freeze. In addition, he wishes to retain control of the use of the property until his death.

19-140.   This example will be used as a basis for discussing a variety of techniques that can be used to freeze the value of an estate. Some of these techniques will achieve all of Mr. Chisholm's goals, while others will only succeed in achieving one or two.

Techniques Not Involving Rollovers

Gifts

19-141.   Mr. Chisholm can freeze the value of his estate without using a rollover. The most straightforward method is to simply gift property to his prospective beneficiaries. The difficulty is that ITA 69(1) treats a gift of property as a disposition at FMV unless the recipient is a spouse, common-law partner, or a trust for a spouse or common-law partner, in which case rollovers apply to override the FMV impact of ITA 69(1). The result would be the recognition of capital gains, recapture, and other income with respect to gifts to the children.

19-142.   In addition, if the individual recipient of the gift is a spouse or minor child the attribution rules would apply, negating any income splitting opportunities. Further difficulties would include the loss of control over the properties and a potential concern that the TOSI rules could apply.

19-143.   While gifts result in a loss of control over property, Mr. Chisholm may want to accelerate donations of property to registered charities. The value of the donation tax credit can more than offset any income tax arising as the result of the gift. In particular, if a gift is made of shares listed on a designated stock exchange, the capital gains are reduced to nil (see Chapter 11).

Instalment Sales

19-144.   Mr. Chisholm could freeze the value of the estate by selling property to the intended family members on an instalment basis. Capital gains could be deferred under a structured arrangement, but the capital gains would need to be included in net income over a five-year period using the capital gain reserve calculations (10 years if a farm or fishing property is involved).

19-145.   Avoiding income attribution would require that the beneficiary provide FMV consideration, which may be problematic if the intended family members do not have sufficient income or property of their own to make the purchase. A carefully structured debt at prescribed rates of interest could also be used to establish FMV consideration, although the ability to make actual payments of interest may be difficult and again depends on the income and property of the individual purchaser. A final difficulty would be that Mr. Chisholm would have no say with respect to the property after giving up ownership.

Establishing a Trust

19-146.   An estate freeze can also be accomplished by establishing a trust in favour of one or more beneficiaries. Opportunities to make income and capital distributions to family members and transfer future appreciation in the value of contributed property to the trust are within the objectives Mr. Chisholm expects to achieve. The trust can be structured so that Mr. Chisholm can retain some control over contributed property while ensuring that the reversionary trust attribution rule of ITA 75(2) does not apply.

19-147.   The difficulty with a trust arrangement, however, is that except in the case of a qualifying spouse or common-law partner trust, a joint spousal or common-law partner trust, or an alter ego trust, there is no rollover provision to defer income tax since contributions of property would be treated as dispositions at FMV as a consequence of ITA 69(1). As a result, if the trust is established for beneficiaries other than Mr. Chisholm or his spouse, Mr. Chisholm will be subject to income tax on any taxable capital gains realized at the time of the contribution of property. As well, any dividends received from a private corporation by related beneficiaries may be subject to the TOSI, whether the shares are held directly or indirectly through a trust.

Use of a Holding Company

19-148.   Mr. Chisholm could dispose of property to a holding company in which intended family members have a substantial equity interest without the use of a rollover. This would freeze the value of his estate and could take place without income tax as long as there was no appreciation in the value of the property disposed of. The use of a rollover such as ITA 85(1) could be used to defer any income tax where the FMV of property exceeds the respective tax costs. Attribution concepts must still be considered in such cases, particularly where the intention of a transfer of property to a corporation with certain family members owning shares is to split income (ITA 74.4(2)).

ITA 86 Share Exchange

Nature of the Exchange

19-149.   Chapter 17 provided an overview of ITA 86, which provides rollover treatment to shareholders in the course of a reorganization of capital. In certain situations such a share reorganization offers the best solution to many estate freeze issues. Specifically, this rollover is most appropriate to an estate freeze where a profitable CCPC is wholly owned by an individual or jointly owned by spouses or common-law partners and a desire is present to pass on future appreciation in corporate value to other family members such as children.

19-150.   The technique involves controlling shareholders exchanging their voting common shares that account for all of the value of the corporation to fixed value preferred shares, effectively locking in that value at a point in time. This method then allows family members to purchase voting common shares for nominal consideration. The locked-in value attributable to the preferred shares cannot subsequently increase in value, leaving any subsequent increases in corporate value to be attributable to the newly issued common shares owned by other family members. In that sense the parent or parents would have frozen their value in the corporation at a moment in time with any future appreciation going to the other family members (e.g., children). Where minor children are involved a discretionary family trust could be established for their benefit. Instead of minor children acquiring common shares directly, the trust would acquire the shares with the children and other family members as beneficiaries. The use of such a trust has many advantages, such as limiting control of the company by children or those not well versed in handling the day-to-day affairs of a corporate business.

Example

19-151.   The main difference between the estate freeze discussed in Chapter 17 and the version discussed here is that a family trust stands between the corporation and the family members. In other words, the family members benefitting from the estate freeze do not actually own shares in the corporation but rather own an income or capital interest in a trust that is the shareholder. The concept is illustrated in the following example.

> **EXAMPLE**   Mrs. Hadley is the sole owner and driving force behind Hadley Inc., a CCPC that carries on a manufacturing business in Alberta. At the end of the current year, the condensed balance sheet of the company is as follows:
>
> **Hadley Inc. — Balance Sheet**
>
> | | |
> |---|---|
> | Net identifiable assets | $10,000,000 |
> | | |
> | Common shares (1,000 shares) | $ 2,000,000 |
> | Retained earnings | 8,000,000 |
> | Total shareholders' equity | $10,000,000 |
>
> On the basis of an independent appraisal, the FMV of the corporation is $15,000,000. Mrs. Hadley has a spouse and three adult children and she would like them to share equally in her estate. The ACB and PUC of the common shares are both $2,000,000.

19-152.   Once the corporation has obtained approval to change its share structure, evidenced by amended articles of incorporation, Mrs. Hadley can exchange all of her common shares for redeemable preferred shares with a redemption value of $15 million. The ACB and PUC of the preferred shares would be the same $2 million as the exchanged common shares, and the disposition of the common shares would occur on a rollover basis without any income tax consequences. The preferred shares would have no participation in the future growth of the company and, as a result, Mrs. Hadley has effectively frozen the value of her estate (i.e., the shares).

19-153.   If Mrs. Hadley wishes to retain voting control of the company, the preferred shares received on the exchange can be voting or she can participate in acquiring a majority of newly issued common shares. Mrs. Hadley can recover her investment value of $15 million by either selling the shares at their FMV of $15 million and realizing a capital gain of $13 million or by having the company redeem the shares, in which case there would be a deemed dividend of $13 million (ITA 84(3)). It is common practice for individuals who have undertaken an estate freeze to have the corporation redeem the shares gradually over a number of years to defer the payment of income tax to the extent possible.

19-154.   At this stage, the redemption value of Mrs. Hadley's preferred shares represents all of the FMV of the corporation, meaning that the value of any newly issued common shares will be equal to what is paid to acquire those shares. This means that common shares can be issued for a nominal amount (e.g., $1 each). It is important, however, that a professional valuation determine the actual FMV to avoid any income tax issues should the value prove to be incorrect.

If we assume that each family member purchased one-quarter of the authorized 1,000 common shares for $1 each, the results would be as follows:

Spouse (250 shares at $1)	$ 250
Child one (250 shares at $1)	250
Child two (250 shares at $1)	250
Child three (250 shares at $1)	250
Total common share legal capital	$1,000

19-155.   The trust option would have Mrs. Hadley establish a family trust with sufficient funds to purchase the common shares. The beneficiaries of the trust would be her spouse and three children. Mrs. Hadley could act as trustee of the trust and therefore retain indirect control of the company in that role. The trust would be the common shareholder, owning 1,000 shares with an ACB and PUC of $1 each. Dividends paid to the trust could be allocated to the beneficiaries, retaining their character as either eligible, non-eligible, or capital dividends.

19-156.   The common shares would benefit from any subsequent appreciation in value attributable to income and appreciation in the value of the corporation. If, for example, in two years the company was valued at $17 million then the common shares would be worth $2 million and the preferred shares $15 million.

19-157.   The use of a trust in the example described above will likely result in the application of the TOSI, meaning that taxable dividends flowed through to beneficiaries would be subject to a 33% federal income tax rate. However, capital gains that qualify for the capital gains deduction are excluded from the TOSI, which provides a considerable income tax advantage where an active business is being carried on by a CCPC in Canada.

Rollovers—ITA 85 vs. ITA 86

19-158.   An estate freeze can be implemented using rollovers under either ITA 85 or ITA 86. In comparing the use of ITA 85 and ITA 86, you should note that ITA 85 provides much greater flexibility than is the case with ITA 86 in that a range of elected amounts can be chosen with the opportunity to receive non-share consideration such as debt in payment. ITA 86, however, is limited to an exchange of shares in the course of a reorganization of capital and provides limited flexibility in choosing an amount that will dictate the income tax consequences. In addition, ITA 86 can result in immediate income tax consequences where non-share consideration is taken back. In practice, share exchanges under ITA 86 are often accomplished on a pure share-for-share exchange basis, avoiding non-share consideration altogether.

19-159.   In terms of formality and procedure, ITA 86 is often easier to implement as there is no formal election required for income tax purposes. ITA 85, however, requires the filing of a formal election on a timely basis. As a rule, there will be some savings in costs using ITA 86 because of not having to file an election, but for the most part an estate freeze involves professional representation that includes valuators, accountants, and lawyers with expertise in estate planning to achieve the income tax and non-tax goals of a family. These costs are generally unaffected by the decision to use either ITA 85 or ITA 86.

Key Terms

A full glossary with definitions is provided at the end of the Study Guide.

Alter Ego Trust	Estate Freeze
Beneficiary	Executor
Capital Interest (in a Trust)	Family Trust
Discretionary Trust	Graduated Rate Estate
Estate	Income Attribution

Income Interest (in a Trust)
Income Splitting
Inter Vivos Trust
Joint Spousal or Common-Law
   Partner Trust
Non-Discretionary Trust
Personal Trust
Preferred Beneficiary
Preferred Beneficiary Election
Qualifying Spousal or
   Common-Law Partner Trust
Reorganization of Capital (ITA 86)

Reversionary Trust
Rollover
Settlor
Split Income
Spousal or Common-Law Partner Trust
Tax Planning
Testamentary Trust
Trust
Trustee
21-Year Deemed Disposition Rule
Will

References

For more detailed study of the material in this chapter, we would refer you to the following:

ITA 70(6)	Transfers to Spousal Trusts on Death
ITA 73(1)	Inter Vivos Transfers to Spousal Trusts
ITA 74.1 to 74.5	Attribution Rules
ITA 75(2)	Trust (Attribution to Settlor)
ITA 85(1)	Transfer of Property to Corporation by Shareholders
ITA 86(1)	Exchange of Shares by a Shareholder in Course of Reorganization of Capital
ITA 104 to 108	Trusts and Their Beneficiaries
ITA 122	Tax Payable by Inter Vivos Trust
ITA 122.1	Definitions (SIFT Trusts)
IC-76-19R3	Transfer of Property to a Corporation under Section 85
S6-F1-C1	Residence of a Trust or Estate
S6-F2-C1	Disposition of an Income Interest in a Trust
IT-209R	Inter Vivos Gifts of Capital Property to Individuals Directly or through Trusts
IT-286R2	Trusts—Amount Payable
IT-291R3	Transfer of Property to a Corporation under Subsection 85(1)
IT-305R4	Testamentary Spouse Trusts
IT-342R	Trusts—Income Payable to Beneficiaries
IT-369R	Attribution of Trust Income to Settlor
IT-381R3	Trusts—Capital Gains and Losses and the Flow through of Taxable Capital Gains to Beneficiaries
IT-394R2	Preferred Beneficiary Election
IT-406R2	Tax Payable by an Inter Vivos Trust
IT-465R	Non-Resident Beneficiaries of Trusts
IT-510	Transfers and Loans of Property Made after May 22, 1985, to a Related Minor
IT-511R	Interspousal and Certain Other Transfers and Loans of Property
IT-524	Trusts—Flow through of Taxable Dividends to a Beneficiary after 1987
T4013	Trust Guide

Self-Study Problems (SSPs)

Self-Study Problems (SSPs) provide practice in problem solving. Within the chapters, we have indicated where it would be appropriate to stop and work on each SSP. The problems can be downloaded by chapter from MyLab Accounting. Solutions are available in the Study Guide. Select problems can also be completed directly in MyLab and auto-graded.

Assignment Problems

Solutions to Assignment Problems (APs) are available to instructors only.

AP 19-1   (Property Transfer to and from a Trust)

Each of the following independent cases involves gratuitous contributions of property to trusts by a settlor. Three of the cases also involve capital distributions from trusts to capital beneficiaries.

A. A gift of non-depreciable capital property is made to a qualifying spousal inter vivos trust. The ACB of the property to the settlor was $45,700. At the time of the transfer the FMV was $51,000. The property is subsequently distributed to the spouse at a time when the FMV is $49,200.

B. A gift of depreciable capital property (a rare violin) is made to an inter vivos trust in favour of the settlor's adult children. The capital cost of the violin to the settlor, a world-renowned violinist, was $125,000. On the date of the gift, the UCC was $72,000 and the FMV was $155,000.

C. A contribution of vacant land that is capital property is made to a qualifying spousal testamentary trust. The cost of the land to the deceased spouse was $200,000, and the FMV at the time of death was $225,500. At the time of death, the deceased had a net capital loss balance of $78,000.

D. A depreciable property is contributed to an inter vivos trust in favour of the settlor's adult children. The capital cost is $17,600, UCC is $9,100, and the FMV is $5,000. It is also the last property in its class.

E. A gift of non-depreciable capital property is made to an inter vivos trust in favour of the settlor's adult children. The ACB of the property to the settlor is $36,900, and the FMV on the date of the contribution is $40,200. The property is subsequently distributed to one of the beneficiaries when the FMV has increased to $51,700.

F. A non-depreciable capital property is contributed to an alter ego trust. The cost of the capital property to the settlor was $101,500 and on the date of the contribution the FMV is $92,300. The property is subsequently distributed to the settlor when the FMV has increased to $100,000.

Required: For each case indicate:

1. The income tax consequences to the settlor as a result of the contribution of the property to the trust assuming any elective options are chosen to minimize income tax to the settlor.

2. The tax cost of the contributed property to the trust.

3. In those cases where trust property is subsequently distributed to a beneficiary, the income tax consequences to both the trust and the beneficiary, including the tax cost of the property to the beneficiary.

AP 19-2   (Inter Vivos Trusts—Income Attribution)

In the process of planning an estate freeze, Glen Marx intends to contribute publicly traded common shares to a trust. The trust documents will direct 50% of the income of the trust to be distributed to his spouse, Greta Petrov, with the remaining 50% split equally between their son, Sergey, and daughter, Anastasia. Sergey is 23 years old and has annual employment income of $35,000, and Anastasia is 19 years old with annual employment income of $25,000.

The trust's income will consist of interest, dividends, and capital gains, none of which will qualify for the capital gains deduction.

The trust documents direct the trustee to distribute all trust property 15 years from the day the trust was established. This distribution will be based on the same allocation used for annual distributions of income.

Required:

A. Identify the type of trust that is being used.

B. Does the trust have a choice in the selection of a taxation year end? If not, what taxation year must be used?

C. The trust allocations of income are made annually to all three beneficiaries. Will the beneficiaries be required to include those income allocations in their own net income or will someone else be required to include the allocations in net income? Would your answer change if Anastasia were 17 years of age? If so, explain how.

D. Explain how your answer to Part C would change if Mr. Marx forms the trust by the settlement of a nominal amount of cash. Mr. Marx then lends money to the trust to purchase the portfolio investments from him at FMV. Assume:

   1. the loan is an interest-free loan;
   2. the trust pays interest at the prescribed rate on the loan.

E. Would the results change if Mr. Marx and Mrs. Petrov were separated due to a breakdown in their marriage? Explain your answer.

AP 19-3   (Trusts and Income Splitting)

Hannah Brood is an engineer with 2021 employment income of $235,000. In addition, she owns investments that earn $65,000 in interest during 2021.

She has a 19-year-old son, Harvey, from her first marriage, which ended when her spouse suffered a heart attack and passed away. Harvey is enrolled in his first year at a Canadian university. It is Harvey's life-long dream to be an accounting professor. Given this, he anticipates that he will be enrolled in university programs for at least six more years. Hannah expects that the cost of his living expenses, tuition, and books will be about $55,000 per year during this period.

Hannah recently remarried and now has a 3-year-old son named Carl. Carl is cared for by a nanny who is paid $17,000 per year. When Carl reaches five years of age, Hannah intends to send him to a private school. She anticipates that the cost of the private school will be similar to the cost of the nanny.

Hannah does not anticipate that either child will have significant income until they complete university.

Hannah would like to contribute the investments to a trust for her children, Harvey and Carl. As her employment income together with the income of her spouse is more than sufficient for their needs, she hopes to use the trust to split income both currently and in future years. Hannah's spouse earns income that also puts him in the same tax bracket as her. She has indicated that, while she wants to support her children fully with the assistance of her personal investments, she does not want the trust to provide the children with any direct payments until they are at least 30 years old. Until then, she wants to direct the trust to pay for their care, education, and other direct expenses.

Required: Outline how a trust might be used to split income with Hannah's children. Ignore the possibility that some of the trust's distributions might be subject to the TOSI.

AP 19-4   *(Graduated Rate Estates—Tax Minimization)*

Mr. Thomas Holt died on March 3, 2020. His will directs that all of his estate is to be contributed to a testamentary trust.

Because of difficulties in locating some of Mr. Holt's estate property, the transfer to a testamentary trust has been delayed past December 31, 2020. Given this situation, the executor of his estate has decided to file a T3 income tax return for the first year period ending December 31, 2020. This return designates Mr. Holt's estate as a GRE.

Due to ongoing delays, the estate of Mr. Holt remains under the administration of the executor at December 31, 2021. A second T3 income tax return is filed for the GRE for the taxation year ending December 31, 2021.

The named beneficiaries of the trust are Mr. Holt's spouse, Renfrew Holt, and their 22-year-old daughter, Roxanne. Renfrew is a successful trial lawyer with an annual income in excess of $275,000. Roxanne has struggled for several years to have a career as a folk singer. She has not enjoyed much success and, as a consequence, she has no net and taxable income for 2021.

In his will, Mr. Holt included a provision that allows the executor to make discretionary income distributions to Renfrew and Roxanne during the administration of the estate.

For the year ending December 31, 2021, the GRE earned the following amounts:

Interest	$43,000
Eligible dividends	31,200
Total income	$74,200

Required:

A. As the estate executor, exercise your discretion to allocate income in the most tax-effective manner for the GRE and the beneficiaries. Determine the amounts and types of income that should be distributed to each beneficiary for 2021 and whether any income should be retained in the GRE and not allocated to beneficiaries.

B. Using the allocations from Part A, calculate the total federal income tax payable for the GRE and the beneficiaries for the taxation year ending December 31, 2021.

Ignore the possibility that some of the trust's distributions might be subject to the TOSI.

AP 19-5   *(Inter Vivos Trusts—Income Tax Payable)*

During 2019, Valerie Larson's parents both died when their private jet was hit by a drone while circling the Toronto Island airport. As an only child, Valerie inherited a substantial estate.

Her parents had transformed the incorporated family construction business from a one-person operation into a successful online marketplace for quality construction services. Valerie and her two sons, Louis and Gabriel, had worked for the CCPC, Larson Services Inc. (LS), all their working lives.

Valerie decided to contribute the investments she inherited into a trust with her two sons as beneficiaries. The taxation year of the trust ends on December 31, and Ms. Larson has no beneficial interest in either the income or capital of the trust. As the president of LS, her employment and other compensation is more than adequate for her financial needs.

Louis is 30 years of age and Gabriel is 25. The trust documents direct the trust to distribute 10% of all trust income to Louis and 50% to Gabriel. Valerie had decided that the trust should allocate a smaller percentage to Louis because he has demonstrated extreme spending habits.

The remaining 40% of unallocated income is to be included in the net income of the trust. Future distributions of after-tax trust funds are to be made to Louis when he demonstrates that he has control over his spending habits.

The trust income for the year ending December 31, 2021, is as follows:

Non-eligible dividends from LS	$450,000
Interest income on corporate bonds	37,000
Rental income before recapture	79,650

During 2021, the rental property was sold. The property consisted of an apartment building and the land on which it was located, all of which was contributed to the trust when Valerie inherited the property. The relevant information related to the disposition of the rental property is as follows:

	Building	Land
POD	$3,200,000	$728,000
UCC	1,881,600	N/A
Capital cost/ACB	2,000,000	500,000

This is the first disposition of capital property by the trust since it was established.

Required:

A. Calculate the taxable income of the trust for the year ending December 31, 2021. In addition, calculate the increase in taxable income for Louis and Gabriel for the same period as a result of trust income allocations.

B. Calculate the federal income tax payable for the trust for the taxation year ending December 31, 2021.

AP 19-6 (Graduated Rate Estates—Transfer and Income Tax Payable)
Sam Cook passed away on September 19, 2020. He had been a successful entrepreneur, operating dozens of unincorporated retail outlets across the country offering vintage music, videos, and art collections. Sam had invested the profits over the previous 20 years into rental properties and investments, including bonds, GICs, and shares of publicly listed corporations. In the last two years, facing declining health, Sam slowly began to sell off all of his retail outlets except for the original location in Burnaby, B.C. Sam also sold some of his rental properties and liquidated many of his investments. Sam used the proceeds to provide cash gifts to employees, friends, family members, and numerous charitable organizations.

Sam was in the process of continuing to sell off most of his assets and pay off any liabilities, including income tax, when he passed away. In anticipation of his death Sam had prepared a will that named a long-time friend as executor to administer the estate by selling off the remaining assets, paying liabilities, filing the necessary tax returns, and making distributions to his two adult daughters, Violet and Trudy.

Unfortunately, the executor was not well versed in the responsibilities, and there were considerable delays in the administration of the estate as a result. In addition, both Violet and Trudy delayed the process by attempting to have the executor removed for lack of competency. A B.C. court ordered the executor to seek legal assistance to complete the estate administration. As a result, the estate administration was completed in August 2022.

Sam's will contemplated delays in the administration of his estate that would likely exceed one year. As a result, Sam provided the executor with discretionary authority to allocate any income to the two beneficiaries with any remainder to be taxed within the estate. The executor designated the estate as a GRE in the first income tax return of the estate for the taxation year ending September 18, 2021.

The following sources of income were earned by the GRE for its taxation year September 19, 2020, to September 18, 2021:

Business income	$68,100
Interest	14,700
Eligible dividends from publicly listed corporations	79,500
Rental income	52,500

Assume that Violet and Trudy's taxable income for the 2021 taxation year before any income allocations from the GRE would have been $32,000 and $98,000, respectively.

Further assume that the only personal tax credits available to both Violet and Trudy are the basic personal credit and any credits that may arise as a result of income allocations from the GRE. Ignore any potential TOSI implications except in Part D of the required.

Required:

A. Determine the taxable income and federal income tax payable for 2021 for each of the GRE, Violet, and Trudy on the assumption that one-third of each source of estate income is allocated to each of Violet and Trudy with the remaining one-third taxed in the GRE.

B. Determine whether you can improve on the result in Part A by minimizing the total combined federal income tax with a different estate income allocation. Explain the basis for the reallocations.

C. Compare the amount of federal income tax payable determined under Part A with Part B and explain the difference.

D. Briefly describe how your answer would change if it were determined that the TOSI would have applied to any business income and rental income allocations to Violet but not to Trudy.

AP 19-7   (Graduated Rate Estates—Transfers and Income Tax Payable)
Martha Dagger was killed in an accident on March 15, 2021. Her will directed that all of her estate be transferred to a testamentary trust. The beneficiaries of the trust will be her 22-year-old daughter, Sharon Dagger, and her 14-year-old son, Morris Dagger. Legal complications have delayed the transfer of the estate, and on December 31, 2021, the estate is still under the administration of the executor.

The executor decides to file a T3 income tax return for the first taxation year of the trust ending December 31, 2021, designating the estate as a GRE. While the executor could have chosen a non-calendar taxation year end, it was decided to use December 31.

Information on the property owned by Martha at the time of her death is as follows:

	Tax Cost	FMV March 15, 2021
Shares in Deadly Dagger Inc. (a CCPC)	$ 897,000	$1,472,000
Corporate bonds	478,000	456,000
Rental property		
Land	562,000	864,000
Building (cost = $1,740,000)	1,390,374	2,476,000

Assignment Problems

The shares of Deadly Dagger Inc. would qualify for the capital gains deduction as QSBC shares. Martha has available capital gains deduction of $250,000 and no CNIL at the time of her death.

Martha's will directs that 70% of any income of her estate (prior to the transfer to a testamentary trust) be distributed on the basis of 40% to Sharon and 30% to Morris. The remaining 30% will be retained in the GRE.

Between March 15, 2021, and December 31, 2021, the following income is earned by the GRE:

Non-eligible dividends		$124,000
Interest on corporate bonds		31,650
Rental income:		
Rental revenues	$251,600	
Rental expenses other than CCA	(172,940)	
CCA claimed	(55,615)	23,045
Total income		$178,695

Required:

A. Determine the increase in Martha's 2021 net and taxable income as a consequence of her death.

B. For the taxation year ending December 31, 2021, determine the net and taxable income for the GRE and the total income allocated to each beneficiary.

C. Calculate the federal income tax payable for the GRE for the taxation year ending December 31, 2021.

AP 19-8   (Business Succession)

Mr. and Mrs. Rohan are 50-50 shareholders of 987456 Ltd., a CCPC incorporated in Manitoba in 1991. The company was formed for the purpose of manufacturing and distributing a wide variety of medical equipment to hospitals across Canada. The company has been very successful, and a recent valuation has determined that the shares of the company are worth $12,000,000. The only shares ever issued by the company were common shares issued on incorporation to each of Mr. and Mrs. Rohan for nominal consideration of $100 each. As a result, the ACB and PUC of the shares are also nominal.

The Rohan's have three adult children, Larissa, Kara, and Julia, all of whom are 25 years of age or older and married or living common-law. In addition, they have a fourth child, Aaron, who is only 16 years old and living at home. Larissa has worked in the family business for the last 10 years along with her husband, Travis. Kara has worked in the business during summers while attending university, and Julia has never worked in the business. Aaron has shown little interest in the family business and has worked summers for a local retailer.

Mr. and Mrs. Rohan have been discussing retiring and passing the business to their children, but they anticipate at least a two-year transition where they would retain some control to ensure that the children who wish to be actively involved in the business are well prepared for the road ahead. Long term, they would also like to provide future financial benefits in connection with the ongoing successful business to each of their children, and indirectly their children's families, regardless of whether they intend to participate in the company business. These financial benefits would include a steady stream of dividend income from the company plus capital gain growth potential on any company shares. In addition, they want to ensure that there are some safeguards in place in case of marital, financial, or health issues among their children.

Mr. and Mrs. Rohan have taken compensation from the company since the beginning, mostly in the form of salary and bonuses with the occasional non-eligible dividend. The annual corporate income has remained below the small business limit throughout as a result of annual bonuses. The company's only activity and source of income has been from an active business.

The Rohan's have told you, as their accountant, that their main objectives are to transition the business to their children with minimal cost to them while maintaining some semblance of control for a few years, to retire with sufficient assets and income, and to minimize income tax throughout the process. They have specifically asked you to provide them with an understanding and the income tax consequences of the various options to transition the company to their children, including whether they should (1) gift their shares to the children, (2) pass the shares to the children on their death through a will, or (3) undertake a standard estate freeze through ITA 86. They have also asked you to explain to them the benefits, risks, and advantages of using a family trust given their objectives.

Required: Provide Mr. and Mrs. Rohan with a brief outline of the important points they should consider that address their objectives, and explain the income tax implications of the three methods they have identified that will result in the children becoming shareholders of the company.

In addition, provide them with an indication of the non-tax and income tax benefits and advantages of using a family trust given their objectives.

Finally, draw a conclusion, with reasons, as to whether an estate freeze with a family trust structure is in the best interests of Mr. and Mrs. Rohan and their children given their tax and non-tax objectives.

AP 19-9 *(Estate Planning)*
One of your clients, Daniel Loh, has read several articles describing the tax advantages of charitable donations. Mr. Loh is 73 years old and has had a successful career in business in Canada. As a consequence, he owns a wide variety of investments in both publicly traded companies and private companies, as well as real estate in Canada and Singapore. You estimate that the value of his estate is in excess of $15 million.

Due to a car accident in Singapore that left him disfigured and made him a recluse, he has never married and has no friends or living relatives. When he dies, he intends to leave all of his estate to his favourite charities.

He has never spent any time on estate planning and has asked you to help him understand estate planning issues and provide him with advice of what he should consider.

Required: Write a brief report providing the advice requested by your client.

CHAPTER 20

International Issues in Taxation

Learning Objectives

After completing Chapter 20, you should be able to:

1. Provide some practical examples of the importance of international tax issues to Canadians (Paragraph [P hereafter] P 20-1 to 20-6).
2. Explain the purpose of tax treaties (P 20-7 to 20-8).
3. Describe the circumstances under which non-residents could be subject to Part I income tax, including the general impact of the Canada/U.S. tax treaty (P 20-9 to 20-37).
4. Explain the purpose of Part XIII tax to non-residents, how it applies, and the impact of the Canada/U.S. treaty with respect to payments from Canada to U.S. residents for interest, dividends, royalties, rents, and pensions (P 20-38 to 20-65).
5. Describe how non-resident shareholders of Canadian corporations are treated when there are shareholder loans or other shareholder benefits (P 20-66 to 20-69).
6. Explain the purpose of the thin capitalization rules and their impact on the Canadian corporation and relevant non-resident shareholders (P 20-70 to 20-71).
7. Explain the purpose, the impact, and the exceptions to the immigration tax rules (P 20-72 to 20-73).
8. Describe the purpose of the emigration rules, their impact on departing Canadian residents, and any elective options available and the circumstances under which they would be used (P 20-74 to 20-83).
9. Explain the reason for legislation that allows the emigration rules to be reversed (P 20-84 to 20-87).
10. Explain how the immigration rules may benefit short-term residents (P 20-88 to 20-90).
11. Describe the foreign investment reporting requirements of form T1135 and explain the reason for these rules (P 20-91 to 20-100).
12. Explain how Canadian residents are taxed in both Canada and the U.S. when they are employed in the U.S., carry on business in the U.S., or dispose of U.S.-based property (P 20-101 to 20-109).
13. Explain the income tax consequences when Canadian resident individuals receive dividends from the U.S. (P 20-110 to 20-117).
14. Describe the Canadian income tax consequences when Canadian resident corporations receive dividends from U.S. corporations that are not foreign affiliates (P 20-118).

15. Explain the concept of a foreign affiliate in your own words and its purpose (P 20-119 to 20-121).

16. Describe the income tax treatment of dividends received from FAs that are not CFAs, including an explanation of both exempt and taxable surplus, the circumstances under which they apply, and their impact on Canadian income tax (P 20-122 to 20-136).

17. Explain the meaning of a controlled foreign affiliate (CFA) and how it differs from an FA (P 20-137 to 20-140).

18. Explain the purpose and meaning of FAPI and how it applies (P 20-141 to 20-147).

19. Describe the income tax treatment when dividends are paid from FAPI (P 20-148 to 20-149).

Introduction

Overview

20-1.   Canada, like most countries, is not self-sufficient and relies on trade with other countries. In general, the annual dollar amount of Canadian imports and exports are often similar. In 2019, for example, Canadian exports amounted to $431 billion while imports totalled $443 billion. Among Canada's many trading partners the United States accounts for roughly 75% of international trade. With this level of trade it is not surprising that Canadian and U.S. business interests are often intertwined in many respects. In addition, it is estimated that upwards of 1 million U.S. citizens call Canada their home, with tens of thousands of Canadians working in the U.S. at any one time and equal numbers of other U.S. citizens working in Canada.

20-2.   Because of the interconnection with the U.S., there are many day-to-day income tax-related questions that relate to (1) how to account for Canadian income tax (including payroll taxes) when non-residents are employed in Canada, (2) how to account for foreign taxes when Canadians work abroad, (3) how to determine Canadian income tax when non-residents invest in Canadian corporations or have interests in partnerships and trusts with activity within Canada, and (4) how to determine the income tax consequences when Canadians invest and carry on business outside of Canada.

20-3.   Other more pressing global international tax matters involve transfer pricing and the associated ever-increasing, onerous reporting obligations; tax havens used to avoid domestic tax; and the foreign affiliate and cross-border surplus stripping rules. In addition, the Organisation for Economic Co-operation and Development (OECD) instituted a study referred to as the BEPS (Base Erosion and Profit Sharing) initiative that has resulted in increased cooperation between member countries such as Canada with a focus on attempts to avoid or evade domestic tax altogether. These initiatives have led to increased complexity as new legislation is drafted to address these ongoing concerns. The 2021 federal budget has introduced legislation consistent with BEPS to limit the deduction of certain cross-border interest and to address concerns with what are referred to as hybrid mismatch arrangements, in which different types of entities between countries has led to tax planning that effectively multiplies income tax deductions.

20-4.   When dealing solely with domestic tax issues the only real concern is Canadian law, specifically either the ITA for federal income tax issues and the ETA *(Excise Tax Act)* for GST/HST issues. In addition, each province has its own income tax legislation that mirrors the ITA. In terms of international tax issues, however, there is an expanded level of knowledge required since any analysis relies on the tax laws of Canada, the tax laws of other countries, and the existence of income tax treaties that often serve to provide tie-breaker rules where the tax laws of two or more countries impose income tax on the same income.

20-5.   While international issues in taxation are of considerable importance, many practitioners choose to limit their practice to domestic income tax and GST/HST, preferring to leave international issues to those who choose to specialize in such matters. This fact is consistent with the CPA competencies for international tax issues, which is generally limited to non-resident issues (competency 6.5, "Income Taxation of Non-residents and Part Year Residents") such as residency, how non-residents are taxed when there is a Canadian source of income, and the impact when Canadians terminate their residency or when non-residents become residents of Canada. The competency level for these international issues in taxation is at a Level C, which is described as the lowest proficiency level that applies to low to moderate complexity but requires candidates to be able to explain, describe, and demonstrate knowledge in routine situations. A greater level of knowledge (Level B) is only required on an elective basis.

20-6.   Our objective in this chapter, as in other chapters, is to provide the necessary CPA competency level while emphasizing the importance of international tax issues and awareness so that any concerns can be identified and addressed when necessary. To that end the international topics that will be covered are briefly summarized as follows:

Residency   The determination of one's residency status is key to the ability of Canada to establish a right to impose income tax. While this topic represents the most important of international issues it was covered in detail in Chapter 1. If you have not recently read that coverage we would encourage you to do so prior to reading further.

Taxation of Canadian Source Income Earned by Non-Residents   While the basic right to impose income tax in Canada applies to residents of Canada, the right to impose income tax also extends to non-residents of Canada who earn income in Canada or dispose of certain Canadian-based property. This basic concept, which is enforced through ITA 2(3), is also discussed in Chapter 1 with additional coverage included in this chapter. Detailed consideration will be given to income tax under both Part I and Part XIII as they are the sections of the ITA most frequently applied to non-residents. We also suggest you read the Chapter 1 coverage titled "Part I Liability for Non-Residents" before proceeding further.

Immigration and Emigration   This topic refers to the Canadian income tax consequences when non-residents become residents of Canada (immigration) and residents become non-residents of Canada (emigration). This topic was very briefly introduced in Chapter 8 but will be expanded on in this chapter.

Taxation of Foreign Source Income Earned by Residents   This broad topic covers foreign reporting requirements when residents own certain foreign property, but more importantly covers the Canadian income tax consequences and analysis when residents earn foreign source income, including employment, business, and property income as well as the taxation of capital gains on the disposition of foreign property.

Foreign Affiliate Basics   The Canadian taxation of foreign dividends depends on whether the dividends represent pure investments such as a portfolio investment in multinational corporations listed on public stock exchanges or whether the foreign dividends represent distributions of foreign business profits in which the ultimate Canadian resident individuals have a stake. The nature of the Canadian tax system and those of other countries favours the foreign incorporation of a foreign business and the holding of an individual resident's interest through a Canadian corporation. This favourable system is referred to broadly as the foreign affiliate (FA) system. While the FA system is extremely complex, the basic principles are not difficult to understand. We have included this coverage to provide a basic understanding and awareness of the FA system. Since a discussion of the FA system is beyond the scope of the CPA competencies, some instructors may choose not to include it in their coverage.

The Role of Income Tax Treaties

20-7.   Income tax treaties generally represent bilateral agreements between two countries for the purpose of facilitating cross-border trade and investment, sharing information relevant to the administration and enforcement of each country's tax system, and avoiding double tax. For example, a Canadian resident employed in the U.S. is subject to Canadian income tax under the residency concept that requires that all worldwide sources of income are subject to Canadian income tax. In addition, the same individual would be subject to U.S. income tax on the basis that the income is sourced in the U.S. Income tax treaties address these and many other issues by providing rules to resolve the potential for double tax.

20-8.   Income tax treaties override the ITA through a combination of legislation that implements the tax treaty, as well as specific provisions within the ITA that recognize the priority given to tax treaties. For example, ITA 2(3) subjects a U.S. resident earning employment income in Canada to Canadian income tax under Part I. Article XV of the Canada/U.S. income tax treaty, however, may, in specific circumstances, restrict Canada's ability to tax that foreign income, giving preference to the U.S. In effect, the income tax treaty overrides ITA 2(3) in specific circumstances. The non-resident would still be required to include the Canadian employment income in a Canadian income tax return, particularly if the goal was to recover payroll withholdings, but ITA 110(1)(f)(i) would allow a taxable income deduction for the same amount to recognize the fact that the employment income is not taxable in Canada as a result of a tax treaty. In this chapter we will focus exclusively on the Canada/U.S. tax treaty.

Canadian Income Tax and Non-Residents

Introduction

Application—ITA 2(3)

20-9.   ITA 2(3) specifies that non-residents are subject to income tax under Part I of the ITA with respect to the following types of income:

- Income from carrying on a business in Canada
- Income from employment in Canada
- Gains and losses from the disposition of taxable Canadian property

20-10.   Part I of the ITA applies to subject the income from employment, business, property, capital gains/losses, and miscellaneous types of income such as pension income of residents to income tax. ITA 2(3), however, is much more limited in scope when it comes to non-residents in that there is no mention of income from property, miscellaneous income, or capital gains/losses on dispositions of property that is not taxable Canadian property.

20-11.   Where non-residents receive income from property or miscellaneous types of income that are paid by a resident of Canada a withholding tax is charged under Part XIII rather than require any amount to be included in net and taxable income of the non-resident as would be the case where Part I applies. The Canadian resident payor is responsible and liable for withholding, remitting, and reporting the amount to the CRA. The Part XIII result can also be altered by the existence of a tax treaty between Canada and the country in which the recipient is resident (e.g., liable for income tax in the other country).

20-12.   Capital gains and capital losses from the disposition of property that does not meet the definition of taxable Canadian property is not subject to Canadian income tax.

20-13.   In summary, non-residents are potentially subject to Canadian income tax (depending on the existence of a tax treaty) under Part I for Canadian employment, Canadian businesses, and capital gains/losses on the disposition of taxable Canadian property, and under Part XIII with respect to income from property and many types of miscellaneous income. Non-residents are not subject to Canadian income tax on dispositions of property that is not taxable Canadian property.

Filing Requirements

20-14.   Non-residents that are liable to Part I income tax are required to file an income tax return in the same manner as residents, although the income tax return is slightly different than that for residents. Non-residents are also required to file an income tax return to obtain a refund or a reimbursement of withholding taxes charged to them. This situation generally occurs where non-residents are sent to Canada by non-resident employers to work temporarily in Canada and

Canadian payroll withholdings have been made by the foreign employer as required and remitted to the CRA. If the Canadian employment income is exempt because of a treaty, then the only method to recover the withheld amounts is by filing an income tax return. This can also occur if a non-resident performs business services in Canada and amounts have been withheld (ITR 105) by the Canadian payor. In such cases, if the tax treaty exempts the business service revenues from Canadian taxation then, in general, the only way to recover the withheld amounts is to file an income tax return.

20-15.   There are other situations where a non-resident may be required to file a Canadian income tax return even though no income taxes are payable. Examples would include that the non-resident has disposed of taxable Canadian property but there was no capital gain. Other examples include that the minister has requested that a return be filed or that the non-resident is an individual that has Canadian income that would create RRSP contribution room allowing the individual to invest in an RRSP. In the latter case the CRA will not recognize any RRSP contribution room unless an income tax return has been filed.

20-16.   If Part XIII applies and a non-resident has paid excessive amounts as a result of an error or the fact that a reduced tax treaty rate was available, then the non-resident must file a special form (NR7-R) to recover the excess. The filing of an income tax return would not be required when the only issue is withholdings under Part XIII.

Taxable Income

20-17.   ITA 2(2) defines taxable income for residents as net income plus or minus amounts included in Division C, such as loss carry overs and the capital gains deduction. The rules for determining taxable income for non-residents are set out in Division D, specifically ITA 115, which is not restricted solely to taxable income deductions. ITA 115 addresses numerous issues, including modifying net income components of ITA 3. For example, ITA 115(1) modifies current-year losses that can be deducted by a non-resident restricting them to Canadian employment losses, Canadian business losses (as long as the business is not treaty exempt), and allowable business investment losses as long as any hypothetical gain from the property would have been included in the non-resident's taxable income. Loss carry overs are restricted by ITA 111(9), which only permits loss carry overs to the extent they originate from Canadian sources that are not exempt because of a tax treaty. Other limited taxable income deductions that may be claimed by a non-resident include Canadian stock option deductions, Canadian dividends received (non-resident corporations only), and charitable donations (non-resident corporations only).

20-18.   If all or substantially all (generally 90% or more) of the worldwide income of a non-resident for a given year is included in her income for purposes of Part I, then all other taxable income deductions become available for that year to the extent they are wholly applicable to income amounts that are required to be included in taxable income. This would include the capital gains deduction for non-resident individuals as long as the particular related capital gain is not treaty exempt.

Tax Payable

20-19.   Non-residents are subject to the federal Part I tax and a quasi-provincial income tax under the ITA that compensates for the fact that non-residents do not generally have sufficient ties to a province to be subject to provincial income tax. This quasi-provincial tax is referred to as the federal surtax on income not earned in a province and is charged at the rate of 48% on the Part I tax. In terms of available tax credits, unless a non-resident individual's Part I taxable income includes 90% or more of his worldwide income for a given year, ITA 118.94 prohibits the use of the majority of non-refundable tax credits for that year. However, the following credits will be available to non-resident filers who are individuals if they have any amount of Canadian source income included in their Part I return:

- Employment Insurance (EI) and Canada Pension Plan (CPP) tax credits
- Charitable donations tax credit

- Disability tax credit (for the disabled individual only)
- Tuition tax credit
- Interest on Canadian student loans tax credit

Carrying on Business in Canada

General Rules

20-20. Non-residents are subject to Part I tax in Canada on income from businesses carried on in Canada. The Canadian income tax rules for calculating business income (see Chapter 6) are equally applicable to non-residents. As a rule, the common law considers a business to be carried on at a specific location where contracts are entered into, purchases are made, services are rendered, goods are manufactured, employees are located, and inventories are maintained. ITA 253, however, expands the meaning of carrying on a business in Canada with respect to non-residents to include a broader range of activities such as the following:

- Producing, growing, mining, creating, manufacturing, fabricating, improving, packing, preserving, or constructing, in whole or in part, anything in Canada

- Soliciting orders or offering anything for sale in Canada through an agent or servant, whether the contract or transaction is to be completed inside or outside Canada

- Disposing of certain property, such as real property inventory situated in Canada, including an interest in, or option on, such real property

20-21. These rules are intended to ensure that certain Canadian activities that are connected to the non-resident's foreign business are potentially subject to Canadian income tax. In the absence of these rules, it could be questionable whether the non-resident person would be considered to be carrying on a business in Canada.

> **EXAMPLE** A U.S. business sends sales representatives to Canada to solicit orders. If the sales contracts can only be finalized in the U.S., under the general rules applicable to business income it could be argued that no business was carried on in Canada. However, ITA 253 makes it clear that the soliciting of orders in Canada is carrying on business in Canada, without regard to where the contracts are finalized.

20-22. Internet-based sales and deliveries of goods to Canadian customers by non-residents, with no physical presence in Canada (office location or employees/agents) where the website is located outside of Canada would generally not be considered to be carrying on business in Canada.

Canada/U.S. Treaty on Business Income

20-23. The treaty allows Canada to tax the business income of U.S. residents provided that business is operated in Canada through what is referred to as a permanent establishment.

20-24. Article V(2) of the Canada/U.S. tax treaty defines a "permanent establishment" as a fixed place of business through which the business of a non-resident is wholly or partly carried on. The treaty provides additional clarification by adding that fixed places of business include a place of management, a branch, an office, a factory, a workshop, a mine, an oil or gas well, a quarry, or other place of extraction of natural resources. Additional rules provide permanent establishment status only if certain conditions are met (e.g., most construction projects are only considered permanent establishments if they last for more than 12 months (article V(3))).

20-25. Article V(6) specifically excludes facilities from being considered a fixed place of business if they are used exclusively for certain activities. These activities include:

- use of facilities solely for storage, display, or delivery of goods;
- maintenance of a stock of goods or merchandise for storage, display, or delivery;
- maintenance of a fixed place of business solely for purchasing goods or merchandise or for collecting information; or

- maintenance of a fixed place of business solely for the purpose of carrying on any other activity of a preparatory or auxiliary character.

20-26.   The tax treaty also deems certain persons to be permanent establishments of a non-resident. Two examples of this are as follows:

- An agent who acts on behalf of a non-resident and who is authorized to conclude contracts on behalf of the non-resident is considered to be a permanent establishment of the non-resident (article V(5)).

- An individual who acts on behalf of a business and meets both a physical presence test (183 days or more in any 12-month period beginning or ending in the year) and a gross revenue test (that more than 50% of the gross active business revenues of the U.S. business are from services performed by that individual during the period the individual is in Canada) is considered a permanent establishment (article V(9)).

20-27.   Article V(7) adds a further exception noting that a non-resident will not be considered to have a permanent establishment in Canada where they conduct business in Canada through a broker, general commission agent, or other agent who is acting in her own independent interests in her own business. In addition, article V(8) clarifies that a non-resident company will not be considered to have a permanent establishment in Canada simply because of the existence of a Canadian corporation that the non-resident controls.

Exercise 20-1

Subject: Carrying on Business in Canada

In each of the following cases, determine whether Jazzco, a U.S. resident corporation, is taxable in Canada.

Case 1   Jazzco, a U.S. corporation, is the parent company of Bluesco, a company incorporated in Ontario. Jazzco produces and sells jazz CDs, while Bluesco produces and sells blues CDs. Jazzco sells CDs to Bluesco, who in turn sells them in Canada.

Case 2   Jazzco sets up a factory in Toronto where they produce CDs for the Canadian market. The CDs are sold exclusively to an independent Canadian franchise retail outlet at a 50% markup.

Case 3   Jazzco manufactures jazz CDs in the U.S. Jazzco ships CDs to a warehouse located in Calgary that they have rented on a five-year lease. Jazzco has employed an individual in Calgary to sell the CDs throughout western Canada. The employee, however, is not allowed to conclude contracts without approval by the U.S. office.

Case 4   Assume the same facts as in Case 3, except that the employee has the authority to conclude contracts on behalf of the employer.

Case 5   Assume the same facts as in Case 3, except that the employee has an office in the warehouse premises where sales orders are solicited.

Solutions to Exercises are available in the Study Guide.

Canadian Source Employment Income

General Rules

20-28.   Non-resident individuals are subject to Part I tax if they are employed in Canada. For this purpose, employment income is calculated using the same rules that apply to residents. The employment income rules were discussed at length in Chapter 3.

20-29.   ITA 115(2) deems certain non-resident individuals to be employed in Canada even when the work is not carried on in Canada. Such individuals include:

- individuals who have become residents of another country and continue to receive employment remuneration from a resident Canadian source, provided a tax treaty exempts that remuneration from taxation in the foreign country (ITA 115(2)(c)); and

- non-resident individuals who have received signing bonuses and other similar amounts that relate to services to be performed in Canada in situations where the resident Canadian employer is entitled to deduct the amounts in computing Canadian income (ITA 115(2)(c.1)).

20-30.   The general policy behind these deeming rules is to ensure that an employment connection to Canada continues to be subject to income tax in Canada. These rules apply a symmetrical approach that looks to whether payments to non-residents are in connection with employment that entitles a Canadian payor to a deduction. The payments will generally be subject to Canadian income tax as long as they are not subject to income tax in the other country.

Canada/U.S. Tax Treaty on Employment Income

20-31.   In general, a country has the right to impose income tax on the employment income of non-residents when it is earned within its borders irrespective of the residency of the employer. This view is reflected in ITA 2(3), which applies where non-resident individuals are employed in Canada. However, the Canada/U.S. tax treaty contains two exceptions:

$10,000 Rule (Article XV(2)(a))   Under this rule if, during a calendar year, a U.S. resident individual earns employment income in Canada that is $10,000 or less in Canadian dollars, then the income is taxable only in the U.S.

183-Day Rule (Article XV(2)(b))   This rule denies Canada the right to impose Canadian income tax on employment income earned in Canada by non-resident individuals who are not physically present in Canada for more than 183 days during any 12-month period commencing or ending in the calendar year. This exemption is conditional on employment income not being paid by an employer with a permanent establishment in Canada who would be able to deduct the amount paid from their Canadian income.

Summary   If the employment income exceeds $10,000 and is deductible in Canada, it will be subject to income tax in Canada, even if the employee is present in Canada for less than 183 days during the year.

20-32.   It is important not to confuse the 183-day employment income treaty rule with the 183-day residency sojourner rule that deems individuals to be resident in Canada for all of a year if they are physically present in Canada in that year for 183 days or more. While the employment income treaty rule applies to any physical presence in Canada, such as crossing the border to work an eight-hour shift, the sojourner rule only applies to actual temporary visits or stays, which implies overnight stays at a minimum. Daily commutes for employment purposes would therefore not count as a day for purposes of the sojourner rule but would be counted as a day for the employment treaty exception.

Exercise 20-2

Subject: Non-Resident Employment in Canada

Dawn Johnson is employed by Alberta Oil Ltd. as an oil well technician in Edmonton. She has accepted a transfer to the Egyptian offices of the company for three years beginning January 1, 2021. Dawn severs her residential ties to Canada on December 31, 2020, and takes up residence in Egypt. Alberta Oil continues to pay her salary. Although the government of Egypt would normally tax such salary, the tax treaty between Canada and Egypt exempts the salary from tax in Egypt. Is Dawn required to pay Canadian tax on the salary paid to her by Alberta Oil? Justify your conclusion.

Exercise 20-3

Subject: Non-Resident Employment in Canada—Canada/U.S. Tax Treaty

In each of the following cases, determine whether the employment income is subject to income tax in Canada.

Case 1   David resides in the state of Washington. He accepted temporary employment as a technician with a Canadian company out of their Vancouver office to do service calls in the Vancouver area for four months beginning September 1, 2021. The Canadian employer agreed to pay David $2,800 Canadian per month. David remained a non-resident of Canada throughout his Canadian employment and was advised that he may be rehired in late 2022.

Case 2   Assume the same facts as in Case 1, except the employer was resident in Washington and did not have a permanent establishment in Canada.

Case 3   Sandra resides in Detroit, Michigan, and has commuted daily to a full-time job in Windsor, Ontario, for the last three years. In 2021, she spent 238 days at her job in Canada. She works for the municipality of Windsor and earned C$50,000 in employment income. Sandra is a U.S. resident throughout the year.

Solutions to Exercises are available in the Study Guide.

Dispositions of Taxable Canadian Property

General Rules

20-33.   ITA 2(3) also adds to the Part I liability of non-residents' capital gains/losses on the disposition of taxable Canadian property. The calculation of capital gains/losses also follows the same rules that apply to residents of Canada.

20-34.   As defined in ITA 248(1), the main categories of taxable Canadian property are as follows:

- Real property situated in Canada
- Certain capital property or inventories of a business carried on in Canada
- A share of a corporation not listed on a designated stock exchange (generally private corporations), an interest in a partnership, or an interest in a trust if at any time within the preceding 60 months more than 50% of the FMV of the share or interest was derived from certain properties, including Canadian real property, Canadian resource properties, and timber resource properties
- A share of a corporation listed on a designated stock exchange (generally public corporations) only if at any time within the preceding 60 months at least 25% of the issued shares of any class were owned by the non-resident taxpayer and/or persons non-arm's length with the non-resident, and more than 50% of the shares' FMV was derived from certain properties, including Canadian real property, Canadian resource properties, and timber resource properties.

Compliance Certificates

20-35.   To ensure compliance with the Canadian income tax laws when a non-resident disposes of taxable Canadian property a certification system has been put in place. The process requires that the non-resident seller obtain a compliance certificate that first requires completing form T2062, "Request by a Non-Resident of Canada for a Certificate of Compliance Related to the Disposition of Taxable Canadian Property." This form, which must be filed within 10 days of the planned disposition, must be accompanied by a payment of 25% of the anticipated capital gain on the disposition of the property (some types of security are acceptable, such as bank guarantees). When these conditions are met, a certificate of compliance will be issued.

20-36.   If the non-resident seller does not obtain a compliance certificate, the purchaser (usually a Canadian resident) is responsible for the 25% or higher tax on behalf of the non-resident, which is based on the purchase price and not the anticipated gain. This can cause considerable issues where the compliance certificate is not obtained. If, for example, a non-resident were to sell land in Canada for $1 million and the ACB of the land was $950,000, the payment required by the non-resident would equal $12,500 [(25%)(POD $1,000,000 - ACB $950,000)]. But if a clearance certificate is not obtained, the purchaser would be liable for $250,000 [(25%)$1,000,000)], which must be remitted within 30 days of the end of the month of the purchase. Failure to remit this on time can result in a penalty under ITA 227(9) of 20%, which in our example would equal $50,000. Note, however, that ITA 116(5) provides an exception to this if, after reasonable enquiry, the purchaser had no reason to believe that the seller was not resident in Canada. We would also add that these rules apply when the purchaser is also a non-resident.

Canada/U.S. Treaty on Dispositions of Taxable Canadian Property

20-37.   Article XIII of the Canada/U.S. tax treaty recognizes that Canada may impose income tax on gains of a U.S. resident arising from only the following specific types of taxable Canadian property:

- Real property situated in Canada
- Property forming part of the business property of a permanent establishment of the non-resident in Canada
- Investments such as shares of corporations resident in Canada and interests in partnerships and trusts where the value of those investments is primarily attributable to real property situated in Canada

---

Exercise 20-4

Subject: Dispositions of Taxable Canadian Property

In each of the following cases the individual is a U.S. resident who is disposing of a property. Determine whether any gain on the disposition is subject to income tax in Canada under Part I of the ITA.

Case 1   In 2021, Nancy Gordon disposed of shares of a widely held Canadian public company that she acquired in 2018. Nancy never owned more than one-quarter of 1% of the outstanding shares of this company. The company's property consists entirely of real estate situated in Canada.

Case 2   In 2016, Joe Nesbitt purchased a condo in Whistler, B.C., that he rented to Canadian residents. He sold the condo in 2021 at a considerable gain. Joe never lived in the condo.

Case 3   Assume the same facts as in Case 2, except that Joe incorporates a private corporation under the *B.C. Business Corporations Act* solely to acquire the condo. At a later point in time, Joe sells the shares at a considerable gain.

Case 4   Assume the same facts as in Case 3, except the corporation is created under Washington state legislation.

Solutions to Exercises are available in the Study Guide.

We suggest you complete SSP 20-1 at this point.

Part XIII Tax on Non-Residents

Introduction

Applicability

20-38.   Non-residents are subject to income tax under Part I with respect to Canadian employment, businesses carried on in Canada, and the disposition of taxable Canadian property. The Part I results may change, however, with the existence of a tax treaty between Canada and the resident country of the non-resident. Other sources of income, including income from property and miscellaneous types of income, are subject to withholding tax under Part XIII, which is set at a flat rate of 25% of the payment but which is often reduced to a lower rate as a result of a tax treaty.

20-39.   Part XIII tax, specifically ITA 212, provides a list of certain types of income that are subject to the withholding tax. The payments fall into the general category of income from property category, such as interest, dividends, rents, and royalties, to the types of miscellaneous income referred to in Subdivision d of Division B of Part I, such as pension benefits, retiring allowances, and payments from an RRSP or RRIF.

20-40.   Three other points are noteworthy with respect to Part XIII:

- Part XIII tax is a non-resident-based tax that is in addition to Part I tax. There are situations, however, in which both taxes could apply to the same income. For example, if a non-resident carries on a business in Canada through a permanent establishment that involves the lending of money, any interest income would be business income. In that case, it would appear that both Part I and XIII would apply to the same income. ITA 214(3)(c), together with ITR 805, gives priority to Part I, meaning that if the non-resident carries on a business in Canada through a permanent establishment then Part I will apply. However, if there is no permanent establishment, Part XIII will apply (this is the CRA position as described in paragraph 12 of IT-420R3, "Non-Residents—Income Earned in Canada").

- Non-residents are not required to file a Canadian income tax return for income that is subject to Part XIII tax.

- In general, it is the Canadian resident who has made a payment to a non-resident of amounts listed in Part XIII who is responsible for (1) withholding the required Part XIII tax, (2) remitting the withheld amounts to the CRA, and (3) filing an information return (NR4) indicating the amounts withheld.

20-41.   Our coverage of Part XIII will be limited to payments of interest, royalties, rents, dividends, and pension benefits to non-residents.

Part I vs. Part XIII Tax

20-42.   Part XIII is a different type of income tax than Part I. Under Part I, the relevant income tax rates are applied to a taxpayer's taxable income, which is composed of different sources of income that have taken related expenses into consideration. For example, investment income is included in net and taxable income after claiming all related expenses. In contrast, Part XIII tax is applied to the gross investment income without allowing for any expenses.

EXAMPLE   Ms. Johnson borrows $100,000 to invest in high-yield bonds. During the current year, the bonds generate $9,000 in interest. Interest expenses with respect to the money borrowed to purchase the bonds total $4,000.

ANALYSIS   If Ms. Johnson were a resident of Canada she would include $5,000 as income from property as part of her net and taxable income for the year for Part I purposes. In contrast, if Ms. Johnson were a non-resident, Part XIII tax would be calculated by applying the relevant withholding rate to the gross amount of interest of $9,000.

Rates

20-43.   Part XIII applies a flat rate of 25% for all payments listed in ITA 212. If the non-resident is resident of a country that does not have a tax treaty with Canada, then the 25% rate will apply. If, however, the non-resident is resident of a country that has a tax treaty with Canada, then the Part XIII rate equals the treaty rate (Income Tax Application Rule (ITAR) 10(6)). Tax treaty rates differ based on the type of payment and the particular treaty.

20-44.   The CRA has added a "non-resident tax calculator" to its website that allows one to choose the non-resident country from a drop-down menu, the type of income payment from Canada (also from a drop-down menu), and to then identify the Canadian dollar amount of the payment. Where there are multiple treaty rates the calculator will provide the rates and information necessary to make the appropriate selection. Once completed, the calculate button will then provide the necessary withholding. The calculator can be found at https://apps.cra-arc.gc.ca/ebci/nrtc/beta/ng/entry.

Interest Payments—ITA 212(1)(b)

Part XIII Rules

20-45.   ITA 212(1)(b) assesses Part XIII tax on only two types of interest:

Participating Debt Interest   Participating debt interest is defined in ITA 212(3) as interest that is contingent or dependent on the use of property (e.g., royalties) or that is calculated by reference to revenue, cash flow, or profit. Although technically interest, the economic nature of participating debt payments is that they resemble distributions of profits and are therefore similar to dividends, which are subject to withholding taxes. This is generally the reason why these payments are not eligible for withholding-free treatment.

Interest Paid to Non-Arm's-Length Non-Residents, Unless the Interest Is Fully Exempt Interest   Fully exempt interest is defined in ITA 212(3) as interest paid or payable on certain types of government-issued or-guaranteed debt (e.g., debt issued by the Government of Canada or a province).

20-46.   In summary, the rules for applying Part XIII tax to interest are as follows:

- Arm's-length interest payments are not subject to Part XIII unless they are interest from participating debt.

- Non-arm's-length interest payments are not subject to Part XIII as long as the interest is fully exempt interest.

Canada/U.S. Tax Treaty on Interest Payments

20-47.   If it is determined that Part XIII applies to interest payments to non-residents then it is necessary to determine the impact of the tax treaty where one exists. Article XI of the Canada/U.S. treaty provides the rules for dealing with interest. The following excerpt from the treaty provides the main rule. We have added bracketed references to the particular country to assist in reading this article:

Article XI(1)   Interest arising in a Contracting State (Canada) and beneficially owned by a resident of the other Contracting State (the U.S.) may be taxed only in that other State (the U.S.).

20-48.   This treaty article means that Canada cannot impose any income tax on U.S. residents who have received interest payments that have originated in Canada. As a result, U.S. residents are exempt from the Part XIII tax, even though Part XIII would otherwise apply. TIP: If you use the CRA's non-resident calculator and choose "other" for the country, you would be dealing with a country in which Canada does not have a tax treaty. In that case two rates are indicated, one for 0% and a second for 25%, both of which are solely dependent on Part XIII as discussed.

Exercise 20-5

Subject: Interest Payments to Non-Residents

In each of the following independent cases, determine whether the interest payments made to non-residents are subject to Part XIII withholding tax, and if so, at what rate.

Case 1 Jason, a resident of a country that does not have a tax treaty with Canada, earned $3,000 in interest from a term deposit in a Canadian bank during 2021.

Case 2 Janice, a resident of a country that does not have a tax treaty with Canada, earned interest of $1,800 on Government of Canada bonds during 2021.

Case 3 Julian, a resident of Canada, acquired a vacation property in a country that does not have a tax treaty with Canada. The property is mortgaged with a bank in the foreign country. Julian paid $12,000 in interest to the foreign bank in 2021.

Case 4 Jasmine, a resident of Canada, paid $5,000 in interest on a loan from her brother, a resident of the U.S., during 2021.

Solutions to Exercises are available in the Study Guide.

Dividends—ITA 212(2)

Part XIII Rules
20-49. Most types of dividends are subject to the 25% Part XIII tax. This includes capital dividends despite the fact that they are not subject to tax when received by Canadian residents. The withholding tax rate applies equally to taxable dividends irrespective of whether they are non-eligible or eligible dividends.

Canada/U.S. Tax Treaty on Dividend Payments
20-50. The Canada/U.S. tax treaty does not exempt dividends paid by Canadian residents to U.S. residents, however the treaty does provide reduced rates. Specifically, there are two different rates that depend on whether the shareholder is a corporation and the percentage of the shares of the dividend-paying corporation that are owned by the non-resident corporate shareholder.

> **5% Rate** If the U.S. resident recipient is a corporation that owns 10% or more of the voting shares of the resident Canadian company, the withholding rate is only 5%. This 5% rate for intercorporate dividends reflects a view that dividend payments between parent companies and their subsidiaries should be less heavily taxed to encourage international trade and investment.

> **15% Rate** Dividends paid by resident Canadian companies to any other shareholders who are U.S. residents are subject to a Part XIII withholding tax of 15%.

Royalty Payments—ITA 212(1)(d)

Part XIII Rules
20-51. Royalties paid or credited to non-residents by a person resident in Canada are subject to the Part XIII flat rate of 25%. However, there are specific Part XIII exclusions that exempt payments for the use of copyrights, payments made under cost-sharing arrangements where the costs are shared with non-residents, and arm's-length payments made that are deductible under Part I against business income earned outside Canada.

Canada/U.S. Tax Treaty on Royalty Payments

20-52.   Article XII of the Canada/U.S. treaty contains the rules with respect to royalties. In general, the rates applicable to royalties are dependent on the nature of the royalty. Royalties for computer software and copyrights are exempt from withholding (a nil or 0% rate), whereas royalties for films are subject to a 10% rate. Royalties for immovable property and natural resources are not subject to reduced rates, so the 25% Part XIII withholding would apply.

Rental Income—ITA 212(1)(d)

Part XIII Rules

20-53.   The situation with rent payments is more complex. While ITA 212(1)(d) lists rents as one of the items subject to Part XIII tax, the *ITA* is designed to give priority to Part I tax over Part XIII tax. However, as we have noted in our discussion on the small business deduction, a taxpayer's rental activities may be so extensive that they may be considered a business. If this is the case, the non-resident taxpayer will be carrying on a business in Canada through a permanent establishment (e.g., Canadian rental properties), which will be subject to Part I tax. If this is the case, the non-resident will be required to file an income tax return under Part I with respect to the rental business. However, there will be no Part XIII tax (ITR 805)).

Rental Income of Non-Residents—Elective Treatment (ITA 216)

20-54.   If the non-resident is not carrying on a rental business in Canada, Part XIII tax will apply at a rate of 25%, which is not reduced by the Canada/U.S. treaty. Part XIII tax can, as a result, create cash flow issues, particularly where the profit margins are small since the tax is imposed on the gross rents ignoring underlying expenses.

> **EXAMPLE** Marcia Dorne, a resident of the U.S., owns a rental property in Canada. The gross rent on this property is $120,000 for the year and is paid monthly at a rate of $10,000. The property is so heavily financed that rental income, as determined for Part I purposes, would only be $12,000 for the year before claiming CCA of $11,000.

> **ANALYSIS** In the absence of an elective option, Marcia would be subject to Part XIII tax of $30,000 [(25%)($120,000)].

20-55.   Under ITA 216, Marcia can elect to apply Part I to her rental activity rather than pay withholding taxes under Part XIII. In the preceding example, this election would result in Part I taxes being paid on the rental income of $1,000 ($12,000 - $11,000 CCA). If Marcia had no other source of Canadian income, this $1,000 would be taxed at the lowest federal rate of 15% and, when combined with the 48% federal surtax on income not earned in a province, the total Part I tax would be $222 [(15%)($1,000)(148%)]. This is significantly less that the $30,000 Part XIII tax.

20-56.   With respect to this election, two other points are worth noting:

- In general, this election can only be made where the rental property is real property situated in Canada.

- If a non-resident taxpayer makes this election, she will file a separate return (CRA form T1159) including only the revenues and expenses related to the rental property. She cannot claim any taxable income deductions and she cannot claim any of the personal tax credits. The individual can, however, claim certain other deductions that reduce net income such as RRSP deductions and deductible support payments.

- Under Part I, the income is not considered to be income earned in a province, so there will be no provincial income tax. Instead there is an additional surtax of 48% of the federal income tax charged under ITA 120(1).

Solution to Potential Cash Flow Problem—ITA 216(4)

20-57.   Unfortunately, use of the ITA 216 election to pay tax under Part I does not relieve the payor from the requirement to withhold Part XIII tax. This will, in many cases, create a significant cash flow problem for the non-resident. Consider the example from Paragraph 20-54. The person paying the rent would have to withhold a total of $30,000 from the payments made to Marcia Dorne and remit each amount withheld to the CRA by the 15th day of the following month. As a result, she would have a negative cash flow of $18,000 [($120,000 - Part XIII tax $30,000) - (expenses of $120,000 - $12,000)]. While the excess tax would eventually be refunded, there is a significant outflow of cash during the rental period.

20-58.   ITA 216(4) provides a method to resolve this issue that requires filing Form NR6, "Undertaking to File an Income Tax Return by a Non-Resident Receiving Rent from Real Property or Receiving a Timber Royalty" by January 1 of each year, which requires filing the ITA 216 return within six months of the end of the year (generally June 30). This method allows the payor to base the withholding on 25% of the estimated net rental income before the deduction of CCA. In our Paragraph 20-54 example, the Part XIII withholding would be reduced from $2,500 per month [(25%)($10,000)] to $250 per month [(25%)(1/12)($12,000)]. Any difference between the amount withheld and the actual Part I liability would be claimed when Marcia Dorne's elective Part I tax return is filed.

Canada/U.S. Tax Treaty on Rental Income

20-59.   Article XII of the Canada/U.S. treaty does not prevent Canada from imposing income tax on U.S. residents with respect to rental income. When the rental property is real property, there is no treaty rate reduction, so the 25% Part XIII tax applies. However, where the rental property is something other than real property in Canada (e.g., equipment or machinery), the Canada/U.S. treaty reduces the Part XIII withholding rate to 10%.

Exercise 20-6

Subject: Rental Payments to Non-Residents

In each of the following cases, determine how the rental activity will be taxed in Canada. In addition, indicate whether an election to pay Part I tax is available and whether the election would be beneficial.

Case 1   Rentco is a U.S. corporation with worldwide rental facilities dedicated to various equipment rentals. Rentco has offices in Saskatchewan, where it rents out farming equipment.

Case 2   In 2018, Jack Foster, a U.S. resident, acquired a hunting and fishing lodge in northern Ontario that he rents out. In 2021, he rented the lodge to Canadian residents exclusively. Jack received $42,000 in gross rents and estimates that expenses, including CCA, totalled $14,000.

Case 3   Assume the same facts as in Case 2, with one additional consideration. Jack acquired three motor boats in 2019, which he rented to guests of the lodge. In 2021, he received $8,000 in gross boat rents and estimates boat-related expenses would be $7,000.

Solutions to Exercises are available in the Study Guide.

Pension Payments and Other Retirement-Related Benefits

Part XIII Rules

20-60.   Amounts received by non-residents as pension or other retirement-related benefits are generally subject to tax under Part XIII. This would include OAS payments, CPP payments, death benefits, certain retiring allowances, as well as payments from RPPs, RRSPs, RRIFs, and DPSPs. Payments from TFSAs are not considered pension payments, but there are special rules for individuals who own TFSAs and become non-resident.

20-61.   There are some exceptions under Canadian legislation that are designed to ensure that a non-resident will only be taxed on amounts that would have been taxable had the non-resident been resident in Canada at the time the benefits were earned. For example, a non-resident may receive a pension from a former Canadian employer, most of which relates to years in which the person was non-resident and worked outside of Canada. Part XIII may exempt the part of the pension that relates to employment outside of Canada.

An Elective Option for Pension Income of Non-Residents—ITA 217

20-62.   The non-resident recipient of Canadian pension income can elect under ITA 217 to be subject to tax under Part I instead of Part XIII. Unlike the ITA 216 election for rental income, this alternative requires that all Canadian pension income that would have been subject to Part XIII be added to other Canadian source income for which the individual is filing a Part I income tax return. The benefit is that the non-resident would also be entitled to claim net income deductions and tax credits normally provided only to Canadian residents. More detailed information is available on the CRA website in the T4145 guide, "Electing under Section 217 of the *Income Tax Act.*"

20-63.   The downside to the election is that the tax rate is based on a calculation that requires adding all of the non-residents' worldwide income (ITA 217(3)). A special tax credit is then provided (ITA 217(6)) to reduce the Part I Canadian income tax on a proportional basis for that other worldwide income that would not be subject to Canadian income tax. The end result is that a low tax rate is generally not attainable using this method. For a low-income individual, choosing to use the ITA 217 election can provide a significant advantage in that it will allow the individual to make use of some of the tax credits that are available under Part I. However, for high-income individuals, the Part XIII rate is likely to be lower than the rate that would apply under Part I of the Act.

Canada/U.S. Tax Treaty on Pension Benefits

20-64.   Article XVIII of the Canada/U.S. treaty applies to pensions and annuities and provides that Canada can tax Canadian-based pension payments to residents of the U.S. The treaty reduces the Part XIII rate to 15% with respect to periodic pension payments from RPPs, RRSPs, and RRIFs. The treaty, however, does not apply to lump-sum payments from any of these plans, meaning that the Part XIII rate of 25% is unchanged.

20-65.   Payments from OAS, CPP, and QPP are also subject to Part XIII tax and eligible for the elective Part I treatment as a result of ITA 217. However, article XVIII(5) of the Canada/U.S. tax treaty limits the taxation of any of these amounts to the country in which the recipient is a resident. As a result, no Part XIII taxes are required.

Shareholder Loans and Benefits to Non-Residents

20-66.   In Chapter 15, we discussed shareholder loans and benefits to residents of Canada. In general, the principal of shareholder loans or the interest benefit calculated under ITA 80.4 and the FMV of shareholder benefits had to be included in a resident shareholder's net income as income from property.

20-67.   Since both shareholder loans and shareholder benefits are income from property, a non-resident shareholder that has benefitted from such amounts would not be subject to Part I tax, which is limited to Canadian employment, Canadian businesses, and certain capital gains on the disposition of taxable Canadian property. Part XIII tax, however, applies to subject the shareholder amounts to withholding tax. ITA 214(3)(a) specifically uses the amounts that would have been required to be included in the income of a shareholder under ITA 15(1), 15(2), or 15(9) (for shareholder loan interest benefits determined under ITA 80.4(2)) had the shareholder been a resident of Canada and treats the amounts as if they represent the payment of a dividend by a corporation resident in Canada. As a result, these shareholder income amounts are subject to withholding taxes that apply to dividends.

20-68.   If a non-resident shareholder has received a loan that would be required to be included in income under ITA 15(2) if the shareholder were a resident of Canada, then any subsequent repayments of the amount included would entitle a shareholder to a deduction for the year of repayment, again if that person were a resident of Canada. Since shareholder loans to non-residents are treated as dividends for Part XIII purposes, any repayments would entitle the non-resident to a refund of the Part XIII taxes attributable to the repayment (ITA 227(6.1)).

20-69.   There is some controversy as to whether deemed dividends are considered dividends for purposes of the Canada/U.S. tax treaty. Article X(3) of the Canada/U.S. treaty defines the meaning of the word "dividend" for purposes of the treaty to effectively include deemed dividends. As a result, the treaty rates applicable to dividends would apply. If, for example, the non-resident shareholder were an individual, the Part XIII rate of 25% would be reduced to 15%.

We suggest you complete SSP 20-2 at this point.

Interest in Thin Capitalization Situations—ITA 18(4)

20-70.   In general, interest paid on debt is deductible to a business, whereas dividends paid on outstanding shares are not. In addition, withholding tax rates on dividends with the U.S. are either 5% or 15%, whereas interest payments are exempt. As a result, there are incentives for non-resident shareholders to invest in Canadian resident corporations by way of debt rather than equity (e.g., shares).

20-71.   To discourage excessive debt financing, ITA 18(4) through 18(6) serve to limit the deductibility of interest paid by resident Canadian corporations in what are commonly referred to as "thin capitalization" situations, which means that non-resident investors have low amounts of equity versus debt. Interest paid or payable to certain specified non-resident shareholders is disallowed as a deduction to the extent it exceeds 1.5 times the sum of the shareholder's share of contributed capital, plus 100% of the corporation's retained earnings at the beginning of the year. In conjunction with this, ITA 214(16) re-characterizes the disallowed interest as a deemed dividend, which will result in Part XIII withholding taxes that will generally be reduced by income tax treaties. For this purpose, a specified non-resident shareholder is defined in ITA 18(5) as a person who owns shares that represent 25% or more of the votes that would be cast at the annual meeting of the shareholders, or 25% or more of the FMV of all issued and outstanding shares.

EXAMPLE   Throughout 2021, Mr. Lane, a resident of the U.S., owns 45% of the shares and holds $3,000,000 of the long-term debt of Thinly Ltd. The capital structure of Thinly Ltd. throughout the year is as follows:

Long-term debt (11% rate)	$5,000,000
Common shares	200,000
Retained earnings	300,000
Total capital	$5,500,000

ANALYSIS   Mr. Lane is a specified non-resident shareholder as he owns 45% of the corporation's voting shares. His relevant equity balance is $390,000 [(45%)($200,000) + (100%)($300,000)]. His debt holding is clearly greater than 1.5 times this relevant equity balance. As a consequence, there would be disallowed interest of $265,650 calculated as follows:

Total interest paid to Mr. Lane [(11%)($3,000,000)] ·	$330,000
Maximum deductible interest [(11%)(1.5)($390,000)]	(64,350)
Disallowed interest (re-characterized as a dividend)	$265,650

Exercise 20-7

Subject: Thin Capitalization

On January 1, 2020, a new Canadian corporation is formed with the issuance of $8,600,000 in long-term debt and $2,400,000 in common shares. On this date, Ms. Sally Johnson, who is a resident of Mexico, holds $4,500,000 of the long-term debt and 30% of the common shares. The long-term debt pays interest at 9%. The company has a December 31 taxation year end. On January 1, 2021, the retained earnings of the company is $900,000. How much, if any, of the interest paid on Ms. Johnson's holding of the long-term debt during 2021 would be disallowed under the thin capitalization rules of ITA 18(4)? What would the Canadian income tax consequences be to her as a result?

Solutions to Exercises are available in the Study Guide.

Immigration and Emigration

Entering Canada—Becoming a Resident of Canada (Immigration)—ITA 128.1(1)

Deemed Dispositions/Reacquisitions

20-72.   When a person becomes a resident of Canada it is important that any Canadian income tax consequences that may occur as a result of dispositions of property that the person owns at the time he enters Canada only consider the change in value (FMV) of those properties from the time he becomes resident. This means that rules must be established to reset tax costs of his property when he becomes resident. ITA 128.1 contains the necessary rules that deem property owned to have been disposed of prior to becoming resident in Canada and then immediately reacquired at FMV. In effect, this means that the tax costs of these properties will equal their FMV.

> **EXAMPLE**   A non-resident individual becomes a resident of Canada and at the time owns investments that cost $100,000 but have a current FMV of $150,000.
>
> **ANALYSIS**   ITA 128.1(1)(b) and (c) provide the disposition/reacquisition mechanism that establishes a Canadian tax cost (ACB) of $150,000. If the investments were subsequently sold for $160,000 Canada would only be entitled to tax $10,000 of the appreciation in value as a gain that occurred while the individual was a resident of Canada. The remaining gain of $50,000 would likely be subject to income tax in the country in which the individual was formerly resident.

20-73.   The deemed disposition/reacquisition mechanism does not apply to all property owned by the person becoming a resident if Canada already has an existing right to tax gains or income with respect to the property. In general, property excluded would include:

- taxable Canadian property;
- inventories and certain other capital property of a business carried on in Canada; and
- **"excluded rights or interests,"** which is a concept defined in ITA 128.1(10) and includes an interest in a RPP, RRSP, RRIF, or DPSP and rights to stock options benefits, death benefits, and retiring allowances, to name some of the more common rights or interests.

Ceasing to Be a Resident of Canada (Emigration)—ITA 128.1(4)

Deemed Dispositions

20-74.   When a taxpayer ceases to be a resident of Canada, ITA 128.1(4)(b) deems the taxpayer to have disposed of all property owned at the time of departure subject to some exceptions. The proceeds of disposition (POD) are deemed to be FMV. If the taxpayer is an individual, the property exceptions are as follows:

- Real property situated in Canada, Canadian resource properties, and timber resource properties
- Property of a business carried on in Canada through a permanent establishment; this would include capital property and inventories
- Excluded rights or interests of the taxpayer as described in Paragraph 20-73

Exercise 20-8

Subject: Ceasing to Be a Canadian Resident (Emigration)

Ms. Gloria Martell owns shares of a publicly listed corporation with an ACB of $28,000 and a FMV of $49,000. During the current year she ceases to be a resident of Canada while still owning the shares. What are the income tax consequences of her giving up Canadian residency, if any, with respect to the shares?

Exercise 20-9

Subject: Ceasing to Be a Canadian Resident (Emigration)

Mr. Harrison Chrysler owns a rental property in Nanaimo, B.C., with a capital cost of $190,000 and a FMV of $295,000. The ACB of the land is $45,000 and the FMV $62,000. The UCC of the building is $82,600. During the current year Mr. Chrysler ceases to be a resident of Canada. What are the current and potential future income tax consequences with respect to this rental property?

Solutions to Exercises are available in the Study Guide.

Canada/U.S. Tax Treaty—Article XIII(7)

20-75. The deemed disposition/reacquisition mechanism applies for purposes of the ITA but may not necessarily be recognized by the new resident country. The result would be a potential for double tax. If, for example, an individual who had ceased to be a resident of Canada was deemed to have disposed of investments for FMV of $40,000 that had been purchased in Canada for $10,000, the individual would be required to pay Canadian income tax on the $30,000 capital gain. If after ceasing to be a resident the individual sold the investments for the same $40,000, the new country of residence would likely also consider there to be a gain of $30,000, which could be subject to tax in that country.

20-76. To alleviate this problem Canada has been renegotiating its tax treaties to add an elective option within the treaties to mirror the Canadian income tax treatment. This would require the other country to recognize the tax cost based on the deemed reacquisition at FMV. In the example in the preceding paragraph this would mean that the other country would accept that the tax cost would be $40,000, eliminating the potential double tax on a subsequent disposition while a resident of that other country. This elective provision is included in the Canada/U.S. tax treaty under article XIII(7).

Elective Dispositions

20-77. We have seen that certain types of property are exempt from the deemed disposition/reacquisition mechanism. There may, however, be circumstances in which an individual wishes to override these exemptions and trigger capital gains or capital losses at the time residency ceases. An important example of this would be farm property that qualifies for the capital gains deduction. Another example would be where an individual wishes to realize a loss on exempt property to offset a gain on non-exempt property.

20-78.   Such situations are provided for in ITA 128.1(4)(d), which allows an individual to elect a deemed disposition on certain types of properties that are exempt from the general deemed disposition rule. The properties on which the election can be made include real property situated in Canada, Canadian resource and timber resource properties, as well as property of a business carried on in Canada through a permanent establishment. Note that, if this election results in losses (capital or terminal), they can only be used to offset income resulting from other deemed dispositions. They cannot be applied against other sources of income, including capital gains from dispositions that occurred in the taxation year but prior to the time at which residency has ceased. Individuals are required to file form T2061A, "Election by an Emigrant to Report Deemed Dispositions of Property and Any Resulting Capital Gain or Capital Loss."

Exercise 20-10

Subject: Emigration

Ms. Gloria Lopez owns shares in a Canadian private company with an ACB of $120,000 and a FMV of $235,000. In addition, she owns a rental property with a FMV of $130,000 ($30,000 of which is attributable to the land) and a cost of $220,000 ($60,000 of which is attributable to the land). The UCC of the building is $142,000. During the current year Ms. Lopez ceases her Canadian residency and becomes a non-resident. Calculate the impact on her net income for the year and whether there is an option to reduce that additional net income with respect to the shares and the rental property.

Solutions to Exercises are available in the Study Guide.

Security for Departure Tax

20-79.   The deemed disposition/reacquisition rules can be burdensome for an emigrating individual. If the individual has substantial amounts of property that have appreciated considerably in value, these rules can result in a sizable income tax liability. This is further aggravated by the fact that there are no actual proceeds to provide funds to pay the liability.

20-80.   In recognition of this problem, ITA 220(4.5) through (4.54) allows individual taxpayers to provide security in lieu of paying the income tax. Similar rules are provided in ITA 220(4.6) through (4.63) for trusts distributing taxable Canadian property to non-resident beneficiaries.

20-81.   ITA 220(4.5) requires the CRA to accept "adequate security." Guidance on what constitutes adequate security is as follows:

> Bank letters of guarantee, bank letters of credit, and bonds from the Government of Canada or a province or territory of Canada are considered acceptable forms of security. Other types of security may also be acceptable, such as shares in private or publicly traded corporations, certificates in precious metals, various other marketable securities, a charge or mortgage on real property, or valuable personal property.

20-82.   If the individual taxpayer elects under ITA 220(4.5), interest does not accrue on the tax that has been deferred until the amount becomes unsecured. This will usually be at the time when there is an actual disposition of the property that was subject to a deemed disposition.

20-83.   ITA 220(4.51) creates deemed security on an amount that is the total amount of taxes under Part I that would be payable, at the highest tax rate that applies to individuals (33%), on taxable income of $50,000. This amount is one-half of a $100,000 capital gain, and the effect of this provision is to exempt individuals who have ceased to be Canadian residents from the requirement to provide security on the first $100,000 in capital gains resulting from deemed dispositions.

We suggest you complete SSP 20-3 at this point.

Unwinding a Deemed Disposition — ITA 128.1(6)

The Problem

20-84. A potential problem can arise when an individual ceases to be a resident of Canada and becomes a resident of Canada at a later time. The following example illustrates the difficulty.

> **EXAMPLE** John Fuller ceases to be a resident of Canada on June 1, 2021. At that time, he owns shares of a private company with a FMV of $200,000 and an ACB of $125,000. As a result of the deemed disposition/reacquisition of these shares, he recognizes a taxable capital gain of $37,500 [(1/2)(deemed POD $200,000 - ACB $125,000)]. In 2022 he becomes a resident of Canada once again. At that time, he still owns the shares and their FMV has increased to $260,000.

20-85. In the absence of any special provision, Mr. Fuller's initial departure from Canada, in which he terminated his residency, would cost him the income taxes payable on the $37,500 taxable capital gain arising on the deemed disposition. On re-establishing Canadian residency, the ACB of the shares would be increased to $260,000. However, the fact remains that his temporary absence has resulted in an out-of-pocket tax cost on $37,500 of taxable capital gains.

The Solution

20-86. ITA 128.1(6) provides relief in this type of situation. With respect to the shares owned by Mr. Fuller, ITA 128.1(6)(c) allows a returning individual to make an election with respect to property that was subject to the deemed disposition/reacquisition rules when the individual ceased to be a resident of Canada. The election effectively reverses the income tax consequences when the individual re-establishes residency in Canada. In general, the election revises the POD to eliminate the initial capital gain and then reduces the ACB of the property by the deferred gain.

20-87. Returning to our example from Paragraph 20-84, if this election is made the 2021 deemed POD would be reduced to $125,000, eliminating the capital gain of $75,000 (revised elective POD $125,000 - ACB $125,000). For 2022 the individual would first be deemed by ITA 128.1(1)(c) to have acquired the property for its FMV of $260,000. ITA 128.1(6)(c) would then reduce the deemed cost (ACB) of $260,000 by the deferred gain of $75,000, resulting in an ACB of $185,000. This means that if the property were immediately sold for $260,000 the deferred gain of $75,000 that accrued while the individual was a resident of Canada would be taxable in Canada. Note that had the individual remained a resident of Canada the capital gain on a sale at $260,000 would have been $135,000 (POD $260,000 - initial ACB $125,000), which is $60,000 higher than the $75,000 deferred gain. This recognizes that since that part of the gain relates to an appreciation in the value of the property that occurred while the individual was not a resident of Canada, then Canada has no right to tax that part.

Short-Term Residents

20-88. With the increasing presence of multinational firms in the Canadian business environment, it has become common for executives and other employees to find themselves resident in Canada for only a small portion of their total working lives. In the absence of some special provision, the deemed disposition rules could be a significant hardship to employees who are in this position.

20-89. For example, if Ms. Eng was transferred from Hong Kong to work in Canada for three years and as a result became a resident of Canada, she could become liable on ceasing to be a resident of Canada because of being deemed to dispose of her properties. The income tax liability could be costly and result in Canadian income tax on personal property such as paintings and jewellery. This could impede the movement of employees to and from Canada.

20-90.   To address this concern, ITA 128.1(4)(b)(iv) provides an exception to the deemed disposition rules that applies to individuals who, during the 10 years preceding the time that Canadian residency has ceased, have been resident in Canada for no more than 60 months. The deemed disposition rules do not apply to these individuals with respect to property that was owned immediately before the individual last became resident in Canada or was acquired by inheritance or bequest during the period of Canadian residency. In summary, the disposition/reacquisition rules will only apply to property acquired other than by inheritance or bequest during the period of residency.

Exercise 20-11

Subject: Short-Term Residents

In 2018, Charles Brookings ceases residency in the U.K. and becomes a resident of Canada for the first time. At this time he owns shares in a U.K. company and vacant land in Canada that he had inherited. The FMV of the shares is $250,000 and the ACB $175,000. The ACB of the land is $95,000 and the FMV is $120,000.

In 2019, he acquires shares of a Canadian public company for $75,000. In 2021, after finding Canada a tad cold for his tastes, he terminates his Canadian residency and resumes residency in the U.K. At this time, the FMV of the shares in the U.K. company is $280,000, the FMV of the shares of the Canadian company are $92,000, and the FMV of the land is $130,000.

What are the income tax consequences of ceasing to be a resident of Canada in 2021?

Solutions to Exercises are available in the Study Guide.

Foreign Source Income of Canadian Residents

Introduction

20-91.   In this section we will begin by discussing the foreign property reporting requirements applicable to Canadian residents. This will be followed by sections dealing with the following:

- Foreign source employment income
- Foreign source income from carrying on a business outside Canada
- Foreign source interest income
- Dividends from non-resident corporations
- Capital gains from the disposition of foreign property

Foreign Property Reporting Requirements—ITA 233.3 (T1135)

20-92.   Page 2 of the individual income tax return (T1) under the heading "Foreign Property" asks the question, "Did you own or hold specified foreign property where the total cost amount of all such property, at any time in 2021, was more than CAN$100,000?" The individual is then prompted to check off a yes or no box. If the answer is yes, the return indicates that s1135 (Foreign Income Verification Statement) must be filed with a warning that there are substantial penalties for failing to do so (a general maximum of $2,500 for each year). Both the corporate income tax return (T2) and the trust income tax return (T3) contain the same question and information.

20-93.   The foreign reporting requirement was introduced to curb the concern that some Canadian residents were not reporting all of their foreign source income. There were numerous examples that were front page news where it was discovered that Canadian residents had used offshore tax havens (low- or no-tax countries) to effectively hide their property and income from the Canadian tax authorities.

20-94.   The filing requirements of the T1135 provides for two reporting methods: the simplified and detailed method. The simplified reporting method applies to taxpayers whose specified foreign property totals more than $100,000 but is less than $250,000 throughout the year. Rather than having to report the complete details, the simplified method allows a taxpayer to identify the general types of foreign property and to indicate a single amount for the total gross income from all specified foreign property, as well as the gain (loss) from the disposition of all specified foreign property in the year.

20-95.   The T1135 supports ITA 233.3, which requires information on what is referred to as "specified foreign property." The more important types of specified foreign property include the following:

- Funds held outside Canada (e.g., funds in a foreign bank account)
- Shares of a non-resident corporation (see Paragraph 20-98 for a streamlined reporting option where foreign shares are held in Canadian brokerage accounts)
- Indebtedness owed by a non-resident
- Real property outside of Canada other than excluded property, such as personal-use or business-use properties
- An interest in a non-resident trust

20-96.   Some of the common property excluded from the definition of specified foreign property are as follows:

- Foreign securities held in Canadian mutual funds or inside a registered account like an RRSP, RRIF, TFSA, or RESP
- A property used or held exclusively in carrying on an active business
- A personal-use property, such as a second home used primarily (more than 50%) for personal use
- A share of the capital stock or indebtedness of a foreign affiliate. Note that a shareholding of 10% or more in a non-resident corporation will be sufficient to constitute a foreign affiliate of an individual. Foreign affiliates are discussed later in this chapter.

20-97.   For taxpayers with specified foreign property equal to $250,000 or more, a great deal of additional information is required, such as:

- the name of the entity holding or issuing the property, or a description of the foreign property;
- the relevant country code (for the country of residence of the bank, corporation, issuer, or trust, or where the property is located);
- the maximum cost amount (e.g., tax cost such as ACB) of the property during the year;
- the year-end cost amount of the property;
- the amount of income or loss related to the property for the year; and
- any capital gain or loss realized on the disposition of the property during the year.

20-98.   Fortunately, in many if not most cases relief is available. To the extent specified foreign property is held in an account with a Canadian registered securities dealer or a Canadian trust company, the only requirements related to specified foreign property are reporting country-by-country aggregate values for maximum FMV during the year, FMV at the end of the year, income for the year, and gains or losses on dispositions during the year. For example, if an individual invests only in U.S. stocks and they are held with a Canadian registered securities dealer, the reporting requirements are greatly simplified.

20-99.   Substantial penalties can result from failure to comply with these reporting requirements. They range from $500 per month for up to 24 months if the failure to file is done knowingly to $1,000 per month for up to 24 months if there is a failure to comply with a demand to file the T1135. After 24 months, the penalty can become more severe, that is, 5% of the cost of the foreign property. This group of penalties is designed to address tax evasion.

20-100.   The most common penalty, however, is for simply overlooking or not realizing that the foreign reporting is required and failing to file the form along with the income tax return. The penalty in this case is determined under ITA 162(7) and is the greater of $100 or a $25 per day the return is late to a maximum of 100 days, or $2,500 in total. The penalty is also subject to interest charges while it remains outstanding. In addition, the CRA can also reassess a taxpayer beyond the normal three-year reassessment period to six years (ITA 152(4)(b.2)). If, for example, an individual failed to report foreign property for six years, the potential penalties would be $15,000 [(6 years)($2,500)] plus interest. Taxpayer relief requests are common in these situations with mixed success. Additional information is provided by the CRA in the form of FAQs at https://www.canada.ca/en/revenue-agency/services/tax/international-non-residents/information-been-moved/foreign-reporting/questions-answers-about-form-t1135.html#h8.

Exercise 20-12

Subject: Foreign Property Reporting

During 2021, Simon Taylor, a resident Canadian individual, has a savings account with the Bank of Scotland. The balance ranged from £4,000 to £52,000 during the year and there is a year-end balance of £41,000. Interest on the account for the year totalled £1,000. In 2020, he made a two-year interest-free loan of £145,000 to his brother-in-law, who is a resident of Scotland. There is no formalized loan agreement. Assume 1£ = $1.70 for 2020 and 2021. Describe Simon's foreign property reporting obligations for 2021 and provide the information required on form T1135.

Solutions to Exercises are available in the Study Guide.

We suggest you complete SSP 20-4 at this point.

Foreign Employment Income

The Problem

20-101.   Individuals who are residents of Canada are taxable on employment income regardless of where the employment duties are performed. This creates a potential problem in that an individual earning employment income in a foreign country could be subject to Canadian income tax because of her residency status and, at the same time, be subject to income tax in the country where the employment services are provided. Income tax treaties are used to resolve this potential double tax issue.

Canada/U.S. Tax Treaty—Foreign Source Employment Income

20-102.   The Canada/U.S. treaty applies the same tie-breaker rules that occur when a U.S. resident individual is employed in Canada. In general, the source country has the right to tax employment income. The Canada/U.S. tax treaty provides two exceptions to this rule. In its application to a Canadian resident employed in the U.S., these exceptions are as follows:

$10,000 Rule   Under this exception if, during a calendar year, a Canadian resident earns employment income in the U.S. that is $10,000 or less in U.S. dollars, then the income is taxable only in Canada.

183-Day Rule   This rule exempts U.S. employment income from income tax in the U.S. provided it is earned by a Canadian resident who was physically present in the U.S. for no more than 183 days during any 12-month period commencing or ending in the calendar year. This exemption is conditional on employment income not being paid by an employer with a permanent establishment in the U.S. who would be able to deduct the amount paid from their U.S. taxable income.

Summary If the employment income exceeds $10,000 and is deductible in the U.S., it will be subject to income tax in the U.S., even if the employee is present in the U.S. for less than 183 days during the year.

We suggest you complete SSP 20-5 at this point.

Foreign Source Business Income

The Problem

20-103.   Canadian residents who carry on a business outside of Canada are subject to Canadian income tax on their foreign business profits. As was the case with foreign source employment income, this creates a potential double tax situation since the country in which the business is carried on would also claim the right to subject the same profits to the income tax of that foreign country.

20-104.   Where there is a treaty between the two countries the issue of whether the country in which the business is carried on has a right to subject the business profits to its income tax is resolved by the tax treaty. This, however, does not mean that the resident country excludes the business profits from the resident Canadian's income, but it does mean that Canada must provide foreign tax relief with respect to that income. In these circumstances, Canada generally uses a combination of foreign tax credits and a foreign tax deduction to address the double tax issue. The following example will demonstrate the foreign tax relief mechanism.

EXAMPLE Ms. Johnson, a Canadian resident, is subject to a Canadian marginal tax rate of 45% on her worldwide income. During the current year, she earns foreign source business income of $1,000, from which the source country assesses and withholds income taxes at a rate of 15%.

ANALYSIS The $1,000 of foreign income would be included in net income for Canadian tax purposes, with the foreign income taxes paid by Ms. Johnson, a Canadian resident, generating a credit against Canadian income tax payable. Applying this to the preceding example results in the following calculations:

Foreign business income received	$ 850
Foreign tax	150
Addition to net income	$1,000
Canadian income tax payable [(45%)($1,000)]	$ 450
Foreign tax credit = Foreign tax withheld	(150)
Net Canadian income tax payable	$ 300
Foreign income tax	150
Total income taxes payable	$ 450
After-tax retention ($1,000 - $450)	$ 550
Overall income tax rate ($450 ÷ $1,000)	45%

Canada would have met its tax treaty obligation of providing foreign tax relief to its resident. The impact is that Canada and the foreign country have shared the income tax on the business profits. Canada will generally restrict the foreign tax credit relief to the maximum Canadian income tax that would have occurred had the income been earned in Canada. Had the foreign tax rate been 50%, then Canada would only have credited 45%.

Canada/U.S. Tax Treaty—Foreign Business Income—Article VII

20-105.   The Canada/U.S. treaty only permits the U.S. to subject business profits of a Canadian resident to income tax if the business is carried on through a permanent establishment situated in the U.S. and only to the extent of the profits attributable to that permanent establishment. This means that if a Canadian resident carries on a business in the U.S. without a permanent establishment, the profits will only be subject to income tax in Canada. Alternatively, if the business income is earned through a permanent establishment in the U.S., it will be subject to income tax in the U.S. with Canada providing foreign tax relief as discussed.

Exercise 20-13

Subject: Foreign Tax Credits

Jason Abernathy is a Canadian resident. During 2020 he carries on business in the U.S. through a permanent establishment, earning $18,000 in business profits. U.S. income tax of $1,800 was paid on those profits. In calculating his foreign tax credit, his adjusted Division B income is equal to $100,000 and his tax otherwise payable is equal to $21,000. All amounts are in Canadian dollars. Jason's marginal combined federal/provincial tax rate is 44%. Determine his after-tax retention and overall tax rate on his foreign business income.

Solutions to Exercises are available in the Study Guide.

Foreign Interest Income

The Problem

20-106.   Residents of Canada are subject to income tax on their worldwide income regardless of where the income is sourced. As was the case with employment income, this again raises the possibility of double taxation where the country where the income is sourced also applies an income tax. Income tax treaties resolve these double taxation issues.

Canada/U.S. Tax Treaty—Foreign Interest Income—Article XI

20-107.   Article XI of the Canada/U.S. treaty provides that interest paid from one country to a resident of the other country will only be subject to income tax in the resident recipient's country. This means that U.S. residents receiving interest from a Canadian source are not subject to any Canadian income tax. Correspondingly, Canadian residents receiving interest income from a U.S. source will only be subject to income tax in Canada.

Foreign Source Capital Gains

The Problem

20-108.   Because of the fact that residents of Canada are subject to income tax on worldwide income, capital gains that arise from dispositions of property anywhere in the world would be subject to Canadian income tax. Dispositions of foreign property, however, may result in the foreign country claiming the right to impose their own income tax on any gains with the potential for double income tax. Income tax treaties would provide rules to address these issues.

Canada/U.S. Tax Treaty—Foreign Source Capital Gains—Article XIII

20-109.   In general, the Canada/U.S. treaty gives priority to the resident country of the seller. Therefore, if a Canadian resident sells property situated or sourced in the U.S., Canada would, subject to any specific exclusions, have a right to impose income tax on that gain. However, the treaty allows the U.S. to impose income tax on gains from the disposition of real property situated in the U.S., as well as gains on most types of property that are used in a permanent establishment through which a Canadian resident carries on business in the U.S.

Foreign Dividends

20-110. Foreign dividends can prove to be extremely complex depending on whether the foreign corporation qualifies as a foreign affiliate (FA) of the shareholder and if it also qualifies as a controlled foreign affiliate (CFA). A non-resident corporation must first qualify as an FA in order to qualify as a CFA. The remaining coverage in this chapter will discuss the basic concepts when residents of Canada that are individuals and Canadian corporations receive dividends from non-resident corporations. There are three different situations:

- When the non-resident corporation is not an FA
- When the non-resident corporation is an FA but not a CFA
- When the non-resident corporation is both an FA and a CFA

20-111. In general, dividends from non-resident corporations are required to be included in the net income of resident Canadian taxpayer's under ITA 12(1)(k) based on rules found in Subdivision i (ITA 90 to 95). When foreign dividends are received by individuals, they are not grossed up nor are they entitled to dividend tax credits. When received by Canadian resident corporations, they are not entitled to a taxable income deduction under ITA 112(1). These favourable concepts are based on integration, which presumes that the underlying corporate income distributed as dividends has been subject to Canadian income tax. This is clearly not the case when non-resident corporations with no permanent establishment in Canada distribute profits as dividends.

20-112. It is important to understand, however, that there are certain tax policy objectives that drive how foreign dividends are treated for Canadian income tax purposes. In very general terms the foreign affiliate concept is designed to allow Canadian corporations to expand and competitively carry on business in other countries. This means that if the foreign country imposes income tax on business profits that the payment of dividends from those after-tax profits to Canadian corporate shareholders should not result in any Canadian corporate income tax until the Canadian company has paid dividends to its Canadian resident individual shareholders. The FA system is designed around this objective and it is relevant when the shareholder of the non-resident corporation that is an FA is a corporation resident in Canada.

20-113. The second important policy objective is similar to Part IV tax that was used to discourage Canadians from using resident corporations to hold personal investments. The foreign equivalent would have Canadian resident individuals establishing a non-resident corporation to hold their personal investments. Investment income earned within the non-resident corporation would not be subject to income tax in Canada until dividend distributions were made. The CFA rules were added to address this particular concern and apply an accrual-based concept to deem the investment income of the non-resident corporation to be income of the Canadian resident shareholders as it is earned but only if the non-resident corporation is a CFA of the Canadian resident taxpayer. This type of income is referred to as FAPI, or "foreign accrual property income." These rules are relevant to both corporations and individuals that are resident in Canada.

20-114. Canadian and foreign reporting obligations with respect to these type of foreign corporate investments are considerable and attract substantial penalties when there are reporting failures. In addition, legislation has been added to the ITA in recent years that allows the CRA to reassess well beyond the normal three- or four-year statute of limitation period. This aspect of Canadian tax is not practised by many Canadian tax practitioners and is thus relegated to foreign income tax specialists.

20-115. In the following material, we will give consideration to dividends from foreign corporations that are received by:

- individuals resident in Canada;
- Canadian corporations where the non-resident corporation is not an FA and CFA;
- Canadian corporations where the non-resident corporation is an FA but not a CFA; and
- Canadian corporations where the non-resident corporation is an FA and a CFA.

Foreign Dividends Received by Individuals

20-116.   If a resident Canadian individual receives a dividend from a foreign corporation that is not a CFA of the individual and there is no withholding of tax by the foreign country, the amount received will be converted into Canadian dollars at the time that it is received. It would then be included in that individual's net income. There will be no gross up or dividend tax credit.

20-117.   Alternatively, if there is withholding tax by the foreign country, the full amount of the declared dividend will be included in the individual's net income. To the extent that the withholding is 15% or less, the individual is entitled to a foreign tax credit. Any withholding in excess of 15% is eligible for a deduction from net income under ITA 20(11).

EXAMPLE   During 2021, Martin Fingle is entitled to $25,000 in dividends from a non-resident corporation in which he is a shareholder. The non-resident corporation is not a CFA to Martin. The foreign country withholds income tax of $5,000 (20%). In addition to the dividend, Martin has Canadian interest income of $22,000. Other than the foreign tax credit, he has other personal tax credits that will reduce his Canadian income tax payable by $2,200. He has no taxable income deductions.

ANALYSIS   Martin's net and taxable income would be calculated as follows:

Interest income	$22,000
Foreign dividends	25,000
Excess tax [(20% - 15%)($25,000)]—ITA 20(11)	(1,250)
2021 net and taxable income	$45,750

His 2021 federal income tax payable would be calculated as follows:

Tax before credits [(15%)($45,750)]	$ 6,863
Less: Personal tax credits	(2,200)
Part I tax payable before foreign tax credit	$ 4,663
Foreign tax credit (see Note)	(2,548)
2021 federal income tax payable	$ 2,115

Note   The foreign tax credit would be the lesser of:

- Amount withheld (limited to 15% of $25,000) = $3,750

- $\left[\dfrac{\text{Foreign Non - Business Income}}{\text{Division B Income}}\right](\text{Tax Payable}) = \left[\dfrac{\$25,000}{\$45,750}\right](\$4,663) = \$2,548$

We suggest you complete SSP 20-6 at this point.

Foreign Dividends from Non-Resident Corporations That Are Not FAs

20-118.   The amount of a dividend distribution received by a Canadian corporation from a foreign corporation is included in the corporation's net income for the year of receipt.

EXAMPLE   Martin Fingle Inc., a Canadian public corporation, is entitled to $25,000 in dividends from a non-resident corporation that is not an FA. The foreign country applies withholding taxes of $5,000 (20%). The corporate tax rate on this income, after the general rate reduction, is 25% (basic rate of 38% - general rate reduction of 13%). Assume that Martin Fingle Inc. has no other income during the year.

ANALYSIS   The corporation's net and taxable income will both be $25,000. Federal income tax payable, before the foreign tax credit, will be $6,250 [(25%)($25,000)]. As a corporation's use of the foreign non-business tax credit is not limited to 15%, the tax credit will be $5,000, the lesser of:

- Amount withheld = $5,000

- $\left[\dfrac{\text{Foreign Non - Business Income}}{\text{Division B Income}}\right](\text{Tax Payable}) = \left[\dfrac{\$25,000}{\$25,000}\right](\$6,250) = \$6,250$

Foreign Dividends from Non-Resident Corporations That Are FAs but Not CFAs

Foreign Affiliate (FA) Defined

20-119.   The status of a non-resident corporation as an FA is unique to each Canadian shareholder. This means that the non-resident corporation may be an FA of some Canadian shareholders but not all. An FA of a Canadian taxpayer is defined in ITA 95(1) as a non-resident corporation in which that taxpayer has a direct or indirect equity percentage of at least 1%. As well, the aggregate equity percentages of the taxpayer and each person related to the taxpayer must be at least 10%. The ownership percentage can be established on either a direct or indirect basis and is defined as the greatest percentage holding in any class of shares of the non-resident corporation.

20-120.   As an example of both the direct and indirect application of this rule, consider the following example.

> **EXAMPLE**   Candoo, a taxable Canadian corporation, owns 70% of the only class of shares of Forco One, a non-resident corporation. In turn, Forco One owns 20% of the only class of shares of Forco Two, a second non-resident corporation.

> **ANALYSIS**   Forco One is an FA of Candoo because of Candoo's 70% direct ownership. Forco Two is also an FA of Candoo because the indirect ownership percentage is 14% [(70%)(20%)].

20-121.   The share ownership thresholds are applied on a shareholder-by-shareholder basis. A non-resident company will be an FA of a resident of Canada only if the resident owns, directly or indirectly, at least 1% of the shares of that non-resident company and, in addition, that resident, together with related persons, owns at least 10% of the shares of that non-resident company.

> **EXAMPLE**   Carson Ltd. and Dawson Inc., two resident Canadian companies, each own 8% of Belgique, a non-resident corporation. While Carson Ltd. is part of a related group that controls Belgique, Dawson Inc. is not related to any of the other shareholders of Belgique.

> **ANALYSIS**   Belgique would be a, FA of Carson Ltd. as Carson Ltd. owns more than 1% of the shares and, in addition, is related with persons, who together with Carson Ltd., own more than 10% of the shares. Belgique would not be an FA of Dawson Inc.

Exercise 20-14

Subject   Identifying a Foreign Affiliate (FA)

Canvest is a resident Canadian corporation that owns shares in three non-resident corporations. For each of the investments described below, determine whether the non-resident corporation is an FA.

Forco 1   Canvest owns 3% of Forco 1. A wholly owned Canadian subsidiary of Canvest owns 8% of Forco 1.

Foreign Source Income of Canadian Residents

Forco 2　Canvest owns 9% of Forco 2. Canvest is not related to any of the other shareholders of Forco 2.

Forco 3　Canvest owns 5% of Forco 3. The spouse of the shareholder who has a controlling interest in Canvest owns the other 95% of the shares of Forco 3.

Solutions to Exercises are available in the Study Guide.

Dividends Received from FAs—Basic Concepts

20-122.　The FA system is designed to exempt dividends received by corporations resident in Canada from non-resident corporations that are FAs from Part I tax in a manner similar to that of intercorporate dividends between Canadian corporations. Dividends between Canadian corporations are excluded from taxable income as a result of a taxable income deduction under ITA 112(1). Dividends between corporations resident in Canada from FAs are also entitled to a taxable income deduction that is claimed under ITA 113(1).

20-123.　While the taxable income deduction of ITA 112(1) is relatively straightforward, the application of ITA 113(1) can be quite complex depending on the nature of the activities of the FA. The policy objective of the FA system is to allow Canadian companies to compete for business in a country with non-residents of other countries by limiting Canadian income tax with respect to business profits. This means that if an FA is involved in earning different types of income, such as business profits, investment income, and capital gains, then a mechanism must be established to separate and track the different income components to ensure that favourable Canadian income tax treatment is specifically targeted to business profits. The tracking mechanism in place is referred to as a surplus system.

20-124.　There are four types of surplus: (1) exempt surplus, (2) taxable surplus, (3) hybrid surplus, and (4) pre-acquisition surplus. Given the basic introductory nature of our coverage, we will restrict our coverage to exempt surplus and taxable surplus.

20-125.　The ITRs contain the many complex rules that include a general surplus ordering rule under ITR 5901 that considers dividend distributions to first come from exempt surplus, then hybrid surplus, then taxable surplus, and finally pre-acquisition surplus.

Exempt vs. Taxable Surplus

20-126.　The exempt and taxable surplus accounts apply different concepts. Exempt surplus is referred to as an exemption-based approach since any dividend distributions to Canadian corporate shareholders are fully exempt from Part I tax. Taxable surplus operates on the basis of a tax credit type system, meaning that if the income tax in the other country on business profits is less than the income tax that would have applied had the business income been earned in Canada there will be some Canadian income tax to make up the difference. In summary, it is preferable to have exempt surplus rather than taxable surplus.

20-127.　The content of these surplus balances requires the allocation of income from four different sources:

- Active business income
- Investment income (e.g., interest and rents)
- Capital gains on dispositions of property used in an active business
- Capital gains on dispositions of property not used in an active business

20-128.　The situation is further complicated in that the classification of a particular type of income will depend on whether the FA is situated in a country with which Canada has a tax treaty or a Tax Information Exchange Agreement (TIEA). A TIEA is an agreement for the exchange of tax-related information for the purpose of administration dealing largely with tax evasion. There are currently 24 TIEAs in effect and 6 under negotiation. A TIEA entitles the other countries to some benefits that are usually restricted to treaty countries. In terms of the surplus system, if active business income is earned in a treaty or TIEA country, active business income becomes part of exempt surplus. Alternatively, active business income becomes part of taxable surplus for all other countries in which there is no treaty or TIEA.

20-129.   The major components of exempt surplus are as follows:

- Income earned by an FA in a country with which Canada has a tax treaty or a TIEA that is:
  - active business income; and
  - the taxable one-half of capital gains on dispositions of property used in an active business.

- For all FAs, without regard to the location of the FA:
  - the non-taxable one-half of capital gains on dispositions of all types of capital property (except shares of other foreign affiliates).

- Less: Foreign income taxes paid on income included in exempt surplus and dividends paid from exempt surplus.

20-130.   The major components of taxable surplus are as follows:

- Income earned by an FA with which Canada does not have a tax treaty or a TIEA that is:
  - active business income; and
  - the taxable one-half of capital gains on dispositions of property used in an active business.

- For all FAs, without regard to the location of the FA:
  - the taxable one-half of capital gains on dispositions of capital property other than that used in an active business; and
  - investment income, which includes income from property and from non-active businesses (FAPI).

- Less: Foreign income taxes paid on income included in taxable surplus and dividends paid from taxable surplus.

Dividends Paid from Exempt Surplus—ITA 113(1)(a)

20-131.   When a dividend is paid from the exempt surplus of an FA, Canada forgoes any corporate income tax, effectively ceding the right to impose income tax to that country. This treatment is only afforded to treaty and TIEA countries on the principle that it is only these countries that apply amounts of corporate income tax that is comparable to that of Canada. In an exemption-based system, there is no foreign tax credit relief provided for the income taxes paid on the underlying exempt surplus income.

20-132.   The key provision of the ITA to enforce this tax-free concept is ITA 113(1)(a), which provides a resident Canadian corporation with a taxable income deduction for exempt surplus dividends received from FAs.

EXAMPLE   An FA makes a dividend distribution of $100,000 to its Canadian shareholder. There is a 10% withholding tax on that dividend, resulting in a $90,000 receipt. The exempt surplus account balance is $100,000, calculated as $120,000 of active business income minus related foreign income taxes of $20,000.

ANALYSIS   The Canadian corporation will include the $100,000 dividend distribution in its net income and will claim a $100,000 taxable income deduction under ITA 113(1)(a). As a result, no Canadian income taxes will be payable on the FA dividend. In addition, however, the Canadian corporation will receive no foreign tax relief for the income taxes of $20,000 on the active business income or the withholding tax of $10,000 on the dividend.

Dividends Paid from Taxable Surplus—ITA 113(1)(b) & (c)

20-133.   When an FA pays a taxable surplus dividend to a corporation resident in Canada the system is designed to allow Canada to impose income tax based on the Canadian income tax rate that would have applied had the foreign income been earned in Canada. If the foreign income tax, which includes income tax on business profits plus any withholding tax on a dividend distribution, is equal to or greater than the Canadian income tax, then the combination of ITA 113(1)(b) and (c) will provide a deduction of the full amount of the dividend, which means Canada does not apply any income tax. If, however, the total foreign income taxes are less than the Canadian income tax, then the taxable income deductions of ITA 113(1)(b) and (c) will be less than the actual dividend, leaving Canada room to impose income tax on the difference. The current Canadian income tax rate equals 25%.

Basic corporate rate (no abatement)	38%
Less: General rate reduction	(13%)
Federal income tax rate	25%

20-134.   The method used in ITA 113(1)(b) and (c) is quite different from ITA 113(1)(a) in that a taxable income deduction is provided that removes from Canadian taxation a converted amount based on the Canadian tax rate of 25%. If, for example, an FA earned $100 that was subject to combined income tax and withholding tax of 10%, Canada should be able to impose an income tax of 15% to account for the difference, which would be $15. A pure tax credit system would apply the Canadian tax rate of 25% or $25 and then allow a $10 foreign tax credit, resulting in Canadian income tax of $15. Instead, ITA 113(1) employs a different method to achieve the same result. The method starts with the $10 of foreign income tax and then determines that it would require $40 in income subject to a tax rate of 25% to result in that $10 of tax. In effect, this is the same as saying that $40 of the $100 of foreign income was subject to a tax rate of 25% and the remaining $60 has not been taxed at all. ITA 113(1)(b) and (c) are therefore designed to reduce the $100 dividend by $40, leaving Canada to impose income tax of 25% on the remaining $60, which would equal $15 in Canadian income tax. This concept will be demonstrated in the following paragraphs.

20-135.   To achieve the desired overall tax rate of 25%, two adjustments are required:

ITA 113(1)(b)   adjusts taxable income to reflect the income taxes paid on the income/profits in the foreign country.

ITA 113(1)(c)   adjusts taxable income to reflect withholding taxes on the dividend payment.

20-136.   An example will serve to illustrate the general details of these two taxable income deductions.

EXAMPLE   Cancor, a taxable Canadian corporation, owns 50% of the outstanding shares of Forco, a corporation located in a country that does not have a tax treaty or a TIEA with Canada. Forco earns $100,000 of active business income and pays 10%, or $10,000, in income tax on that income. The taxable surplus account balance of Cancor would therefore be $45,000 [(50%)($90,000)]. Forco declares a dividend of $90,000 to its shareholders and is subject to a 5% withholding tax. Cancor receives $42,750 with $2,250 [(5%)($45,000)] representing the dividend withholding taxes.

ANALYSIS   From a policy point of view, foreign income tax and withholding tax total $7,250 and the Canadian income tax would have been $12,500 [(25%)($50,000)]. This means that the Canadian income tax should equal the difference of $5,250 ($12,500 - $7,250), which is shown in the table below:

Required Canadian income tax [(25%)($50,000)]	$12,500
Foreign income tax paid by FA	(5,000)
Foreign withholding taxes on the dividend	(2,250)
Required Canadian income tax	$ 5,250

The calculations to achieve this same result under ITA 113(1) are complex. There are two central adjustments. The first (ITA 113(1)(b)) is related to the $5,000 in foreign income tax paid, which is referred to as the UFT, or underlying foreign tax. This is the portion of the total income taxes of $10,000 paid that represents the 50% interest of the Canadian corporation. Converting this income tax of $5,000 would suggest that it is the equivalent to 25% tax on $20,000 of income. However, this does not take into consideration the fact that income has already been reduced by $5,000, from $50,000 to $45,000 by these taxes. Given this, ITA 113(1)(b) requires that the $5,000 in foreign taxes be multiplied by a relevant factor of 3 [(1 ÷ 25%) - 1]. This deduction therefore equals $15,000.

ITA 113(1)(c) determines a deduction with respect to the withholding taxes on the dividend of $2,250. Since this tax is already based on the net $45,000 dividend payment, the amount is determined by multiplying by 4 (1 ÷ 25%). This results in a deduction of $9,000, which when multipled by 25% equals the withholding tax of $2,250.

Putting all of this together results in the following calculation of the federal income tax payable:

Net income	$45,000
ITA 113(1)(b) deduction for foreign income taxes	(15,000)
ITA 113(1)(c) deduction for foreign withholding tax	(9,000)
Taxable income	$21,000
Required Canadian tax rate	25%
Federal income tax payable	$ 5,250

This, as expected, is the same amount that we calculated in the preceding table using a more intuitive approach that is not based on the ITA 113 legislation.

Dividends Received from a CFA

Controlled Foreign Affiliate (CFA) Defined—ITA 95(1)

20-137.   ITA 113 reinforces the tax policy objective of supporting the expansion of Canadian companies into foreign countries by limiting Canadian income tax when foreign business profits are repatriated to Canada as dividends. ITA 113, however, does not directly address the issue of using a non-resident corporation to defer Canadian taxation on investment income. The concept of a "controlled foreign affiliate" (CFA) is designed to deal with this particular issue.

20-138.   In general terms, ITA 95(1) defines a CFA of a Canadian taxpayer as an FA that is:

1.   controlled by the Canadian taxpayer; or

2.   controlled by the Canadian taxpayer together with:

   • persons (residents or non-residents) who are not at arm's length with the Canadian resident;
   • up to four Canadian residents who are not related to the taxpayer (referred to as "relevant" shareholders); and
   • any other persons (residents or non-residents) who are related to the "relevant" Canadian shareholders.

EXAMPLE Cantext, a Canadian public company, owns 11% of the voting shares of Fortext, a company located in Germany. Two other resident Canadian corporations that are not related to Cantext each own an additional 15% of the voting shares of Fortext. A French subsidiary of one of these other Canadian companies owns 20% of the voting shares of Fortext.

ANALYSIS   Fortext is an FA of Cantext since Cantext holds more than 10% of the voting shares of Fortext. It is also a CFA in that:

- Cantext owns 11%;
- two unrelated Canadian companies (relevant shareholders) own an additional 30%; and
- a company related to one of the relevant shareholders owns another 20%.

This result is a total ownership interest of 61% , which is sufficient to constitute control of Fortext. Note that Fortext is also a CFA of both the other Canadian corporations.

20-139.   The significance of the CFA concept is that, if a non-resident corporation is a CFA of a Canadian taxpayer, then that taxpayer must annually accrue its portion of certain investment-type income referred to as FAPI (foreign accrual property income) prior to its actual distribution as a dividend.

20-140.   There is a de minimus exception that allows Canadian residents to avoid the FAPI reporting requirements if the FAPI does not exceed $5,000 (ITA 95(1) definition of "participating percentage"). The $5,000 exception applies a cost/benefit compliance aspect in recognition that FAPI calculations and reporting can be quite complex and therefore should not be required where the FAPI amount is small. Since FAPI income is included in income as it accrues, subsequent-year dividend distributions of previously taxed FAPI are not included in net income.

Foreign Accrual Property Income (FAPI)—ITA 95(1)

General Rules

20-141.   In simplified terms, FAPI is the passive income of a CFA. FAPI includes income from property (e.g., interest, portfolio dividends), income from non-active businesses (e.g., rental income), as well as the taxable one-half of capital gains resulting from the disposition of properties that are not used in an active business. An important distinguishing feature of this type of income is that, with the exception of rental income, its source is mobile in that it can be easily moved from one country to another.

20-142.   The property income definition for FAPI also includes income from a foreign investment business. This type of business is analogous to the specified investment business that is used in determining income eligible for the small business deduction (see Chapter 12).

20-143.   As is the case with the specified investment business rules, an FA would be considered to be earning active business income if it either employs more than five full-time employees or the equivalent of more than five full-time employees to earn income that would normally be considered property income. This "five-employee" exception is especially important in determining whether foreign rental income is active (exempt from the FAPI rules) or passive (subject to the FAPI rules).

Taxation of FAPI

20-144.   If a non-resident corporation is a CFA of a Canadian taxpayer, FAPI must be accrued as it is earned by the CFA and included in the net income of the Canadian taxpayer. This is a separate issue from the distribution of dividends from CFAs, which will be discussed in the next section.

EXAMPLE   Paul Peterson, a Canadian resident taxpayer, owns 80% of the shares of Tabasco Ltd., a company that is incorporated in Trinidad. During 2021, the company has income of $100,000, all of which is earned through passive investments. No income taxes are paid on this income in Trinidad, and no dividends are paid out of this income to Mr. Peterson.

ANALYSIS   Tabasco Ltd. is a CFA to Mr. Peterson since he controls the company. Further, all of its income is from passive income and would therefore be considered FAPI. Given this, under ITA 91(1), Mr. Peterson will have to include $80,000 [(80%)($100,000)] in his Canadian net income for 2021.

20-145.   The preceding example was simplified by the fact that Tabasco Ltd. was not subject to any income taxes in the foreign country. If there had been foreign income taxes, ITA 91(4) provides a net income deduction that is designed to compensate for foreign income taxes that are attributable to the FAPI. In effect it represents a form of foreign tax relief to prevent double taxation.

20-146.   The ITA 91(4) deduction recognizes this difference by multiplying the foreign taxes paid on FAPI by what is referred to as a relevant tax factor (RTF). As defined in ITA 95(1), the RTF for individuals is different than it is for corporations.

Canadian Resident Individual   If the Canadian taxpayer is an individual, the RTF is 1.9. This is based on the notional assumption that the Canadian tax rate on this income would have been about 52.63% (1 ÷ 1.9 = 52.63%) if the income had been earned in Canada.

Canadian Resident Corporation   If the Canadian taxpayer is a corporation, the RTF is 4. This RTF is based on 1 divided by a notional tax rate that would have applied to the income (1 ÷ 25% = 4). The 25% rate is equal to the basic federal corporate rate of 38% less the general rate reduction of 13%. The 10% federal tax abatement would not be taken into consideration since the income would not have been earned in a province.

20-147.   If the income of the CFA is subject to foreign income tax at the rate of 52.63% for individuals or 25% for corporations, the ITA 91(4) deduction will completely offset the FAPI inclusion. In most cases, however, the foreign income tax rate will be less than those notional Canadian income tax rates, resulting in some net FAPI being included in net income. The ITA 91(4) deduction cannot exceed the FAPI, which is consistent with the notion that Canada will allow foreign tax relief up to the Canadian tax equivalent and no more. In other words, the Canadian government will not compensate Canadian taxpayers for excessive foreign income tax.

EXAMPLE CONTINUED (Foreign Income Tax Paid)   Paul Peterson, a Canadian resident, owns 80% of the shares of Tabasco Ltd., a company that is incorporated in Trinidad. During 2021, the company has income of $100,000, all of which is earned through passive investments. The company pays Trinidadian taxes at a rate of 20%. No dividends are paid out of this income to Mr. Peterson in 2021.

ANALYSIS   The income tax consequences to Mr. Peterson would be as follows:

FAPI [(80%)($100,000)]	$80,000
Deduct lesser of:	
• FAPI = $80,000	
• ITA 91(4) deduction [(1.9)(80%)(20%)($100,000)] = $30,400	(30,400)
2021 FAPI addition to net income	$49,600

Exercise 20-15

Subject: FAPI

Forco is a wholly owned foreign subsidiary of Canco, a resident Canadian company. Forco earns $100,000 of investment income in 2021 and pays 18% in income tax in the foreign country. No dividend distributions are paid to Canco in 2021. Determine the income tax consequences to Canco for its 2021 taxation year.

Solutions to Exercises are available in the Study Guide.

Dividends from FAPI

20-148.   A final issue remains when a CFA subsequently distributes the FAPI to the Canadian resident shareholders as a dividend. While these dividends must be included in income, the *ITA* provides a deduction to reflect the fact that all or a part of the dividend may have already been included in income in an earlier taxation year as FAPI.

20-149. The deduction is provided through ITA 91(5) in the case of individuals and a combination of ITA 91(5) and ITA 113(1)(b) in the case of corporations. The deduction is equal to the lesser of the dividends received and the FAPI previously included in the income of the shareholder net of the ITA 91(4) deduction. Any foreign withholding taxes on the payment of foreign dividends to corporate shareholders are eligible for a deduction under ITA 113(1)(c) as described in Paragraph 20-136.

> **EXAMPLE CONTINUED (Dividend Paid)** Paul Peterson, a Canadian resident, owns 80% of the shares of Tabasco Ltd., a company that is incorporated in Trinidad. During 2021, the company has income of $100,000, all of which is earned through passive investments. The company pays Trinidadian taxes at a rate of 20%. Tabasco Ltd. declares and pays dividends of $40,000 in January 2022. There are no withholding taxes on this dividend.
>
> **ANALYSIS** Mr. Peterson's addition to 2021 net income was $49,600 (Paragraph 20-147). The income tax consequences of receiving the dividend in 2022 would be nil, as shown in the following calculation:

Foreign dividends [(80%)($40,000)]	$32,000
Deduct lesser of:	
• Previous FAPI after ITA 91(4) deduction = $49,600	
• Dividend received = $32,000	(32,000)
Addition to 2022 net income	Nil

Exercise 20-16

Subject: Dividends from FAPI (An Extension of Exercise 20-15)

Forco is a wholly owned foreign subsidiary of Canco, a corporation resident in Canada. Forco earns $100,000 of investment income in 2021 and pays 18% in income tax in the foreign country. In 2022, Forco distributes its net after-tax FAPI of $82,000 to Canco as a dividend. Assume that there are no withholding taxes on the dividend payment. What is the effect of the receipt of the foreign dividend to Canco with respect to its net income for 2022?

Solutions to Exercises are available in the Study Guide.

We suggest you complete SSP 20-7 at this point.

Key Terms

A full glossary with definitions is provided at the end of the Study Guide.

Business Income	International Taxation
Capital Gain	Non-Resident
Controlled Foreign Affiliate (CFA)	Permanent Establishment
Dividends	Person
Double Taxation	Resident
Employment Income	Sojourner
Exempt Surplus	Tax Haven
Foreign Accrual Property Income (FAPI)	Taxable Canadian Property
Foreign Affiliate (FA)	Taxable Surplus
Interest Income	
International Tax Treaty	
(a.k.a., International Tax Convention)	

References

For more detailed study of the material in this chapter, we would refer you to the following:

ITA 2(3)	Tax Payable by Non-Resident Persons
ITA 20(11)	Foreign Taxes on Income from Property Exceeding 15%
ITA 90	Dividends Received from Non-Resident Corporation
ITA 91	Amounts to Be Included in Respect of Share of Foreign Affiliate
ITA 95	Definitions [Foreign Accrual Property Income]
ITA 113	Deduction in Respect of Dividend Received from Foreign Affiliate
ITA 115	Non-Resident's Taxable Income in Canada
ITA 116	Disposition by Non-Resident Person of Certain Property
ITA 118.94	Tax Payable by Non-Resident (Tax Credits)
ITA 126	Foreign Tax Credits
ITA 212	Tax in Income from Canada of Non-Resident Persons (Section in ITA Part XIII that deals with Canadian property income of non-resident persons)
ITA 216	Alternatives Re: Rents and Timber Royalties
ITA 217	Alternative Re: Canadian Benefits
ITA 248(1)	Definitions (Taxable Canadian Property)
ITA 249	Definition of "Taxation Year"
ITA 253	Extended Meaning of "Carrying on Business"
IC 72-17R6	Procedures Concerning the Disposition of Taxable Canadian Property by Non-Residents of Canada—Section 116
IC 75-6R2	Required Withholding from Amounts Paid to Non-Resident Persons Performing Services in Canada
IC 76-12R6	Applicable Rate of Part XIII Tax on Amounts Paid or Credited to Persons in Countries with which Canada Has a Tax Convention
IC 77-16R4	Non-Resident Income Tax
S5-F2-C1	Foreign Tax Credit
IT-137R3	Additional Tax on Certain Corporations Carrying on Business in Canada
IT-173R2	Capital Gains Derived in Canada by Residents of the United States
IT-176R2	Taxable Canadian Property—Interests in and Options on Real Property and Shares
IT-262R2	Losses of Non-Residents and Part-Year Residents
IT-303	Know-How and Similar Payments to Non-Residents
IT-420R3	Non-Residents—Income Earned in Canada
IT-451R	Deemed Disposition and Acquisition on Ceasing to Be or Becoming Resident in Canada
IT-465R	Non-Resident Beneficiaries of Trusts
IT-468R	Management or Administration Fees Paid to Non-Residents

Self-Study Problems (SSPs)

Self-Study Problems (SSPs) provide practice in problem solving. Within the chapters, we have indicated where it would be appropriate to stop and work on each SSP. The problems can be downloaded by chapter from MyLab Accounting. Solutions are available in the Study Guide. Select problems can also be completed directly in MyLab and auto-graded.

Assignment Problems

Solutions to Assignment Problems (APs) are available to instructors only.

AP 20-1 (Part I Tax on Non-Residents)

The following material describes six independent cases that involve U.S. residents or U.S. companies that have some Canadian source income.

Case 1

Flager is a U.S. manufacturing company. To facilitate Canadian sales, the company ships its product to a warehouse located in Moncton, New Brunswick. The warehouse is rented on a monthly basis, with a clause in the lease that allows cancellation on 90 days' notice.

Flager has made an arrangement with Jack Martin to sell their products in the Maritime provinces. Jack works out of an office in his home. He does not have authority to conclude individual sales contracts without approval from the head office in the U.S.

Case 2

Flager is a U.S. manufacturing company. To facilitate Canadian sales, the company ships its product to a warehouse located in Moncton, New Brunswick. The warehouse is rented on a monthly basis, with a clause in the lease that allows cancellation on 90 days' notice.

Flager has made an arrangement with Jack Martin to sell their products in the Maritime provinces. Jack works out of a large office in the warehouse, which takes up a considerable portion of the total floor space. He has the authority to conclude individual sales contracts without approval from the U.S. head office.

Case 3

Genevieve Boulud is a U.S. resident. Because she speaks fluent French, her U.S.-based employer transfers her to an affiliate's Montreal office for four months. Her employment income during this period is US$36,000, all of which is paid by her U.S. employer.

Case 4

Ruby Nash is a U.S. resident. During the current year she accepts an employment contract that requires her to work in Calgary for a period of three months. Her salary is C$11,000 per month. The contract is with a Canadian corporation that is responsible for paying the salary.

Case 5

Ada Taylor is a U.S. resident. She owns all of the shares in a U.S. company, which are not listed on any stock exchange. This corporation's only activity is buying and operating vacation rental properties in Canada. In order to support her increasingly decadent lifestyle, she sells all of her shares in the company during the current year. She realizes a gain on this sale of $250,000.

Case 6

Cynthia Edwards is a U.S. resident. She is a minority shareholder of a Canadian resident corporation that is a CCPC. The corporation's only activity is buying and operating rental properties in major Canadian cities. Because of her concern about the inflated prices in both Toronto and Vancouver, she sells her shares in the company during the current year. The sale results in a gain of $785,000.

Required: For each case, indicate whether the U.S. resident would be subject to Canadian income tax under Part I.

AP 20-2 (Permanent Establishments)

A U.S. manufacturer of furniture is considering entering the Canadian market. The company will use one of the following alternatives to expand into Canada:

A. Direct sales to wholesalers by full-time salespeople who report to a sales office in each of three Canadian provinces. The sales offices will coordinate marketing and shipping of products from two warehouses located in Canada. However, formal approval of contracts will be administered in the U.S. head office.

B. The sales offices described in Part A would be independent profit centres with regional credit managers. The two warehouses from which orders are filled will be near the sales offices.

C. Company online sales would be expanded to include shipping to Canada.

D. Sales to wholesalers through non-exclusive independent agents. The agents will represent other suppliers as well.

E. Direct sales to wholesalers through full-time salespeople in each of three Canadian provinces. No sales offices will be opened, and the furniture will be shipped from a warehouse in the U.S. Shipment will be made only after a customer's credit and contract are approved by the U.S. head office.

F. Selling furniture to Canadian distributors. The distributors pay the shipping costs on the furniture from the U.S. port or border crossing closest to them.

Required: For each market expansion alternative, determine whether or not the U.S. manufacturer will be considered to have a permanent establishment in Canada. Justify your conclusion and identify any other information required in support of your position.

AP 20-3 *(Part XIII Tax on Non-Resident Corporations and Individuals)*

The following two cases involve a non-resident corporation (Case A) and a non-resident individual (Case B) earning multiple sources of Canadian income. Assume that all amounts are in Canadian dollars and that neither of the non-residents are considered to be carrying on a business through a permanent establishment in Canada.

Case A—Non-Resident Corporation

All of the shares of Alberta Inc. are owned by its U.S. parent company, Blazes Corporation (Blazes), which is incorporated in the state of Delaware. Blazes manufactures and wholesales specialty equipment for firefighters. Its products are sold and leased in Canada through Alberta Inc. The following transactions took place between the two companies in 2021:

1. Blazes loaned Alberta Inc. $20 million at favourable interest rates in 2019, which was exclusively used in its business operations. Alberta Inc. paid Blazes interest of $310,000 for its 2021 taxation year that ended December 31. Assume that the interest is not "fully exempt interest."

2. There is a royalty agreement between Blazes and Alberta Inc. with respect to firefighting equipment made available to Alberta Inc. for lease to its customers. Blazes receives ongoing fees for such property that are calculated on the basis of the value of the property, the term of the underlying lease, and a wear and tear factor. In 2021 Alberta Inc. paid a fee of $189,000 to Blazes as a result of that agreement.

3. In December 2020 Alberta Inc. declared and paid a dividend of $600,000 to Blazes.

Case B—Non-Resident Individual

Tara Johnstone is a U.S. resident with friends and family in Canada. During relatively recent visits she learned that there are many interesting investment opportunities, particularly given the favourable currency exchange rate. As a result she made the following Canadian investments:

1. She made two loans in 2020 to businesses situated in Ontario. The first loan was made to an arm's-length CCPC for business purposes at interest rates slightly above the market rate to account for various risks. The company paid her $12,750 in interest in 2021. The second loan

was made to her sister to start a clothing boutique in Toronto. The terms of the loan call for a minimal rate of interest plus an additional amount based on a percentage of gross sales. Her sister paid her $11,220 in 2021.

2. Tara owns shares in two Canadian companies. The first is a listed Canadian public company in which she owns 100 Class A common shares representing a fraction of 1% of all outstanding shares, and the second is an 18% shareholding in the CCPC in which she loaned money to as mentioned in point 1 above. In 2021 she received $7,700 in eligible dividends from the public company and $16,300 from the CCPC, $10,000 of which is a non-eligible dividend and the remaining $6,300 a capital dividend.

3. Tara also purchased two lakefront cottages—one in Alberta and one in British Columbia. Both properties were rented throughout 2021 to Canadian residents. The monthly rent on the Alberta property was $2,500 and total expenses in 2021 totalled $36,800, excluding maximum CCA of $6,200. The monthly rent on the B.C. property was $4,250 with expenses in 2021 totalling $19,000, excluding maximum CCA of $6,800.

Required:

Case A: Determine the Part XIII income tax implications of each of the three payments made by Alberta Inc. to Blazes. Include in your analysis the impact of the Canada/U.S. tax treaty. Explain how your answers would or would not have changed if Blazes had been a resident of a country that did not have a tax treaty with Canada.

Case B: Determine the Part XIII income tax implications of each of the three types of Canadian investments made by Tara. Include in your analysis the impact of the Canada/U.S. tax treaty. In addition, provide any advice with respect to the dividends and whether an election under ITA 216 for the rental properties would be recommended.

AP 20-4 (Emigration—Tax Planning)

Harlen Holt, a resident of Nova Scotia, will emigrate and therefore cease to be a resident of Canada on December 31, 2021. On that date, he owns the following property:

Automobile Harlen owns a BMW 750 that cost $135,000. The FMV on December 31, 2021, is $52,000.

Interest in an RRSP The December 31, 2021, balance in Harlen's RRSP is $973,000.

Shares of Canadian Public Companies Harlen owns a portfolio of publicly traded shares that have an combined ACB of $460,000 and a FMV of $535,000 as of December 31, 2021.

Shares of a CCPC Harlen is a minority shareholder of a CCPC. The CCPC owns and operates five apartment buildings. More than 80% of the FMV of the shares is derived from the value of these buildings. The ACB is $287,000 and the FMV $300,000 as of December 31, 2021.

Principal Residence This property was purchased for $430,000 with $150,000 attributable to the land and $280,000 to the building. The FMV of the property on December 31, 2021, is $540,000 with $200,000 attributable to the land and $340,000 to the building.

Cottage This property was purchased for $345,000 with $95,000 attributable to the land and $250,000 to the building. Because a large nearby development has flooded the market with low-priced units, the FMV of the cottage on December 31, 2021, is only $300,000 with $50,000 attributable to the land and $250,000 to the building. Harlen has rented out this property since its purchase and realizes a small rental profit every year. He has never claimed CCA on the property.

Savings Account The balance in this account is $45,600 in Canadian dollars.

Required:

A. For each of the listed properties, indicate the income tax consequences, including any amounts of deferred income, that would result from Harlen ceasing to be a resident of Canada. Assume that he does not make any elections at the time of his move. Ignore the capital gains deduction.

B. Under ITA 128.1(4)(d), taxpayers who are individuals can elect to dispose of certain property that would otherwise not be deemed to have been disposed of on terminating Canadian residency. Determine if Harlen could use this election to minimize his income tax obligation that arises as a result of ceasing to be a resident of Canada. Determine any reduction in his net income that would result from this election.

AP 20-5   *(Comprehensive Review Problem — Residency of Individuals)*

Note   This problem covers material from several other chapters of the text.

Elaine Brock is employed as a marketing manager by a multinational corporation that is resident in the U.S. While she has always been a Canadian resident, working out of the corporation's Toronto office, she has been offered a promotion that would require that she relocate to Tampa, Florida. As this is intended to be a permanent change, Elaine has applied for and received the documentation that will allow her to live and work in the U.S. She will be moving to Tampa on July 1, 2021.

The corporation provides a $40,000 moving allowance that will be paid by the Toronto office prior to her move. While the corporation does not require documentation of this amount, Elaine estimates that she will incur $32,000 in actual moving costs.

The state of Florida does not charge a state income tax on its residents, largely because of the high level of tax revenues generated by Disney World. Assume that the marginal federal (U.S.) rate for Elaine would be 35%. This rate would only be applied to income earned in the U.S.

On July 1, 2021, the date that Elaine ceases to be a resident of Canada, she owns the following properties:

Description	Date Acquired	Original Cost	FMV
Interest in an RRSP	N/A	$235,000	$452,000
Canadian paintings*	Various	125,000	232,000
Principal residence in Toronto	2008	360,000	480,000
Huntsville cottage	2011	225,000	175,000
Automobile	2016	85,000	62,000
Sailboat	2018	28,000	32,000
Shares of Brock Inc., a CCPC	2006	98,000	156,000
Shares of the Bank of Nova Scotia	2014	56,000	85,000

*None of the paintings had an ACB or a FMV that was less than $1,000.

Elaine owns 100% of the real property. She has rented out the cottage since its purchase and reported a small rental profit every year. She has never claimed CCA on the property. The loss in value is related only to the land as the waterfront has been severely damaged by flooding. The value of the land has decreased from $130,000 at purchase to $80,000.

Elaine plans on renting both the principal residence and the Huntsville cottage for at least three years. She plans on selling any other remaining property as soon as possible.

Required: Explain to Elaine the income tax consequences of ceasing to be a resident of Canada. Assume the following:

*   Elaine ceases to be a Canadian resident when she departs for the U.S. on July 1, 2021.
*   Any additional income that Elaine earns in 2021 while a resident of Canada will be subject to a combined federal/provincial rate of 47%.

In addition, advise Elaine as to any tax planning opportunities to minimize her Canadian income tax payable for the current and future years. Ignore the capital gains deduction.

AP 20-6   *(Foreign Investment Reporting Rules—T1135 (ITA 233.3))*

Note to Instructors: We have endeavoured to include some of the more common practical situations together with frequently asked questions that have been put to and answered by the CRA concerning the T1135. We have broken down the situations into three categories: (1) shares of non-resident corporations, (2) personal-use property, and (3) miscellaneous. We suggest that you choose two from each category to illustrate the concepts.

For each of the mutually exclusive situations presented, indicate whether foreign reporting is required for the 2021 taxation year and provide reasons in support of your answer. Assume that all amounts are expressed in Canadian dollars and that the persons identified do not own any other foreign property. Assume that all references to foreign reporting requirements are only to the T1135.

Shares of a Non-Resident Corporation

1. A Canadian resident individual taxpayer purchased shares in a U.S. public corporation in January 2021 for $95,000. Additional shares of the same U.S. company were purchased in late December 2021 for $10,000. No dividends were received on the shares in 2021.

2. Would your answer to #1 change if the Canadian resident individual had instead acquired shares in a non-public U.S. corporation that resulted in the individual owning a 15% interest in that company?

3. Would your answer to #1 change if instead of acquiring shares in a U.S. public company the Canadian resident individual acquired, for $105,000, an interest in a U.S. mutual fund that owned shares in the U.S. public company?

4. Would your answer to #1 change if instead the Canadian resident individual owned an interest in a Canadian mutual fund that owned shares in the U.S. public company?

5. Would your answer to #1 change if the shares of the U.S. public company were acquired by your self-administered RRSP?

6. A Canadian resident individual owns all of the shares of her own corporation, which was incorporated in Alberta years ago. Would your answer to #1 change if the shares of the U.S. public company were acquired by the individual's Canadian corporation?

Personal-Use Property

1. A Canadian individual residing in Newfoundland acquired a vacation home in the Dominican Republic for $178,000 in March 2021. The individual plans to spend the long Canadian winters living in that home each and every year starting in September 2021. The property will remain vacant for the months it is not used.

2. A Canadian resident individual residing in Nunavut purchased a condo in the Turks and Caicos in January 2021 for $240,000. The individual plans on spending one month every year at that property. The individual has contracted with a real estate management company to oversee the property, ensuring it is well maintained and secure. To offset the management fees the individual has agreed to allow the condo to be rented for a few months every year.

3. Would your answer to #2 change if it was determined that the individual planned to use the property for one month each year during the low season and would rent the property throughout the high or busy season, making a considerable profit every year?

4. A Canadian resident individual residing in the Yukon acquired an apartment building in Hawaii for $995,000 in mid-January 2021. An additional $840,000 was spent on renovations. The apartment contains five equal-sized apartment units. The individual plans on spending a minimum

of three months each year living in the apartment with the best view. When not being occupied that unit will remain empty. All of the other four units will be rented throughout the year.

5. A Canadian resident individual residing in Vancouver acquired three time shares in Las Vegas at a deep discount. The total cost was $150,000. Each of the three time share units allow the holder to spend two months each year in properties along the famous Las Vegas strip. The individual plans to use the time share units personally a few weeks each year and to rent the remaining time to arm's-length persons. The individual anticipates a substantial profit that should allow recovery of the investment in as little as three years.

6. Would your answer to #5 change if it was determined that the time share units were owned 50-50 by spouses who contributed their own funds to the purchase? Both spouses are Canadian resident individuals.

Miscellaneous

1. A Canadian resident individual living in Halifax, Nova Scotia, was advised of an inheritance from a family member living in Regina, Saskatchewan, who passed away in August 2021. The individual inherited a half acre plot of land located in Tampa, Florida, that was valued at $600,000. The family member had acquired it in 1972 for $12,000.

2. A Canadian resident individual living in Saint John, New Brunswick, frequently vacations in the U.S. The individual is contemplating acquiring a U.S. currency account to avoid the fluctuations in Canadian versus U.S. currency. Assuming that the account balance will exceed $100,000 in Canadian funds, would foreign reporting be required if the individual (a) opens an account with a U.S. bank or (b) an account with a Canadian bank?

3. A U.S. resident commutes to Canada five days a week for employment purposes in 2021. The individual is a non-resident of Canada but is required to report Canadian employment income by filing an individual income tax return and paying Canadian income tax. The individual owns property in the U.S. the cost amount of which exceeds $100,000. Is the individual required to report the foreign property?

4. A Canadian resident individual residing in Ottawa, Ontario, has been asked by a sibling living in Colorado for assistance in acquiring a home near Boulder. The sibling is a non-resident of Canada. The individual agrees to help and advances the sibling an interest-free loan of $200,000 in May 2021 payable over a 10-year period.

5. A Canadian resident individual living in Surrey, B.C., owns a rental property in Seattle, Washington, that was acquired 30 years ago for $75,000. No capital additions or renovations have ever been made to the property and no CCA was ever claimed for Canadian income tax purposes. The property is rented throughout 2021. In October 2021 the individual opens a small store in Seattle to sell Whistler mountain souvenirs. The store, including furniture, equipment, and fixtures, are all leased. The only assets owned are the inventory. Initially the maximum cost of the inventory in 2021 is $30,000. The year-end inventory value at December 31, 2021, however, is only $8,000.

6. Would your answer to #5 change if no business was established in the U.S. and the rental property was sold for $700,000 in November 2021? The proceeds net of miscellaneous legal costs were deposited in a U.S. bank account in the name of the Canadian resident individual and transferred to a Canadian bank account seven days later at which time the U.S. account was closed.

AP 20-7 *(Foreign Source Investment Income and the T1135)*

Vickey Gateley works and resides in Niagara Falls, Ontario. She has built a well-diversified portfolio of shares of British companies. At December 31, 2021, Ms. Gateley owns shares with a cost of £800,000. She also has a British bank account with a London bank that has a balance that fluctuates between £25,000 and £50,000.

Ms. Gateley's boyfriend lives in Buffalo, New York. Three years ago, when she started spending many of her weekends there, she decided to purchase a condo in Buffalo. Because the building she chose had construction problems, the prices were depressed and she purchased four units for US$200,000 each. She has rented out the other three units.

During 2021, she earned the following amounts of investment income:

Dividends from British public corporations net of 15% withholding tax	£54,400
Interest on British bank account	£ 1,300
Gross rental income from U.S. rental properties	US$86,000
Expenses of U.S. rental properties	US$45,000

Other Information

1. Ms. Gateley has left the interest in her British bank account and has not transferred it to Canada.

2. Ms. Gateley believes her condo units are undervalued. Because of her concern with respect to future recapture, she does not claim CCA on her rental properties.

3. The dividends from the British corporations were paid on a quarterly basis.

4. Assume that the exchange rates throughout 2021 were £1 = C$1.70 and US$1 = C$1.30.

Required:

A. Indicate the amount of investment income that would be required to be included in Ms. Gateley's 2021 net income, as well as any tax credits that would be available to Ms. Gateley to offset the income tax on this income.

B. Is Ms. Gateley required to file a T1135? If yes, what properties have to be included? Assume that detailed reporting is not required.

AP 20-8   (Foreign Dividends Received by a Resident Canadian Individual)
Matthew Fortin is a Canadian resident who lives in London, Ontario. During the year ending December 31, 2021, he has the following sources of income:

Employment income	$121,300
Taxable capital gains	11,400
Dividends from Canadian public companies	27,350
Dividends from foreign companies:	
Country One—Saxon Ltd. (before withholding tax of $8,000)	40,000
Country Two—Selena Ltd. (before withholding tax of $1,800)	18,000

His business and investment activities have been unsuccessful in previous years and, as a consequence, he has the following loss carry over balances available:

2019 net capital loss	$16,760
2020 non-capital loss	13,480

His only tax credits are the basic personal credit, employment-related credits, and any credits with respect to dividends received.

Required: Determine Matthew's 2021 federal income tax payable.

AP 20-9   (Taxation of Foreign Affiliate Dividends)
CTP is a Canadian public corporation that owns 15% of the shares of FTP, a corporation that was created in a foreign country. During the year ending December 31, 2020, FTP earns $20,000 in

investment income, $70,000 from an active business, and $20,000 of capital gains from the sale of investments.

In early 2021, FTP distributes all of its 2020 after-tax income as a dividend to all of its shareholders. FTP has no income in 2021.

In both 2020 and 2021, assume that CTP is subject to a Canadian federal income tax rate of 25%.

In the following six cases the information above is modified to some degree with additional or alternative assumptions that principally address the Canadian income tax impact of dividends received by residents of Canada from non-resident corporations.

Required: Provide the information that is requested in each of the following cases.

Case 1 FTP is a foreign affiliate (FA) of CTP but not a controlled foreign affiliate (CFA). Assume that it is located in a country that does not have a tax treaty or TIEA with Canada, that this country does not assess income taxes on corporations and does not assess withholding taxes on dividend payments to non-residents. What are the income tax consequences for CTP resulting from its investment in FTP during 2020 and 2021? Include the increase in net and taxable income and the total income tax payable for both years in your solution.

Case 2 Assume the same facts as in Case 1, except that FTP is a CFA of CTP. How would the tax consequences for CTP differ from the income tax consequences described in Case 1 for 2020 and 2021?

Case 3 Assume the same facts as in Case 1, except that CTP does not own sufficient shares such that FTP is not a foreign affiliate. How would the tax consequences for CTP differ from the tax consequences described in Case 1 for 2020 and 2021?

Case 4 Assume the same facts as in Case 1, except that FTP is located in a country that has a tax treaty with Canada. How would the income tax consequences for CTP differ from the tax consequences described in Case 1 for 2020 and 2021?

Case 5 FTP is an FA but not a CFA of CTP. Assume that FTP is located in a country that has a tax treaty with Canada, that this country assesses income taxes on active business income at a rate of 10% and does not assess withholding taxes on dividend payments to non-residents. The income taxes paid by FTP in the foreign country total $7,000 [(10%)($70,000)]. What are the income tax consequences for CTP resulting from its investment in FTP for its 2020 and 2021 taxation years?

Case 6 Assume the same facts as in Case 5, except that the foreign country levies the 10% income tax on all of FTP's 2020 income. This income tax would total $11,000 [(10%)($110,000)]. In addition, a further 8% withholding tax of $7,920 [(8%)($110,000 - $11,000)] was assessed on the dividend paid in 2021. The resulting dividend payment was $91,080 ($110,000 - $11,000 - $7,920). What are the income tax consequences for CTP for its 2020 and 2021 taxation years?

AP 20-10 (Canadian Source Income — Short Cases)
Case A
Mr. Jack Holt is a U.S. resident and employee of Stillwell Industries, a U.S. resident corporation. During the period June 15 through December 6 of the current year, Mr. Holt worked in Canada providing technical assistance to a Canadian subsidiary of Stillwell Industries. His salary was US$5,500 per month. During the period that Mr. Holt was in Canada, Stillwell Industries continued to deposit his salary into his normal U.S. bank account. Both his salary for this period and all of his related travelling expenses were billed to the Canadian subsidiary.

Required: Explain Mr. Holt's tax position.

Case B

Mr. John McQueen was for many years a resident of Ontario. On his retirement 10 years ago, he returned to his native Scotland and has not since returned to Canada. However, he has retained considerable investments in Canada, as follows:

- **Common Shares** He has a large portfolio of common shares that are registered in the name of his Toronto broker. The broker receives all dividends and periodically sends a cheque to Mr. McQueen in Scotland.

- **Mortgage Portfolio** He has a large portfolio of second mortgages. All collections on these mortgages are made by a Toronto law firm and are deposited into a Toronto bank account in the name of Mr. McQueen.

Required: Who is responsible for withholdings of Part XIII tax and on which amounts must withholdings be made?

Case C

Hotels International is a U.S. resident corporation with hotel properties throughout the world. It has recently developed a property in Nova Scotia that will open during the current year. A long-term lease has been signed with Hotel Operators Ltd., a Canadian company specializing in the management of hotels. Under the terms of the lease, Hotel Operators Ltd. will pay all of the operating expenses of the hotel and, in addition, make an annual lease payment of $1,250,000 to the U.S. owners of the new hotel.

Required: Will the U.S. corporation, Hotels International, be subject to Canadian income taxes on the annual lease payment, and if so to what extent?

Case D

The Maple Company, a public company resident in Canada, has 2,400,000 common shares outstanding. Sixty percent of these shares are owned by its U.S. resident parent company, Condor. The remaining shares are owned by Canadian residents. In addition to the common shares, the Condor Company owns holds all of Maple Company's bonds. Two of the five directors of the Maple Company are Canadian residents, while the remaining three are residents of the United States. During the current year, the Maple Company paid a dividend of $1 per share on its common stock and interest of $900,000 on its outstanding bonds.

Required: Calculate the amount of Part XIII taxes to be withheld by the Maple Company with respect to the interest and dividend payments to its U.S. parent.

CHAPTER 21

GST/HST

Learning Objectives

After completing Chapter 21, you should be able to:

1. Describe, in general terms, the GST and HST and how it applies across Canada in all provinces and territories (Paragraph [P hereafter] 21-1 to 21-17).
2. Describe the different ways in which transaction-based sales taxes can be applied and the approach used by the GST/HST (P 21-18 to 21-38).
3. Explain the basic charging provision for GST/HST, who is liable for the tax, and the concept of a supply (P 21-39 to 21-43).
4. Outline the difference between fully taxable supplies, zero-rated supplies, and exempt supplies (P 21-44 to 21-58).
5. Explain the place of supply rules and how the GST/HST is applied to tangible goods, real property, and services (P 21-59 to 21-67).
6. Explain who is responsible for collecting and remitting the GST/HST (P 21-68 to 21-71).
7. Determine whether an entity is required to register for GST/HST and, if so, at what point in time registration is required. Explain the concept of a small supplier and its impact on registration (P 21-72 to 21-90).
8. Apply the rules for calculating input tax credits (ITCs) on current and capital expenditures (P 21-91 to 21-97).
9. Explain some of the basic restrictions on claiming ITCs (P 21-98 to 21-99).
10. Explain how the ITC concept applies to vendors of exempt supplies (P 21-100).
11. Explain some of the differences and similarities as to how amounts are accounted for accounting, income tax, and GST/HST purposes (P 21-101 to 21-105).
12. Determine the GST/HST payable or refund when fully taxable, zero-rated, and exempt supplies are provided (P 21-106 to 21-109).
13. Describe and apply the quick method of accounting for GST/HST and compare it to the regular method to determine the optimum choice (P 21-110 to 21-121).
14. Determine the income tax consequences of claiming ITCs and the use of the quick method (P 21-122).
15. Describe and apply the simplified method of accounting for ITCs (P 21-123 to 21-127).
16. Outline the basic compliance and administration of the GST/HST, including reporting periods, filing returns, payments and instalment obligations, the assessment of penalties and interest, and general resolution of disputes with the CRA (P 21-128 to 21-151).

17. Explain the purpose of the employee and partner GST/HST rebate and calculate the rebate for an employee (P 21-152 to 21-160).
18. Explain how the GST/HST applies when residential homes are purchased and the circumstances where a new housing rebate is available, including a general description as to how the rebate is calculated in a non-HST province or territory (P 21-161 to 21-167).
19. Describe the possible GST/HST implications resulting from the sale of a business as either a sale of assets or a sale of shares (P 21-168 to 21-171).
20. Briefly explain the GST/HST implications when rollovers under ITA 85, 87, and 88(1) apply (P 21-172 to 21-175).
21. Briefly describe how the GST/HST applies to holding companies, to intercompany transactions between members of a closely held corporate group, and the general implications when a GST/HST registrant ceases to carry on a business (P 21-176 to 21-179).
22. Briefly describe how the GST/HST applies to certain types of organizations, such as charities, NPOs, and governmental organizations (P 21-180).
23. Describe the GST/HST implications related to partner expenses, dispositions of partnership interests, transfers between a partnership and its partners, and the reorganization of partnerships (P 21-181 to 21-188).
24. Briefly explain how GST/HST applies to trusts (P 21-189 to 21-192).

Introduction

Background

Introduction of the GST

21-1.   Each province and territory has the right to charge their own sales tax even though some choose not to apply any sales tax. The federal government also possesses that same right to charge sales tax in each province and territory. These sales taxes are generally applied on goods and services sold within the province or territory and often vary between provinces in terms of rates and the goods and services to which they apply.

21-2.   A federal sales tax, the goods and services tax (GST) was introduced in Canada on January 1, 1991, as a replacement for the antiquated federal sales tax system. The GST is a sales tax that applies to those participating in the production, manufacture, and distribution of goods and services, effectively making each participant at each stage responsible for the GST on any value added. The ultimate tax, however, is essentially paid by the consumer. The initial GST rate was set at 7% but was subject to a few reductions. The current rate of 5% has remained unchanged since 2008.

21-3.   The initial concepts underlying the GST were simplification and fairness applying to all goods and services. Unfortunately, the rules, which are set out in the *Excise Tax Act* (ETA), can be quite complex and in many cases reminiscent of the complexity found in the ITA. Complexity typically results in increased compliance costs, which is contrary to the initial tax policy objectives. However, the basic concepts are relatively straightforward.

21-4.   One of the potential redeeming features of the GST was the hope that the Canadian sales tax system could be overhauled and simplified into one generic system that would apply one set of rules to both the provincial/territorial and federal sales taxes. In that regard the federal government pursued discussions and entered into negotiations with some provinces to encourage them to combine or to harmonize their sales tax system with the GST. This could have resulted in substantial savings in both compliance and administrative costs. The attempts to harmonize, however, were only partially successful.

21-5.   Only the province of Quebec showed any early signs of cooperation. Quebec introduced the Quebec Sales Tax (QST), a similar but not identical transaction tax, in 1992. As part of the arrangement with Quebec it was agreed that both the QST and all GST collected in Quebec would be administered by the province of Quebec. While negotiations were underway with

Quebec, several other provinces were launching court challenges on the basis that the GST was constitutional. These challenges ultimately proved unsuccessful.

Harmonized Sales Tax (HST)

21-6.   In 1997, three of the Atlantic provinces, New Brunswick, Nova Scotia, and Newfoundland and Labrador, implemented a harmonized sales tax (HST) that combined their provincial sales tax with the GST to form one provincial sales tax rate. On April 1, 2013, Prince Edward Island agreed to harmonize its provincial tax with the GST. As a result, all four Atlantic provinces apply the HST.

21-7.   The HST is, in effect, a combination of the 5% GST rate plus a provincial rate that is either 8% in Ontario or 10% for each of the four Atlantic provinces. As a result, the HST rate in Ontario is 13% (GST 5% + provincial rate of 8%) and is 15% (GST 5% + provincial rate of 10%) in each of the four Atlantic provinces. The HST was introduced in British Columbia in 2009, but it was defeated and reversed as a result of a provincial referendum in 2011. While the GST represents the federal sales tax rate in all provinces and territories, the three territories (Yukon, Northwest Territories, and Nunavut) and the four western provinces (British Columbia, Alberta, Saskatchewan, and Manitoba) have not harmonized their territorial/provincial sales tax with the GST.

21-8.   A major advantage of the HST is that it is administered by the federal government (specifically the CRA), eliminating the need for the dual administrative system that is required in those provinces that collect both GST and PST.

Current Sales Tax Rates in Canada

21-9.   The inability to reach a consensus on a harmonized sales tax system has left Canada in a state where the sales tax rules can vary considerably from province/territory to province/territory. Figure 21-1 summarizes the various sales tax rates in each province and territory, including identifying the level of government responsible for administering the sales tax.

Figure 21-1 Transaction Taxes in Canada as of July 1, 2021			
Type of Tax	**Province**	**Rates**	**Tax Administration**
GST Only	Alberta	5% + 0%	Federal
	Northwest Territories	5% + 0%	Federal
	Yukon	5% + 0%	Federal
	Nunavut	5% + 0%	Federal
GST and PST	British Columbia	5% + 7%	Federal and provincial
	Manitoba	5% + 7%	Federal and provincial
	Saskatchewan	5% + 6%	Federal and provincial
HST	New Brunswick	15%	Federal
	Newfoundland and Labrador	15%	Federal
	Nova Scotia	15%	Federal
	Ontario	13%	Federal
	Prince Edward Island	15%	Federal
GST and QST	Quebec	5% + 9.975%	Provincial

NOTE: There is a general sales tax rate in B.C., Manitoba, Saskatchewan, and Quebec, however the provincial rates can vary in certain circumstances for specified goods and services (e.g., the B.C. sales tax rate for liquor is 10%).

21-10.   This table illustrates the variation in provincial and territorial rates and the overall administration of the tax system. Within each jurisdictional sales tax system there are additional complexities that provide for rebates (i.e., refunds) of a portion of the provincial sales tax component on select items. These additional complexities can increase the compliance costs for businesses that must be made aware of the different rules that apply in each of those provinces and territories in which they carry on business (i.e., provide goods and services).

How This Text Deals with the Complexity

21-11.   The purpose of our coverage is to ensure that the basic concepts are well understood to provide students with a general knowledge of the GST/HST impact of particular transactions, including ensuring that all reporting and remittance and other compliance-related obligations are respected. This overall objective is consistent with the CPA competencies for GST/HST, the majority of which are rated as Level C, meaning a level of comprehension sufficient to be able to "explain, describe, and demonstrate knowledge that is low to moderate in complexity for a routine situation."

21-12.   CPA competencies rise to Level B for GST/HST compliance-related concerns. This added emphasis recognizes the role that CPAs can fulfill with respect to service and advice to clients in terms of tax compliance. Level B includes the demonstration of knowledge, problem analysis, and the related ability to draw conclusions with respect to low to moderate complexity in routine situations.

21-13.   The GST is applicable to all provinces and territories either as a separate tax or as a component of HST. Fortunately, many of the provisions for the HST are identical to those for the GST. This means that, in general, the concepts and procedures involved are the same for both the GST and the HST.

21-14.   Given this situation, our discussion and examples will focus on one of two scenarios:

- Situations where only the GST is applicable. Alberta and the three territories are the only jurisdictions to which this situation applies.

- Situations where the HST is applicable.

21-15.   Most of our examples will not involve provinces where both GST and PST are in effect, nor will detailed attention be given to the unique situation in Quebec.

21-16.   With the exceptions of a brief Chapter 3 discussion of the GST/HST component of taxable employee benefits and a limited presentation on the impact of GST/HST on business income, all of our material on GST/HST is included in this chapter. This includes discussion of the employee and partner GST/HST rebate, as well as the application of GST/HST to the purchase and sale of capital property. We have also included GST/HST compliance issues, procedures, and administration in this chapter.

21-17.   The majority of businesses in Canada are required to file GST returns. In addition, many organizations, such as charities and businesses carried on by partnerships, must file GST returns even though they are not required to file an actual income tax return. The importance of the GST/HST to Canadian businesses cannot be overstated. An understanding is an essential component of the knowledge base of each professional accountant and business person in understanding one's tax obligations to ensure full tax compliance with respect to both income tax and GST/HST.

Transaction Tax Concepts

General Description

21-18.   While taxes like the GST and HST are often described as a commodity tax, the description is not necessarily appropriate because the term "commodity" does not include services. When the provision of goods and services are subject to a sales type tax, the tax is imposed on a transaction-by-transaction basis as opposed to the broad taxation of an accumulation of income over a period of time, as is the case with income tax.

21-19.   In Canada, the bulk of federal tax revenues are raised through the taxation of the income of individuals and corporations. However, sales taxes account for a larger percentage of provincial tax revenues excluding federal transfers. In addition, there has been a worldwide trend toward increased use of sales taxes, with many industrialized countries relying heavily on sales taxes.

21-20.   Some of the factors that favour the use of transaction-based sales taxes are the following:

- **Simplicity**   Transaction taxes are generally easy to administer and collect, particularly in comparison with income tax. Consumers are not required to file any tax forms, the determination of the tax is straightforward, and if the individual wishes to acquire a particular good or service it is difficult to evade payment.

- **Incentives to Work**   An often-cited disadvantage of income taxes is that they can discourage individuals' initiative to work and invest, particularly in a progressive income tax system where the tax rates increase with increases in income. Transaction taxes do not exhibit this characteristic.

- **Consistency**   Transaction taxes, with their flat-rate system, avoid the fluctuating income and family-unit problems that are associated with progressive income tax systems. In effect, sales tax revenues tend to be much more stable than taxes raised on income, which can fluctuate significantly in economic downturns.

- **Keeping the Tax Revenues in Canada**   While some types of income are prone to planning that can move the source of income outside of Canada, sales taxes on the provision of goods and services within Canada generally remain within Canada. The 2021 federal budget proposed legislative changes to the GST/HST that would ensure that the provision of goods and services to Canadians by anyone, made anywhere in the world, would be subject to the GST/HST.

21-21.   Given these GST/HST preferences, one may ask why income tax is still used; would a tax system based solely on sales tax be preferable? The answer to this question largely involves the question of fairness. In general, transaction taxes relate to consumption. When this is combined with the fact that low-income individuals usually spend a larger portion of their total income on consumption, transaction taxes represent a larger portion of an individual's income than would be the case for high-income earners. It is in this sense that the GST/HST is viewed as regressive. The tax system, however, does attempt to level the playing field to some degree by providing a GST/HST credit to refund a portion of these consumption taxes for low-income individuals as well as ensuring that basic necessities such as most groceries and medications are GST/HST exempt.

21-22.   While a sales tax represents an integral part of a country's revenues, Canada is not willing to abandon the income tax, which is based on an important tax principle that income tax burdens should be based on one's ability to pay. Therefore, individuals with high levels of income should pay a larger share of the tax. This tax policy objective is best achieved through the use of a progressive income tax system that applies an increasing income tax percentage as income rises.

Types of Transaction Taxes

Alternative Methods

21-23.   A transaction-based sales taxes can be structured and applied in different ways. In this section we will consider the alternative sale tax approaches, the Canadian sales tax system, and how it compares to sales tax systems of other countries.

21-24. In discussing the various approaches, we will use a simple example as shown in Figure 21-2. The example looks at the production and distribution chain of a product from the manufacturing stage through to the consumer stage. The example begins with a manufacturer who produces 1,000 units of a given product at a cost of $4 per unit for a total cost of $4,000. The 1,000 units are then sold to a wholesaler for $10 per unit. The wholesaler then sells all of the units to a retailer for $25 per unit. The retailer, in turn, sells all of the units to consumers for $50 per unit. In effect, value is added at each stage, represented in this example by the profit component.

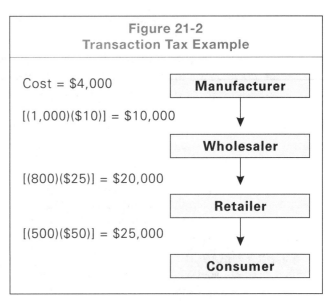

Figure 21-2
Transaction Tax Example

Single Stage Transaction Taxes — Retail Sales Tax

21-25. A single stage transaction tax could be applied at any level in this example. The most common type of single stage tax is applied at the consumer level. This would be the familiar retail sales tax that is collected in several Canadian provinces. For example, if the transactions depicted in Figure 21-2 took place in Manitoba, a 7% retail sales tax would be assessed on the $25,000 price that the retailer charged the consumer, resulting in a provincial sales tax of $1,750 paid by the consumer.

Multi-Stage Transaction Taxes — Turnover Tax

21-26. Referring back to Figure 21-2, it would be possible to impose a multi-stage transaction tax at any combination of the various levels of the production and distribution. For example, the tax could be applied only at the wholesale and retail levels or only at the manufacturing and wholesale levels. If a sales tax is applied at each stage the tax is referred to as a turnover tax, which is an indirect tax, which generally means that when the good or service is purchased by the end consumer the price reflects taxes paid at each previous stage.

21-27. The problem with such a turnover tax is that it involves the pyramiding of taxes when there is no credit for taxes paid earlier in the chain. For example, if there were a 5% turnover tax in place, the manufacturer in Figure 21-2 would charge the wholesaler $10.50 per unit. When the wholesaler applies its normal markup of 250% of cost ($25 ÷ $10), the price would be $26.25 per unit [($10.50)(2.5)]. Of this $26.25, $0.025 [($0.50)(5%)] would represent a tax on the tax that was charged to the wholesaler by the manufacturer. If the 5% tax were also applied to the transfers to the retailer and to the ultimate consumer, there would be further additions of tax on previously assessed amounts of tax. The turnover tax in this case applies in a manner similar to the compounding of interest. Given this pyramiding problem, turnover taxes are not widely used.

Value Added Tax (VAT) — Types

21-28. VATs are multi-stage transaction taxes that can be assessed in two basic ways:

Accounts-Based Method In this approach, the tax is assessed on the basis of the value added at each production and distribution stage. It is usually based on some type of accounting-based determination of income (e.g., value added).

Invoice-Credit Method In this approach, tax is assessed on gross sales. The taxpayer is then provided with a credit based on purchases made. No accounting-based determination of income is required.

21-29. These two approaches will be illustrated using our basic example from Figure 21-2.

Accounts-Based VAT

21-30.   Internationally, the most common type of VAT uses the accounts-based method. Using this method, transactions are taxed at each level in the distribution chain. Using whatever rate is established, the VAT is applied to the value added by the business to goods and services, rather than to the gross sales of the business.

21-31.   If we assume a 5% rate of tax in the example presented in Figure 21-2, this method would require the raw materials supplier to charge tax on the sale price of $4 per unit. The manufacturer would then charge tax on the difference between the sales price of $10 per unit sold and the related input costs of $4. The wholesaler would then charge the 5% on the difference between the manufacturer's invoice of $10 per unit sold and the wholesale price of $25 (i.e., the value added by the wholesaler). Finally, the retailer would charge the VAT on the difference between the retail sale price of $50 and the wholesaler's cost of $25. The total tax calculation is as follows:

Raw materials [(5%)(1,000)($4)]	$ 200
Manufacturer to wholesaler [(5%)(1,000)($10 - $4)]	300
Wholesaler to retailer [(5%)(800)($25 - $10)]	600
Retailer to consumer [(5%)(500)($50 - $25)]	625
Total value added tax	$1,725

Invoice-Credit VAT—The Canadian Approach

21-32.   This is the approach that is used in Canada for GST/HST purposes. Under this approach, each vendor charges tax on the full selling price. This tax is then offset by a credit for the tax that was paid on the costs incurred by the business (these are referred to as input tax credits or ITCs).

21-33.   Continuing to assume a 5% rate of tax is applied to our basic example from Figure 21-2, the invoice-credit VAT calculations would be as follows:

Raw materials supplier	
GST collected [(5%)(1,000)($4)] (no ITC)	$200
Net GST payable	$200
Manufacturer	
GST collected [(5%)(1,000)($10)]	$500
GST paid on costs = ITC [(5%)(1,000)($4)]	(200)
Net GST payable	$300
Wholesaler	
GST collected [(5%)(800)($25)]	$1,000
GST paid on costs = ITC [(5%)(1,000)($10)]	(500)
Net GST payable	$ 500
Retailer	
GST collected [(5%)(500)($50)]	$1,250
GST paid on costs = ITC [(5%)(800)($25)]	(1,000)
Net GST payable	$ 250
Net tax—Raw materials supplier	$ 200
Net tax—Manufacturer	300
Net tax—Wholesaler	500
Net tax—Retailer	250
Total net tax—All levels	$1,250

Comparison

21-34. The overall results for the two approaches are as follows:

Total tax—Accounts-based VAT	$1,725
Total net tax—Invoice-credit VAT	(1,250)
Difference	$ 475

21-35. In this example, using the invoice-credit approach results in less tax being paid. The reason for this is that, when the invoice-credit approach is used, the business receives tax credits for all purchases irrespective of whether the goods are sold. In this example, at both the wholesale and retail levels, the number of units purchased exceed the number of units sold. This means that there is a cash flow advantage when purchases exceed sales. In contrast, under an accounts-based VAT system, the tax to be paid only considers units sold and no credit is received with respect to unsold items in inventory until they are actually sold.

21-36. If all goods purchased are sold, the sales tax under an invoice-credit VAT system is the same as the sales tax under an accounts-based VAT system. This can be seen at both the raw materials and manufacturer level in our example. In the case of the manufacturer, the 1,000 units purchased were all sold. As a result, the two VAT approaches resulted in exactly the same $300 of net tax.

21-37. Both approaches to a VAT apply the tax at each production and distribution stage when sales occur. The central difference is the point in time an ITC is provided with respect to purchases. The Canadian approach is to allow a credit to the purchaser as soon as the purchase is made that matches the sales tax charged by the seller as opposed to only providing a credit for purchases when goods are actually sold. In Figure 21-2 sales by the manufacturer to the wholesaler and from the wholesaler to the retailer result in a charge of 5% on the sale and a corresponding immediate and matching tax credit (ITA) to the purchaser. The net result is that the government does not economically benefit until the sale is made to the end consumer, which is when the production and distribution process comes to an end. During the process, the system applies a general uniformity in terms of cash flow, requiring that GST collected on sales be remitted to the government and that the government reimburse any GST paid on purchases.

21-38. Finally, as a rule this Canadian approach is income tax neutral. GST/HST collected on sales does not affect income, and GST/HST paid on purchases is not a part of the cost of inventory since the amounts are reimbursed through ITCs. The overall impact is that businesses in the production and distribution process simply act as agents of the government in the GST/HST collection and remittance process by collecting taxes that belong to the government. It is also the reason why the CRA takes a hardline position when GST/HST amounts collected are not remitted on time.

Exercise 21-1

Subject: Alternative VAT Approaches

At the beginning of the year the cost of the opening inventory of Darvin Wholesalers (Darvin) was $180,000. Darvin purchased additional inventory for $233,000 during the year. Sales during the year totalled $416,000, and the cost of the inventory sold was $264,000. All of these amounts are before the addition of any sales tax. Assuming a rate of 5%, determine how much sales tax would be paid by Darvin under an accounts-based VAT system and under an invoice-credit VAT system.

Solutions to Exercises are available in the Study Guide.

We suggest you complete SSP 21-1 at this point.

Liability for GST/HST

Basic Charging Provision

21-39.   The basic charging provision for GST is found in the ETA:

> **ETA 165(1)   Imposition of goods and services tax**—Subject to this Part, every recipient of a taxable supply made in Canada shall pay to Her Majesty in right of Canada tax in respect of the supply calculated at the rate of 5% on the value of the consideration for the supply. [Note that ETA 165(2) adds the provincial component for the HST provinces.]

21-40.   In order to understand this charging provision, it will be necessary to give attention to the concept of a taxable supply, which will be covered in the next section of this chapter.

21-41.   It is also important to recognize that the legislation imposes the tax on the recipient of the taxable supply rather than the provider. As we shall find in a later section of this chapter, responsibility for collection of the tax is the responsibility of the provider of the taxable supply who is identified as the GST registrant.

The Concept of a Supply

21-42.   The term "goods and services tax" implies that it is a tax that is applied to goods and services or, more specifically, transactions that involve the provision of goods and services. The term that is used by the ETA in referring to goods or services is "supply." This term is defined as follows:

> **ETA 123(1)   Supply** means the provision of property or a service in any manner, including sale, transfer, barter, exchange, licence, rental, lease, gift or disposition.

21-43.   The definition is comprehensive and would include amounts that would be considered revenues for accounting purposes but is actually much broader. It would include all of the following:

- The sale, rental, or transfer of goods
- The rendering of services
- Licensing arrangements for copyrights or patents
- The lease, sale, or other transfer of real property
- Barter transactions or gifts

Supply Categories

NOTE ON GST/HST DIFFERENCES   While the HST provinces use the same categories of supply that are used in the ETA, some fully taxable items are given point-of-sale rebates for the provincial component of the HST (e.g., Ontario provides an 8% point-of-sale HST rebate for children's clothing). In effect, purchasers pay only the federal GST rate of 5% on these goods. In the harmonization process, many HST provinces wished to preserve certain sales tax exemptions in their pre-existing sales tax system. These exemptions are often maintained through point-of-sale rebates that generally apply to books, children's clothing and footwear, child car seats, and certain other goods.

A full description of these differences for all of the HST provinces goes beyond the scope of this text. Given this, the examples that are described in the following discussion include items that fall into the fully taxable category under the federal GST legislation. Because of provincial rebates in the HST provinces, purchasers of some of these items will not pay the full HST rate.

Taxable Supplies

General Rules

21-44.   The ETA defines "taxable supplies" as follows:

ETA 123(1)   Taxable supply means a supply that is made in the course of a commercial activity.

21-45.   Expanding on this definition, "commercial activity" is defined as:

ETA 123(1)   Commercial Activity of a person means

(a) a business carried on by the person (other than a business carried on without a reasonable expectation of profit by an individual, a personal trust or a partnership, all of the members of which are individuals), except to the extent to which the business involves the making of exempt supplies by the person,

(b) an adventure or concern of the person in the nature of trade (other than an adventure or concern engaged in without a reasonable expectation of profit by an individual, a personal trust or a partnership, all of the members of which are individuals), except to the extent to which the adventure or concern involves the making of exempt supplies by the person, and

(c) the making of a supply (other than an exempt supply) by the person of real property of the person, including anything done by the person in the course of or in connection with the making of the supply.

21-46.   For GST/HST purposes the term "business" has the following meaning:

ETA 123(1)   Business includes a profession, calling, trade, manufacture or undertaking of any kind whatever, whether the activity or undertaking is engaged in for profit, and any activity engaged in on a regular or continuous basis that involves the supply of property by way of lease, licence or similar arrangement, but does not include an office or employment.

21-47.   In summary, if goods or services are provided in the course of a business activity irrespective of whether the activity is conducted in the pursuit of profit, or the selling or leasing of real property, then taxable supplies are being provided unless:

- the business does not have a reasonable expectation of profit (this criterion only applies to businesses run by individuals, certain partnerships, or certain trusts);
- the supplies are exempt supplies; or
- the services are employment services.

21-48.   In the ITA, an activity would not be considered to be a business in the absence of a profit motive. The ETA, however, provides a broader concept that is directed at the underlying activity, which allows GST/HST to be charged in circumstances that would not apply in the ITA. An example would be a charitable organization or a non-profit earning income where profit is not the motive.

21-49.   Taxable supplies fall into two categories. The first category is supplies that we will refer to as fully taxable supplies. The second category is supplies that are referred to as zero-rated.

Fully Taxable Supplies

21-50.   Fully taxable supplies are goods and services subject to the 5% GST rate or the appropriate HST rate (13% or 15%). Examples of fully taxable supplies include the following:

- Transportation within Canada, including taxi or commercial ride-sharing services
- Hotel accommodation
- Restaurant meals and beverages
- Clothing and footwear

- Furniture
- Admissions to concerts, athletic events, and other events
- Car repairs
- Legal and accounting services
- Haircuts
- Cleaning services

Zero-Rated Supplies

21-51. The ETA provides a list of taxable supplies that are designated as zero-rated. While these supplies are said to be taxable, they are taxed at a 0% rate rather than the regular GST rate of 5% or the HST rates of 13% and 15%.

21-52. At first glance, this concept seems a bit confusing in referring to a 0% rate as a taxable supply. The purpose of labelling a zero-rated supply as a taxable supply is to allow the underlying commercial activity to recover any GST/HST paid as an ITC since such credits are restricted to taxable supplies. In contrast, while providers of exempt supplies do not charge and collect GST/HST they are also not eligible for ITCs.

21-53. In addition, as zero-rated supplies are considered taxable at a rate of 0%, they are included in the threshold amounts for determining the filing frequency of a GST or HST return. This is covered beginning in Paragraph 21-131.

21-54. Common items included in the category of zero-rated supplies include the following:

- Prescription drugs
- Medical devices such as wheelchairs, eye glasses, and hearing aids
- Basic groceries
- Most agricultural and fishery products
- Goods and services exported from Canada
- Foreign travel and transportation services

21-55. Some elaboration is required for the meaning of foreign travel. Surface travel by ship, bus, or train is zero-rated when the origin or termination point is outside Canada (e.g., a train trip to the U.S. is zero-rated). Domestic surface travel is fully taxable.

21-56. In the case of air travel, the GST/HST rules can be complicated. International air travel is zero-rated only when flights are deemed to be outside of continental North America, not just outside of Canada. As an example of the possible complications, this broader definition can make Canadian air travel to and from the United States fully taxable.

Exempt Supplies

21-57. As was the case with zero-rated supplies, the ETA provides a list of supplies that are exempt from GST. Persons providing exempt supplies do not collect GST/HST and are not eligible for ITCs for GST/HST paid on related purchases. This means that suppliers of exempt supplies pay GST/HST that is not refundable to them on the goods and services required to carry on their business. As a consequence, the non-recoverable GST/HST paid is a cost of doing business that is likely to be passed on to consumers in the form of higher prices.

21-58. Some common goods and services that are exempt supplies include the following:

- Basic health care and dental services provided by licensed physicians or dentists for medical reasons (would not include cosmetic surgery)
- Financial services provided by financial institutions to Canadian residents
- Sales of used residential housing and long-term residential rents including condo fees (e.g., rentals for more than 30 days)
- Most land sold by individuals where the land was not used in a business
- Educational courses leading to certificates or diplomas, tutoring for credit courses, and music lessons

- Child care services provided to children 14 years of age and younger for periods of less than 24 hours per day
- A wide variety of services provided by charities, not-for-profit, and government organizations (see discussion under "Specific Applications" at Paragraph 21-180).

Applying the GST/HST Rate

Place of Supply

The Problem

21-59.   The rate at which GST or HST will be applied varies from a low of 5% in a province where only the GST is applicable (e.g., Alberta and the three territories) to a high of 15% under the HST regime (e.g., the four Atlantic provinces). This range of rates makes the question of which rate to apply to a particular supply of goods and services quite significant.

21-60.   A further question relates to whether the tax should be based on the location of the registrant providing the supply or, alternatively, the location of the recipient of the supply. Prior to 2010, the place of supply rules were mostly based on the location of the supplier. The current rules rely more heavily on where the recipient is located and are based on a policy that it is the location where goods are consumed or the benefits of services are received that should generally apply. This means that a supplier must be able to determine the transaction taxes in any province where goods are delivered or services are provided, as well as the transaction taxes in the province where the supplier is located.

21-61.   The legislation provides for a wide variety of situations, some of which can be quite complicated. Our coverage is limited to a basic overview of how the rules are applied in the most common situations.

Tangible Goods

21-62.   The rules for tangible goods are relatively straightforward. A GST registrant will calculate GST/HST based on the rate in effect in the province where the goods are delivered. The following example illustrates the application of this method.

> **EXAMPLE**   An Ontario HST registrant sells shirts online and ships them to purchasers in Ontario, Prince Edward Island, Alberta, and Quebec.
>
> **ANALYSIS**   The GST/HST rate charged on the sales will vary as follows:
>
> - Ontario recipient—HST will be charged at 13%.
>
> - Prince Edward Island recipient—HST will be charged at 15%.
>
> - Alberta recipient—Only GST at 5% will be charged.
>
> - Quebec recipient—Only GST at 5% will be charged. This example makes the point that Quebec is using a separate transaction tax (QST) rather than harmonizing with the federal GST. If the Ontario registrant was a QST registrant as well, QST would also be charged on this sale. Note that Quebec consumers are required to voluntarily pay the relevant QST to Revenu Quebec (the provincial equivalent of the CRA) on purchases shipped from outside Quebec that do not have QST charged.

Real Property

21-63.   As real property (e.g., land and buildings) cannot generally be moved across provincial and territorial borders, there are few complications in this area. The GS/HST will be based on the rates in effect in the province where the real property is located. For example, on a taxable sale of real property in Ontario, HST of 13% is charged regardless of where the seller resides.

Services

21-64.   Unlike tangible goods and real property, the determination of the place of supply for services can be complicated at times since it depends on many factors, including the nature of the services provided (personal, professional, etc.). The general rule is that the place of supply is the province or territory in which a person or location benefits from the service.

> **EXAMPLE**   A professor at a Manitoba university is also a freelance editor of a widely used accounting text. He does his editing in his office in Winnipeg. His editing fees are consistently in excess of $50,000 per year. Because of this, he is a GST registrant (Manitoba does not participate in the HST program). His work is sent to the Toronto office of the publisher and cheques for his fees are issued from that office.

> **ANALYSIS**   As the services benefit a location in Ontario, the editor would bill HST at 13%.

Applying the Rate

Consideration Received

21-65.   To determine the amount of GST/HST to be charged, the appropriate rate is applied to the amount of consideration received in return for taxable supplies. In most cases, the consideration will be monetary and the amount matches the sales price. If the consideration is non-monetary (e.g., a barter transaction), GST/HST is still applicable. In this case, however, an estimate will have to be made of the FMV of the consideration received.

21-66.   The GST/HST is calculated based on the sales price or service fee, which may indirectly include other charges and fees such as any non-refundable federal taxes, provincial taxes other than retail sales taxes, and duties and fees that are imposed on either the supplier or recipient in respect of the property or services supplied. In that case these additional amounts add to the cost of the goods sold or services provided, which is then indirectly passed on to the recipient through an increased price or charge for services. Where both the GST and a provincial sales tax apply, the GST calculation would not include the provincial sales tax, which is separately calculated. If, for example, an item priced at $100 is purchased in Manitoba by a Manitoba resident, GST will be 5% or $5 and the Manitoba sales tax will be 7% or $7 for a total of $112.

Effect of Trade-Ins

21-67.   Where a good owned by a person that is not registered for GST/HST is traded in toward the supply of a new good, GST/HST is calculated on the net amount after the trade-in. The most common occurrence of this type of trade-in is when an individual consumer trades in a used car for a new one with an automobile dealership.

> **EXAMPLE**   John Bailey, a resident of Alberta, purchases a new Tesla at a cost of $92,000. He is given a trade-in allowance of $21,000 on his used car.

> **ANALYSIS**   The GST would be $3,550 [(5%)($92,000 - $21,000)].

Collection and Remittance of GST/HST

21-68.   Income tax is generally collected from the taxpayer who is liable for that income tax. A corporation, for example, determines its income tax liability and remits that amount directly to the government.

21-69.   The situation is different with GST/HST. We noted previously that GST/HST charges the tax to the recipient of the taxable supply. However, the responsibility for the collection and remittance of the GST/HST falls on the provider of the taxable supply. This responsibility is legislated by obliging providers of taxable supplies to become GST registrants, which then legally requires the supplier to act as an intermediary on behalf of the government in collecting and remitting the tax. Registration requirements are discussed in the following section.

21-70.   As a rule, the amount of the GST/HST is fully disclosed on the invoice when a good or service is provided. In some instances, however, some retailers have used a promotional practice of advertising that certain goods can be purchased for a limited time with no GST/HST. This gives the recipient purchaser the impression that the supplier seller has somehow managed to avoid the GST/HST, but this is not the case. Special regulations describe how the GST/HST is to be determined when there is one price without any breakdown of a GST/HST component. The regulations apply a fraction based on the GST or HST rate. The fraction would be 5/105 for GST provinces and territories, 13/113 for Ontario, and 15/115 for the four Atlantic provinces.

> **EXAMPLE**   An Alberta store advertises a GST-free promotion. A customer pays the no-GST sales price of $2,500 for a new appliance. The invoice does not identify any GST.

> **ANALYSIS**   From the customer's point of view, it appears that no GST has been charged. However, the retailer will have to treat the $2,500 as a GST-inclusive amount and remit GST of $119.05 [($2,500)(5/105)] to the government.

21-71.   You should note that, while the supplier is responsible for the collection of GST/HST, this does not relieve the purchaser of the responsibility for payment if GST/HST has not been charged when it should have been. If a supplier fails to charge and collect the tax, the CRA can, in some cases, technically assess the purchaser; however, this is not practical in most circumstances.

Registration

Meaning of a Person for GST/HST

21-72.   For GST/HST purposes, the ETA defines a "person" as follows:

> **ETA 123(1)   Person** means an individual, a partnership, a corporation, the estate of a deceased individual, a trust, or a body that is a society, union, club, association, commission or other organization of any kind.

21-73.   While both the ITA and ETA define a "person," the ETA definition is much broader given that it is identifying potential suppliers of goods and services that do not necessarily fit the mould of a person in the ITA, which is generally restricted to individuals, corporations, and trusts. The ETA definition, for example, includes partnerships and non-profit organizations (NPOs), which are not required to file income tax returns although they are required to file information returns for income tax purposes.

Who Must Register

Basic Requirement

21-74.   As we have previously indicated, the collection of GST/HST is administered through a registration requirement for providers of taxable supplies. This requirement is as follows:

> **ETA 240(1)**   Every person who makes a taxable supply in Canada in the course of a commercial activity engaged in by the person in Canada is required to be registered for the purposes of this Part, except where
>
> (a)   the person is a small supplier;
> (b)   the only commercial activity of the person is the making of supplies of real property by way of sale otherwise than in the course of a business; or
> (c)   the person is a non-resident person who does not carry on any business in Canada.

21-75.   This requirement contains several terms and concepts that require further elaboration that is covered in the following section.

Commercial Activity

21-76.   ETA 240(1) requires registration only when "taxable supplies" are delivered in the course of "commercial activity." In simple terms, any person who provides taxable or zero-rated supplies in the course of a business is required to register for the GST/HST unless one of the exceptions listed in ETA 240(1) applies.

21-77.   Specific commercial activity exclusions include the following:

- Business activity that is carried on by an individual without a reasonable expectation of profit (e.g., a hobby)
- The provision of exempt supplies (e.g., child care services)
- The provision of employment services

21-78.   Registration for GST/HST is not required or permitted if a person is involved solely in an excluded activity. If, for example, a hobby would qualify, an individual would be able to claim a GST/HST refund through ITC claims on what amounts to personal expenditures.

Exemption for Non-Residents

21-79.   The ETA 240(1) requirement to register, in general, excludes non-residents. The major exception to this would be when a non-resident person carries on business in Canada. This exception would apply, without regard to whether the business is carried on through a permanent establishment, which is generally the income tax test to determine liability of a non-resident with respect to a business. For GST/HST purposes, however, a non-resident with a permanent establishment in Canada (a branch office) is deemed to be a resident of Canada with respect to activities carried on through that location. In addition, Canadian residents with permanent establishments situated outside Canada are deemed to be non-residents with respect to activity carried on through that foreign location.

21-80.   In general, the concept of factual residency (see Chapter 1) is the same for GST/HST purposes as it is for the ITA. ETA 132(1) sets out some deemed residency rules that apply. For example, corporations are deemed resident if incorporated in Canada; partnerships, societies, clubs, and so on are deemed resident if a member that exercises control is resident in Canada or the majority of members are resident in Canada; and individuals are deemed resident if they are deemed resident by ITA 250(1)(b) to (f) (this would not include the 183-day sojourner rule).

Exemption for Small Suppliers

Overview

21-81.   The ETA 240(1) registration requirement does not apply to "small suppliers." A small supplier is a person whose revenues (before expenses) from taxable supplies, including those of associated persons, is less than $30,000 per year. This small supplier rule is intended to provide compliance relief to very small businesses. It applies to businesses that meet the commercial activity criteria and would include business carried on by a sole proprietor, a partnership, or a corporation.

21-82.   Since the small supplier rules contemplate revenues of associated persons, a general understanding of associated persons is important. The associated person rules are set out at ETA 127 and rely on the associated corporation rules in the ITA (ITA 256) when associating corporations, but there are many additional rules for other situations. For example, some of the main rules with respect to individuals can be summarized as follows:

- Individuals who alone or together with associated persons control a corporation would be associated with that corporation.
- Individuals who alone or together with associated persons are entitled to more than half of the profits of a partnership would be associated with that partnership.
- Individuals whose interest in a trust alone or together with associated persons exceeds half of all the value of the trust would be associated with that trust.

21-83.   The basic test for qualification as a small supplier is based on calendar-year quarters (i.e., January to March, April to June, July to September, and October to December). Under this test, a person qualifies as a small supplier in the current quarter and the month following the current quarter if the person, together with associated persons, did not have cumulative taxable supplies exceeding $30,000 in any single calendar quarter and in the last four consecutive calendar quarters. The four consecutive calendar quarters are not required to be in the same calendar year. In effect there are two separate tests that establish whether small supplier status has been lost. The first is when the total of the last four consecutive calendar quarters exceed $30,000 and the second is where the $30,000 limit has been exceeded in one calendar quarter.

Last Four Calendar Quarters Test (Cumulative)

21-84.   If taxable supplies accumulate to $30,000 at any time within the last four consecutive quarters, the person remains a small supplier for those calendar quarters plus one additional calendar month. The person is required to begin collecting GST/HST beginning with the first sale made after the additional calendar month. The supplier must formally register within 29 days from that deemed registration day (e.g., the date of the first sale).

EXAMPLE   Supplier A opened for business on January 1, 2021. The following table indicates the revenues from taxable supplies for each calendar quarter in 2021. The first sale in November 2021 was made on November 4.

Quarter	Months	Taxable Supplies
One	January to March	$ 7,000
Two	April to June	8,000
Three	July to September	20,000
Four	October to December	9,000
Total		$44,000

ANALYSIS   To determine if small supplier status has been lost we can look to the two tests. Since there are no calendar quarters that exceed $30,000, the four calendar quarter test is the only remaining test that could impact small supplier status. Supplier A's revenues accumulate to more than $30,000 in the third quarter of 2021 ($7,000 + $8,000 + $20,000 = $35,000). This means that Supplier A is considered a small supplier for the month of October 2021 and is only required to register and begin collecting GST/HST starting with the first taxable supply made from November 1, 2021. As a result, effective registration is considered to begin November 4, 2021, and GST/HST must be collected from that day. Official registration is required within 29 days of November 4, 2021, or by December 3, 2021.

Calendar Quarter Test (> $30,000 in a Single Quarter)

21-85.   An alternative to the "last four calendar quarters" test is the "single calendar quarter test," where the $30,000 threshold is exceeded in a single calendar quarter. The calendar quarter test overrides the four calendar quarter test. When a sale results in the $30,000 threshold being exceeded in a single quarter, the person is immediately deemed a registrant and must collect GST/HST on the supply (sale) that caused the limit to be exceeded, even though she is not yet registered. The supplier must formally register within 29 days from that deemed registration day.

EXAMPLE   Supplier B began carrying on business January 1, 2021. The business is an art gallery and Supplier B had only two sales in 2021, one for $39,000 on May 15 and the other for $5,000 on August 28.

Quarter	Months	Taxable Supplies
One	January to March	Nil
Two	April to June (May 15)	$39,000
Three	July to September (August 28)	5,000
Four	October to December	Nil
Total		$44,000

ANALYSIS Supplier B would be deemed a registrant as of the May 15 sale, reflecting the fact that this single sale pushes the sales for that quarter past the $30,000 threshold amount. Starting with that sale, GST/HST should be collected on all taxable supplies made. While Supplier B does not have to register until June 13, 2021 (29 days after the May 15 sale), the collection of GST/HST is required starting with that sale on May 15, 2021.

21-86.   In comparing the two preceding examples, note that Supplier A and Supplier B each had revenue from taxable supplies of $44,000 in the four calendar quarters for 2021. Supplier B, however, exceeded the $30,000 threshold in Quarter Two. This results in Supplier B being deemed to be registered starting with the May 15, 2021, transaction whereas Supplier A will not have to start collecting GST/HST until November 4, 2021, using the last four calendar quarters test.

Exercise 21-2

Subject: Requirement to Register

Ms. Sharon Salome and Mr. Rock Laughton begin separate businesses on April 1, 2021. The quarterly sales of taxable supplies for both businesses are as follows:

Calendar Quarter	Sharon Salome	Rock Laughton
April to June 2021	$10,000	$ 8,000
July to September 2021	4,000	13,000
October to December 2021	35,000	4,000
January to March 2022	40,000	17,000

At what point in time will Ms. Salome and Mr. Laughton have to begin collecting GST? At what point will each be required to register?

Solutions to Exercises are available in the Study Guide.

Voluntary Registration

21-87.   The small supplier exemption can represent an advantage to persons with limited commercial activity whose clients are consumers who cannot claim ITCs. If the vendor is not registered, the goods or services can legally be sold without charging GST/HST, which would result in savings for consumers.

21-88.   There is, however, a disadvantage to this exemption. If a person does not register, they are not entitled to ITCs for any business-related GST/HST paid. They are effectively treated as the final consumer with respect to their own purchases and expenses. This means that the business must either absorb the GST/HST paid on its costs or, alternatively, pass the GST/HST paid on purchases and expenses on to its customers in the form of higher prices.

21-89.   Given this problem, voluntary registration is an alternative. Any person engaged in commercial activity in Canada can apply to be registered, even if taxable sales are less than the $30,000 small supplier threshold. In deciding whether this alternative is viable the person must consider the amount of ITCs that would be available. However, the person must also consider whether charging GST/HST will reduce product or service demand, especially if the competition does not charge GST/HST.

Registrants Ineligible for the Small Supplier Exemption

21-90.   Certain taxable suppliers are prohibited from avoiding registration as small suppliers. Specifically, those who provide taxi services, commercial ride-sharing services (e.g., Uber), and non-resident performers selling tickets to performances, amusement (carnivals), seminars, and other events are required to register for the GST/HST.

We suggest you complete SSP 21-2 at this point.

Input Tax Credits (ITC)

Vendors of Fully Taxable and Zero-Rated Supplies

General Rules

21-91.   A GST/HST registrant must collect and remit GST/HST on sales of fully taxable supplies. In the process of supplying these goods and services, the registrant will incur costs, some of which are likely to include GST/HST. To the extent that these costs have been incurred in commercial activity (i.e., supplying either fully taxable or zero-rated goods and services), the registrant can claim a refund of the GST/HST that has been included in these costs.

21-92.   The GST/HST refunds that are available to registrants are called input tax credits (ITCs). If the available ITCs for the period exceed the GST/HST collected during the period, the registrant can claim a GST/HST refund for the net amount.

21-93.   As will be discussed in the sections that follow, the rules for claiming ITCs vary depending on whether the GST/HST was paid on current expenditures (e.g., business expenses and inventory purchases) or, alternatively, capital expenditures (buildings, machinery, etc). In addition, the rules also vary with the type of capital expenditure on which the GST/HST was paid.

21-94.   In claiming ITCs, there is no matching of costs and revenues. ITCs on inventory purchases become available at the time of purchase, not when the goods are sold. ITCs on capital expenditures generally become available when the property is acquired, not spread over the useful life of the property.

Current Expenditures

21-95.   With respect to current expenditures, if all or substantially all (90% or more) of a current expenditure is related to commercial activity, then all of the GST/HST that was paid can be claimed as an ITC. In contrast, if 10% or less of an expenditure is related to commercial activity, no ITC can be claimed. If the percentage of the current expenditure used for commercial activity is between 10% and 90% , the ITC available is calculated by multiplying the total GST/HST paid by the percentage of commercial activity usage. Because commercial activity is limited to taxable supplies and zero-rated supplies, any use toward an exempt activity that exceeds 10% could reduce the amount of the ITC with respect to a particular expenditure.

Capital Expenditures

21-96.   The GST/HST paid on purchases of capital property used in commercial activities is eligible for an ITC at the time of purchase, irrespective of whether the purchase is paid in full or financed and regardless of how the capital property is depreciated for accounting purposes or depreciated for income tax purposes.

21-97.   In general, capital property for GST/HST purposes has the same meaning that is used for income tax purposes. However, for GST/HST purposes it is generally categorized as either capital real property or capital personal property. In situations where a capital property is not solely used in a commercial activity, the method used to determine the available ITC will depend on the type of capital property:

> **Capital Real Property (Land and Buildings)**   For this type of property, the ITC available is in proportion to the extent to which the property is used in commercial activities. That is, if the building is used 35% for commercial activities, the ITC will be equal to 35% of the GST/HST paid. This is reflected in Figure 21-3, which summarizes that (1) if the commercial use is 10% or less there is no ITC, (2) when the commercial activity is 90% or more a full ITC is allowed, and (3) where the use falls between 10% and 90% it is the actual use that is applied to the GST/HST paid.

	Figure 21-3 Maximum ITCs	
Taxable Purchase	**Percentage Used in Commercial Activities = X%**	**Input Tax Credit**
Current expenditures* and capital real property	X% ≤ 10% 10% < X% < 90% X% ≥ 90%	Nil X% 100%
Capital personal property (excluding passenger vehicles*)	X% ≤ 50% X% > 50%	Nil 100%
*Special rules apply to certain items. See Paragraph 21-98.		

Capital Personal Property (Capital Property Other Than Real Property) In order for the ITC to be available on capital personal property, the property must be used "primarily" in commercial activities, which means more than 50% of the time. This is also reflected in Figure 21-3. If commercial activity is 50% or less, none of the GST/HST paid can be claimed as an ITC. If commercial activity exceeds 50%, all of the GST/HST is eligible for an ITC.

Restrictions on Claiming ITCs

21-98. The rules of the ETA are generally separate from those of the ITA but there are certain restrictions imposed in the ITA on what may be claimed as an expense, including CCA, that carry through to the ETA in terms of what is permissible with respect to ITCs. Some of the more common restrictions are as follows:

Passenger Vehicles No ITCs are available for GST/HST paid on the portion of the cost or lease payment of a passenger vehicle that is in excess of the prescribed amounts for income tax purposes (see Chapter 6). In addition, if the vehicle is owned by a registrant who is an individual or a partnership and the vehicle is used partly for business (more than 10% and less than 90%) and partly for personal use, the ITC is pro-rated based on the annual CCA claimed, applying the rates of 5/105, 13/113, or 15/115 depending on whether the province or territory applies only GST or is an HST province.

Club Memberships No ITCs are available for GST/HST paid on membership fees or dues in any club whose main purpose is to provide dining, recreational, or sporting facilities.

Provision of Recreational Facilities No ITCs are available for the GST/HST costs of providing certain types of recreational facilities to employees, owners, or related parties.

Business Meals and Entertainment ITCs on most meals and entertainment expenses are limited to 50% of the GST/HST paid. This restriction follows ITA 67.1, which only allows 50% of most meals and entertainment to be claimed as an expense. Where the ITA does allow a 100% deduction for income tax, GST/HST also allows 100% ITCs.

Personal or Living Expenses ITCs cannot generally be claimed on costs associated with the personal or living expenses of any employee, owner, or related individual.

Reasonableness Both the nature and value of an expenditure or purchase must be reasonable in relation to the commercial activities of the registrant before an ITC can be claimed. This is similar to the reasonableness test found in ITA 67.

21-99. There are time limitations for claiming ITCs, which is important if some ITC claims were understated. For large businesses whose sales are less than 90% taxable but in excess of $6 million and listed financial institutions, the time limit is generally two years from the filing date for the GST/HST period in which the ITC relates. For all other registrants the time limitation is four years from the filing date.

Vendors of Exempt Supplies

21-100.   Vendors of exempt supplies cannot claim any GST/HST paid on expenditures or purchases that relate to exempt supplies. In some situations, vendors are involved in making fully taxable or zero-rated supplies as well as exempt supplies. Since these businesses can only recover GST/HST paid on their fully taxable or zero-rated activities, they must apportion their ITCs on a "reasonable" basis. This applies to both current and capital expenditures that cannot be directly identified with particular exempt or taxable activities.

Accounting vs. Income Tax vs. GST/HST

Differences

21-101.   The concept of matching is integral to the determination of business income for both accounting and income tax purposes. For GST/HST purposes, the matching concept is not relevant. GST/HST is collected when taxable supplies are provided and ITCs become eligible when expenses and costs of commercial activity are incurred. No attempt is made to match the ITCs claimed with respect to the related sales of taxable supplies, and the notion of receivables and payables is not generally relevant. The question is whether an expense or cost has been incurred and whether revenue has been earned.

21-102.   Other significant differences between accounting, income tax, and GST/HST include the following:

- Most accounting and income tax allocations, for example amortization or CCA, are largely irrelevant for GST/HST purposes except for the determination of ITCs on passenger vehicles. GST/HST paid on capital expenditures that are eligible for ITCs can generally be claimed in the period in which the expenditure is made.

- Many deductible expenses for income tax purposes do not affect GST/HST. For example, GST/HST does not apply to employee wages, interest, property taxes, or educational services. While such costs are usually fully deductible in the calculation of net income, they do not require the payment of GST/HST and, as a consequence, do not generate ITCs.

Similarities

21-103.   In contrast to these differences, there are some similarities that are common to both GST/HST and income tax. For example, GST/HST is normally collectible and revenue is generally recognized for income tax purposes when a timely invoice is issued for the provision of goods or services. The actual payment of the invoice is not generally a relevant consideration for either income tax or GST/HST purposes.

21-104.   Similarly, if an account receivable becomes uncollectible, an adjustment is required for both income tax and GST/HST purposes. The adjustment for GST/HST purposes is equal to GST/HST multiplied by the proportion of the total sales price (including GST/HST and any provincial sales tax) that is determined to be uncollectible. In addition, some of the restrictions that apply in the deductibility of certain expenses for income tax purposes (e.g., 50% of business meals and entertainment and the $800 monthly leasing restriction for passenger vehicles) are also part of the ETA.

Financial Statement Presentation

21-105.   The revenue issue is covered in ASPE 3400 and IFRS 15. In general these accounting standards recognize that GST/HST should not be included in revenue. There is no corresponding statement with respect to expenses. However, it would be logical to assume that any GST/HST paid that is eligible for an ITC would not be included in the reported expense. Note, however, that even though the revenues and expenses are reported net of GST/HST, the net GST/HST recoverable as a refund or payable would be reflected in the balance sheet.

Example 1—Fully Taxable and Zero-Rated Supplies

21-106.   In this example we will assume that the company sells only fully taxable and zero-rated supplies (no exempt supplies).

EXAMPLE   Marson Ltd. is located in the province of Alberta, which does not have a provincial sales tax and does not participate in the HST (see Figure 21-1). In the following income statement of Marson Ltd. for the year ending December 31, 2021, the sales and expenses are all reported net of any GST. In other words, none of the amounts include GST.

Sales	$9,500,000
Expenses:	
Cost of goods sold	($6,500,000)
Amortization	(900,000)
Salaries and wages	(1,500,000)
Other expenses	(200,000)
Total expenses (excluding GST and income taxes)	($9,100,000)
Net income for accounting purposes	$ 400,000

Other Information:

1.   Of the total sales, $6,800,000 were fully taxable supplies and $2,700,000 were zero-rated.

2.   Purchases of merchandise totalled $8,700,000 without GST. All of the merchandise sold and purchased is attributable to fully taxable supplies.

3.   All of the other expenses were subject to GST. Of the total, 80% relate to fully taxable supplies and 20% to zero-rated supplies.

4.   During 2021, capital expenditures totalled $7,500,000 without GST and the amounts have not yet been paid. These consisted of $5,000,000 for an office building and $2,500,000 for furniture and fixtures. The office building was used 60% for fully taxable supplies and 40% for zero-rated supplies. The furniture and fixtures were used 55% for fully taxable supplies and 45% for zero-rated supplies.

ANALYSIS   Based on this information Marson Ltd. is eligible for a GST refund calculated as follows:

GST collected [(5%)($6,800,000)]	$340,000
Input tax credits:	
Purchases [(5%)($8,700,000)]	(435,000)
Amortization expense	N/A
Salaries and wages	N/A
Other expenses [(5%)(80% + 20%)($200,000)]	(10,000)
Building [(5%)(60% + 40%)($5,000,000)]	(250,000)
Furniture and fixtures [(5%)(55% + 45%)($2,500,000)]	(125,000)
GST refund	($480,000)

21-107.   While Marson Ltd. reports positive income for accounting purposes, the company is nevertheless eligible for a GST refund. This example illustrates the fact that GST reporting is not based on the matching principle. The company is entitled to full ITCs with respect to the capital expenditures irrespective of amortization expense, and full ITCs are available with respect to the inventory purchases regardless of whether the inventory has been sold.

Example 2—Fully Taxable and Exempt Supplies

21-108.   In this example, we have revised the Marson Ltd. example so that the company sells fully taxable and GST exempt supplies (no zero-rated supplies). The revised information is repeated for your convenience.

EXAMPLE   Marson Ltd. is located in the province of Alberta, which does not have a provincial sales tax and does not participate in the HST (see Figure 21-1). In the following income statement of Marson Ltd. for the year ending December 31, 2021, the sales and expenses are all reported net of any GST. In other words, none of the amounts include GST.

Sales	$9,500,000
Expenses:	
Cost of goods sold	($6,500,000)
Amortization	(900,000)
Salaries and wages	(1,500,000)
Other expenses	(200,000)
Total expenses (excluding GST and income taxes)	($9,100,000)
Net income for accounting purposes	$ 400,000

Other Information:

1. Of the total sales, $6,800,000 were fully taxable supplies and $2,700,000 were exempt supplies.

2. Purchases of merchandise totalled $8,700,000 without GST. All of the merchandise sold and purchased is attributable to fully taxable supplies.

3. Of the other expenses, 80% related to fully taxable supplies and 20% to exempt supplies.

4. During 2021, capital expenditures totalled $7,500,000 without GST, and the amounts have not yet been paid. These consisted of $5,000,000 for an office building and $2,500,000 for furniture and fixtures. The office building was used 60% for fully taxable supplies and 40% for exempt supplies. The furniture and fixtures were used 55% for fully taxable supplies and 45% for exempt supplies.

ANALYSIS   Based on this revised information, the GST refund for Marson Ltd. would be calculated as follows:

GST collected [(5%)($6,800,000)]	$340,000
Input tax credits:	
Purchases [(5%)($8,700,000)]	(435,000)
Amortization	N/A
Salaries and wages	N/A
Other expenses [(5%)(80%)($200,000)]	(8,000)
Building [(5%)(60%)($5,000,000)]	(150,000)
Furniture and fixtures [(5%)(100%)($2,500,000)]	(125,000)
GST refund	($378,000)

21-109.   In this example, where some of the costs relate to the provision of exempt supplies, only 80% of the GST on other expenses is eligible for an ITC. Similarly, only 60% of the GST paid on the building is eligible. However, because the furniture and fixtures are capital personal property and used more than 50% for commercial activity (e.g., taxable supplies), all of the GST paid is eligible for an ITC, even though 45% of their usage was attributable to exempt supplies.

Exercise 21-3

Subject: HST Calculation

March Ltd. carries on business in Ontario, where the relevant HST rate is 13%. During the current period, March Ltd. has taxable sales of $1,223,000. Its cost of goods sold for the period was $843,000 and its inventory purchases totalled $969,000. Other expenses for the period included salaries and wages of $87,000, interest expense of $16,000, and amortization expense of $93,000. No capital expenditures were made during the period. None of the amounts indicated include HST. Determine the HST payable or HST refund for the period.

Exercise 21-4

Subject: HST Calculation

Ms. Marsha Stone resides and works in Nova Scotia, where the relevant HST rate is 15%. During the current year, she earns business revenues of $224,000.

Office rent for the year totals $25,800, and she pays a clerical assistant an annual salary of $28,500. Her capital expenditures during the year are $36,000 for new office furniture and $20,000 for computer hardware and software. None of these amounts include HST. Of the capital expenditures, 100% are attributable to the provision of taxable supplies.

Determine the HST payable or HST refund for the year.

Exercise 21-5

Subject: ITCs on Capital Expenditures

Modam Ltd. carries on business in Alberta, a province that does not participate in the HST and has no provincial sales tax. During the current period, Modam Ltd. purchases an office building and land for $1,200,000. The company also purchases office equipment for $226,000. The building will be used 40% for taxable supplies and 60% for exempt supplies. The office equipment is to be allocated in the same 40-60 proportion. For accounting purposes, the building will be amortized over 40 years, while the office equipment will be amortized over a four-year period. None of these amounts include GST.

Determine the ITCs that Modam Ltd. can claim as a result of these capital expenditures.

Solutions to Exercises are available in the Study Guide.

We suggest you complete SSP 21-3 and 21-4 at this point.

Relief for Small Businesses

Quick Method of Accounting

General Rules

21-110.   Eligible businesses, defined as businesses with annual GST/HST-included taxable sales, including those of associated businesses, of $400,000 or less during the year, can elect to use the quick method of determining the net GST/HST remittance. Both fully taxable and zero-rated supplies are included in calculating the $400,000 threshold, while exempt supplies, supplies made outside of Canada, sales of capital real and personal property, and provincial sales taxes are excluded. In addition, certain businesses are excluded from using the quick method, including legal, accounting, and financial consulting services.

21-111.   If the quick method election is filed (Form GST74), the registrant charges GST or HST at the normal rate on taxable sales. The major advantage of this method is that the business is not required to keep detailed records of current expenditures that are eligible for ITCs. When this method is used for current expenditures, the registrant can still claim ITCs on capital expenditures. This means that there will continue to be a need to track the details of capital expenditures for ITC purposes.

21-112.   In the absence of detailed records on current expenditures eligible for ITCs, a specified percentage, the remittance rate, is applied to the GST/HST-inclusive total of fully taxable sales to determine the amount of GST/HST to be remitted.

21-113.   The remittance rate is not an alternative GST/HST rate. It is based on an assumed relationship between revenues subject to GST/HST and expenses and costs on which ITCs are available with respect to a specific type of business. For example, the quick method remittance rate for service providers in Alberta is 3.6%. The following example illustrates that the rate is based on the assumption that, for service providers subject only to GST, eligible expenses and costs are equal to 24.4% of fully taxable sales.

EXAMPLE   An Alberta GST registrant who is providing fully taxable services to residents of Alberta has taxable revenues of $50,000 in each of its second, third, and fourth quarters. Its eligible current expenditures for these quarters are $5,000 (less than 24.4% of revenues) for Quarter 2, $12,200 (equal to 24.4% of revenues) for Quarter 3, and $30,000 (more than 24.4% of revenues) for Quarter 4.

ANALYSIS   The GST payable calculated under the quick method for each quarter is $1,890 [(3.6%)(105%)($50,000)]. The quick method results are the same for each quarter as the calculation is based on revenues and is not affected by the amount of current expenditures. GST payable under the regular and quick method would be as follows:

	Quarter 2	Quarter 3	Quarter 4
GST on revenues [(5%)($50,000)]	$2,500	$2,500	$2,500
ITCs on costs at 5%			
[(5%)($5,000)]	(250)		
[(5%)($12,200)]		(610)	
[(5%)($30,000)]			(1,500)
GST payable—Regular method	$2,250	$1,890	$1,000
GST payable—Quick method (Note)	(1,890)	(1,890)	(1,890)
Advantage (disadvantage) quick method	$ 360	Nil	($ 890)

Note   There is a 1% credit on the first $30,000 of GST/HST-inclusive taxable and zero-rated sales. The credit generates a maximum of $300 for each year. Quarterly filers would claim this credit in the first quarter to the extent of the $30,000 limit. If the limit was not reached in the first quarter, then any excess limit can be applied in subsequent quarters. In our example we have assumed that taxable sales are at least $30,000 in that first quarter, therefore there is no additional credit for the remaining three quarters.

In Quarter 3, when current expenditures are equal to the assumed 24.4% rate of fully taxable sales, the regular method and the quick method results are the same. In

Quarter 2, when current expenditures are less than 24.4%, the quick method results in a lower amount payable. In contrast, in Quarter 4, when current expenditures are greater than 24.4%, the quick method results in a higher amount payable.

Quick Method Categories

21-114.   Conceptually, there is an argument that there should be multiple rates for each type of business; however, this would be counterproductive given that the purpose of the quick method is to simplify the compliance burden of the process with respect to ITCs on current expenditures. The government instead opted for only two broad categories.

21-115.   The categories to which the two rates are applied are as follows:

Businesses That Purchase Goods for Resale   These businesses have a lower remittance rate to reflect a higher percentage of eligible expenses and costs. In order to use these rates, the cost of goods purchased for resale (GST/HST inclusive) in the previous year must equal 40% or more of the revenue from sales of taxable supplies for that same previous year (GST/HST inclusive). Examples of types of businesses that generally qualify for this low rate include grocery and convenience stores, hardware stores, gas stations, antique dealers, and clothing stores.

Service Providers   These higher rates (double the reseller rate) apply to service businesses such as consultants (other than financial), hair salons, restaurants, dry cleaners, travel agents, campgrounds, cleaning services, painting contractors, photographers, and taxi drivers.

Specific Quick Method Remittance Rates

21-116.   In addition to the GST rate of 5% that is used in non-participating provinces, there are two different HST rates:

- 13% in Ontario
- 15% in New Brunswick, Newfoundland and Labrador, Nova Scotia, and Prince Edward Island

21-117.   The quick method is designed to approximate the results under the regular method of calculating GST or HST regardless of whether the rate is 5%, 13%, or 15%, and therefore the remittance rate will vary depending on the GST/HST rate in effect. The remittance rate will also vary where the place of supply is different than the permanent establishment of the business. Figure 21-4 illustrates the remittance rates where the place of supply is in the same province or territory where the permanent establishment of the business is located. If, for example, a business in Manitoba were to sell goods to residents of New Brunswick, the remittance rate would be 10.4%. These cross-border situations are not reflected in Figure 21-4 but are listed in CRA guide RC4058, "Quick Method of Accounting for GST/HST."

Figure 21-4 Quick Method Remittance Rates from January 1, 2019 (Excluding Quebec)		
GST/HST Rate	**Businesses That Purchase Goods for Resale**	**Service Providers**
GST at 5% (B.C., Alberta, Manitoba, Saskatchewan, and the three territories)	1.8%	3.6%
HST at 13% (Ontario)	4.4%	8.8%

HST at 15% (Newfoundland and Labrador,
    Nova Scotia, New Brunswick, and Prince
    Edward Island)
	5.0%	10.0%

Quick Method Example

21-118.   As an example of the quick method, consider a supply store located in Alberta that files its GST on a quarterly basis. Annual GST-inclusive taxable sales have never exceeded $400,000. Its current-year first quarter taxable sales were $40,000, resulting in GST-included sales of $42,000 [(105%)($40,000)]. Purchases of goods for resale totalled $26,600 before GST. Qualifying capital expenditures used exclusively for taxable supplies during the first quarter were $3,000 before GST. Under the regular method, the first quarter GST payable would be calculated as follows:

Sales [(5%)($40,000)]	$2,000
Purchases [(5%)($26,600)]	(1,330)
Capital expenditures [(5%)($3,000)]	(150)
First quarter GST payable—Regular method	$ 520

21-119.   Under the quick method, the first quarter results are as follows:

Basic tax [(1.8%)(105%)($40,000)]	$756
Less: Credit on first $30,000 [(1%)($30,000)]	(300)
Subtotal	$456
ITC on current expenditures	N/A
ITC on capital expenditures [(5%)($3,000)]	(150)
First quarter GST payable—Quick method	$306

21-120.   Determining whether the quick method is preferable over the regular method would require calculating the results of both the regular and quick method with respect to specific business information including revenues and a breakdown of costs and expenses into current and capital expenditure categories. In general, a person must have been in business for at least one year to be eligible to use the quick method, although there are exceptions for new registrants based on reasonable estimates that the GST/HST-inclusive revenues will not exceed $400,000. An election is made by filing form GST74.

21-121.   In some instances the benefits of the use of the quick method are readily determinable and clear without the need for extensive analysis. For example, a freelance writer, operating out of his principal residence, is not likely to have significant current expenditures that qualify for ITCs. In this case, the quick method will likely result in a smaller GST/HST payment than the regular method. In addition, it will certainly be less time consuming to file a GST/HST return since ITC information on current expenditures will not be required. This latter concern may not be a significant issue since information with respect to current expenditures must be determined and compiled for the purposes of filing income tax returns.

ITCs and Income Tax

21-122.   When a business claims expenses or makes purchases that include GST/HST, those costs and expenses are deductible for income tax purposes. ITCs claimed by the business, therefore, effectively compensate the business by refunding any GST/HST component. As a result, the ITC amount for current expenditures and purchases of inventory must be included in income. In the example in Paragraph 21-118, this means that the current expenditure ITC of $1,300 is required to be included in business income. The ITC of $150 for the capital expenditures would reduce the capital cost of the capital property in the following taxation year, which reduces CCA claims. Finally, when the quick method is used and results in a saving, the difference between the GST/HST that would have been collected under the regular method and the quick method is also required to be included in business income. Based on the comparison of the results of the example in Paragraphs 21-118 and 21-119, $214 ($520 regular method - $306 quick method) would be required to be added to business income for income tax purposes.

Exercise 21-6

Subject: Quick Method

Robbins Hardware operates as a sole proprietorship in Alberta and sells only fully taxable supplies to customers in Alberta. During the first quarter of the year, the business has sales of $42,500 and taxable purchases of $21,000, both of which do not include GST. There are no capital expenditures made during the first quarter. Using the quick method, determine the GST payable for the quarter.

Exercise 21-7

Subject: Quick Method

Guy's Boots operates as a sole proprietorship in Ontario and sells only fully taxable shoes and boots to customers in Ontario. During the first quarter of the year, Guy's Boots has sales of $56,100 not including HST. Current expenses, all of which were subject to HST, total $23,400 (not including the HST). Due to a major renovation of the store, Guy's Boots has capital expenditures of $42,000 (not including the HST). Compare the use of the quick method and the regular method for this first quarter.

Solutions to Exercises are available in the Study Guide.

We suggest you complete SSP 21-5 and 21-6 at this point.

Simplified Input Tax Credit (ITC) Method

21-123.   A method for claiming ITCs and rebates is available to registrants with annual GST/HST taxable sales, including those of associated businesses, of $1,000,000 or less in the preceding year. An additional requirement is that annual GST/HST taxable purchases total no more than $4,000,000.

21-124.   Rather than tracking GST/HST paid on each purchase, the simplified method bases ITCs on the total GST/HST-inclusive amounts of fully taxable purchases. This amount would also include any non-refundable provincial sales taxes paid on taxable supplies. Once this total is established, it is multiplied by the following factor:

> **Factor**   Applicable GST/HST rate of either 13/113 (Ontario), 15/115 (Atlantic provinces), or 5/105 (all other provinces and territories)

21-125.   The method begins with all of the eligible business expenses (current and capital), including purchases, but excludes the following amounts:

- Capital expenditures for real property (these are tracked separately for ITC purposes)
- Purchases of zero-rated supplies, such as groceries and prescription drugs
- Purchases of exempt supplies, such as interest payments
- Purchases made outside Canada, which are not subject to GST/HST
- Purchases from non-registrants
- Refundable provincial sales taxes (only in Quebec)
- Expenses not eligible for ITCs (e.g., 50% of the cost of meals and entertainment)

21-126.   There is no election required to use this method and it does not affect the calculation of the GST/HST on sales that must be remitted. The following example illustrates this method as applied in the province of New Brunswick.

EXAMPLE Georgia Steel Ltd. carries on a business solely in New Brunswick and Nova Scotia. Its only activities involve the provision of fully taxable supplies. During the current year, current expenditures are $75,000, real property expenditures are $145,000, and expenditures for capital property other than real property are $25,000. None of these amounts include HST, although HST was charged on all amounts. In addition, the company paid salaries of $200,000.

ANALYSIS The company's ITC for the current year would be as follows:

HST-included amounts for taxable expenditures other than real property [(115%)($75,000 + $25,000)]	$115,000
Factor (for New Brunswick and Nova Scotia)	15/115
ITC on taxable expenditures	$ 15,000
ITC on real property expenditure [(15%)($145,000)]	21,750
ITC for the current year	$ 36,750

21-127. The simplified method base only includes purchases of fully taxable goods. A further restriction on the amounts claimed is that credits can be claimed only to the extent that the purchases included in the simplified method base are used to provide fully taxable or zero-rated goods and services. Where a specific supply is used to provide both taxable and exempt goods and services, the ITC claim must be pro-rated so that only the portion that applies to taxable goods and services can be claimed. The proration does not apply if 90% or more of the supply is attributable to taxable supplies, in which case a full ITC (100%) can be claimed.

Exercise 21-8

Subject: Simplified ITC Method

Simplicity Inc. carries on business in Alberta. For the current year, the company has GST-inclusive sales of $315,000 and GST-inclusive purchases of merchandise and other current expenditures of $189,000. Capital expenditures consist of real property (land and a building) costing $650,000 and capital personal property totalling $50,000. The capital expenditure amounts do not include GST. Using the simplified method of accounting for ITCs, determine Simplicity's GST payable or GST refund for the current year.

Solutions to Exercises are available in the Study Guide.

GST/HST Compliance and Administration

GST/HST Returns and Payments

Timing of Liability

21-128. In general, the supplier becomes responsible for the tax at the earliest of when the invoice for goods or services is issued, when payment is received, or when payment is due under a written agreement. Following this rule, a registrant usually becomes responsible for remitting GST/HST in the reporting period in which a customer is invoiced, even if this is not the same period in which the cash is actually received. These general rules assume that goods or services have been provided that legally entitle the supplier to payment. If, for example, a customer deposits $100 as a down payment on a good that is not actually delivered until the following month, then the supplier would have no claim until the good is delivered. In that case the supplier would not be liable to GST on the deposit until the purchase is actually made in the following month.

21-129.   Similarly, ITCs for GST/HST payable to suppliers can be claimed in the reporting period invoices are issued, even if the supplier is paid in a later period. Again, the supply must have been made for an invoice to be issued.

Taxation Year for GST/HST Registrants

21-130.   Every registrant is required to have a "fiscal year" for GST/HST purposes. This fiscal year is the rough equivalent to the taxation year for income tax purposes. However, if registrants are allowed to use a non-calendar year for income tax purposes, they have the option of either using the calendar year or the same year used for income tax purposes. For example, a company with a taxation year ending on January 31, 2021, and with a quarterly filing requirement could choose to base its reporting using the same year of January 31 or could choose to use a calendar-based fiscal year. The first quarterly reporting in 2021 would either end January 31, 2021, or March 31, 2021, depending on which year was selected. The GST/HST fiscal year determines the reporting periods and filing deadlines for GST/HST returns.

Filing Due Date

21-131.   All persons registered to collect GST/HST are required to file a GST/HST return on a periodic basis, even if there is no activity during the relevant period. The CRA's My Business Account service can be used to file GST/HST returns online. Filing frequencies for the remittance of GST/HST are determined by the total annual taxable supplies made by the registrant and associated persons. The normal reporting periods, along with the options that are available on an elective basis, are shown in Figure 21-5.

21-132.   A registrant may elect to have a shorter filing period than the one that is assigned for their amount of taxable supplies. This may be advantageous for registrants who normally receive a GST/HST refund, such as businesses with significant exports or zero-rated sales (e.g., pharmacies and grocery stores). It may also be advantageous for some annual filers to choose to file quarterly as it reduces the burden of compiling all the necessary information for a whole year. In addition, as discussed in the next section, filing on a quarterly basis eliminates the requirement to pay GST/HST instalments.

21-133.   For monthly and quarterly filers, GST/HST returns are due one month after the end of the reporting period. In general, for annual filers, GST/HST returns are due three months after the year end. There is an extension to June 15 for annual filers who are individuals with business income that use a calendar year as the fiscal period of a business for income tax purposes. This exception allows individuals carrying on a business to match the GST/HST reporting requirements with that of the ITA.

Payments and Instalments

21-134.   In general, payment of amounts owing are due when the GST/HST returns are due. This is one month after the end of the reporting period for monthly and quarterly filers and three months after the year end for annual filers. For annual filers who are individuals earning business income that uses a calendar-based fiscal period, the GST/HST payment due date is April 30. This means the filing due date and payment due date are the same for both income tax and the GST/HST for these qualifying individuals.

Figure 21-5 Assigned and Optional Reporting Periods		
Threshold Amount of Annual Taxable Supplies	**Assigned Reporting Period**	**Optional Reporting Period**
$1,500,000 or less	Annual	Monthly or Quarterly
From $1,500,000 to $6,000,000	Quarterly	Monthly
More than $6,000,000	Monthly	None

21-135.   Instalment payments are not required for monthly or quarterly filers. However, annual filers are required to make quarterly instalments if the GST/HST remitted for the previous fiscal year was $3,000 or more and is $3,000 or more in the current year. Each instalment will usually be one-quarter of the net tax owing from the previous year, however the instalment payments can be based on the current year where the net tax owing is expected to be less than the previous year (ETA 237(1) to (3)). These instalments are due one month after the end of each quarter. For example, calendar-year filers are required to make instalments by April 30, July 31, October 31, and January 31. For annual filers below the $3,000 threshold no instalments would be required and any remaining net tax is due at the usual time of March 31 or April 30.

Interest

21-136.   If the GST/HST return shows an amount owing and it is not paid by the due date, interest is assessed. Interest is also assessed on late or deficient instalments. The applicable rates are the same as those used for income tax purposes:

- On taxes owed to the government, the rate is the prescribed rate plus 4%.
- On amounts owed to taxpayers other than corporations, the rate is the prescribed rate plus 2%.
- On amounts owed to corporations, the rate is the prescribed rate only.

21-137.   As is the case with interest on late income tax instalments, interest paid on late GST/HST payments is not deductible for income tax purposes (ITA 18(1)(t)(ii)).

Late Filing Penalty

21-138.   The GST/HST late filing penalty is equal to 1% of the amount owing, plus 0.25% for each complete month to a maximum of 12 months. Unlike the late filing penalty for income tax, there is no doubling of this penalty for a second offence. There is, however, a penalty of $250 where the CRA has made a demand to file the GST/HST return that has been ignored.

Associated Persons

21-139.   Associated persons were first discussed in Paragraph 21-82. While associated persons file separate GST/HST returns, they must combine their total taxable sales of goods and services in certain situations, such as when determining:

- whether they qualify for the small supplier's exemption,
- whether they are eligible for the quick method of accounting,
- whether they are eligible for the simplified method of calculating ITCs,
- the required filing frequency of their returns (i.e., monthly, quarterly, or annual).

Refunds and Rebates

21-140.   In a period during which ITCs, instalment payments, and other adjustments exceed GST/HST collections, a refund may be claimed in the GST/HST return for that period. Provided all required returns have been filed and are up to date, interest on unpaid refunds generally starts accruing 30 days after the later of the last day of the reporting period and the day after the registrant's return is filed.

21-141.   The ETA also provides for a number of rebates of the GST/HST paid by consumers under certain circumstances. For example, if a GST/HST amount is paid in error, or by a foreign diplomat, a rebate of the GST/HST may be claimed on a General Rebate Application Form. Our coverage of the GST/HST rebate for new housing begins at Paragraph 21-161.

Books and Records

21-142.   For GST/HST purposes, every registrant must keep adequate books and records that enable the CRA to be able to determine the registrant's liabilities and obligations under the ETA.

Such records must be maintained at the registrant's place of business or at the individual's residence in Canada.

21-143.   All books and records, along with the accounts and invoices necessary to verify them, must be kept for a period of six years from the end of the last taxation year to which they relate. This is the same record retention threshold that is applied for income tax purposes. Failure to maintain adequate books and records can result in interest and penalties. The CRA will issue what is referred to as an "inadequate books and records" letter to those businesses that fail to meet their requisite level of adequacy. Failure to comply can result in penalties and interest.

Appeals

Informal Procedures

21-144.   As is the case with income tax disputes, the usual first step in disputing an assessment or reassessment is to contact the CRA. In many cases the proposed change or error can be corrected or resolved through communications with the CRA, often by simply providing supporting documentation. In order to authorize a person or firm to represent a GST/HST registrant in such disputes, an authorization can be made online through CRA's My Business Account.

Notice of Objection

21-145.   If the informal contact with the CRA does not resolve the issue in question, the taxpayer should file a formal notice of objection (form GST159). The notice of objection must be filed within 90 days of the date on the notice of assessment. A request for an extension is permitted as long as it is made within one year of the expiration of the 90-day period and it is justifiable and equitable given the facts.

21-146.   On receiving the notice of objection, the minister is required to reply to the GST/HST registrant:

- vacating the assessment (meaning that all of the assessment/reassessment is reversed);
- confirming the assessment (upholding or stating that they are unwilling to change the assessment); or
- reassessing (allowing the assessment in whole or in part).

21-147.   Unresolved objections will be subject to review by the chief of appeals in each Tax Services Office. The appeals division generally operates independently of the audit and assessing divisions and should provide an unbiased, objective opinion. If the matter remains unresolved after this review, the registrant must either accept the minister's assessment or, alternatively, continue to pursue the matter to a higher level of appeal. The taxpayer has the option of bypassing this notice of objection process with the CRA and may appeal directly to the courts.

21-148.   The CRA is restricted from taking collection action in many situations involving income tax excluding a number of exceptions such as payroll taxes. The restriction prevents any collection action until the appeal process has come to an end. There are no collection restrictions, however, with respect to the GST/HST. The justification for this is that GST/HST collected represents funds that belong to the government that are held in trust by registrants who are simply acting as go-betweens or intermediaries on behalf of the government. This is the same justification as to why there are no restrictions on collecting overdue payroll taxes (e.g., income tax, EI, and CPP/QPP).

Tax Court of Canada, Federal Court of Appeal, and the Supreme Court of Canada

21-149.   Procedures for handling GST/HST disputes through the courts are generally the same as those for income tax disputes. The procedures are described in Chapter 2 and will not be repeated here.

General Anti-Avoidance Rule

21-150.   The GST/HST legislation includes a General Anti-Avoidance Rule (GAAR). This rule is found under ETA 274 and is similar in many respect to the GAAR found in ITA 245.

21-151.   While the GST/HST GAAR is intended to prevent abusive tax avoidance transactions, it is not intended to interfere with legitimate commercial transactions. If a transaction is considered by the CRA to be an avoidance transaction, the tax consequences of the transaction may be adjusted to reflect the economic reality. This could involve denying an ITC, allocating an ITC to another person, or recharacterizing a payment. The anti-avoidance rule does not apply if there is no misuse or abuse of the provisions of the ETA. In addition, any transaction that is undertaken primarily for bona fide purposes other than to obtain a GST/HST tax benefit cannot be considered as part of the anti-avoidance analysis. Unlike the ITA there have been very few court cases involving the GAAR under the ETA.

Employee and Partner GST/HST Rebate

General Concept

21-152.   Many of the expenses employees can deduct against employment income include a GST/HST component. If the individual were a GST/HST registrant earning business income, these GST/HST payments would generate ITCs. However, employment is not considered to be a commercial activity and, as a consequence, employees who have no separate commercial activity cannot be registrants. This means that they will not be able to recover any GST/HST on deductible employment expenses as ITCs. A similar analysis applies to partners who have partner expenses that they are entitled to deduct from their share of partnership income or loss.

21-153.   The employee and partner GST/HST rebate allows employees and partners to recover the GST/HST paid on their employment- or partner-related expenses, including vehicles, in a way that is similar to ITCs that they could have claimed if they were GST registrants. Form GST370 is used to claim the GST/HST rebate and is filed with the employee's or partner's income tax return.

21-154.   To qualify for this rebate, the individual must be either an employee of a GST/HST registrant or a member of a partnership that is a GST/HST registrant. Employees of financial institutions are not eligible for the rebate nor are employees who receive allowances that are not required to be included in their employment income. However, employees of charities, not-for-profit organizations, universities, school boards, and municipalities are eligible as long as the employer organizations are GST/HST registrants. In addition, employees of provincial governments, Crown corporations, and the federal government also qualify for the rebate. To claim the rebate, the individual must have unreimbursed expenses on which GST/HST was paid that are deductible against employment income or loss or the partners' share of partnership income or loss.

Calculating the GST/HST Employee Rebate Amount

21-155.   The GST/HST rebate is based on the GST/HST amounts included in those expenses that can be deducted in the determination of employment income. In terms of calculations, this is accomplished by multiplying the GST/HST and non-refundable PST included in the cost by the rate of 5/105, 13/113, or 15/115.

> **EXAMPLE**   Marcia Valentino is employed in British Columbia. She has deductible cell phone expenses of $2,240, which includes the 5% GST of $100 and 7% non-refundable PST of $140. She is not reimbursed nor does she receive a non-taxable allowance for these expenses. She deducted $2,240 in her calculation of employment income.
>
> **ANALYSIS**   Ms. Valentino's rebate would be $107 [($2,240)(5/105)]. This is more than the $100 in GST she paid as the rebate base includes the non-refundable PST. She will include the $107 in her employment income for the subsequent year in which she receives credit for that amount when she files her income tax return.

21-156.   Eligible expenses exclude expenses for which a non-taxable allowance was received, zero-rated and exempt supplies, supplies acquired outside of Canada, supplies acquired from non-registrants, and expenses incurred when the employer was a non-registrant.

Example

21-157.   The following simple example illustrates the calculation of the GST/HST rebate for an employee.

> **EXAMPLE**   Tanya Kucharik is a successful sales manager employed in Ontario. She used her car 93% and her cell phone 80% for employment purposes during 2021. She claimed the following expenses on form T777, "Statement of Employment Expenses," for 2021 (all HST taxable amounts include applicable HST at 13%):
>
> | | |
> |---|---:|
> | Cell phone charges (80%) | $ 1,200 |
> | Gas, maintenance, and car repairs (93%) | 17,500 |
> | Insurance on car (93%) | 1,023 |
> | Capital cost allowance (CCA) on car (93%) | 3,100 |
>
> The car on which the CCA was deducted was purchased in 2021. She did not own a car prior to that time. Note that car insurance is an exempt supply and therefore no HST is charged.
>
> **ANALYSIS**   The HST rebate would be as follows:
>
> | | Eligible Expenses | HST Rebate (13/113) |
> |---|---:|---:|
> | Eligible expenses other than CCA ($1,200 + $17,500) | $18,700 | $2,151 |
> | Eligible CCA on which HST was paid | 3,100 | 357 |
> | Totals | $21,800 | $2,508 |

21-158.   Ms. Kucharik will deduct the employment expenses of $22,823 ($1,200 + $17,500 + $1,023 + $3,100) in her 2021 income tax return. The GST/HST rebate is a refundable amount for the year in which the expenses relate. In this example the rebate of $2,508 is treated as income taxes withheld or instalments paid and is added to line 45700 of the T1 income tax return to reduce income taxes payable or to increase a refund.

21-159.   Since the rebate acts as a form of assistance that allows the recovery of part of the cost of deductible expenses it is understandable that the rebate amount should affect income for income tax purposes for the year in which the rebate claim is made. Based on the example, if Ms. Kucharik claimed the rebate when filing her 2021 income tax return in 2022 she would receive the benefit of that rebate in 2022. As a result the rebate must be reflected in her 2022 income. The part of the rebate amount that relates to current expenses ($2,153) is added to her 2022 employment income, and the remaining $357 that relates to capital expenditures through CCA will reduce the capital cost of her car, which will reduce subsequent-year CCA claims.

21-160.   While the rebate is normally claimed in the return in which the expenses are deducted, it can be claimed in any income tax return submitted within four years of the year in which the expenses are claimed.

We suggest you complete SSP 21-7 at this point.

Residential Property and New Housing Rebate

General Rules for Residential Property

21-161.   Residential real estate is an area of considerable importance to most Canadians. Given this, it is not surprising that residential real estate is provided special treatment under the ETA.

21-162.   In general terms, GST/HST applies to residential property only on the first sale of a new home. If an existing home is sold in substantially unaltered condition, no GST/HST will be charged. If the homeowner undertakes renovations to an existing home, such as a kitchen, GST/HST will be charged on the materials and other costs of the renovation. If an existing home is acquired and substantially renovated before the home is occupied by the purchaser, the acquisition will be treated as a new home purchase and the transaction will be taxable for GST/HST purposes. The CRA considers a substantial renovation as one in which 90% or more of the interior of an existing home is removed or replaced.

New Housing Rebate

Calculating the Rebate

21-163.   While sales of new homes attract both GST and HST at the applicable rates, rebates of the amount paid are available. In provinces and territories that do not participate in the HST, the rebate is equal to 36% of the GST paid. However, the situation with participating HST provinces is much more complex, including provincial variations in the HST rebate percentage, as well as the eligibility thresholds. Because of this additional complexity, we will deal only with non-HST provinces in this section. The CRA has a detailed guide covering the many complexities in this area titled "GST/HST New Housing Rebate" (RC4028).

21-164.   The maximum GST rebate for a non-HST province is $6,300, the amount of the GST rebate on a $350,000 home [(36%)(5%)($350,000) = $6,300]. In addition, the rebate is phased out for homes costing more than $350,000 and completely eliminated for homes costing more than $450,000. The cost for calculating the rebate does not include the GST.

21-165.   The rebate is calculated as follows:

$$[A][(\$450,000 - B) \div \$100,000], \text{ where}$$

A = The lesser of 36% of the GST paid and $6,300; and
B = The greater of $350,000 and the cost of the home.

21-166.   A simple example will illustrate the mechanics of this calculation.

EXAMPLE   Gilles and Marie Gagnon purchase a new home with a cost of $420,000 plus GST of $21,000 [(5%)($420,000)] for a total of $441,000.

ANALYSIS   As 36% of the GST paid is $7,560, an amount in excess of the limit of $6,300, the rebate available to Gilles and Marie will be $1,890 {[$6,300][($450,000 - $420,000) ÷ $100,000]}.

Implementing the Rebate—Practical Considerations

21-167.   While the GST could be included in the price paid by the home purchaser, with that individual claiming the rebate, this is not the usual industry practice. The usual practice is for the builder to charge the purchaser an amount that is net of the rebate, with the purchaser assigning rights to the GST rebate to the builder. In the case of our example, the builder would charge Gilles and Marie $439,110 ($420,000 + $21,000 - $1,890).

We suggest you complete SSP 21-8 and 21-9 at this point.

Sale of a Business

Sale of Assets

21-168.   The sale of a business can be made by selling all of the assets of the business. This constitutes a taxable supply for GST/HST purposes and applies irrespective of whether the business is carried on by a sole proprietor, partnership, or corporation. If, however, "all or substantially all" (i.e., 90% or more) of the assets that are required to be able to carry on the business of the vendor are acquired, a special election is available that allows the vendor and purchaser to elect to treat the supply as if it were zero-rated. This means that no GST/HST would be charged. The election form is GST44.

21-169.   The use of the election is not permitted when the vendor is a registrant and the purchaser is a non-registrant. However, without regard to the type of business, the election can be used when both the vendor and the purchaser are not GST/HST registrants.

21-170.   If the election is made, the vendor does not collect GST/HST on the sale of taxable supplies, and the purchaser cannot claim an ITC. As a result, a sale of the assets of a business can be made without payment of GST/HST. If the election is not made, GST/HST will be collected on the sale and offsetting ITCs are then available to the purchaser. One main advantage of the election is that it preserves cash flow, particularly with respect to the purchaser who would have to wait for the processing of an ITC claim for the GST/HST reporting period in which the purchase occurred to recover the additional GST/HST cost.

Sale of Shares

21-171.   The business of a corporation can also be sold by selling its shares. As a general rule, the sale of shares in a corporation is considered the sale of a financial instrument, which is an exempt supply. As a result, the sale of shares does not result in GST/HST.

Other Situations

ITA 85 Rollovers & ETA 167

21-172.   The incorporation of a business carried on by a sole proprietor or partnership is accomplished by selling the assets of the business to a corporation. ITA 85, which is discussed in Chapter 16, allows a joint election with the corporation to treat the sale price for each asset to be set at amounts that can avoid income tax altogether. The election, however, does not change the commercial reality that a business is incorporated and the corporation is paying full FMV. In the absence of any rollover, the base for the GST/HST would be the sale price of each asset regardless of the income tax treatment afforded the seller and purchaser for income tax purposes.

21-173.   If the business provides taxable supplies, then the sale of the assets to a corporation would be subject to GST/HST to the seller with the corporate purchaser eligible for ITCs in the same manner as discussed throughout this chapter. The ETA election referred to in Paragraphs 21-168 to 21-170 is equally applicable in this case where a business is being incorporated. Any other use of ITA 85 to sell individual assets to a corporation would be subject to GST/HST in the same manner as a regular sale.

Amalgamations and Wind-Ups

21-174.   Where two corporations are amalgamated or the business of a corporations ends because it is wound up/dissolved into a parent corporation, the new amalgamated corporation or the remaining parent company is generally treated for GST/HST purposes as a separate person.

21-175.   If the amalgamation qualifies for rollover treatment under ITA 87 or the wind-up qualifies for the rollover under ITA 88(1) the ETA deems any transfer of assets not to be a supply and therefore there are no GST/HST consequences.

Supplies within Closely Held Corporate Groups

21-176.   The supply of taxable goods and services between members of closely held corporate groups is subject to GST/HST. However, an election can be made to have such supplies deemed to be made for nil consideration for GST/HST purposes with the result that there is no required payment of GST/HST.

21-177.   The conditions for this election are quite strict and require either the ownership of at least 90% of the voting shares of one corporation by the other, or that the corporations are sister corporations where 90% or more of the voting shares of each corporation are owned by the same corporation. In addition, the electing corporations must be Canadian residents and the supplies involved must be used exclusively (more than 90%) in a commercial activity (e.g., for taxable or zero-rated supplies).

Holding Companies

21-178.   Many holding companies act as intermediaries between individuals and operating companies. These holding companies generally only own shares or debt and do not carry on a "commercial activity" in the usual sense. The ETA allows holding companies to register for the GST/HST and claim ITCs with respect to transactions that relate to the shares or debt it owns. To qualify, the shares or debt owned by the holding company must be in respect of a company that the holding company controls (more than 50%), and 90% or more of the assets of that controlled corporation must be used exclusively in commercial activity. These provisions allow holding companies to obtain refunds of GST/HST paid on the purchase of property or services solely related to the ownership of shares or debt.

Ceasing to Carry on Business

21-179.   When a person ceases to carry on a commercial activity, or becomes a small supplier and as a result ceases to be a registrant, the person is deemed to have sold all assets at FMV upon deregistration. If the assets were used for commercial purposes, GST/HST will be payable on the deemed dispositions. The effect is that all or part of any ITCs previously claimed on these assets will be recaptured (i.e., required to be repaid).

Specific Applications

21-180.   There are many GST/HST rules that apply to a wide array of transactions and organizations. Detailed coverage of these rules goes beyond the scope of an introductory text. However, we do believe it is useful to provide some general information on some of the more common situations.

- **Imports**   In general, imports are subject to GST/HST.
- **Exports**   In general, exports of goods and services from Canada are zero-rated. This means that while no GST/HST is charged on exports, ITCs can be claimed by the Canadian resident registered exporter.
- **Charities**   In general, the revenues of registered charities are exempt from GST/HST. However, revenues from commercial activities (e.g., museum gift shop revenues) are fully taxable subject to an increased small supplier threshold of $50,000. A special provision provides a 50% rebate of the federal GST paid on purchases that relate to exempt supplies. In the HST provinces, there is a 50% rebate of the federal portion of the HST on such purchases, as well as an additional rebate of the provincial portion of the HST. The provincial rebate varies from province to province.
- **Non-Profit Organizations (NPOs)**   In general, the revenues of NPOs are fully taxable (in contrast to the situation with registered charities). However, exemptions are provided for such services as subsidized home care and meals on wheels. As was the case with registered charities, qualifying NPOs receive a 50% rebate of the federal GST paid on purchases related to exempt supplies. In the HST provinces, there

is a 50% rebate of the federal portion of the HST on such purchases, as well as an additional rebate of the provincial portion of the HST. The provincial rebate varies from province to province.

To be classified as a qualifying NPO, the organization must receive at least 40% of its funding from government sources.

- **Government Bodies**   All federal government departments receive a full rebate of the GST/HST paid on purchases by means of a tax remission order. Each provincial and territorial government is registered as a separate entity for the GST/HST and uses "certificates" to receive point-of-purchase relief from the GST/HST.

- **Crown Corporations**   Crown corporations are not GST/HST exempt and are registered as separate persons for purposes of the GST/HST.

- **Municipalities, Universities, Schools, and Hospitals (MUSH)**   These organizations are classified as "public institutions" in the ETA and, except where there are specific exemptions, their revenues are fully taxable. Examples of exemptions include property taxes for municipalities, course fees for universities, and medical services for hospitals. Rebates for the federal GST paid on purchases related to exempt activities are available, with the rates varying from 67% for universities to 83% for hospitals to 100% for municipalities. In the HST provinces, the same rebates are available for the federal portion of the HST, as well as an additional rebate of the provincial portion of the HST. The provincial rebate varies from province to province.

- **Financial Institutions**   The ETA defines financial institutions to include "listed" financial institutions, such as banks and insurance companies, as well as deemed financial institutions (e.g., businesses with financial revenues exceeding specified threshold levels). Revenues from providing financial services are designated as exempt. This means that, for an institution where the bulk of its revenues is from the provision of financial services, only limited ITCs are available.

Partnerships and GST/HST

General Rules

21-181.   The ITA treats a partnership as a person only for the purpose of computing income or loss to its partners. The ETA considers partnerships to be separate persons that are generally required to register for the GST/HST with respect to commercial activities. In addition, anything a partner does with respect to partnership activities is considered done by the partnership and not by the partners themselves.

21-182.   The result is that it is the partnership, and not the partners, that is required to register for the GST/HST with respect to partnership business. Given this, partnerships are required to collect and remit GST/HST on taxable supplies and are eligible for ITCs. Partners are jointly and severally liable, however, with respect to GST/HST that relates to the partnership business.

Partner Expenses

21-183.   Non-reimbursed expenditures for property or services incurred personally by individual partners, which relate to the partnership business and that are deductible for income tax purposes by the partners, are generally eligible for the employee and partner GST/HST rebate. Such property and services include office expenses, travel expenses, meals and entertainment, parking, lodging, and CCA on certain capital property such as automobiles. This rebate was discussed beginning in Paragraph 21-152.

21-184.   A partner can only claim a rebate to the extent that the partnership could have otherwise claimed an ITC if it had incurred the expense. This means that, if a partnership provides only exempt goods or services, the partners would not be eligible to claim a GST/HST partner rebate for expenses they deduct from their share of partnership income or loss.

Disposition of a Partnership Interest

21-185.   A partnership interest may be disposed of or acquired in many situations. These include the admission of a new partner or retirement of an existing partner. A partnership interest, like a share of a corporation, is considered a "financial instrument" and is exempt from GST/HST. In addition, any legal and accounting fees related to the acquisition or disposition of a partnership interest are not eligible for an ITC since they relate to a financial instrument and not to the partnership's business. Finally, drawings and capital contributions that specifically relate to a partnership interest are considered "financial services" and are also exempt from the GST/HST.

Transactions between Partners and Partnerships

21-186.   ITA 97(1) and ITA 98(2) deem property dispositions between partners and a partnership to be made at FMV subject to limited rollovers and elections that allow income tax to be avoided and deferred. The ETA contains similar rules that treat supplies of goods or services as supplies made for consideration at FMV depending on the circumstances. While there are exceptions, caution should be exercised since the ETA views the partner and the partnership as two separate persons for GST/HST purposes. GST/HST does not apply to transfers of cash, accounts receivable, or debt, however, since these are exempt financial services.

Reorganization of a Partnership

21-187.   The admission of new partners or retirement of existing partners that legally terminate the old partnership and result in the creation of a new partnership will not cause the new partnership to register for GST/HST as a new person unless the registration of the old partnership is cancelled.

21-188.   There are no GST/HST implications to a new partnership that has formed as a result of an old partnership ceasing to exist if certain conditions are met. The conditions are as follows: That the members of the old partnership together owned interests that represented more than 50% of the capital of the old partnership; the members represent more than half of the members of the new partnership; and the members have transferred 90% or more of the property they received on the termination of the old partnership to the new partnership. The new partnership is considered to be a continuation of the old partnership for GST/HST purposes, meaning that there are no GST/HST implications.

Trusts and GST/HST

21-189.   A trust or an estate is included in the definition of "person" under the ETA and, as a consequence, a trust that is engaged in commercial activity is required to register and collect GST/HST on taxable supplies. However, an interest in a trust is considered to be a financial instrument, so the sale or other disposition of an interest in a trust is an exempt supply and is therefore not subject to GST/HST.

21-190.   A distribution of trust property by a trustee to a beneficiary of a trust is treated as a supply by the trust. The consideration is equal to the proceeds of disposition determined under the ITA. Therefore, distributions in satisfaction of an income interest of a beneficiary are deemed to have occurred at FMV, whereas distributions in satisfaction of capital interest of a beneficiary are deemed to have taken place at the cost of the property to the trust or estate.

21-191.   Distributions of property not used in a commercial activity by a trust in the process of the settlement of an estate are GST/HST exempt. Similarly, a distribution of financial securities or cash is also exempt from GST/HST. The GST/HST only applies to property acquired by the trust that is used in a commercial activity where the trust is a registrant.

21-192.   Where property is settled through the use of an inter vivos trust, including an alter ego or joint spousal or common-law partner trust, the consideration for the property transferred is deemed to equal the amount determined under the ITA, which is generally the FMV of the property. GST/HST is payable where the supply was made in the course of a commercial activity. However, when an estate is settled, an election can be filed to distribute any property of a deceased registrant without the payment of GST/HST. In this situation, the beneficiary of the deceased's estate must also be a registrant, and the beneficiary is deemed to have acquired the property for use exclusively in a commercial activity.

Key Terms

A full glossary with definitions is provided at the end of the Study Guide.

Capital Personal Property	New Housing GST/HST Rebate
Commercial Activity	Quick Method
Commodity Tax	Registrant
Employee and Partner GST/HST Rebate	Simplified ITC Accounting
Exempt Goods and Services	Small Suppliers Exemption
Fully Taxable Goods and Services	Supply
Goods and Services Tax (GST/HST)	Transaction Tax
Harmonized Sales Tax (HST)	Value Added Tax (VAT)
Input Tax Credit (ITC)	Zero-Rated Goods and Services
MUSH	

Self-Study Problems (SSPs)

Self-Study Problems (SSPs) provide practice in problem solving. Within the chapters, we have indicated where it would be appropriate to stop and work on each SSP. The problems can be downloaded by chapter from MyLab Accounting. Solutions are available in the Study Guide. Select problems can also be completed directly in MyLab and auto-graded.

Assignment Problems

Solutions to Assignment Problems (APs) are available to instructors only.

AP 21-1   (Turnover Tax vs. GST)

You have been appointed tax policy advisor to a country that has never used sales taxes on goods or services. Because of the increasing need for revenues, the finance minister, Maximus Surplus, is committed to introducing a sales tax. He is considering two alternatives:

- A 5% value added tax using the same invoice-credit approach that has been incorporated into Canada's GST/HST.

- A turnover tax that is applied as goods move from the raw materials supplier to the manufacturer to the wholesaler to the distributor to the retailer and finally to the consumer. Minister Surplus would like you to calculate the turnover tax rate that would produce the same amount of revenue as the alternative 5% VAT.

  In illustrating this to Minister Surplus, he would like you to assume a sale price of $250 plus tax by the raw materials supplier to the manufacturer. At this and subsequent turnover points, he would like you to assume a markup by each seller in the distribution and supply chain of 40% of their before-tax cost.

Required: Provide the requested information together with an explanation of your calculations.

Assignment Problems

AP 21-2   (Registration Requirements — Small Supplier Exemption)

Clarisa Cole commenced carrying on a business as a sole proprietor February 4, 2021. The business makes specialty sandwiches plus provides catering services. The business is solely carried on in a non-HST province. Clarisa decided not to voluntarily register for the GST.

Calendar quarterly sales of taxable supplies from January 2021 to the end of June 2022 are as follows:

January 1 to March 31, 2021	$ 6,200
April 1 to June 30, 2021	9,000
July 1 to September 30, 2021	10,200
October 1 to December 31, 2021	27,500
January 1 to March 31, 2022	42,300
April 1 to June 30, 2022	31,700

Required: Clarisa wants to delay registering for the GST as long as possible. As her accountant, based on the following assumptions, advise her as to (1) when she has lost small supplier status, (2) when she is required to begin charging and collecting GST, and (3) when she is officially required to register for the GST with the CRA.

Situation 1:   Assume that all sales occur evenly throughout each calendar quarter and that the first sale in February 2022 occurs on February 3.

Situation 2:   Assume that Clarisa catered a New Year's Day event on January 1, 2022, billing $32,000 without GST. The remaining $10,300 of sales in the first calendar quarter of 2022 was earned evenly throughout February and March 2022 after Clarisa returned from a January winter vacation.

Situation 3:   Assume that the sales in the fourth calendar quarter of 2021 (October 1 to December 31) were $37,500 instead of $27,500 and that the sale that exceeded the $30,000 small business limit took place December 14, 2021.

AP 21-3   (Registration Requirements and GST Collectible)

After years of study, Martin believes that he has developed a process for making perfect macaroons. He also believes that there is significant demand for these tasty treats. Martin follows through on his belief and begins to carry on a business as a sole proprietor on March 1, 2021, on the opening of a retail store under the name "Martin's Macaroons" in a mall in Edmonton, Alberta. All sales are at this mall, where customers may purchase macaroons either singly or in packages of three.

His business will have a calendar-based fiscal period ending December 31. All of his sales will be in Alberta. Martin wishes to delay registering for GST for as long as possible.

Martin's Macaroons had monthly sales for 2021 as follows:

Month	Sales
March	$ 2,420
April	4,650
May	13,780
June	13,240
July	13,780
August	15,760
September	16,480
October	16,670
November	18,490
December	21,750

Required:

A. Indicate the date on which Martin's Macaroons will be required to start collecting GST and the date by which Martin will be required to register.

B. Assume that Martin's Macaroons has elected to file GST on a quarterly basis. Calculate the GST collectible for each quarter of 2021 and specify the due date of each GST return and payment.

C. Assume that Martin's Macaroons files GST on an annual basis. Calculate the GST collectible for 2021 and specify the due date of the GST return and payment.

D. Assume that in January 2021 Martin comes to you for advice on when he should register for the GST. What factors should he consider?

AP 21-4 *(Regular GST Return)*

Lotor Inc. (Lotor) is a CCPC that was incorporated in Alberta in 2013. Lotor operates exclusively within the province and is registered for GST purposes as an annual filer.

The income statement for the current year is shown below. None of the amounts include GST.

Sales		$2,980,000
Less expenses:		
Cost of fully taxable goods sold	($471,200)	
Cost of zero-rated goods sold	(288,500)	
Amortization expense	(350,000)	
Salaries and wages	(232,000)	
Interest expense	(142,000)	
Other expenses	(427,000)	
Income tax	(223,000)	(2,133,700)
Net accounting income		$ 846,300

Other Information:

1. Reported sales for the year are broken down as 12.5% for exempt supplies, 20.5% for zero-rated supplies, and 67% for taxable supplies.

2. All of the cost of goods sold represents either taxable or zero-rated supplies. During the year, purchases of taxable goods amounted to $419,100 and purchases of zero-rated goods were $296,400. These purchase amounts are net of any GST charged.

3. Lotor purchased a new office building in the year for $2,075,000 plus GST of $103,750 [(5%)($2,075,000)]. The company estimated that the office building will be used 53% for the provision of fully taxable supplies, 29% for zero-rated supplies, and 18% for exempt supplies.

4. The company also purchased furniture, fixtures, and office equipment for the new office building totalling $1,145,000 plus GST of $57,250 [(5%)($1,145,000)]. The company estimated that these capital expenditures will be used 64% for the provision of fully taxable supplies, 32% for zero-rated supplies, and 4% for exempt supplies.

5. Other operating expenses includes $28,000 for a corporate golf club membership, $41,000 for life insurance premiums on the lives of company executives, and $63,000 for meals and entertainment with customers. None of the exceptions to the 50% rule of ITA 67.1 apply to any of the meals and entertainment expenses. The remaining expenses of $295,000 are business related and can be broken down as 68% for the provision of fully taxable supplies, 17% for zero-rated supplies, and 15% for exempt supplies.

6. The company also estimated that 93% of the salaries and wages are either for the provision of fully taxable or zero-rated supplies.

7. All of the interest expense represents mortgage interest on the purchase of the new office building.

Required: Calculate the net GST payable or net GST refund that Lotor will remit or receive for the current year. Show all supporting calculations and, where you excluded a particular item, provide the reason for the exclusion.

AP 21-5   (Regular HST Return)

Conan Barbarian carries on a business as a sole proprietor. The business is located in New-foundland and goes by the name Conan's Comics. All of the business is carried on solely in Newfoundland.

The business is an HST registrant that sells both fully taxable and zero-rated goods. In addition, Conan's Comics provides exempt services. The business is an annual filer for HST purposes.

The income statement for the current year is as follows. All amounts are before the addition of any HST.

Revenues:		
Fully taxable goods	$643,431	
Zero-rated goods	311,412	
Exempt services	416,253	$1,371,096
Less expenses:		
Cost of fully taxable goods sold	($489,567)	
Cost of zero-rated goods sold	(203,642)	
Amortization	(106,911)	
Salaries and wages	(62,435)	
Interest expense	(16,243)	
Other expenses	(28,968)	(907,766)
Income before taxes		$ 463,330
Less: Federal and provincial income tax		(157,243)
Net accounting income		$ 306,087

Other Information:

1. Purchases of fully taxable goods amounted to $464,917 and purchases of zero-rated goods were $222,885.

2. Capital expenditures for this period amounted to $1,950,000, with HST being paid on all amounts. Of this total, $1,260,000 was for a building that will be used 35% for the provi-sion of fully taxable supplies, 25% for zero-rated supplies, and 40% for exempt supplies. The remaining $690,000 was for equipment that will be used 38% in the provision of fully taxable supplies, 27% for zero-rated supplies, and 35% for exempt supplies.

3. Of the other expenses, 62% were related to the provision of fully taxable supplies, 24% for zero-rated supplies, and 14% for exempt supplies.

4. Of the salaries and wages, 65% were attributable to employees involved in providing exempt supplies.

Required: Calculate Conan Comic's HST payable or HST refund for the current year.

AP 21-6   (Quick Method)

John, Alice, Alex, and Jerry Rangi are siblings that each carry on their own business as a sole proprietor.

All of the businesses are located in Ontario and all of the revenues are earned from doing busi-ness in Ontario. All of the businesses are registered for the GST/HST.

The siblings provide you with the following annual information for each of their businesses. All amounts shown include HST. None of the sales or purchases are zero-rated or exempt, and none of the businesses made any capital expenditures during the year.

	Type of Business	Sales	Purchases
John	Computer sales, repairs, and tutoring	$ 103,960	$ 26,160
Alice	Bicycle sales and service	194,360	159,330
Alex	Menswear sales and custom tailoring	126,560	47,460
Jerry	Hair styling service and hair product sales	84,750	41,810

The HST rate in Ontario is 13%. The quick method remittance rates are 4.4% for resellers and 8.8% for service providers. When calculating the applicable remittance rate, assume the sales and purchases of the previous year were equal to those of the current year.

Required: Recommend whether any of the businesses should use the quick method to calculate HST remittances. Show all of your calculations.

AP 21-7   *(Regular and Quick Method GST/HST Returns)*

Johnny Dangerous has successfully engaged in criminal activity since he was 12 years old. Financially, he has been very successful and, to date, he has no criminal record. All of his activity is carried out in Ontario. The HST rate for Ontario is 13%. The Ontario quick method rates are 4.4% for businesses that purchase goods for resale and 8.8% for service providers.

Early in his career, his father taught him that the notorious Chicago gangster Al Capone was sent to jail not for his many murders and other illegal acts, but for tax evasion. Taking this lesson to heart, Johnny has been very diligent about filing both income tax returns and GST returns on time. For the 2021 taxation year, his activities fall into three categories:

Contract Assassinations   Johnny accepts contracts for assassinations at a base rate of $15,000. He charges higher fees for particularly difficult cases. Johnny handles all of this activity personally.

During 2021, his revenues from this work totalled $323,000. While he does not specifically advise his clients that they are paying HST, he files his GST return on the basis that the amounts charged include HST.

Export of Illegal Drugs   A growing part of Johnny's activities involve exporting illegal drugs. His 2021 revenues from this activity totalled $113,000.

Loan Sharking   As a service to his clients, he offers extremely high interest rate loans to individuals who cannot find other sources of financing. Revenue from this source totalled $87,000 for 2021.

Johnny has an assistant, Cruella Ratched, who works on a full-time basis for his business. Since he lost his driver's licence two years ago, her duties include driving him to his jobs using her car. Her salary for 2021 is $85,000, which includes a $12,000 car allowance.

Johnny maintains an office that he rents for $4,000 per month plus HST. During the year, miscellaneous office costs total $6,900 plus HST. The office costs include $400 for business insurance. The furniture, fixtures, and art in the office are leased at a cost of $2,000 per month plus HST. Telephone and internet cost $125 per month plus HST.

Johnny has calculated that these costs should be allocated to his three business activities as follows:

Contract assassinations	65%
Export of illegal drugs	20%
Loan sharking	15%

Expenditures specific to his various activities are as follows:

Contract Assassinations   Johnny uses a Glock 9mm for this activity. He disposes of each gun after a single use, making this a significant cost of doing business. On January 1, 2021, he had five of these guns on hand. Their total capital cost was $3,101, plus HST, and they had been categorized as class 8 property for income tax purposes. They were the only property in this class and on January 1, 2021, the UCC was $2,792. During 2021, Johnny acquires an additional 19 guns at $549 each, plus HST. After using each weapon once, he disposes of 20 of his guns. There were no proceeds associated with the disposals.

His only other costs associated with this activity were for travel. Airline, hotel, and taxis totalled $12,000 plus HST. Meals while travelling totalled $7,492 plus HST.

Export of Illegal Drugs   Costs associated with this activity are as follows:

Purchases of processing equipment (includes HST)	$11,300
Security service for lab (includes HST)	5,650
Shipping costs (no HST—Using undocumented immigrants)	3,000
Bribes to customs officials (no HST)	4,500
Cost of goods exported (no HST)	21,700

Loan Sharking   Johnny used bank loans to finance these loans. Interest on these loans for 2021 was $12,600. When he experienced difficulties with collections he used a former World Wrestling Entertainment champion to enforce the payment of the loans. Costs for this service for 2021 were $4,800 (no HST—small supplier).

Required:

A. Determine Johnny's HST payable or HST refund for the year ending December 31, 2021, using the regular HST method.

B. Determine whether Johnny can use the quick method for 2021.

C. Determine Johnny's HST payable or HST refund on the assumption that he can use the quick method for the year ending December 31, 2021.

AP 21-8   (Regular and Quick Method HST Returns)
For the year ending December 31, 2021, the income statement of Sloan Inc. is as follows (all amounts are without the addition of the HST):

Revenues:		
Sales of fully taxable goods	$291,600	
Provision of exempt services	105,300	$396,900
Less expenses:		
Cost of goods sold	($166,050)	
Amortization expense	(75,600)	
Salaries and wages	(16,200)	
Rent	(56,700)	
Interest expense	(12,150)	
Other expenses	(36,450)	(363,150)
Income before taxes		$ 33,750
Less: Federal and provincial income tax		(10,800)
Net accounting income		$ 22,950

Other Information:

1. Sloan Inc. is a retail business located in Ontario where all of the company's revenues are earned and expenses incurred. The HST rate in Ontario is 13%. The quick method rates are 4.4% for businesses that purchase goods for resale and 8.8% for service providers.

2. For the previous year ending December 31, 2020, Sloan's cost of goods purchased for resale totalled $148,500 and the revenue from sales of taxable supplies totalled $407,700. Both amounts are before HST.

3. Purchases of taxable goods in 2021, before HST, cost $155,250.

4. All of the other expenses involved the acquisition of fully taxable supplies and were acquired to assist in the provision of fully taxable supplies.

5. Of the salaries and wages, 52% were paid to employees involved in providing exempt services and 48% for fully taxable supplies.

6. A capital expenditure was made during the year at an HST-inclusive cost of $83,620. The expenditure was for furniture and fixtures that will be used 60% for the provision of fully taxable supplies. HST was paid on the acquisition of all depreciable property on which amortization is claimed.

Required: For the year ending December 31, 2021:

A. Determine if Sloan is eligible to use the quick method and the applicable quick method remittance rate.

B. Calculate Sloan Inc.'s HST payable or HST refund using regular HST calculations.

C. On the assumption that Sloan Inc. is eligible to use the quick method, calculate the HST payable or HST refund using the quick method.

AP 21-9 *(Employee HST Rebate Including CCA)*

Sarah Martin is a resident of Ontario. She is employed by a large public company with all of its business carried on in Ontario.

Sarah's employment duties require that she travel extensively on behalf of her employer. She uses a second car she recently purchased for much of the travel. The first car is used for personal purposes while the recently acquired second car will be used 100% for employment purposes. The second car was purchased in 2020 at a price before HST of $27,500 and $31,075 [(113%)($27,500)] with HST. In 2020 she claimed maximum CCA of $13,984 [(1.5)(30%)($31,075)]. The portion of her HST rebate related to her car's CCA is $1,609 [(13/113)($13,984)]. Sarah plans on claiming maximum CCA in 2021.

Sarah does not receive any reimbursement or non-taxable allowance from her employer for her travel- or car-related expenses.

In her 2021 income tax return, Sarah deducts the following amounts in the calculation of her net employment income:

Accommodation (includes HST of $1,560)	$13,560
Business meals and entertainment—Deductible amount (includes HST of $1,170)	10,170
Automobile expenses:	
Gas and maintenance (includes HST of $1,430)	12,430
Interest on automobile loan	1,805
Insurance	1,460
Total before CCA	$39,425

Required: Calculate the maximum CCA that Sarah can claim on her car for 2021. In addition, calculate the 2021 HST employee rebate that Sarah can claim.

Assignment Problems

AP 21-10   *(Regular and Simplified HST Returns)*

Adeedas Sports is a retail business situated in Nova Scotia where all of its revenues are earned and expenses incurred. There are no associated businesses and the HST return is filed on an annual basis.

Adeedas' income statement for the current year is shown below with no HST included in any of the amounts:

Revenues:		
Fully taxable goods	$397,523	
Exempt services	109,564	$507,087
Less expenses:		
Cost of goods sold (all taxable)	($201,372)	
Amortization expense	(34,784)	
Salaries and wages	(25,679)	
Rent	(27,841)	
Interest expense	(75,964)	
Other expenses	(31,478)	(397,118)
Income before taxes		$109,969
Less: Federal and provincial income taxes		(21,489)
Net accounting income		$ 88,480

Other Information:

1.   Purchases of taxable goods amounted to $181,811 before HST.

2.   A capital expenditure was made during the year at an HST-inclusive cost of $105,294. The expenditure was for equipment that will be used 60% for the provision of fully taxable supplies and 40% for exempt supplies. All of the amortization expense relates to capital expenditures on which HST was paid.

3.   All of the other expenses are attributable to the provision of taxable supplies.

4.   The rent was not subject to HST as it was paid to a non-registrant. The rented property is used 80% for taxable supplies and 20% for exempt supplies.

5.   Of the salaries and wages, 60% are attributable to taxable supplies and 40% to exempt supplies.

Required:

A.   Calculate the net HST payable or HST refund of Adeedas Sports for the current year using regular HST calculations.

B.   Calculate the net HST payable or HST refund of Adeedas Sports for the current year using the simplified ITC method.

AP 21-11   *(New Housing GST Rebate)*

An individual residing in Alberta purchases a newly constructed home from a builder. GST is charged on the sale price at 5%. Since Alberta does not have a provincial sales tax nor does it participate in the HST, the only sales tax obligation to the individual is the 5% GST.

Required: Calculate the GST new housing rebate and the percentage of GST paid that is rebated in each of the three following situations:

Case A   The sales price is $200,000.

Case B   The sales price is $300,000.

Case C   The sales price is $400,000.

INDEX